——————————————————— psychology for the classroom

JANICE T. GIBSON

University of Pittsburgh

Prentice-Hall, Inc., Englewood Cliffs, New Jersey 07632

THE PSYCHOLOGY FOR THE CLASSROOM

SECOND EDITION

Library of Congress Cataloging in Publication Data

Gibson, Janice T.
  Psychology for the classroom.

  Bibliography: p. 529.
  Includes index.
  1. Educational psychology.   2. Child development.
3. Teaching.   I. Title.
LB1051.G484   1981   370.15   80-20911
ISBN 0-13-733352-8

PSYCHOLOGY FOR THE CLASSROOM
second edition
Janice T. Gibson

Editorial supervision: Serena Hoffman
Interior design: Judy Winthrop
Cover design: Lucy H. McCargar
Photo research: Anita Duncan
Manufacturing buyer: Edmund W. Leone

Chapter opener photographs: page 4: Alice Kandell, *Photo Researchers, Inc.;*
  page 38: Lew Merrin, *Monkmeyer;* page 72: Chuck Iossi;
  page 114: Lynn McLaren, *Photo Researchers, Inc.;*
  page 158: Chuck Iossi; page 202: Bettye Lane, *Photo Researchers, Inc.;*
  page 240: Bettye Lane, *Photo Researchers, Inc.;* page 296: Kenneth Karp;
  page 334, Hugh Rogers, *Monkmeyer;* page 372, David S. Strickler, *Monkmeyer;*
  page 404: Miriam Reinhart, *Photo Researchers, Inc.;*
  page 442: Arthur Grace, *Stock, Boston;* page 480: Paul Conklin, *Monkmeyer*

Cover photographs: left: Suzanne Szasz, *Photo Researchers, Inc.;*
  center: Owen Franken, *Stock, Boston;*
  right: Kenneth Karp, *Photo Researchers, Inc*

© 1981, 1976 by Prentice-Hall, Inc., Englewood Cliffs, New Jersey 07632

Printed in the United States of America
10 9 8 7 6 5 4 3 2

PRENTICE-HALL INTERNATIONAL, INC., *London*
PRENTICE-HALL OF AUSTRALIA PTY. LIMITED, *Sydney*
PRENTICE-HALL OF CANADA, LTD., *Toronto*
PRENTICE-HALL OF INDIA PRIVATE LIMITED, *New Delhi*
PRENTICE-HALL OF JAPAN, INC., *Tokyo*
PRENTICE-HALL OF SOUTHEAST ASIA PTE. LTD., *Singapore*
WHITEHALL BOOKS LIMITED, *Wellington, New Zealand*

To my students at the University of Pittsburgh,
who, for so many years, have showed me
again and again, in many different ways,
what a wonderful experience it is to be a teacher.

OUTLINE OF CONTENTS

CONTENTS

motivation and the humanized classroom *203* 6

guidelines for teaching *241* 7

THE EFFECTS OF INDIVIDUAL DIFFERENCES ON LEARNING AND TEACHING 293

classroom management of aggression and other problem behaviors 297 8

teaching students with special needs 335 9

mainstreaming 373 10

PROLOGUE: SO YOU WANT TO BE A TEACHER?

This text is designed to help people who are preparing to be teachers. Its basic premise is that the discipline of educational psychology is primarily concerned with improving the teaching/learning process—in all of its facets and in all types of schools and training institutions. Prospective teachers need information that will help them understand what children and adolescents and adults are like—information that will provide insight into how individuals learn. Teaching is a complicated task and a difficult one. As those of us who have been involved in teaching know, it can be an extremely rewarding task as well, particularly when we succeed at what we set out to do with our students.

what makes a successful teacher?

We all know that some teachers are unquestionably more effective professionally than others—regardless of the particular philosophies of education they follow, the particular modes of instruction they use, or the particular environments in which they teach. Research has shown that teacher ability is related to student ability; that is, effective teachers can produce achievement gains from students of all levels of ability, whereas the reverse is true for ineffective teachers. Some teachers are able to make classroom learning exciting. Others, even though they hold advanced degrees in specific subjects or in education, have difficulty providing students with learning experiences that are exciting and that can be applied directly to real life. Unfortunately, the less successful teachers frequently tend to outnumber the better ones, not only in elementary and high schools, but also in institutions of higher learning.

How many really excellent teachers can you recall today from your elementary and high school years? All of us, as we set out at the task of learning to be teachers, want to be remembered by our students as one of those really outstanding teachers. What is it that makes a teacher be remembered this way?

Historically, educators and psychologists have described the difference between successful and unsuccessful teachers in terms of what was considered the "art of teaching." This assumption that teaching is an "art" is important because it minimizes the significance of teacher education. According to this assumption, the successful teacher simply has a "knack for teaching"; the unsuccessful teacher does not. According to this view, there is little to be done to change the situation—a pessimistic assumption indeed!

Psychology for the Classroom, Second Edition is based on an entirely different and much more optimistic set of assumptions: (1) that good teaching is not due to a "knack," but rather to the acquisition of teaching skills, and (2) that these skills can be defined and taught.

The skills required of teachers are as varied and complex as the environments in which they work. To specify all the behaviors needed in each teaching situation is hardly possible; and even if it could be done, it would actually be detrimental to the teacher, as we shall see later. What is needed is to learn general categories of skills that lead to good teaching.

Let us therefore begin by examining the major attributes or skills of the successful teacher. Then we shall discuss the role that educational psychology can play in strengthening these attributes, or, more specifically, what this text can do to help prepare you, the prospective teacher, for a purposeful and exciting career.

Knowledge of subject matter The first attribute of a successful teacher—skill in subject-matter content—is so critical to good teaching that it hardly needs comment. No teacher can perform well without a solid background in the subject he or she is teaching. Imagine for a moment having to stop to find out what something means while a classroom full of youngsters waits for you to answer. Of course, there will be times when you will have to say, "I don't know. Give me a little while to check that answer for you. I'll begin tomorrow's class with a discussion of the answer." You should never be afraid to admit that you don't know the answer when you don't. But you cannot do a successful job if such situations occur every few minutes.

By itself, knowledge of subject matter is not enough to make a successful teacher. Really good teachers, the ones students remember later in their lives, have acquired a variety of related skills that make learning a valuable experience for their students. These skills include the fundamentals of language and writing. It is impossible to teach a subject if you cannot communicate your ideas clearly and concisely to your students.

Application of psychological principles Subject matter and communication skills are important, but are still not sufficient to produce a good teacher. Skill in applying psychological principles to the teaching process constitutes another important attribute of the successful teacher.

Two kinds of research form the basis of these psychological principles. First, through research conducted under controlled (regulated) conditions and often in laboratory settings, psychologists have identified principles that can be applied in instructional settings in other contexts as well to explain human behavior. Second, through research in classroom settings, educational psychologists have identified principles of effective teaching.

This book emphasizes the practical application of psychological principles and theories discovered both in the laboratory and in the classroom. For example, the work of developmental and child psychologists is critical to predicting the behavior of schoolchildren of different experiences, backgrounds, and ages. The psychological background that teachers need to predict and understand behavior at each age level and for each background is described in *Part 1, The Developing Individual.*

Part 2, Principles of Learning and Teaching, provides useful tools for predicting how these same students will respond to specific types of instruction and, more generally, how children respond to the teacher's manipulation of the teaching-learning environment.

Psychologists and educators have long known that differences exist among people in abilities, interests, attitudes, and expectations. *Part 3, The Effects of Individual Differences on Teaching and Learning,* explores these differences and the methods that have been found effective in dealing with them. One new and controversial method of dealing with individual differences, *mainstreaming,* is discussed at length.

Knowing how to find out and interpret what students know and do not know is crucial to good teaching. Principles of measurement provide tools for evaluating student progress; without evaluating progress, teachers have little direction for furthering instruction. *Part 4, Uses and Methods of Evaluation,* provides measurement and evaluation expertise.

The teaching-learning process can be viewed from a variety of theoretical positions, and the choice of any given viewpoint by a teacher is very likely to affect his or her behavior in the classroom. For this reason many points of view are discussed throughout this text. Underlying each position is the same question: How can we present instruction and instructional materials in the most meaningful ways?

Understanding of the instructional process Familiarity with the total instructional process is also essential to good teaching. Too frequently new teachers enter classrooms unprepared for what they will find there. This lack of preparation leads to disenchantment and to the large number of teacher dropouts during the first year in the classroom. It also leads to poor teaching.

To prepare new teachers for classroom instruction, many schools of education have designed classroom-observation and practice-teaching programs for their students. But to be prepared for the "real world" of education, the prospective teacher must become aware of many more facets of education than can be encountered through relatively brief observations in nearby schools. The teacher must also become aware of the psychological, sociological, political, and economic forces acting upon the teaching-learning process. For this reason, some teacher-preparation programs give students the opportunity to participate in school and community activities, thereby focusing on significant issues in the communities where they will be employed. The Student Study Guide accompanying this textbook provides a series of field studies to allow students to get out into the field, talk with teachers, students, and parents, and, through a series of real-life experiences, find out just "what it's all about."

Adaptability to new situations A truly successful teacher is skillful in adapting to new situations. In recent years teachers have been bombarded with instructional innovations: individually prescribed instruction, competency-based teaching, and open-classroom methods, among many others. In addition, they have been inundated with new teaching devices, such as teaching machines and computer-assisted instruction.

Vast political, social, and economic change throughout society has led to rapid and often unpredictable changes in planning and policy-making in the schools. It is impossible to determine today what the specific problems of tomorrow will be. One thing, however, remains clear: Teachers with narrow instructional expertise cannot be effective in the diverse situations they are likely to meet. Teachers need to identify and resolve new problems each new day as they arise.

Successful teachers of the future must approach teaching as more than an "art" or a "knack." They must also be more than just technicians whose specialty lies in the details of a particular subject. Instead, successful teachers must be capable of adapting whatever instructional procedure is available to the particular learning situation and to the individual needs, goals, interests, aptitudes, and developmental stages of their students. They must be prepared for what Toffler (1970) once called "the unknown society of tomorrow." Knowledge of the principles of educational psychology can provide the skills that make such adaptability possible.

Preparing for adversity More than at any time in our past, teachers can expect that there will be increasing violence in the schools. Viewers of the television program "Sixty Minutes" on March 18, 1979, were not surprised to hear the effect on teachers of adversity in the schools being compared to battle fatigue of soldiers during wartime. By the end of the 1970s, attacks on teachers and even rape had become common in many urban schools. Newspaper articles appeared regularly describing the physical dangers of being a teacher. Teachers and teachers' unions reported that there was danger simply in remaining alone in the halls. Delinquency and violence, originally found only in inner-city schools, had become a pervasive part of American education.

In general, attempts at integrating the schools have failed, even though research shows that, when performed successfully, integration increases self-image and achievement of both black and white students (For a good discussion, see Rubin, 1976). Today adversity comes from the results of that failure, as well as from the failure of society to socialize its children adequately. Adversity comes as well as from disgruntled adults who charge that the lack of discipline and learning is due to teachers "who are not doing proper jobs." Teachers are accused, first, of not teaching and, second, of covering up by inflating grades (Winsor, 1977).

Love of children The day of social approval and high social status meted out to the school teacher is long past. Teachers who remain in public school classrooms must look elsewhere for their rewards. In spite of all the problems associated with teaching, rewards for teachers still exist, as they have for as long as there have been teachers and students. These rewards come from watching children grow, from finding small changes in behavior due to the often grueling efforts of the teacher, from seeing children learn how to use new ideas and how to find meaning in their life experiences. The schoolteacher who succeeds today is unafraid of changes and unafraid of adversity. He or she is prepared for the failures that might come, and learns from the successes.

what can this book do to help?

In the past, educational psychology courses have been criticized for their failure to prepare teachers for actual classroom experiences. The first edition of *Psychology for the Classroom,* published in 1976, was designed to make clear the *link between theory and classroom*—to tie knowledge of psychological principles to the real world of teaching. To that end, it provided up-to-date coverage of research, as well as the current educational, social, and economic controversies that affect students and teachers. It attempted, also, through the use of classroom examples, to explain relevant psychological theories that can be generalized to cover a wide range of practical situations.

How is this Book Organized? The second edition of *Psychology for the Classroom* has been designed to provide prospective teachers with the new skills needed to deal with today's problems. Where the first edition dealt intensively with fundamentals of psychology as they apply to classroom use, the second edition provides more extensive applications and examples to show teachers how to act in different teaching situations.

Since most prospective teachers take additional courses in child or adolescent psychology, *Part I* of this book provides brief overviews of topical aspects of development and discusses how these aspects affect classroom learning. Chapter 1, for example, deals with personal-social development and the ways that teachers can expect children of different ages to interact with one another and with the teacher in instructional situations. Chapter 2 deals with language and cognitive development and their effects on ability to learn at all ages, with particular emphasis on the effects of bilingualism. Today, as in earlier periods of our history, immigrants arrive on our shores daily; more and more children enter public school without English language proficiency—a serious but not insurmountable problem for the teacher who is prepared.

Psychology for the Classroom, Second Edition examines various approaches to learning in light of their direct classroom applications: behavioral approaches to classroom management (Chapter 3); cognitive psychology to specific curriculum designs (Chapter 4); and motivation to humanizing the classroom (Chapter 6). Ways to improve student memory and to help students transfer learned material to real-life problems are discussed in Chapter 5. Chapter 7 reviews both new and basic instructional designs tested in the 1960s and 1970s that can be expected to be in use through the next decades.

Terrel H. Bell, former U.S. Commissioner of Education, reported that "the true challenge of American education is to bring out the best in each student with respect to individual differences" (1977, p. 16). Individualization of instruction is emphasized in *Part III*. Research has shown that certain types of students benefit from one type of instruction, while others benefit from another. Clearly, it is important to differentiate children on the basis of individualized needs. Children with special needs—from mentally and physically handicapped to gifted children—are described in Chapter 9, together with instructional methods that have proven effective with these children. With discipline one of the most important problems facing the teacher in the 1980s, an entire chapter has been devoted in this new edition to management of aggression and other problem behaviors in the classroom (Chapter 8). Ways to implement mainstreaming under Public Law 94-142 are described in Chapter 10.

The uses and methods of evaluation, a topic under considerable debate currently, is the subject of *Part IV*. Chapter 11 shows prospective teachers how to design their own classroom tests and check them for reliability and validity. When standardized tests are used, the teachers must be able to interpret the results. This is particularly important at a time when the public is concerned about downward slide of performance on standardized tests of achievement. Ways to deal with this problem are discussed in Chapter 12.

How Should this Book Be Used?

Each chapter of *Psychology for the Classroom, Second Edition* is self-contained. That is, students and instructors can use the chapters *in any order* that best meets the needs of their own individual group. Each chapter begins with a tinted panel in which an actual teaching situation is described. Students should study these *chapter-opening case histories* carefully, and later apply the concepts discussed in the chapter to the situation described in the first few pages. *Additional case histories* and examples of practical application of educational and psychological theory are interspersed throughout the chapters; they are readily identified by their tinted background.

To assist the reader in organizing and retaining the main ideas presented in this book, each chapter concludes with a *summary* that enumerates the key points covered in that chapter. For students who wish to read further on any given topic, there is an *annotated bibliography* at the end of each chapter; readings included in these bibliographies were selected on the basis of their relevance to education today.

A complete list of *references* appears at the end of the book to document significant works in the fields of education and psychology that were summarized in the text. Finally, an updated and expanded *glossary* at the end of the book will help the student to understand unfamiliar or technical terms; such key terms appear in boldface type within the text to signal that they can be found in the glossary.

Supplementary materials are also available for students desiring further assistance in preparing for examinations. The *student workbook* provides self-help sections, questions that students may use to test their comprehension, and other study aids. Exercises for use in group learning situations and an up-to-date list of films and readings are provided in the *instructor's manual*.

acknowledgments

In preparing this up-to-date edition of *Psychology for the Classroom*, I relied not only on my own experience in education psychology, but on the team efforts of other people as well. Timothy Murphy did the background research, providing new data that was incorporated in both the new and revised chapters. Rachel D. Morton and Shirley Wilson Roby contributed various anecdotes and examples of student/teacher conflicts. Jerry Bergman, Bowling Green State University; James E. Klahn, Central Washington University; J. Blair Stone, University of Utah; John Lutz, East Carolina University; John D. Hampton, Oklahoma State University; Leonard B. De Fabo, Indiana University of Pennsylvania; William E. Roweton of James Madison University; and Gioia Castiglione reviewed portions of the rough draft of the manuscript and helped with useful suggestions

Yvonne Irvin and I wrote the Student Workbook; Pam Meadowcroft and Claudia Van Arsdale prepared the Instructor's Manual. The Prentice-Hall staff, including Bob Sickles, Susan Katz, Serena Hoffman, Judy Winthrop, Anita Duncan, and Gert Glassen, provided valuable supportive services. Sandra Poore did a most excellent job of editing the rough manuscript. Elsie Squitieri prepared the typed manuscript swiftly and accurately, and assisted with editorial comments.

To all these people, I owe a sincere debt of gratitude.

Janice T. Gibson

THE DEVELOPING INDIVIDUAL

To be effective in the classroom, teachers need to understand the ways that children change as they get older. Children and adolescents have different capacities for learning and view their worlds in different ways. For this reason, most student teachers take at least one college course in child or adolescent psychology. If you have not had such a course, Part I will provide you with a basic understanding of the developmental process. If you have already completed a course in child or adolescent psychology, these next two chapters can be used as a review of basic theory. In either case, you will learn specific ways to apply developmental psychology to classroom situations and to put your students' stages of development to best use in learning.

Chapter 1 describes the personal, social, and physical changes that take place as students get older and the ways that these changes can affect classroom learning. Personality and social development are described as they take place at home, as well as in the classroom. The relationships between students and their families, peer groups, and teachers are important influences on the classroom experience.

Chapter 2 deals with the development of language and cognition. Education is aided by the fact that human beings are able to use language to pass their knowledge on to the next generation. Moreover, while all living things can react to the environment, only human beings are able to think about it in abstract terms. These two related abilities, speaking and thinking, are essential for classroom learning. Because all teachers, regardless of the subject they teach, are indirectly concerned with teaching language skills and thinking, ways to help students improve these skills are also described.

PERSONAL AND SOCIAL DEVELOPMENT

The Case of Peggy P.

Thirteen-year-old Peggy P. was a student in the eighth grade of Stover School, a middle school in a large eastern city. When Peggy's teachers became concerned about what they described as "developing problem behaviors," the counselor for the eighth grade called her parents in for a conference.

Peggy had always been considered a model student by her teachers. Even during the period of her parents' separation and divorce, she had maintained an A average, always did her homework, and seemed interested in what was going on in school. But, recently her grades had dropped. She had been getting to school an hour or more late, had not done her homework assignments, and had been daydreaming through classes. The week that the counselor called her parents, she had been caught cutting class and smoking marijuana in a vacant lot about a block from the school. One of the boys caught with her had had some hard drugs in his locker.

Peggy's parents were horrified. Mrs. P. didn't get home from work until after 6 P. M. She hadn't noticed any change in Peggy's behavior at home. She noted that Peggy had been spending more time at night in front of the TV, but had assumed that her work was done as it had always been in the past. Mrs. P. couldn't explain Peggy's being late in the mornings; she always left the apartment on time.

Peggy's father was particularly shocked that his daughter was found smoking pot with boys. But he didn't live at home and didn't know how he could help. He and Mrs. P. disagreed about many things, but they both felt that Peggy wasn't old enough to be dating boys and that marijuana was not to be tolerated. "What's wrong with you?" Mr. P. shouted. "We've given you everything we could."

Peggy looked at the floor and nervously picked at a fingernail. "What difference does it make to you what I do? What do you know about my feelings? All you ever do is work. Working on homework never brought *me* any fun. And you can't tell me that either of you *ever* had fun."

Peggy's father was so distraught that he would have struck his daughter then if the counselor hadn't intervened. "Let's talk this over and see what we can figure out as a group," she suggested. "It's time we began seriously to think about why this is happening. Then maybe we can come to some solutions. Understanding just what Peggy is doing as she grows and develops will help us become better parents and teachers."

What do we know about the personal and social development of children like Peggy? As children grow and develop, their bodies and behaviors change. They grow physically larger; their body proportions change; they gradually become stronger; their interests, attitudes, and values develop; they become more and more capable of solving complex problems and making intricate responses. Sometimes the changes that take place occur smoothly. Other times, problems develop that affect the ways children think, solve problems, and interact with others.

Many psychologists (called **developmental psychologists**) are concerned with describing and explaining the changes that take place in children as they get older. These psychologists view what they see in terms of series of developmental stages characterized by progressively more complex ways of doing things. They stress that understanding children's behavior depends on knowing what stages they are passing through. For example, the counselor who talked with Peggy and her parents was familiar with other children of Peggy's age and understood the ways that their social world affected them at that level. In the meetings that followed the initial session, Peggy, her parents, and the counselor explored the ages and stages through which American children pass as they grow up. They also discussed the ways that family life, peer groups, and school pressures affect that particular stage that Peggy was getting ready to enter: adolescence.

Some changes that take place with age are due simply to our biological inheritance as human beings. For example, we know that a kitten will grow to be a cat and that a baby will grow to be an adult human being—regardless of its environment. We call this type of development, which is controlled by the genetic material in our bodies and is independent of our environment, **maturation.** Developmental psychologists have shown that many human behaviors depend solely on maturation. The ability to learn a relatively simple behavior such as walking is affected only minimally by learning experience. Unless we deprive children of all opportunity to practice walking, we can expect them to learn to do so without any special training at all. Learning more complicated behaviors such as reading or morality, on the other hand, may require a certain amount of maturation but primarily depends on specific learning experience.

Sometimes the interaction between maturation and learning leads to the development of useful skills, as when a child first learns to master a new type of arithmetic problem satisfactorily. At other times, this interaction leads to less useful learning. A good example of this is social misbehavior among adolescents like Peggy.

Most psychologists, from Freud on, have seen adolescence as a time of storm and stress. A good number of adolescent boys and girls manage to become young adults without a lot of tension and fuss, but, for many others, the fight for independence is tinged with emotional and even physical violence. A warm accepting relationship between adolescents and their parents seems to minimize the stress, but the barriers set up by society often serve to increase adolescents' frustration by keeping them from chances to practice being adults. Today, middle schools and high schools regularly employ counselors to help children who, like Peggy, need guidance in working out their problems. The most important part of counseling focuses on encouraging adolescents to talk about their problems with their parents.

Of course, developmental psychologists are concerned with more than conflicts. They are concerned with describing in detail the unvarying sequence through which much of our development goes as we progress from early childhood to adolescence and adulthood. This knowledge is important for teachers; without it, we could not predict how groups of children will behave at any given age, or explain why one child differs in any significant way from the others. We do not teach just minds—we teach whole beings, and it is important for us to understand all the ways in which our students are growing.

Physical and Motor Development

The immense physical changes that take place in children from the earliest school grades until graduation from high school have been studied by many developmental psychologists. The changes from birth to five years alone are so dramatic that it is hard to believe that we are dealing with only one kind of creature (see, for example, Gesell, Ilg, Ames, and Rodell, 1974, pp. 19-20). By the time they reach school age, children have developed the ability to control their motor responses in complex ways, to communicate, and to question, while developing individual personality identities.

Physical and motor development is particularly important to school-age children. Many of the tasks they must master during the school years, beginning in the first grade when they are required to print their names, require motor coordination. The abilities of high school students to drive a car or learn the new steps at the local disco also depend on perceptual-motor coordination. In fact, psychologists who study perceptual-motor coordination have called for special instruction in motor-skill learning simply because of its importance in other aspects of development. The child who has difficulty with motor coordination is also likely to have difficulty at other tasks. Such a child, unfortunately, is also likely to be made fun of by other children.

The rate of physical growth is also important in understanding behavior. Over the past one hundred years, American children have not only been getting bigger, they have been getting bigger earlier. The age of puberty has declined dramatically in America, as it has in other societies where socioeconomic conditions have improved, although there is some recent evidence that this trend is finally decreasing in industrial nations (Krogman, 1972; Tanner, 1968; Winter et al., 1978). Researchers have attributed the decreasing age at puberty to the decline of growth-retarding illnesses among large segments of our population; better nutrition, medical care, and personal health practices; and improved living conditions in general. In countries where socioeconomic conditions have not improved, as in impoverished areas where malnourishment is widespread, children's physical size and their growth rate have either decreased or remained the same.

Peggy, like most girls in her class, reached puberty by age 13. Today, however, girls as young as 10 years old have been known to experience puberty (Goldfarb, 1977). Going through puberty often becomes something of a race among adolescents. Being the first to need a shave or wear a bra confers a special sort of status, while being last often means consignment to social oblivion. The lowest person on the totem pole of puberty is usually the late-maturing boy. To the adolescent, the physical changes associated with puberty often are a source of anxiety, partly because they are new and strange and partly because society regards adolescents in contradictory ways: It recognizes their developing physical maturity, but limits their freedom to exercise it; it recognizes their abilities to take care of themselves and demands that they do so, but limits the extent to which they are free to make many decisions.

As a result of the progressively younger ages at which puberty occurs, school children must cope with sex-related problems at earlier ages. The general feelings of malaise and search for identity that often accompany puberty are increased, particularly for children whose parents do not seem to have found their own happiness, or who are unavailable to them for communication.

Earlier puberty is just one of the reasons for the recent establishment of middle schools in America. Today's middle schools usually encompass sixth through eighth grade, as contrasted with the earlier traditional junior high school's seventh through ninth grade. In addition, rather than "miniaturizing" the high school curriculum as the traditional junior high school did, the middle school employs a special

Hella Hammid, Photo Researchers, Inc.

Learning to control your muscles gives you the power to make things behave as you want them to.

curriculum and staff designed to deal with the social and sexual problems of newly emerging adolescents. Special staff, such as the counseling psychologist who met with Peggy and her parents, is just one of the different special services designed for this age group.

*Personality
Development*

Developmental-stage psychologists view the process of growing up as a sequence of maturational stages that occur in fixed and predictable order. A child must successfully complete one stage before advancing to the next. This is most obvious in physical development, where we all must walk before we can run. Beginning with Freud, psychologists have applied this stage approach to the development of other human attributes such as thinking and personality.

According to Freud, all children acquire their basic personalities, including their identities, by age 5. Freud considered it unlikely that any major personality change would take place after this. This is an extremely fatalistic and deterministic conclusion, especially for teachers, who do not get to work with children until they are past the age of 5. Fortunately, research by many developmentalists on personality development has shown that many aspects of our personalities do continue to develop throughout adolescence and adulthood.

The psychosocial approach of Erik Erikson Erik Erikson (1963, 1968), a leading developmental-stage theorist, studied individuals growing up in a variety of different cultures and used his data to expand on Freud's version of personality development. Erikson describes eight stages, each of which centers around a different type of developmental crisis (see Table 1-1). According to Erikson, personality development is a life-long process, influenced by the tug between positive and negative poles.

The preschool years are characterized by what Erikson refers to as *initiative* or *guilt*, depending on the responses of parents or caregivers to the child's experimentation with the environment. The early school years, ages 6 to 11, are the years during which the child devel-

Table 1-1 Erikson's Eight Stages of Personality Development

STAGE	DEVELOPMENTAL CRISIS
Infancy	Trust versus mistrust
First three years	Autonomy versus shame
Ages 3 to 6	Initiative versus guilt
Ages 6 to puberty	Industry versus inferiority
Adolescence	Identity versus role confusion
Adulthood	Intimacy versus isolation
Middle age	Generativity versus stagnation
Old age	Integrity versus despair

From *Childhood and Society* (2nd ed.), by Erik H. Erikson, with the permission of W. W. Norton & Company, Inc. Copyright © 1950, 1963 by W. W. Norton & Company, Inc.

The early school years are the ones in which children first develop feelings of industry or inferiority.

Christa Armstrong, Photo Researchers, Inc.

ops feelings of *industry* or *inferiority*. It is in these years that the child learns to relate to peers, to play by rules, and to perform academic tasks. Reward for learning and assistance in learning lead to industry. Excessive criticism or overly high standards, on the other hand, lead to feelings of failure and inferiority.

Erikson probably is best known for his descriptions of adolescent development. According to Erikson, individuals use adolescence, the period from about 12 to 18 years, to discover their identities. The development of identity begins in early childhood, but until we are adolescents, we are not aware enough to notice it.

Finding out how we have been shaped by our childhood is often a shock. Pulling together our various qualities to form an integrated adult personality and taking responsibility for its future growth are the major developmental tasks of adolescence. Specifically, the goal is to develop what Erikson calls a *positive ego identity*. This is a reality-based conviction that one is a competent person who can achieve pleasure and prestige through mastery of the environment, and that one is moving forward toward a meaningful future. A high school student who has begun to think of possible future careers and is studying successfully in preparation is said to have a positive ego identity. A student who merely questions the relevance of everything society has to offer succeeds in accomplishing nothing toward achieving some control over the world and usually has trouble sorting things out. Such an individual is said to be in a stage of **identity crisis.** Only when positive ego identity is finally attained are firm ideological and interpersonal commitments possible. At that point, which may not occur until well into adulthood, the identity crisis of adolescence is said to be over.

Many adolescents unable to successfully resolve the identity crisis suffer what Erikson calls *identity diffusion,* or confusion about their roles. Part of this confusion can be explained by taking a look at the world surrounding the adolescent. It is almost overwhelmingly complex, disquieting, and disjointed; members of our society frequently lack a common body of experience or a sense of group involvement and continuity; adult models of character and identity seem vague or disorganized; the number of available roles has vastly multiplied; and authority figures do not seem to merit the respect they once did.

Evidence of identity diffusion can often be seen in the American classroom. Asking students for analysis and evaluation of a particular issue often results in their giving stereotyped responses that they have learned from those around them. The teacher's response—"Yes, but what do *you* think?"—is met simply with bafflement or hostility.

The adolescent may also exhibit identity diffusion in following the behavior of peers. While peers at least seem to have some kind of identity that he or she can adopt, that identity may not be a good fit. For example, an adolescent may cut a class when friends do, even though he or she may actually like the subject.

Often, in an attempt to come to terms with what they think, believe, or desire, adolescents reject all the values of adult society. As a consequence, they may become apathetic and refuse to attend school, or, having no alternative choices left, become frustrated and hostile. Both behavior patterns are familiar in American schools today, for both are signs of acute distress in the adolescent. Erikson, for one, feels it is a grave mistake to pin the label "criminal" on these adolescents without regard for the underlying personality dynamics that help to explain their behavior.

Value development: Piaget and Kohlberg   Jean Piaget, another major developmental-stage theorist, is mainly concerned with children's cognitive development, but he has also studied the way children develop the ability to make judgments about morality. According to Piaget (1933, 1965), development of moral judgments and other values proceeds according to a system of rules and reflects specific kinds of attitudes acquired at a particular stage of development. From an investigation of children's attitudes and behavior with respect to social rules, Piaget has concluded that children go through a series of stages of moral development. These stages correspond to the stages of cognitive development.

Piaget found that children crystallize their definitions of right and wrong as they grow older. When Piaget presented some children under age 9 with stories in which a child did something wrong, they tended to evaluate the act solely in terms of its consequences, without any consideration of motives. They felt that a child who broke five cups accidentally was worse than a child who broke a single cup deliberately. Older children, on the other hand, tended to evaluate the apparent motives for the behavior before deciding how bad it was (Flavell, 1963).

The same tendency holds true for lying. Young children define a lie as any statement that is untrue, regardless of whether it is told unknowingly or deliberately, and they judge the severity of a lie solely in terms of its consequences. An unintentionally untrue statement that hurts somebody seems worse to them than a deliberate deception that does no appreciable damage. Older children, by contrast, seek to understand other aspects of a situation, such as intent.

Lawrence Kohlberg is another developmental-stage theorist with deep interest in moral development. Kohlberg's theory of moral development also involves developmental sequences, and in many ways it adapts and further illustrates Piaget's concepts.

Kohlberg's theory (1964) of progressive stages of morality is derived from a study in which he interviewed boys 10 to 16 years of age on ten hypothetical moral dilemmas. For instance: Joe's father promised Joe that he could go to camp if he earned the $50 for it; he then changed his mind and asked Joe to give him the money he had earned. Joe lied and said he had earned only $10 and went to camp using the rest of the money he had earned. Before he went he told his younger brother Alex about lying to their father. The boys were then asked: If you were Alex, would you tell your father? From the boys' responses, Kohlberg defined six developmental types of value orientations, which he grouped into three moral levels (Table 1-2).

In Level I, children determine if an act is right or wrong entirely by its consequences for themselves. A child at Stage 1 of this level would respond to Alex's hypothetical dilemma in terms of its physical consequences: "If I don't tell on my brother, and Dad finds out, he might get mad and spank me." Or: "I should keep quiet or my brother will beat me up." Later at this level, at Stage 2, the child would respond on the basis of anticipated rewards: "If I don't tell on Joe, maybe he'll give me his BB gun when he gets back from camp."

In Level II, children conform to stereotyped standards in order to gain approval. They have very strong respect for authority and are moved by a sense of duty to behave as society dictates. Children at this level most likely would think that Alex should tell his father about Joe's lie because his father "knows what's best."

In Level III, the individual's notions about right and wrong reflect general principles or laws agreed upon by society. At the same time, however, he or she now makes judgments on the basis of a personal value system and may rationally decide that disobedience may be more desirable than blind obedience. The individual's conscience and self-chosen, abstract, moral principles do the guiding. He

Table 1-2 Kohlberg's Levels of Morality

LEVEL AND STAGE	ILLUSTRATIVE BEHAVIOR
Level I. Premoral	
Stage 1. Punishment and obedience orientation	Obeys rules in order to avoid punishment
Stage 2. Naive instrumental hedonism	Conforms to obtain rewards, to have favors returned
Level II. Morality of conventional role conformity	
Stage 3. "Good-boy" morality of maintaining good relations, approval of others	Conforms to avoid disapproval, dislike by others
Stage 4. Authority maintaining morality	Conforms to avoid censure by legitimate authorities, with resultant guilt
Level III. Morality of self-accepted moral principles	
Stage 5. Morality of contract, of individual rights, and of democratically accepted law	Conforms to maintain the respect of the impartial spectator judging in terms of community welfare
Stage 6. Morality of individual principles of conscience	Conforms to avoid self-condemnation

Based upon L. Kohlberg, The development of children's orientation toward a moral order: Sequence in the development of moral thought, *Vita Humana*, 1963, 6, 11-33.

or she conforms to these principles in order to integrate what is morally relevant in a given situation and make a decision. People at this level would probably think that Alex should not tell his father, who had broken his promise in not letting Joe go to camp.

In evaluating this evidence, Kohlberg (1963) points out that it is inadequate to view moral development solely as a process of socialization, or the internalization of the rules of society. Rather, changes in moral thinking result from a continual interaction between individuals and their environments. Thus, classroom experiences appropriately matched to children's levels of moral development can serve as teaching devices and help pave the way toward the next stage of development.

personal and social development: an environmental approach

Although many psychologists have stressed the importance of understanding children through the examination of developmental stages, other psychologists point out that the picture is incomplete without an understanding of the environments in which that development takes place.

In his theory of moral development Kohlberg stressed that the best way to help a child reach the next stage is to correct wrong behavior by methods that appeal to that higher stage. Researchers have interpreted this to mean that teachers of preschool-age children must be careful not to equate obedience with moral development (Brody and Henderson, 1977; Muuss, 1976). When Susie stops knocking down Joanie's pile of blocks after her teacher tells her that she has been naughty, this doesn't necessarily mean that Susie knows why she has been naughty, or, in fact, that it is "wrong" to knock down another child's blocks. Susie may learn to behave properly simply because she is afraid of being punished (Stage 1, obedience and punishment) or expects praise from the teacher for her behavior (Stage 2, hedonism).

In order to determine at what level Susie is responding, her teacher must pay close attention and find out just *why* she is behaving as she is. If necessary, the teacher can ask Susie herself. Then and only then can the teacher be sure how best to appeal to the next stage.

Let's assume Susie's teacher had the following conversation with Susie on the playground:

Teacher: Susie, who knocked down Joanie's pile of blocks?
Susie: I don't know who did it.
Teacher: Did you do it?
Susie: If I say yes, will you be mad at me?
Teacher: Nobody will be mad. I just want to know who did it.
Susie: I did it, but I won't do it again.

At what level and stage of Kohlberg's model of moral development is Susie responding? How can you tell? What should the teacher do to teach Susie not to knock down piles of blocks that other children build? Why?

Human beings learn to become social animals by adapting to the environment in the process we call **socialization.** Through socialization, certain patterns of behavior characteristic of a commonly shared culture are transmitted from one generation to the next.

Imagine for a moment a society that failed to teach its young the behaviors and values on which it is built. That society as such would cease to exist. Socialization, therefore, is not only a way for an individual to adapt to the environment; it is also the process by which society perpetuates itself. For a society to survive, it must pass on its economic, political, and social foundations.

Socialization has both universal and specific effects. The effects are universal in the sense that each developing child, regardless of culture, learns certain similar skills—using a language, for example. The effects of socialization are specific in the sense that children from different parts of the world adopt patterns of behavior that are unique

to their society and characteristically different from those of other societies (Caudill and Weinstein, 1969; Harrington and Whiting, 1972). Thus, American children learn a language that is different from the one learned by Masai children in Africa. How we grow up, the kind of people we become, and how we behave are largely determined by the socialization process in the culture in which we are reared.

The essence of socialization is learning. Children learn what behavior is socially acceptable: what to eat, how to dress, how to treat property, how to deal with other people. They learn what religious and moral beliefs and value systems are acceptable to their social groups. For example, a premium is placed on education in middle-class American society.

Children learn first to imitate the acceptable (and socially rewarded) behaviors of those around them. Later, this **imitation** turns to **identification** when they behave in new situations just as they would have expected their models to behave. The child who identifies with a model has adopted and internalized the model's standards and uses them to judge his or her own behavior. Socialization begins the moment we are born, and it has its strongest influence during our formative years as young children.

Enculturation is the process by which a child adapts to a culture and adopts its values. How a child is enculturated in any society depends on the interaction of various factors. Parents and other family members, peer groups, day-care centers, and the mass media (especially television) all transmit and interpret the culture for children. The relative importance of these influences will vary according to the cultural environments in which a child is reared. Thus, a child's biological parents have a greater impact on socialization for American children reared in a nuclear household than for children reared in a children's center on a kibbutz in Israel. Furthermore, socialization is greatly influenced by variables such as sex, race, and the family's educational level and socioeconomic status. All this takes place even before children are old enough to enter the formal institution responsible for socialization in our society, namely the school.

In this section we examine the various factors that socialize the young child. Bear in mind that no factor is completely independent of the others. Rather, these factors interact, and it is this interaction that produces the unique socialization of one child in a particular culture.

The Family: The Child's First Teachers

In America, the family is considered to be the child's first teacher of socialization. For Americans in past generations, the term *family* referred to the **extended family,** which consisted of parents, children, and other close relatives all living together. Today, changes in mobility patterns have led to the predominance of the **nuclear family,** which traditionally consisted of two parents and their offspring. In recent years, higher divorce rates have led to a significant number of tem-

Well-designed classrooms and good teachers can provide opportunities for children to learn many important skills by imitation.

Bruce Roberts, Photo Researchers, Inc.

porary or permanent single-parent families. These changes in family structure have contributed significantly to changing our patterns of child rearing (Toffler, 1970).

Systems of care-giving   Much recent research has compared different types of households. Data gathered so far suggest that the amount of kindness and attention shown to the child varies directly with the number of adults in the home: the larger the number of adults in the household, the greater the kindness and attention given to the children. Thus, there is a greater tendency to treat the young indulgently in extended families, where children are raised simultaneously by many adults, than in households with only one or two parental figures (Whiting, 1961). Observations of children raised communally with many care-givers, as, for example, on kibbutzim in Israel or in day-care centers in the Soviet Union, have generally supported the view that carefully planned multiple care-giving systems do not have harmful effects on the child (see, for example, Bronfenbrenner, 1969, 1977). In fact, these systems can serve certain useful functions.

Both the extended family and the collective society have a unique advantage absent in the typical nuclear household: They offer children the availability of several care-givers who can take turns responding to their needs. In such arrangements—when the child's mother is pregnant, for example, or busy taking care of a new baby—the older children stand less chance of being neglected. In the nuclear family, on the other hand, a parent with several children simply may not have enough time or energy to care adequately for all of them (Margolin, 1974). Furthermore, losing a parent might be less traumatic for a child accustomed to other care-givers than for a child who has depended on one parent exclusively (Ainsworth, 1967).

American families are becoming more aware of these advantages of multiple care-giving. Exposing children to the stimulation of preschool is now seen as a good way to prepare them for elementary school. Divorce, economic necessity, and the desire for an independent identity are bringing an increasingly large percentage of mothers of young children into the labor force. When a mother works, other competent people must be available, whether in the home or in day-care centers, to help care for the young child.

Characteristics of good care-givers   What characteristics of care-givers are most important to personality development? Research shows that the most important factor in personality development is not simply the presence of the care-giver but his or her reaction to the child. In some nuclear families, the mother provides a constant physical presence, yet she may rarely interact with her children in a playful, affectionate, and stimulating manner. Mothers who do interact may not be consistently responsive to their children. Unfortunately, recent studies have shown that American mothers tend to interact less frequently with their children in day-to-day situations than mothers in other cultures do. (Gibson, Wurst, and Cannonito, in preparation; Wurst, 1978).

According to many psychologists, the ideal care-giver is one who is warm, loving, consistent, and nonrejecting. This type of care-giver is sensitive to the child's needs and distress signals and responds promptly and appropriately. He or she spends considerable time in the same room with the children, looking at them, stimulating them, and playing with them. He or she is free from emotional problems like anxiety and depression and thus is able to attend to the children's needs. Interactions with the children are mutually pleasurable (Ainsworth, 1967; Clarke-Stewart, 1973). Care-givers should be more than just available to children; they should interact in specific and direct ways and have general competence.

Developing self-esteem What components of family life cause a child to behave in a manner reflecting a certain level of self-esteem? In one study of self-esteem (Coopersmith, 1967), boys 10 years of age and older were categorized as low (sure they had no worth), medium (unsure), or high (thought they were good) in self-esteem on the basis of their self-evaluations, evaluations by others, and clinical evaluations. It was found that the boys' evaluations of self-esteem reflected those of their parents more than the boys' actual ability. For example, boys whose self-esteem was low had mothers who rated themselves as below average on such characteristics as poise, assurance, and emotional stability. On the other hand, boys who had more favorable views of themselves had parents whose self-esteem and stability ratings were also high.

The mothers of the boys with a high self-esteem level seemed to accept the responsibilities of motherhood realistically. They were neither punitive nor overly permissive; above all, they set clear and consistent standards for behavior. It was also apparent that the boys with high self-esteem tended to have closer relationships with their fathers. The mothers of boys with low and middle levels of self-esteem tended to act in an inconsistent manner, being both highly punitive and permissive.

The boys with low self-esteem reported that their parents' values centered around such attributes as obedience, helpfulness, and good manners; the boys' desire to be acceptable and pleasing to others reflected these values. The boys with high self-esteem said that their parents stressed achievement; thus, they were more inclined to feel that their parents valued their abilities and accomplishments.

These findings tell us that when parents are well adjusted, interested in their children (and their friends), and basically accepting (but within reasonable, clearly defined, and consistent limits), the children

Young children living in poverty homes often headed by only one parent may be left alone for large parts of their day—without important stimulation provided by day care and preschools.

are more likely to want to identify with and try to emulate parentally approved behaviors. Equally important, they will have a much more positive attitude toward themselves.

Parental deprivation Having looked into cases of child-rearing in which either one or several parental figures guided the socialization, let us now examine what happens to the child who is deprived of contact with a parent.

In now-famous experiments with infant rhesus monkeys, psychologists showed that effects of maternal deprivation varied under different conditions (Harlow, 1958; Harlow and Zimmerman, 1959). Monkeys reared with artificial surrogate mothers made of wire or of soft terrycloth tended to display abnormal sexual and maternal behaviors as adults (Harlow and Harlow, 1966).

Close physical contact with a mother or mother-substitute is necessary for normal social and emotional development in human infants, too. During World War II, babies institutionalized under crowded, understaffed conditions were seriously affected by being deprived so early in life of adequate contact with biological or substitute parents (Freud and Burlingham, 1943, 1944; Spitz, 1945, 1946). Spitz, for example, reported that infants who had been institutionalized since birth soon began to exhibit unusual behavior. At first they would cry continuously, but later they simply stared vacantly into space, totally uninterested in their surroundings or the people who approached them.

They became retarded in every aspect of development—physical, intellectual, and social.

Today in America almost 6 million families are like Peggy's family—headed by only one parent because of divorce. In 1975, there was nearly one divorce for every two marriages. Since that time, divorce has increased. What effects has this had on personal and social development of American children?

Obviously, it is necessary to understand a particular situation before the effects of divorce or separation per se can be understood. Research shows that divorce need not necessarily cause serious emotional problems. Children of divorce generally are not more disturbed than their counterparts coming from intact two-parent families. However, the period of divorce can produce many types of stress for all family members. In some situations, like Peggy's, behavioral manifestations may not occur until well after the divorce has taken place. The children's age at the time of divorce seems to be correlated with ease of adjustment. Preschool children are generally less affected than children who are older (Landis, 1960).

In addition to the increasing number of American families headed by one parent as a result of divorce, the 1970s brought with them an increasing number of unmarried teenaged mothers, many of them still in school. Problems frequently abound in the relationships between these mothers and their children. Young mothers report ambivalence in their feelings toward their babies and tend to exhibit insecure, inconsistent maternal behaviors. The results often lead to problem behaviors that are reflected in these children once they enter school themselves (Gibson, 1978; Williams, 1974).

Preschool Programs Around the World

The design of a preschool program will reflect the child-rearing patterns of the particular society. For example, as soon as infants and toddlers are enrolled in Soviet preschools, they are exposed to the responsibilities of collective living and collective stimulation.

Learning to become self-reliant is emphasized. By the time the children have reached the age of 18 months, they are expected to have completed toilet training and to be learning how to dress themselves. In time, the teacher ceases to play an active role in leading the group, and the children supervise themselves in much of their activity. According to many researchers (Bronfenbrenner, 1970, 1977; Gibson and Vinogradoff, in press), the effect of this system has been generally desirable, due to the amount of consistent warm attention given youngsters. Soviet youngsters, especially those in elementary school, do, indeed, exhibit behavior that we normally consider happy and honest; they exhibit few behaviors normally associated with emotional problems.

In the People's Republic of China, although day-care staffs toilet-train, bathe, and teach children their basic skills, mothers are allowed time off from work to nurse their babies, and youngsters spend evenings and weekends with their families. But these early experiences in the basics of group living teach children the prime importance of peer approval, which will influence them throughout their lives (Alston, 1975).

Communal child-rearing programs are not limited to socialist societies; they exist in Western societies as well. The goal of Swedish day-care programs is the development of open expression, individuality, and freedom from repression. They avoid excessive prohibition and supervision, so as to nurture natural curiosity (Passantino, 1971).

America has generally not kept pace with these other nations in the provision of day-care services. Educators as well as laymen are now recognizing the need for greatly expanded preschool facilities, but there are at present too few day-care centers to meet the growing demand. The increasing proportion of working mothers who need day care for their children has made the situation acute. Facilities for infants and toddlers are in particular need, since many states have laws that do not permit their licensed centers to accept children at such early ages.

A report by M.D. Keyserling, *Windows on Day Care* (1972), summarized the results of a study into the extent and quality of the existing day-care facilities in the United States. The report noted that approximately 6 million American children under age 6 have mothers who work. The quality of our nation's day-care centers was found to vary considerably. Only 25 percent offered what was described in the report as superior quality "developmental care." Five years later, the noted psychologist Urie Bronfenbrenner (1977) reported that substitute care for children, regardless of its form—nursery school, group day care, family care, or just a warm body to babysit—fell far short of need.

A day care center in Vietnam teaches preschoolers important skills for socialization and adaptation to later life.

As our society becomes more complex, it becomes more difficult for the family, particularly the nuclear family, to teach a child everything that is necessary for adjustment. The school must thus assume a major role. For families of children under the age of 6 in which there is only one parent in the household or in which both parents work, the preschool becomes the first outside teacher of the child.

The teaching of personal and social development, begun in the preschool years, continues in the school years. Educators generally recognize that the schools' responsibility is more than the teaching of specific subjects; part of their job is to educate children in character and morals as well. However, because the ethical standards of our society are complex, confused, and extremely relative, even if a teacher presents the concepts of right and wrong unambiguously, there is no guarantee that the students' actual behavior will reflect those standards.

Does knowledge of right and wrong in fact produce moral behavior? Hartshorne and May's (1930) character education inquiry was a classic study designed to answer this question. Its goal was to measure the correlation between children's level of moral consciousness and their behavior. First, Hartshorne and May described a situation and asked the children what they would do if it were to occur—for example, what would they do if a fight broke out on the playground? Next, they placed the children in a test situation that would allow them to cheat, in order to see if there was a correlation between social (moral) perceptions and the incidence of cheating. In essence, they asked: If children have high moral consciousness, are there still situations in which they will display immoral behavior, such as cheating? The results showed that there was no correlation between the children's knowledge of right and wrong and cheating, nor between either age or sex and cheating, although children from higher socioeconomic backgrounds and those with higher IQs did tend to cheat less.

Value teaching in our schools stresses the trait of obedience, which, in many ways, is necessary for social cohesion and functioning. Children are taught to obey the rules proclaimed by parents, teachers, or government. But terrible crimes and great injustices have been committed in the name of obedience. The Nazis were "obeying orders" when they killed millions of Jews in concentration camps. How do we explain this? Is obedience always right? Or should character training provide room for conflicts between obedience and other values in certain situations? Clearly, a teacher who is overly concerned with obedience training for its own sake can do damage to a child's moral development. Being blindly obedient means not having to take responsibility for one's own actions. An individual who is blindly obedient may be blind to humanity as well.

Aspects of the environment other than the school also have strong effects on a child's personal and social development. Among these are two examples we discuss here—peers and television.

The peer group It is generally acknowledged that the child's peer group contributes to his or her personality and social development. Two reasons exist for the importance of peer groups in our society. First, parents today are spending significantly less time interacting with their children than parents of the previous generation did (Gibson, Wurst and Cannonito, in preparation; Wurst, 1978). Second, there is an increasing tendency among people of all ages in our country to spend a greater proportion of their time in the company of their peers.

Peer interaction during the preschool years consists primarily of what we call *play*. **Parallel play,** in which children perform the same activities at the same time, aware of one another and, at the same time, independent of one another, is the first stage. Later, but still during preschool years, **imitation** and **role play** begin. Preschool children in the Soviet Union use role play to act out common situations they might expect to encounter in their everyday lives, and American children, when they play house, for example, do the same thing. Role play contributes to socialization by providing children with an opportunity to act out and study their relationships to other people.

Peer play among preschoolers may also involve **model building,** which is most prominent between ages 4 and 8. Children incorporate toys, costumes, and other props into their play to make it more realistic and meaningful. This imaginative aspect of model play can be a useful outlet for self-expression. According to some researchers, model play may also help children to establish and reaffirm their self-images. Children are, in effect, rehearsing for particular roles they may actually assume later on in life. In addition, model play aids the child in developing a system of values and morals, including a basic sense of what is right and wrong.

Play is a very individual activity, but it reflects the attitudes and values characteristic of a particular culture. Although play in the general sense is a universal phenomenon, the specific activities that children select for their play tend to vary among cultures.

At what age does peer-group influence begin to assert itself? According to Bowerman and Kinch (1959), children start to shift their attention from their parents to their peers at about age 12. Hamm and Hoving (1969), on the other hand, indicate that children are strongly influenced by their peers as early as age 7. The tendency to lean on the peer group gradually increases toward adolescence. At this period, teachers see peers exhibiting tremendous control in all group interactions in classroom situations. When tasks are clear, children increasingly stand on their own two feet as they get older, even when their peers disagree with them. But, when tasks are confusing, children are more apt to do whatever they see their peers doing (Hoving, Hamm, and Galvin, 1969). Thus, although peer-group conformity seems to depend on the child's age (Costanzo and Shaw, 1966), it also depends on the type of task at hand.

Many researchers have pointed out that American adolescents must confront a complex social world in which they are largely segregated from adults who might guide them (see, for example, Newman, 1976). In the face of such a confusing array of alternatives, conformity to the social rules of the peer group isn't surprising. Adolescents, deeply concerned with establishing their own identities and achieving a high place in the high school pecking order, emulate group members who seem to be the most popular and successful. Effective communication with teenagers thus depends on an understanding of the value system of the peer group and the in-group/out-group structure that reflects it (Newman and Newman, 1976).

According to Ausubel (1954), the adolescent peer group performs three critical functions. First, it gives or denies individuals status in their own right—that is, they are no longer identified by the status they obtain from their parents. Second, the peer group has the potential for letting an adolescent know that he or she is important. Third, the peer group can provide a useful anchor and source of comfort during a difficult and troublesome period in which most adolescents share similar problems and feel misunderstood by older people.

The relationship between peer-group influence, on the one hand, and parental and teacher influence, on the other, also has a considerable impact on adolescents. School teachers have greater influence on adolescents, particularly in their value development, when they display a clear and sincere interest in them (Newman, 1976). Generally, adolescents tend to choose as friends those people who have the same basic attitudes and values as their parents, though perhaps in a somewhat more liberal form. When parental or teacher attitudes and those of the peer group conflict, however, the latter often win out. Reiss (1968) found that adolescents' attitudes about sex resemble those of their friends more than those of their parents. On the other hand, adolescents are likely to trust and be guided by their parents with regard to decisions about education and a career (McCandless, 1970). Obviously, peer-group influence gradually declines as adolescents grow into young adults, leaving old friends behind and venturing out on their own into new experiences.

Television, imitation, and identification Without doubt, one of the most potent influences on socialization is television. TV predominates among the mass media available to young children. American preschool children watch television for an average of 54 hours a week—

more time than they spend in any other activity except sleep (Brozan, 1975). This means that the average 3-year-old will watch more than 2,800 hours of television, almost the equivalent of 4 months, 24 hours a day—all in one short year of life. Although children tend to spend less and less time in front of the TV until they reach the end of adolescence, an enormous number of hours is still spent in front of the picture tube.

Television is so popular among American children that parents, other adults, and even peers may be given second priority to a favorite television program. Psychologists and laymen alike question the effects of this huge amount of television viewing on the part of impressionable children, particularly in light of the increasingly violent nature of our society. An analysis of the content of prime-time commercial television programs in the late 1960s showed that physical violence occured in 80 percent of the programs, with an average of five violent episodes every hour. Cartoons had an even greater proportion of violence—25 episodes per hour (Gerbner, 1972).

The relationship between violence depicted on television and the behavior and values of children is an area much studied today. An attempt to determine what effects violence on television has on children's behavior was made in an experiment (Friedrich and Stein, 1973) in which nursery school children were shown one of three types of television programs: aggressive cartoons; prosocial programs providing examples of positive, nonaggressive behavior; and neutral films. The children viewed these programs over a four-week period. In order to evaluate the effect the experience had on the children, they were observed in free play before, during, and after their exposure to the programs. The results showed that the children exposed to the violent television programs tended to increase their aggressive behavior. Much of this increased aggression was interpersonal in nature, indicating that the children did not simply imitate what they had seen; rather, they generalized their aggression to fighting among themselves. The children exposed to the prosocial programs, on the other hand, increased their cooperation and exhibited other positive behaviors, again on an interpersonal basis.

A six-year investigation of 1,565 adolescent boys in London provided similar and perhaps more frightening information: Boys who were shown to be habitual watchers of violent TV programs tended to commit significantly more violent acts than those who did not. A few of the more serious acts committed and described by the boys were "I deliberately dropped a lighted match into a shopper's bag"; "I busted the telephone in a telephone box"; "I kicked a boy in the crotch as hard as I could" and "I took a hammer to a car and laid into it" (Muson, 1978).

Television, of course, is not the only source of violence in a child's environment. Children are surrounded by other models of aggressive behavior. The effects of continued exposure to violence on the socialization of children have been interpreted in terms of imitation (Bandura, 1969). In Bandura's experiments, preschool children were brought individually into a playroom where another person (either another child or an adult model) was already engaged actively in aggressive play. As the children entered the room, they saw the model hitting dolls, throwing and breaking objects in the room, and employing aggressive language. Later, the children were brought into another room and allowed to play freely with any of the toys there. Some of the toys resembled those they had seen being used previously in an aggressive manner. In this second situation, however, no one was present to influence the children. Bandura found that the play of the children in this part of the experiment matched the aggressive behavior of the model they had watched earlier. Presumably, these children learned aggression through imitating the behavior model. It can be assumed that these same children will later internalize their behavior so that they will respond in similar ways in other situations. Then imitation will have changed to identification.

Dealing with Social Behaviors Generated by Environmental Interaction

We now shift our attention from the factors influencing the socialization process to the children themselves and to the social behavior they exhibit as they develop.

Because our society is a competitive one, it is considered particularly important that children develop such qualities as initiative, independence, and properly channeled aggression. Furthermore, in our culture, adaptation to society is based more on achieved status (characteristics developed by the individual, such as talents, skills, and a likable personality) than on ascribed status (characteristics predetermined at birth, such as sex, race, and religion). Consequently, children brought up in the United States are often encouraged to develop self-reliance and to become independent and assertive. Even so, the model child must also learn to exercise self-control and restraint. Thus, a delicate balance exists between the popular ideal of developing one's potential and accepting and conforming to one's position in the social structure.

Dealing with dependency and attachment Two types of behavior that psychologists are interested in in young children are dependency and attachment. An **attachment** is a durable tie of affection oriented toward one particular person and is seen in such behaviors as clinging, following, smiling, and crying. **Dependency,** on the other hand, consists of such behaviors as seeking help, attention, and approval from another person.

Neither type of behavior necessarily indicates helplessness. The child who is dependent may be attempting to secure attention, express affection, and obtain assistance through his or her behavior. The ways in which dependency is expressed vary with the child's age. Chronic and persistent crying episodes are common in infants, but they are a sign of a possible problem in preschool children. Also, as children get older, dependency becomes two-sided; that is, children give as well as receive. As their world grows beyond the environment of their homes, their dependency broadens to include people other than family—teachers and peers, for example. When they reach adolescence, their dependency on peers develops greater importance than at any other time in their lives.

We can never separate behavior from the variables determining it. Thus, when we see a high level of childhood dependency, we must recognize that it often reflects the attitudes and behavior patterns of the parents, particularly the mother. Specifically, dependency tends to be greatest among children with permissive, indulgent parents whose use of discipline is love-oriented, but who give little firm direction (Smart and Smart, 1972).

Developing trust   Another type of behavior that may be manifested early in life, which is probably learned in the first year or two, is *trust*. Overprotective parents interfere with the normal development of trust in their youngsters. First, overprotection seems to imply that the parents think the child is incompetent and gives children reason not to trust themselves. Second, children whose parents' overprotection is inconsistent come to mistrust their environment. Physical and emotional abuse also cause a lack of trust, as can the early loss of a parent through death or divorce.

Too much trust on a child's part can be dangerous. Children need a degree of trust that is realistic and will enable them to cope with an unpredictable world. For example, most children are taught not to accept gifts and rides from strangers. On the other hand, children whose parents raise them to fear everything will be as severely damaged as those who are taught to blindly trust everyone and everything. To prepare their children to deal realistically with potential dangers in the environment, parents should teach them not only what to avoid but also what to do if danger does occur. But it is only through their own experiences that children will learn that there are many people in their environments they can count on, not least of all themselves.

Developing altruism and cooperation   Kindly, unselfish behavior that has no apparent reward other than the intrinsic one of feeling good is what we call *altruism*. Children do not exhibit this trait until they have developed some ability to appreciate the attitudes, feelings, and experiences of other people. Thus, truly altruistic behavior is rarely seen in preschool children. However, its foundations are often laid early in life.

Cooperation, like altruism, is an important component of moral development, but, unlike altruism, it begins much earlier in life, often in infancy. For example, infants learn to "help hold" their own bottles at an early age. Toddlers on Israeli kibbutzim learn to cooperate and share in games and play. In all societies, children who wish to play with their peers must cooperate by conforming to the rules of the group.

Teachers can teach both of these behaviors by providing children with appropriate models, opportunities to practice altruistic behavior, and rewards, such as praise, when the altruistic behavior occurs (Hartup, 1970; Hoffman, 1970; Rosenham, 1969).

Dealing with anger and aggression Two behavioral traits with important consequences for later development are anger and aggression. *Anger* is a feeling of distress that surfaces when individuals are restrained or blocked in their effort to accomplish something. Toddlers and preschool children at first have little control over their anger and typically display it by crying, kicking, and throwing things. **Aggression** is a way to cope with anger by increasing power or status. At certain times, anger can be productive and useful, but at other times it is destructive and dangerous. By the time children reach the middle school years, they are expected to know how to control their anger.

Learning the necessary controls of both anger and aggression is an important aspect of growing up. Care-givers and teachers can aid a child in learning such controls if they follow certain guidelines. For example, providing basic needs like food and rest on a regular but flexible routine can keep a child's distress from becoming overwhelming. Children's calls for assistance should be answered promptly. As children get older, their opportunities for decision-making and doing things on their own should be increased. Finally, when a child does exhibit hostile aggression, care-givers or teachers should quickly express disapproval and insist that the behavior be stopped.

Handling jealousy and rivalry Jealousy and rivalry are feelings of anger based on the belief that someone else is receiving the love, attention, or success we would like for ourselves. A child will often experience feelings of jealousy when a new baby in the family receives a good part of the attention formerly reserved for the older child. Behavior patterns in this case vary. Young children might inform their mother that she should get rid of the baby, and when she doesn't, they might start crying or lash out physically, hitting the baby or the mother. Older children may exhibit other, equally destructive behaviors.

This special form of jealousy is called *sibling rivalry*. The older child must now compete with the new baby for the parents' time.

Likewise, the baby, as it grows up, may come to feel resentful that he or she is not given all the privileges accorded the older child.

Through the school years, jealousies and rivalries develop based on many other factors such as the affection of peers. Children who are sufficiently mature learn to control these emotional reactions and seek approval through socially acceptable ways.

Helping children cope with fear Parents and educators should understand that no child is free from fears. Recognition of a child's fears will better equip the care-givers to assist the child in learning how to cope with them.

Different types of fears appear at different stages of development. Infants' fears are basic ones related to their needs for food and protection. Gradually, most infants learn that these fears are groundless and proceed to develop new ones. They become increasingly attached to their mothers and are afraid of losing them. At the same time, they become very fearful of strangers and unfamiliar situations. A child of preschool age who has positive experiences with new situations becomes better able to cope with them (another beneficial result of early placement in day care).

Many childhood fears emerge as the result of conditioning and modeling (which we discuss at length in later chapters). For example, preschool children in America most commonly fear animals and the dark and may develop a fear of dogs simply by hearing their parents talking about a child who was bitten by a dog. Coincidence accounts in only small measure for the fact that children's fears parallel those of their parents. Constant exposure to parental apprehensiveness in certain situations affects the child. Violent episodes on television and the child's own exploration and discoveries can lead to fears as well.

Many parents and teachers attempt to help fearful children by reasoning with them or by showing them that no harm will come to them. Sometimes this works, though forcing children to encounter things they fear—by turning out the night light, for example—is almost always counterproductive. So is telling children that their fears are "silly," that they are "afraid of nothing, " or are "stupid" for not listening to rational explanations. The world is a very mysterious and unpredictable place to children, and most children express their insecurity as fear. A very good way teachers can help children of all ages to cope with fears and insecurity is to have an open class discussion about fears. The children should all be encouraged to talk about their fears, or even to act them out. The teacher might discuss coping techniques with the class, though often simply knowing that he or she is not the only person in the world who is afraid can do much to calm a fearful child.

Also, because children's most desperate fear involves being abandoned by their parents, separation from people to whom children are attached should be done gradually. When children are ill, their fears may magnify; therefore, loved ones should be available to provide sick children with comfort and reassurance.

Teaching sex-role identification The way in which children learn to feel and act the role of one sex or the other is known as **sex-role identification.** Children normally start to learn sex-appropriate behavior very early in life. Two things contribute to this process: rewards that parents and later teachers provide, and the processes of imitation and modeling discussed earlier. We see these rewards all around us. Boys are praised for learning how to throw a ball and frowned on for crying; girls are applauded for playing house and punished for punching someone. Children are most likely to imitate a model who appears to be nurturant and/or has power or status. For toddlers, this figure is most apt to be the mother, but, as the child gets older, the father becomes an influential model, too.

In our society, masculinity and femininity are associated with one's degree of aggressive behavior. Bronfenbrenner (1961) points out that parents are generally more indulgent with girls and less permissive with boys. This is also true in the relationship between teachers and boys and girls. Starting as early as 18 months, boys are expected to be and, in fact, are more aggressive than girls of the same age (Maccoby, 1974). The difference cuts across many behavioral situations—in free play as well as in the laboratory, in verbal aggression as well as in physical aggression.

Compliance, too, is generally sex-typed in American children. Boys are expected to have, and indeed do have, a greater tendency than girls to resist giving in to immediate demands. Usually, boys need greater pressure to obey orders than is necessary for girls (Maccoby, 1974).

In the past, when children did not exhibit behavior considered appropriate for their sex, they were looked on as deviant or immature. This view transcends what is learned in the family and is the result of cultural stereotypes. Until recently, sex-role stereotypes were generally accepted. What was inside or outside the boundaries was clearly defined. Today, however, our views are broadening. An overall raising of our consciousness has caused us to reevaluate our traditional notions about sex-typed behavior. The old stereotypes are giving way to new ideas of what is appropriate. Die-hard views toward sex differences in clothing, hobbies, and occupational choices are being modified. Many children today are brought up in an environment of what we might call unisexuality. For example, girls as well as boys of all ages wear jeans, and if a girl prefers a truck to a doll, or a boy finds a stove more interesting than a football, this behavior is no longer regarded as peculiar (Margolin, 1974).

Teachers and parents have both been concerned with developing ways to enhance moral growth. Just as Peggy's parents and her counselor are concerned with her use of marijuana and possibly other more dangerous drugs, other parents and other counselors are concerned with other problems among schoolchildren, such as delinquency and truancy.

Both Piaget and Kohlberg have many points to make concerning the development of moral maturity and how it can be taught. For example, both theorists assume that during each stage of development toward moral maturity the individual interacts with his or her environment. Applying their theories to formal education requires the introduction of educational experiences that reflect real-life moral issues of direct concern to students as members of society, either as individuals or as a group. A social science or literature course seen in this way should be designed to develop both logical and moral thought.

Using a Stage Approach to Teach the Development of Values

According to stage theorists, such experiences must be matched to the students' present stage of moral and intellectual development. A teacher should never presuppose a student's capabilities for reflective or critical thinking and for problem-solving. The concepts of matching and timing enter here as they do in cognitive development. All too often, parents and teachers alternate between abstractions that children cannot comprehend and explanations that underestimate their true grasp of a situation.

According to Kohlberg, associating with people whose moral judgments reflect a higher stage in the developmental sequence causes the child to experience cognitive conflict. This conflict stimulates introspection and results in the child's achieving a more advanced stage. To provide the opportunity for this to take place, the teacher must make time for group discussion and clarify advanced levels of moral reasoning without resorting to preaching (Kohlberg, 1971). Students must be given the opportunity to stretch their own moral capacities, to experiment through interaction with others, without having arbitrary standards that reflect the teacher's personal moral biases imposed on them.

Formal character education classes in which teachers tell students how to act responsibly do not appear to have a demonstrable effect on children's moral conduct. For example, Peggy's counselor realized that Peggy's hostility toward her parents and probably everyone else in authority would have made her unresponsive to a lecture on the impropriety of her behavior. Peggy's problem involved understanding the changes and urges that she was going through at age 13. It dealt also with her inability to discuss these matters with her parents, who were not only busy and usually tired, but who also had been involved for a long time with their own problems related to their marriage and divorce.

The problems of divorce and the fear of growing up confront many adolescents today, who, like Peggy, frequently seek refuge in "acting-out" behaviors. Many middle and high schools have developed programs to deal with the problem. One such program, Contemporary Family Life, a twelve-week course that begins with students pretending to get married and ends with them pretending to get divorced, was begun at the Parkway High School in Portland, Oregon, about ten years ago. It achieved such success at helping adolescents that it was described in *Time* ("Divorce course," 1974). Students taking the course experienced simulations of the social, economic, and moral problems of real married life—they searched for an apartment, looked for a job, prepared a budget, "had" a baby, bought a house, and saw a lawyer for a divorce. Guests from the community—insurance agents, realtors, bankers, clergymen, marriage counselors, and lawyers—frequently met with the class. Issues pertaining to the development of identity were discussed personally and openly. Although the insights that students gained were often disillusioning ("and they lived happily ever after" isn't always the case in real life), one thing was certain—these students learned. Curriculum designs like this demonstrate the excitement of intelligently planned reality orientation.

Using an Environmental Approach to Increase Self-Esteem and Decrease Alienation

Schools influence self-esteem by providing variables that contribute to or diminish a student's feeling of self-worth. In school, each child has many opportunities to see how he or she measures up against others in terms of intelligence, physical skill, and popularity. Although such opportunities can contribute to the development of self-esteem, too much emphasis placed on grades and conformity and the suppression of individual creativity can have the opposite effect.

Teachers can help a child to develop self-esteem in several ways. They can set expectations that are appropriate for the age level and intellectual functioning of each of their students. They can stress positive activities and play down negative ones. They can also convey the feeling that they anticipate success. It is especially important for teachers to act in a rewarding, unpunitive, and consistent manner.

Often, understanding the stage of development through which a child is passing is helpful in planning a proper social environment for learning. For example, when teachers are dealing with adolescents, they should make a special effort to understand the point of view of this age group (Felker, 1974). The adolescent needs opportunities to act independently but, at the same time, he or she needs to feel a sense of belonging. A student who misbehaves in class may have selected a not very constructive way to act independently. Teachers

American students are encouraged to develop skills that make them self-reliant, independent, and assertive, as well as help them in their socialization.

David R. Frazier, Photo Researchers, Inc.

should not see such misbehavior as a threat to their authority and punish the student because of it. Rather, the teacher should try to grasp the student's need and respond as he or she would to another adult. Teachers can also help adolescents by explaining what is happening to them physically, socially, and emotionally at this often confusing period in their development. Early-maturing girls and late-maturing boys need reassurance that there is nothing wrong with them. Probably most important, teachers should point out that there is nothing wrong with having conflicts, frustrations, and other emotional difficulties. Such feelings are not part of adolescence alone; they occur throughout life. Dialogue with young people should emerge from the day-to-day encounters in the classroom, if and when the students express a need to discuss the things that are troubling them. Furthermore, such dialogue must come from a teacher's geniune interest; all children have an acute ability to detect phoniness, but adolescents are particularly sensitive to insincerity and are mistrustful of adults.

Bronfenbrenner (1972), who sees most American children as neglected, has made a number of suggestions that involve utilizing all our social institutions as a support system for them. For younger children, his recommendations include modifying work schedules so that parents will have more free time to interact with their children and establishing day-care centers that provide adequate stimulation, actively involve parents, and reach out into the home and community.

Bronfenbrenner suggests that a major job of the day-care centers should be to teach children what the world is like outside of their own small communities by using adult models of all ages and occupations.

The experiences that children have in school should help them to develop a sense of responsibility and self-esteem. According to many psychologists like Bronfenbrenner, American education, with its almost exclusive emphasis on achievement in academic subjects, seems peculiarly one-sided in comparison with other educational systems. Not only do American schools pay little attention to developing children's character; they regard the classroom as somehow sacred, as the only place where learning can take place, which virtually eliminates the opportunity for interaction among the school, home, and community. This segregation of the school from the rest of society is one of the factors contributing to the sense of alienation felt by so many students. As one remedy for this problem, Bronfenbrenner suggests developing neighborhood and family centers that are open to everyone—parents, teachers, children, and the rest of the community as well—where people of all ages can meet and establish a dialogue through which they may hear and understand viewpoints other than their own. Bronfenbrenner suggests reacquainting schoolchildren with the adult world by teaching them about the field of work. He has described a Soviet program in which a series of visits was arranged between groups of adults (working together in a shop, office, or factory) and groups of children, whom they "adopted." This brought the generations together: The adults had the opportunity to see the kinds of things children were doing, and the children became familiar with how and where adults made their living.

Bronfenbrenner strongly urges that we involve children in genuine responsibilities, not "make-work." They should be given tasks that have meaningful means and ends and that involve independent thinking and decision-making. Children do not automatically acquire good judgment when they graduate from high school; it is like a muscle that needs early and frequent exercise. It is therefore important to integrate the school into the broader social realities.

summary

1. Understanding the process of development is an important part of understanding and predicting children's behavior.

2. Some developmental changes are strictly biological; others occur as a result of biological and environmental influences. The type of development that occurs independent of the environment is called maturation.

3. Physical and motor development is particularly important to school-age children. American children have been growing bigger and going through puberty earlier than other cultures. Today's middle schools have been designed to help children cope with the stresses of early adolescence.

4. Sigmund Freud was the first to describe development in terms of stages, and his work in describing personality development has been extremely influential, even though his views are more rigid about these stages than those of many other developmental psychologists.

5. Erik Erikson divides personality development into eight stages, each of which involves a crisis that has to be resolved before the next stage can be attained. The major task of the early school years involves developing industry and coping with feelings of inferiority. The major task of adolescence is the development of identity and the acceptance of responsibility for its future growth. Adolescents who cannot successfully resolve the identity crisis experience identity diffusion.

6. Jean Piaget has described stages in the development of morality that parallel his stages of cognitive development. Younger children tend to evaluate behavior in terms of its consequences, while older children take motives and intentions into account.

7. Lawrence Kohlberg's approach to value development involves three levels, each of which is composed of two stages. As children grow up, they pass from a premoral stage, in which they interpret actions on the basis of their consequences, to a blind repetition of stereotyped social standards, to the development of a more personal and consistent system of values.

8. Environmentalists insist that such descriptions of development are inadequate because they do not take into account the environment within which that development takes place.

9. Socialization is the process by which a culture is transmitted from one generation to another. Agents of socialization include parents, peers, teachers, and the media. The process of socialization involves the imitation of a model's behavior and the identification (or internalization) of that model's standards.

10. The family has traditionally been the first and primary agent of socialization for American children. In the past, the family was an extended family, but recent years have seen the dominance of the nuclear family and the emergence of the single-parent family.

11. Advantages of the extended family or communal approach to child-rearing include more attention for the child, increased security due to the formation of multiple attachments, and greater stimulation.

12. The most important quality in a care-giver is consistency. The care-giver should not be merely available to the child; he or she should always be responsive and supportive. American mothers do not typically spend as much time with their children as mothers in other cultures do. Divorce, economic necessity, and temporary relief from parental responsibilities have motivated many women to seek day-care services for their pre-school-age children.

13. Children's levels of self-esteem depend on how their care-givers feel about themselves as well as how they react to the children.

14. Close physical contact with a mother or mother-substitute is an important factor in children's social and emotional development. Increased rates of divorce and teenage pregnancies have resulted in a growing number of single-parent families. Children deprived of parents through divorce are not necessarily more disturbed than children from intact families. The youth and immaturity of adolescent mothers often leads to problems for their children.

15. The child's first outside teacher is generally the school, which bears a responsibility to educate the child morally as well as academically. Unfortunately, value teaching in our schools sometimes stresses obedience rather than independent thinking.

16. Peer groups have increased their influence on children as parents have come to spend less time interacting with their youngsters. Peer play can be broken down into several types. In parallel play, children do the same things but don't interact. Imitative play and role play allow children the opportunity to act out adult roles. Model building involves the use of props to make play more realistic and meaningful.

17. Children begin to rely heavily on their peers at about age 12. Peer conformity, which depends on the child's age and on the type of task at hand, is a common feature of adolescent behavior.

18. Young children spend a great deal of time watching television, and many studies have found a relationship between television and aggression.

19. Social behaviors generated by environmental interaction include dependency, attachment, trust, altruism and cooperation, anger and aggression, jealousy and rivalry, fear, and sex-role identification.

20. Teachers who understand the stage approach can encourage moral development by matching classroom experiences to a child's current level (following Piaget) or by exposing children to models whose judgments reflect a slightly higher stage (following Kohlberg). Simply telling children about right and wrong has a negligible effect on value development.

21. Setting appropriate standards, emphasizing positive achievements, and anticipating success are all things teachers can do to help their students to develop self-esteem. Adolescents particularly need the sincere interest of their teachers. Urie Bronfenbrenner has suggested that integration with the larger community would greatly improve the school's effectiveness in moral education.

for students who want to read further

BRONFENBRENNER, U. *The Worlds of Childhood.* New York: Pocket Books, 1973. This short text compares and contrasts two methods of raising children in two very different societies: the United States and the Soviet Union. Problems related to social development in America are discussed extensively, and Bronfenbrenner provides some provocative solutions.

CLARKE-STEWART, A. *Child Care in the Family.* New York: Academic Press, 1977. Clarke-Stewart's book is a review of research on the effects of different types of early environment on the development of young children. The author provides advice on a variety of useful early environments that supply adequate psychological development as well as supervision.

COOPERSMITH, S., AND FELDMAN, R. "Fostering a positive self-concept and high self-esteem in the classroom." In R. Coop and K. White (Eds.), *Psychological Concepts in the Classroom.* New York: Harper & Row, 1974. This article discusses methods that teachers and parents can use to encourage self-esteem in children.

2

LANGUAGE
AND
COGNITIVE
DEVELOPMENT

Tommy Sanchez:
A Second Grader Who Wouldn't Speak in Class

Tommy Sanchez, an 8-year-old Chicano child, refused to speak in class. Tommy spoke English well, unlike many of the other Chicano youngsters coming from his area of the city. He had been tested by an audiologist who had reported that his hearing was excellent. The school psychologist found Tommy's intelligence to be normal and reported no emotional problems. Tommy's second-grade teacher asked the first-grade teacher what she remembered of Tommy's behavior the previous year. The first-grade teacher was surprised. "Why, I hardly remember Tommy at all. He was a quiet boy—almost never talked in class. He did all right on his written work, though. I gave him mostly Cs—good for a Chicano kid—and I assumed everything was okay."

The school social worker, Mr Thorpe, went to Tommy's home. He spoke with Mr. and Mrs. Sanchez in Spanish (Tommy was the only family member who was fluent in English). Mrs. Sanchez told Mr. Thorpe that their next-door neighbor, a "native-born American," had been Tommy's babysitter when he was very small and had spoken English to him, and that Tommy had picked up the language easily before he was even 3 years old. Mr. and Mrs. Sanchez expected Tommy to do well in school. Tommy enjoyed studying, and they thought their son might grow up to be an important man one day. "Why have you come, Mr. Thorpe?" Mrs. Sanchez spoke anxiously. "Tommy's a good boy, isn't he?"

"Mr. Thorpe's worried because I won't talk in class, Mama," Tommy said. "But I do all my homework. And I get most of it right. What difference does it make?" He paused and looked up at the social worker. "I hate to talk English in front of the other kids. I understand what they're saying, and I know what I'm reading. But when I talk, it sounds different from when they talk. Sometimes I can't think of the right word to use, and they make fun of me."

Mr. Thorpe answered, "You're learning much less than you would if you let your teacher know what you're doing, and ask questions when you don't understand. You need to be able to communicate if you want to learn the things you've come to school to learn. You need to talk to work out many problems." Mr. Thorpe pointed out that understanding spoken and written English is crucial to learning, but that communicating one's own thoughts orally is equally important. He suggested to Tommy that, even though Tommy had passed the language exam in English, he should join an English conversation class to help overcome his shyness in speaking.

Language, thinking, and understanding are often referred to as the **cognitive processes.** We can see a clear relationship between thinking and understanding. But is there a connection between thought and speech? Is Mr. Thorpe right? Or can Tommy learn to think and solve problems without learning the language skills necessary for social interaction? Because language is our basic medium of communication, it is impossible to talk about thinking and problem-solving without discussing verbal ability and speech. Theorists have argued for years, however, about the specific way in which these are related.

An important theory about the relationship between language and cognitive development is that of Jean Piaget, the influential Swiss researcher. According to Piaget, cognitive development proceeds on its own, in a series of discreet stages that increase in complexity. The development of thinking is followed by, or, at least reflected in, children's language. Piaget thus assumes that cognitive growth is the necessary prerequisite for the development of language skills.

Piaget was mainly interested in the functions of language and thinking and the manner in which they affect the development of children. In his studies of the spontaneous speech of kindergarten children, he determined that they exhibit two major classes of utterances: **egocentric speech** (undirected speech, not aimed at others for the purposes of communication) and **socialized speech** (speech directed toward communication). Piaget further hypothesized that egocentric speech always precedes socialized speech (Piaget and Inhelder, 1969). In other words, we learn to talk to ourselves before we talk to other people.

A different approach to the relationship between language and cognitive development was taken by John B. Watson (1913). Watson, the so-called father of American behaviorist psychology, said that "thought processes are really motor habits in the larynx." Thus, for Watson, thought and speech were one and the same; when we think, we are in fact talking to ourselves.

Lev Vygotsky (1934, 1962) has stated that the development of speech causes the development of cognition. According to Vygotsky, if you haven't learned to talk, you haven't learned to think either. The implications of this theory are important to teachers: If we haven't learned a word or words for a concept, then we can't think about it. In this context, language teaching becomes extraordinarily important for a boy like Tommy, who may not have developed as extensive a speaking vocabulary as others around him.

For Vygotsky, cognition and the development of language are intertwined from the very beginning. All new language development is related in some way to the development of new thinking processes. Vygotsky believes that egocentric or undirected speech is not simply related to an early developmental stage of thinking, as Piaget describes it. Rather, according to Vygotsky, the speech of very young children is private speech—a tool that they use to help them to direct their own cognitive processes, not to practice communicating with others.

understanding language development

Just as there are different approaches to interpreting the personal and social development of children, there are different approaches to interpreting the development of verbal ability. Developmental-stage theorists, such as Piaget, explain language development in terms of a series of stages. Environmental theorists, such as Vygotsky and the American behavioral psychologist B. F. Skinner, attribute much greater importance to the effects of learning experiences and the environment.

*Developmental-
Stage Approaches
to Explaining
Language
Development*

Developmental-stage theorists view language development primarily as a function of the cognitive maturity of the child. They point out that similarities occur in the kinds of meanings expressed in children's language at various stages of their development, regardless of the language being learned (Slobin, 1972). For example, the number of different sounds made in a given verbal communication increases with age and stage.

The developmental-stage approach of Jean Piaget   Jean Piaget points out that children's speech parallels their developing interests. As we have discussed, children under 3 years of age tend to use language for private purposes. Early efforts toward communication generally express needs and desires: "Want Mommy!" "Want cookie!" After age 3, children's speech is characterized by descriptions of what they are doing and how they feel about it. Some examples: "Johnny bad boy!"

"Bad doggy eat ice cream." Piaget refers to these more mature utterances as **socialized speech**.

The innate capability approach of Noam Chomsky   Noam Chomsky, the famous linguist, has taken the developmental-stage approach one step further. Chomsky theorizes that language development involves early learning of what he calls **kernel grammar** or elementary grammar. This grammar consists of the main parts of speech and the rules for creating simple sentences. According to Chomsky, children then develop the capability to learn more complex grammatical rules. Using these rules, even young children are able to create an infinite number of sentences from simple ones. Children like Tommy, who learn very early to be bilingual, find this task easier and develop the ability to learn the second language with greater ease than do people who learn a second language when they are older.

In order to explain the infinitely large number of sentences that even young children are able to construct, Chomsky has hypothesized that we are born with the ability to process language, construct language rules, and understand complex speech (Chomsky, 1957).

Environmental psychologists maintain that language, along with most other behaviors, develops first through operant conditioning, a basic form of learning.

Environmental Approaches to Explaining Language Development

The behavioral approach of B. F. Skinner   According to B. F. Skinner, infant vocalizations that happen to sound like adult words first are reinforced (rewarded) selectively by parental attention. Later, Skinner theorizes, the process changes and becomes more complex. Parents and teachers continue to reinforce more complex speech responses, but reinforcement also comes from the child's increasing ability to obtain desired objects through communication.

Other environmental approaches   Some learning theorists who essentially agree with Skinner feel, however, that parental approval and attention are not sufficient to explain the highly complex process of language development. Lovaas, Varni, Koegel, and Lorsch (1977), for example, point out that sensory reinforcement is inherent in verbalization: Children enjoy hearing themselves talk. Learning theorists have also noted the extreme importance of imitating and modeling in language learning (Whitehurst and Merkur, 1977). Children copy and model what they see and hear whether they are rewarded or not. It is well known that children whose parents spend a great deal of time talking with them before they enter school tend to learn more easily and certainly communicate with greater ease than children who have less opportunity in their early years to hear and imitate the language later used in school. It is easier for children to learn a second language when this imitation process is begun at an early age. Thus, children of bilingual parents who hear and practice both languages spoken at home from the time they are infants have an easier time learning the second language than children who, like Tommy, hear only one language at home and later learn another language outside the home.

Jerome Bruner's consideration of language development in the context of daily needs   Another researcher interested in cognitive development, Jerome Bruner (1978), points out that, although the acquisition of language appears miraculous, close observation indicates that children and their earliest teachers (usually their mothers) work together, and that the role of the teacher-mother is crucial. Bruner has suggested that we consider language development in the context of children's everyday needs and activities. For instance, a game of "peek-a-boo," which we regard merely as a cute way to pass the time, can in fact make a significant contribution to the child's development of language. Bruner (1975) calls such interactions *exchange games* and suggests that they are an important part of a child's first mastery of language. Through such games, "young children learn to signal and recognize certain expectancies. . . . And they learn to manipulate features of language that they must later put together in complicated ways" (p. 83).

An example described by Bruner involved Nan, a 9-month-old child. Nan was learning to play an exchange game with her mother,

Exchange games are an important part of a child's first mastery of language.

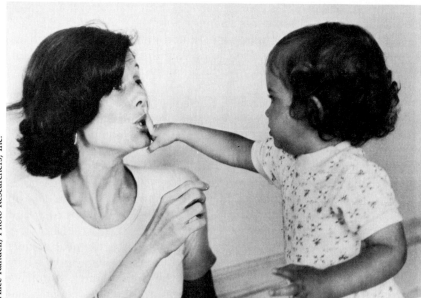

Alice Kandell, Photo Researchers, Inc.

but she had not yet learned the adult language code for giving and receiving. Thus, she said "Kew" (her version of "Thank you") as she handed an object to her mother, although she might not say "Kew" when her mother handed it to her. Later, at 12 months, "Look" replaced "Kew" in the giving phase of the game, and "Kew" moved to its proper position in the receiving phase. According to Bruner, "Nan has used the order of steps in the game to sort out the proper order for the language she uses now in play and will use later to communicate" (p. 83).

---

understanding cognitive development

The development of cognition, the ability to think and understand, has also been examined closely by developmental-stage and environmental theorists.

Piaget's Developmental-Stage Approach to Explaining Cognitive Development

Jean Piaget is probably the single most influential stage theorist concerned with describing how children's thinking and problem-solving change as they get older. According to Piaget, the development of thinking proceeds in a clearly defined, fixed sequence of stages. Each stage is relevant to a specific chronological age. For example, we can expect children aged 7 to 11 to have difficulties conceptualizing certain kinds of problems, such as algebraic equations, unless the teacher has first provided some kind of concrete stimuli. Only when children are older (according to Piaget, 11 or older) can they perform these formal operations without the use of concrete aids. But these abilities do not appear naturally at certain ages. A child will not attain a new level of development until he or she has mastered the tasks of earlier levels; more mature methods of problem solving presuppose success with earlier methods.

Piaget emphasizes the fact that children act on their environment. Thus, experience will affect their movement from lower to higher levels of cognitive development. Environmental stimulation either at home or in the classroom increases the development of the ability to solve problems. A teacher who provides stimulation appropriate to the child's cognitive level helps the child to learn to solve problems at his or her level of thinking and thus provides the child with the means to proceed to the next level.

How cognitive development takes place: Assimilation and accommodation   According to Piaget, cognitive development involves two processes: **assimilation** and **accommodation.** We assimilate when we take in a new stimulus from the environment and respond to it with a behavior we have already used for a familiar, and in some way similar, stimulus. For example, when a little boy encounters an orange for the first time and rolls it like a ball, he is assimilating his experience with balls to the new stimulus. He fits the orange into his concept of "ball" without regard for its important non-ball-like qualities.

We accommodate when we add a new activity to what we already know or when we modify an old behavior. For example, our little boy already knows that a ball rolls; when he learns to bounce it, he has added a new behavior. His concept of ball matures as he adds new information (it bounces) to his preexisting ideas (it is round and it rolls). This new response to a stimulus to which he has been exposed in the past increases the number of reponses the child can make to the old stimulus and later to new and different stimuli as well.

Piaget has stressed that assimilation and accommodation occur only when an environmental stimulus (the ball in our example) is appropriately matched with the particular level of cognitive development attained by the child. Bouncing a ball in front of a newborn, for example, would not increase cognitive development, since the baby could not respond to it. Presenting a series of abstract mathematical problems to kindergarten children who have never before worked with abstractions would be equally inappropriate.

Piaget further states that children's interactions with their environment will be most meaningful to their development only when assimilation and accommodation occur equally and continually. If at any time a teacher or parent ceases to provide new lessons matched to the child's level of understanding, both processes will stop, and the development of the thinking processes will end.

Piaget's stages of cognitive development   Piaget hypothesizes a series of stages through which all children pass as they develop their cognitive abilities (see Table 2–1). The rate at which children complete these stages is dependent on their biological maturation and their experiences in their environment. Some children, of course, will advance faster than others because of differences in both these factors. Thus the chronological ages ascribed to each stage vary somewhat.

Table 2–1   Piaget's Stages of Cognitive Development

AGE	STAGE
Birth–2 years	Sensorimotor
2-7 years	Preoperational
2-4 years	Preconceptual
4-7 years	Intuitive
7–11 years	Concrete operations
11 years on	Formal operations

Each advance to a new stage of cognitive development integrates and transforms the learning of the previous stages.

The earliest stage, which Piaget calls the **sensorimotor stage,** consists of several substages. At this point, children's intellectual development consists largely of action schemas, since they cannot use language yet. During the first month of life, they go through the reflexive stage, in which their innate responses (reaching, grasping, sucking) become efficient. They later begin to perform more and more complex behaviors through a series of circular (repetitive) reactions. First they repeat actions for their own sake; then they repeat actions to watch the results. The coordination of these actions is evident in later means-end behavior, where they use their reponses to achieve a goal, and motivation becomes a factor. Still later (11 to 18 months), children use active trial and error; they also become aware that objects can be hidden and make attempts to find them.

Mental combinations (18 months on) occur when children are able to think before they act, that is, when they can represent to themselves the outcome of their actions before they take them. At this period, they also develop what Piaget calls the object concept; they realize that objects have a permanence and identity of their own, that the objects exist even when they cannot be seen. At this point, children begin to use language, first to imitate and then to represent reality.

The next stage of development, the **preoperational stage,** includes two substages: preconceptual and intuitive thought. In the **preconceptual stage** (ages 2 to 4), stimuli begin to take on symbolic meaning to a child. A little girl, for example, will treat her doll as a real baby. In the **intuitive stage** of intellectual development (about ages 4 to 7), direct perceptions still dominate thought. A child cannot yet understand that a given quantity remains the same regardless of changes in its shape or position in relation to other objects. According to Piaget, children in this stage focus on one quality of an object at a time; a little girl who wants two cookies is satisfied even when she sees her mother break one cookie in half and give her the two halves. At this stage, Piaget says, children have difficulty seeing viewpoints other than their own. They cannot put themselves in someone else's place. Abstract relationships present a problem, yet preoperational children are constructing more complex images and more elaborate concepts. The use of language facilitates this process.

By the next stage of development, the stage of **concrete operations** (about ages 7 to 11), children are in school, where they are expected to pay attention. And they do, or, rather, they can. They are aided in this ability by their development, at this time, of reasoning and logic with respect to concrete objects. A child of this age treats an abstract such as "'God," for example, as a real—that is, concrete—

person. Juliet Lowell (1961) has included these two delightful examples of "concrete abstractions" of 7- to 11-year-olds in her book *Dear Folks:**

Dear Aunt Fannie,

We are riding home in a plane tomorrow. The plane is going to ride very high. I hope we wont hit the cloud God's sitting on and bump him off.

Love,
Babs

Dear Aunt Renee,

We had a nice time flying in the plane back to France. All the way I keep looking out of the window for angels. I did want to see them, they would have looked so pretty floating through the air with their little pink wings. Maybe it was just to windy for them to be out.

Marie

At the concrete operations stage, children begin to develop the concept of quantity based on many dimensions. They are able to differentiate between part and whole, between greater and lesser. They will no longer accept a cookie broken in half as two cookies. They also learn **conservation,** the idea that mass remains constant regardless of its changes in form. At this stage, they finally understand that an amount of clay remains the same whether it is rolled into a ball or smashed flat on the table. Thus, they can think about concrete things in systematic ways, although they cannot yet think abstractly. **Seriation,** which involves the ability to order a series of objects along some dimension, develops at this time. Children at the concrete operations stage can learn to pile blocks according to size. They are also ready to begin to understand cyclic order so that they can learn to tell time (Friedman, 1977). **Classification** involves ability to sort according to some quality, and children at the concrete operations stage are able to classify things according to color or size. Later, they will learn to classify according to more abstract attributes such as value judgments.

In the stage of **formal operations,** according to Piaget (from about age 11 onward), children are ready to learn abstract concepts. They now develop the capacity to reason through the use of hypotheses and to make logical deductions from data. They no longer need concrete stimuli to help them solve problems in subjects such as algebra, because at this stage abstractions match their level of mental development.

Adolescence and formal operation, Piaget notes, are marked by other emerging abilities as well. Adolescents can think about their own

*Reprinted by permission of G. P. Putnam's Sons from *Dear Folks* by Juliet Lowell. Copyright © 1961 by Juliet Lowell.

thoughts as well as recognize possibilities and actualities. Just as the formal operations stage initiates the ability to think about one's own thoughts, it also creates the ability to think about the thought of others. This is often a mixed blessing. Adolescents commonly have trouble differentiating between their own concerns and those of others—just one more cause of adolescent storm and stress.

Another ability that develops during adolescence is the ability to reflect on one's own mental and personal traits. This new capacity for introspection is manifested by adolescents' new secretiveness about their private thoughts, a characteristic that often drives teachers and parents to distraction!

For the teacher, the concept of **matching** is extremely important. Because children go through this fixed sequence of stages in cognitive development, the teacher must plan experiences and stimuli that are consistent with the students' maturational level. For instance, Piaget has stressed that sophisticated mathematical and symbolic concepts

Children at Piaget's concrete stage of development can begin to learn to read using letters they can touch.

When Piaget conducted his research, he often used tasks that could easily be performed at the kitchen table. The following Piagetian-type tasks were developed by an educational psychologist at the University of Pittsburgh to be used with young American children (Vasudev, 1976). To try out these tasks, find two children between the ages of five and ten. Use for your subjects children whose ages are as far apart as possible. Ask them, one at a time, to perform the tasks described below. Write down their responses to your questions. When you are finished with both children, answer the questions that follow the tasks.

Task 1: Conservation of Mass

Step 1 Take two balls composed of equal amounts of clay or dough. Show them to the child and ask, "Are they both the same?" (If the child does not think that they are the same, allow opportunity for manipulation of the balls sufficient to demonstrate that this is the case.)

Step 2 Roll out one of the balls, in view of the child, into a "hot dog." Ask the child, "Is there the same amount of clay in the ball as in the hot dog?"

Step 3 Ask the child to explain his or her answer.

Task 2: Conservation of Continuous Quantity

Step 1 Take two glasses and fill them with the same amounts of water. Ask the child, "Is there the same amount of water in both glasses?" (If the child does not think that they are the same, demonstrate that this is the case.)

Step 2 In front of the child, pour the contents of one glass into a glass that obviously is taller and slimmer. Make sure the level of water is high in the tall glass. Ask the child, "Do the tall glass and the shorter glass have the same amount of water?"

Step 3 Ask the child to explain his or her answer.

Questions

1 Did the children respond differently to the questions you asked them? If yes, describe these differences fully.

2 Look back to descriptions of Piaget's stages of cognitive development described in this chapter. According to these descriptions, at what level of development is each of these children responding? What evidence can you give to support your answer?

cannot be taught before a child reaches the stage of formal operations (Piaget, 1964).

Environmental Approaches to Explaining Cognitive Development

Environmental theorists agree with Piaget that language and cognitive development appear in a series of stages, but environmentalists are much more interested in manipulating teaching to see what changes they can create in a child's learning. American researchers have designed a variety of teaching methods and new curricula that they feel

Recent Soviet research in cognitive development has produced findings that seem to show clearly that given certain specified lessons, very young children can solve extremely complex mathematical concepts. Psychologists at the Institute of General and Pedagogical Psychology in Moscow under the direction of C. V. Davydov have developed methods of teaching mathematics and other subjects to very young children in which they report very young children are able to solve abstract problems without ever having gone through a concrete stage (J. Gibson, 1980). Children as young as preschool age using this method are able to solve problems such as the following:

> A collective farm has a large amount of grain at the harvest season. Some of it is taken away to be used for the people in the city. How much is left in the warehouse for the peasant?

To solve this particular problem the children decided that:
a = number of sacks of grain
b = amount taken away
c = sacks of grain left

The correct answer, provided on the board by one preschooler, was the abstract equation:

$$a - b = c$$

Soviet preschoolers work out algebraic equations on form boards at their desks.
The complexity of the work is shown in a sample page from a preschooler's notebook.

can increase the rate at which children learn. Two of these researchers serve as excellent examples of this particular approach to cognitive development: Jerome Bruner and Robert Gagné.

Jerome Bruner views development as proceeding through a hierarchy of stages, as Piaget does, but Bruner does not see these stages as fixed and critical. In a statement that appears to refute Piaget's concept of fixed developmental stages, Bruner (1960) says that "any subject can be taught effectively in some intellectually honest form to any child at any stage of development." Piaget would agree that you can teach a child at any age by using stimuli appropriately matched to the child's level of cognitive development; in such a manner, assimilation and then accommodation can occur. But, for Bruner, noting a child's stage of cognitive development and then arranging a curriculum around it are most important. By providing the proper curriculum, the teacher can increase the child's ability to think. Bruner's **spiral curriculum** is designed to match each learning step with the child's stage of cognitive deveopment.

Robert Gagné, a learning-environmental psychologist, is also disturbed by what he sees as Piaget's indifference to the role of learning in intellectual development. Gagné believes a child's cognitive skills develop because he or she learns an ordered set of abilities. As learning moves along, these abilities build on each other in a progressive fashion. Thus, a child who learns to solve simple problems improves his or her ability to solve more complex problems at a later time (Gagné, 1968). Gagné's research involves, therefore, the designation

Some children need to master certain simple prerequisite skills, such as learning the sound of the letter h, before they can succeed at a remedial reading task.

Lynn McLaren, Rapho/Photo Researchers, Inc.

of prerequisite skills for each task to be learned. Researchers have shown, for example, that cognitive development in adolescence is strongly affected by learning experiences in middle childhood (Barenboim, 1977). This is true whether one considers problem solving in academic or interpersonal situations.

Abilities may also expand through self-initiated thinking activity. For teachers, this implies that the teacher does not necessarily have to organize activities for learning to take place; children may reach a higher level of problem-solving by themselves. According to Gagné, stages of development are not correlated with chronological age, except in the sense that learning takes time.

using developmental research in classroom teaching

Piaget's theoretical work can be linked to classroom practices in several ways. First, his basic idea of a progression through specific cognitive stages has clear relevance for educational planning. Teachers should design curricula to take a child through a logical sequence of steps so that his or her cognitive development may advance from one stage to the next.

Second, Piaget's work in the concept of matching is also relevant to education. It is important for teachers to realize that two children of the same chronological age may be functioning at different levels of development. A child in the sensorimotor stage of development should be provided with experiences that are action-linked; a child in the formal operations stage can be exposed to more theoretical experiences that match his or her ability to cope with complex and abstract problems.

Compensatory preschool education programs, whose aim is to better prepare a child for later school experiences, place a special emphasis on giving a child the opportunity to act directly on concrete objects. This preparation has a particular connection with the development of language: As children are developing their ability to use language, the teacher must be aware of their level of thinking and verbalization and speak at this level. Teachers who do not invoke the principle of matching by selecting stimuli that their students can use and understand will find that their students will likely perform poorly and be frustrated, apathetic, or bored.

An aspect of environmental stimulation that teachers have learned to take into account in planning programs is that new events interest children, but extremely different or strange happenings frighten them. When a new event is familiar enough to be assimilated without distortion into the student's current cognitive level and novel enough to produce some degree of conflict, then interest and learning

Using Developmental-Stage Approaches to Increase Language and Cognitive Development

are promoted. The child is ready to learn. Since children of the same chronological age may behave on different cognitive levels, some teachers believe that children should be given the freedom to work individually at tasks of their own choosing. This does not mean that the learning situation should be unstructured; the teacher must provide interesting materials for each student to work on.

Piaget stresses the child's interaction with the environment, because the processes of assimilation and accommodation can occur only in a stimulating environment. Teachers are aware that children from different backgrounds do not solve problems in the same ways. Some may come from environments that have not provided sufficient or appropriate types of stimulation. Programs such as Head Start have been developed to compensate for this lack.

It is possible to increase the rate of the assimilation-accommodation process by giving children opportunities to practice their reasoning skills. An example of a preschool program designed to do this is described by Kamii (1972). Each phase of this program is planned so that the child can advance from one set of mental operations to the next. The curriculum is designed to develop the child's internal processes of cognitive growth rather than his or her external behavior and to increase his or her opportunities eventually to attain the formal operations stage of thinking. According to Kamii, this goal is accomplished by promoting the child's natural curiosity and initiative through active exploration, experimentation, and questioning. By providing curriculum materials that cover physically observable knowledge, social knowledge, logic and mathematical knowledge, and encouraging their use, teachers can enhance the children's creativity and their confidence in their growing capabilities.

Should the application of Piagetian principles stop at the level of preschool education? One proposal suggests that the entire elementary school curriculum could be based on the development of Piagetian thought structures (Furth, 1970). The curriculum would be geared to building the thought structures of the concrete operations stages by providing the child with exercises to trigger mental operations that develop and stabilize these structures. Its aim would also be to develop spontaneous thinking that would lead the child to the beginnings of formal operational thought. Operational steps and stages in development are the key elements in such a curriculum.

One impressive program designed to give school-age children the opportunity to practice reasoning skills was described in *Time* ("Grade School Philosophers," 1974, p. 74).* Children in this program took part in an experimental class in philosophy. First graders learned to categorize: "Four stores and three men make seven things in the world we can touch." Sixth graders learned to make distinctions between things and beings: "If you have a friend who is only your friend when you

*Reprinted by permission from *Time*, The Weekly News-magazine. Copyright Time Inc., 1974.

are lonely, then you are using your friend as a thing." The class also covered deductive reasoning (for example: all birds are warm-blooded; robins are birds; therefore, robins are warm-blooded), universal and particular sentences, logic, differences of degree, relationships, and styles of thought. One teacher reported that "by the end of the course . . . (the children) were going to the library and taking volumes of the encyclopedia home." The class was so successful that it is being introduced for fifth and sixth graders in other schools.

The **open classroom,** an approach to teaching that discards the traditional elementary classroom setup in which the children sit at their desks, with everyone doing (or trying to do) the same thing as the teacher instructs from "center stage," is still another example of curriculum design that can make use of Piaget's stages of development. In the open classroom, the room is divided into funtional areas rich in learning resources. The child is free to roam about the room and use these materials as he or she wishes. Individualization of instruction allows each child to work at his or her own level. A teacher and aides work with the children individually or in small groups, rarely presenting the same material to the class as a whole. The children must be able to try things out to see what happens, manipulate objects and symbols, pose questions and seek their answers, reconcile what they find at one time with what they find at another, and test their findings against the perceptions of others their age. Activity essential to intellectual development includes social collaboration, group effort, and communication among children. Only after a good deal of experience is the child ready to move on to abstract concepts.

Stage theories of cognitive development have relevance for teachers of middle school and high school students as well. By focusing on the emergence of formal operations during adolescence, teachers can gain a perspective on characteristics of adolescent development that they might otherwise miss. The apprehension, idealism, self-consciousness, and introspection that take up so much of the adolescent's time (often when teachers would prefer concentration on mathematics, physics, or chemistry) can be viewed as both a function of and natural corollaries to the newly acquired cognitive skills that characterize the formal operations stage. Some researchers have described the attitudes of adolescents as those of "emerging scientists." Okun and Sasfy (1977, p. 378) report, for example that,

> similar to new scientific theories, the new self-theory (of adolescents) is particularly vulnerable to disconfirming evidence. Alternatively, we see in the adolescent the concern for gathering critical evidence to support the developing self-theory. Thus, getting a driver's license or "the first date" can become immensely significant and emotional affairs because they are critical empirical evidence for important postulates in the self-theory; for example, "I am competent" and "I am desirable to the opposite sex." These experiences parallel the critical experiments upon which new scientific theories are often built.

What can teachers do to make use of these students' new way of looking at the world? For one thing, teachers can help adolescents to reduce their fears that they are different by demonstrating to them that their new concerns are really not unusual. Free discussion of emerging sexuality, competency, and social roles should be encouraged whenever possible. English teachers, for example, could take advantage of creative writing classes to give adolescents the opportunity to express their feelings about themselves and the world. Giving students the assignment of keeping a daily journal is a useful device to do this. At a time when teachers and the public are concerned about teaching literacy, such experiences can be used to teach reading and writing skills and the ability to think out new ways to solve new problems.

Finally, teachers can help adolescents, as well as younger children, by allowing them to do their own learning. It is clear that children cannot be taught to increase their language or cognitive abilities simply by having teachers talk to them. Good teaching must involve presenting students with situations in which they themselves are al-

Good teaching allows students to do their own learning, pose questions, and seek answers, rather than listen impassively.

Ray Ellis, Photo Researchers, Inc.

lowed to experiment, in the broadest sense of the term. Students should be encouraged to try things out to see what happens, manipulate symbols, pose questions, seek their own answers, reconcile what they find out at one time with what they find at another, and compare their findings with those of other students. It is through these processes, rather than through passive listening, that the assimilation-accommodation process that Piaget describes takes place in the classroom.

Making Practical Use of Piaget in the Classroom

A good understanding of Piagetian principles can be very useful to the busy teacher. With the current glut of new methods and new curricula, it is often difficult to separate out those programs that really work from those that won't. The following suggestions have appeared in a variety of manuals for parents and for teachers and are said to be accepted in common classroom practice (Gibson, 1978, p. 326). Do you agree or disagree with them? Why? Can you come up with different ideas to help the classroom teacher?

1. In the past few years, a number of manuals have suggested that "there is no such thing as a bad child, only bad behavior." These manuals warn teachers that when disciplining children they should always be careful to punish "the behavior, not the child."

   The preschool years, according to Piaget, are characterized by egocentricity. Children under 3 have difficulty separating themselves from their actions. In light of this fact, how relevant is this message to preschool teachers? To elementary school teachers? At what school grade do you think these manuals might make a difference? Why?

2. In recent years, Americans have become more and more concerned with teaching both the basics—reading, writing, and arithmetic—and moral reasoning. Many manuals point out that one reason for low skill level in the basics and for increased immoral behavior on the part of children is the lack of adult models. Teachers themselves, these manuals point out, sometimes cannot read or spell very well. In some cases, they provide less than adequate models of moral behavior for children to imitate, as, for example, when they behave differently to black and white children in urban schools.

   It is believed by many developmental psychologists that children are able to learn through the use of concrete objects long before they are able to understand abstract symbols. Considering what we learned about Piaget's stages of cognitive development in this chapter and about his stages of moral development in Chapter 1, do you believe that the best way to teach children either basic cognitive skills or moral reasoning is through the use of concrete models? At what age would you prescribe concrete stimuli for teaching? At what age would you suggest an appeal solely to reason? Why?

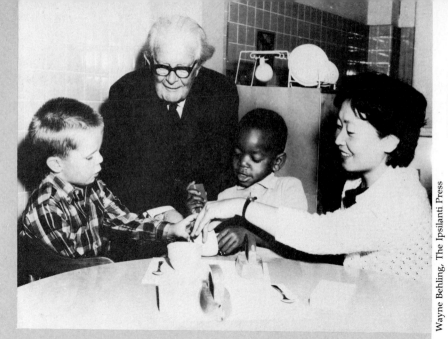

Jean Piaget (shown here) has demonstrated that children of the same age often do not reach the same level of cognitive development.

Wayne Behling, The Ipsilanti Press

3. Many manuals suggest appealing to children's pride and making use of secondary reinforcers such as social approval in the classroom, as, for example, by saying, "What a good paper! You'll be proud to take a high grade home on your report card next month." These same manuals suggest, conversely, that busy teachers might appeal to parental authority, as in the threat, "Wait till your bad report card goes home!" or "What shall I tell your mother when she comes to the PTA meeting next week?" It is true that environmentalists suggest that a very effective way to teach young children to behave in desired ways is to reinforce them for desired behavior. But, according to Piaget, young children still have only a hazy understanding of the concept of time. Long-term goals are meaningless. At what age can a teacher begin to use delayed rewards (or punishments) as aids in classroom teaching?

Reprinted from *Growing Up: A Study of Children* by Janice Gibson. Copyright © 1978. By permission of Addison-Wesley Publishing Co., Reading, Mass.

Using Environmental Approaches to Increase Language and Cognitive Development

Piaget (1972) and other developmental-stage theorists suggest that all children do not achieve the most complex level of formal operational thinking. Why? Environmental theorists attribute these children's lower level of development to environmental factors—specifically, poor, insufficient, or inappropriate environmental stimulation. For environmental theorists, language acquisition and cognitive development are dependent primarily on teaching. They emphasize that proper teaching procedures can assist the development of early skill learning, thus raising the otherwise lower levels of cognition of some children.

Most American children today are raised at home by parents or care-givers who individually select learning experiences for their

charges. Environmental theorists point ou
are more fortunate than others, in terms
made available to them in their early year:

But, considering the cognitive skills
is formal education prior to age 5 appropri
psychologists would answer yes. They be
tions for later intellectual development are
five years of life. Thus, supplying system;
essary in the preschool years to aid cogni
This intervention would be particularly vi
relatively restricted environments where a
provided (Glaser and Resnick, 1972).

Robert Gagné and Jerome Bruner w
of cognitive development can be influenced
The implication of their position is that a ch
and as fast as he or she could be taught. C
depends on the availability of a sequence o
capitalize on their emerging cognitive capac
biological factors. If children cannot perform
reading, their teacher must go back, identify
have not yet mastered, develop an educatio.... sequence that leads to
its acquisition, and then begin to teach them reading again. This is
similar in one way to Piagetian approach, in which a teacher might
first identify the signs of potential competency in the child and then
arrange a curriculum that capitalizes on it and leads him or her to
higher levels of cognitive development.

Teaching language acquisition   Perhaps the most striking instance of
the emphasis environmental psychologists place on the role of training
and instruction in cognitive development is with respect to language
acquisition. For environmental theorists, the way in which language is
used in the child's early environment is all important. Jerome Bruner
has in fact suggested that language is culture-bound; that is, the
words that children first learn to describe their worlds are determined
by the culture in which they grow up. His cross-cultural studies (Bruner, Olver, Greenfield, et al., 1966) indicate that the specific language
a child speaks is not as important a factor in cognitive growth as the
training he or she receives in the uses of that language.

In the United States, preschool children's first teachers are often
their mothers. Learning takes place at home. Socioeconomic conditions, education, intelligence, general experience, and attitudes of
such parent-teachers clearly affect the language as well the cognitive
development of children (Dlugokinski, Weiss, and Johnston, 1976;
Hall and Kaye, 1977).

Children like Tommy Sanchez, who learn a different language at
home from the one used later in school, sometimes are treated by

they have never learned important concepts in any
thers of such children should be able to speak their lan-
ter to determine just what they do and do not understand.
eason, in 1968 Congress passed the Bilingual Education Act,
calls for teaching in both English and the native languages of
dren unfamiliar with standard English. Since 1968, experimental
bilingual education programs have proliferated in the United States.

If children live in a cultural setting that hinders their cognitive growth because their language skills are poorly developed in that setting, then formal language programs can be used to unlock their cognitive capacities and release their full potential.

According to Bruner, children must be trained through formal instruction to use language symbolically and abstractly. Children have relatively little trouble in grasping the concepts inherent in words for simple concrete objects (bottle, table, ball) at the age which they usually learn these words because they can manipulate those objects. But it is much more difficult for them to grasp abstractions such as time (before, after), direction (underneath, between), and relative judgments (warmer, heavier). An extremely articulate and well-trained teacher is needed to offer the necessary elaboration, corroboration, or negation of a child's emerging ideas.

In homes that provide instruction and support, the child's development of abstract thinking is facilitated. In homes where support is not provided, the development of this kind of thinking is hindered because the child has not been given the essential language experience necessary to develop it (Bernstein, 1960). A study of the effects of teaching language skills to children on a tutorial one-to-one basis (Blank and Solomon, 1968) concluded that children could develop a firm language base for thinking when they were given consistent guidance and frequent reinforcement of new skills. Studies of this kind reflect the recognition that language holds a central position in the process of cognitive growth.

In order to meet the problems of preschool children who are not provided adequate stimulation at home, educators have developed two basic kinds of programs. One is child-centered: The child is given compensatory training at centers outside the home. The other is parent-centered: The parents are taught skills to use in educating their children at home. The programs can, of course, be combined. One evaluation of the parent-centered type of program suggested not only the need for early and continuing education of the child, but also the need for early and continuing support for parents in their roles as educators of their children (Schaefer, 1972).

Teaching cognitive skills Many different methods have been designed by environmental theorists to teach thinking and problem-solving skills to children from preschool age to high school. The recent interest in preschools in this country reflects the growing realization that traditional methods of education have scarcely tapped children's abilities to learn, while, in many cases, more modern methods have dramatically increased children's mental development. A basic assumption on which modern preschool programs are based is the all-important understanding that children's needs differ from those of adolescents or adults. Facilities and programs in the past focused on the children's physical, social, and emotional development. Today they have shifted to cognitive development. For example, American preschooler have been exposed to the strategies needed to solve algebraic problems and spell complex words.

The **Montessori method** of teaching is one example of a preschool method designed to increase cognitive development by providing special experiences and special skill learnings. It is one of the oldest and most successful methods of increasing cognitive development in preschool children. Although this approach has only recently become popular in the United States, the Montessori movement has been in use in Europe for decades.

*Montessori,
Head Start,
and Other
Teaching Methods*

Maria Montessori, an Italian doctor, developed her theories of education through extensive work with slum children in Italy. After observing the turbulence and chaos of the children's home conditions, Montessori determined that they could be successfully educated only in a carefully manipulated, orderly environment. Through her efforts to structure such classrooms and her work in creating materials that build sensory and cognitive skills, Montessori developed a theory of teaching and learning. Her ideas became the basis for a network of schools that spread across Europe during the early 1900s and are in use today throughout the world.

A key notion in Montessori teaching is the **planned environment.** The cleanliness, neatness, and stability of the classroom are of prime importance. Everything in the classroom, from the dimensions of the furniture to its arrangement, is carefully designed with the youngster in mind. Ideally, the program allows for freedom of movement within the room, but the children must be orderly and must use materials properly. The teacher carefully demonstrates how to handle the materials in order to prevent random, disruptive, or destructive use of them by the children.

Montessori education emphasizes motor and sensory training, as well as overall cognitive and social skills. Dr. Montessori saw all these areas of education as interconnected; she believed that the child must master sensory and motor tasks in order to succeed in such intellectual areas as reading and writing. Montessori created letters and shapes out of brightly colored sandpaper with which she taught cognitive skills to 4-year-olds. The children were given a letter, told its name, and then encouraged to repeat the name while rubbing their fingers over the letter and tracing its pattern. Through the use of such materials and methods, 4-year-olds learned to read and write in a month and a half.

Montessori believed that preschool children have an almost insatiable thirst for new words and an almost inexhaustible capacity for learning them. She demonstrated that young children could learn and retain difficult scientific and technical terms. Montessori believed that the word-learning process could be stimulated even further by presenting words that related most directly to the objects and experiences in the child's home environment.

Montessori programming allows for the teaching of mathematics at early ages using uniformly colored and shaped blocks or cylinders. More advanced mathematical concepts can be taught by employing sequentially sectioned rods such as Cuisinaire or Sterms blocks. Even value concepts can be taught through use of Montessori decimal blocks, which symbolically represent units, tens, and hundreds (Havis and Yawkey, 1977).

Montessori felt that preschool children should not be segregated by age for the purpose of learning. Thus, a typical Montessori classroom includes children of ages 3 to 6. Montessori believed that the learning atmosphere is more interesting if children of different ages are in the classroom together. Younger children often ask for and receive assistance from older ones; this is satisfying to the older child and at the same time allows the younger child to learn by observing others.

In Montessori schools, separate classrooms are normally arranged for the 3- to 6-year-old group and for the 7- to 9-year old group. But even in this arrangement, the children pass freely from one classroom to another. They observe each other's behavior and learning, work on certain common projects, and learn to relate to children of different ages. Sometimes the younger children are surprised to discover that they can understand material being taught to the older children.

Montessori (1967) summarized all these points in a description of the classroom atmosphere in her schools:

> The child's progress does not depend only on his age, but also on
> being free to look about him. . . . Our schools are alive. To
> understand what the older ones are doing fills the little ones with
> enthusiasm. The older ones are happy to be able to teach what they
> know. There are no inferiority complexes, but everyone achieves a
> healthy normality through the mutual exchange of spiritual energy.
> (p. 228)

Private Montessori schools, usually serving middle- and upper-income children, have been established in many cities in the United States. In one sense this development is ironic, since the Montessori method was originally designed to meet the needs of low-income slum children in Italy. However, many urban school systems have developed preschool programs that rely heavily on the Montessori method.

A different approach to preschool programs aimed at increasing cognitive development in children deprived of early learning experiences was taken by Bereiter and Engelmann (1966). Their program was designed to provide direct instruction in cognitive areas only, rather than a total environment, and it deals specifically with highly structured drills and practice in language, arithmetic, and reading. The learning procedures move at a rapid pace, especially in language learning, and rely heavily on imitation and reinforcement. Although some critics argue that social and personality development are not given consideration in this program, its supporters note that IQ gains of 10 to 30 points in one year justify it sufficiently.

Probably the best-known enrichment program for children who have not had adequate stimulation in the preschool years is Head Start, which was created and funded by the federal government. Since 1964, when the program began, millions of these disadvantaged preschool children have been enrolled in various programs designed to prepare them to enter first grade on a cognitive level on a par with that of middle-class children. The programs have not been standardized throughout the country. Each community determines for itself which needs are most important and then devises its own materials and methods to meet those needs. For example, some Head Start educational centers have stressed cognitive growth through programs

David S. Strickler, Monkmeyer

that develop language skills, reading, and number concepts; others have concentrated on cultural aspects of development by means of planned trips, art projects, and creative play. In this sense, Head Start is considered child-centered; but it is also parent-centered in its efforts to teach parents the importance of later educational and intellectual stimulation.

Assessments of the effectiveness of Head Start, when it was first begun, showed mixed results. Some studies concluded that, although children in Head Start programs achieved cognitive gains initially, the gains were not long-lasting (Cicirelli et al., 1969; Rosensweet, 1971). The authors of the early studies concluded that the main problem was that the short-term gains that the children made while in the program were not followed through when they entered regular school systems. The past decade, however, has produced more extensive programs as well as the opportunity for longitudinal research. In 1979, the Consortium for Longitudinal Studies was able to report lasting effects beyond preschool, particularly when such factors as assignment to special education classes and retention during the school years was taken into consideration (Lazar and Darlington, 1979).

Special techniques that stimulate the cognitive development of elementary, middle school, and high school students have also been developed in the past decade. Some have had greater success than others. Useful technological aids include educational TV, individual-ized tape cassette recordings, films, teaching machines, and comput-ers. A new array of technological devices, for example, now help classroom teachers to increase skill learning and individualize instruc-tion to meet student needs. Methods that individualize instruction are particularly useful during adolescence, when students develop a new, but frequently changing, interest in future careers at the same time that basic literacy skills assume critical importance.

Teaching basic literacy skills with particular emphasis on reading has received widespread attention in recent years. Learning to read is a long stride toward eventual full cognitive growth for a child. In ad-dition to being a valuable source of stimulation, reading has a psycho-logical impact on children. Whether they can read or not is a crucial factor in their self-esteem, and their ability to handle other develop-ment tasks is strongly affected by their performance in reading (Havig-hurst, 1952). This is of particular importance because many American children reach high school without having learned to read. Clearly, in a text-oriented educational system such as ours, the ability to read should be a necessary condition for academic achievement.

One innovative program found particularly useful is Project PLAN (Klaus, 1971). Begun in 1967, it provides a system of programmed learning for language arts, science, social studies, and mathematics for grades 1 through 12. Behaviorally oriented objectives are built into **teaching-learning units (TLUs),** modules of instruction representing 10 to 15 hours of instruction for an average student, each designed to be used over a two-week period.

The materials in the TLUs vary; they are tailored to each stu-dent's particular background, aptitude, and interests. Before students begin to use the modules, they are tested extensively to determine their abilities, interests, and previously acquired knowledge. All stu-dents proceed at their own pace. The teacher's role is to help them to overcome specific difficulties and to check their progress on complex assignments. Students are tested to see if remedial steps are necessary and to provide students and their teacher with a flow of information—feedback—about their accomplishments and aspirations. Project PLAN also uses a computer to collect, organize, and analyze the information from the tests to assess the performance of each student on each module.

Finally, alternative high schools in major urban areas have exper-imented in recent years with freer school philosophies in which emo-tional and expressive development are given as much emphasis as for-mal academic learning. Alternative schools run the gamut from politically active "liberation schools" in inner cities to rural utopian en-vironments. In all the environmentally oriented programs, however, although teaching methods vary, teaching of basic skills is designed as a preliminary step to the teaching of high-order skills.

summary

1. There are several theories about the relationship between thinking and speech. Piaget feels that language development follows cognitive development. Watson considered thought and speech to be parallel developments. Vygotsky has stated that we have to have a word for things before we can think about them, so that cognitive development is intertwined with language development in a very complex manner.

2. Piaget's finding is that young children have two basic types of verbal expressions: egocentric speech, which is not meant for other people, and socialized speech, which is used for communication with others. According to Piaget, egocentric speech develops first. Vygotsky, on the other hand, says that the speech of young children is a tool that they use to direct their own cognitive processes, not to practice communication skills.

3. Developmental-stage theorists view language development in relation to cognitive maturity. Piaget has identified stages of language development that parallel the stages of cognitive development. Chomsky believes that we have an inborn ability to process language, as witnessed by children's seemingly effortless acquisition of kernel or elementary grammar.

4. Environmentalists believe that language acquisition is the result of learning. B. F. Skinner states that children learn to speak through selective parental reinforcement of utterances that resemble adult speech. Other environmentalists stress the sensory reinforcement inherent in verbalization and the importance of modeling and imitation. Jerome Bruner, the cognitive psychologist, has pointed out the many occasions for language learning in a child's everyday interactions with parents or care-givers.

5. According to Piaget, probably the most influential stage theorist concerned with cognitive development, cognitive development occurs in a series of stages relevant to specific ages. Cognitive growth depends on the assimilation of new experiences and the revision of established concepts to accommodate them. If these processes do not occur equally and continually, cognitive growth will cease.

6. As Piaget describes it, cognitive development proceeds through a fixed series of stages keyed to a large extent to the child's chronological age. The sensorimotor stage (birth to about 2 years) consists largely of action because children at this age cannot use language. During this stage, children develop the ability to make circular reactions, use trial and error, make mental combinations, acquire the object concept, and begin to use language. The preoperational stage (from about age 2 to about 7) is characterized by the child's giving symbolic meaning to concrete objects (preconceptual stage, from about age 2 to 4), focusing on one aspect of an object at a time, and difficulty in seeing other people's point of view (intuitive stage, age 4 to 7). Children at the concrete operations stage (about age 7 to 11) are capable of reasoning and logic with concrete objects, focusing on more than one aspect of an object, and understanding conservation, seriation, and classification. During the formal operations stage (approximately age 11 and up), children finally are ready to learn abstract concepts.

7. Environmentalists stress the effect of learning on cognitive development and have devised a variety of teaching methods that are aimed at increasing children's rate of learning. Bruner believes that a child's stage of development is not as fixed or critical as Piaget suggests. Robert Gagné believes that cognitive skills develop as children learn an ordered set of skills. Researchers have also suggested that children may teach themselves by actively seeking more stimulating experiences.

8. Piaget's stage theory can be used in planning curricula to provide learning experiences matched to a child's particular level of development, programs incorporating novel (but not overly strange) stimuli, and learning methods based on individualized instruction. Such programs can be applied in preschool as well as in higher grades.

9. Environmental theorists emphasize the effect that proper teaching methods can have on children's cognitive development. They recommend formal education in the preschool years, because they feel that children develop as fast as they can be taught.

10. Psychologists such as Bruner emphasize the effect on language acquisition of formal instruction, particularly on the more symbolic and abstract uses of language. Educators have used many of Bruner's ideas to devise child-centered and parent-centered programs to compensate for inadequate home environments.

11. Preschool programs such as Head Start and those using the Montessori method seem to help children make gains in cognitive ability. A variety of other techniques to stimulate the cognitive growth of older children, such as Project PLAN for grades 1-12, have also been developed.

**for students
who want to read
further**

CHALL, J. *Learning to Read: The Great Debate.* New York: McGraw-Hill, 1967. This book, based on laboratory research as well as classroom studies, discusses the controversies that have arisen in regard to different methods of teaching reading. In the light of new concerns regarding literacy, Chall's arguments are particularly incisive and to the point.

DALE, P. *Language Development: Structure and Function.* Hinsdale, Ill.: Dryden Press, 1972. Dale's book is an interesting and fairly easy-to-read summary of psycholinguistics and the development of language in school children. The chapters on reading, early education, and black English should be of special interest to teachers.

FURTH, H. *Piaget for Teachers.* Englewood Cliffs, N. J.: Prentice-Hall, 1970. This is an easy-to-read and yet comprehensive summary of Piaget's views of how teachers can relate most effectively to school-age children.

FURTH, W., AND WACHS, H. *Thinking Goes to School.* New York: Oxford University Press, 1975. The book describes how Piaget's principles were implemented in an experimental school program conducted by Furth and Wachs. Of particular use to teachers is a detailed description of almost 200 exercises and activities designed to increase children's cognitive development.

PIAGET, J. *To Understand Is to Invent.* New York: Grossman, 1973. This easy-to-read book is one of the very few written by Piaget for the general public.

II

PRINCIPLES OF LEARNING AND TEACHING

Teachers can use the principles of learning in many different ways. They can use them as guides to interpret what they see their students doing in school. They can also use information provided by learning psychologists to design new and more effective curricula. Teachers need to understand the principles of learning for a very simple reason: If you don't understand how children learn, how can you select the best ways to teach them? Educational psychologists define learning as a relatively permanent change in behavior that results from a student's interaction with the environment. Because the learning process is not directly observable, we must base our assumptions that something has been learned on indirect measures such as test scores. Thus, learning is often thought of as some sort of change within a student that occurs some time between the classroom experience that set it in motion and the test answers from which the process is inferred.

The first four chapters in this section, Chapters 3–6, deal with different approaches psychologists have taken in order to explain learning. Each approach has contributed in a unique way to classroom curriculum design. Chapter 3, for example, deals with behaviorism, which describes learning in terms of students' observable behavior. Behaviorism has given rise to innovative curricular designs such as programmed instruction. It is also the basis of behavior management, an approach used widely in the schools today. Behavior management and specific ways it can be implemented are described in detail in Chapter 3. Chapter 4 presents cognitive psychology, which describes learning in terms of thinking changes that take place in students and that intervene between learning exercises and student responses. Cognitive psychology has led to classroom approaches like discovery teaching. Memory is an important part of learning. If students don't remember what they have been taught, we can't really say they have learned. Chapter 5 discusses how to help students transfer information learned in school to real-life problems, as well as how to increase their memory of those skills. The final chapter in this series, Chapter 6, deals with the motivation process. Motivating students to learn and ways that teachers can "humanize" their classrooms—both important aspects of effective teaching—are discussed in detail.

The final chapter in this part, Chapter 7, contains guidelines for effective teaching of specific skills. General aids to good teaching such as learning objectives and task analysis are described in detail. The second part of the chapter discusses ways to teach students the perceptual, motor, language, concept, and problem-solving skills they will need to master any academic subject as well as the attitudes conducive to learning in general.

3

BEHAVIORISM
AND
CLASSROOM
MANAGEMENT

Michelle, A Preschooler Afraid to Fail

Michelle is the only child of a middle-aged couple who run a poultry farm. When Michelle was 4 years old, her parents enrolled her in a developmental day-care center to reduce her anxiety about being with other children her own age.

The program was designed to increase children's cognitive skills, but the teachers noticed that Michelle had very little interest in this aspect of their program. Michelle said that she did not want to tackle an individual learning task. She also said that she was afraid that she might fail. The teachers were concerned that Michelle was not interested in learning new things and that she had too little ability to follow through on tasks.

After talking with Michelle and her mother, the teachers decided to abandon the tasks they had initially set for the little girl. While the other children were given daily brief lessons in which they practiced language skills and the manual dexterity necessary for later learning of reading and writing, Michelle was allowed free play. The teachers noticed what Michelle did during that free time. She played with blocks, building houses and fences. "What are those for?" her teacher asked. "The kittens will live in the little house over there, and the puppy will stay in the big house," Michelle responded. "Those little tiny houses are for the chickens." Sometimes she knocked the blocks down. "Why did you do that?" her teacher asked. "Just because I felt like it," Michelle answered. "That's all right," her teacher responded.

Then the teacher told Michelle that she could bring one of her pets to school. The next day, she and her father carried one of the kittens into the class.

"Today we're going to play with Michelle's kitten," announced the teacher. "But first, Michelle is going to tell us all about him." Michelle held up the kitten to show the children. "Spooky is extra special," Michelle began. "He has six toes."

"Let's see," said the teacher. "Can you count them?"

"See! One-two-three-four-five, and there's one more little one, six."

The teacher planned a series of tasks for Michelle built around pets and games with other children. To assure success, she first presented tasks that she knew Michelle would be able to do. She did not ask Michelle to count *all* the kitten's toes on the first day because she knew that Michelle could count only as far as ten. That task would come later. She carefully praised Michelle for her good work in front of the other children. Later, she increased the complexity of each task, always being careful to do so in small steps so that Michelle could get them right.

The result? A happy, involved, more self-assured little girl began to learn new facts about things that interested her very much. Michelle was helped through this sequence: observation of her behavior during free play and interviews with her mother at home; concern for both short- and long-term goals of development (commitment to a task and following it through); intervention (planning different programs); encouragement; and praise. What Michelle's teacher did was to use the best principles of behaviorism in helping Michelle learn how to interact with her environment in new and meaningful ways.

behaviorist approaches to learning

Psychologists have developed several different explanations of how human beings learn. The one we discuss in this chapter is called **behaviorism** because the explanation of learning is based on people's observable behavior. This approach to learning has also been called **associationism** and the stimulus-response approach (S-R) because it is based on the idea that learning occurs when people associate their behavior with stimuli in the environment. For example, we stop our cars at a red light (a stimulus in the environment) because we have learned to associate that stimulus with the particular response of stopping. By explaining the link between stimulus and response, the behaviorists posed one explanation of why we behave as we do.

Behaviorism originated in the United States many decades ago. John B. Watson, an early leader of the behaviorist approach to psychology, stated that psychologists couldn't and shouldn't concern themselves with the whole human being because it was just not possible to make scientifically valid statements about what goes on inside people. Instead, psychologists should concentrate on behavior that can be directly observed. Human behavior, Watson insisted, is real, objective, and practical. You cannot see someone thinking, so consciousness cannot be a factor in behavior. Watson restricted his research to what he could observe himself and concluded that human behavior is based on learned responses to stimuli in the environment.

Watson's first task was to specify the links between those responses (an individual's behavior) and the stimuli in the environment. He asked himself questions such as, "How do school children come to associate the ringing sound that occurs in the late afternoon with joyous excitement, and the smell and sight of a dentist's office with trepidation?"

Operating on the assumption that humans can be taught specific responses through the use of specific stimuli, Watson trained an 11-month-old baby he called Little Albert to fear a white rat. Watson first showed Little Albert a white rat to prove that the child was not afraid of it. Another time, Watson suddenly banged two rods together behind Little Albert's head to show that the child was afraid of loud noise. His next step was to present the child with the rat and immediately bang the rods together so that the child experienced fear of a loud noise together with the sight of the rat. Watson did this many times, and soon Little Albert screamed and cried whenever he saw the rat. In fact, after a while, Little Albert would scream and cry at the sight of almost any white furry object. Watson had demonstrated that you can teach people to be afraid and that responses can be generalized to other similar stimuli in the environment.

Behaviorists today view **school phobia,** a generalized fear response to school situations, in much the same way that Watson viewed Little Albert's learning. They suggest that, in many cases of school phobia, children have been frightened by their teachers' or peers' aggressive or hostile responses and that the resulting fear has generalized to the school situation itself.

*Classical
(Respondent)
Conditioning*

Little Albert did not have to be taught how to scream and cry when he heard the sticks banging together behind him. His crying was a reflex action; he cried automatically. This is an example of what behaviorists term an unconditioned stimulus (noise) and an unconditioned response (crying). An **unconditioned stimulus** produces a response without learning having to take place. An **unconditioned response** is one that takes place automatically in the presence of an unconditioned stimulus.

One of the first systematic and objective accounts of these phenomena was reported by Ivan Pavlov, a Russian psychologist, in the early twentieth century. Pavlov's experiments involved training a subject to respond to a neutral stimulus—one that by itself would be incapable of eliciting a response—by repeatedly associating it with an unconditioned stimulus. The white rat was a neutral stimulus until Little Albert learned to associate it with the loud noise (unconditioned stimulus). The white rat then became a **conditioned stimulus.** Crying at the presentation of the white rat is an example of a **conditioned (learned) response.** This simple form of learning is called **classical conditioning;** it is also called **respondent conditioning** because the subject does not respond until after the stimulus has been presented.

Pavlov demonstrated classical conditioning in the simplest and clearest way possible by conditioning (training) dogs to salivate at the sound of a bell. A hungry dog will not naturally salivate at the sound of a bell, but it will salivate at the sight and smell of food. Pavlov presented the food and rang the bell almost simultaneously a number of times so that eventually the ringing bell alone was enough to make the dog salivate. Once this had taken place, the ringing bell had become a conditioned stimulus. By pairing conditioned and unconditioned stimuli many times, Pavlov was able to elicit the response of salivation to a conditioned stimulus (ringing bell). Salivation at the sight and smell of food was an unconditioned response; salivation at the sound of the bell became a conditioned response.

Pavlov discovered that time had an important effect on the strength of the dogs' responses. The dogs salivated much more when he presented the food approximately half a second after he rang the bell. If he waited longer, the association between the food and the bell was weaker, and the dogs salivated less.

This finding has useful implications for the classroom teacher who wants to know why children behave as they do. On the first day at school, young children may not respond in any particular way to the school bell. They may continue to talk and play after the bell has rung. Teachers often condition young students to come to attention immediately after the bell has rung by using a voice that children will automatically respond to—the tone of voice in this case is the unconditioned stimulus. Not many pairings of the voice and the school bell are needed before the class will come to order on hearing the school bell alone. Another example is the way children respond to three short sounds that indicate that there is a fire drill. Almost immediately, older children who have experienced many such drills rise to their feet, close windows and doors, and proceed down prearranged exit routes, along with their teachers. Children similarly become conditioned to grading systems when high grades are associated with parent and teacher approval, and low grades are associated with disapproval. This conditioning may last well into adulthood.

Using Pavlov's procedures, V. M. Bechterev (1928) conditioned dogs to raise their paws in response to a bell or a light by administering a small electric shock to their paws immediately after flashing the light or ringing the bell. The dogs raised their paws automatically when given the shock (the unconditioned stimulus) alone. By pairing the shock with light or sound (the conditioned stimulus) a number of times, Bechterev could make the dogs raise their paws in response to either the light or the bell alone. Bechterev found that the dogs raised their paws more quickly when the shock followed the light or bell by a short interval. The dogs had learned that they could avoid the shock that was sure to come by raising their paws right after the conditioned stimulus was presented. This type of classical conditioning is called **avoidance learning.**

Bechterev's finding is also useful to the teacher. Children are afraid of people who yell in anger or scowl constantly. Teachers who cannot control their tempers or show a dour, unsmiling face all the time are certain to instill fear responses in children. Some feel that the only sure time to obtain obedience and respect from students is at the very beginning of the school year. "Do not smile at them," these teachers say, "not at the beginning! Give them the idea that you are tough and stern and they will get the message of what is in store for them during the rest of the year." Unfortunately, these teachers very often have the highest incidence of "morning stomach aches" among their pupils and the largest number of resentful parents who have to cope with this problem every morning of the first three or four weeks of school, sometimes even longer. Bright, well-adjusted youngsters will survive and progress in spite of a negative environment, but the weaker ones will very often mentally wilt and resist any enriching experience presented by such a teacher.

As we have seen, learning occurs when the unconditioned and conditioned stimuli occur close together in time, and a response is made. But something else happens that determines whether or not the same response will occur again. Edward L. Thorndike (1913) proposed a principle called the **law of effect** to explain the association process more fully. This law states that the association between a stimulus and a response is strengthened or weakened depending on whether a "satisfier" or an "annoyer" follows the response. If a satisfier (a reward) follows, the bond will be strengthened; if an annoyer (punishment) follows, the bond will be weakened.

Thorndike's early studies were based on observing the behavior of chickens, cats, and dogs as they learned to escape from a specially constructed box (Thorndike, 1898). At first an animal made a series of random movements. Eventually, it made the required response that opened the box and revealed food—the satisfier. When the animal was placed in the box again, it took less time to make the required response and get the food. The reward determined how fast the animal learned to make the right response; the stimulus and response simply occurring together did not determine how rapidly the learning process occurred.

Thorndike believed that humans learn by trial and error, or, better, by trial and success. When confronted with a new problem, people stab in the dark, hit or miss, until they find an approach that works. When they finally do arrive at a correct solution, they stop trying alternatives; they think they have discovered the key and will use it again when confronted with the same problem. For example, Felix, age 3, was being introduced to the game of hide and seek. After unhappily being found immediately many times, Felix found a better spot to hide—behind the teacher's desk. To his great joy, he was one of the last to be found. Because this pleased him, he continued to hide gleefully in the same spot even though, by now, the other children knew where he would be.

In a typical experiment, high school students who had no knowledge of Spanish were shown a list of Spanish words and were asked to match them with the English equivalent. (Thorndike, 1932). After students had guessed, the experimenter told them whether their answers were right or wrong. Thorndike assumed that correct answers would be satisfying and that wrong answers would be annoying and thus, a very mild form of punishment. Because of this, he assumed that the students would be more likely to repeat the right answer when presented with the same Spanish word, and to change their answers if they were wrong. In fact, however, students who made wrong guesses were more apt to give the same wrong answer when presented with the same word again later.

The students' behavior led Thorndike to develop a second law of effect, which he called the **truncated law of effect.** Thorndike stated that, although satisfiers always strengthen the bond between stimulus and response, annoyers (punishment) do not necessarily weaken it; in fact, they could have very little effect on it at all. Thorndike had established that punishment does not automatically weaken or inhibit a response—an observation that educators have been very slow to understand.

*Operant
(Instrumental)
Conditioning*

In classical (respondent) conditioning, the key to learning is what happens *before* a response is made. When Little Albert was classically conditioned to fear a white rat, the animal was presented *before* he made his fear response. According to the law of effect, on the other hand, learning also depends on what happens *after* the response. Thorndike's animals learned to get out of the box *after* they made the correct response. Similarly, students learn to study properly when high grades come afterwards.

One of the first psychologists to take this approach to learning was B. F. Skinner. Skinner is considered to be one of the most influential contemporary psycholgists in America. He is the author of many extremely important and controversial books dealing with learning, behavior, and the effects of both on society. He systematically applied Thorndike's findings to human learning, pointing out that people make an overwhelming number of responses to the overwhelming number of stimuli around them. Many responses are emitted spontaneously at first, and the type of stimulus that follows a response determines whether or not that response is repeated or discarded. Because Skinner sees people as actively operating on the environment, this type of learning came to be called **operant conditioning.** It is also called **instrumental conditioning** because one response (or *instrument*) is most likely to lead to a reward (or *reinforcement*).

In order to study operant conditioning in its simplest or purest form, Skinner designed an enclosed box (subsequently called a **Skinner box**) that contained a bar or lever and a device for providing reinforcers such as food pellets, candy bars, or water. Pressing the bar would release the reinforcer. Skinner then deprived rats and other animals of food before he put them in the box. At first, the hungry animals made a variety of random movements. At some point, by chance, a rat would press the bar and immediately receive a pellet of food. This reward naturally led to another bar-pressing and another pellet. The number of bar-pressings could be used to measure the strength of operant response, which Skinner called **operant strength.** Operant strength is one way to describe the amount of learning that has taken place.

We can see many real-life examples of how people modify their behavior, depending on what happens after they make their responses. For example, any young child demands love, attention, food, and objects. Her mother, however, is free to ignore all of them until her daughter says "Please." In this way, children learn to say "Please" in order to get what they want. Their demands are really **operants;** they are attempts to create change in the environment. A mother wants to teach her child to phrase requests politely and responds only when the child utters the polite word. When she does make the operant response of saying "Please," she is rewarded by getting what she wants. The situation works much the same way in school. In the story that opened this chapter, Michelle learned to solve cognitive problems when she received praise following the successful completion of a task.

This child is learning to read by working with a special typewriter that provides reinforcement in the form of letters flashed on a large screen in front of him whenever he makes a correct response.

Toje Fujihira, Monkmeyer

Reinforcement As we have seen, the critical element in the operant conditioning approach to learning is what happens after a response has been made. Responses that are rewarded tend to be repeated and strengthened. The psychological term for this type of reward is **reinforcement.**

Some reinforcers are physiological. These reinforcers are called **primary reinforcers** because they are of prime importance to the physical survival of the organism. Food and water are examples of primary reinforcers. Reinforcers not necessary to the physical survival of the organism are called **secondary reinforcers.** Secondary reinforcers are not rewarding until they become associated with primary reinforcers. For example, a baby learns to associate food and touch-contact with its mother's presence. Later, the mother's presence alone becomes a secondary reinforcer. Young students find their teacher's social approval reinforcing. Later, many students associate this approval with high grades; high grades alone become secondary reinforcers to these students.

Reinforcement in the classroom may be informal and spontaneous or carefully structured and formal. A hard candy, a colorful sticker on a good paper, stars on charts for students who have exhibited certain desired behaviors, special reward learning centers, and student-of-the-day or of-the-week are all effective reinforcements for younger students. Older students may find acceptance into special learning groups such as gifted groups or Beta Clubs, invitations to serve on publications' staffs, or opportunities to speak at community club meetings reinforcing.

Psychologists have pointed out that infants whose parents smiled, cooed, and gurgled at them at the same time as feeding and touching them tend later to become children who seek approval from others. Approval in this example has become a secondary reinforcer through association with earlier satisfaction of needs. But what about infants whose parents scowled, threatened, and perhaps slapped and abused them when they fed them? What behaviors are likely to become secondary reinforcers for these infants as they get older? Infants and children who are continually brutalized by the same people who provide them with primary reinforcers are likely to perceive this brutalization as a secondary reinforcer. This example helps us understand why battered children often defend and even love the parents who have brutalized them and seem, in many cases, to almost want to be hurt. In this case, painful behavior serves as a reinforcer, that is, a stimulus that follows a behavior and increases its frequency.

Negative reinforcement and punishment   So far, we have discussed only **positive reinforcers**—stimuli that follow operant behavior and increase its frequency. In the case of the battered child, brutalization can be a positive reinforcer when it increases the frequency of the behavior it follows. A teacher may have a problem with a disruptive student who does not pay attention in class. The teacher can begin to correct this behavior by watching the student closely and giving praise immediately after he or she does pay attention, however briefly. If the student's moments of attention are followed by praise often and regularly, he or she will gradually become more and more attentive in class. Praise, in this case, is a positive reinforcement. It's not always so simple. Sometimes children are disruptive because they want attention. In this case, the teacher must do much more than simply supply praise for good behavior; he or she must be extremely careful not to supply attention of any kind—even criticism—to the unwanted behavior. Needless to say, this is often a very difficult task.

Reinforcers may be negative as well as positive. Negative reinforcement, like positive reinforcement, increases the frequency of operant behavior, but the operant behavior it reinforces consists of *escaping* from the **negative reinforcer.** For example, a high school girl has not been doing her homework and thinks she may fail an upcoming examination. If she fails this examination, she will probably receive a low grade for the course. This possibility frightens her because she has had a good scholastic record so far and is proud of it. She therefore decides to study the course material regularly every day and passes the exam with a fairly high grade. By studying regularly, that is, by increasing a certain kind of operant behavior, she escapes the threat of the failure and lowered self-esteem, both of which are negative reinforcers in this case.

Negative reinforcers are effective when there is an opportunity to escape them by adopting constructive behavior and that opportunity is obvious to the individual. The teacher who is faced with a severely disruptive student is in a very difficult situation. Sometimes, unfortunately, the teacher's frustration leads to the use of an aversive stimulus in the attempt to suppress the disruption. Such a teacher might choose to use corporal punishment, for example, when there doesn't seem to be any other way out.

Punishment in any form is the administration of an aversive stimulus, that is, something undesirable, for the purpose of suppressing the immediately preceding response. Teachers who strike children or scream at them believe that such punishment will stop the child from acting in an undesirable way. Unfortunately, the actual effects of using aversive stimuli in this way are variable. The child might temporarily suppress the unwanted behavior. On the other hand, as Thorndike's studies of high school students suggest, he or she might not.

Negative reinforcers, although they may in fact be the same noxious stimuli, differ from punishment in their purpose. Unlike punishment, negative reinforcers are designed to strengthen an escape response, not to inhibit an undesirable response. The high school girl we described earlier was generally conscientious and was reinforced

Teachers sometimes resort to punishment to deal with disruptive students.

Tass from Sovfoto

for her behavior by receiving good grades (positive reinforcer). Had her teacher chosen to use the threat of poor grades as a negative reinforcer, she probably would have said something like "You'd better study harder or you might not pass the test." The girl might choose to study in order to escape this threat. But she could also choose some other escape response—for example, dropping the course. But what would happen if she decides not to drop the course but doesn't study and as a result can't answer the questions on the test? She would probably get a failing grade. This bad grade is designed as punishment for her after she has not studied, in order to teach her to study in the future. But what escape is available? The lack of studying has already occurred. If the student can't take the test over again, no escape is possible. She might just give up and drop out, one of the responses to negative reinforcement listed in Figure 3-1.

There are ways to make negative reinforcement effective in some classroom situations. One fourth-grade teacher and her class had a discussion on the danger everybody faced if physically violent attacks by students were allowed to go uncontrolled. The teacher asked the class to write suggestions for a penalty for fighting. The unsigned suggestions were read out loud, and the class settled on ten weeks without going ouside at recess. The teacher tried to reduce the penalty, but the students insisted that they were concerned about their safety and wanted a stiff penalty to make sure that the class bullies would get the message.

In this case, allowing students to participate in setting penalties and making sure that the penalty would apply equally to all offenders

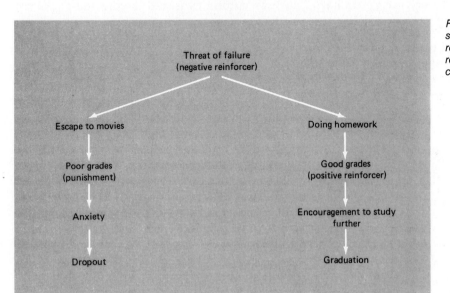

Figure 3–1 Flow chart showing possible responses to negative reinforcement in the classroom.

made it a highly effective way to reduce undesirable behavior. Potential bullies got the message: There was an effective and socially desirable response they could make in order to escape the penalty. That was to behave in nonviolent ways. Doing homework and studying may be two other positive escape responses to negative reinforcement, as Figure 3-1 shows. Such positive escape responses, however, occur much less frequently than the less desirable ones do.

Negative reinforcers follow the same learning principles as positive reinforcers—with one important distinction. The *introduction* of a positive reinforcer increases the probability that the immediately preceding response will occur again, while the *termination* of a negative reinforcer does the same thing. There is a second important difference that the teacher ought to consider carefully: The response that is caused by a negative reinforcer is an escape response, but the escape is not always the response that the teacher intended to reinforce, and, in fact, may be just the opposite. Instead of studying as a means to escape the teacher's anger, the student might decide to cut class and, in so doing, successfully escape the negative reinforcer at least for a short time. Teachers are very well acquainted with the very serious problem of cutting class. Each successive cut makes it more difficult for the student to come to class the next time. Once a student gets into the habit of cutting, the probability of his or her becoming a real dropout increases significantly.

Other common forms of negative reinforcement currently in vogue in our schools are ridicule, sarcasm, criticism, and detention. The termination of these negative reinforcers always reinforces escape responses. Some of these are desired by the teacher, but some of them are not so desirable, such as cutting class and daydreaming. All too frequently, the teacher does not notice which escape response was reinforced because of the erroneous assumption that punishment alone was operating to inhibit the inappropriate behavior. Negative reinforcers used by classroom teachers increase the probability that whatever the child was doing when the negative reinforcer stopped will be repeated. The story is told of a principal who promised his teachers that if their charges did not do their homework, they could send them to his office where he would paddle them. The same young girl appeared in his office regularly for this penalty. When asked about its effectiveness by an outside observer, the teacher countered, "Well, you can see how poor a student she really is, since even repeated spankings by the principal have not gotten her to do her homework." Truancy, dropping out of school, even physical counterattacks are not uncommon escape responses adopted by school children. Recently there have been increasing numbers of students involved in attacks on teachers.

Continuing negative reinforcement can also lead to extreme anxiety, an emotional response that makes complex problem-solving much more difficult. Each of us can recall preparing at great length for exams but doing poorly because we feared the outcome.

The anxiety caused by punishment (with no escape response available) or negative reinforcement (with an escape response) often suppresses other desirable responses. For example, a child enthusiastically raises his hand to answer a question asked by the teacher, but responds incorrectly. There is laughter, not only from the child's classmates but from the teacher as well. This type of reaction helps to create the high levels of anxiety found in our schools. Occasionally, children become too frightened to answer or to ask any questions—even to ask for permission to use the toilet.

Danielle, age 12, was sure she knew the answer to "What does the word *corps* mean?" in her book. She waved her hand wildly to capture the teacher's attention. When she answered, "A dead body," there was some scattered laughter, but the teacher was quick to respond, with a smile, "Good thinking! Those words do look a lot alike. Let's look at them." She wrote both words, "corps" and "corpse," on the board, and the students discussed the differences and similarities in spelling, pronunciation, and meaning. Danielle was spared embarrassment; her teacher reduced the negative reinforcement and turned the situation into a positive learning situation.

Because of unique past experiences that each child has, each child will respond differently to negative reinforcement. In addition, each child considers different stimuli as aversive and uses different methods to avoid them. Because it is usually difficult for the teacher to know all the variables necessary to predict behavior accurately, using aversive stimuli is much riskier than using positive reinforcement to obtain the desired results.

Should teachers use negative reinforcement in the classroom? Yes, they probably should consider it sometimes. However, the circumstances under which it is effective are so rare that student teachers would be wise to seek other methods of teaching whenever possible. In one study, Hall and his colleagues (1971) found that using very mild aversive stimuli in a classroom setting could remove undesirable responses. In this study, children were assigned five-minute detentions each time they left their seats without permission. They learned very rapidly to stay in their seats. Even five days after the detentions were discontinued, the children's out-of-seat behavior remained significantly below the initial rate. The authors commented that aversive stimuli should not be "physically or psychologically abusive." However, since what is abusive to one child may not be to another, the teacher assumes great responsibility in using the technique.

Extinction   The rat in the Skinner box was reinforced with a food pellet every time it pressed the bar; this positive reinforcement led the rat to press the bar again in order to get another pellet. How long would

Cheating: One Response to Continued Negative Reinforcement

A popular escape from negative reinforcers in the classroom is cheating. Teachers and parents often wonder how young people can steal answers from each other so regularly and so glibly without any obvious twinges of conscience. A learning psychologist might explain cheating by saying that in many classrooms this particular escape response is stronger than any other.

Cheating can also happen in a classroom where academic achievement is not regarded as self-rewarding, but as a means of displaying superior ability, which quite often promotes a position of prestige in the peer group. By nature, youngsters need to distinguish themselves and be appreciated, but they very seldom possess enough maturity of character to be modest and demure about their achievements. In individualized systems, where students advance at their own pace on the basis of their ability to organize their work and master concepts independently, advancing beyond everybody else becomes a status symbol, not an academic goal. The pressure of achieving becomes a negative reinforcement that very often leads to cheating in order to keep the momentum while advancing from one skill to another. It takes a very alert teacher to become aware of potential trouble spots in the system, spots that may be open to cheating opportunities, and try to work around them by means of personal input.

it take the rat to stop pressing the bar if no food pellet were delivered each time? Likewise, did the high school girl mentioned earlier stop studying immediately after passing her exam because she knew she would not have to take another one for several weeks?

It has been demonstrated that behavior, if not reinforced, will gradually occur less and less frequently and will eventually return to the rate of occurrence before conditioning was first begun. This process is called **extinction.** Extinction may take a long time, depending on how strong the response was originally; the time it takes is a good indication of operant strength. A good example is David, a bright but troubled boy, who insists constantly that he hates people—teachers, classmates, siblings. He also hates school, including seatwork, homework, and anything connected with it. Although his teachers have to bite their tongues not to remind him that hating his world does not help his plight, they are attempting to ignore his constant whinings and capitalize on what he does of worth. If they are always extremely careful to ignore his unwanted behavior, they know that, gradually, it will diminish because they will no longer reinforce it with their attention.

Operant conditioning procedures, including extinction, can be put into effect without people being aware of them. Two colleagues and I conducted an experiment some years ago with college students to demonstrate that behavior can be changed quite unconsciously (Bachrach, Candland, and Gibson, 1961). The students were first reinforced for speaking rapidly during a conversation. The experimenters used positive reinforcement such as verbal approval and head nodding to show that they agreed with everything the students said. In this situation, the students increased their speaking rates dramatically (as measured by the number of words spoken per minute). After an extinction period, during which the experimenters ignored the students' comments in conversation by not responding and apparently not even listening, the students' speaking rate slowed down considerably. During both reinforcement and extinction periods, the students were totally unaware that they had increased or decreased their rate of speech and, in fact, were shocked to learn that their behavior had been manipulated in such a manner.

Teachers should use extinction instead of either negative reinforcement or punishment whenever possible. Simply ignoring the child's undesirable responses, while positively reinforcing the child's desirable responses, is more effective and predictable in its results. Few children can stand being ignored for any length of time. Some may go to great and unpleasant lengths to get the teacher's attention, so this technique does take patience and a lot of self-control.

How fast or how often reinforcers are given after a person's response determines the strength of the responses (operant strength).

Schedules of Reinforcement

Continuous reinforcement In the simplest schedule, called **continuous reinforcement,** reinforcement follows every response. This schedule produces a regular pattern of responding. Giving a gold star to a student every time he or she hands in a neat paper is an example of continuous reinforcement. In everyday life, however, it is usually impossible to reinforce desired responses continuously. The person responsible for the reinforcement is usually involved in other affairs and often misses the performance of a correct response. For example, a mother who has regularly praised her daughter whenever she cleans her room may sometimes be away and therefore not present to give reinforcement. Her daughter may then fall back into the habit of leaving her room messy. Desired behaviors that were learned on continuous reinforcement schedules are thus especially vulnerable to extinction.

Intermittent reinforcement Reinforcement given less frequently is called **intermittent reinforcement.** There are two types of intermittent reinforcement schedules—ratio and interval. On a **ratio schedule,** reinforcement is given only after the person has made a specified number of desired responses. If a teacher rewards a child with a gold star each time the child reads three books, the teacher is using a 3:1 ratio schedule.

Reinforcement on an **interval schedule** depends on the amount of time between reinforcements, not on the number of responses an individual makes. Individuals on an interval schedule quickly learn that it is not worthwhile to give the correct response until it is time to be reinforced. An example of an interval schedule would be announcing a quiz to be given every Friday. Most students wait until Thursday night to study for a Friday quiz.

Ratio and interval schedules can either be fixed or variable. On a **fixed schedule,** reinforcement is given according to a consistent and set pattern. A *fixed ratio schedule* provides reinforcement each time the person gives a specified number of desirable responses. A father who gives his son a dollar for every two A's on his report card has placed him on a fixed ratio schedule. A teacher who gives quizzes each and every Friday puts the students on a *fixed interval schedule.*

An individual who cannot accurately predict which response will be followed by reinforcement is said to be on a **variable schedule of reinforcement.** On a *variable ratio schedule,* reinforcement is given for an average number of responses rather than for some specified number. A man may be aware that, on the average, he will get a ticket 50 percent of the time if he parks in a no-parking zone. The other 50 percent of the time he will not receive a ticket, but he cannot predict the actual instance when he will or will not be ticketed.

The teacher who calls on her students to answer in rows does not understand the concept of variable ratio scheduling. If children know that they may be called on at random several times or not at all, they are more likely to study harder to have their answers ready. A by-product is that students will listen to the answers of others and will stay involved in the discussion, rather than daydreaming after they have answered.

The time period between reinforcers on a *variable interval schedule* may be short or long. A mother may praise her child "every once in a while" just because she "happens to feel like it." The responses established on variable reinforcement schedules, both ratio and interval, resist extinction and occur at a higher rate than those established on fixed schedules. Unannounced quizzes at irregular intervals will encourage students to study more frequently than quizzes that are always given on Fridays.

Delayed reinforcement A general principle of operant conditioning is that reinforcement is most effective when it immediately follows a response. This is particularly true with young children. The traditional grading system in schools is based on the dubious assumption that children will benefit even though there are long delays in reinforce-

Miriam Reinhart, Photo Researchers, Inc.

ment, and that grades are effective secondary reinforcers. Even if they were, their effectiveness as reinforcement is damaged because report-card grades are usually given at intervals of six to eight weeks, and papers are rarely graded immediately. Teachers should be aware of the fact that the grades they give out may have little or no effect on study habits if they are given too late.

Many teachers would like to provide immediate reinforcement, but simply don't have enough hours in the day to mark the never-ending stacks of papers generated by their students. Several answers to this problem have been suggested: select perhaps one-third of the papers at random to mark on a given night; have the students mark their own papers under group guidance and supervision; have students exchange papers; upgrade the quality of assignments so that thinking skills are developed and downgrade the quantity of problems or items; mark only one aspect of a paper or assignment (making sure that the students realize ahead of time which aspect will be marked); have students give their responses orally and mark them as they read or explain them.

The argument over grading goes on. Operant theorists point out that high grades do not serve as reinforcers for many students. In addition, they say, the delays involved in reporting grades make them ineffective. Others criticize grades as competitive, undemocratic, negative, subjective, inequitable, inaccurate, and frustrating. Furthermore, grades are considered to be punitive—they reduce or obliterate interest in a subject and tend to reward the plodding conformer and penalize the imaginative student. Opponents have suggested and devised alternatives such as evaluations and portfolios. Those in favor of grades argue that such alternatives at least imply grading—especially, for instance, if a portfolio contains only a student's best work. To them, students not graded on their measures of achievement are in for a rude shock when they enter the real world. Thus, a nonjudgmental system such as pass/fail is, for these proponents of grades, a fraud and an illusion. One spokesman for grades suggests that the problem lies not in the system itself but in its abuse. "The failure," he says, "is with the teacher" (Moulds, 1974, p. 503). Do you agree? What suggestions would you make to improve the system? Are there yet other alternatives educators may have overlooked?

Operant Conditioning and Higher-Order Learning

Operant conditioning reinforces desired responses that are at first given out spontaneously. The person responds correctly by chance and, when only the correct response is reinforced, learns to modify his or her behavior. According to learning theorists, even complex, higher-order learning occurs in this way.

Shaping   Learning more complex behavior can be achieved through a process called **shaping.** In the shaping procedure, the teacher begins by reinforcing *all* responses that are somewhat similar to, or that approximate, the desired response. Each successive reinforcement increases the probability that the student will spend more time doing what the teacher wants. In Michelle's case, when that happened, the teacher then gradually limited reinforcement so that finally she was reinforced only when she solved complex learning tasks.

Mathematics, languages, reading skills—any traditional school subject—can be taught more effectively if the teacher has a basic understanding of the technique of shaping. When the student first enters a new and difficult subject area, the teacher should begin by rewarding any improvement. As the student progresses, the teacher should reinforce only those responses that reflect an understanding that goes beyond the basics. In teaching a child to write the alphabet, for example, the teacher first reinforces all attempts to draw letters, whether they are correct or not; later the teacher withholds praise until the letters are more correctly drawn.

Discrimination and generalization During the course of learning, an individual comes to respond in a certain way to one set of circumstances and in a different way to another set of circumstances. Psychologists call this phenomenon **discrimination.** Discrimination occurs when the individual responds to two or more stimuli in different ways. Discriminations are continually being made in our everyday lives, as well as in the classroom. Babies learn to discriminate among the overwhelming number of sounds they hear. Children, in learning to read, discriminate among the letters in the alphabet. College students learn very fine distinctions among abstract concepts.

The opposite of discrimination is **generalization.** In **stimulus generalization,** the same response is made to two or more stimuli. A child bitten by a dog might come to respond to all dogs with fear. Here the same response, fear, is generalized from one particular dog to all dogs in general. On the other hand, if a child has a rewarding experience with a dog, he or she might generalize this enjoyment and learn to love other animals.

How many of us can remember our first-grade teacher? We either loved her dearly or feared her. Seldom did we remain neutral about her. Her effect on us was devastating or gratifying, and whatever we came to feel about teachers in general probably was generalized from our feelings about that first-grade teacher.

Response generalization occurs when a particular stimulus evokes responses that are similar or related to the desired response. A student who is conditioned to stop talking and sit quietly when the bell rings will probably also exhibit a variety of other related responses. For example, he or she may pick up pencils, check to see that all books and papers are available, and look attentive.

Sometimes a generalization occurs to such an extent that it distorts reality. We call such a phenomenon **overgeneralization.** Any rigid and detailed stereotype involves an overgeneralization. For example, not all blondes are dumb, and not all of them have more fun.

Chaining Thus far we have discussed how to reinforce only one desirable response in operant conditioning. It is also possible to teach a series of responses that must be performed in a specified order before they are reinforced. This kind of higher-order learning is called **chaining.** Skinner taught rats and pigeons to perform very complex acts by this process. One of his most famous examples involved teaching pigeons to play a highly competitive form of modified ping-pong.

Daily life often consists of sequences of stimulus-response connections that work together in a larger, overall pattern. For example, the sequence that makes up the morning ritual might run as follows: The alarm clock goes off; the person rises from bed and puts water on the stove to boil; he or she then washes up; the water boils and the person makes coffee, whose aroma stimulates the appetite; he or she then prepares breakfast and eats it; the cat in the meantime begins to cry for food, a signal for the person to feed it, and so on. Chains like this are common in everyday life. We do not learn such behavior chains all at once. Most of us learn one part at a time and then find the most effective way to put them together. You might not be able to find the bathroom before having your coffee, but someone else might prefer to get all dressed before sitting down to relax with a morning cup of brew.

Superstitious behavior involves the same chaining process. Skinner (1948a) put pigeons into a box and reinforced them with grain once every minute regardless of what they did. Each pigeon tended to repeat whatever it had been doing just before it was reinforced. For instance, one pigeon circled continually to the left while another pecked in a certain corner before going to the food box. Because these responses were not related to reinforcement, Skinner termed this superstitious behavior.

People develop superstitious responses in much the same way that lower animals do. Any chained series of responses that occurs before a reinforcement will tend to occur more frequently in the future, whether those responses actually caused the reinforcement to be administered or just happened to occur before it. Students who receive high grades on an exam sometimes superstitiously wear the same clothes when they come to take the next exam.

Other explanations for higher-order learning Behavioral research shows that students learn more effectively when teachers use appropriate operant techniques such as shaping or chaining. However, all psychologists do not feel that doing a good job of conditioning automatically ensures that students will become good problem-solvers. Many psychologists agree that proper use of operant procedures usually makes learning easier. But, they point out, a great deal of learning is so complex that we cannot begin to describe it without delving into the thinking process itself. For these psychologists, strict operant approaches provide a simplistic view of learning.

using behaviorist approaches in the classroom

*Classical
Conditioning*

Classical (respondent) conditioning occurs continually in the classroom, although the teacher and the students are usually not aware of it. As we noted earlier, Watson conditioned Little Albert to fear a white rat by pairing the sight of the rat with a loud noise, a stimulus that instinctively evokes a fear response in babies. The baby then generalized his fear of white rats to other white furry objects. A parallel situation often exists in the classroom.

Teachers and parents frequently create high levels of anxiety in children by threatening them with failure. This threat represents the unconditioned stimulus in classical conditioning. Every other activity that is accompanied by the threat becomes a conditioned stimulus by association. The highly anxious student stops wanting to study, come to school, or, in fact, do most things associated with the anxiety. Sometimes a student manages to perform well in spite of the threat because the subsequent reinforcement overrides the effect of the conditioning.

Unfortunately, many children experience great anxiety not only about wrong answers but about school in general. The simplest means at a teacher's disposal to overcome anxiety is to discontinue threatening or punishing the students. The teacher can also try to recondition a student by creating a pleasurable situation whenever the student begins to grow anxious or frightened—for example, the teacher can encourage the anxious child to talk about hobbies or pastimes. One student, Heidi, knew she was intelligent, and she knew the material, but she got so nervous that she just couldn't concentrate on tests. Her teacher was unaware of her fear of testing until Heidi's mother mentioned it during a conference. With this helpful information, the teacher was able to give Heidi support and reassurance by talking to her calmly before tests and by giving her an occasional friendly pat on the shoulder during tests. Testing became less of a problem for Heidi because she knew the teacher understood.

Conditioned anxiety in students can often be reduced by allowing children to act out their anxiety or anger in ways that teachers let them know are acceptable. Little Michelle, for example, acted out her feelings in free play. The teacher told her that knocking down her blocks was "all right, " and then, later, Michelle was able to perform more constructive tasks.

Reinforcement also occurs regularly in the classroom. Its effects depend on the type of reinforcers used.

*Operant
Conditioning:
The Effects of
Reinforcement*

Using reinforcement procedures with the lecture method   In traditional classrooms teachers lecture to their students for large portions of the day. The lecture method has a number of drawbacks, according to behavior theory. The most important is that frequently the teacher does not give students time to respond and therefore the learning is not reinforced. What can the alert teacher do about this? One teacher provided a list of suggestions that work, she says, even with large classes: (1) Make up a list of questions to intersperse with the lecture material. It's best to prepare many questions to make sure that you have enough, and also to be sure that they are simple enough for your students to answer correctly. Stop every few minutes to ask the questions, always being careful to choose different children who are paying attention and who should be able to give the right answer.

Teachers reward students in various ways. A teacher's attention to an interested student is a potent tool for learning.

Remember always to reinforce—perhaps with praise, perhaps with another question. (2) Arrange to have your students do some of the lecture themselves. Assign them topics ahead of time. It's best to make these mini-lectures brief, both to give as many students as possible time to provide lecture material to the class (and, of course, be reinforced for their responses), and to keep interest level high. (3) Give your students the task of making up lists of questions based on what you're talking about. With each lecture, provide opportunity for students to ask their questions. Reinforce good questions by assigning the class the task of answering them, or answer them yourself. Remember, as long as your students have opportunities to respond to what you are saying and doing in class, and as long as you reinforce the good responses, learning will continue. If you spend your day lecturing to note-taking students, and if you don't allow for responding and reinforcing, learning won't take place. The result will be simply a tired teacher and a group of bored students.

Positive reinforcement, negative reinforcement, and punishment One researcher (Feshbach, 1972) examined the styles of reinforcement used by mothers with their 4-year-old children. She found that working-class mothers employ negative reinforcement far more frequently than middle-class mothers do. This finding is significant for two reasons. First, psychologists have shown that children tend to adopt their parents' behavior. Children whose mothers frequently use negative reinforcement are more likely to use negative reinforcement in their dealings with other children. Second, the type of reinforcement used in the home relates to learning skills. Feshbach found that poor readers tended to have parents who used a great deal of negative reinforcement, while the parents of better readers used positive reinforcement more often.

All sorts of teacher behaviors have been shown to affect student learning in the classroom. Woolfolk (1978), for example, pointed out that teachers' tone of voice and facial expression (pleasantness) can serve as positive reinforcers for sixth graders. Simple praise has been shown highly effective in increasing reading and math achievement (Walker and Hops, 1976).

The teacher's reinforcement style also has a strong effect on student behavior. Feshbach (1972) had children observe two 4-minute films in which a teacher gave a brief geography lesson. In one film, the teacher used positive reinforcement to motivate the children, while in the other the teacher used negative reinforcement. Feshbach found that middle-class children imitated the mannerisms of the teacher who used positive reinforcement significantly more than the teacher who used negative reinforcement. This is further evidence that the negative reinforcement that is so prevalent in our public schools does not promote desired behavior.

In another classroom study, Cooper (1977) showed that teachers' negative criticism of academic work of first and second graders was related directly to decreased academic initiations. Children who received negative criticism simply didn't try as hard.

Two major drawbacks to the use of negative reinforcement and punishment in the classroom are: (1) they both raise anxiety levels in children and (2) in the case of negative reinforcement it may lead children to adopt undesirable escape responses. The child may also interpret the negative reinforcement as an indication of personal failure. In such a case, the child's levels of performance and aspiration may both be reduced.

"Yes," the future teacher may respond, "but *some* anxiety increases the child's attention span." This is true, but with important qualification. A low level of anxiety does enable a child to sustain attention and make other conditioned responses. However, a high level of anxiety greatly interferes with complex learning processes. Furthermore, once established, anxiety is very difficult to extinguish. Finally, the child generalizes anxiety to other situations.

"But," the future teacher may continue, "negative reinforcement allows me to control my classes more effectively." This argument is inaccurate and misleading. Under aversive stimuli children often adopt a method of escape that is even more difficult for the teacher to control. They may withdraw completely, or in very extreme cases, they may attack the teacher physically. The teacher may very well end up with less control than he or she had to begin with.

The teacher's voice and facial expression can serve as a positive reinforcer.

Corporal punishment Corporal punishment carries with it many problems that make it an ineffective and undesirable method of controlling behavior. Corporal punishment is associated by those who receive it with pain, anxiety, and, more often than not, resentment and open hostility toward the grown-up who slapped, whacked, or beat them. Still, some school administrators and teachers insist on seeing physical punishment as necessary and valuable. One principal had three paddles in his office in different sizes for affluent, middle-class, and slum children. He justified this biased treatment of children by saying, "I try to go along with parents' preferences" (Ramella, 1973, p. 26).

During a parent-teacher conference, Mr. Lewis showed concern about his son Eric's disruptive behavior in class. "Just sock him a good one across the head. He'll behave then!" The teacher tactfully explained that he would rather deal with the situation without hitting the child. The father responded that Eric was often bad at home and that all he needed was "a good belt." Obviously, the frequent punishment at home had not improved the boy's behavior. The teacher wisely looked elsewhere for an answer to Eric's problem.

Corporal punishment is, of course, not the only kind of noxious stimulus the student might encounter in the classroom. Psychological punishment—criticism, ridicule, or sarcasm that occurs after a child makes an improper response and from which he or she cannot escape—can be equally devastating. Standing behind the classroom door as a punishment or wearing a dunce cap might not have hurt our bottoms, but they left——for those of us who received them—indelible and unpleasant images in our memories.

Delayed reinforcement in the classroom   Some teachers do not reinforce their students' good performances until days and weeks later when report cards are issued. They may assume that students provide their own self-reinforcement when they do well on a paper, and that this self-reinforcement should suffice until report card time. In fact, research has shown that students do sometimes reinforce themselves for good work. However, this occurs most frequently with high achievers and not with low achievers (Ames, 1978), a fact that teachers frequently do not consider. On the other hand, these same teachers very often strengthen children's bad behavior by reinforcing it immediately. For example, as teachers, we tend to pay attention to the child who talks out loud and hits his or her neighbor and not notice the child who sits quietly and does everything we expect.

Ability to learn through use of delayed reinforcement is partly a function of age. Sturges (1978) showed that, under some conditions, college students who received informative feedback from a multiple-choice computer-assisted test remembered more with delayed (20-minute to 24-hour) feedback than when feedback was immediate. However, these results cannot be generalized to other groups of students. Those who eventually enter college constitute a select group and by the time they reach college age, students usually have learned to deal with delayed reinforcers in the grading system.

programmed instruction and behavioral technology

In his observations of the Boston public schools during the 1940s, B. F. Skinner noted a number of common, but ineffective, teaching techniques. Classes were large, and the teachers taught all students the same thing at the same time without regard for individual abilities. They could provide very little immediate feedback to the students and had to leave reinforcement primarily to chance.

Skinner designed a mechanical teaching device that instructed each student individually and provided immediate feedback. He programmed the machine to present the student with progressively more complex problems step by step. Each step (or frame) contained a question, and the machine could immediately tell the student whether the answer was right or wrong. Skinner phrased the questions so that the student would most likely make correct responses, which the machine immediately reinforced, thereby increasing the probablity of more correct responses. In this manner, students proceeded through a subject area from simple to complex problems and received continual immediate feedback (J. Gibson, 1972).

Although Skinner's teaching machines were not the first, their demonstrated success motivated educators to further develop and popularize them. Today teaching machines, programmed textbooks, and technological aids that provide immediate feedback to the student, as for example, computers used in computer-assisted instruction, are used in the teaching of many different subjects. In each case, the purpose of the *behavioral technology*, as it is called, is to offer individualized plans of study based not only on students' interests and needs, but also on reinforcements that are effective in teaching. Behavioral technology's significant contribution to education lies in its ability to tailor instruction individually for each student.

*Programmed
Instruction*

There are two basic types of programming used in **programmed instruction:** linear and branching. In *linear programming,* the questions are arranged in a single line from simple to complex. Every student answers the same questions in the same order. Norman Crowder introduced branching programming in 1959 in order to suit the needs of a wide range of students. *Branching programming* routes each student individually, depending on his or her responses at preselected choice points. If a student answers incorrectly at one of these points, the program supplies more material on the subject and asks another question. If the student answers correctly at the choice point, the program simply goes on to a more difficult question (see Figures 3–2 and 3–3).

Many teachers agree that programmed instruction is useful in teaching *some* subject matters. Because programmed material can present a logical sequence of questions, starting with the most simple and going to the most difficult, these teachers point out that it is ideally suited to teach complex concepts such as in mathematics, geometry, or economics, where a thorough understanding depends on the mastery of certain basic ideas.

However, skeptics persist in asking if programmed instruction can really teach a student to think. Some psychologists would answer that if teachers can define behaviorally what they want students to do, they can use programmed instruction to teach anything, even poetry. All learning involves a rational process that is governed by environmental consequences. The act of writing poetry consists of responses the writer makes to very complex elements in the environment. Programmed material, many behavioral psychologists conclude, can even teach poetry appreciation and creative problem-solving (Hilgard and Bower, 1975).

Figure 3-2 An example
of a linear program.
(J. Gibson, Educational
Psychology, 2nd ed.,
p. 187. © 1972.
Reprinted by permission
of Prentice-Hall, Inc.,
Englewood Cliffs, N.J.)

7 Growth is directional, proceeding from head to foot. At birth the head is large in comparison to the rest of the body. As the child grows older, the rate of growth increases in the lower extremities of the body. As this occurs, the head gradually begins to look (larger/smaller) in comparison to the rest of the body.[2]

•

7   smaller

8 A child is able to manipulate his arms and hands before he learns to coordinate his legs. He can hold a rattle and bring it to his mouth long before he can control the movements of his legs and feet to walk.
Development, as well as growth occurs in a h_____ to f_____ direction.

•

8   head to foot

9 Frequently it is difficult for a child below the age of six, whose arm may be sufficiently powerful to swing a baseball bat, to make the finer finger manipulations required for printing or drawing. When this happens we know that:

a. motor development probably has not yet developed sufficiently in his fingers. As teachers, we should be helpful rather than punitive; therefore, when he turns in sloppy printing or drawing on a paper.
b. he must have a partial paralysis of the arms.
c. he is not developing properly.
d. we should train the muscles by requiring him to create "neat" and very small but intricate drawings.

•

9   a

Figure 3-3 An example
of a branching program.
(D. L. Ramsey and L. M.
Solomon, Simulations in
Dermatology, p. 124.
New York: Appleton-
Century-Crofts, 1974.)

IN INITIATING THERAPY, YOU WOULD BE PARTICULARLY INTERESTED TO ORDER (SELECT AS MANY AS YOU CONSIDER ESPECIALLY PERTINENT):

144	Topical paintings with nitrogen mustard (mechlorethamine)	144	[Steady and real improvement, but patient's skin becomes very reactive, and it is necessary to discontinue the medication. Eventually lesions reappear. MAKE ANOTHER CHOICE FROM THIS SECTION.]
145	Prednisone 50 mg p.o. q.d.	145	[Some improvement noted, but patient develops a gastric ulcer and it is necessary to discontinue the medication. Lesions reappear. MAKE ANOTHER CHOICE FROM THIS SECTION.]
146	Methotrexate 37.5 mg IM q. wk	146	[Improvement. MAKE NO FURTHER CHOICES FROM THIS SECTION. TURN NOW TO SECTION 10–F.]
147	Goekerman regimen	147	[No improvement.]

Computers are a relatively recent addition to the educational scene. Yet they have been used and tested at all educational levels, from kindergarten through graduate school. The computer has a remarkable capacity for collecting, processing, storing, and retrieving large amounts of information. This is its key asset in an educational program. Individualized instruction methods in particular need computer assistance. The computer can provide background data for each student and can store test results; it can provide a complete listing of the materials used by each student during each class; it can evaluate and score student responses with remarkable speed; it can develop special plans of study geared to the individual learner. Finally, the computer can suggest how close a student is to his or her individually prescribed level of achievement.

There are almost no limits to the potential uses of computers in education. Currently, computers are being used as laboratory computing devices. Many schools also use computers for information storage and retrieval, enabling teachers and administrators to record and process important data regarding students and curriculum. Computer science can also be applied in locating references and serving as audiovisual aids for teachers. Another development has been the grading of essay tests and compositions by computer. At the University of Connecticut a computer analyzes a whole essay for ideas, organization, style, mechanics, and creativity. It makes comments similar to those of a teacher and assigns a grade—all within a total time of 30 seconds! Of course, only the teacher can determine the variables that the computer measures in analyzing the essay.

Often the primary function of the computer in individualized instruction is to assist teachers and students in planning and record keeping. The instruction itself is not generally automated; this type of instruction is called **computer-managed instruction (CMI).** In some instances, though, the computer itself prescribes learning materials on an individual basis; this type is called **computer-assisted instruction (CAI)** (Cooley and Glaser, 1969).

Most CAI systems in use today are equipped with a small television screen, which serves as the display apparatus, and with a typewriter keyboard, which students use to respond to test items. CAI involves continual interaction between the student and the program. The computer functions as a teaching machine; it presents information, asks questions, and records and evaluates responses.

Some CAI programs suggest appropriate topics and materials for students, but the actual selection is made by the teacher. In other programs (such as tutorial systems), the computer determines the nature and sequencing of material. Since this requires elaborate and extensive equipment, school systems have rarely been able to afford such computer programs.

Computers also have been used to provide novel sources of classroom reinforcement. One famous computer used in a New York City public school was designed to look and act like a robot. Leachim, as the robot was called, could provide individualized and specialized instruction. Leachim had reference books, including a dictionary, processed into his data bank, and he could recall whatever pages were necessary for aiding a student. He could evaluate a student's performance and then reprogram his tapes to fit the student's new learning needs. He has infinite patience, and he often complimented the children with little jokes. "Today Leachim said he saw smoke comin' out of my ears cause I was thinkin' so hard," one boy proudly declared (Randolf, 1974, p. 29). Leachim didn't hesitate to tell the students when they were doing badly either. A headset permitted students to work with Leachim without disturbing the rest of the class. And a child's success with the robot built confidence for his later efforts in the classroom. According to Leachim's developer, the robot spared a child psychological trauma of failing in front of a teacher and his peers.

Clearly, computer technology can be an important part of American education. Some experts believe that computers have still greater potential for assisting instructors and administrators, and also for managing individualized instruction programs. But there is also criticism of the use of the computers in education. Controversy has resulted from the inordinate amount of time, energy, and money required by computer systems. In particular, CAI programs require a great deal of equipment at high installation costs. The use of computers has also been attacked for contributing to social problems in the schools. A study by Brod (1972) found that junior high school students (mostly from low-income, Mexican-American families) in a CAI program had a reduced perception of the teacher's authority. Such attitudes are traditionally considered "undesirable" by school administrators. Furthermore, machines cannot show concern for the learner in a human way. Critics point out that children are aware that even the most humanlike instrument is still a machine.

It is difficult to speculate about CAI's future. If cost and maintenance problems can be minimized, improved technology will probably reshape education dramatically. The critical question of how to adapt instructional techniques to individual needs remains. Computers may accumulate information over time that will help solve this problem.

classroom management: what the teacher can do

Behavioral psychologists take the position that most behavior is learned. Behavior that is reinforced will grow stronger, and behavior that is ignored will disappear. This process is a vital part of everyday life and takes many different forms. Teachers reward students with

grades and praise; employers reward employees with salaries, bonuses, and promotions; adults reward each other with smiles, compliments, and wedding rings.

When we intentionally reward desirable behavior and ignore or
punish undesirable behavior in the classroom, we are engaging in
what is called classroom management. In using classroom management techniques, we are taking conscious and active control of our
learning environment rather than letting it unthinkingly control us. In
this respect, the teacher is similar to an architect. Just as the architect
selects the building materials that will go into a house, the teacher
determines the kind of behavior he or she wants students to adopt.

Before setting any long-term goals, the teacher employing classroom
management techniques must carefully study the students' current
repertoires of behavior. The student's current behavior always provides the starting point for any succeeding stage of learning. A teacher
cannot reinforce behavior that does not exist in the first place. Shaping
is necessary.

*Selecting Desirable
Behaviors*

Teachers often describe their students as being "enthusiastic,"
"belligerent," "lazy," "shy," "accommodating," and so on. These
words convey some information, but not enough to be useful in behavior management. They are imprecise and must be broken down
into more exact components. Behavior is reinforced, not personal
qualities. How do students show that they are enthusiastic or belligerent?

The teacher must also observe the environment. What conditions
encourage students to work and which are distractive? Having gotten
this information, the teacher can make the most of the stimuli that
motivate children to work and remove those that distract them.

Mrs. S., a fifth-grade teacher, is by nature an outgoing, pleasant person with a ready smile, generally prompted by her liking of people.
Her colleagues think of her as kind and considerate, while her students seem to love and respect her. Yet, in the school system, Mrs. S.
has the reputation of being a very demanding teacher who can control
her students and lead most of them into accomplishing very advanced
social, academic, and personal tasks. She believes in two particular
principles of professional behavior: consistency and honesty. She uses
them at all times in her dealing with her students.

*Selecting Proper
Reinforcers*

At the beginning of the school year, she states the rules that are
to be followed by her class. These rules are few, but they are very
important to the students' relationship with each other and with their
teacher. Mrs. S. also warns them about the type of work they will be
doing during the year. The impact of all these announcements is softened by the statement of what she will do for her students, namely,

standing by them, helping them, and cheering them all the way through, because working together will make projects easier and more pleasant. At the end of her "speech," she starts acting in her normal way, and within a few days, her students come to enjoy her presence and directions and are able to relax. The atmosphere in the classroom becomes favorable to the satisfactory completion of learning projects. The students feel free to come very close to the teacher if they want the warming touch of the teacher's arm around the shoulders for a hug and an extra smile while receiving individual instruction. Meanwhile, the recalcitrant few will realize that if they break the rules, the smile on Mrs. S.'s face will quickly disappear, and the punishment will come as promised at the beginning of the year. Because their behavior is strictly monitored, and their work and effort checked and praised or criticized openly and honestly as it deserves, these students will learn that nobody is allowed special privileges. New rules may be given daily by Mrs. S. under the form of general directions or as necessary requirements while preparing a particular project, but the original ones are consistently upheld. It is much easier to be consistent with a few, basic principles, rather than many confusing ones. Mrs. S., by being true to her personality of warm and loving feelings, yet firm in her principles, conveys an impression of honesty and consistency in her actions and behavior toward her students.

However, the teacher's job is complicated by the fact that no single stimulus will reinforce all children equally. Praise, attention, and encouragement are the most effective reinforcers for school children, but even these stimuli are sometimes ineffective. Some children get a thrill out of irritating the teachers. They stop any behavior that the teacher praises and deliberately behave in a way to make the teacher lose his or her temper. Teachers, therefore, have to choose the stimuli they use as reinforcers so that they suit each individual child.

Two methods for individualizing classroom reinforcers are student-selected reinforcers and token reinforcers.

Student-selected reinforcers In using this type of reinforcement the teacher may use a principle first developed by Premack (1959): observing the students to see how they spend their free time. For example, a student may spend 15 minutes playing with a tape recorder, 5 minutes with a deck of cards, and 8 talking to a friend. If the child keeps to this pattern for several days, the teacher can expect that the tape recorder will work most effectively as a positive reinforcer and can then make the tape recorder available whenever the child behaves in a desirable way.

Another way to select the reinforcer, often most effective with older students, is to ask each student what he or she would like. The teacher in this case would select the reinforcement by choosing something from the student's list. Becker and his colleagues (1975) stated the following principle of student-selected reinforcers: "You do what I want you to do before you get to do what you want to do."

Use of **token reinforcers** is another way to allow students to select their own reinforcers. In this method, the teacher immediately rewards desirable behavior with a token. After the child has accumulated several tokens, he can cash them in for a variety of privileges or things. Token reinforcers are especially effective because they can be automatically adjusted to a child's changing desires. The child can buy time with the tape recorder one day and may use the next day's tokens to spend time with a friend. Token reinforcers seem to be more effective with younger than older students in classroom situations (Kolesnik, 1978).

Contingency contracts Once a reinforcer has been selected and found to be effective, it may be used in a variety of ways. Teachers may simply elect to use it after desirable behavior occurs. Or they may use it in connection with specific agreements arranged with the students in the class. **Contingency contracts** stipulate specific reinforcers for specified behaviors or levels of achievement. For example, a teacher may select a grading system as the reinforcement in a contract with students in the class. Such a teacher might say, "I will give an A to anyone who turns in two acceptable projects and five acceptable book reports. I will give a B to anyone completing the two projects, but turning in only four reports." Contingency contracts might also involve specified numbers of questions answered correctly on a test as the desired behavior. Token reinforcers or student-selected reinforcers can be used as well as grades. In all cases, however, agreement on desired behaviors and reinforcers must be reached *prior* to the beginning of the lessons.

Group reinforcement and competition Group reinforcement and competition can both be used as reinforcers in school. In **group reinforcement** a group—either a whole class or a section of it—is rewarded for what the group or section has accomplished as a unit. For example, a teacher might assign 100 arithmetic problems to each row of students in the classroom. The row that solves all the problems first might then be rewarded with a few minutes of extra recess time.

Research on team reinforcement has shown it to be effective in increasing effort expended by students. Group reinforcement may stimulate cooperation in these situations because the brighter students become motivated to help the poorer ones in order for the entire team to win.

An eighth-grade math teacher found that his class was gradually getting more careless about bringing pencils to class. He set each row of students in competition with every other row to be completely prepared with books, paper, and pencils each day. It was a good-natured competition, working toward the prize of 10 minutes of free socializing on Friday afternoon. After a few weeks the entire class was enjoying the Friday social group.

How Teachers May Contribute to Student Discipline Problems

In a study of discipline problems in a San Francisco high school, a former teacher and school principal noted that many problems were caused by specific teacher behaviors (Duke, 1978).

1. *Inconsistent rule enforcement.* This behavior was exhibited by teachers who sometimes neglected certain rules and other times enforced them. Situations in which rules were enforced by some teachers and not by others created similar problems. According to Duke, students at the school were particularly sensitive to inconsistent rule enforcement. The result: disrespect for the school as a rule-governed organization.

2. *Noncompliance with discipline policies.* Duke reported that, at the school studied, teachers frequently didn't comply with regular school policies, such as checking admission slips, basing student grades on conduct, monitoring hallways. The result? According to Duke, some students didn't know what to expect and therefore stopped basing their own behaviors on discipline policies.

3. *Insensitivity.* Teachers who exhibited this behavior were all business. They showed little patience for the students' personal concerns. By failing to help the individual problems, these teachers contributed to student feelings of isolation, resentment, and low self-esteem. Sending a student to the principal over each rule infraction may get the teaching job done, Duke reported, but it frequently reinforces other unwanted behavior.

4. *Lack of data.* Teachers concerned about student discipline in Duke's study frequently reported that they knew little about which students were behaving inappropriately. Without a data base, it is impossible to build an adequate classroom management program.

5. *Lack of classroom management skills.* Duke reported that few teachers had received specific training in classroom management, although many complained about discipline problems. In the San Francisco high school studied, most teachers lacked skill in diagnosing behavioral problems and in prescribing appropriate instructional techniques.

6. *Inadequate administration of disciplinary policies.* Teachers and administrators in Duke's study frequently failed to get together over student problems. Sometimes teachers took matters into their own hands because they felt that sending students to the administrators provided no solution. Sometimes administrators took major roles in handling discipline problems. The greatest energy, whatever the problem being handled, seemed to be expended on attendance problems, smoking, or disrespect for authority. Rarely were discipline problems affecting students—extortion, fighting, name calling, theft of personal property—treated with equal zeal. The result? Students often felt that they were second-class citizens.

What can be done? Duke made a number of suggestions, all of which are consistent with behavioral principles. Students, teachers, and principals should develop school rules together and enforce them consistently. Teachers should be provided with information concerning behavior problems and with training in effective ways to deal with them. Special attention should be given to rewarding students for behaving properly, not simply punishing those who misbehave. Classroom management works two ways.

Reprinted with permission from *The American School Board Journal* (June, 1978), the National School Boards Association. All rights reserved.

Making Use
of Extinction
in the Classroom

Extinction is an effective technique for decreasing a response rate to its preconditioning level. Under this procedure, you simply withhold reinforcement for a response that has been previously reinforced. To extinguish the bar-pressing response in a trained rat, for example, the researcher would stop the food pellets from coming out whenever the rat pressed the bar. In the classroom, the same principle should follow. To extinguish unwanted behavior such as disruptive behavior, a teacher should ignore it. Attention is reinforcing, so ignored behavior is no longer being reinforced.

In this case, the teacher can easily identify the stimulus that is reinforcing the unwanted behavior. However, teacher attention is certainly not the only source of reinforcement in the classroom. Sometimes, the teacher cannot control the responsible stimulus. The disruptive student is often reinforced by attention from other students, and this factor is hard to eliminate. Undesirable behavior can also be self-reinforcing—chewing gum is a case in point.

When the teacher cannot control the effective reinforcer, he or she must positively reinforce behavior that is incompatible with the unwanted behavior. If a child is daydreaming in class, the teacher can begin to reinforce attentive behavior. The child will gradually spend more time paying attention. Since the child cannot pay attention and daydream at the same time, he or she will eventually stop daydreaming.

Melanie was a sullen, argumentative child in a small class of remedial readers. For an undetermined reason, she started angrily kicking the chair of the girl in front of her. Her teacher calmly picked up Melanie's books and told her to move to the rear of the classroom. The little girl was angered by this until the teacher told her that she could return to her seat just as soon as she was ready to behave properly. Melanie wasn't convinced. But she did behave, and after class the teacher complimented her on her behavior. Similar incidents happened during the first few months of school. Sometimes she sat at the back of the room for a half hour, shouting and making comments. Each time her behavior was ignored except for the separation from the other students. Gradually the episodes became less frequent, and during the second semester, there were few occasions for separation.

The teacher who chooses to extinguish undesirable behavior by ignoring it should remember five important points. First the child may interpret the teacher's silence as a form of approval. The teacher can avoid this pitfall by specifying which kind of behavior is appropriate and which is not. Second, ignoring the child may cause even more disruptive behavior as the child tries even harder to get attention and recognition. The teacher must remain steadfast in withholding anything that could be interpreted as a reward. Third, extremely destructive behavior cannot be ignored. It should not be positively reinforced either. Fourth, important reinforcement for unwanted behavior often comes from the applause of fellow students. The teacher, perhaps through the use of reinforcement, must learn to control such behavior. Fifth, the teacher must be absolutely consistent in rewarding good behavior and ignoring bad behavior. As was pointed out before, behavior learned under an intermittent reinforcement schedule is most difficult to extinguish—a problem the inconsistent teacher faces daily in the classroom.

*Problems in
Classroom
Management*

Classroom management can be a highly efficient way to deal with disruptive behaviors, as many studies have shown (see, for example, Kirschner and Levin, 1975), but it is not without its problems. According to Skinner (1969), a major problem is caused by the improper arrangement of social reinforcers. "Unfortunately, social contingencies are hard to arrange. To induce the members of a classroom community to behave well with respect to each other, additional reinforcers may be needed. . . . The main problem is to make these reinforcers contingent on desired behavior. They are often not available on the spur of the moment" (p.23).

Are reinforcers bribes?   Some educators argue that reward systems, like the token economy, are nothing more than a form of bribery. They also point out that the teacher can use student-selected reinforcers to make students work for what the teacher used to allow them to do freely. Furthermore, these methods sometimes make the children do things that they do not really want to do. To some extent, this argument is invalid. Reinforcers, even when they occur accidentally, determine the child's whole repertoire of behavior. Reinforcers of one sort or another *always* exist. So why is it bad to use reinforcement in a rationally controlled way? In classroom management, teachers do not artificially create reinforcers; they use them.

Many psychologists have criticisms of this view. Lindsey and Cunningham (1973), for example, charge that classroom management essentially makes discipline a system of rewards rather than progress toward mutually established and worthwhile goals. Further, classroom management limits the possible healthy expression of student discontent and denies human reasoning.

Bad habits (like good ones) are learned. After a time we repeat these behavior patterns without thinking; they become involuntary. That is why bad habits are so hard to break. Will power is often not enough, as any habitual smoker can tell you. A booklet (free for the asking) is available from the American Cancer Society (1970) describing ways to extinguish the smoking habit. Following is one method that is suggested. Can you think of others? What principles of operant conditioning are evident here? Could classical conditioning also be used? In what ways?

Keep a Track Record

Many smokers have found that a useful step in understanding their smoking is the keeping of a daily record on a scale like that below.

In your gradual withdrawal you may decide to eliminate those daily cigarettes that you find are rated 1, 2, or 3, i.e., ones you want less. Or you may wish to give up first the cigarettes you like most. In any case keeping a smoking log will give you information about yourself, make you more aware of what your smoking habits are.

You may find that you are largely a social smoker, that smoking makes you feel closer to others, more welcome at a party, that you seem to have more friends. A cigarette may play a surprisingly large part in your picture of yourself as a mature and successful person. How do you convince yourself that people like and respect you for more important reasons than for your cigarette? Try not smoking and see.

Plus and Minus

Write down carefully, after some thought, in one column reasons why you smoke and in another all the reasons why you should give up cigarettes.

As you turn this exercise over in your mind, new material will occur to you for one or the other columns. Thoughtful concentration on your reasons for giving up cigarettes is important in changing your behavior.

Score Card

Copy this record sheet seven times for seven days. Make a check for each cigarette you smoke, hour by hour, and indicate how much you need it: a mark in the box opposite 1 shows low need, a mark opposite 6 high need; opposite 4, moderate need, etc. Then decide which cigarette you wish to eliminate.

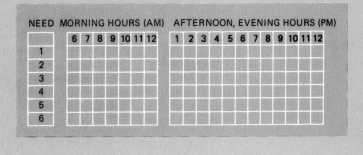

NEED	MORNING HOURS (AM)							AFTERNOON, EVENING HOURS (PM)											
	6	7	8	9	10	11	12	1	2	3	4	5	6	7	8	9	10	11	12
1																			
2																			
3																			
4																			
5																			
6																			

Students can use behavior management, too Researchers have shown that students can shape their teachers' behavior as well. In one study (Gray, Graubard, and Rosenberger, 1974), a California teacher worked with a special class of so-called incorrigible students aged 12 to 15. These students were given instruction and practice in behavior management for one class period a day. They learned how to shape their teachers' behavior by using various reinforcers. These included smiling, making eye contact, and sitting up straight. They also practiced ways of praising a teacher—"I like to work in a room where the teacher is nice to the kids"—and ways of discouraging negative behavior—"It's hard for me to do good work when you're cross with me" (p. 44). Then they were moved into regular classes for two periods a day. Many of the students had difficulty in smiling or in learning to praise the teacher with sincerity. They also had to develop the ability to make small talk; after considerable training, they excelled at it. They learned to identify positive teacher behavior accurately by role-playing and studying videotapes. They also kept formal records of teacher responses in their other classes. (Trained adult aides also kept records of teacher behavior in the classes.) The results of the study showed that during the five weeks of shaping, the positive comments of the teachers increased and the negative comments decreased. Later courses in which gifted students practiced behavior management on peers, parents, and teachers were equally effective. Beyond these changes was a more important outcome for all: a more positive environment in which to live and learn.

The story was told of a psychology class in a large West Coast university that decided to use behavior shaping on their young graduate student instructor. With the character of Napoleon as their target, they began reinforcing any behavior that appeared to them to be Napoleonic. They would sit up, take notes, look interested, and smile when the instructor spoke in short, clipped sentences or when he happened to stand with his hand across his chest. However, when he rambled on or walked about, they stopped their note taking, gazed out the window, and yawned. By the end of the semester, they had so shaped the behavior of their instructor that he was lecturing to them in short, staccato sentences with his hand inserted in his shirt, totally unaware of what had happened to his behavior.

The Ethics of Classroom Management

Day and Mowrer (1972) pointed out that Skinner had failed to discuss fully the possibility that the scientists, or controllers, may abuse their power in applying behavioral techniques. These critics did not intend to diminish the social importance of behavioral technology; they only wanted to raise the important ethical issues of who should do the controlling and who should control the controllers (Lindsey and Cunningham, 1973). Other psychologists also question the morality of turning a classroom into a place where children are taught to be mercenary and are considered primarily as unreasoning beings.

In response, Holland (1974), a University of Pittsburgh psychologist, asked two important and sensitive questions: "Who has the moral right to decide what behavior people should or should not adopt?" and "Who is a behavioral program really designed to benefit, the modifier or the modifiee?" The two questions are connected; one cannot answer the first without resolving the second. Critics have pointed out that behavioral technologists have too often ignored both these questions before instituting programs. In many cases, the subjects of these programs have had no say at all about how they were being conditioned. For example, the spread of behavior modification units in our prisons has been the subject of much criticism and controversy. Prison specialists have designed programs to eliminate so-called disruptive behavior and enhance appropriate behavior. They have frequently used negative reinforcement on prisoners and deprived them of positive reinforcement in order to create behavior that meets only the needs of the prisons.

These ethical considerations also arise in the classroom. What do we mean by "desirable" and "undesirable" behavior? To answer this question, Winett and Winkler (1972) analyzed every study on classroom management published in the *Journal of Applied Behavior Analysis* between 1968 and 1970.

The subtitle of their study reveals their findings: "Be Still, Be Quiet, Be Docile." Teachers consistently defined desirable behavior as keeping quiet, keeping still, and looking either at a textbook or at the teacher. They defined undesirable behavior as running around the room, talking excessively, and making too much noise. As in prison programs, the teachers wanted above all to instill submissiveness in all their students; they punished any child who was too active, or too self-reliant, or too creative.

Winett and Winkler suggested that, rather than changing the student to fit into the environment, educational planners should focus on the environment.

> There is another role, however, for the behavior modifier that involves changing the social system that maintains the behavior, thereby creating new environments instead of patching up the results of the existing environments. In the present context, such a role involves changing the educational system. (p.502)

Community members most concerned with the welfare of students should become involved in formulating the objectives of behavioral programs. Parents, teachers, and children should jointly discuss what the objectives should be and the methods for reaching them. Certainly children would take a more active role in reinforcing each other to achieve objectives they had had a voice in establishing.

Classroom management techniques have become increasingly popular in our society, and many people have become involved in their use and design. Thompson and his colleagues evaluated the effects of a one-week training course in these techniques (Thompson, Brassell, Persons, Tucha, and Rollins, 1974). The trainees were teachers who were being taught how to reinforce quiet and submissive behavior in their students. By the end of the course, the trainees were able to increase significantly the behavior they desired—one more bit of evidence to prove that we as psychologists and educators have a grave responsibility and should examine closely the questions of what behavior we should reinforce, who should make these decisions, and what our purposes are.

Behavioral theories have far-reaching implications for educators and, in fact, for all of society. Though Skinner's reflections on the role of the environment are by no means new, and though many critics point out that the simplicity of the Skinnerian approach is restrictive and does not handle all problems of learning, still systematic application of behavioral psychology clearly can affect classroom behavior in many advantageous ways.

summary

1. Behaviorism explains learning in terms of people's observable behavior. This view of learning is also called associationism and the stimulus-response approach (S-R) because learning is said to occur when people associate their behavioral responses with stimuli in the environment.

2. John B. Watson, an early leader of the behaviorist approach, said that a scientific study of human behavior was impossible unless psychologists restricted themselves to studying human qualities and abilities that could be directly observed and objectively measured. Thus, learning had to be based on observable behavior instead of some internal and unobservable process like thinking. Watson's teaching Little Albert to fear a white rat proved that humans could be taught specific responses through the use of specific stimuli.

3. The type of learning involved in Watson's experiment with Little Albert is called classical conditioning. Classical conditioning depends on the association of a response an individual makes automatically (unconditioned response) with a previously neutral stimulus (conditioned stimulus). This association is accomplished through pairing the conditioned stimulus with an unconditioned stimulus that automatically elicits the unconditioned response. After enough pairings, the individual will make a conditioned response when presented with the conditioned stimulus alone. The first systematic studies of classical conditioning were done by Ivan Pavlov, who trained dogs to drool when a bell rang by pairing the sound of the bell with food. Classical conditioning is also called respondent conditioning because the individual does not respond until after the stimulus has been presented. Using Pavlov's procedures, V. M. Bechterev studied a type of classical conditioning called avoidance learning.

4. Edward L. Thorndike proposed the law of effect, which states that the association between a stimulus and a response will be strengthened or weakened depending on whether a "satisfier" or an "annoyer" follows the response. Thorndike believed that, essentially, humans learn by trial and success; success is satisfying and thus leads us to perform the same response again in later situations. After studies showed that this explanation was inadequate, Thorndike proposed another law, the truncated law of effect, which added the idea that, while satisfiers always strengthen the bond between a stimulus and a response, the effect of annoyers is much less predictable; sometimes they weaken the bond, but sometimes they don't.

5. B. F. Skinner agrees with Thorndike's view that what happens after a response is made is critical to learning. Skinner's approach to learning is called operant conditioning because, in effect, we operate on the environment in order to cause certain consequences. It is also called instrumental conditioning because certain responses or instruments are essential in leading to a reward. Skinner studied operant conditioning in its simplest form by observing the behavior of rats in a specially constructed box called a Skinner box. The number of times a rat pressed a bar to get a food pellet is a measure of the response's operant strength.

6. Reinforcement increases the operant strength of a response and makes it more likely to occur again. Primary reinforcers satisfy the individual's basic physiological needs; secondary reinforcers become effective rewards through their association with primary reinforcers.

7. Positive reinforcement increases the frequency of the response that immediately precedes it. The cessation of negative reinforcement also increases the frequency of a response occurring. This time, however, it is the response that leads to escape from the negative reinforcer. Negative reinforcers are effective only when there is a chance to escape them and that chance is obvious to the individual. Punishment is the administration of an aversive stimulus for the purpose of suppressing the immediately preceding response. The effects of using either negative reinforcement or punishment are unpredictable. Because both punishment and negative reinforcement have undesirable side effects such as increasing anxiety among school children, teachers are advised to use positive reinforcement in the classroom.

8. When a response is no longer followed by positive reinforcement, it is performed less and less often until extinction occurs. This principle is the basis for advising teachers simply to ignore undesirable behavior whenever possible.

+ #19

9. There are several different schedules of reinforcement. Each has a different effect on operant strength. In a continuous reinforcement schedule, reinforcement is given after every correct response. This schedule produces a regular pattern of responses, but the learning is particularly vulnerable to extinction. Intermittent reinforcement is given on the basis of a certain number of correct responses (ratio schedule) or a certain period of time (interval schedule). The number of responses and the length of

the time period may be fixed or variable. On fixed ratio and fixed interval schedules, reinforcement consistently occurs after a specific number of responses or after a specific amount of time, while reinforcement given on variable ratio and variable interval schedules occurs unpredictably. Responses learned on either of these variable schedules are more resistant to extinction than responses learned on fixed schedules.

10. Reinforcement is generally most effective when it immediately follows a response. Unfortunately, most teachers rely on delayed reinforcement such as that provided by traditional grading systems.

11. Operant principles also apply to complex, higher-order learning. A gradual approach to the learning of complex behavior is shaping, in which responses similar to the desired response are reinforced. The standards on which reinforcement depends gradually narrow until the individual is reinforced only for the correct response.

12. Discrimination occurs when the individual learns to respond to two or more stimuli in different ways. The opposite of discrimination is generalization, in which the same response is made to two or more stimuli (stimulus generalization) or a particular stimulus evokes responses that are similar to the desired response (response generalization). Overgeneralization occurs when generalization gets out of hand and distorts reality.

13. The sort of higher-order learning in which a series of behaviors must be performed before reinforcement is given is called chaining. Many everyday behaviors, including superstitions, are composed of such behavior chains.

14. Despite the fact that operant procedures make learning more efficient, some psychologists still feel that leaving out the thought processes gives an oversimplified view of complex human learning.

15. One example of classical conditioning in the classroom is the development of conditioned anxiety among school children. This anxiety can generalize to the total school experience and may develop into a school phobia.

16. Using negative reinforcement or punishment in the school can increase children's anxiety levels and lead to the adoption of undesirable escape responses.

17. Delayed reinforcement can be effective with some students, but generally immediate reinforcement is better. Programmed instruction is a teaching technique that provides individualized instruction as well as immediate and continuous reinforcement.

18. Classroom management involves the use of behavioral principles to shape students' behavior. The first step is to select desirable behaviors and the most effective ways to positively reinforce them. Student-selected reinforcers, token economies, and contingency contracts all increase the chances of selecting appropriate reinforcers. Group reinforcement and competition can also be effective ways to increase learning.

19. Ignoring disruptive behavior can lead to extinction of that behavior. For this approach to work, the teacher must be steadfast, patient, and absolutely consistent.

20. Some critics of classroom management say that reinforcements are bribes. But because reinforcements always exist, using them in a rationally controlled way may be sensible rather than unethical. However, serious ethical questions in classroom management remain: Who should decide what sort of behavior is desirable? Who is the behavioral program primarily designed to benefit? Teachers should seriously consider the answers to these questions before implementing a program of classroom management.

BUELL, M. A. A peaceful coexistence? Behaviorism vs. humanism. *Delta Kappa Gamma Bulletin*, Vol. 44 (2), Winter 1978, pp. 29-31. Buell's brief argument presented in this journal for educators points to the impracticality of a teacher's selecting a behavior management approach as opposed to a humanistic approach in the classroom. Buell, in discussing some of the implications for classroom use of both approaches, suggests a coexistence of the two approaches and describes a series of effective classroom procedures that she says employs aspects of both.

GRAUBARD, P. AND ROSENBERG, H. *Classrooms that Work.* New York: Dutton, 1974. Graubard and Rosenberg's easy-to-read text describes classroom situations in which teachers have employed classroom management strategies in successful ways.

SKINNER, B. F. *Beyond Freedom and Dignity.* New York: Knopf, 1971 (also available from Bantam Books). This book is important for students who wish to understand behavioral approaches to classroom learning and their implications for teachers. Dealing with the issues of control and personal freedom, Skinner's book is a major contribution both to psychology and education and is useful also for those who oppose Skinner's approach.

SKINNER, B. F. *Walden Two,* New York: Macmillan, 1948. This novel describing a utopian society based on behavioral principles is useful reading for those who want to understand not only behavior management principles, but also why some other societies planned as modern-day utopias failed at meeting their goals. *Walden Two* is useful reading for students wanting to understand, for example, why the American religious cult community in Guyana had such a horrendous ending in 1978.

STAINBACK, W. C., ET AL. *Establishing a Token Economy in the Classroom.* Columbus, Ohio: Charles E. Merrill, 1973. This is a brief and practical text designed to explain the steps a teacher must go through to establish an effective token economy in a classroom situation. The authors give excellent arguments for use of token reinforcers with children.

for students
who want to read
further

4

COGNITIVE PSYCHOLOGY AND CURRICULUM DESIGN

Learning to Think

"Our students frequently have trouble carrying through an idea in writing; they have no idea what a paragraph is; worst, they are unable to string details in a logical sequence so as to communicate their thinking to others." The instructor in the Special Program at Midtown City Junior College was describing problems characteristic not only of students enrolled in that program, but also of large numbers of students enrolled at Midtown and at the four-year colleges in the city.

"The problem is pervasive," the instructor pointed out. "We realize that by beginning to work with it at the college level, we are missing out on the most important learning years. It would be far better to begin at the high school, middle school, or elementary school level. Unfortunately, at those levels teachers seem too concerned with immediate educational objectives stated in terms of specific desired behaviors, rather than in terms of learning how to learn."

To illustrate her point, the instructor pulled out at random the file of one student. Pete was 18 years old and had graduated the previous year in the top half of his high school graduating class; his scores during his senior year on the Scholastic Aptitude Test were above the fiftieth percentile. "But," the instructor pointed out, "scores on the standardized aptitude and achievement tests have decreased annually across the country in the past twenty years in a frightening way. Pete's scores, even ten years ago, would have been below average."

During his first semester at Midtown, Pete enrolled in a series of liberal arts courses: psychology, sociology, art, mathematics, English literature. He was shocked to discover that he had trouble sometimes understanding the long sentences in the textbooks and was dismayed at the grades he received on his written work. He had an above-average IQ, and both his parents had gone to college. What was wrong? His counselor advised him to enroll in the special program before taking any more courses.

"Don't worry," the counselor told him. "There are a lot more students just like you. See what you think of the program. I think you'll like it. Later, you can take the regular courses."

The Special Program provided a set of learning experiences different from any Pete had ever encountered. On the first day, the instructor announced that the class had to decide what to do. "The purpose of education," she pointed out, "is to teach people to think. So, let's think."

"About what?"

"About anything you want. What's on your mind?"

"Nothing," laughed a young girl.

"What's nothing? Is it empty space . . . blankness?"

"Not really, but the thoughts aren't relevant to anything in particular."

"Do they float by? Are they pleasant or unpleasant?"

"I don't know how to describe it."

"That's a good place to begin."

That first lesson was a surprise to Pete. If they couldn't describe "nothing" (they all tried, but none of them could come up with a definition they were satisfied with), what *could* they describe? The assignment for the next class was to think about "nothing." Students were given the choice either of writing an essay about it or preparing some form of presentation to the class in which they demonstrated its meaning.

Midtown City Junior College began offering the Special Program about a year ago; it's currently one of the most popular on campus for students like Pete who strongly dislike the regular courses, as well as for students who simply think it's fun to learn that way. Thus far the faculty is pleased with the results. They point out that early inability to use the basic tools of learning leads later to inability to think, solve problems, and communicate the results to others.

"That's what it's all about," said the Special Program instructor. "We aren't ever sure any day exactly what we will say or do, but one thing we know for sure. Our students must learn to think. To do that we can't hold up grades as rewards and just wait for them to do it. We've got to allow them to discover for themselves what they're thinking about, and what they want to say. Then, and only then, will they be able to make use of their abilities."

what is cognitive psychology?

Many psychologists believe that learning is more than the result of a series of stimulus-response connections, which is the position taken in Chapter 3. Cognitive psychologists do not necessarily disagree with behavioral explanations of learning. They see them as incomplete rather than wrong. Behavioral theories, they feel, are incomplete because they leave out the human element, rather like saying that driving a car is simply a matter of turning the key and watching the car drive away. Few of us would set foot out of the house if our roads were indeed full of two-ton metal monsters undirected by human intelligence. Unlike behavioral psychologists, cognitive psychologists do not ignore internal processes such as thinking that can only be inferred because they cannot be directly seen and measured. These psychologists feel that learning can best be understood by looking at those processes that serve as mediators between the stimulus and response, for example, how we process and organize information.

Cognitive psychologists are concerned with many different areas of psychology—learning and reasoning, perception, physiological and comparative psychology, and the psychology of personality. Many cognitive psychologists are particularly interested in the higher levels of learning (for instance, concept formation and problem solving), but the ultimate goal of cognitive psychology is to be able to explain all types of learning, from the simplest trial-and-error learning and conditioning to the most complex forms of human reasoning. Educational psychologists who take a cognitive approach design curricula that specify the organization of the thinking steps involved in the learning process as well as the desired outcomes of learning.

Foundations of Cognitive Psychology: Gestalt Psychology

Contemporary cognitive psychology is based on Gestalt psychology which originated in Germany in the early part of the twentieth century. **Gestalt psychology** began primarily as a reaction against what were considered the excesses of stimulus-response behaviorism. The German psychologist Max Wertheimer is credited with having started the Gestalt movement in 1912, but there were other influential spokesmen such as Kurt Koffka and Wolfgang Köhler. These early researchers believed that **perception**—how we learn to make sense of our sensory impressions of the environment—is the basis of behavior. The term *Gestalt* first used by Wertheimer in 1912, means "form," "shape," or "configuration" in rough translation.

A basic principle of Gestalt psychology is that perception is a continuous process of forming and responding to relationships. As one example of perception and its importance in real life, consider a classroom of 50 students. In terms of an image on his or her retina, each student senses the door of the classroom as a slightly different shape. This is because each student's seat in the classroom is in a slightly different position in relation to the door. However, if you asked what shape the door was, each student would probably say it was rectangular, regardless of the image on his or her retina. This happens because the students have learned that doors are rectangular, and our perceptions (how we interpret sensory experiences) are affected by past learning.

Researchers studying perception are concerned with the many ways in which meaning is attached to sensation, or the ways in which different perceptions are developed. One of the major characteristics of this approach is what we call *relativism*. In order for any new perception to develop—that is, for a sensation to acquire meaning for us—we must first relate it to, or integrate it with, material that we are already familiar with; we must perceive it in relation to past experience.

Because all students have had different past experiences, they

a door is shaped as it is from where you're viewing it and regardless of image on retina

begin school with different perceptions. Effective teachers put these different perceptions to work in developing meaningful experiences for their students. Like the instructor at Midtown City, they continually adjust the curriculum in light of each student's new perceptions and build on them to produce new learning. This is why the Special Program instructor doesn't use rigid lesson plans. She doesn't know from day to day exactly what she will do or say in the classroom because that depends entirely on her students. In addition, whenever possible, she integrates material being taught in one class with those being taught in others. For example, she may use common themes or concerns to coordinate social studies and literature, or physical education and biology. When students can see structure, relevance, and purpose in their curricula they take a much more active interest in learning because they can attach more meaning to the learning process.

Insight Learning

When a person perceives a situation in a new way that results in a meaningful change in his or her cognitive structure, or reorganization of relationships, we say that he or she has achieved insight. **Insight** is a form of discovery learning in which the end results are finding a solution that works and developing an understanding of why it works. Developing insight implies grasping an idea; the individual clearly understands the concept and is not simply responding without knowing why. Learning that involves insight is less likely to be forgotten than learning that is based on memorization without understanding.

Insight involves taking in information from the environment and transforming it into some kind of new understanding. Psychologists have theorized that this process requires analyzing, synthesizing, formulating, and testing hypotheses, then accepting or rejecting them and integrating the results into a meaningful solution. However, going through this process does not automatically guarantee that a person will achieve insight. He or she may lack the ability to make meaningful inferences from his or her investigations, or may not use the correct hypotheses. It is possible to arrive at a solution that will work by chance or by imitation, but, without understanding, the change in cognitive structure necessary for insight learning will not take place. Older children and adults, with their greater experience in problem solving, are more likely to achieve insights than younger children are. The development of insight depends on more than maturation, but more experienced individuals are better able to differentiate and restructure a constantly expanding world and use that understanding as a guide for their behavior. One problem that led to the formation of Midtown City's Special Program, for example, was that high schools, middle schools, and elementary schools were not providing enough opportunities for children to develop insight learning.

The notion of insight learning as a distinct learning process was first popularized by the publication in 1925 of the English translation of Kohler's *The Mentality of Apes,* which described his extensive research into problem-solving behavior. Köhler's experiments were conducted with chimpanzees. In a typical experiment, a banana was hung from the top of the animal's cage. Other things were put in the cage, too, such as sticks, balls, and a box. The banana was hung too high for the chimp to reach, but if he moved the box and climbed on top of it, he could reach the banana. Köhler called such a solution to the problem "insight." The animal's chance exploration of its immediate environment may have given rise initially to the idea to use the box. But Köhler also observed that sometimes an ape would pause after failing to reach the banana by familiar methods and then, as if saying "Eureka!,"suddenly see the solution. After seeing the ape pause in this way, Köhler came to the conclusion that insight learning had occurred. In this problem, all the stimuli necessary to solve it were clearly visible, but Gestalt psychologists have maintained that insight learning is possible even when such stimuli are not visibly present, such as when a rat searches out food in a maze, although the development of insight in those cases will be more gradual.

Classroom researchers often refer to this same phenomenon in the classroom as the "Aha!" syndrome. We have probably all had this experience some time in our lives. We may hear the same concept explained half a dozen times or more with no effect on our understanding, until, one day, we are suddenly able to put the pieces together in a new way. We sit up straight, our mouths open, our eyes widen, and we may even say "Aha!" out loud. The old comic-strip notion of the light bulb lighting up over someone's head conveys some of this, but it leaves out the rush of energy and even pure joy that insight brings.

Insight learning can be verbal, preverbal, or nonverbal. When very young children learn how to put food in their mouths, pull themselves to a standing position in a playpen, and crawl across the floor, they acquire insight into solving these problems without ever putting any of the issues into words.

Insight as product and process   If insight cannot always be verbalized, how can we recognize it when it occurs? In answer to this question, psychologists describe insight as both a product and a process (Ausubel, Noraka, and Hanesian, 1978). As a *product,* insight refers to the end results of meaningful problem-solving. For example, a boy realizes that the stains on his new shirt were put there when his younger brother wore it last night. Subjectively, this leads to a feeling of overall satisfaction: So he borrowed it, did he! If so, he is responsible for the stain! Objectively, it includes the practical application of the newly obtained solution: He'll pay the cleaning bill!

As a *process,* insight is the steps a person takes in solving a problem. According to cognitive psychologists, the process of insight depends on the structure of the problem and the learner's past experiences. This points to one major difference between cognitive psychology and behavioral psychology. Behavioral psychology implies that, in order to solve a problem (to give the correct response), a person needs certain prior learning experiences. People solve problems by associating past and present behavior with past and present environmental stimuli. Cognitive psychologists would agree that certain learning experiences are necessary in order to solve new problems, but they believe that the structure of the present learning situation is important, too. Some environmental arrangements lead more easily to insight than others.

The gradual development of insight and the role of serendipity
Solutions based on insight may often appear to occur suddenly and unexpectedly, but this is not actually the case. The instructor at Midtown City's Special Program planned experiences in which seemingly brand-new problems were presented to the students. When initially confronted with these problems, the students' behavior seemed to be exploratory, unsure, and largely unproductive. They did not appear to be doing anything to solve the problems; they were just sitting around. During this period of apparent inactivity, however, they were busy restructuring their perceptions in order to arrive at a solution. We may say "Eureka!" as though surprised when we hit upon a solution, but the insight really does not come abruptly, as Pete and the other students in Midtown City's Special Program learned as they worked on their first assignment. Insight learning involves a gradual process of testing hypotheses and progressive clarification.

Serendipity, finding valuable or agreeable things not specifically sought after, plays a role in insight learning. Yerkes (1943) first illustrated this point in an experiment in which a chimpanzee watched the experimenter insert a banana into a tube that was open at both ends. The chimpanzee's task was to get the banana out. His initial efforts were unsuccessful. There happened to be a hoe handle in the room, which the chimpanzee by chance threw in the direction of the tube. The animal stopped playing, reflected for a moment, then picked up the handle and used it to push the banana out of the tube. From a chance event came a valuable hint that ultimately led to the solution of the problem. Similar things happen in human experience all the time.

The test for insight: Transposition The only true way to determine whether or not a person has developed insight is to present him or her with a situation that has the same basic characteristics as the original but is not exactly the same in every detail and see if he or she can apply the same principles to the new situation. If the person can do this, **transfer of learning** or, in Gestalt terms, **transposition** has occurred. This process is important in much of human learning, including concept formation and problem solving.

Productive Thinking

Wertheimer's *Productive Thinking* (1945/1959), published posthumously, has been a widely read and influential book. Wertheimer was particularly interested in the thinking of school children and in the practical applications of Gestalt theory to education, and this emphasis is found throughout his writings.

In *Productive Thinking*, Wertheimer distinguished between two types of attempted solutions to a problem. Type A solutions involve originality and productive thinking. They indicate that the learner understands the meaning and use of previous experience, as well as the essential structure of the problem itself. Type B solutions also use past experience, but they are blind solutions, really no more than trial and error. Type B solutions which were acceptable earlier but are not appropriate to solving the new problem, are applied mechanically without understanding.

Wertheimer (1945/1959) turned to the field of geometry to compare these two approaches to problem-solving. In one study, children were first taught how to find the area of a rectangle by watching Wertheimer divide a large rectangle into many small squares. The children did not need to memorize a formula; they were given visual evidence that the area of the rectangle was equal to the number of squares in each row multiplied by the number of rows.

The children were then presented with an unfamiliar figure—a parallelogram without right angles—and asked to find its area. Some protested that they could not solve the problem without another demonstration of what to do. Others blindly tried to follow the same procedure they had learned for finding the area of a rectangle, but, of course, they obtained incorrect answers to the problem. Some children were able to get the correct answer (multiplying base times altitude) by trial and error, but they had no clear understanding of why the method worked. In all these cases, the children were giving Type B responses to the problem, indicating no productive reasoning on their part.

A few children did arrive at Type A solutions to the problem. One child noticed that the source of difficulty was the two projecting ends, but that the part that was "no good" on one side was "right" on the other side (Wertheimer, 1945/1959). She asked for scissors, cut off the left end of the figure, and then placed it at the right end, thus converting the parallelogram into a rectangle (see Figure 4-1). Another child, also showing conceptual understanding, converted the piece of paper into a ring, so that the two ends fit together. She then cut the ring vertically so it became a rectangle. These two children integrated the parallelogram problem with what they had previously learned. This reflected their ability to reorganize an unfamiliar and puzzling perception into one that was familiar and meaningful. By changing the parallelogram into a better gestalt—a rectangle—they gained an understanding of its structural relationships and discovered a logically correct and original means for achieving the goal they were seeking.

The same type of learning occurs frequently in classrooms. In a high school math class, one teacher allowed his students to discover for themselves the formula for the sum of the interior angles of a polygon. The students first learned that the sum of the angles in a triangle equals 180°. Next, a quadrilateral was drawn on the board. A student was asked to divide it into two triangles, and he realized that the sum of the angles must be 360°. Next, a pentagon was drawn, and the teacher formed three triangles within it, leading the student to discover that the sum is 540°. The formula then became one he could use because he understood it.

According to Wertheimer, education should lead to genuine understanding and productive thinking. This goal can best be achieved by deemphasizing rote memorization and presenting material in such a way that children have to fill in the necessary gaps themselves instead of being spoon-fed by a teacher. Unless a teacher allows students to discover the essential nature of a problem for themselves, they will continue to respond mechanically instead of productively. Programs that train teachers to develop productive thinking in their students are now under way throughout the country.

Jerome Bruner, whose theory of cognitive development we discussed in Chapter 2, has been greatly influenced by Gestalt psychology. Bruner also emphasizes insight learning, though he refers to it as "intuition." According to Bruner, the primary purpose of education is to learn skills and be able to use them in other situations (Bruner, 1964, 1965, 1966). School curricula should be organized so that children's mastery of the basic skills of a subject will make learning more advanced skills easier.

In his famous critique *The Process of Education,* Bruner (1960) used examples from the teaching of scientific and mathematical concepts to illustrate basic principles that are applicable to all areas of teaching and learning. Four central themes, each of which assumes a major role in Bruner's theory, are detailed here.

The first theme is that learning involves understanding basic relationships in the *structure* of a subject, rather than merely knowing facts and techniques. According to Bruner, being able to effectively relate one aspect of knowledge to another gives students a sense of direction that makes learning more exciting. This understanding of relationships also helps students to remember the material and transfer it to new learning situations.

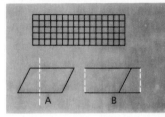

Figure 4-1 Wertheimer's parallelogram problem. (top) Rectangle divided into small squares showed the children how to find the area of the rectangle. (bottom) A and B represent the child's solution to the problem of finding the area of a parallelogram.

Bruner's Theory of Learning: Insight and Discovery

123

Years ago, English teachers taught grammar and the parts of speech by teaching students how to diagram sentences. This process fell into disrepute for a generation but has seen a revival in recent years. Diagramming provided a meaningful structure—both a product and a process—that demonstrated a logical relationship of words to the student. One English teacher asserts, "When I am writing, I still close my eyes and see the sentence in diagram form in my mind's eye. That way, I know if it is correct and can often find a more expressive way of putting my thoughts."

Readiness for learning is Bruner's second theme. The concept of readiness does not mean that instruction in certain subjects must be postponed until the student has reached a certain level of maturity. According to Bruner, the foundations of any discipline can be taught in a form simple enough to be meaningful even to very young children. In this respect, he agrees with Piaget, who maintained that we can teach effectively only so long as we match the subject matter to the student's cognitive level.

Too often, however, teachers apply rigid rules to decide specific chronological ages at which pupils are capable of learning certain subjects. Such teachers interpret the stage-dependent approach to cognitive development as meaning that a child should not be taught certain tasks until he or she has reached the necessary stage of cognitive development.

Learning problems develop when kindergarten students who have failed to pass reading-readiness tests are required to repeat kindergarten so that they might mature sufficiently before entering first grade and beginning to learn to read. Many educators have pointed out that it is a mistake to leave such children alone and simply wait for them to mature; with stimulation and teaching methods that require a lower mode of representation, they will be ready to learn to read much earlier than if they are ignored and allowed only to repeat what they have already done. Bruner believes that a student should not have to wait in order to learn: Rather, the concept of readiness should take the subject matter into account as well as the child. Furthermore, by providing children with challenging problems a step ahead of their development, a teacher can actually lead them to higher levels of reasoning at a more rapid rate than they would ordinarily be expected to display.

Bruner's third theme is his insistence that schools place much more emphasis on the development of *intuitive thinking*. Intuitive thinking involves the ability to arrive at reasonable but tentative formulations, prior to any actual formal analysis. It results in the "hunch" or educated guess, which may, of course, be either correct or incorrect. Bruner is not suggesting that students should rely exclusively on guessing, but he is saying that students should not be penalized for such responses. In daily life, we must often make decisions and take action on the basis of incomplete knowledge, and so Bruner feels that students should have early training in creative thinking and in recognizing the value of their guesses.

Motivation is the essence of the fourth theme. According to Bruner, a child can be motivated to learn. The teacher is essential in stimulating such a desire, and, if he or she is effective in this role, the student's desire to learn will carry over from the environment of the classroom to the rest of the world. Bruner feels that the best way teachers can stimulate learning is by making the material interesting so that students will want to learn it. For example, a teacher can show high school students how important reading is by showing the student the "job-wanted" ads in the newspaper. Students who spend money daily in stores and do not want to be cheated can be made to see how worthwhile it is to learn to add and subtract properly. Because Bruner's approach emphasizes the application of classroom learning to real life, artificial goals such as grades have little meaning and should be deemphasized.

Bruner is also concerned with the practical problems that occur in the implementation of his theories. Creating curriculum materials that will reflect the basic principles of a subject is the first problem. The second is developing teaching methods that will best utilize the capacities of students of different ages and abilities.

Bruner's Views on the Structure of Curricula

The Gestalt concepts of perceptual organization are also basic to Bruner's learning theory. According to Bruner, it is necessary to understand how a student perceives what he or she is learning. In order to make these perceptions most meaningful, Bruner suggests that the teacher structure the curriculum to "give a student as quickly as possible a sense of the fundamental ideas of a discipline—in other words, to convey the structure of a subject" (Bruner, 1960, p. 3). The subject's fundamental ideas and the relationships among them must be understood if the subject is to be used. Teachers can also help students to understand the subject by showing them how it relates to other subjects in meaningful ways.

Structure is both a product and a process because it includes the subject's fundamental ideas as well as a way of perceiving the logical relationships between those ideas. In this way it aids learning and memory: We understand more if the material is logically organized, and remember more if we can see how the various ideas relate to each other.

The structure and the sequence of the structured material are important topics in Bruner's learning theory. He maintains that the basic structure of any body of knowledge depends on three related aspects of learning: the mode of representation, economy, and power. These vary not only with the nature of the material but also with the age and the ability of the learner.

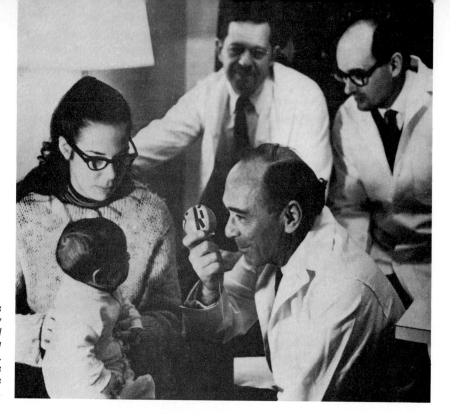

Dr. Jerome Bruner's theories lead to very direct and practical methods for teaching children of differing ages. Here Bruner concerns himself with an infant's perceptual organization.

Mode of representation The **mode of representation** refers to the basic method by which people understand and make use of their environments. Bruner calls these modes enactive, iconic, and symbolic. Infants are capable of using only the **enactive mode.** This basic mode involves processing information using only one response, such a motor response. An infant crawling across a room to reach a doll is an example of this mode.

The second mode of representation develops as the child increases in age and is called the **iconic mode** (pictorial representation). A young child drawing a picture of a doll he or she has seen is an example of the iconic mode.

The most advanced mode of representation is the **symbolic mode,** because it provides a means of going beyond what is immediately perceptible in a situation. Language plays a major role in this mode; for example, an adult describing a doll he has seen is using symbolic representation.

Bruner believes that teachers can combine the knowledge of developmental stages and modes of representation to determine the language and context appropriate for teaching the structure of a discipline at different periods of childhood. Consider, for example, Bruner's modes of representation in teaching very simple economic theory. Young children are thought to learn best by the enactive mode. Because they are not yet ready for abstract thinking, they should be introduced to ideas by "acting them out." A group of preschool children might be introduced to some basic principles of economics by playing "store." These same ideas can be taught to older children by using pictures or diagrams that show flow and distribution of money and goods from consumer to storekeeper and back to the consumer. This is Bruner's iconic mode of representation. Finally, the child is ready to learn and express ideas on an abstract or symbolic level. Now he or she is ready to learn about economics through mathematics. The symbolic mode of representation not only is the most sophisticated way of learning something new—in this example, microeconomics—it can also be the most powerful way if the child is ready to learn in this mode.

Economy   Economy is related to the structure of a subject and concerns the amount of information a student must learn and remember in order to understand that subject. The larger the amount, the less the economy. If, for example, we asked a child to memorize all the multiplication tables from 1 to 9 at the same time without developing a series of steps that provided meaning, there would be little economy of learning. In order to learn economically, we should not only acquire new information but get the maximum use out of it (Bruner, 1959, 1966). When a school curriculum is organized around atomistic or "episodic" units—for example, students first learn addition, then separately learn multiplication—the result is uneconomical. The earlier learning (addition) is not being used effectively to facilitate the later learning (multiplication). To learn multiplication, the students in a sense must begin all over again because they were not shown the relationship between the two units when they started out. A much more economical way of teaching, according to Bruner, would be to divide learning into a series of steps to explain why both parts of the curriculum—addition and multiplication—make sense. Thus what is learned as addition would be used to teach multiplication.

Power   The power of the material being learned is its value in terms of its applicability. Although a summary of a topic is a very economical means of presentation, it won't be as powerful as a more thorough description of the same material that teaches meaning and use. Using addition concepts to teach multiplication is a good example of this concept. Material can thus be economical in its presentation although it lacks power. However, the reverse is quite unlikely; if material is presented uneconomically, the emphasis on meaning and use will be dissipated, and some of its power will be lost (Bruner, 1966).

Proper sequencing of information   The *sequence* of structured material is the order in which the component parts of the subject are presented. Bruner believes that, because each situation is different, there is no one sequence that will apply to all learners in all situations. Among the factors that determine which sequence will work best are the learner's stage of development, past experiences, individual preferences, the nature of the materials themselves, and the criteria by which learning will be measured.

In one respect, Bruner firmly agrees with behavioral psychologists: Whatever sequence of learning materials is adopted, at some point the teacher must provide the learner with feedback about the appropriateness of his or her responses. Both specificity and the timing of feedback are important to learning. Feedback is necessary whenever the student compares what he or she has done with some criterion of what he or she hopes to achieve. The teacher must be specific in telling a student how he or she is doing. The teacher must provide the student with detailed information on his or her immediate activities as well as on his or her progress toward ultimate goals. Timing is critical: If feedback is given too early, before a student has had a chance to respond, it might not be understood; if it is given too late, long after he or she has responded, it might result in forgetting and wasted effort.

Unfortunately, with all the other duties that teachers have in the classroom, it is not always possible for them to follow Bruner's advice. When they don't, Bruner points out, the bad results they get are understandable. An eighth-grade history teacher was bemoaning the fact that there was so little time for her to mark her papers. "When I return the papers the next day after a class assignment, the discussion is lively and all the kids want to examine their answers—it's great. But I have so many students it takes many hours to mark papers properly. When I return them a week later, the children have forgotten what the assignment was about, and most of the papers are left in their desks or thrown in the wastebasket."

The act of learning According to Bruner, the process of learning a subject takes place in a series of episodes, each of which involves three integrated steps: acquisition, transformation, and evaluation. The first step, **acquisition,** is the process of obtaining new information that can be used to either replace or refine something previously known. The second step, **transformation,** is the manipulation of information to make it fit new situations. The third step, **evaluation,** is the process of checking whether the acquired information has been manipulated appropriately. The teacher can tailor the nature of these learning episodes to the needs and capacities of the individual student by shortening or lengthening the time spent on a particular step.

Transfer The application of knowledge from one area to another, or **transfer,** is one of Bruner's major concerns. In today's complex world, vast amounts of information are necessary in order to cope with day-to-day interactions. It is important that teachers provide more opportunities for students to transfer what they have learned in the classroom to the outside world.

The manner in which material is taught affects the student's ability to use it in new ways in new situations. According to Bruner, the more organized and integrated a teacher's presentation is, the more the student can use the material as a base on which to add further information. For example, isolated facts may become outdated, but their basic meanings, the relationships among them, and the methods of inquiry used to acquire them are all still valuable and relevant. If this approach is used in the classroom, the teacher can help the student to become a scholar instead of a parrot.

The important issue for Bruner is not so much what we learn, but what we can do with it. In order for a child to understand relationships and transfer knowledge to new situations—that is, to cross the barrier from learning to thinking—the learning that takes place in the classroom must be clearly related to everyday life. Bruner deplores the "passivity of knowledge-getting" that characterizes much of the learning that takes place in schools. He is extremely critical of the traditional American system of education. In his view, the schools encourage students simply to gather facts, learn formulas, and memorize by rote, without considering the importance of understanding meaning; the schools do not stimulate an inclination or enthusiasm to pursue knowledge. One problem with current education, according to Bruner (1959), is that

> the emphasis is upon gaining and storing information, gaining and storing it in the form in which it is presented. We carry the remainder in long division so, peaches are grown in Georgia, transportation is vital to cities, New York is our largest port, and so on. . . . There is little effort indeed which goes into the process of putting the information together, finding out what is generic about it.
>
> So knowledge-getting becomes passive. Thinking is the reward for learning, and we may be systematically depriving our students of this reward as far as school learning is concerned. (p. 184)

Bruner's Theory Applied to the Classroom

The teaching of one unit of the health curriculum in a middle school, as organized by one teacher, illustrates Bruner's theory clearly. The unit deals with the body systems, their relationship to each other, their function, and their position in the human body.

1st step—The teacher explains the topic in a general way, relating to the students' previous knowledge of the major organs in the body. After explaining how each organ is part of a system, the teacher stimulates the students' reasoning ability by assembling a guideline for them to follow in their research about each system. The guideline will eventually read as follows:

1. Description of the main organ.
2. What does it do?
3. How does it work?
4. Are there other important organs in the system and what do they do?
5. Where are the organs and other parts of the system located in the human body?
6. What would happen to your body if that system did not work properly?
7. What can you do to keep the system working effectively?

The outline of the report may vary slightly according to the grade level. This step represents Bruner's structure of the topic.

2nd step—Bruner's mode of representation is shown by the establishment of the format of the completed report. It requires a properly formulated written part (symbolic mode), a diagram of the main organ, and a view of its location in the human body (iconic mode).

3rd step—The concept of economy, better illustrated at the end of the activity, is the separation of the students into small groups, each of which is to study one of the systems. For the time being, the reason for the grouping is the limited amount of informative material that needs to be shared by every member of each group.

4th step—Bruner's power step is provided by the actual use of the material in relation to the guideline. Comprehending what each student is reading or using and selecting the needed information gives power to the report, which will present paragraphs coordinated in a meaningful sequence that clearly discuss the topic. Each section will naturally connect with the next one in an articulate, explanatory way, as required by Bruner's stress on the proper sequence of information.

5th step—We come now to transfer. After collecting, checking, and marking the reports, each group is called on to explain to the rest of the students the function of each organ and how it works. The final practical transfer will happen when each student will have the outline of his or her body traced on a large piece of paper, his or her skeleton cut out and glued in the proper position within the outline, and finally each organ also cut out of colored paper, glued in the proper position and, depending on age level, showing the proper connections among the various systems. This is also an illustration of economy, since the students use up all they have learned from their previous work.

The whole project can be adjusted to the specific degree of difficulty that the age level, the grade, and the ability of the students require by eliminating or adding more specific sections in the guideline or in the transfer activity.

Bruner's Views on Insight: The Act of Discovery Bruner, like the Gestalt psychologists discussed earlier, stresses how *insight* contributes to learning with understanding. Although he prefers the terms "intuition" or "intuitive thinking," the basic concept is the same.

By **intuition,** Bruner means "immediate apprehension or cognition" (Bruner, 1960, p. 60). Intuitive thinking is characterized by the development of hunches and hypotheses, by perceptions that seem to appear suddenly and dramatically. The child appears suddenly to understand the solution to the problem. Maybe he yells, "Aha!" or "Oh boy!" Then he proceeds to solve easily what had seemed to be a very difficult task just a few moments before. Bruner distinguishes *intuitive thinking*—which can precede and does not depend upon formal analysis—from the *analytic approach*—in which the steps taken to solve a problem are well thought out and clearly defined, and in which the learner is usually fully aware of the procedure he or she is following. In intuitive thinking, the learner thrashes about looking for shortcuts instead of proceeding methodically, and once having arrived at a tentative solution, he or she may have difficulty explaining how this new understanding was reached.

One reason that developmental psychologists have been able to show that children's free play increases cognitive ability, is that it provides excellent opportunity to try combinations of behavior that children would never try under formal pressure (Bruner, 1974, p. 22). In free play situations, children are allowed to discover for themselves what will work or not work without fear that they are making mistakes.

The *act of discovery* in the classroom, as Bruner described it (1961), involves intuitive thinking in which the teacher gives the student as firm a grasp of the subject as possible, while at the same time keeps him or her autonomous and self-propelled. The advantages involve an increase in intellectual potency, a shift to intrinsic rewards in which students begin to learn for their own enjoyment, a learning of the heuristics of discovery, and an aid to increased memory. All of these were goals of Midtown City Junior College's Special Program.

Bruner feels that teachers have encouraged children to develop analytical ways of thinking at the expense of intuitive thinking (Bruner, 1960). This is not to suggest that analysis (learning to solve a problem by breaking it down into its component parts) is necessarily undesirable or that intuitive thinking is always preferable. The ideal learning situation is one in which analytical and intuitive thinking complement one another. We cannot determine the value of a new hypothesis by relying on intuition alone, but neither can we expect to generate many new hypotheses only on the basis of analytical thinking.

Scholars, scientists, and others use both intuitive and analytic reasoning to solve problems. For example, a physician might first ask the patient questions, then examine the patient briefly, and finally make a probable diagnosis. If this preliminary diagnosis (intuitive thinking) suggests a possibly serious condition, the physician would then proceed systematically by ordering tests, recommending hospi-

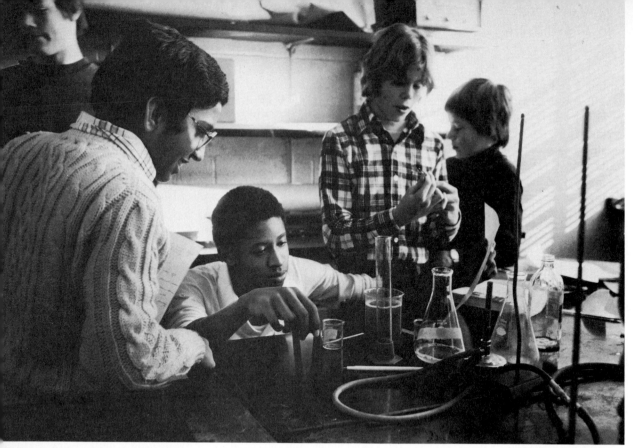

Discovery learning often takes a great deal of time, but can produce some of the most exciting memories that students have of their classroom experiences.

talization, or telling the patient to return for another checkup (analytic reasoning). In this way the two approaches are combined. Similarly, a scientist might make a preliminary hypothesis about the cause of an event (intuitive thinking), then follow it with an experiment in which all possible causes are tested systematically and scientifically (analytic reasoning).

Bruner contends that children can also use both of these approaches to problem-solving. He regrets, for example, that geometry is not included in the elementary school curriculum. The axioms, theorems, and proofs of this discipline are not presented until high school, and students are often bewildered by these new concepts because they have not been taught the fundamentals. At the same time, teachers too frequently reward these students for simply memorizing without necessarily understanding the concepts being taught. To Bruner, a more productive approach would be to introduce children at a much earlier age to simple geometric configurations and fundamentals and to the intuitive strategies for dealing with them. With this background in their elementary school years, adolescents could then presumably draw on that knowledge to go beyond mere memorization of proofs and formulas to the type of thinking in which scholars engage—discerning relationships and discovering their own proofs.

Teachers may find it difficult to get their students to engage in intuitive thinking because students are often unwilling to risk making mistakes. One problem is that teachers themselves often provide extrinsic rewards in the form of praise, good grades, and so on to students who memorize the material as presented and then reproduce it in similar form on an exam. In so doing, they encourage their students to develop rote-learning abilities or, at best, analytic thinking exclusively, but at the same time they inhibit the children from developing the ability to learn through insight. Probably this approach is less taxing for teachers than waiting for their students to arrive at what Bruner terms the "magic moment" of insight. Whatever the cause, American schools do emphasize extrinsic rewards as opposed to the intrinsic rewards of discovery, and it is this practice that Bruner finds so unfortunate.

Bruner's theories suggest that the schools must drastically alter their curricula in order to truly contribute to the intellectual development of the child, and that teachers are capable of implementing these changes.

The traditional practice of teaching specific facts or skills, without imparting the underlying principles that give structure to the subject,

Fixation: Enemy of Insight

We all love that moment when "the light comes on" as we're trying to solve a problem. Gestalt psychologists call this *insight*. But sometimes we feel stymied, unable to perceive the essential elements required for a solution. This condition is called *fixation*. Martin Scheerer (1963) has found that it operates in several ways. Often we cling to an incorrect assumption. For example, when asked to assemble six matches to form equilateral triangles each side of which is equal to the length of the matches, most people assume—incorrectly—that the matches must lie flat. The correct solution—building a three-dimensional pyramid—calls for a *reformulation* or *recentering* of one's thoughts. His studies also indicate that any type of fixation can be strengthened by too much motivation. Strong ego involvement, for example, makes for overmotivation and is detrimental to the process of finding a solution. A final factor affecting fixation is habit. We use habitual ways of responding because they're most available to us; this makes it much harder to approach a problem with a fresh perspective. Scheerer concludes: "If insight is the essential element in intelligent problem-solving, fixation is its archenemy. Fixation is overcome and insight attained by a sudden shift in the way the problem or objects are viewed . . . precisely what brings [this] about is still unknown. It remains the central problem of problem-solving" (p. 128).

makes long-term retention and transfer extremely difficult. Furthermore, the practice offers little intellectual excitement to the learner (Bruner, 1960). Instead, schools should stress the general principles that make up a subject. Teachers must make a subject seem interesting and worthwhile; if they don't, learners are apt to quickly forget the material, and much of their learning will have become wasted effort. This belief has led Bruner to formulate his ideas on discovery teaching, discussed later in this chapter.

The act of discovery and cheating   Bruner's writings do not deal with the problem of cheating, so prevalent in American schools today. But teachers concerned with the day-to-day problems of how to prevent classroom cheating point out that it is impossible to cheat at discovery learning. Either the student grasps the concept or does not. Unlike rote learning, he or she cannot put down on the test paper something that is correct but is really not understood at all. For teachers who have had to learn to cope with crib sheets tucked into shirts and short answers written on arms, this more than compensates for any "taxing" effects of waiting for insight to appear.

Information-Processing Approaches to Learning and Memory   Psychologists who approach the processes of learning, remembering, and forgetting as information processing compare the functioning of the mind with what they suggest are similar processes in computers. This is termed the **cybernetic theory** or **information-processing approach** to cognition. Encompassing a large number of theories, the general feature of this approach is its central focus on how information flows from its initial input into memory storage to its final output as retrieved memory. A theoretical model has been developed by these theorists to account for what happens when we remember and forget. The model can then be used to help to identify and understand the possible mechanisms involved in memory.

In generating a theoretical model, advocates of an information-processing approach examine the general requirements a computer must meet in order to be able to solve certain types of problems, (see, for example, Newell and Simon, 1972). For instance, a computer must have some sort of analyzer that examines incoming information before it is processed by another part of the computer. This kind of general feature in computers is incorporated into the theoretical model of human memory.

This model of information processing is used to answer two questions: How is information placed into storage? and How is this information retrieved at a later time? Interest in the first question centers on which perceptual attributes of an item are extracted for storage in memory. For example, when you are looking for a new car, you store a great deal of information about the cars you see: the color, number of doors, engine size, manufacturer, and so on. Each fact is a variable that you must use in deciding which car to buy. The relevant aspect of each car is then stored under each of these categories. This process has been described as analogous to a cross-referencing system in a library, in which a book may be found catalogued under a variety of categories. This storage process is important because how carefully we put something away determines how easily we'll find it when we need it later.

Encoding is an interesting phenomenon that occurs during storage (Tulving, 1972). This process enables us to reduce or abbreviate the amount of information stored for a particular item. For example, when we see a cat, we notice that it has four legs, whiskers, two eyes, and so on. But we do not have to store each of these bits of information separately. We form an image of the cat that includes all this information in a chunk, and we store this chunk instead. Chunks of information are sometimes stored independently of one another (Miller, 1956), but they are sorted, filed, and cross-indexed in meaningful ways. "Cat," for example, is stored with "animals," "household pets," "furry critters," and so on.

Organization is another aspect of storage. In this process, bits of stored information are related to one another (Tulving, 1972). It is possible, however, that the way we organize information will lead to interference: One piece of information may disrupt another piece of information while it is being stored.

Information-processing theorists see the storage and retrieval of information as two distinct processes. The storage process is concerned with input, while the retrieval process is a search for information activated by a memory task. However, retrieval is not simply a matter of searching through all the items in the memory storage until the appropriate one is found. That could take forever. The manner in which the searching proceeds depends on the cues that are available to guide the search (Wood, 1972). Let us assume, for example, that you are asked to remember a list of eight items, but you can recall only five of them. If I provide you with a category for the forgotten items (a cue), you will be more likely to remember them. If the cue is "fruit," you might be able to remember that the three missing items are "apple," "pear," and "banana." The items had been stored in your memory, but to retrieve them your search had to be initiated by a cue. Teachers can provide cues to aid retrieval if they word their questions carefully in the classroom and on tests. The help provided by cues is one reason why many students find multiple-choice questions easier than essay questions on a test.

Is information processing an accurate description of what goes on in the human brain? The issue has been hotly debated. Dreyfus (1972), for example, has pointed out that information-processing theories do not account for all levels of human performance, that they lack generality, and that they do not represent the steps that humans consciously go through when they solve problems. Some information-processing theorists agree that the basic theory may be oversimplified. Kirby and Das (1978), for example, suggest that information-processing theories that explain only one way that information is stored in the brain probably are an oversimplification of what is taking place. They suggest, instead, that information is stored in at least two different ways, through simultaneous and successive processing. Other advocates of information processing respond by pointing out that information-processing descriptions of cognition could be complete if it were possible to store all past learning of a human being. They do not see information processing's failure to describe conscious thinking as important. They point out (Pylyshyn, 1974, 1975) that the processes that enable people to solve problems should not be confused with the processes people are aware of.

Information-processing advocates give teachers advice that is similar to that of other cognitive psychologists: Help students to understand by presenting information so that it can be stored in meaningful chunks; show how some pieces of information are related to others so that they can be chunked; and, in testing situations, provide cues to help with retrieval.

Ausubel's Approach to Problem-Solving

Cognitive psychologists agree that information should be taught in ways that make it most meaningful. The manner in which this can be done, however, is disputed. Some specialists suggest discovery learning or open classroom methods. Other cognitive psychologists are more interested in the specific teaching/learning process. Some of these suggest that students learn and retain most effectively if they are taught general, all-inclusive concepts first.

Ausubel's theory of subsumption According to David Ausubel, a leading cognitive psychologist, and his colleagues (Ausubel, 1963, 1968; Ausubel et al., 1978), learning general concepts first allows students to use these concepts as anchors onto which subsequent details, illustrations, and examples can be attached. According to information-processing theory, Ausubel's principle, which he termed **subsumption,** means that learning general principles is the best way to help a student organize new material.

Some psychologists believe that Ausubel's subsumption approach is not the most effective way to work with all students. They point out that because of their past histories of learning experiences, some students learn better initially and retain their knowledge longer when taught in the opposite sequence, from specifics toward principles and concepts (McDade, 1978). Clearly there are major differences between students in their preferred manner of learning.

Meaningful learning   Ausubel's prime interest in the past decade has been to demonstrate that what he terms "meaningful learning" is most beneficial in classroom instruction. One common measure of meaningfulness is the number of associations or the familiarity a particular subject has for a student. Ausubel's version of meaningful learning involves concepts that come from everyday meaningful discourse (Ausubel et al., 1978). According to Ausubel, children learn concepts in much the same way as adults do, but they use fewer abstract concepts and fewer higher-order abstractions in their thinking. Thus, children can learn in much the same manner as adults as long as the material presented to them has meaning, that is, as long as proper allowance is made for the smaller number of higher-order concepts the children can handle (Ausubel, 1968).

The use of concrete props   Ausubel and his colleagues (1968, 1978) believe that autonomous discovery, learning without a teacher's assistance, is not necessarily the best or only way to teach children to solve problems. During the early elementary schools years, for example, when children are responding at what Piaget termed the concrete operations stage of development and with what Bruner called the iconic and then symbolic modes of representation, concrete props are very useful teaching tools. Teaching a first grader to solve a simple algebraic problem is not impossible or even difficult, if the child is presented

Concrete props are helpful in making each step of the learning process clear when students are young.

Alice Kandell, Photo Researchers, Inc.

first with a series of blocks or other stimuli to make each step of the process clear.

Cognitive Styles We all have our own ways of doing things, from combing our hair to processing information. The particular styles with which individual students process information in the course of learning are known as **cognitive styles.** Your cognitive style includes your individual preferences in perceiving, thinking, remembering, and solving problems. Ausubel, (1968), along with many other investigators, believes that, to a great extent, cognitive styles reflect individual differences in personality and motivation.

The importance of paying attention to individual differences in cognitive style has been emphasized ever since the advent of progressive education. However, more often than not, recognition of individual differences has simply meant giving each student different amounts of time to do the same required work. Teachers have learned how to adapt their methods of instruction to differences in pace, but not to differences in style.

A case in point is Judy, an exceptionally bright student, who often finished her work before the other students did. Until the fifth grade, she had been encouraged to spend her extra time reading. Her fifth-grade teacher, however, felt Judy could spend her time more productively and suggested independent math projects, science reports, and so on. The teacher was disappointed when Judy seemed willing, but simply didn't do these assignments. Next, the teacher tried being more specific. She set up a structured project with exact short- and long-term goals. Now Judy knew just what to do, and she completed several satisfying and worthwhile projects. As bright as she was, she needed a lot of guidance and structure.

Reissman (1966) was one of the first to emphasize the importance of cognitive styles. He pointed out that each individual has a distinct style of learning in much the same way that each individual has a distinct personality. Cognitive styles are learned early in life and are difficult to change once they have been learned. The three basic styles Reissman identified are visual (reading), aural (listening), and physical (doing). According to Reissman, most people show a distinct preference for one of these methods as compared with the others. For example, many socially disadvantaged children have cognitive styles that are characterized by hyperactivity, distractibility, and difficulty in settling down. Often these children have more difficulty performing tasks that require reading or listening than performing tasks that require "doing."

In addition to the cognitive styles identified by Reissman, other aspects of behavior that might also be classified as cognitive styles are the mode of response and the thinking pattern (Nations, 1967). *Response mode* in this sense refers to whether an individual prefers to work alone or in a group. *Thinking pattern* refers to the tendency of some individuals to gather details first and organize them later, as compared with the tendency of others to look for the overall picture first and to obtain supporting information afterward.

Reissman's position with regard to cognitive styles is that they are developed early in life as a result of a combination of predisposition and environmental experience, and are not later subject to fundamental change. Consequently, teachers should help their students to discover the style that is most effective for them and should use this information in designing the curriculum activities. For example, a student who likes to learn by actively doing might begin to take more of an interest in reading if it were combined with role-playing activities. The instructor at the Special Program in Midtown City Junior College gave her students choices among different projects to do about "nothing" because she was trying to take different cognitive styles into consideration.

Psychologists have identified many factors related to personality and temperament that influence a student's performance in the classroom.

First of all, children vary greatly in their level and *span of attention*. There are important individual differences in depth and scope of attention that determine how vividly a child experiences what he or she is learning. Children also differ in their ability to select relevant environmental cues and ignore extraneous ones. Some children can pay attention for long periods of time, while others are easily distracted or frequently daydream. Still others pay attention only to what interests them. By observing such differences in the way students pay attention, a teacher can determine which children need to be monitored during class instruction and which children can handle long assignments.

The *capacity for independent work* also varies greatly from child to child. Some can work with very little supervision, some need a little help only at the beginning of an assignment, some need help sporadically, and some need it constantly. Teachers who are aware of these differences can budget their time much more effectively. Many children also have to be taught how to manage the time they spend on a project.

A child's rate of learning is not necessarily the same as his or her capacity to learn—some pupils work slowly but still manage to learn a great deal. A child who works slowly may be overcautious or sluggish but still have high ability. A child who works quickly may be very intelligent and able to comprehend a great deal, but he or she can also be impulsive, impatient, and disorganized. Many children work at various rates depending on the assignment, and the teacher should take this into account when assigning homework. There is a danger in forcing a child to learn at a rate incompatible with his or her natural rhythm and abilities.

A good way to find out about your students' cognitive styles, attention spans, needs for supervision, and so on, is to watch them prepare a report. The guidelines for the report should be decided on in advance—how long it should be, number and type of diagrams, use of research materials, and so forth. Then bring in the widest possible variety of research materials, and let them go to it. Some students will go straight to the books; others will want to use the audiovisual materials. Watch them at their desks: Some will become engrossed in their work, while others will fidget and look up a lot. Some will spend so much time on the "fun part" of the report—drawing the diagrams and collecting the data—that they may not get around to writing the report until the last minute. And every class probably has a "can't" or two—students who "can't" find the research they need, "can't" understand the assignment, "can't" draw anything, "can't" work without the teacher's continual guidance and support. Direct observations like these can help you to plan your time and provide activities that suit your students' different personalities and learning styles.

A child's readiness to learn and his or her expectations of what the learning situation will be have a powerful effect on what he or she actually does learn. The child's typical style of *perceiving* also largely determines what and how he or she learns. Shortly after World War II, Asch and Witkin and their associates at Brooklyn College first identified important differences in children's modes of perceiving. They found that some children have the ability to make fine discriminations and isolate items from a surrounding context; they called this kind of active analysis **field independence.** Other children tended to be overwhelmed by the complex organization of a field or object and could not discriminate between figure and ground; the researchers called this kind of passive, unanalytic acceptance of a problem **field dependence** (Messick, 1970; Witkin et al., 1962; Witkin et al, 1967).Students tend to do better at subjects that are compatible with their preferred style (Witkin et al., 1977b). Field-dependent children might have difficulty picking out which factors to solve in a mathematical factor-analysis problem; field-independent children would probably have an easier time.

Children's memories also work in different ways: Some children tend to confuse and blur present objects and events with similar ones in the past; other children can't see any similarities between present and past events, even when the events are almost identical (Holzman and Klein, 1954).

Researchers have also found a wide variation in children's willingness to accept new perceptions, experiences, and surroundings (Klein, Gardner, and Schlesinger, 1962; Messick, 1970; Sperry, 1972). This is particularly noticeable in children's reactions to the first day at school and to new and unfamiliar activities. Some children accept new experiences as a challenge and seem relaxed and receptive almost immediately; more apprehensive children develop headaches and stomach aches, or panic when the teacher introduces new subject matter and new routines.

Children have many different styles of forming concepts, solving problems, and thinking. In studying the ways in which children select hypotheses and process information, researchers have isolated tendencies toward impulsiveness (**impulsivity**) and reflectiveness (**reflectivity**). Because of a desire for quick success, impulsive children make immediate responses that are often wrong; they blurt out the first answer that occurs to them without stopping to think through a problem and consider alternatives. Reflective children, on the other hand, are more anxious about making mistakes. They tend to think about a problem first and consider various possibilities before deciding on an answer. In a classroom in Utah, a teacher conducted research that demonstrated that many children are never given "thinking time" when a question is asked by a teacher. Those who think quickly—or answer quickly—are usually the ones called on. Reflective children, who may never be called on, early during their school years may stop raising their hands or find it more gratifying to meditate on things other than those being taught in the classroom. Problems may also exist for the impulsive child: Children with average intelligence often do poorly in school because of their impulsivity and distractibility.

There are also great differences in children's views of the world and of other people's behavior. Some children see others in a rather elementary, one-dimensional way, while other children are capable of seeing the world in a discriminating and multidimensional way. Researchers have also studied children's tendencies to use either broad or narrow classifications (Messick, 1970; Pettigrew, 1958) and have attempted to determine whether these classifications are based on concepts that have been thought through in an orderly, discriminating manner.

Peer Teaching: A Motivator for the Classroom

One clever way that teachers have found to increase classroom motivation is to make use of *peer teachers*, students who are either older or more advanced in their subject matter than the students they teach. Peer teaching is used regularly in Soviet schools, where selected peer teachers help out students who are having difficulty each day after class. Teachers report that peer teaching is motivating both for the tutors and for their pupils. Tutors perceive the assignment as a source of great pride; their pupils enjoy individual attention, an opportunity to work with someone their own age, a look at the problem from the perspective of another student.

American psychologists and educators have tried out peer teaching experimentally with excellent results, although the method is not being used frequently in traditional public school classrooms. Researchers have found the method very effective in experimental education and community programs. For example, self-help groups such as Alcoholics Anonymous and Recovery, Inc. are based on the principle that people with similar problems can help one another. In Mobilization for Youth, high school students tutored peers and younger students; in Flint, Michigan, sixth-graders with reading difficulties tutored fourth-graders with similar problems. Both groups showed substantial improvement as a result of the tutoring program (Riessman, 1965). More recently Oakland and Williams (1975), using same-aged tutors, showed that tutors the same age as their charges have good effects on learning when adequately supervised by teachers.

Studies show that the helper role is a particularly valuable one for the students (Rosen et al, 1978; Becker, 1978). It contributes to their feelings of self-esteem and to eventual leadership potential. When a child realizes that others think highly of him or her, it leads to higher self-expectations. Thus, peer teaching may be a useful means of strengthening the confidence of students with learning difficulties.

Peer teaching is not the only way that students can be used to help each other in the classroom. Learning teams and instructional games in which groups of children participate have been tried out experimentally in urban classrooms in America. In these experiments, reinforcements are meted out to groups, rather than to individual students. Studies have shown that such student teaming improves both academic performance and student attitudes. In situations in which the student groups are biracial, researchers suggest that this method provides an effective way to increase cross-racial friendships (DeVries et al, 1978).

The helper role is a particularly valuable one for students; both the peer teacher and the student being helped have been shown to profit tremendously by this method.

Cognitive theories have direct application for curriculum development. In teaching subjects that require perceptual skills, such as reading, the Gestalt laws of perceptual organization play a major role. Organization of the curriculum and learning tasks is also all-important, in the teaching of subjects that require the development of abstract thinking and problem solving.

Teachers should not develop a curriculum on their own; teachers, subject-matter specialists, and psychologists should all work together. Moreover, any basic changes in the curriculum should be tested by careful observational and experimental methods. A successful curriculum does not simply lead to increased achievement. The criterion of success is whether the children can make sense of the material and organize it into a meaningful whole (Bruner, 1966).

Planning the Curriculum

In addition, curriculum planners must pay more attention to individual differences among students. Students vary considerably not only in general ability but also in specific skills, subject-matter preferences, approaches to solving problems, and need for external reinforcement.

> If a curriculum is to be effective in the classroom it must contain different ways of activating children, different ways of presenting sequences, different opportunities for some children to "skip" parts while others work their way through, different ways of putting things. A curriculum, in short, must contain many tracks leading to the same general goal. (Bruner, 1966, p. 71).

Bruner's **discovery teaching** requires the rearrangement of subject matter structure so that the learner is able to go beyond the evidence presented to new insights (Bruner, 1962). According to Bruner, the ideal teaching program for accomplishing insight learning is the **spiral curriculum.** This curriculum is designed to teach specific agreed-upon and fundamental ideas and principles. It is constructed so that students at different ages and developmental stages can approach it at varying levels of complexity. In the spiral curriculum, early learning, which requires a simple level of understanding, serves as preparation for later learning and deeper understanding (Bruner, 1966). For example, in the spiral curriculum, elementary school children would not be required to read Shakespeare's original works, but they might be prepared to pursue this activity later by first being introduced to the significance of human tragedy and the various ways it has been depicted in literature.

Discovery Teaching and Insight Learning

Discovery teaching and reinforcement Discovery teaching is not incompatible with the behavioral position that reinforcement is important to learning. Bruner and his colleagues concede that students need regular feedback on the appropriateness of their responses, but they fear that feedback will make students dependent on the teacher's corrections. Learners need to develop self-sufficiency so that when a teacher is not available they can take over the task of correcting themselves. Bruner believes that reinforcement inherent in the subject matter itself is critical to learning.

Tackling a problem independently, correcting oneself as one goes along, and, most important, deriving satisfaction from the resulting discoveries are behaviors characteristic of scientists and scholars. It is no coincidence that Bruner urges teachers to develop the same abilities in their students. A major purpose of discovery teaching is to bridge the gap between the world of the scholar and the classroom world of the student, a point Bruner makes in *The Process of Education*.

> Intellectual activity anywhere is the same, whether at the frontier of knowledge or in a third grade classroom. What a student does at his desk or in his laboratory, what a literary critic does in reading a poem, are of the same order as what anybody does when he is engaged in like activities—if he is to achieve understanding. The difference is in degree, not in kind. (1960, p. 14)

Discovery teaching and transfer Research with preschoolers has demonstrated that **guided discovery teaching** does increase transfer of school learning to real-life situations (Solter and Mayer, 1978). In guided discovery teaching, the teacher allows students to solve problems by themselves, rather than providing the correct answer for them and then "allowing" them to duplicate the process. In Solter and Mayer's study, preschoolers were taught to match poker chips according to different characteristics (number, size, closeness to one another, color, and so on). Children who were guided by the teacher to pay attention to the important aspect of the task, but who still solved the problem for themselves, transferred this information later to conservation task problems. They did so significantly more effectively than children who learned by watching the teacher solve the matching problem and then imitating the correct response.

Discovery teaching does have a couple of possible negative side effects. School children of all ages realize that they are dependent on adults, and most of them resent it. Being able to do anything independently is exciting, and the feelings of freedom and power that accompany the independent achievements provided by discovery teaching sometimes go to children's heads. Some youngsters do not have the emotional maturity to be humble about their abilities and successes, and teachers must be alert to ensure that the brighter, more aggressive students don't trample on those who are slower or need more help from the teacher. Thus, reinforcements such as praise must be carefully tuned to minimize competition among the students.

Allowing students to solve problems on their own also may be harmful if students are not required to verbalize or put in writing, what they have learned. Oral recitation polishes a student's vocabulary, shows mastery of the subject and its terminology, and aids retention. Oral presentations may take the form of informal answers to teachers' questions, individual reports and speeches, small-group discussions, and even formal debates. All these techniques show that students have learned how to use what they have discovered.

In Bruner's view, discovery teaching would be a vast improvement over present teaching methods. In addition to learning and remembering more from their classroom activities, children would derive more pleasure from the experience. Testing hypotheses and solving problems would become an exciting adventure for them. Their reward would be their increased understanding of the structure of the subject as well as the realization that understanding was obtained in large measure through their own discoveries.

Practical implementation of discovery teaching Researchers have provided a variety of practical ways in which discovery teaching might be implemented in an actual classroom. Two suggestions that clearly illustrate the nature of the discovery approach are considered here.

Bigge (1964) has proposed an application of insight teaching to a multiplication lesson. In a fourth-grade class about to learn how to multiply by 9, the teacher first asks the pupils to review the multiplication tables they have already learned—2s, 3s, 5s, 10s—and makes sure that they understand the basic relationships. As the teacher begins to write the new table on the blackboard, he or she asks the class to supply the answers based on the knowledge they already have of the other multiplication tables. Thus, for example, since they have already learned in the multiplication table for 3s that 3 x 9 = 27, they can be led into the discovery that 9 x 3 equals the same amount.

The discovery method might also be applied to a history unit, a collection of poetry, or any other aspect of the curriculum. Bruner offered an illustration pertaining to an actual sixth-grade geography lesson (Bruner, 1960). In this lesson, each student in the class was given a map of the central states that showed only bodies of water, agricultural products, and natural resources. Based on that information alone, the students were asked to locate Chicago. One child reasoned that a large city required lots of water and so placed Chicago at the junction of three lakes. Another child reasoned that a major city, because of its large population, would need to have a good food supply, and thus placed Chicago in what would be Iowa. Other children had different hypotheses, and a lively discussion ensued about where Chicago belonged on the map. The fact that no one in the class produced the correct response was not as important, Bruner felt, as the excitement and reward of learning by discovery.

Unfinished stories are also good ways to encourage thinking in students. When a child is presented with a set of characters, a situation, a setting, and a few other details and is carried to a certain point in a story, he or she quickly learns the excitement of finishing up the action and wrapping up the suspense.

Naturally, no child will be able to produce the response that the original author intended, but often the child's conclusion far surpasses in worth and interest the original one pointed so formally in the textbook.

An evaluation of the approach Bruner sees several important advantages to the discovery method of teaching.

1. It leads students to a better understanding of the basic ideas and concepts of a subject—its structure.
2. It aids students in applying both memory and transfer to new learning situations, as well as in original learning.
3. It encourages students to think and work on their own, without having to rely on directions and feedback from another person.
4. It encourages students to think intuitively and to formulate and test their own hypotheses. Thus, they can deal more effectively with unstructured situations, not only in school but in everyday life.
5. It provides students with a sense of inner satisfaction, independent of extrinsic rewards.
6. It makes learning intellectually stimulating to students, who will approach difficult subject matter and time-consuming problem activities with interest and enthusiasm.

Bruner's enthusiasm for discovery teaching is not shared by all psychologists. Some feel that many of his claims are exaggerated and that the arguments made to support the method are based more on intuitive conviction than on well-established empirical evidence from properly controlled studies (Ausubel, 1968; Smedslund, 1964; Travers, 1972). The main drawback, however, is that discovery learning is extraordinarily time-consuming. A student may take four hours to discover something he or she could learn by direct teaching in five minutes.

Ausubel has been highly critical of Bruner, primarily for conveying the impression that discovery teaching is the only way that classroom learning should take place. Ausubel does acknowledge that discovery learning may be useful to concept formation during the child's early years of schooling, but he feels that meaningful learning can occur in many situations without it (Ausubel, 1963, 1967a, 1968; Ausubel and Sullivan, 1970).

During the last twenty years, classroom procedures based on rigid, authoritarian disciplinary measures have been widely challenged. One alternative known as the open classroom advocates an informal style of teaching.

The open method of teaching was originally a key recommendation of the 1967 **Plowden Report,** a comprehensive analysis of modern British primary school practices conducted by the British Central Advisory Council for Education. The Plowden Report was concerned with the quality of instruction in the British "infant schools," schools for children from age 5 to age 7 or 8. One of the critical findings was that the most successful schools tended to be "open" in their approach to teaching. Administrators allowed a considerable amount of freedom both in daily classroom activities and in curricular planning. Children in such schools showed increased interest in schoolwork and excellent rapport with teachers.

Open classrooms contain many different kinds of learning materials for children in order to stimulate curiosity and interest. The major responsibility for choosing materials rests with the teacher, who continually talks with students about their interests and preferences. Resnick (1971) suggested that the open classroom teacher, by questioning the students and giving them individual attention, serves as a powerful model for building a positive attitude toward free inquiry and environmental exploration.

The open classroom in England   The open educational system in England is often described as the *integrated day program,* because there are very few fixed time periods for which a specific activity is compulsory. Instead, individual teachers and students organize the school day as they wish. Each child is generally free to perform the particular activity that interests him or her at any given time. The children can either explore a certain part of the room or remain in a familiar work area. They can work alone or in a group. Teachers will normally move around the room, working for a certain period of time with one child or a group of children, then moving on to another area. Within any given day, one child may work on a variety of different projects, sometimes alone, sometimes with various friends, and sometimes with the teacher.

This is not to suggest that the role of an open classroom teacher is an easy one. In fact, the open classroom teacher has enormous responsibilities. He or she must be sensitive to the needs of a large number of children and must be able to develop individualized instructional tasks for each of them. Rather than formulating one lesson plan for 30 children, the open classroom teacher needs to develop 30 separate lesson plans every week. A good open classroom teacher does not ignore a defiant or uncooperative child. Instead, the teacher attempts to learn why the misbehavior occurred and how it can be avoided in

The open classroom allows children to take on different learning tasks, when and where they want to.

Stan Wakefield

the future. The use of arbitrary punishment as a means of suppressing disobedience is discouraged in open education. For the open classroom to be successful, the relationship between teachers and students must be one of mutual trust and respect.

Observers unfamiliar with the characteristics and rationale for the open classroom sometimes find the atmosphere noisy and chaotic. Many are accustomed to seeing students seated at their desks, quietly doing their work. It can be startling, at first, to see students constantly moving about the room on their own initiative. But when the curriculum is geared to the children's interests, when they have a say in selecting their own materials, and when the teacher has an accepting attitude, the discipline problem can be minimal.

The open classroom in the United States The trend toward informal education has spread from England to the United States. Both urban and rural school systems have instituted a variety of open classroom methods and techniques. In addition, a number of university-based teacher-training programs have shifted toward this approach. As a result, a growing number of American teachers operate in open classrooms, which are spreading from elementary to middle school and high school programs.

Since the late 1960s, more than half the new schools built in the United States have been open-space schools (Seidner, Lewis, Sherwin, and Troll, 1978). These schools are identified by specific architectural characteristics: limited use of interior walls, large open spaces, and few physical barriers to interaction among students of various ages and grade levels. Although not all teachers in these schools have made extensive use of open methods, such methods are easier to implement in these settings.

Using and evaluating open classrooms American teachers have developed a variety of methods to "open" the American classroom, including encouraging children to bring pets to school and using them as stimuli to teach other subjects. The Alexander Lindsay Jr. Museum in Walnut Creek, California, for example, opened the Pet Library Club some years ago. The Pet Library is a club in which children can "check out" a bunny, a rat, a guinea pig, or even a chinchilla. These are among the 250 animals youngsters can take home for a week. A primary (but not exclusive) purpose of the library is to give children the opportunity to develop the responsibility needed in taking care of a pet. The library provides a cage and food. The only requirements to join the pet-lending program are that a child be 6 years old and that the parents sign a consent form (Clifford, 1975).

Another important aspect of the program involves the schools. The museum director, Sam Smoker, notes, "People have fears regarding certain animals and by getting to know them these fears can be overcome" (Clifford, 1975, p. E2). Claire, the resident boa constrictor, is taken by adult volunteers on tours to classrooms where the children can pet her. Black vultures are also visitors, staff members insisting that "to know a vulture is to love a vulture." Creative teachers in open classrooms can provide many innovative learning experiences from visits of this sort.

One major problem of opening American classrooms has been that American children may have more difficulty than British youngsters in adjusting to the open classroom atmosphere. Perhaps as a result of the long history of centralized schools in the United States, American youths seem more accustomed to authoritarian methods both at home and in school; the same seems to be true of American teachers. It is clear that not all teachers feel comfortable with the informality and lack of structure of the open classroom. Many advocates of informal education do not recommend its use by teachers who are more comfortable with an authoritarian style.

One of the major questions about open education involves the role of the teacher. Madden (1972) has emphasized that one of the teacher's responsibilities in an open classroom is to exercise control and to provide systematic positive reinforcement. He recommends helping students to develop responsible freedom of choice and self-direction in small, sequential, reinforced steps. When this procedure is followed, "the result can and should be the development of a humane classroom culture in which each child can learn not only to be free and independent but how to reconcile the demands of social learning upon freedom" (Madden, 1972, pp. 106-107).

Ausubel and Robinson (1969) distinguish between discovery teaching, in which students discover and give structure to the subject matter themselves, and **reception teaching** in which the material to be learned is presented to the student in "more or less final form." The multiplication tables are usually learned by reception learning; reading an eyewitness account of a historical event is another example of this form of learning. Ausubel maintains that, although reception learning is not characterized by the independent search that Bruner considers so important, it can still be an important, meaningful, and active learning experience. Reception learning can lead the student to do any or all these active steps.

*Ausubel's
Reception
Teaching*

1. Relating new material to relevant ideas already established in the student's cognitive structure.
2. Seeking to understand similarities and differences between new material and related concepts and propositions.
3. Translating what the student has learned into a frame of reference that reflects his or her own experience and vocabulary.
4. Reorganizing the student's existing knowledge so that he or she can formulate new ideas.

Ausubel contends that not all reception learning is necessarily rote, and that not all discovery learning is necessarily meaningful. The conditions under which learning takes place determine whether it is rote or meaningful.

Both Bruner and Ausubel support their contradictory positions with strong arguments. Since valid arguments can be made for both the discovery and the guided instruction methods, teachers have no golden rule to follow. Empirical evidence generally suggests that guided learning does increase immediate learning and retention. The evidence of long-term retention is not nearly as clear, however. The discovery approach, on the other hand, does facilitate the transfer of basic principles to new situations, but at present we have no evidence from which to conclude that the techniques and strategies associated with discovery learning are subject to similar transfer, although Bruner has said that original learning by discovery leads to the ability to learn more by discovery. The teacher who wants to be as effective as possible in the classroom will make use of both approaches—depending on the subject matter, the student, and the time available for learning.

Because time is so limited—no teacher has time to teach everything he or she has planned—teachers use discovery learning in some subjects rather than in others. For example, spelling and English have clear-cut structures and rules that would be very difficult to discover; they can be learned through reception teaching. But only a minimum of preparation may be sufficient for the students to discover forms of expression in literature and most of the rhetorical forms of composition, because they are a basic means of communication. Math can be learned quickly through reception teaching at the beginning, as it is exact; discovery learning may be effective to teach increasing degrees of difficulty of specific mathematical skills. Given adequate preparation, social studies may become more enjoyable if discovered through individual reading and observation of material. As far as science is concerned, even if we think of experiments and therefore discovery when we think of science, a teacher has to consider curriculum requirements, the students, extent of scientific background, and age level before using the discovery technique.

This is another illustration of the first rule in a teacher's code: Adjust your method of teaching to the variable in each class, which is, and always will be, the students, both as individuals and as a group. An experienced teacher knows that this adjustment is made not only at the beginning of every school year, but also many times within the year, the month, the week, and often within each day.

Information Processing and Curriculum Design

Psychologists who explain learning in terms of the ways the human mind places information into storage and later retrieves it stress the importance of helping students to understand information so that they can store it in meaningful chunks. To do this, psychologists have suggested providing students with *structural outlines* of what they are to learn before learning begins. Research with college students has clearly shown that presenting students with detailed outlines before they read their textbooks does indeed increase recall of specific facts (Glynn and DiVesta, 1977). Similarly, provision of paragraph headings and instructions to generate sentences about paragraphs has been shown to increase reading comprehension in sixth graders (Doctorow, Wittrock, and Marks, 1978). Because cues for chunking material clearly help students, we have put detailed outlines at the beginning of each chapter in this book.

A principal of a small middle school was discouraged with his teachers' lack of attention to announcements made during their faculty meetings. He planned a simple and straightforward agenda for the next session on which were printed the major items for discussion and ample spaces for notes beneath each topic. He found that providing this simple structure helped his teachers pay attention, encouraged them to keep a few notes, kept his remarks brief and to the point, and left everyone with a record of what went on in the meeting.

Advocates of information-processing approaches tell us that telling students in specific terms what they are supposed to learn helps them process information more efficiently. Cognitive psychologists who are interested in instructional design tend to agree. According to Scandura (1977), for example, defining behavioral objectives alone is really tantamount to leaving the "guts" out of learning; defining the specific process that the student must go through in order to learn is necessary for instruction to be effective.

Economy and Concept Learning

Does the simulation of reality help or hinder information processing? Francis Dwyer (1972) conducted a study to find out. He compared four groups of students taking a course in the anatomy of the human heart. All groups heard the same tape-recorded lecture, but the visual aids differed. Group 1 saw no pictures, only the names of the parts of the heart flashed on a screen as they listened; Group 2 saw abstract line-drawings; Group 3 saw more detailed, shaded drawings; and Group 4 saw realistic photographs.

Those who saw only simple line drawings retained the most. Those who saw the realistic photographs (the least economic) retained the least of the four groups. Evidently, reality can be uneconomical. It often introduces irrelevant and distracting details that can interfere with concept learning.

"Stick to the basics" thus finds experimental support—at least in initially clarifying the critical features of a concept. Studies such as this suggest something more (as studies tend to do): that teachers need to intelligently evaluate the aids they utilize in the classroom. As a famous architect once noted, less is often more.

The implications of different cognitive styles for curriculum design are far-reaching and should be understood by the teacher. Witkin et al. (1977a) give many examples of how field dependence and field independence should cause the teacher to use different techniques in the same classroom. For example, field-dependent children have been found to be more socially oriented than field-independent children. While most field-dependent children will "discover" the social material in a subject by themselves, the teacher needs to bring it to the attention of field-independent children. Because field-dependent students tend to have more difficulty at structuring material than field-independent students do, teachers need to provide far more structure in designing lessons for them.

Because students show such vast differences in cognitive styles and because evidence has shown that students do better in subjects that are taught by methods that are compatible to those styles (Witkin et al., 1977b), it is clear that teachers must not teach all children by the same methods. Instead, they must make every possible attempt to accommodate for students' differences in preferred style. Since factors such as capacity for independent work and attention span vary greatly from student to student, these must be taken into consideration in curriculum planning. Some students learn most easily when taught from general concepts to specific facts, as Ausubel's theory of subsumption suggests; others learn most easily when teaching goes from specific facts to general principles (McDade, 1978).

Some students learn most effectively by reading; some learn most effectively by listening; some, like the ones in this picture, learn most effectively by doing.

Elizabeth Hamlin, Stock, Boston

There is a great deal of evidence that class size is related to student achievement: The smaller the class, the more effective the teaching—when the teacher takes advantage of small class size to interact more extensively and freely with students and to individualize instruction to meet individual needs (Olson, 1971; Vincent, 1968).

Lecturing and different cognitive styles   The lecture method does not lend itself easily to helping all students learn by the cognitive style that comes most easily to them. The teacher who prepares the lecture assumes that the students in the class learn more effectively by listening. Many, however, learn most effectively by reading or by going over the material in groups. Teachers can best accommodate these students by allowing them opportunity to break up into small groups for at least part of the instructional period and by planning these groups according to the students' cognitive styles. Students who learn best by reading might work individually with the option to read materials related to the subject. Aural learners might prepare recitations based on important components of the teacher's lecture to present to the rest of the class.

Departmentalization   Many schools have adopted a system called departmentalization as a way of accommodating students' differences in cognitive styles without overburdening the teachers. Students are assigned to departmentalized groups on the basis of certain types of achievement. On each grade level, a departmentalized group will be formed by a cross section of the whole grade. Two subjects in particular, reading and math, lend themselves to the departmentalization approach. In reading, the students usually are grouped according to their comprehension ability. There are usually three reading groups: top, average, and low. The top and average groups receive the largest percentage of the students, while the low reading group is purposely kept small. Each group is thus fairly homogeneous in ability, so that the diversity among the youngsters is less pronounced, therefore simplifying the teacher's lesson planning.

In math, the groups may be based on differences in computing ability. One class will be for students of average and above-average achievement, the other for those who are below average. Both classes may use the traditional approach to teaching math, relying on textbooks, workbooks, and written exercises. A third class might use an individualized math system, for which the requirements are the ability to work independently at skills and the ambition to do one's best. With the help of a parent who checks some pre- and posttests, the teacher has adequate time for individualized instruction. This method, if properly organized and handled, may be rewarding, motivating, and academically satisfactory for the students.

Many teachers find that it is much easier and more suitable to teach a more homogeneous group than a heterogeneous one for several reasons: better use of time, wider range of teaching techniques, amount of subject matter, less pronounced differences among students, and, often, more uniform motivation.

Educational and instructional television Departmentalization provides one way to make it easier for teachers to provide instruction that matches individual students' achievement levels and cognitive styles. Another is **instructional television** or educational television.

As a method of instruction, educational television (ETV) is a popular and welcome medium combining sight, sound, motion, and instantaneous transmission. ETV and instructional television (ITV) are often used interchangeably, but the terms do not mean the same thing. The ETV designation is generally reserved for programs on noncommercial channels that the Federal Communications Commission has specifically allocated for educational purposes. ITV, on the other hand, refers to special broadcasts that provide formal course instruction in a logical sequence. Whereas ETV programs are usually transmitted in open-circuit systems available to the public at large, most ITV programs are transmitted via cable in a closed-circuit system, thus restricting their availability. Many college campuses and some school districts receive ITV.

Students who learn most effectively by sight and sound do well with instructional television, particularly when teachers prepare lessons in conjunction with the TV watching. Instructional TV allows teachers to break down their classes into smaller groups and provide individualized instruction. While Johnny and Phyllis are watching an advanced program in physics, for example, the teacher can spend time with another group of children who are still learning basics. The advanced program can be shown later with the same TV teacher and the same message—when the second group of students is ready for it.

summary

1. Cognitive psychologists who study learning emphasize the importance of how students process and organize information. Curricula designed on cognitive principles specify the organization of the thinking process involved in learning as well as desired behavioral objectives.

2. Contemporary cognitive psychology is rooted in Gestalt psychology, which was developed by the German psychologists Wertheimer, Koffka, and Köhler in the early 1900s. The Gestalt psychologists emphasized the importance of perception in learning. One of the key factors in this approach is relativism—the integration or relation of new sensations with what the person already knows. Teachers can help students to learn by planning lessons around what they already are familiar with.

3. Insight occurs when a person perceives a situation in a new way that results in a meaningful change in his or her cognitive structure. Learning

that involves insight is less likely to be forgotten than rote learning. Insight is described both as a product (the result of meaningful problem solving) and a process (the steps taken to solve the problem). Insight learning involves a gradual process of testing hypotheses and progressive clarification. Another factor in insight learning is serendipity—the chance finding of something pleasant or valuable. The only true test for insight is transposition, the transfer of learning from one situation to another.

4. According to Wertheimer, there are two types of solutions to problems: Type A solutions involve originality and productive thinking, while Type B solutions are essentially trial and error.

5. Jerome Bruner also emphasizes insight learning, which he calls intuition. According to Bruner, school curricula should be designed so that early learning makes later learning easier and transfer, the primary goal of education, is enhanced. Bruner's theory of teaching emphasizes the importance of teaching the structure of a subject as well as facts and techniques; adapting the presentation of a subject to the student's level of readiness instead of basing curricula on certain arbitrary chronological ages; emphasizing the development of intuitive thinking as well as analytical thinking; and increasing children's motivation to learn.

6. According to Bruner, the basic structure of any body of learning depends on the mode of representation, economy, and power. An individual's mode of representation is the basic method he or she uses to understand the world. The enactive mode, used by infants, is based on processing information through motor responses. In the iconic mode, used by older children, understanding is expressed through pictures. The symbolic mode, the most advanced, is based on symbols such as letters and numbers. Economy is defined as the amount of information a student must learn and remember in order to understand a subject. A subject's power is its value in terms of applicability to other situations.

7. The sequence of structured material is the order in which the component parts of the subject are presented. According to Bruner, the learning process involves three integrated steps: acquisition, obtaining new information that replaces or refines previous learning; transformation, manipulating information to make it fit new situations; and evaluation, checking to see if the new material has been manipulated properly. The more organized and integrated a teacher's presentation is, the more transferability the learning will have.

8. The cybernetic or information-processing approach focuses on the flow of information from input into memory storage to output as retrieved memory. Encoding allows us to reduce the amount of information we need to store into more manageable chunks. Another aspect of storage that determines the efficiency of retrieval is organization, the relationships between stored bits of information.

9. David Ausubel's principle of subsumption states that learning proceeds best from the general to the specific. Meaningful learning depends on the number of associations a student can make between what is being taught and what he or she already knows. Ausubel advises that concrete props

are useful tools in teaching younger children whose cognitive development is not advanced enough for discovery learning.

10. Cognitive styles are individual ways of processing information and reflect individual differences in personality and motivation. Cognitive styles are learned early in life and are very resistant to change. According to Reissman, most people show a distinct preference for either visual, aural, or physical methods of learning. Other personal preferences that affect cognitive style are response mode (whether an individual prefers to work alone or in a group) and thinking pattern (whether an individual gathers details first and organizes them later or looks for an overall picture first and then obtains supporting information).

11. Other factors that affect a student's performance in the classroom include attention span, capacity for independent work, rate of learning, style of perceiving (field-dependent or field-independent), the way the memory works, willingness to accept new experiences, the tendency toward impulsivity or reflectivity, and tendency toward using broad or narrow classifications.

12. Curriculum development should be a collaborative effort among teachers, subject-matter specialists, and psychologists. A successful curriculum will lead to increased achievement, aid children in organizing what they have learned into a meaningful whole, and take individual differences into account.

13. According to Bruner, the ideal program for accomplishing insight learning is the spiral curriculum, in which early learning prepares students for later learning. Bruner recognizes the value of teacher-supplied reinforcement, but prefers to see students find reinforcement in the material itself. Guided discovery teaching has been shown to increase transfer of school learning to real life, which Bruner considers the most important goal of education.

14. The major drawback to discovery teaching is the greater amount of time it takes. Ausubel and other psychologists also take issue with Bruner for saying that discovery teaching is the only effective way to teach. Ausubel's approach, called reception teaching involves presenting information to the student in more or less final form. Ausubel says that the conditions under which learning occurs have more of an impact on meaningfulness than whether it occurs through discovery or reception.

15. Information-processing theorists stress the importance of presenting information to students in ways that make storage and retrieval more efficient. Telling students what they will be learning before learning begins is an effective way to increase learning and retention.

16. Because students have different cognitive styles, teachers cannot teach all their students by the same methods. Students' different capacities for independent work, attention spans, and thinking patterns should all be considered by curriculum designers. Departmentalization is an approach in which students in each grade are grouped in smaller classes on the basis of achievement level, so that teachers can limit the diversity they find among their students.

BRUNER, J. S. *Toward a Theory of Instruction.* Cambridge, Mass.: Harvard University Press, 1966. In this text, Bruner discusses his theory of instruction with specific applications for the classroom. This book is especially relevant for teachers of future teachers of social studies, English, arithmetic, and elementary school subjects in general, as Bruner uses examples of instruction in these disciplines.

MORINE, H., AND MORINE, G. *Discovery: A Challenge to Teachers.* Englewood Cliffs, N.J.: Prentice-Hall, 1973. This is an easy-to-read and very practical book that explains to the teacher just what he or she should do to make discovery teaching work. Illustrations of successful uses of the method are given.

SHULMAN, L. S. AND KEISLAR, E. R. (Eds.). *Learning by Discovery.* Chicago: Rand McNally, 1966. A collection of papers about discovery learning that should be helpful to anyone trying to determine whether or not he or she wishes to use this method in the classroom.

WITKIN, H. A., ET AL. Field-dependent and field-independent cognitive styles and their educational implications. *Review of Educational Research,* Vol. 47 (1), Winter 1977, pp. 1–53. This is an excellent review of research in cognitive styles. The authors provide clear evidence that cognitive styles exist and spend perhaps half of the article providing tips to teachers as to how to make use of them in solving instructional problems. The article is not easy to read, but does provide good material for the student who wants more information about this very important concept.

for students
who want to read
further

5

REMEMBERING AND TRANSFERRING LEARNING: From the Classroom to Real-Life Situations

Two Scholars with Exceptional Memories

We have all heard about people who have the ability to remember long lists of names or of numbers after seeing or hearing them only once or twice. We think such people have exceptional memories, but we really don't know what they do that makes them exceptional. We don't know how these people remember more effectively than the rest of us, or whether the methods they use are the same for all people with excellent memories.

A British professor, A. C. Aitken, and a Russian intellectual, S. V. Shereshevskii, both possessed amazing abilities to memorize (Hunter, 1977). Both men's memories were far beyond what average people are able to do, although they used entirely different methods of memorizing. As a result, the two men had different types of abilities to think and solve problems.

Aitken, a mathematician, was an unusual scholar. He could "produce a host of recondite facts about numbers, calculative methods, mathematics, and mathematicians; play, on the violin, many pieces by heart; recall many musical compositions; securely identify many snatches of music heard or seen in written notation; quote extensively from English literature; and recite tracts of Latin and English verse. He could recall details of many events he had witnessed, so many that committees often consulted him as an official minute book" (Hunter, 1977, p. 68). He could recall facts even after years of neglect.

Shereshevskii also had many admirable traits. He was an outstanding mnemonist (someone who can memorize long, haphazard strings of items). His technique involved pairing each item with a mental image. "If given a 25 word list, he might take an imaginary walk along a street that has a vivid succession of landmarks. He would represent the first word by a distinctly imaged picture which he would 'locate' on the first landmark; the second word would be another mental picture 'located' on the second landmark, and so on" (Hunter, 1977, p. 162). In this way, he was able to memorize a slowly read list in a single trial. His mental landmarks even enabled him to recall the list years later.

The chief similarity between these two cases lies in the fact that both men comprehended material in terms of its unconventional properties, knitted those properties into unconventional (therefore memorable) patterns, and retained the encoded patterns in storage for later retrieval. The chief difference between them lies in the types of patterns that the two men designed for such storage. Aitken's patterns were conceptual; his kind of pattern is called the panorama or map. Shereshevskii's patterns did not involve conceptual imagery.

Even with his great ability to memorize, Aitken had some difficulty using his method to memorize meaningless lists. On the other hand, while Shereshevskii could memorize long and complicated mathematical formulas, he comprehended them in terms that had no mathematical meaning. As a result, he could not use his formulas to solve new or different problems. Despite these limitations, both scholars were clearly exceptional. The vast majority of us, no matter what training we receive, will never be able to repeat either feat.

If we want to remember material learned in the classroom and apply it to new concepts, we clearly need to group conceptually, as Aitken did. However, as long as teachers continue to test for facts that are unimportant conceptually or have little meaning for their students, students would do well to put their money on Shereshevskii's methods. But which approach is more effective for later learning? That is one of the questions we consider in this chapter.

Few people are consistently happy with the way their memories work. Nearly every day, most of us have trouble remembering something, and all of us know someone who could benefit from a memory transplant. Our irritation at our own and other people's memory lapses is evidence of our deep consciousness that, if we lose our memories, we lose ourselves and the world as we know it. Our memory of what we have learned is our hold on the past. Our ability to transfer what we have learned to new situations gives us a hold on the future.

Teachers often neglect this vital aspect of learning. If a student fails to retain what he or she has been taught, few teachers think of teaching that student more effective ways to remember; they usually just give the student a poor grade. Teachers need to recognize that unless students can remember what they have been taught, learning has not really occurred. Thus, helping students to train their memories is an important part of the teaching process.

Showing students how to transfer what they have learned from one situation to another is also important. To learn a foreign language—French, let us say—students must transfer to French the general concepts that they have already learned about the English language—sentence structure, spelling, verb tenses, and so on. They may easily learn that "maison" means "house," but to be able to converse in French, they must transfer the learning that in French as in English, "maison" is a noun, that it can be pluralized, that it can be modified by an adjective, that it can be the subject or the object of a sentence, and so on.

Transfer of learning in the classroom also means transferring what is learned in school to real-life situations. For example, learning to add a column of figures in school can be transferred to keeping track of the runs, hits, and errors in a baseball game. When the student grows up, he or she will transfer that skill to balancing a checkbook. These simple examples point to the significance of transfer of learning: What we learn and remember is valuable to us only when we are able to use it in new situations.

remembering classroom learning

Remembering and its opposite, forgetting, have long been major concerns of psychologists and educators. Hermann Ebbinghaus (1913) was a pioneer in this field. His studies concerned how much we forget during various time intervals after the termination of learning. Using himself as a subject, Ebbinghaus learned a list of nonsense syllables (combinations of letters totally without meaning). He waited set periods of time—minutes, hours, days—and then relearned the nonsense syllables. By varying the intervals between the original learning of the lists and the relearning, and by comparing how much he retained, Ebbinghaus found that he forgot the largest amount during the first few hours after learning, and that after about 24 hours he hadn't forgotten much more. Numerous studies since that time by other experimenters have confirmed this finding that the greatest amount of forgetting occurs immediately after learning.

Of course, the length of time after learning is not the only factor that affects how much we retain. Another factor is the meaningfulness of the material. Meaningful material is remembered better than meaningless material such as the nonsense syllables that Ebbinghaus learned.

The manner in which the material is originally learned also affects retention. Psychologists have shown that learning in which trials are spaced over time is more likely to be retained than learning massed into a single session (Ciccone, 1973). Indeed, experience tells us that we remember more material for an examination if we space our studying over several days than if we cram it all into one all-night session right before the examination—a very important fact many of us forget when exam week rolls around.

Types of Memory   Psychologists who approach the processes of learning, remembering, and forgetting in terms of the storing of learned material and its retrieval for later use are advocates of what we call **cybernetic theories** or **information-processing** approaches to cognition. Advocates of this approach compare the functioning of memory to similar processes in computers, which are also supposed to receive information, put it away, and give it back to us later when we need it. Information processing is a useful tool to study the types of classroom memory with which teachers and students are involved. Psychologists taking this approach to understanding memory agree that there are at least three distinct types of memory: **sensory information storage, short-term memory,** and **long-term memory.**

Sensory information storage Sensory information storage refers to our perception of the world through our senses—that is, what we see, hear, feel, smell, and taste. This type of memory is extremely short-lived. Several experiments have shown that we can retain an accurate sensory image for only one second at most (Simon, 1972). For example, if you tap your fingers against your arm several times, you will find that the feeling of the taps—the sensory image—lasts only for a split second. Or listen to the taps; the image of the sound will also fade quickly. You might also open and close your fist and see how long you retain the resulting sensory image on your skin.

The important distinguishing feature in sensory information storage is that, although you retain the knowledge that you tapped your fingers or heard the tapping or smelled a daffodil on a rainy day, you do not retain the actual sensation of feeling or hearing or smelling. For this reason, cognitive memory does not fall into the category of sensory information storage.

Short-term memory In short-term memory, we store material as an immediate and direct interpretation of sensory stimuli, that is, we remember an interpretation of an event, not the event itself. For example, when you look up a number in the telephone book, you remember the number, not the way it looks on the page. Short-term memory is direct, retains only a small amount of information, and is short-lived unless rehearsed, that is, mentally reviewed. Most of us say phone numbers out loud after we look them up because we have learned that, unless we make an effort to remember that phone number, we will quickly forget it.

Long-term memory Of the three memory types, long-term memory is perhaps the most important and complex. To remember thoughts, ideas, or information for a long time, you must make a concerted effort. Examples of long-term memory are remembering the meaning of words, procedures involved in complex problem-solving, and events long past. Professor Aitken remembered snatches of songs for years. Although most of us do not have this extraordinary memory ability, we do remember some details for years. For instance, we might remember a book that we read and enjoyed as a child—its title, who gave it to us, something of the plot, how we felt about it at the time. The capacity of long-term memory for storing information is thought to be huge, much greater than most of us normally make use of. Researchers have also shown that our capacity to retrieve information from long-term memory increases during the school years (Foellinger and Trabasso, 1977).

If a teacher informs a class that a certain piece of information is interesting but not crucial to remember (for example, the current population of New York City) and that another piece of information is important to remember (for example, the factors that affect family patterns in the United States and the ways that these factors can be expected to affect their own lives), the students will store the first item in their short-term memories and the second in their long-term memories for retrieval later when needed.

Long-term memory clearly is an important phenomenon in day-to-day living. People tend to remember information such as names and places much longer when they use it regularly. For example, psychologists have found that people remember the names and faces of their classmates for years, even decades, even when they have physically and psychologically moved away (Bahrick, Bahrick, and Wittlinger, 1974).

Methods for Measuring Long-Term Classroom Memory

Memory can be measured in a variety of different ways in the classroom. Psychologists have found that the method the teacher uses will strongly affect the apparent ability of students to remember. In this section, we discuss several methods that teachers might use to measure student's memories.

Recall The **recall** method is the most familiar measure of remembering. It requires the student to remember information with only a minimum number of cues or hints to the correct answers. This method is used by foreign-language teachers when they ask students to translate words from a foreign language into English, or when they ask students to recall the foreign-language equivalent of an English word.

Recall can be tested through the use of various types of questions. One type is the essay question: "Explain the interference theory of forgetting and tell how interference can be prevented in the classroom." Another type is the fill-in question: "_____ was the name of the first President of the United States." A third type is the identification question: "Identify three states in New England."

Of the common testing methods, the recall method is least capable of measuring very small amounts of retained information. It is less likely than other methods to detect a difference between students who know nothing and those who simply have trouble remembering.

Recognition In assessing **recognition,** the teacher provides the student with many cues. The multiple-choice question is the most frequently used type of recognition question. You have all seen multiple-choice questions in which you were required to recognize the correct answer in a list of possible responses. Here is an example of a recognition question of the multiple-choice type:

> A student who cannot remember some French pronunciations because a lesson on them was followed immediately by one on English pronunciation is said to have experienced
>
>   a. retroactive inhibition.
>   b. proactive inhibition.
>   c. overlearning.
>   d. transfer of learning.

Recognition provides more cues to remembering than the recall method, in which the answer has to be constructed totally from memory. Age is a variable affecting the success of these two methods: The additional cues provided in recognition tests are more necessary for children than for adults (Hall and Pressley, 1973).

Relearning Relearning, in which a student relearns previously learned material that apparently has been forgotten, is probably the most sensitive measure of long-term memory. If a student takes 80 trials to learn the multiplication tables originally, and only 20 trials to relearn them later, we would say that there was a savings of 75 percent over the trials necessary to learn the tables originally. Relearning is clearly a more effective method than either recall or recognition in measuring material that seems to be forgotten.

> Jacob had been quite a hit when he recited T. S. Eliot's "Growltiger's Last Stand" for his seventh-grade poetry class. His expression and gestures were perfect. Four months later, when the seventh graders were planning a variety show assembly program for the entire school, one of the committee members remembered Jacob—"How about asking Jacob to give that funny poem of his?" The other students agreed that it was a fine idea, but when they asked Jacob, he realized he had forgotten it completely. He also remembered the many nights he had worked on it to get it "just right." He told the committee that he just didn't have the time to relearn it. That evening, though, he thought about it and took out his copy of the poem—just to look at it. In less than an hour, he had relearned it. He told the committee the next morning that he would recite the poem. We can explain this only by assuming that, although he had no awareness of the memory, Jacob had in fact retained some of what he had learned.

Being able to remember information over great lengths of time is really a remarkable ability. Most of us take it for granted and don't see memory as a skill. Forgetting is seen as a sign of weakness, instead of as normal.

Psychologists have developed several explanations for remembering and forgetting, depending on their approach to learning in general. As we look at these theories, we should remember that, although we know *what* memory does, no one is really sure *how* it works. Because no one is sure how memory works, no one really knows what happens when it doesn't work.

Behavioral Explanations of Remembering and Forgetting

One way to explain learning is to say that we learn because we make associations between stimuli and responses, and we build upon these associations for later learning. From this perspective, "a memory is nothing more than a response produced by a stimulus" (Osgood, 1953, p. 550), and forgetting is a weakening of a stimulus-response association.

Psychologists adopting this approach seek to determine which factors influence this weakening of associations after learning (conditioning) has occurred. Their research involves specifying why forgetting occurs, the degree to which it occurs, and the circumstances that affect the amount of forgetting.

Fading One of the simplest explanations of why forgetting occurs is known as the **fading** theory. This theory proposes that learning creates actual changes in the brain. The structural changes in the nervous system associated with learning are called **memory traces.** These traces can be reactivated at a later time, but, with time, unused traces are

Figure 5–1 Ebbinghaus's curve of remembering and forgetting seems to support the theory that memories fade with time.

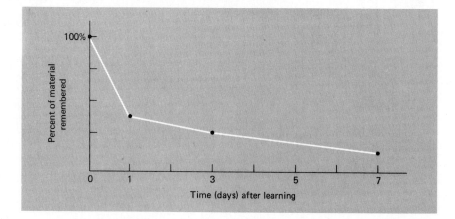

said to gradually fade, and forgetting occurs (Lindsay and Norman, 1972). In this explanation, time would appear to be the variable accounting for forgetting.

Ebbinghaus's findings are consistent with this approach. He found that the degree of forgetting increased with and was directly related to the time elapsed since the original learning. However, this relationship between time and forgetting is not linear—the memory traces did not fade gradually. Instead, the forgetting was rapid at first and then slowed significantly. When the percent of material remembered is plotted on the Y axis and the time after learning on the X axis, Ebbinghaus's curve of remembering and forgetting looks like the curve in Figure 5–1.

Extinction Forgetting differs from another behavioral concept often confused with it, the concept of **extinction.** Extinction, the reduction of a learned response, is the result of the removal of reinforcement from a learning situation. Forgetting, according to behaviorists, is caused by the passing of time, not by lack of reinforcement. Depending on the schedule of reinforcement that had been used, extinguished behavior may drop off rather suddenly, while memories fade gradually. Furthermore, extinguished behavior frequently reappears spontaneously—clearly not "forgotten" by the individual at all.

Cognitive explanations of remembering and forgetting (and thinking and problem solving as well) have their roots in Gestalt psychology. According to **Gestalt psychologists,** the main determinant of remembering is good organization, not time. Material that is poorly organized when originally learned will fade more quickly than material that is well organized. In fact, if the material was poorly organized when it was originally presented, our memory can transform it into a more organized entity. For example, if you took a course in modern European history, then a course on Greece and Rome, a course on the French Revolution and Napoleon, then one on the Middle Ages and the Renaissance, you would still be able to rearrange all this material into a coherent survey of Western civilization in your memory.

*Cognitive
Explanations of
Remembering and
Forgetting*

Information-processing explanations of memory Advocates of information processing explain memory in terms of two basic responses: **storage** and **retrieval.** According to the information-processing approach, learners do not store chunks of information in the memory in isolation. Instead, they sort, file, and cross-index them in meaningful ways. Through a process called **encoding,** learners reduce or abbreviate the amount of information stored for a particular item, storing all the information related to that item in a single chunk. Ability to encode, or organize the material to be learned according to some basic

One of the keys to Professor Aitken's extraordinary memory abilities was the ease with which he used present cues to evoke past events. Psychologists have shown that, in addition to the cues we use to remember an event, our expectation of what that earlier event should be strongly affects our abilities to remember it. Even the questions we are asked about an event can alter our memory of it. In fact, changing even one word in a single question can systematically alter an eyewitness account.

Loftus (1974) conducted an experiment to examine the influence of an interrogator's language on people's memories. Students were shown films of automobile accidents and told that they had to remember and report what they saw. After viewing a film, each student filled out a 22-item questionnaire containing 16 irrelevant and 6 critical questions. Three of the 6 questions asked about items that had been present in the film, while the 3 others asked about items that had not actually been present. For half the subjects, the critical questions began with "Did you see *a*" as in "Did you see *a* broken headlight?" For the rest, the critical questions began with the words "Did you see *the* . . ." as in "Did you see *the* broken headlight?" Results showed that those witnesses who received questions with "the" were much more likely to report having seen something that had not appeared in the film. Those who received questions with "a" were more likely to respond "don't know," whether the object had been present or not. Following another film, the experimenters conducted a test on judgment of speed resulting in an accident. The subjects reported higher rates of speed when the questions used words such as "smashed," "collided," and "bumped" rather than "hit" and "contacted." A week later, the subjects of this test, without viewing the film again, were asked whether they had seen any broken glass, although, in fact, there had been none in the film. More than twice as many subjects who had answered questions containing the word "smashed" reported seeing the nonexistent glass than those queried with "hit."

This experiment clearly demonstrates the power of suggestion that words carry. In addition, it shows our strong tendency to try to complete a not-so-clear memory, even to the extent of remembering things that weren't there.

set of categories, is probably the key to good memory. Increased ability to encode large amounts of material increases the ability to remember more material far longer (see, for example, Miller, 1956, or Tulving, 1972).

Remembering is also dependent on our ability to retrieve what we have stored. Retrieval involves encoding, too. Imagine how long it would take to remember things if we had to search through all the items in our memory storage until we found the appropriate item. Thus, usable memories depend on being able to retrieve already chunked information and sorting through only that information for the desired bit. Students who have learned to effectively encode learned

Information that has been stored in the memory in a meaningful way can be retrieved at a later time when needed.

Ed Lettau, Photo Researchers, Inc.

material into meaningful chunks will also be able to retrieve the largest amount of material later when needed.

Interference   Another cognitive approach explains forgetting in terms of the phenomenon of **interference.** This theory proposes that new and old learning compete: They interfere with each other and thus limit our ability to remember either of them. Interference theory has special relevance to classroom learning, where students learn so many subjects every day.

The classic study first documenting interference in the memory process was conducted by Jenkins and Dallenbach (1924), who found that people remembered more when learning was followed by sleep than when it was followed by activity. In their study, people learned lists of nonsense syllables and were tested for retention after time. One group learned the nonsense syllables prior to regular working activities; the second, prior to sleep. At the end of a specified period of time, both groups were tested. The people who slept after learning retained more. Jenkins and Dallenbach reasoned that, since we learn more when we are awake, the inability to remember after activity was due to the interference of new learning.

The term applied to interference in which subsequent learning interferes with earlier learning is **retroactive inhibition.** For example, you might have difficulty remembering an algebraic concept you have just learned if you follow it immediately by learning a geometric concept; this difficulty would be due to retroactive inhibition. Learning the geometric concept would retroactively inhibit your ability to remember the algebraic concept.

A second type of interference has also been proposed. In this case, prior learning interferes with the ability to remember new learning. This is called **proactive inhibition.** Proactive inhibition can occur simultaneously with retroactive inhibition. Suppose that a student prepares a chemistry lesson immediately before studying a physics assignment. If he or she later confuses the chemistry concepts with physics concepts, we would say that proactive inhibition has occurred. That is, earlier chemistry studying interfered with ability to learn and retain the physics concept later. At the same time, retroactive inhibition may take place, and the student may find that studying physics interferes with learning chemistry.

According to these two principles of interference, the way teachers present material to students has a significant effect on learning. The extent of interference between two tasks depends on the similarities and differences of the subject matter and the responses the learner must make in the learning situation. If the subject matters of two tasks are similar, the amount of interference depends on the difference between the required responses in the two situations.

For example, suppose that a French teacher tells his or her students to translate a list of words into French. An hour later, in Spanish class, the same students are asked by their Spanish teacher to translate an almost identical list of words into Spanish. In this situation, we could expect a great deal of interference. Because the tasks and required responses are so similar, a number of French words are apt to pop up on the Spanish list. It would clearly be better for the students if the two language teachers could make their assignments less similar. A teacher can limit the results of such interference more effectively by sequencing material so that dissimilar subjects follow one another; for example, follow an English lesson with an art lesson.

Humanistic-Motivational Explanations of Remembering and Forgetting

Explanations of memory by motivation theorists focus on the individual's motivation to learn and remember material. Why can a young boy remember the starting lineups of all the baseball teams in the American League, but not the multiplication tables? Why do people forget the name of someone they have just met at a party but can still remember who they sat next to in third grade? According to researchers into motivation, people are better able to remember material that is meaningful to them (see, for example, Ellis, 1972).

Teaching to complete goals Motivation theory has been used to explain the finding that a person is able to recall an uncompleted task more readily than a completed one. This phenomenon is known as the **Zeigarnik effect.** Motivation theorists assume that we are less motivated to remember a completed task simply because it is finished, while we need to remember an uncompleted task in order to finish it. Thus, encouraging students to finish what they start frees their memories for more important things.

Reducing classroom anxiety   While most forgetting seems to be accidental, sometimes people are motivated by anxiety to forget certain painful experiences. According to Sigmund Freud's theory of **repression,** we push painful experiences out of our conscious mind and into our unconscious mind as a way of preserving the status of what he called the ego. Learning that is associated with painful experiences is similarly repressed. According to this approach, a student who has a great deal of fear and anxiety in the classroom would probably consciously remember very little of what was taught there; he or she would repress the memory of the learning. Teachers can counteract repression and increase conscious memory by making the classroom a less fearful place, thus making learning more pleasant.

Memory as a function of the time of day   Another factor related to memory is the time of day in which studying occurs. According to educational researchers, morning seems to be the best time for learning, and children who study early in the day remember learned material more effectively than children who study later. Much of the early work in this area (reviewed by Freeman and Hovland, 1934) was aimed at laying down guidelines for the optimal arrangement of school timetables. The message was clear: Mental work should be given to students early in the day, and the afternoon should be relegated to motor learning. This conclusion was based on a very early study by Gates (1916) that showed that tasks requiring short-term memory were performed best in the morning.

Gates suggested that school children's relatively lower ability to perform these same tasks in the afternoon was probably related to mental fatigue. More recent studies, however, have noted that the human body actually is in a higher state of arousal in the afternoon. Instead of being fatigued or depressed, researchers have shown that the human body increases both temperature and performance on immediate processing tasks (see, for example, the work of Kleitman, 1963, and Colquhoun, Blake, and Edwards, 1968). The reason that children tend to perform less well on short-term memory tasks in the afternoon, according to researchers, may be due to the fact that increased body arousal actually decreases their ability to perform this type of task, rather than the fact that mental fatigue has set in (McClean, 1969).

More recent research has corroborated this finding. Craik and Blankstein (1975) showed that physical arousal (as measured by body temperature and activity) decreased short-term memory. Folkard, Monk, Bradbury, and Rosenthal (1977) concurred with this finding, but demonstrated that the phenomenon occurs for short-term memory only. The researchers read stories to 12- and 13-year-old school children at 9:00 AM and 3:00 PM, and then tested them both for short-term (immediate) and long-term (one week) memory. The children did much better at the short-term memory task in the morning and at the long-term task in the afternoon. Clearly, deciding when to teach a particular subject is a complex problem. Interference and the positioning of a subject in the context of the entire school schedule need to be taken into consideration, but so does the teacher's goal—long-term or short-term memory.

the improvement of memory

How Teachers Can Help Students to Increase Long-Term Memory

Often the goal of long-term memory is not achieved. For example, cramming for an exam the night before may possibly place enough information in your short-term memory for you to pass the exam and maybe even get a good grade. But this material will not be retained for any length of time, and so, though you may have passed, you have not really learned. Furthermore, it will be more difficult on the next test to rely on past learning. You are likely to get farther and farther behind.

In one college English class, two hundred lines of poetry had to be memorized and quoted to the professor before a grade would be assigned. For most of the students, the semester flew by, exams loomed, and still the lines had not been learned. High anxiety was evident in each class member. Asked about the memorization activity after reciting successfully, one student said, "I knew that I had to learn the lines, so I found a tiny closet beneath the dorm stairs and closed myself up in it. I know that it's hard to believe, but I learned— well, I memorized—those lines within two hours, went directly to the professor's office, recited them accurately, and came back to the dorm. I doubt I could recite any of them now."

What can classroom teachers do to enhance long-term memory? Several techniques have been shown to help teachers to achieve this goal.

Providing immediate feedback According to behavioral psychologists, immediate **feedback** is essential for optimal learning and retention because feedback is a reinforcer for most students. Feedback is most effective when it is immediate, because then there is less possibility for erroneous associations. If feedback is delayed, a child may associate the feedback not with the correct response, but perhaps with an irrelevant or incorrect response.

What can teachers do to provide immediate feedback? One thing is to give diagnostic tests that pinpoint problems that students might encounter in a particular area. Following their analysis of the students' tests, they can let the students know immediately what they have done correctly and what they still have to work on. Teachers can respond promptly to student performance on exams, and they can help students to evaluate their own performance on exams.

Providing overlearning The work of Ebbinghaus showed that increased practice leads to increased memory (J. Gibson, 1968). **Overlearning** is learning that continues even after the material appears to be learned and remembered. Such review has been found to reduce forgetting, especially of factual material. Overlearning is not

Many different ways can be used to provide overlearning. A good example of overlearning is the special music education program directed by Dr. Robert Pace at Teachers College, Columbia University, and the National Piano Foundation. Pace's method uses a form of group instruction that is so successful it is being adopted all over the world.

> A pair of youngsters get a private lesson together once a week, plus a weekly group lesson—with several other pairs of students—in the fundamentals of music—harmony chords, improvisation, writing music, and ear training. In these groups one child may play notes on the piano while another listens and evaluates his work, and still another writes on the blackboard the notes he hears the first child play. This audio/visual/tactile approach helps each child to actually feel the notes while he's seeing and hearing them. (Brooks, 1974,p. 48)

The system works because it allows children to benefit from one another's strengths; a child strong on rhythm, for example, can help a child who is weak in that area. Knowledge is shared, and reliance on one another motivates the children to practice.

A teacher can guide students in overlearning in the classroom by teaching them how to practice, although the burden of practice is the students' responsibility. The teacher can provide contexts in which students can use skills and abilities learned earlier. For instance, on completion of a reading unit about children in other countries, a teacher can have students select library books on similiar themes to read at home. Each time students engage in these activities—that is, engage in overlearning—they increase the probability of long-term retention.

The teacher should keep in mind that the amount of overlearning students achieve is related to the number of trials it takes them to learn the material initially. A student who learns quickly may be bored by too many practice homework assignments. On the other hand, a student who learns slowly may grasp the material only at the end of a series of homework assignments and so will need more opportunities to practice and overlearn. Thus, teachers should take individual differences in learning rates into consideration when they provide opportunities for overlearning.

the same as drill or rote learning. It does not have to take these forms, although sometimes it may. For example, practicing addition learned in school by checking a supermarket receipt is overlearning; doing dozens of exactly the same type of addition problems as those done in class is drill. Each time you read a book or magazine you are engaging in overlearning how to read, although obviously that is not your purpose in reading. Similarly, when you practice a skill such as swimming or skating, you are overlearning that skill. People say that once you have learned how to swim, you never forget; that is because every time you swim you are overlearning.

Providing recitation Behaviorists emphasize the importance of active responses in learning. Many students learn more by actively doing than by passively listening. Thus, teachers should provide opportunities for recitation. Recitation allows students to practice what they have learned and to receive feedback and reinforcement for their achievement.

American education makes use of recitation. But, in comparison with education in some other countries, American teachers often neglect this important aspect of learning. Children in Soviet schools, for example, learn to recite in front of their classmates while they are still in kindergarten. By the time they reach the end of elementary school, they are often accomplished speakers.

Research with sixth-grade students learning ecology showed clearly that recitation teaching is more effective in promoting student learning than nonrecitation instructional experience lasting the same period of time (Gall et al., 1978). Through recitation, students learned more information and retained it better. In addition, students allowed to recite improved their ability to respond orally and in writing to higher-level questions about what they had learned.

Recitation can increase learning memory in another way: Psychologists have shown that when students are allowed to design questions about what they are learning and ask other students in the class for the answers, the questioners remember considerably more information (Ross and Killey, 1977). One variation of this approach might be letting students participate in designing tests for the class.

How successful oral recitation is in increasing long-term memory depends on several factors: the degree of abruptness in introducing new material, the rate at which students are paced, the type of subject matter, and the ability and temperament of the students. The best way to find the optimal amount of oral recitation to use in the classroom is to experiment.

Constructing the curriculum properly Curriculum structure often reflects the organization found in textbooks. How should text material be structured to aid long-term retention? Placing questions within a body of text material facilitates learning, but the location of those questions is an important variable. Locating questions before a text section is helpful, but the effect of those questions on retention appears to be limited to the specific information called for by the questions. Locating questions after a text section, however, facilitates retention of both specific and general text material (Glaser and Resnick, 1972; Sagaria and DiVesta, 1978).

How many questions should the teacher ask? Too many questions presented before the introduction of a new subject seem to decrease retention because they disrupt the continuity of the discussion. But frequent questions presented after the material seem to increase retention. The type of question preceding the material also seems to affect recall. Specific questions were found to aid retention more than general questions (Glaser and Resnick, 1972).

The organization of the text material itself also affects retention. For example, structuring material by object names rather than by attributes seems to facilitate retention (Glaser and Resnick, 1972). For example, in a unit about transportation, retention would probably be increased if the material were organized by object names (boats, cars, planes) rather than by the attributes that those objects share (motor, speed, passenger capacity). Text material organized around introductory topic sentences has been found to be retained better than text material that is well integrated throughout but lacks topic sentences (Gagné, 1969). (Note, for example, the first sentence of this paragraph; it is the topic sentence around which the paragraph is organized.)

Teachers should pay attention to the arrangement of tasks for increased retention. In the past, research in this area focused on the effects of presenting the parts of a task separately versus presenting the task in its entirety. Although the research has not always provided definitive answers about which method is most effective, some suggestions can be made about subdividing learning and arranging it into parts. Subdivisions should adhere to the laws of organization expressed by the Gestalt theorists.

First, *the individual parts should not exceed the memory span of the students.* The length of the segments should be appropriate for the student's cognitive level. In order to determine the optimal length of each part, the teacher must be familiar with the cognitive level of the child.

Second, *the parts should reflect the logical structure of the material as a whole.* Thus, if the student's task is to learn the major cities of the United States, the cities might be organized into groups or parts according to geographical location, thus reflecting the overall geography of the country—for example, all the cities on the East Coast. If, for some reason, the parts in a particular learning situation do not reflect the whole, they should contain some organization of their own that makes sense to the student.

Third, *the type of material should determine the way in which it is divided into parts.* Some material can be organized into a hierarchy of skills or information. Easier skills or pieces of information can be grouped together and presented before more difficult skills or facts are introduced. Sometimes, it is useful to introduce the task in its entirety first so that students can get an overall picture of what the task involves.

One sixth-grade class provided a good example of how this can work. The students had been given newspapers to glance through in preparation for a newspaper unit. Georgia, with an anxious expression, asked the teacher, "What are we going to do with this? There are so many pages. Are we going to read all of it?" Clearly, she was disturbed by the thought of reading an entire newspaper every day for several weeks. Her teacher asked her and the class if they would like to know what they were going to do with the newspaper. They said yes, they would. She then proceeded to give them a brief overview of what they would be learning in the unit. They needed this immediate reassurance that the unit would be limited to tasks they could understand and could do. According to advocates of information processing, this procedure helps the encoding process. Such an introduction to a task can be limited to a brief presentation; detailed presentations can be left until the component parts are introduced.

totally unfamiliar to them. But taking them to a play that is produced specifically for youngsters and that uses the language level they have mastered would be effective. It is particularly important for teachers to understand this when working with socially disadvantaged children. Such children's learning difficulties may stem from unfamiliarity with the middle-class language used in the schools, not from any deficiency in cognitive ability. Presenting materials chosen specifically for their level of language ability and in their own dialects will provide them with something familiar and thus something that will be better retained. In order to make learning most meaningful to all students, it is important to *individualize instruction* so that each individual student is presented with material in a way that is most familiar and that allows him or her to make the most sense of it (Hart, 1978).

A third measure of meaningfulness is the degree to which facts in the material are related to an overall rule or principle. To aid retention, a teacher should present an understandable principle before giving students the factual information explained by that principle. Within such a framework, the facts will be better remembered. For example, in beginning a unit on transportation in the early primary grades, a teacher could provide a framing question such as "How do

---

**Operation Upgrade: Stories Told in the
Language Level and Dialect of Students**

Once upon a time there was a boy name the great John. He was so great he had a lion for a pet. One day the great John saw a man in the river so I swooped down and got the man out of the river. And so the same day I saw a plane falling so I flet up to catch the plan and I took the plan to the airport. And when the great John put down the plane he fixed it with his laser gun. And that same night the great John hear a rattling noise in bed so he looked out the window and saw some thives. And so the great John got on his suit and flew out the window and got the thieves and took them to jail. And the great John went back home. So that morning the captain of the air-force called the John and said he seen some flying sacers and he wanted me to fly up and see what was the matter the next episode tomorrow.

There was this man he always thought of money he would always play pitch. I know how to play it 2 to 5 people can play every one gets a penny and throw it to the line whose ever penny gets to the line closer. Wins the rest of the people's money. He was a grambler. His mother name him money, because very time he say some money he would always take it. Until people start asking for money. He wanted to change his life. But he couldn't so he started to gramble. And gave almost all his money away.

Johnson, N. J. A., *Four Steps to Precision Teaching.* (Unpublished manuscript, Western Illinois University, 1973).

people get from one place to another?" before proceeding to the specifics—boats, cars, planes, and so forth.

A last way to consider meaningfulness is in relation to the goals of learning. A great deal of research has been done on preparing students for specific goals and outcomes before learning takes place (Barnes and Clawson, 1975). Students learn more easily and remember longer when they understand why they are learning a subject and what the specific learning outcome will be (Gagné, Bing, and Bing, 1977). To aid retention, the teacher should let the students know at the outset what they will accomplish in a given learning task. Goals can be stated as principles or as skills.

Making learning exciting You can't have come this far in school without finding out that learning that is interesting and fun will be remembered for a longer time than learning that is dull and boring. Psychologists have pointed out that learning that contains an element of surprise is remembered considerably longer than other types of learning. A surprised student becomes personally involved in learning and thus has a personal memory to associate with the memory of the material. A special term has been coined for such memories—*flashbulb memories*. Flashbulb memories occur when an event carries with it a high level of surprise, a high level of consequentiality, and emotional arousal (Brown and Kulik, 1977). The teacher who begins a college lecture on reinforcement by suddenly marching up to a student, handing him a jelly bean, and saying, "You're paying good attention!" can be sure that this is one class the student won't forget.

The ultimate responsibility for increasing long-term memory rests with the student. How a student studies and whether he or she is a fast or a slow learner will determine his or her achievement in school. Although there are many ways to improve study habits, only the student can decide to adopt them. No teacher or parent can force a student to study properly. These adults can guide and encourage; the rest is up to the student.

How Students Can Increase Their Own Memory

Developing proper study habits Ellis (1972) outlined five interrelated techniques to improve study habits. First, *survey the material* to get an overall idea of the author's direction. For example, in this book, you might read the chapter outlines and the chapter summaries before beginning to read the chapters.

In the second technique, you "*focus your attention on your task* and eliminate irrelevant stimuli" (Ellis, 1972, p. 131). If you are studying this chapter while watching television, turn the set off.

Third, *set a goal* in advance and *give yourself a reward* after you have achieved it. This is called "self-management of contingencies" (Ellis, 1972, p. 132), and it operates to reinforce your achievement in studying. For instance, you might schedule a five-minute coffee break after you have finished the material on "How Students Can Increase Their Own Memory," keeping in mind that you have achieved only one goal and must still return to study the next section.

The fourth technique involves further *organization of the material*. Even if a text is well organized, you must be able to impose your own structure on the material, whether by taking notes, writing an outline, or by some other method that suits you.

As the fifth technique, *practice what you have learned* to keep the items in your memory storage from fading. Do not simply measure how much you have studied, but concern yourself with putting the material to use. For instance, you may complete this chapter in record time, but your studying will not be effective in facilitating long-term retention unless you can retrieve the information discussed here and put it to use later—in this case, when you become a teacher.

Spacing and timing study sessions Massed studying is less effective in promoting long-term retention than studying distributed over a number of sessions. There are several reasons for this. First, one long cramming session leads to boredom and mental and physical fatigue, which interferes with your ability to learn and remember material. Second, you have a greater buildup of frustration in massed studying. If you attempt to study a difficult concept in one unbroken effort, you

Cramming, a universally popular study technique, has been shown by research to be ineffective and inefficient.

Jan Halaska, Photo Researchers, Inc.

are overdoing it. Without any pauses, your frustration will grow even more. Frustration at being unable to master a complex topic may grow in any studying situation, but if you can get away from the topic entirely and return to it later, you will be fresher and better able to conquer it. Bigge (1964) cited the case of a man in his forties who, after years of watching others, finally attempted to learn to swim. Throughout that summer, he encountered a great deal of frustration and remained a very poor swimmer. But, after a winter's break, he was able to catch on and learned to swim with ease the following summer. Without that break, the man's attempt to learn to swim would probably have ended in dismal failure because of his continual frustration.

Massed studying is also inefficient for long-term retention because it does not allow for much feedback. Spaced studying, through the processes of repeated review and feedback, provides a way to overlearn, which is probably the best method for enhancing long-term retention. In this course, for example, you might read a chapter in this text and compare it with your class notes on the topic. In class the next day, you could ask your instructor any questions you might have. When you return to the chapter and your notes the next night, any problems you might have had with the material will have been resolved, and you will find it easier to review at exam time. Similarly, when a teacher gives a homework assignment to a class and then reviews it and returns it, the students are provided with feedback. Their next study session is more effective because they know what is correct or incorrect in what they have done.

The effectiveness of spaced studying varies with the type of material to be learned. Spacing seems to facilitate the retention of meaningless material to a greater extent than meaningful material. Nevertheless, both types of material are always retained significantly better if the studying is spaced rather than massed.

Spacing learning can be a deliberate act on the part of a student. Teachers can also organize classroom learning so that trials are spaced properly. For example, Fern was a happy but flighty fifth grader with a short attention span. She often sought her teacher's approval by erasing the boards or straightening the books on the shelves. She was having a particularly difficult time in learning syllabication of words. Her teacher asked if she would like to stay for a bit after school to help with a new bulletin board. While she was there, they could go over syllabication. "Oh, yes, but I don't think it'll help much," Fern laughed. After the other students had left, the teacher wrote a few words on the board and assisted Fern in syllabicating them. The teacher then asked her to help staple some pictures on the new bulletin board. She alternated the work and the play. Fern found that it "wasn't too hard" to concentrate when she didn't have to work continuously.

Providing for overlearning Overlearning requires effort and diligence. Without practice, even the most basic skills can be forgotten. An extreme example of this occurred during World War II, when it was revealed that many illiterate armed forces inductees had previously learned to read (Travers, 1967). It is apparent that they had not practiced their reading skills after leaving school. Remember—use it or lose it.

Utilizing oral recitation There are many ways in which you can use oral recitation to help you remember. You can participate actively in class discussion, which will enhance your retention of the material as well as give you feedback on the correctness of your responses. You can also talk to a friend or relative about your classwork. This will enable you to get a better idea of what you know and to retain the information for a longer time.

Practicing mnemonics Psychologists have recently become interested in special strategies for memorization that can be of great use to students who need to memorize large amounts of information. **Mnemonics** are mental contrivances that enable us to impose meaning on material that is otherwise meaningless to us. They typically involve comprehending the material in terms of perceptual chains (Hunter, 1977). As we saw earlier, the Russian scholar Shereshevskii used mnemonics to remember long lists of words—meaningless as well as meaningful—for years at a time.

Shereshevskii's method was described at the beginning of this chapter. A similar procedure for memorizing lists of nouns depends on associating each noun with part of another, (Miller, Galanter, and Pribram, 1960). As an example, let us look at the following word-number pairs:

one/bun	six/sticks
two/shoe	seven/heaven
three/tree	eight/gate
four/door	nine/line
five/hive	ten/hen

Once each of the numbers in this list is paired with a rhyming noun and studied together, the task of remembering any list of ten nouns becomes much easier. All one has to do is associate each of the nouns in the noun-number pairs with the new noun to be remembered. For instance, if the new word is "house," you might visualize a house squashed inside a bun. You might try this technique yourself to see how really effective it can be.

A similar strategy known as the *loci method* was developed long ago by the Greeks and analyzed in some detail by Bower (1970). In this method, you do not have to remember any initial list of basic words. All you have to do is take a particular geographical location and visualize each word to be remembered in a particular place in that location. For instance, you might choose the block on which your home is located and place items at various points from one end of the block to the other. Say one item is "banana." You might then visualize the tree at one corner of your block as a banana tree, and continue from there.

Crawford (1969) edited an entertaining and easy-to-read manual (CORD) with guidelines for instructional planning using these mnemonic devices to good advantage. The writers of the manual have broken down the important components of any learning objective into ABCDs—*Audience, Behavior, Condition,* and *Degree.* In other words, a properly written learning objective, according to this manual, should answer each of the following questions as clearly and precisely as possible.

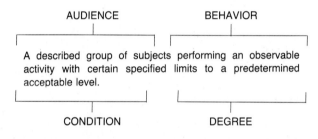

A. For what *audience* of people is the specified instructional outcome intended?
Examples: Third-grade students with average reading ability; eleventh-grade students in an American history class.
B. What observable and measurable change in *behavior* will be used to demonstrate that the desired learning has taken place?
Example: Third-grade students with average reading ability will be able to read aloud any designated paragraph in their textbook.
C. Under what *conditions* should the desired behavior change be expected? (If possible, the conditions should be generalized to real life.)
Example: Third-grade students with average reading ability will be able to read aloud any designated paragraph in their textbook which their teacher has assigned for homework.
D. What *degree* or performance criterion signifies an acceptable level of performance?
Example: Third-grade students with average reading ability will be able to read aloud any designated paragraph in their textbook which their teacher has assigned for homework with 100 percent accuracy.

Mnemonics are demonstratively effective in increasing memory, and most students are glad of their help on occasion. But students ought to use mnemonics with great caution. Mnemonics focus attention on the kind of property and pattern in material that has severely limited utility for productive thinking. When a student memorizes a mathematical formula using mnemonics, he or she comprehends it in terms that have no mathematical meaning, and so nothing the student has learned can be used in solving any other type of mathematical problem. Shereshevskii, with all his unusual talent, could not use his memorized material to solve new problems (Hunter, 1977). It is probably best, therefore, to rely on such strategies only when it is necessary to remember material that does not require conceptual understanding.

transferring classroom learning to the world outside

Remembering what is learned in the classroom and applying it in new situations later is essential if education is to be meaningful. What is transfer? **Transfer of learning** occurs "whenever the existence of a previously established habit has an influence upon the acquisition, performance, or relearning of a second habit" (McGeogh and Irion, 1956, p. 299). This concept, which is important in understanding learning, is a significant one for teachers. Our purpose in examining this phenomenon here is to pinpoint the conditions under which classroom teaching influences other situations. We want to know how learning simple skills influences later learning.

Positive and Negative Transfer

There are two forms of learning transfer: positive and negative. **Positive transfer** occurs when learning in one activity facilitates learning in a new or similar activity. Positive transfer will take place under the following conditions (Ellis, 1972):

1. The two activities have identical elements in them.
2. The two activities have similar required responses.
3. The two activities have similar required techniques.
4. The two activities have similar principles of action.

There are many classroom applications of the principles of positive transfer. For instance, a student's learning of arithmetic may be positively transferred when he or she takes up accounting at a later time. Reading-readiness programs offer a rather good example of positive transfer. These programs provide young children with exercises that develop the basic skills needed in learning how to read—for instance, discriminating among letters that look alike. If the programs are successful, these identical skills are transferred to learning to read.

In terms of subject matter, teachers have many opportunities to aid positive transfer in their students. English lessons are one obvious instance. Students will have to speak and write every day of their lives, and they should learn how responses required in English composition and oral recitation tasks resemble those they will perform later in life. Greek mythology, with its emphasis on the tragic consequences of pride, has much to teach students about human relationships. The teacher should point out the similar elements in all people (and in the Greek gods who, after all, have human qualities) that students need to understand if they are going to be successful in their dealings with other people.

The teacher's basic task in facilitating positive transfer is bringing activities into the classroom that relate to real life, whether they are cognitive skills that exercise the mind and allow it to grow, or subject matter and experiences that will occur in later life.

Negative transfer (also called interference) is said to take place when learning in one area interferes with or impedes learning in another area. Negative transfer is another term for retroactive and proactive inhibition, which were discussed earlier. Examples of negative transfer in the classroom are numerous. We discussed several in the earlier section on inhibition. We mention several more here, not to be heavy-handed or dull, but to emphasize how common such situations are. Perhaps if you overlearn this concept a little, you will find it easier to avoid such problems when you begin teaching.

For example, a teacher presenting a unit on poetry discusses the sonnet, noting its unique length and rhyme scheme. For homework, he or she assigns several poems to be read and asks the class to find the rhyme scheme in them. However, the assigned poems are not sonnets; they may contain fourteen lines, but they do not have the sonnet rhyme scheme. Because the students are being asked to use the same responses on their homework as they used in class, they may well become confused. The teacher's lack of foresight has resulted in negative transfer.

Another example of this phenomenon: Americans usually have difficulty adjusting to driving on English roads because the English drive on the left side of the road, and we have learned to drive on the right. Here, similar tasks (driving) provide the setting for transfer. However, because the responses are different (driving on different sides of the road), the chances of negative transfer are increased.

A Historical Look at the Concept of Transfer

The earliest formulation of the concept of transfer was embodied in the doctrine of **mental discipline.** According to this doctrine, the mind is composed of faculties such as memory, will, attention, reasoning power, and judgment. These faculties are analogous to muscles and need exercise to function adequately and become strong. Though acknowledged today as theoretically and empirically unsound, this doctrine had a profound effect on American education from its inception in the middle of the last century to the early part of the twentieth century.

The following statement, written in 1865 by a state superintendent of public instruction in Pennsylvania, illustrates how influential these ideas were in the United States:

> The intellectual faculties can receive culture only by judicious exercise . . . . No means are known whereby the faculties of the mind can be developed but by exercising them. By the potent spell of the magic word Exercise, is evoked all human power. (Bigge, 1964, p. 249)

What sort of exercise did these educators recommend? Latin, Greek, mathematics, and other difficult subjects were considered ideal material for the training of the mind. The intrinsic worth of the subject matter itself was considered to be unimportant, for long after the subject was forgotten, the effects of the training were thought to remain. These educators believed that the mind as well as the study habits of the student were generally strengthened so that they could function better in any subject toward which they were applied.

The first psychologist to seriously question the doctrine of mental discipline was William James in his classic work *Principles of Psychology*, published in 1890. James himself first memorized over one hundred lines of Victor Hugo's poem *Satyr*. Then he extensively exercised his faculty of memory by memorizing Book I of Milton's *Paradise Lost*. Finally, he tested the theory by once again committing to memory the same number of lines in a different passage from *Satyr*. He found it took longer the second time then it did on his first attempt. Exercise had apparently not strengthened his mind at all. (This is not to say that experience has no effect on one's ability. Experience with different mnemonic devices does help because the devices help, not because one has "strengthened" the mind by experience.)

Following James's work, more scientific experiments were undertaken, which led eventually to the demise of the mental discipline doctrine. Edward L. Thorndike's monumental study was particularly important in this area. This study (Thorndike, 1924) involved a comparison of scores of high school students on a test of reasoning before and after a year's study of the regular high school curriculum. Thorndike reasoned that, if classical studies improved the mind, then those students who had taken classics during the previous year would perform better on the test than students who had taken courses in subjects such as drama or home economics. However, the classics group performed only slightly better on the reasoning test than the other group did. Thorndike accounted for this very slight difference by the initial differences in IQ scores between the two groups, not by any differences in the subjects they studied. Subjects designed to improve the mind did not, in fact, increase mental ability. His findings dealt a fatal blow to the traditional belief that classical subjects enhanced a student's general reasoning power.

How does transfer take place? Two broad theories of transfer—identical elements and generalized principles—attempt to specify exactly what is transferred from one activity to another.

The theory of identical elements Thorndike's evidence refuted the mental discipline doctrine. What did Thorndike suggest as a replacement?

On the basis of numerous experiments, Thorndike believed that transfer occurred only within a very restricted range of conditions. This range was defined in his now-famous **theory of identical elements.** According to this theory, each activity was composed of many precise movements and connections. Transfer occurred to the extent that two activities shared certain elements. Thorndike was never very precise in specifying exactly what he meant by identical elements, but, even though his theory was never completely developed, it contains some basic educational implications.

In general, the amount of transfer from one learning situation to another depends on the degree to which they both involve responses using the same concepts, operations, and/or symbols. For instance, more positive transfer will take place if you study mathematics rather than French literature in preparation for a career in accounting. This theory provides a good starting point for constructing sequences of courses. For example, it is obvious why algebra is taught before calculus: Algebra is less complex, and it contains many of the symbols and symbolic relations found in calculus.

Notice how Thorndike's rationale for teaching certain material differs from the rationale in the doctrine of mental discipline. Latin, for example, is important because it facilitates learning in other subject areas, not because it is good mental exercise. Latin might be introduced because its grammatical constructions and vocabulary enable students to gain better insights into the English language as well as other languages they might study.

The theory of identical elements also provides a rationale for bringing more courses into the curriculum that deal with real-life situations. Such topics as community problems or family and personal living can help to bridge the gap between the classroom and the everyday world. So can students' field trips to museums, business establishments, zoos, and farms. Present-day educational costs, unfortunately, frequently force cutbacks in such trips.

One enterprising teacher of a junior high science class has found a way to circumvent the loss of her students' field trips to a farm or zoo to observe live animals and to increase transfer to real-life situations. Her work was important enough to be described in the local newspapers. What did this teacher do? Instead of taking students on field trips, she brought animals to school. One such guest of honor was Gretchen, a goat, and her newborn kid, Heidi Ho Ho. The visit was timed so that it fit into the students' study of the life cycle of mammals. Said Suzanne Glencer, the teacher: "I kept the umbilical cord of Heidi to show the youngsters an example of the relationship between mother and child before birth" ("Animals Go to Northgate School," 1975, p. 9). During the visit some of the students also got a chance to milk Gretchen. When the class studied the biology of egg-laying animals, Suzanne brought in three different types of chickens.

In general, Thorndike's theory suggests that teachers should not assume that transfer is a magical process that occurs frequently and readily from one subject area to another. Instead, the theory suggests that teachers ought to gear their instruction to very specific topics. According to this framework, the direction of teaching is best when it goes from specific to general, and not the other way around.

The theory of generalized principles   Charles Judd's (1908) **theory of generalized principles** contrasts in many ways with Thorndike's theory of identical elements. Judd suggested that the process of transfer is based on an understanding of the principle or generalization underlying the responses made in two or more activities. If a general principle is understood, Judd claimed, all the instances of the principle will be put into perspective and readily understood. Judd (1939) defined this type of general principle as "a kind of summary of many experiences. It makes possible the proper interrelating and interpreting of a whole body of varied experiences" (p. 496).

Judd's classic dart-throwing experiment (1908) illustrates the power of his theory. Two groups of 11-year-old boys were trained in trying to hit a target placed approximately 12 inches under water. Their training differed in one respect. The principle of refraction (the distortion of light under water) was explained to one group and not to the other. Both groups, however, were allowed to master the task to an equal proficiency.

Two new tasks were then presented to the boys in both groups. These tasks simply involved a change in the depth at which the object was placed under water, first to 4 inches and then to 8 inches. The results clearly supported Judd's theory. The group that had been instructed in the principle of refraction performed significantly better in both new tasks. Thus, transfer was exhibited only when the boys understood the principle underlying the tasks they were engaged in.

Support for Judd's theory comes from an early study comparing different methods of teaching Latin (Hamblen, 1925). The measure of transfer in this experiment was the degree to which the study of Latin facilitated a student's ability to understand English derivatives. Three teaching conditions were employed. In the first one, no effort at all was directed toward promoting transfer. In the second, many examples of derivations were introduced. In the third, these examples were related to the principles of derivation. The degree of transfer was found to be significantly greater under the third condition. Again, we see that identical elements were not sufficient to induce transfer, although an understanding of the principles involved was.

More recent research suggesting that finding identical elements in two learning situations does not always lead to positive transfer was reported by Timko (1977). Timko showed that kindergarten children learning to discriminate letters of the alphabet had more trouble recalling them in later learning sessions when they were more similar in appearance than when they were distinctive. These children looked for similarities in shapes of letters in making their responses and therefore made mistakes. In this particular example, looking for general principles on which to base discriminations might have helped the children. Other recent research in relation to discrimination learning supports Judd's model. Fourth and fifth graders, for example, benefited in discrimination tasks by first selecting a general problem-solving rule, and then using that rule in later problems.

Numerous classroom examples can be generated to fit Judd's model. The main criterion is the student's recognition that two situations are related by and organized under the same principle. For example, the principle of division, illustrated in the context of short division, should transfer to the learning of long division. Similarly, if this text teaches principles of educational psychology properly, you should be able to apply the principles you learn to a variety of situations you will encounter in your student teaching and later in your classrooms.

Accepting Judd's theory doesn't mean that you should throw Thorndike's out. Teachers can use both. For example, in some cases it may not even be necessary for two tasks to share any common elements, as long as they are related through some common principles. Learning how to drive a car, for example, may, facilitate learning how to operate a motorboat. The mechanics and instrumentation differ in the two tasks, yet because of some shared principles, there is a possibility for some transfer to occur.

The problem of specifying more precisely when transfer will occur even if two tasks share a principle in common still needs to be elaborated. One significant step in this direction was made in the context of an experiment conducted by Haslerud and Meyers (1958). Simply stated, they found that a principle was more likely to effect transfer if a student derived the principle independently, as opposed to merely hearing the principle stated by the teacher. This conclusion is essentially another recommendation of the discovery method of teaching.

In general, though, the educational implications derived from

Judd's theory are quite different from, and even contrary to, those derived from Thorndike's theory. Instead of proceeding from the specific to the general as Thorndike advised, Judd recommended that teaching ought to proceed from the general to the specific. For Judd, generalized principles enable a student to relate a wide diversity of facts and concepts. Rather than studying a large number of fractions to understand how they operate, one would simply use a few illustrative examples to explain the theory behind the operation of fractions. In economics, the notion that single-crop economies can lead to disaster enables the student to put into perspective numerous historical and present-day examples. Judd, as should be obvious by now, considered transfer a most pervasive phenomenon.

Judd's position is similar to the Gestalt position. The Gestalt psychologists stress that organization is basic to learning. Thus, both the Gestalt psychologists and Judd differ from Thorndike in emphasizing the importance of higher-order principles over particular features. In fact, the only source of meaning details have is found in organization and higher-order principles.

*How Teachers Can
Increase Positive
Transfer to the
World Outside the
Classroom*

Regardless of the theory you use, the necessity for positive transfer from the classroom to other situations or other classes cannot be overemphasized. The goals of education cannot be realized unless what is learned in the classroom is related or transferred to situations outside the classroom. This is one reason that orienteering is becoming popular, as a classroom activity as well as a sport. The students in a sixth-grade science class start with enlarging small maps by using graph paper. They learn to follow simple maps of the woods adjoining the play area of the school by using signs and compasses. By spring, they have become expert enough to explore town and county reservations and parks with confidence. In this example, positive transfer has reduced the amount that students had to learn by providing the means to facilitate learning from the classroom to the outdoors.

Making tasks similar   Although similarity between tasks can be defined in a number of ways, it is still an important factor in the process of transfer. In general, one would be safe in assuming that positive transfer will be increased to the extent that two activities are similar or, more precisely, have similar stimuli or responses.

One way in which similarity has been defined is in terms of a known physical scale such as size or brightness. Let's say we changed the traffic rules so that cars would be required to stop at an orange light instead of a red light. There would be a high degree of positive transfer between the two conditions, and drivers would probably have little difficulty obeying the new signal. The similarity between the two stimuli—their color resemblance—would be the condition that would facilitate positive transfer between the two situations. The results, of

Reducing interference In general, teachers should avoid situations in which similar learning materials that require different responses follow one another. For example, to increase retention, the teacher should not follow a lesson on English grammar with one on French grammar. It would be much better, as we said earlier, to follow the English grammar lesson with art, or perhaps chemistry, leaving the French lesson for another day or part of the day.

Timing learning effectively Teachers who want their students to remember learned material for as long a time as possible should consider the time of day when learning occurs. Whenever possible, learning tasks requiring mental activity should be taught in the afternoon rather than at the beginning of the school day, if long-term retention is desired.

Making learning meaningful The more meaningful material is to a person, the more motivated he or she will be to remember it. How do we define "meaningfulness"? One measure of meaningfulness is *association*. The more associations an idea brings about, the more meaning that idea is said to have for a person. In this sense, the concept of "weather" might be meaningful to a fourth grader, since he or she has many associations with it, but the concept of "nuclear physics" will not.

Another measure of meaningfulness is *familiarity*. In one study in which people were asked to remember different kinds of sentences, it was found that the closer a sentence was to the way an individual usually speaks, the better it was remembered (Miller, 1973).

Classroom examples of this phenomenon are numerous. In one class, for example, students were given the task of learning a list of strange and unfamiliar Greek names. The students were positive they would never remember them until one boy mentioned that he had a Venus pencil in his notebook—he'd remember that. Another boy remarked that he had some miniature Aurora cars. The teacher started writing these words on the chalkboard as the students looked for more and more names they did recognize. Everyone knew echo, of course, and Mercury and Pluto, which are planets. From this awareness, the teacher took them one step farther with derivatives. She explained that much of mythology lives on today in our language, and she gave them other words—Arachne, Tantalus, Rhea—to research to find the similarities between the original Greek words and our modern derivations.

The fact that more frequently occurring words and common word order are more familiar, more meaningful, and thus better retained has important implications for teachers. Teachers should be aware that students' lack of familiarity with the language used in a lesson may hinder their learning and retention. For example, taking most young children to see Shakespeare's *Romeo and Juliet* in the original version would not help their learning because the language used would be course, would be just the opposite if the drivers had to learn to stop at a green light and go ahead at a red light. Similarity has also been viewed in terms of the judgments people must make in response to stimuli (Ellis, 1967). Two or more stimuli are presented to each subject, who then rates the stimuli according to their perceived similarity. The variety of dimensions that can be employed is almost unlimited.

Notice that these two methods of assessing similarity parallel the difference between Thorndike's theory and Judd's theory. Thorndike's theory of identical elements would be more compatible with a definition of similarity in terms of objective, externally established criteria, while Judd's theory of generalized principles would be more compatible with a subjective determination of similarity. Subjective similarity, in Judd's theoretical framework, would reflect the degree to which a person related two different stimuli because of familiarity with a given principle.

Whichever criteria one adopts, the teacher should try to arrange the curriculum so that the concepts and information introduced are similar in nature. This strategy will optimize the degree of positive transfer that takes place. On the other hand, the teacher should definitely try to avoid situations where different responses to very similar stimuli are learned.

If principles that work in the laboratory also work in outside situations, then positive transfer will occur.

Chester Higgins, Jr., Rapho/Photo Researchers, Inc.

For instance, an elementary school teacher might teach a unit on energy production. The subject could be introduced with a general account of how energy makes things work. Then a waterwheel and a windmill, each running a simple engine of some sort, could be shown. The general principle that energy makes things work would bring about positive transfer in Judd's sense from the first example to the second. In teaching an elementary school unit on drawing skills, a teacher might first ask the students to produce their own drawings. As a homework assignment, they could be required to make up a list of examples of art they see around them in their daily lives. In class, they could be asked to relate their lists—posters, graffiti, pictures on the walls at home, and so on—to their own work. Positive transfer will occur through their perception of similarities, and they will come to see something of what goes into making a drawing, whether their own or someone else's.

On the high school level, an English teacher could present two different works of literature—for example, a poem and a play—that illustrate similar themes. He or she could also present two works of literature by the same author—for example, *A Tale of Two Cities* and *Great Expectations* by Charles Dickens—and point out that, although the plots and themes of the two differ, similar elements deriving from the author's unique style and point of view tie the two together. Thus, positive transfer would occur, and the students would understand what is meant by an author's "style." Further positive transfer would occur if the English teacher could assign *A Tale of Two Cities* at the same time that the history teacher was assigning the French Revolution.

Pointing out similarities between the classroom and the real world
The process of transfer from classroom to applications outside school has been stressed throughout this chapter. Needless to say, the teacher should not assume that such transfer will occur automatically. Transfer occurs only when students have the expectation that it will. In fact, merely pointing out the possibility of transfer can significantly enhance its occurrence.

In an experiment conducted more than fifty years ago (Dorsey and Hopkins, 1930), two groups of people received comparable training in a specific area. Then they were all given a test on which they could show the benefit of that training. One group had been given explicit instructions on how to apply the previously learned material to the test material; the second had not been given such instructions. The group that received transfer instructions performed significantly better on the test.

By pointing out how concepts discussed in class can actually be applied in outside situations, the teacher can help to increase students' positive transfer to these later situations. In teaching addition and subtraction, for example, an elementary school teacher could have students make up sample checkbooks. At a higher level, a high school economics teacher, in presenting a unit on the stock market, could have his or her students invest imaginary money in a sample portfolio of stocks and bonds and have them follow the fluctuations in the market value of their holdings in the daily newspaper. At both the elementary and high school levels, teachers could develop economics concepts by using examples of the inflation-recession cycle as they affect the students' daily lives: Has the high unemployment rate made it difficult for you to get a summer job? Why? Has your mother told you that you'll have to wait until next year to get a new bicycle?

One major problem that teachers have in helping their students transfer what they are learning in the classroom to the outside world is that too many teachers themselves have not had opportunity to transfer much information to real life. One way for teachers to solve this problem is to get out and see what the real world is like. The more experience teachers have, the easier it is to make classroom learning meaningful to students.

A good example of classroom learning made meaningful in this way is the program of psychology offered at Fort Lewis College in Durango, Colorado. Dr. John Hale, professor of psychology and chairman of the psychology department at Fort Lewis, for many years taught a course in abnormal psychology to local policemen. He got tired of hearing remarks like, "That's okay for you to say, Doc. But go out into the street and find out what it's really like."

Dr. Hale goes about his daily police duties.

Dr. John Hale, Fort Lewis College, Durango, Colorado

Dr. Hale did just that. He took off five weeks during the summer to become a policeman because "I wanted to experience what being a policeman is like on a day-to-day basis." Also, "I'm interested because of the application psychology is supposed to have on law-enforcement" (Fort Lewis College, *Information*, July 7, 1977). He continued being a policeman after the summer ended because he enjoyed learning as well as teaching. Hale's duties as a policeman included knocking on colleagues' doors to inform them that neighbors were complaining about barking dogs or that they were watering their lawns illegally. Hale reported that he acquired useful knowledge for his Fort Lewis classes through being a policeman. "I hope it won't be the case of telling a lot of war stories," he said. "However, I have gained kind of a different view of what to expect of people under different circumstances. That is a good thing for a psychologist to know. It can be passed along to classes in the area of abnormal behavior" (Fort Lewis College, *Information*, July 7, 1977).

Teaching for general transfer: Learning to learn Thus far we have tried to pinpoint the specific dimensions of similarity that facilitate positive transfer. Transfer can also occur between two situations that share general factors. Through practice on related tasks, students become progressively more capable of solving new tasks, although the new tasks may be more difficult (Ellis, 1972). They have learned general techniques of problem-solving or modes of attack, regardless of the specific content of past situations. In effect, through general transfer, they are *learning to learn*.

The existence of this phenomenon was documented by Henry Harlow (1949) in his work with monkeys. Harlow taught a monkey to discriminate between two objects. If it picked the one arbitrarily chosen as correct, it received a reward. Eight monkeys engaged in 344 different discrimination tasks, each of which was run for a predetermined number of trials. The critical finding was that the monkeys gradually performed better on each new task, despite the fact that the correct solution of the task was different. For instance, a red ball might be correct in one task, the attribute being "redness"; and in the next task, a red triangle and not a red ball might be correct, the attribute being "triangular shape." With practice, the monkeys improved their ability to solve this general type of problem. In other words, they had learned to learn.

Teachers can find many ways to put this principle into action. In general, practice in problem-solving can enable a student to solve problems better in the future, although the teacher should always be aware that practice for its own sake is of no value. Let us say that a teacher has his or her class learn how to figure out percentages. He or she can then present them with specific instances that involve percentages—for example, interest on a bank account, sales tax, a tip on a restaurant check, and so on. In this way, they will transfer the general problem-solving ability to new tasks without rote practice.

However, learning sets are sometimes detrimental to learning in new situations. A good example of this is the difficulty most of us are having as America converts to the metric system. The system of weights and measures used in the United States has been described as "a medieval hodgepodge" ("The Metrics Are Coming! The Metrics Are Coming!" *Changing Times*, 1974). With the exception of Burma, South Yemen, an island or two in the Caribbean, and the United States, this is a metric world. Teachers, unfortunately, are having a great deal of difficulty helping their students to overcome their previous learning sets—to think of meters, kilos, and degrees Celsius, instead of feet, pounds, and degrees Fahrenheit. Educators as well as politicians and business people have pointed out that we need to get in step with the rest of the world, but learning thus far has been slow, and adults have served as very poor models for children. Negative transfer in this situation is not surprising. How can this be changed? Practice, practice, and more practice—overlearning in metric conversion.

Overlearning can be done in a variety of ways that increase retention without boring students. One high school math teacher introduces the metric system with familiar objects. The students use a meter stick to measure such things as a paper clip, pencil, stick of gum, length and width of the desk, books, and paper. Next they progress to clothing sizes and the heights of the students in the class. The teacher attempts to limit the objects to things whose sizes are known and recognized by most of the students.

Providing sufficient practice In general, overlearning ensures transfer in the same way that it increases long-term retention: Once having mastered a task, a student is more likely to transfer his or her skills to another task. For instance, a biology student who masters the techniques involved in dissecting a frog will be better able to move on to a more complicated specimen such as a fetal pig.

One needs to approach overlearning with some caution, however. In some cases, initial practice on one task may increase the probability of negative transfer to another task. Some studies have also shown that children who have had opportunity to overlearn certain tasks do not necessarily do better than their counterparts who have not overlearned, at least in relation to transferring to new problems (see, for example, Gilbert, Spring, and Sassenrath, 1977).

There are, of course, many explanations for why overlearning may not work in a given classroom situation. If the two tasks require different responses to similar stimuli, for example, then negative transfer will occur. However, if the first task is sufficiently well learned, positive transfer will usually occur, even in these cases.

As Judd demonstrated long ago, the outcome of practice depends on the context in which it occurs. More recently, an experiment extended this idea and determined that the manner in which a principle is introduced affects the extent of transfer (Overing and Travers, 1966). The results of the experiment indicated that transfer is best facilitated when the introduction of a principle is preceded by a practice problem. This "warm-up" practice problem enables the individual to better comprehend the principle than if it were introduced "cold."

"Practice" does not mean doing the same thing over and over. The more variety the student encounters as he or she engages in overlearning a given task, the better the chances that there will be positive transfer to other tasks. For this reason, we emphasize once again that repeated drills on the same material have little value. By presenting problems to students from a number of perspectives, a teacher can facilitate positive transfer. For instance, in teaching students to use punctuation correctly in compound sentences, the teacher can present different types of sentences on which students can practice. This varied practice will serve to stabilize learning and thus make it more transferable.

Developing meaningful generalizations   Although we have stressed how important it is to learn principles, such learning is not a goal in and of itself. If students can only apply a principle in a restricted number of contexts, the principle is not meaningful. Teachers should present a principle to their students in several ways and in several contexts, so that it will be generalized. As Andrews and Cronbach (1950) commented: "One may memorize Caesar's biography, or may observe it in the consequences of concentrated power" (p. 304).

There are many ways teachers can avoid overemphasizing the particulars of a subject at the expense of the meaningful implications of the material. For instance, teachers can present *Macbeth, King Lear, Hamlet,* and *Othello* to point out the general nature of the tragic hero in Shakespeare. Although the particular qualities of each man should be discussed, the outcome of the study of this subject should be an understanding of the general concept of Shakespeare's treatment of the tragic hero. Similarly, a discussion of American foreign policy should not deal solely with the United States' relations with one nation—for example, the Soviet Union—but with how our philosophy of foreign relations is manifested in our dealings with a number of nations—for example, the Soviet Union, France, Spain, Japan, and others.

Recognizing individual differences in positive transferability Psychologists have long been aware that individual differences tend to affect the facilitation of positive transfer. Relationships have been found between certain personal characteristics and positive transfer, although it should be noted that this does not mean that these characteristics *cause* positive transfer.

1. Age—in general, the older the child, the more capable he or she is of positive transfer.
2. IQ—the higher the child's IQ, the more capable he or she is of positive transfer.
3. Motivation—anxiety, for example, tends to hinder positive transfer.

Teachers need to take these factors into consideration when they plan curricula to enhance positive transfer.

Decreasing negative transfer (interference) Negative transfer is more likely to occur when different responses are associated with the same or very similar stimuli in two learning situations. Negative transfer does not occur when the stimuli in two tasks are very different. Rather, it occurs when the stimuli in the two tasks are only slightly different. For instance, we would not expect negative transfer to occur between algebra and English literature, but we would expect it to occur between algebra and geometry.

The meaningfulness of the material also appears to affect the degree of negative transfer. In general, negative transfer is reduced by making material more meaningful (Ausubel, 1968). In fact, this reduction of negative transfer might clearly have been what Bruner was advocating in his discussion of discovery learning, which requires that a subject be organized in a way that is meaningful to the student.

Negative transfer is also related to the storage and retrieval processes. Greeno, James, and DaPolito (1971) have suggested that negative transfer involves two processes. The first is concerned with interference in storage. It is their hypothesis that it is difficult to store a stimulus-response association if the stimulus has been stored previously in association with a different response. For instance, if "Benjamin Franklin" has been stored as the discoverer of electricity in lightning, interference will occur when trying to store him as a United States ambassador to France unless special attempts are made on the part of the learner.

The second process in negative transfer is concerned with the retrieval process. The hypothesis is that negative transfer will occur with the same stimulus acts as a cue in two different retrieval systems. For example, if "Benjamin Franklin" is a retrieval cue for "famous American scientist" and for "famous American diplomat," there might be interference.

summary   1. Unless students retain what they have been taught and can transfer their knowledge to new situations in school and real life, learning has not really occurred. Therefore, it is important that teachers understand how memory works and how it can be improved.

2. Memory research began with the work of Hermann Ebbinghaus, who found that time is a critical factor in retention—people do the most forgetting during the first few hours after learning. Later researchers have found that retention is also affected by the meaningfulness of the material and the way in which it was learned. Meaningful material learned in several spaced trials is retained better than meaningless material learned in a single session.

3. The cybernetic or information-processing approach to memory compares human storage and retrieval of learned material to similar processes in computers. Psychologists who take this approach break memory down into sensory information storage, short-term memory, and long-term memory.

4. Sensory information storage registers our sense organs' impressions of the world. It is extremely short-lived and does not encompass cognitive memory.

5. In short-term memory, we store material as an immediate and direct interpretation of sensory stimuli. The small amount of information that can be stored in short-term memory quickly fades unless it is rehearsed.

6. Long-term memory is the basis for our civilization. Its capacity is thought to be huge, and it is implicitly a major goal of education.

7. Long-term memory can be measured through recall, recognition, and relearning. Recall, in which material must be remembered with a minimum number of cues, is the least sensitive measure of retention. Recognition is exemplified by the multiple-choice question in which remembering is stimulated by many cues, rather than the few typical of recall situations. Relearning, in which the person learns previously learned but forgotten material, is the most sensitive measure of long-term memory.

8. Psychologists have developed several explanations for remembering and forgetting, depending on their approach to learning in general. Behaviorists feel that forgetting occurs when a stimulus-response association is weakened. According to the fading theory, learning creates structural changes in the brain called memory traces which gradually fade if they are not strengthened by use. The fading of memory traces is often confused with extinction, which is caused by the removal of reinforcement instead of by the passing of time. Extinction occurs suddenly, instead of gradually, and recurs spontaneously, instead of being lost forever like forgotten memories.

9. Cognitive explanations of remembering and forgetting are rooted in Gestalt psychology, which emphasizes organization rather than time as the primary determinant of memory. Information-processing approaches explain memory in terms of storage and retrieval. Memories that are encoded in meaningful ways before being stored are more easily retrieved. Cognitive psychologists explain forgetting in terms of interference between old and new learning. In retroactive inhibition, new learning interferes with old learning; in proactive inhibition, old learning interferes with new learning. Thus, the order in which teachers present material to students has important effects on learning.

10. Motivation theorists remind us that people are better able to remember material that is meaningful to them. The *Ziegarnik effect* is explained by the motivation to finish incomplete tasks. Students who are highly anxious in school may unconsciously repress the source of anxiety as well as the learning they are exposed to there. Motivation theorists also emphasize the effect of the time of day when learning takes place. Higher levels of physical arousal in the afternoon hamper short-term memory but seem to improve long-term memory.

11. Teachers can help students to increase their long-term memories by providing immediate feedback, opportunities for overlearning, recitation, and properly constructed curricula; reducing interference; timing learning effectively; and making learning meaningful. Meaningfulness depends on the number of associations between new material and past learning, the material's familiarity, its relevance to some general principle, and its relationship to the overall goals of learning. In addition, learning that is exciting—that elicits flashbulb memories—is remembered for a long time.

12. Students are ultimately responsible for the efficiency of their memories. Students can improve their long-term retention by developing proper study habits, carefully spacing and timing study sessions, overlearning, taking advantage of oral recitation, and practicing mnemonics.

13. Transfer of learning involves using what we have learned in new situations. Positive transfer occurs when past learning facilitates new learning. Negative transfer, which is also called interference, occurs when past learning gets in the way of new learning. The earliest form of transfer, the doctrine of mental discipline, led to the idea that the effort involved in learning certain subjects strengthened the mind and made later learning easier. This doctrine was first questioned by William James and was finally undermined by research stimulated by James's work. We now know that a course's content is transferred, not its quality as a mental exercise.

14. There are two broad theories of transfer. Edward L. Thorndike's theory of identical elements stated that the amount of transfer depended on the extent to which two activities shared certain common movements and

connections. This theory is a good basis for the construction of curricula in which courses are arranged in order from the simple to the complex. Courses that use the same concepts, operations, and symbols would be unified; and more real-life situations would be introduced. In general, Thorndike's theory reminds us that teachers need to plan for transfer and teach from the specific to the general, not the other way around.

15. Charles Judd, in contrast to Thorndike, suggested that transfer is facilitated when students understand the general principles behind two or more activities and, thus, that teaching from the general to the specific is more effective. Both Judd and the Gestalt psychologists emphasize principles over particulars.

16. Teachers can increase specific positive transfer by making tasks similar and pointing out similarities between the classroom and the real world. A way to encourage positive transfer in general involves students' learning to learn. However, while learning sets can make problem solving more efficient, they can also decrease flexibility and creativity. Overlearning also contributes to transfer, when it involves variety rather than repetitive drill. Teachers should also help their students to make meaningful generalizations about what they have learned. Teachers also need to consider the child's age, IQ, and motivation in planning for positive transfer.

17. Teachers can reduce negative transfer by avoiding the use of similiar stimuli in different learning situations and making material more meaningful. Negative transfer may also be a result of interference in the way students store and retrieve information from their memories.

**for students
who want to read
further**

ELLIS, H. C. *The Transfer of Learning.* New York: Macmillan, 1967. Ellis does a good job of covering all aspects of transfer of learning. The final section contains reprints of original articles by well-known theorists such as Underwood and Harlow.

HALACY, D. S. *Man and Memory.* New York: Harper & Row, 1970. This is an easy-to-read book on the difficult memory theories covered in this chapter. Halacy also reports on ways to improve long-term memory, as well as on physiologocial and computer memory models.

HART, L. *How the Brain Works.* New York: Basic Books, 1975. In this book and in the article that follows, Hart describes his interpretation of learning and memory that takes into consideration neurophysiological aspects of the brain as well as psychological knowledge of classroom learning. The approach that he calls "proster theory" is a compilation of knowledge that has been helpful in classroom situations.

HART, L. The new 'brain' concept of learning. *Phi Delta Kappan,* February, 1978, 59 (6), 393–396. Hart's proster theory is described in terms of a series of hints to the teacher. Hart suggests that school learning today is largely "brain-antagonistic," but that, with creative work on the part of the teacher, it can be made "brain-compatible."

LORAYNE, H., AND LUCAS, J. *The Memory Book.* New York: Ballantine Books, 1974. This book describes a series of ways that students can increase their memories, from thinking up associations by using methods similar to mnemonics in the memorizing of words to methods for remembering faces of acquaintances.

NORMAN, D. A. (ed.). *Models of Human Memory*. New York: Academic Press, 1970. This collection of readings contains detailed descriptions of memory and forgetting prepared by the theorists covered in this chapter. Other models are also discussed.

MOTIVATION AND THE HUMANIZED CLASSROOM

A Case Study of an Unmotivated Eighth Grader

Carlos is 13¹/₂ years old and in the eighth grade. He is the oldest of five children, all males. His four younger siblings are in grades one, two, four, and six in an elementary school near the family apartment. All the children appear to be in good health, but none is doing well academically. Mrs. DelVara is a widow who supports the family by doing housework. Carlos works as a newspaper boy and donates all the money he earns to the family's support. The DelVara apartment consists of three small rooms, sparsely furnished but clean. Mrs. DelVara takes in boarders.

Carlos entered first grade at age 6. His father, who worked as a laborer, taught him English, and Carlos was one of a very few students in his class to begin school with a speaking knowledge of the language. He did very well in his first three years. When he was in the fifth grade, however, his father was killed in a fight at a local bar. The police never found the murderer. Carlos's mother went out to find work. Carlos often stayed at home to take care of the younger children. Mrs. DelVara reported her fear that Carlos spent most of his time thinking about his father's murderer and ways to avenge his death when he grew up. She cautioned her son that it was dangerous to think that way. Good schoolwork, she pointed out, is the only way out of the barrio. That June, Carlos's grades went down. His teacher thought of failing him, but decided against this action because she didn't want to make him afraid of school. She asked Mrs. DelVara to help Carlos with his reading over the summer months, so that schoolwork the next year would be easier, but Mrs. DelVara could not read English. Carlos spent that summer babysitting. He earned a small amount of money running errands for neighbors.

When Carlos was in the seventh grade, his teacher made a note in his anecdotal record, the first the caseworker found in the file: "Carlos seems to be a bright boy. However, he simply isn't interested in anything. He does a small amount of work—just enough to pass. With his ability level, he no doubt could do much better. *Carlos isn't motivated to learn.*"

His eighth-grade counselor advised Carlos to enter a vocational program. Carlos was very skillful working with his hands. He had received a C + in his shop course—the highest grade he had received in any course he had taken in the past several years. The counselor pointed out to Carlos that the boy could easily change that grade to an A. His shop teacher had reported extraordinary talent. Carlos had sat quietly through the interview. When the counselor was finished, he said, "Register me in whatever program you want." The counselor said, "But I want it to be one that will interest you." Carlos stood up to leave. "A C is average—average for Anglos—excellent for Chicanos. Register me in whatever program you want." The counselor's reported ended with this statement: *"Carlos DelVara is unmotivated."* The counselor predicted that he would not succeed. He did recommend, however, that Carlos be placed in the vocational program.

For the present, Carlos is not in serious trouble. There is no reason that he should not be able to successfully complete the ninth grade, if he tries. But there is a strong question as to whether Carlos will try. According to his present teacher, Carlos attends class regularly, sits quietly through the lessons, and never asks any questions. After school, he hurries back to the barrio. He reportedly has joined one of the Chicano gangs. The teacher feels that Carlos could succeed *"if he were motivated."* The psychologist, however, reports that Carlos *would be motivated if he were succeeding at learning in school."*

---

what is motivation?

Carlos's teacher and the psychologist writing his case history clearly disagree about the reason for Carlos's low interest in schoolwork. The teacher thought that Carlos was not learning because he was not motivated. The psychologist suggested that Carlos was not motivated because he was not learning. Who is correct? To answer this question, we must decide just what **motivation** is, and how it develops.

Behaviorists explain learning in terms of stimuli in the environment and responses made by the individual. Cognitive psychologists and motivation theorists, however, are interested in what takes place *between* the stimulus and the response. Cognitive psychologists concern themselves with individual's *perceptions* of the world, while motivation theorists emphasize the connection between behavior and needs, drives, goals, and motives.

According to motivation theory, what goes on inside us—our internal state, how we "feel"—largely determines the energy we expend and how we behave. This internal state—or "feeling" of the person—cannot be seen or measured directly; we must infer its presence from the quality of the person's observable behavior.

A basic assumption in motivation theory is that people behave as they do to reduce their needs. A **need** is a requirement that must be met for optimal adjustment to the environment. There are several kinds of needs. Certain needs, such as those for food and water, must be met simply to survive. Because of their essential nature, these physical requirements are called **primary needs.** Most learning experiments conducted with animals have made use of these primary needs by first

Needs, Drives, Goals, and Motives

depriving the animals of food or water and then using the satisfaction of these needs as reinforcers.

Other sorts of needs are call **secondary needs** because they are not essential to physical survival but their fulfillment does make a significant positive contribution toward our adjustment. In other words, satisfying our primary needs keeps us alive, but satisfying our secondary needs makes us happy. Some secondary needs, like companionship, are personal, while others, such as the need for high-status possessions, are cultural. As civilized people living in an affluent society, most of our needs are secondary rather than primary.

According to motivation theorists, individuals who have needs, whether primary or secondary, are compelled to act in ways that reduce or satisy those needs. This compulsion to act is called **drive.** Like all variables intervening between stimulation and the individual's response, drive is inferred from measurable circumstances. Let's take the example of a hungry newborn baby who cries and squirms. One could assess the strength of the baby's drive in terms of either the number of hours since its last feeding (degree of need) or the vigor of its crying and squirming (activity level). These two measures of **drive strength** are usually closely related.

This example illustrates an important point about drives. No matter how strong a drive is, it cannot provide need reduction by itself. A drive tells us that something is needed, but it doesn't tell us what it is or how to get it. These things must be learned as part of the socialization process. Our newborn baby, for instance, knows that it is hungry, but, because it has never experienced feeding through its mouth, we cannot asume that it knows it wants its mother's breast or a bottle. Because it takes time to learn the best ways to channel our drives, motives usually develop gradually rather than all at once.

For example, a 9-year-old boy whose parents have associated social approval with success in school may well develop a secondary

Jeanne Tifft, Photo Researchers, Inc.

Showing approval and attention is one way a teacher can satisfy an important secondary need of students.

need to achieve. However, until he learns to behave in certain ways in class, he will have an unmet need compelling him to some activity. School children with histories of poor grades might want to learn. Unfortunately, they have not learned how. They may never experience need satisfaction and thus may continue to express their drive as undirected behavior in the classroom.

Motivation thus includes both *energy* (drive) and *direction* (learned ways to satisfy our needs). Teachers who think that one of their students is unmotived need to analyze the child's behavior to see which of these two aspects is involved. Is the child indifferent to learning (low-drive strength)? Or, does the child want to learn, but not know how (lack of direction)? Observation of the child's behavior in school is probably more effective than asking the child directly. If Carlos were asked if getting A's in school was important to him, he would probably laugh, leaving the teacher to conclude that Carlos's drive toward learning was weak, which is not really true. He is discouraged, not indifferent.

Having a strong drive does not necessarily make learning more efficient. Children will not always perform best under conditions in which their drive strength is highest. Children who are intensely driven are often so determined to achieve their goals that they lose patience with the work required to achieve them and may do very poorly as a result.

The effectiveness of drive strength in children's learning also depends on the complexity of the tasks at hand. Children who are highly aroused usually perfom better on simple rather than complex assignments. High levels of arousal or drive strength usually cannot be maintained for the length of time required to accomplish a very complex task. High levels of anxiety also interfere with complex problem-solving.

Maslow's Hierarchy of Needs

Human motivation is clearly a complex process. One of the most original attempts to deal with the complexity of the problem as well as to propose educational solutions that take student needs into consideration can be found in the work of Abraham Maslow (1943, 1954, 1968a, 1968b). Maslow, considered one of the foremost humanistic psychologists, has suggested that human nature has been sold short by psychological theories that do not take into consideration the reality of higher human needs, motives, and capacities. Maslow's approach to these higher humanistic qualities is discussed in detail in a later section of this chapter. Now, we examine his interpretation of basic human motivation, which he has portrayed in terms of satisfying a hierarchy of needs.

Maslow's hierarchy of needs is composed of a number of different types of needs. These needs are arranged in a pyramid. Higher

Figure 6-1 Maslow's hierarchy of needs.

needs become dominant only when lower needs have been gratified. Maslow's hierarchy is shown in Figure 6-1.*

Maslow did not believe that each need must be absolutely and fully gratified in order for the next higher need on the pyramid to be operative. Rather, he believed that each basic need gradually emerges as its predecessor is relatively, but not completely, fulfilled. As Maslow (1943) explained: "A more realistic description of the hierarchy would be in terms of decreasing percentages of satisfaction as we go up the hierarchy" (p. 338). In other words , the average adult has a greater percentage of his or her lower needs satisfied and a lesser percentage of his or her higher needs satisfied. None of his or her needs may be completely gratified at any given time.

Physiological needs, in Maslow's framework, are the most basic of all; they must be gratified before any higher needs can fully emerge. The thoughts and fantasies of a starving man will be dominated by images of food. Even his dreams, more often than not, will center on food-oriented themes. If the man were given a choice between a steak dinner and a college education which do you think he'd pick? Later though, when his stomach was full, he might jump at the chance to go to college.

Educators know that hungry children are less able to pay attention in school than those who had enough to eat. In fact, children who are physically uncomfortable for any reason are less likely to be attentive students. During a period of chilly weather recently, children in a southern school found the school's furnace broken and the classrooms frigid. For three days, teachers attempted to teach under these conditions. Each teacher reported that little if any learning had occurred, that students had been unusually apathetic, that absenteeism had been above average, and that the instructional programs had suffered a setback. The principal reported that teacher morale was also at an all-time low.

Next in the hierarchy are *safety needs*. These needs do not generally have much impact on adults, but sometimes they do. Saving yourself from a flood would occupy most or all of your attention until the danger was past. Many totalitarian governments subject their citizens to illegal imprisonment and torture. Most people suddenly arrested, tortured, or deprived of food quickly lose interest in self-actualization.

Although safety needs occasionally dominate adults lives, infants and children have to satisfy such needs almost every day. During their early years, human beings are relatively helpless and thus most in need of stable and orderly environments. When a child's world is dis-

---

*Figure 6-1 illustrates five basic needs as Maslow originally defined them. In some of Maslow's and other researchers' writings, a seven-level presentation of these same needs is given; for our purposes now, however, we shall discuss the five most basic needs.

rupted, as Carlos's was when his father was murdered, safety needs come to dominate his or her growth and development. Carlos could not worry about school grades when he was preoccupied with fears of death.

The third level in Maslow's hierarchy of needs is *love and belonging*. Once people feel safe in their environment they will turn toward others in order to achieve fulfillment. Friendships, love relationships, and group acceptance emerge as the dominant concerns at this point. According to Maslow, when a person is thwarted in satisfying this need, maladjustment and even severe psychopathology may result. Teachers and child psychologists are both keenly aware of the importance of this need in the lives of school-age children. Children who have trouble getting along with their classmates and teachers also have trouble reaching their academic potential. For young children, school is the first real testing ground for establishing their place among other children. If they fail in their social relationships, school can become a hostile environment associated with much fear and anxiety.

Teachers regularly deal directly with their students' needs for love and belonging. One day, a school secretary noticed a sixth-grade girl standing at the counter in the office crying. She was aware that the girl was new in the school and attempted to find out what the matter was. The girl sobbed, "My stomach hurts whenever I go into the classroom and I want to go home." For three days these symptoms recurred. Yet when the child was in the office, she appeared to feel fine and even offered to run errands or help the secretary in her duties. When forced to face the classroom and deal with reality, the girl found that her teachers were just as sympathetic as the secretary, and within a week or two she settled down to learning with her peers.

Children probably have an easier time adjusting to school if they have had a chance to practice establishing social relationships in preschool. Being away from home is hard for most children, but the older they are, the harder it is and the longer it takes them to feel comfortable. It seems much more sensible to allow children to get used to being with other children in preschool and kindergarten instead of in first grade, when their lives are further complicated by having to learn to read, write, and do math at the same time.

Next in Maslow's hierarchy are *esteem needs*. In this category he includes the need for self-respect as well as the need for respect from others. From self-respect comes confidence, independence, and freedom. From the respect a person receives from others comes a sense of prestige and appreciation. If these needs are not satisfied, people become preoccupied with their own inadequacies and with possible rejection by others.

The last and most far-reaching need is what Maslow termed *self-actualization*. Self-actualized people, according to Maslow's definition (1954), are happy people. They perceive reality easily and are comfortable with it. They accept themselves and others. They feel free to think and act spontaneously. They approach problems with no personal biases. They value time they can spend by themselves as well as time they spend with others. Their thinking is not rigidly tied to cultural values, and they feel brotherhood among all human beings. They enjoy a small number of rich relationships with people of both sexes. They enjoy work involved in achieving goals. They are relatively free of prejudice and jealousy. They have a sense of humor and an ability to be creative. They have a real sense of joy in experiencing life.

According to Maslow, these characteristics make up a composite picture of a well-adjusted individual that could serve as a goal toward which all people might strive. Self-actualization is possible through education that supplies students with acceptance of their basic natures and reduces fear, anxiety, and defense to a minimum (Maslow, 1968b). Each person has to find his or her own path toward actualization, but sensitive teachers can help by encouraging students to understand and value experiences important in this process rather than viewing students as passive learners who can be manipulated by rewards and punishments. Even with such help, however, some people find self-actualization harder to reach than others.

Although Maslow's hierarchy of needs is a useful way to understand an aspect of human behavior, it does oversimplify matters somewhat. For example, no behavior can be described exclusively in terms of a single need. Behavior in Maslow's framework can be multimotivated. To use one of Maslow's own examples, making love may be partially motivated by each of the basic needs in the hierarchy. We may have a physiological need for sex, feel safer with the other person, wish to satisfy our need for love and belonging, feel better when we make someone else feel better, and feel more actualized when we express our emotions in physical terms.

Second, psychologists point out that not all behavior can be analyzed in terms of motivational factors alone. Some behavior, such as the smile of a happy person or the brisk gait of a person taking a morning walk, can be more adequately described as expressive than as motivated behavior. Incidental or accidental learning (such as knowing the color of your next-door neighbor's front door) cannot be explained in terms of motivational factors either. And rote habits or mannerisms—such as the way you carry your books or get dressed in the morning—often cannot be sufficiently explained simply in terms of ungratified needs.

Finally, there is evidence that Maslow's hierarchy does not always hold true for all people. From Joan of Arc to the more recent martyrs of the Gulag Archipelago, there have always been individuals who, under torture or threat of death, have held firmly to their higher values and ideals.

Achievement motivation is a persistent attempt to secure what our culture describes as success. For students, achievement motivation is usually considered in relation to persistent attempts to do well in school, which we measure by high grades. Achievement motivation is a vital factor in successful teaching; increasing achievement motivation in students like Carlos, for example, would aid learning considerably. Achievement motivation among college students has been related to a number of personal factors such as a desire for self-improvement, positive attitudes toward school, desire for self-esteem, enjoyment of learning, and so on (Doyle and Moen, 1978). Achievement motivation can also be affected by the teacher.

David McClelland and his associates (1965, 1972) are pioneers in the study of achievement motivation. According to McClelland, giving students concrete ideas about how to reach their goals increases their motivation to achieve. For example, McClelland has raised the achievement motivation of junior high school and high school students by simply teaching them to think, talk, and act like people with high achievement motivation. Abstract advice, such as "Work hard," isn't very helpful unless the person is given a clear idea about what to work hard at.

Because it takes a lot of effort to satisfy the need for achievement, McClelland emphasizes that the individual must be able to see the numerous benefits to be had by increasing his or her achievement motivation. For example, reaching a goal leads to a heightened sense of self-respect as well as greater respect from others. McClelland believes that such practical, everyday rewards are more motivating than pie-in-the-sky goals such as "living up to one's potential." McClelland has recognized that people just developing a need for achievement often have past histories of failure and recommends that they avoid becoming discouraged by keeping a written record of the concrete tasks they have successfully accomplished.

Although teachers generally try to encourage achievement motivation by giving students easier tasks at first, sometimes achievement motivation can be increased by making the learning task more difficult. "Oh, Peter you forgot your paper again today?" Peter nodded and slouched in his seat. His teacher knew he wasn't the only one in this remedial class who frequently forgot the newspaper. The eighth-grade English classes were working on a newspaper unit, and the teacher was finding it difficult to teach the unit to this class when so few students brought their papers with them. After class, the teacher asked Peter why he and his classmates forgot their papers so often. Pete answered that they didn't like to carry the "dumb local paper" because the other kids (in the nonremedial class) were using *The New York Times* and "they make fun of us." The teacher realized that *The New York Times* had become a status symbol. The next year, the teacher

Achievement Motivation in the Classroom

This Russian child's persistent efforts to achieve are rewarded by the approval of his classmates.

Tass from Sovfoto

used the same paper in all classes. What the students lacked in comprehension skills, they made up for in other areas.

Another psychologist interested in achievement motivation, John Atkinson, stated that the concept of achievement motivation is relevant only in those situations in which students both perceive themselves as responsible for the outcome and understand that their achievement will be evaluated against some standard of excellence. Thus, teachers who want to increase achievement motivation ought to specify student roles clearly and spell out in detail what is wanted (Maehr and Sjogren, 1971).

Achievement and failure orientation: Positive and negative self-concepts Atkinson (1958) pointed out that there are two conflicting motivations involved in the achievement of goals: achieving success, and avoiding failure. Some people are more concerned about how successful they will be. An **achievement- or success-oriented** person, such as a student who wants badly to graduate *summa cum laude,* has self-assurance and feels that he or she can do well— in short, he or she is likely to have a positive self-concept.

Other people are more concerned about failing. A good example would be the student whose prime concern in studying for an examination is getting a passing grade and not having to repeat a course. Carlos DelVara is a case in point. In Atkinson's terms, Carlos would be considered a **failure-oriented** student with a negative self-concept.

Research has shown that students with high self-concepts engaged in more positive self-reinforcement after succeeding at tasks than students with low self-concepts did (Ames, 1978). It is not surprising that Carlos, with his low opinion of his work and his experience of failing at school, was not impressed with his teacher's assumption that he could do A work and that he was, after all, a bright student.

Atkinson postulated that a student's motivation to learn was influenced by his or her perception of the difficulty of the task. Achievement-oriented individuals consistently preferred tasks that they considered to be moderately difficult (Maehr and Sjogren, 1971). Tasks perceived as too difficult or too easy were less preferred. This tendency can be generalized to include preferences for jobs and school curricula that present moderately difficult challenges.

Not only do achievement-oriented students prefer tasks they consider moderately difficult, they also tend to work longer at these tasks than others. In a study in which people experienced failure in a task they had been told was easy, achievement-oriented individuals were significantly more persistent than people who were failure-oriented (Feather, 1963).

The implications of all these findings for the teacher are obvious. Students whose teachers individualize their learning tasks to make sure that students are moderately challenged rather than overwhelmed or bored will have students with higher achievement orientation. One way to motivate all students at an optimal level might be to allow them to set their own goals and then grade them accordingly. A study conducted by Alschuler (1968) provides empirical support that this suggestion will work. In his study, students were presented with a learning task in the form of self-competition game. The students set their own goals; they were evaluated according to the terms they set for themselves. This procedure was found to significantly increase their levels of achievement in the task.

Sex differences and achievement motivation   Many researchers in the past thirty years have studied the effects of sex differences on achievement motivation. Studies using tasks that people perceived as reflecting individual intelligence or leadership ability have shown significant differences in achievement motivation between men and women. Such tasks consistently aroused and heightened men's achievement motivation (McClelland, Atkinson, Clark, and Lowell, 1953). Women, on the other hand, failed to exhibit this expected increase in their achievement motivation (Fontana, 1971). Classroom evidence gathered over the years that male students tend to achieve more in accepted "masculine" subjects such as mathematics is consistent with these findings. Studies have also shown that female college students achieve more in mathematics courses when individual reinforcement rather than male-stereotyped competition is used to assist motivation. The opposite has been found true for male college students (Michaels, 1978).

Matina Horner (1972) found that women she studied felt that academic success would threaten their femininity and possibly lead to social rejection. Two-thirds of her subjects expressed feelings of anxiety and guilt in response to a story about a woman who was at the top of her class in medical school. In Horner's words, they experienced a "fear of success."

This fear of success was strongest in highly intelligent women reared in an atmosphere in which achievement was valued. Because of their backgrounds and abilities, these women had high need for achievement at the same time as they were afraid of success. Horner suggested that this dilemma resulted from two contradictory pressures. These women, who were encouraged to do their best in school, were also expected to get married before they graduated from college. At that period in our history, those two goals were difficult to accomplish simultaneously. The women felt that academic success would make them appear less feminine and consequently less likely candidates for marriage. Many women still feel this way, although evidence indicates that men's attitudes toward academic achievement by women are gradually changing.

Sex-typed attitudes toward achievement are learned early. Teachers and parents have been known to reinforce quiet, gentle, nonaggressive, noncompetitive, "feminine" behavior in girls while criticizing the same behavior in boys as early as the preschool years (Fagot, 1977). Education of women through recent civil rights laws and the increase in strength and popularity of the women's liberation movement are expected to change this attitude and lead to increasing achievement strivings among American women. Although female students in American public schools and colleges are expressing the belief that achievement strivings are just as appropriate to women as to men, role changes in professional careers and personal lives among both men and women are occurring very slowly.

Level of aspiration and achievement motivation Among the variables affecting achievement motivation and achievement itself is **level of aspiration**—an individual's expectations of his or her own future successes or failures.

Some students have levels of aspiration that might be considered too high. Based on their past performances, these students expect to perform more than they can realistically achieve. These students tend to be dissatisfied with their current levels of performance, no matter what those performance levels are. These are the students who hound their teachers for extra-credit projects, who bring in pages and pages of homework when it is not assigned, whose work is often characterized by quantity instead of quality, and who worry constantly about their grades and whether or not a certain discussion will be on the next test.

Other students have levels of aspiration that might be considered too low. Such students are, for the most part, insecure individuals with histories of failure who expect to continue failing and therefore do not try to achieve. People who have moderately positive levels of aspiration, however, are able to set realistic goals and are generally successful achievers.

Students' levels of aspiration can also be influenced by other factors besides personality. The application of systematic social reinforcement has been shown to be highly successful in modifying school children's level of aspiration. The teacher's behavior influences the student's self-evaluation and can affect student behavior as well. Such a chain of events has been termed the **self-fulfilling prophecy.** In one of the early studies on this topic, Rosenthal and Jacobson (1968) first administered nonverbal intelligence tests to a large group of children in grades 1 through 6. The teachers were told that the purpose of the test was to discover which students would be most likely to show substantial academic progress in the coming year. Each teacher was given a list of students who, based on the test results, were the most likely candidates to exhibit such academic growth. Actually, the students on this list were chosen totally at random and made up 20 percent of the entire school population. Rosenthal and Jacobson tricked the teachers in order to prove their theory that students singled out as possible intellectual whizzes would show significantly greater gains than other students. At the end of the school year, Rosenthal and Jacobson once again administered intelligence tests to the children. According to the researchers, the children teachers had expected to do well did in fact show greater gains on the test than their classmates, even though there was originally no difference between the two groups. This effect was strongest in the first and second grades. Rosenthal and Jacobson reported that these results showed that teacher expectations affected performance as well as students' self-evaluation.

Although a number of other researchers have repeated this study with similar results (see, for example, Barber, Calverley, Forgione, McPeake, Chaves, and Bowen, 1969; Barber and Silver, 1968; Claiborn, 1969; Fleming and Anttonen, 1971; José and Cody, 1971; Leacock, 1969; Rothbart, Dalfen, and Barrett, 1971; and Shore, 1969), many researchers disagree with Rosenthal and Jacobson's findings. Some have reported research design problems. For example, Rosenthal and Jacobson did not examine how the teachers conveyed their expectations to the students. R. L. Thorndike* (1968) questioned the validity of the specific tests used and the IQ scores obtained. Still, sufficient evidence has been provided to demonstrate to teachers that their attitudes are certainly an important influence on their students' self-evaluation and learning, just as teachers' use of social reinforcers such as verbal approval or smiles is (Andrews and Debus, 1978).

A group of college students involved in a teacher-training program visited an innovative project in thinking skills on a given day. The project director was in the process of doing several classroom demonstrations for the visitors and had no time to brief them about the students who would be involved.

As the director, the college students, and the children left one highly motivated period, the students commented on how sharp these youngsters had appeared, how deep their thinking had been, and how involved each child was in what was going on.

"It must be nice," mused one of the future teachers over lunch, "to work with a highly gifted group like that. How responsive they all were! Wouldn't it be nice if all students were motivated to learn the way they were?"

The project director smiled as she answered, "Highly gifted? Not quite. That group was made up of what the teachers here labeled 'the bottom of the barrel.' They can hardly read, are usually involved in disruptive behavior in the classroom, and each of them has repeated at least one year——some of them two. You see, it all had to do with

---

*R. L. Thorndike is the son of E. L. Thorndike, the Columbia University psychologist who was responsible for formulating the "law of effect" in 1913.

what you as a teacher expect of these young people. They think they're a special group to me—and they are!"

Earlier, we defined needs as either primary or secondary and indicated that secondary needs are derived from analogous primary needs. In general, this is true, but researchers have described several behaviors that don't seem to fit this scheme. These behaviors are not related to survival and seem to be done for their own sake, for no direct gain beyond the pleasure of the activity itself.

For example, Harry Harlow and his associates (1950) found evidence of what they called an independent **manipulation drive.** They noted that rhesus monkeys actively and persistently took apart and manipulated puzzles when no external reward was provided. Further, they found no evidence to indicate that the monkeys had learned to associate this manipulatory behavior with any primary drive. They concluded that manipulation is not a secondary drive; rather, it is, in a sense, an independent drive.

Along these same lines, Berlyne (1957) suggested the existence of an **exploratory drive** in humans. In one experiment, he had each subject sit alone in a dark room. By pressing a key, the individual could project a picture onto a screen for about a quarter of a second. In this way, the subjects were able to view a number of different slides and could repeat any particular slide as often as they wished.

In reviewing his data, Berlyne noticed that his subjects consistently preferred those pictures that were most novel or incongruous. In one series of pictures, for example, a depiction of an elephant's head attached to a dog's body was repeated more often than other more conventional pictures. Berlyne concluded that human beings had an intrinsic need to explore new or unfamiliar situations. Interpretation of these studies for classroom use is clear. The findings suggest that human beings often seek stimulation rather than avoid it. Dull, boring classes are not nearly so likely to produce activated students as classrooms full of exciting stimuli or ideas.

There are many ways that teachers can make lessons exciting and stimulating. In one class, for example, a stack of *National Geographic* magazines had laid untouched for months in the corner. The teacher, in setting up a center on Halloween, looked through the magazines and found a rather frightening article on the vampire bat. She cut out the pages, bound them with yarn into a booklet, and placed them in the center with activities to be pursued. To her gratification, she found the students fighting for a chance to read her vampire brochure.

In another center, the same teacher always had a burlap bag with something unusual in it. Students were allowed to feel the object in the bag but not to look at it or talk about it to others. Then during the

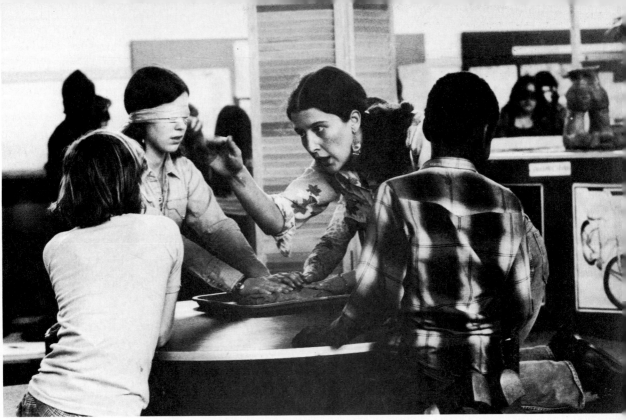

day, they expressed their feelings and guesses on paper or through some other means of communication. Needless to say, her homeroom students were always waiting at her door when she arrived at school.

Teachers can draw upon the human need for stimulation and exploration as the basis of exciting classroom learning.

We have already discussed Erik Erikson's concept of identity in the context of developmental theory. We reexamine this concept here briefly—this time as a motivational construct. In terms of motivation theory, identity can be viewed as a psychosocial need that the adolescent must satisfy.

Identity: A Strong Student Need

Erikson defined identity as a subjective feeling of selfness. The individual's identity is attained by answering the questions "Who was I?", "Who am I?", "Who am I not?" Psychologists have shown that children often learn the answers to these questions in the classroom. The same students who perceive that their teachers rate them highly also evaluate themselves highly (Curtis and Altman, 1977).

According to Erikson, although one's identity is formed throughout childhood, it is not until adolescence that it becomes the individual's primary psychological concern. The adolescent's identity is not established in one dramatic moment; the answer to "Who am I?" develops gradually. How does this process work? In part, the adolescent learns to adapt to a changing body and to the increased social demands that accompany this period of rapid change. During this time, preparation is made to enter the adult world with all its many responsibilities. During this period, the adolescent does a great deal of thinking in which past achievement and crises are integrated with present interests, desires, and expectations.

Ideally, the adolescent achieves identity through interactions with peers, teachers, and family. In many cases, however, this process does not go smoothly. Some adolescents become confused or overwhelmed, perhaps as a result of their inability to measure up to the ideals expressed by parents or friends or settle on a satisfying vocation; possibly there has been a traumatic relationship with another person. Despite such setbacks, the adolescent's need to establish an identity remains. According to Erikson, this need is not unlike a primary need, which leads in turn to a drive state. The reduction of this drive and the restoration of psychological balance are essential for successful adjustment.

In some instances, adolescents assume what Erikson termed a negative identity. Adolescents usually reveal this negative identity by rigidly assuming a role that is inconsistent with the roles they were taught were highly acceptable. As Erikson (1959) described it: "Many a late adolescent, if faced with continuing diffusion would rather be nobody or somebody bad, or indeed, dead—and this totally, and by free choice—than be not-quite somebody," (p. 132). Jim K. is a good example of an adolescent with a negative identity.

Jim is a highly creative boy whose parents split up when he was young. He was sent to live with an elderly but kindly grandfather. When the parents were reunited, they collected Jim's two siblings, but left him with his grandfather. Jim always passed his schoolwork but rarely did much more. He often found himself in the principal's office for discipline during his early childhood years. The friends he chose were always those on the brink of failing.

Yet Jim's name always came up when teachers gathered to discuss innate giftedness or creativity. Jim always had the unique answer or question in class discussions. His projects were always different from anyone else's. His behavior, though questionable, always exhibited ingenuity. For example, he was without a doubt the most devious cheater in the school.

When a program for gifted children begun, Jim was asked to be a part of it. Teachers dubiously welcomed him into their classrooms, expecting him to be a misfit. For two months, a battle raged between what Jim really was and the way he saw himself. Teachers bit their tongues and waited. Although the outcome is inconclusive at this point, all indications point to the emergence of a new Jim with a positive identity.

Other adolescents seeking identity become class clowns. Every-

Students often seek attention and approval from their teachers in their drive for identity.

Paul Conklin, Monkmeyer

one knows a class clown—the student who jokes a lot and makes everyone in the class laugh. Class clowns often get themselves into trouble by poking fun at the teacher or the administration. Teachers report that they are usually males, that they tend to be more assertive, unruly, and attention-seeking than their counterparts, and, perhaps because so much of their energies are spent in clowning, they also tend to be low achievers. Clowns, on the other hand, tend to see themselves as leaders, intelligent, nonconforming, and active group participants. Clowns feel more need for parental understanding than do nonclowns (Damico and Purkey, 1978).

Teachers need to understand that the search for identity is a very strong drive, and that some adolescents may take rather desperate means to reduce their internal discomfort. Most adolescents try on various personalities until they find one that works, and some change their choices as often as they change their clothes. No one can give a person an identity, but a teacher's understanding and positive reinforcement can be gentle guides to troubled adolescents.

Anxiety, according to motivation theorists, is an internal fear response that has generalized from an original feared stimulus to many other stimuli. Anxious people tend to exhibit many noticeable indicators of their anxiety, such as increased perspiration or nervous gestures. People generally feel better when their anxieties are reduced. Thus, in the context of drive-reduction theory, anxiety can be considered as a drive.

Fear and Anxiety: Drives Detrimental to Learning and Conducive to Cheating

The evidence indicating that the anxiety response is generalized to many stimuli comes from a variety of sources. For example, the behaviorist John Watson conditioned an 11-month-old boy he called Little Albert to fear a white rat (Watson and Rayner, 1920). Little Albert's fear response soon generalized to other white furry objects as well. He became afraid of white rabbits, a fur coat, and even a Santa Claus mask.

As a drive, anxiety can be very difficult to extinguish. In a classic study, Neal Miller (1948) trained rats to go from a white compartment into a black compartment in order to escape electric shocks. He then discontinued the shocks completely. However, the rats continued to stay out of the white compartment and showed signs of distress when placed there, no matter how long it had been since they were last shocked.

What happened? According to Miller, fear of actual shocks generalized to anxiety about possible shocks whenever the rats were placed in the white compartment. Going into the black compartment had at first stopped the shocks; later it reduced the generated anxiety. Each escape to the black compartment resulted in drive reduction, even though shock was no longer present.

Unfortunately, a great many teachers still believe that fear and anxiety are effective tools to curb undesirable behavior. They reason that, if children are punished or at least threatened with punishment each time they misbehave, their fear of punishment will soon cause them to stop such behavior. What these teachers don't realize is that children treated this way often generalize their fear response to other school-related activities and develop an overall anxiety associated with being in school.

Students with such fears will find learning very difficult and often impossible. Some anxious students sit woodenly in class, too nervous to absorb very much of what is going on. Others get Monday-through-Friday stomach aches and stay home a lot. Still others avoid the anxiety-producing situation by cutting classes.

One result of high levels of anxiety, in addition to those already listed, is cheating. American teachers wonder at the amount of cheating going on in classes, frequently never stopping to think of the high levels of anxiety produced by their teaching methods and the terrible fear of many students of the results of doing poorly on their tests. Interestingly, cheating is a behavior exhibited not only by students who are actually failing, but also by students who are afraid of doing worse than they, their parents, or their peers expect of them. The student who fears failure and the prospect of repeating a grade or a course might cheat in order to keep this from happening. The highly anxious serious student might cheat in order to receive an A instead of an A−.

Providing structure can be helpful; routine is a great calmer of anxiety. Constant feedback is of great assistance in reducing some forms of extreme anxiety—particularly on test performance, and particularly with low IQ students. Programmed instruction that provides immediate knowledge of the correctness of one's responses increases subsequent test scores (Petty & Harrell, 1977) and also reduces anxiety. Another method of reducing extreme anxiety is simply to avoid criticizing students, particularly low-achieving students (Cooper, 1977).

Not all anxiety harms learning. With some students, a little anxiety serves to increase the adrenalin and keep them interested and alert. Students who are a little anxious about a test are likely to remain alert to possible errors and stay awake in class before the test. Teachers' goals should be to reduce extreme anxiety, but not eliminate this low-level excitement.

*Group
Reinforcement
and Competition:
Sources of
Classroom
Motivation*

In school systems in socialist countries, the primary emphasis, especially in the early years, is on teaching sharing and group cooperation. Soviet children, for example, are taught from very early ages to be self-reliant group members and to always value the interests of the group above those of the individual. This orientation continues throughout a child's entire education.

In the United States, on the other hand, this kind of group support is usually secondary to individual competition. However, one experimental attempt to use group reinforcement proved quite successful (Cohen and Filipczak, 1971). The National Training School for Boys is a residential treatment center for male adolescents who have had extended histories of failure at home and at school. Its directors feel that a child continues to fail because he has experienced so few successes and has received so little support from others. Consequently, they decided to set up schedules of reinforcement that were individually tailored to allow each boy numerous successes, whatever his level of proficiency. To keep individual competition at a minimum in the classrooms, programmed texts and teaching machines were used.

But the key to the program's success can probably be found in its use of group reinforcement. Everyone in the school supported the progress made by each boy. If a boy showed marked improvement in his studies, the teacher pointed this out to his classmates, who then gave their congratulations. Even the correctional officers—in effect taken out of their traditional role as punishers and put into the role of encouragers—provided support. They were also encouraged to give the boys special bonuses for good behavior. According to Cohen and Filipczak, both the boys and the officers enjoyed this setup. Eventually, the boys came to realize that their fellow students, as well as the entire staff, were always behind them.

If cooperative activity and group support are beneficial, one might ask if and when competition has any redeeming qualities. Competition varies in its effects from situation to situation and from individual to individual. For example, competition as a teaching device has been shown to be more beneficial in simple or mechanical tasks than in more complex problem-solving tasks (Ahlstrom, 1957; Clifford, Cleary, and Walster, 1972; Shaw, 1958). The effects of competition in this case must be evaluated in terms of the complexity of the task at hand. The possiblity of continued failure leading to high levels of anxiety and possible learning difficulties must always be taken into consideration. A teacher would be wise to rely on competition in the classroom as an effective source of motivation only when dealing with fairly straight forward learning tasks.

Competition is most effective if it is treated as fun. Teachers should emphasize participating as well as winning. The student's feeling of self-worth is always more important than whether he or she wins. One fourth-grade teacher uses a reading comprehension game in her class that stimulates strong competition but not hard feelings. The class is divided into three groups. The first student in group A reads a paragraph aloud; the first student in group B asks any question about the paragraph; and the first student in group C must answer to everyone's satisfaction. The groups are rotated for each new paragraph.

If grades are awarded competitively, the teacher should allow a variety of procedures to use in determining the grades. Some students do better at tests than papers; others excel at projects. Teachers should keep grades confidential. The self-concept of the poor student is at stake, and sacrificing a student's self-concept often means sacrificing learning as well.

Competition appears to be an effective source of motivation when the competitors have a chance to succeed and when they are fairly evenly matched (Strong, 1963). The implication of this finding for teaching is that competition is most beneficial to those children who need it least—the ones who are already doing well. They will be the ones who will tend to succeed in competitive situations and get the best grades. Only the winners become highly motivated to achieve by competition. Regular losers tend to lower their levels of aspiration and simply stop trying.

Thus, while competition can sometimes motivate achievement, it can also be a two-edged sword that may hurt as many students as it helps. Because of its potentially negative effects on those students whose self-images are the weakest, teachers should probably think twice before introducing frequent competition into their classrooms. Slow and shy students will be trampled by it, while brighter and more aggressive students may create competitive situations on their own without the teacher's connivance.

Finally, if used at all, competition should be used as a learning device—to help students test themselves, discover strengths and weaknesses, make career plans, and so on. Competition should never be used as punishment. Remember the drive reduction model discussed at the beginning of this chapter: Motivation occurs after drive reduction takes place; it never occurs in the absence of drive reduction. Spelling bees have been a favorite form of competition for many years. Some teachers today use them only as team competition to foster friendly rivalry rather than to establish one winner and many losers. Often bonus words and extra credit are added to enhance the game-learning aspect of it.

Humanistic Approaches to Classroom Motivation

Abraham Maslow felt that human nature had been sold short by psychological theories that did not take the reality of human needs, motives, and capacities into consideration. As a first step in taking these qualities into consideration, Maslow proposed the hierarchy of needs discussed earlier in this chapter. Understanding this hierarchy is basic of Maslow's conception of humanistic education–the helping of the student by the teacher to find out "what's already in him rather than to reinforce him or shape or teach him into a prearranged form, which someone else has decided upon in advance" (Maslow, 1968b, p. 688).

The hierarchy of needs and classroom learning According to Maslow's theory, if lower, more "primitive" needs are not met, individuals will not attempt to meet needs more advanced in the hierarchy.

Thus, it is foolish to attempt to teach children who are hungry. They simply will not be interested in higher-level needs. Yet large numbers of American children come to school hungry every morning.

As a child's nutritional needs are satisfied, safety needs, according to Maslow, then become dominant. The teacher must keep in mind that children, especially young children, can easily be frightened by a strange and hostile environment. If children are reprimanded persistently for each mistake they make, and if they feel that such reprimands threaten their safety, they will soon protect themselves by withdrawing or becoming very defensive. Only when they are accepted for what they are can children feel safe. And only when they feel safe can they grow and develop.

Love and belonging needs are next in Maslow's hierarchy. It is important that a teacher perceive school not only as a place where children learn facts and skills, but also as a place where they develop numerous interpersonal relationships. The teacher should encourage children to work and play together, especially during their free-time activities. Projects that require the cooperative activities of several students strengthen the child-to-child network.

Watch the classrooms after the final bell sounds in the afternoon, and you will see which teachers care about their students. Young people will be hanging around. Students who have passed on to other schools will return to chat with the caring teachers. Years later, these same students will return to catch these teachers up on their progress, and when their own children find themselves in the same classrooms, the parents will breathe more easily.

One of the most important roles a teacher plays is to serve as a model for students to follow. If a teacher relates to each student honestly and respectfully, students will tend to adopt this same attitude among themselves. If a teacher experiences and displays enjoyment in getting to know each of his or her students, students begin to see that everyone has something special to offer.

Next in the hierarchy are the esteem needs. In addition to giving each student respect, teachers must also provide opportunities for students to develop self-respect. This is a most difficult task. While acknowledging that there are individual differences between students, teachers should try to convey the idea that struggles to achieve deserve as much respect as the achievements themselves.

Offering false praise to a child for his or her work is undoubtedly one of the worst things a teacher can do. Children are amazingly adept at perceiving this sort of insincerity and tend to resent it deeply. Children more often prefer honest feedback, even if it is negative. Children will be more motivated to try to do their best when they know that a teacher can differentiate between their half-hearted attempts and their utmost efforts.

Finally, we arrive at Maslow's highest need—the need for self-actualization. Some educators believe that the qualities Maslow incorporated into the concept of self-actualization can serve as useful ideals toward which education ultimately should be aimed. Others argue that, given all the other concerns teachers have, self-actualization is not a viable school goal. Self-actualization is a concept that is not easily put into words, much less translated into specific educational practices. Although teachers may not be able to do much to foster self-actualization specifically, there is much that they can do to satisfy the lower needs on the hierarchy, thus leaving their students free to explore ways to become self-actualized.

Maslow's self-discovery approach   According to Maslow's humanistic view of education, the role of the teacher is to help students discover "what they are" and "what they can become." The process involves self-discovery, self-acceptance, and self-making. Teachers can help students to satisfy their need for self-actualization by leading them to discover both their commonness and uniqueness compared with other humans.

How does Maslow propose that this be done? If we want to be good teachers, he suggests, we must first learn to accept people as they are. We must understand their styles of learning, their specific aptitudes, and their potentialities. We must learn what we can build upon. To do this, we must be nonthreatening and reduce anxiety to its minimum in learning situations. Finally, we must teach, not to reach a certain set of external criteria, but to reach self-actualization.

Instead of lecturing *to* students, the humanistic teacher discusses problems *with* them. As two humanistic psychologists point out, "discussions are more than alternatives to lectures; they are the place where personal exploration is not only encouraged but expected, where student and teacher become colleagues involved in the search for meaning" (Welch and Usher, 1978, p. 21). For centuries, students have been priding themselves on the ability to get their teachers off the subject. Recently, however, teachers have begun to learn how to "let themselves be gotten off the subject." Inquiry and discovery teachers find that the best learning goes on when students and teacher wander from the prescribed learning task into that magical unknown termed "off the subject."

Is it possible to develop a humanistic approach to classroom teaching while still taking into consideration the learning principles accepted by traditional educational psychologists? Certainly, humanists such as Maslow have disagreed with behavioral traditions in which psychologists and educators have manipulated external reinforcers in order to increase specified desired behaviors. Humanists also have disagreed with cognitive approaches to teaching. Cognitive approaches recognize a series of internal processes occurring between stimulus and response, but they continue to specify desired outcomes as well as desired routes to these outcomes, rather than allowing students to work these routes out for themselves.

Roger's learner-centered approach   The major thrust of the humanist approach to teaching is regard for the internal life of the student, and the belief that the student should determine and be responsible for his or her own behavior. This position is described by the term **learner-centered approach** (as opposed to teacher-centered), as used first by the counseling psychologist Carl Rogers. Teachers who use this approach trust and value their students and are sensitive in devleoping warm, personal relationships with them. With the help of such teachers, students eventually become capable of educating themselves (Rogers, 1967 1; 1975).

Comb's self-concept approach   Arthur Combs (1965, 1975), a third major advocate of a humanistic approach to motivation, took this process one step further. He pointed out that the way students perceive themselves is of major importance in developing their abilities to learn. For this reason, Combs suggested that teachers should concentrate on helping their students to develop positive self-concepts. Simplifying Maslow's hierarchy, Combs proposed that the single most important need that teachers should consider is **self-adequacy.**

Humanizing the Classroom

Some final advice for teachers comes from the advocates of a humanistic approach to classroom learning. Humanistic teachers encourage search and personal exploration. They allow students time to express involvement or interest, prepare them to handle current problems, and talk with them, not to them.

Being a humanistic teacher does not mean that you let students learn only what they want to learn. Certain skills are essential for a satisfying life, and teachers should set their goals to ensure that students learn those skills. After all, "what could be more dehumanizing than not possessing the competencies to adequately function in the society?" (Buell, 1978, p. 31)

Individualized instruction is a basic tool of humanistic education. Although not appropriate for all situations or for all students, it does express humanism's concern for the individual. When students must be taught in groups, they should be encouraged to act democratically rather than competitively. Teachers should positively reinforce their students as often as possible in both individual and group teaching situations.

Humanistic education's concern for the individual extends to the teacher as well as the students. Humanistic teachers consider themselves as a human textbook that their students learn from. As students learn accurate facts from their printed textbooks, they can learn constructive behavior from their human teachers.

What do these concerns suggest for classroom teaching? What specific actions can teachers take to increase motivation and learning in the classroom?

Increasing Achievement Motivation

Teachers frequently complain that many school children, like Carlos DelVara, are simply not motivated to learn in school. How can the teacher create a classroom climate in which students see themselves as originators of their own actions and controlers of their own acitivities? David McClellenad, whose work on achievement motivation was discussed earlier, suggested that the answer can be found in Jacob Kounin's work on classroom management techniques.

Kounin (1970) found that several approaches are involved in promoting a classroom climate that will increase student involvement and allow students to control, design, and participate in classroom activities. First, the teacher must provide a sufficient challenge to his or her students through a variety of approaches in order to interest and excite them. Second, the teacher must insure participation and require student responsibility for activities. And third, the teacher must, through letting the students know that he or she knows what's going on regarding the children's behavior, make each student feel accountable for what he or she accomplishes in the classroom.

Increasing Levels of Aspiration

Students' levels of aspiration—their expectation of future success or failure based on their past performances and desire to improve—exert strong influences on their choices of tasks and on their feelings about which tasks are too difficult. Teachers should aim to raise their students' aspiration levels so that the children approach new problems enthusiastically and realistically. To accomplish this, they should structure their classroom activities so that every student has a chance to succeed in most of what he or she does. However, the teacher should not eliminate failure altogether in classroom experience. A child who experiences no failures in school will develop a distorted image of his or her own abilities, which will be a poor preparation for the real world, where, as we all know, failure is as much as part of life as success.

Motivational approaches to classroom learning stress that a teacher's expectation of how well each student will perform in school may in itself influence students' aspiration levels. If a teacher expects a student to perform well in the classroom, his or her behavior toward that student will probably be consistent with that expectation. The teacher's behavior may then influence the student's self-evaluation and perhaps his or her behavior as well. Remembering the quality of each student as a unique human being, therefore, and seaching for abilities to aid the student in self-discovery are two important teacher goals. Teachers should particularly remember that female students might want to be as highly successful in academic fields as males are. Until teachers recognize that male and female students have the same potentials, female achievement motivation will be more difficult to foster than male achievement motivation.

Let Me Do It: Achievement Motivation

Evaluation of students' performance is traditionally part of a teacher's duties. But a study (Klein and Schuler, 1974) reveals that student self-evaluation can effectively reduce the time teachers spend on this task as well as improving academic performance. The subjects of the study were students in two third-grade math classes in an inner-city public school in Pittsburgh, Pennsylvania. The students were using the Individually Prescribed Instruction (IPI) Math Program, under which they complete workbook pages and take a test that measures skill performance per unit of work. Ordinarily, the teacher evaluated their workbook performance. However, the students were told that if they passed the first test in the present skill they would earn the right to evaluate all workbook pages for their next skill. The children were also free to proceed at their own pace and to attempt to master their next skill test at any time they chose. Failure on a test meant loss of self-evaluation privilege. Students apparently wanted the privilege of evaluating their own work: Both the percentage of tests passed and test scores were higher. The study suggests that the opportunity to be more autonomous, as demonstrated in self-evaluation rather than teacher evaluation, is a strong motivating factor in academic performance.

Reducing Classroom Anxiety

The reduction of extremely high levels of student anxiety is a very difficult task. It is extraordinarily important, however, particularly when we value creativity. Not only are high levels of anxiety disruptive in learning situations, but children with lower levels of anxiety tend to be more creative, particularly in nonstructured situations (Klein, 1975).

Although we can advise a teacher to refrain from using punishment as a source of motivation on the basis of what we know about learning theory, it is not as easy to provide a teacher with a list of "do's and don'ts" concerning anxiety caused by other aspects of classroom life.

Let us take the case of the anxiety generated by taking tests. Such anxiety interferes with a student's ability to think rapidly and clearly. Students who have a record of past failures and students who usually do well in school are equally likely to be anxious about tests. In an experiment with college students, Goldberg (1973) studied only those students who had maintained at least B averages. He found that test anxiety is particularly detrimental to those students whose self-images rest heavily on school performance. Their anxiety reactions to testing tended to generalize to a wide variety of school-related activities. Furthermore, they tended to have relatively low opinions of themselves as measured on tests of self-esteem.

In an attempt to reduce the amount of anxiety experienced by college students, some colleges have offered the pass-fail grading option to their students. It is thought that this grading method will relieve the constant pressure to maintain or better one's grade-point average. Some faculty and students feel that with this pressure relieved, students ought to feel freer to explore a subject without fear.

To examine the effects of the pass-fail system on the behavior and attitudes of college students at a large midwestern university, a team of researchers administered several hundred questionnaires to students who had selcted this option (Hales, Bain, and Rand, 1973). The results of this study were somewhat contradictory. On the one hand, a great majority of students reported less anxiety in their pass-fail courses than in their regularly graded courses. But this was counterbalanced by student reports that they were less motivated to learn and work in their pass-fail courses than in their regular graded courses. Thus, the pass-fail system seems to reduce anxiety, but it also seems to reduce motivation for students who are used to being reinforced by grades.

Another technique that has been proposed for reducing anxiety is put to work in the context of **competency-based instruction** also called mastery learning (Young and Van Mondfrans, 1972). The main principle here is to provide students with specific information about what they must do to complete their education. In some forms of competency-based education, not only are students told precisely what behaviors they must exhibit in projects and in examinations, they are also allowed to examine the test before they actually take it. Competency-based education makes the assumption that students and faculty agree on what constitutes competency in any given subject. All students agree to meet a certain level of competency, although each student may take different amounts of time to meet his or her goal. This procedure does not appear to have the pitfalls that sometimes accompany the pass-fail option. Telling students in advance exactly what they need to know (as, for example, an outline of what is to be on the test) appears to have two benefits: It reduces anxiety and, at the same time, increases motivation to learn.

*Making Classes
Nongraded*

One way to increase learning and at the same time reduce anxiety is to get rid of the rigid grading system that frightens children who think they might be left behind if they are not capable of keeping up with the others.

The basic principle behind nongraded classes is that not all children of the same age are capable of learning the same things; consequently, age segregation is not always conducive to learning. For example, in a typical class of 6-year-olds, a few children may be able to read materials designed for 8- or 9-year-olds; others may not yet know how to read; and still others may be able to read introductory materials. If all of these children are required to complete similar tasks, the slower children can become overwhelmed, while the brighter children become bored. By contrast, in a nongraded classroom different levels of reading matter are available for each group of children.

There are no rigid criteria for nongraded education. Each child works at his or her own pace, according to his or her own capabilities. Failure is minimized, since students are not forced to attempt overly difficult tasks. Instead, they are presented material that is within their ability range. At the same time, teachers do not bore children with work that is too easy for them.

Nongraded classes fulfill both educational and social objectives. The teacher in such a class recognizes that "people learn from differ-

TV Can Make Learning Fun

Sometimes TV can be used to provide motivation and make learning fun. A good example is a course taught at the E. Washington Rhodes Middle School in North Philadelphia, which has attracted national attention. The Language Arts TV Program is an experimental project devised by two Philadelphia teachers who were concerned about the reading problems that underlie most academic failure. Most inner-city children, they found, are not interested in the reading texts prescribed for them. They provide neither motivation nor relevance, with the result that "three out of four students in most major urban schools read below grade level" (Water, 1974, p. 7).

The course features one class per week using television sets and three follow-up classes per week without them. In the TV-reading classroom, children sit before a small videotape recorder and two television monitors. The *Lucy* show, for example, progresses by starts and stops; the children glance up at the screen to take in a visual joke, then attend to the scripts on their desks. The teacher switches off the TV to introduce a new fact, make an observation, or ask questions that prompt class discussion. The children often read and "act" parts in a script. During the course of a year, each student works his way through six 35- to 80-page scripts (provided by the shows' producers).

With the emphasis still on reading, the program includes other subjects (which utilize various teaching materials in conjunction with the TV shows). A segment of *Sanford and Son* might lead to a discussion of racial attitudes; *Kojak* and *Police Woman* might lead to a study of courts, law enforcement, the judicial system; and *The Waltons* might serve as the text for a class on history, psychology, philosophy, economics, or religion. The possiblities are limitless for the inventive teacher.

ences as well as similarities and . . . from meeting and living with different kinds of people" (Clark, 1967, p. 260). The mixture of ages helps create a diverse and lively atmosphere, which can be as educational for children as any set of materials. Of course, the nongraded classroom has disadvantages for slower students who will perpetually be left behind by more rapid students, but they will be relieved of the pressure to go more rapidly than is possible for them.

Managing and teaching a nongraded class is a difficult job. Teachers must place children in appropriate instructional groups and must assume a large degree of responsibility for what each child learns. Unlike the traditional teacher, the teacher in a nongraded class cannot rely on a particular textbook or syllabus to find the "normal" curriculum. The specific needs of each student must be determined, and materials that will meet that student's needs must be prepared.

*Improving
Lecturing to
Increase Motivation*

Teachers cannot always find innovative devices like TV sets to increase motivation of their students. Often they find themselves with large classes, no assistants, and long lesson plans that their principals expect them to follow. How can teachers in this situation motivate their students to learn? For one thing, they can remember that sitting in a class for forty-five or fifty minutes listening to a teacher talk and having no opportunity to respond is boring. Teachers can make the time they spend lecturing more interesting to students by remembering not to talk in monotones, by asking questions as frequently as possible, and by remembering to use questions to attract the attention of the quiet students in the class. Those students who sit obediently taking notes might actually be daydreaming or even asleep if no one requires them to come alive and think.

*Learning by
Discovery*

According to Jerome Bruner, discovery learning—finding things out for ourselves rather than being told everything by the teacher—is intrinsically motivating for students. Students learn because they enjoy it, not because they are graded. Like the motivational theorists discussed in this chapter, Bruner believes that ideal rewards in learning should be intrinsic to the learning situation itself rather than extrinsic or external. Proponents of discovery learning and intrinsic motivation point to a rather sizable literature concerned with the possible negative effects of extrinsic incentives (Maehr, 1976), as well as to the basic logic inherent in discovery learning (Strike, 1975). They point out that certain properties in materials that teachers present to students to help them learn, among them complexity, novelty, change, incongruity, and surprise, seem to produce intrinsic motivation. This kind of stimulus (for example, a jigsaw puzzle or something much more intricate) apparently causes a discrepancy or conflict between what is expected or known and what is presented. Discovery learning can involve activities characterized by minimal teacher guidance, intervention, direction, exploration, and supervision. These activities place maximum reliance on student experience, observation, intuition, hunches, and deductive reasoning.

Some writers have suggested that the student using discovery learning is motivated to solve the problem by a need to reduce tension. Others have stressed the enjoyment of discovery. However, whatever the mechanisms involved in this process, discovery does seem to be a pervasive source of motivation. Students generally do not find the extremely familiar and the known very stimulating, but new material interests them because it raises questions instead of resolving them. This type of material sets up a sort of symbolic conflict in their minds, most often resulting in what we could call intrinsically motivated behavior. Intrinsic motivation can be the source of a student's preoccupation with certain kinds of problems for hours on end, when no external reinforcements are provided.

Let us look at some suggestions made by Berlyne (1966) for ways in which intrinsic motivation can be effectively created in the classroom through "conceptual conflict." In natural science, for example, the teacher can use experiments to contradict student expectations. Many experiments have been devised that result in particularly surprising outcomes. Students not only enjoy demonstrations presented by their teachers (as, for example, dropping objects of different weights or sizes so that students can see them fall at the same rate of speed), but, just as important, tend to remember the explanations or principles behind them.

Teachers can also intentionally produce a state of doubt in their students by presenting them with a general proposition that may or may not be true. The students may try to resolve their doubts by investigating the evidence for and against the proposition. Once again, according to the advocates of intrinsic motivation, the student is primarily motivated by the problem itself, rather than by a desire to obtain an external reward of some kind.

Evaluation is one area where thinking skills can be developed. For instance, suppose a class has read a certain short story and the teacher wishes to evaluate its comprehension of it. Instead of asking the same mundane questions, he or she might try some of these:

> What were the choices available to the main character? If you had been that character, what would you have done?

> Suppose the last three pages of the story had been cut from your book? How would you have finished it?

> Suppose the setting in your story had been in your home or school? How would the action have been different?

> How do you think the main character's actions were changed in the future by the happenings in the story?

Write a brief letter to the author and tell him what kind of sequel you would like for him to write.

Well-thought-out answers to these questions not only demonstrate high comprehension of the story, but also provide an opportunity for creative thinking and writing by the students.

In a similar manner, the teacher can create a state of uncertainty in his or her students by presenting them with a problem that has a number of possible solutions. Berlyne (1966) referred to a geography lesson in which students had to "guess the locations of cities on a map showing only the natural features of the territory." In order to resolve their uncertainty, the students had to gradually eliminate possibilities until the correct solution became apparent.

Another technique a teacher can use to motivate students is to ask them to imagine themselves in a very difficult practical situation. For example, if a lesson concerns adaptation to the environment, have the students describe what they would do if they were lost in the middle of a deep forest with only enough water to get them through one day. (Of course, in order for them to visualize themselves in this sit-

Just sitting and listening to the teacher can become boring. Asking provocative questions is one way to revive interest and increase motivation.

Susanne Anderson, Photo Researchers, Inc.

uation and to come up with any solution, they would need sufficient information about the nature of the forest.)

The possibilities for classroom activities such as these are limitless. Every teacher should keep in mind that the main goal in designing such activities is to maximize intrinsically motivated behavior, behavior that is engaged in for its own sake rather than to obtain an external reward.

teaching creativity and self-actualization

Creativity, the ability to solve problems in innovative ways, is a stated goal of most classroom teachers and one characteristic of Maslow's self-actualized individual. Creative thinking plays an important role in acquiring knowledge, whether in fine arts, business, homemaking, engineering, or any other field of human endeavor. If a person is flexible and original in his or her thinking, he or she can approach new material from a wider number of perspectives and interpretations. Creativity, even when distinguished from intellectual ability, also seems to be an important factor in achieving vocational success (Bayard-de-Volo and Fiebert, 1977; Milgram and Milgram, 1976). Creativity, like the motivation to achieve, is a distinguishing feature of people who are at the top in their fields. For all these reasons, it is highly important to identify creative students and promote creative thinking in all classroom activites. Unfortunately, probably because of all their other duties, teachers often forget this.

E. Paul Torrance (1960, 1975) has developed a number of innovative methods to identify creativity in the classroom. One method involves presenting a child with a group of toys and allowing the child to play freely. The child is then asked to think of ideas for improving each toy so that it would be more fun to play with. The child's responses to this suggestion provide a basis for evaluating his or her inventiveness, flexibility, and constructiveness.

Another method is Torrance's "Ask-and-Guess Test." Here children are presented with a picture and asked to think of as many questions as they can that would help them to better understand the action or event presented in the picture. A child's ability to formulate hypotheses is then assessed by examining his or her responses to two questions posed by the investigators. First, the child is asked to make as many guesses as he or she can about the possible cause of the event shown in the picture, and, second, he or she is asked to guess the possible consequences of the event.

Promoting creativity is more difficult than finding it. Researchers have shown that, with young children at least, rigid authoritarian upbringing decreases creativity (Bayard-de-Volo and Fiebert, 1977). On the other hand, parental aid in developing imaginative play fosters creativity (Freyburg, 1975). By encouraging children's fantasies, parents and teachers can allow them to express themselves as individuals. The preschool years are particularly significant, because youngsters tend to show their imaginativeness in observable play; in later years, children are more apt to keep their imaginative activities to themselves and become more set in their ways. Freyberg offers these suggestions for encouraging imaginative ability: Enact stories in which adult and child add both sound effects and voice changes, stories to which a child can make up his or her own ending; synchronize activities and pretending (for example, suggest going on a boat voyage at bath time); give a child free-form items from which he or she can make "pretend" objects; and encourage a child's role playing. According to Freyberg make-believe play enhances creative thought and helps children to achieve an integration of their experiences.

Because make-believe play may not be appropriate for older children, Sillick (1977) suggests using students' daydreams as the basis for creative thought. As Sillick reports, daydreams are characterized by "freedom of the imagination, unbounded by the conscious, undominated by the familiar. Rarely are the people in the students' daydreams people they know or places they've been. Everything is new. Also since the students are reporting what they see rather than interpreting or summarizing it—the detail they use tends to be very visual. Small touches grace their descriptions that are absent in their conventional writing" (P. 34). Daydreams can be used as a classroom activity to teach fiction writing, but they can also serve to show teachers a side of their students' interior lives that they seldom get to see.

A good open classroom has proven particularly useful for fostering creative activity among school children. Where individual freedom

David Strickler, Monkmeyer

Children can be helped to enhance their creativity by spontaneous dramatizations with hand puppets.

and innovation are stressed in nonstructured situations, children develop the ability to express themselves, produce more ideas, and communicate them to others (McCormick, Sheehy, and Mitchel, 1978). In an open classroom, a student might draw up a poster or make a slogan to use to further a cause in which he or she is interested. A student might describe his or her version of Utopia, or perform any of a variety of activities that allow free personal expression. Because such activities are expressive rather than academic, and personal rather than competitive, they may elicit greater involvement and effort than purely intellectual tasks. With involvement and effort comes relaxation, and, with relaxation, laughter. Classroom situations in which laughter frequently appears tend to produce more creative responses in adolescents than traditional "straight-and-serious" lecture classes (Ziv, 1976).

Unfortunately, even though it is often stated as a major goal, creativity is not encouraged in most American schools. In fact, highly creative students often become alienated from their teachers and their peers. Why? One reason is that teachers are often threatened and intimidated by the numerous questions that the creative student asks. What if they don't know the answers? Will the students think they are stupid? Teachers who are not creative themselves are made extremely uncomfortable by original and novel questions for which they have no prepared answer. Teachers generally find the motivated student more desirable than the highly creative student. Creative students often provide interesting questions or answers, but, at the same time, they cause the teacher to change the prepared lesson plan regularly. If given the choice between a student who is both highly intelligent and highly creative and a student who is highly intelligent but not quite as creative, teachers (particularly those teaching in rigid, traditional classrooms) will more often than not choose to teach the less creative student.

A second factor contributing to the alienation of the creative student is that classroom tests often emphasize recall of facts and discourage creative thinking. Creative students are particularly penalized by standardized tests, for on these tests they are asked to provide one, and only one, appropriate answer. Original and novel answers are considered inappropriate and thus given less or no credit. (This problem is compounded by colleges and universities' use of standardized achievement tests to assess prospective students. Intelligent but less creative children receive reinforcers throughout their school career for their more limited, although highly successful, test-taking achievement.)

A final factor is the popular stereotype that all creative students are artists, writers, or musicians. As a result of this stereotype, many students who show creativity in the natural and social sciences are given little recognition. However, the art student often does not benefit from this attitude, either. On the contrary, although the artist may be lavished with attention, he or she may be expected to produce too much too quickly and many thus feel as stifled as the creative science student who is ignored.

Teachers need to become more aware of the contribution that their creative students can make. They should learn to recognize and reward creativity when it appears in their classrooms, even when it is easier to ignore it. When all is said and done, whether creativity will blossom or fade depends to a great extent on whether teachers, parents, and others decide to reward or punish it.

summary

1. Motivation theorists emphasize the effect that needs, drives, and goals have on behavior. A need is a requirement that must be met for optimal adjustment to the environment. Some needs are necessary for physical survival, some are cultural, and some are personal. Because they are essential to survival, physiological needs are called primary needs. Needs whose satisfaction has a strong positive effect on our adjustment but is not essential for survival are called secondary needs.

2. According to motivation theorists, individuals who have primary or secondary needs are compelled to act in ways that reduce or satisfy those needs. This compulsion to act is called a drive. The strength of a drive must be inferred from the strength and frequency of the individual's overt behavior. Until we learn how to satisfy our needs, drives are manifested in undifferentiated, undirected behavior. Because it takes time to learn the best ways to reduce our needs, motives usually develop gradually.

3. Motivation includes both energy and direction. Simply having a strong drive does not necessarily make learning more efficient. Children who feel a great deal of pressure often become impatient and do less than their best work. High levels of drive strength also interfere with complex tasks and problem solving.

4. Abraham Maslow's hierarchy of needs is one attempt to analyze the relationship between motivation and behavior. The needs in Maslow's hierarchy are arranged in a pyramid; lower-level needs must be satisfied before higher-level needs can become dominant. Starting at the base of the hierarchy, the needs Maslow defined are basic physiological needs, safety needs, love and belongingness needs, esteem needs, and self-actualization. These needs are not exclusive; behavior may often be multimotivated. In addition, some behavior may be expressive rather than motivated, incidental or accidental, or simply habitual.

5. Achievement motivation is defined as a persistent attempt to secure whatever the culture defines as success. According to David McClelland, concrete suggestions are more effective than abstract advice in stimulating achievement motivation. According to Atkinson, achievement motivation operates only when people feel responsible for the result of their efforts and know that their performance will be evaluated. He noted that the achievement of goals depends on the motive to avoid failure as well

as the motive to achieve success. Success-oriented people prefer moderately difficult tasks and are much more persistent in completing them. Individualized instruction and student goal-setting are two effective ways to raise achievement motivation.

6. Clear sex differences have been found in the expression of achievement motivation. Achievement motivation among males is heightened by competition, while females' achievement motivation is not. According to Matina Horner, women are raised to fear success because of the stress placed on being a desirable marriage partner and the traditional negative attitude toward women's achievements in nondomestic areas. As attitudes toward women change, women's own attitudes toward achievement can be expected to change as well.

7. Achievement motivation can be affected by people's levels of aspiration—their expectation of future success or failure. Generally successful achievers have moderately positive levels of aspiration and are able to set realistic goals. The influence that teachers' expectations can have on a student's level of aspiration has been called the self-fulfilling prophecy.

8. Certain motives, which are not primary or secondary motives, seem to be done for their own sake rather than for any direct gain. The manipulation drive was first described by Harry Harlow and his colleagues. D. E. Berlyne reported evidence for an exploratory drive that leads humans to seek out complex and novel stimuli. Identity, described by Erik Erikson, is a strong need among adolescents. Adolescents who become confused or overwhelmed in their search for identity may assume a negative identity by behaving in ways that are inconsistent with what they have been taught.

9. Anxiety is a generalized fear response that was rooted in a specific stimulus but has since spread to other stimuli. Teachers who use fear and anxiety to curb undesirable behavior run the risk of making their students anxious about school in general. Routine is a good antidote for anxiety, and constant feedback can reduce anxiety about tests. Teachers should also avoid criticizing their students, particularly those who are low achievers.

10. Group reinforcement can be a more effective motivator than competition, though competition is more common in American schools. The few redeeming qualities in competition are generally outweighed by its negative effects. The children who benefit most from competition are those who need it least.

11. The hierarchy of needs is the basis for Maslow's conception of humanistic education, which is based on teachers' acceptance of students as they are and teaching aimed at self-actualization rather than simple recall of facts. Discussion is a more humanistic technique than lecturing because there is more opportunity for student self-discovery. Carl Roger's approach to education is learner-centered rather than teacher-centered. Arthur Combs advises teachers to concentrate on helping their students to develop positive self-concepts. According to Combs, our most important need is self-adequacy.

12. Teachers can increase achievement motivation by creating a classroom in which students see themselves as originators of their own actions and controllers of their own activities. Assignments should be challenging, student participation must be assured, and students must be held responsible for what they do in the classroom.

13. Teachers can raise their students' levels of aspiration by structuring classroom activities to allow students to succeed on most tasks. Although success is an important factor in increasing aspiration as well as achievement, a certain amount of failure is necessary, too. In addition, teachers must realize the effect their expectations have on students' self-images and thus on their levels of aspiration and achievement. Teachers need to deal with students as unique individuals and search for ways to aid each student's self-discovery.

14. Reducing high levels of student anxiety is an extremely difficult task. Although teachers can easily avoid the use of punishment, relieving anxiety caused by other aspects of school life such as test taking is more difficult. Pass-fail grading systems reduce incentive along with anxiety. Telling students what they need to know in advance does increase motivation as well as reduce anxiety.

15. Jerome Bruner has emphasized the intrinsic motivation in discovery learning. New material that raises questions instead of answering them is also intrinsically motivating for students. Berlyne points out that the conceptual conflict inherent in unfamiliar material is an effective way to increase intrinsic motivation in the classroom. Teachers can encourage conceptual conflict by using demonstrations that contradict students' expectations, presenting students with general propositions that may or may not be true, avoiding commonplace and stale questions on tests and assignments, and creating problems that have a number of possible solutions.

16. Identifying and enhancing creativity in school children are important aspects of education. However, many teachers seem to find docile, less creative children easier to teach, while authoritarian parents find them easier to raise. Parents and teachers can promote creativity by allowing young children to express their fantasies and encouraging make-believe play. Older students' daydreams can also serve as a basis for creative thought. Teachers need to avoid being intimidated by highly creative students, realize that tests that emphasize recall of facts stifle creativity, and recognize creativity in fields other than music, art, and literature.

**for students
who want to read
further**

HOLT, J. *How Children Learn.* New York: Pitman, 1967. Holt's lively description of how children can grow to enjoy learning if given the appropriate opportunities includes many examples of intrinsic motivation in action.

MASLOW, A. H. *Toward a Psychology of Being* (2nd ed.). New York: Van Nostrand Reinhold, 1968. In this book, one of the best accounts of this famous theorist's position on motivation, Maslow discusses at length his concept of self-actualization.

SILLICK, J. Is anything happening under their hair? *American Educator,* Vol. 1 (1), 1977, pp. 32-34. This brief article written by a school teacher in upstate New York points to the use of daydreams in teaching creativity.

Sillick's interest in listening to young people and recognizing the importance of their interior lives can best be classified as humanistic teaching.

STACY, J., ET AL. (EDS.). *And Jill Came Tumbling After: Sexism in American Education.* New York: Dell, 1974. This is a compilation of 42 articles dealing with motivation and achievement, with particular emphasis on the effects of sex stereotyping on female achievement motivation in our schools.

TORRANCE, E. P. Motivation and creativity. In E. P. Torrance and W. F. White (Eds.), *Issues and Advances in Educational Psychology.* Itasca, Ill.: Peacock, 1975. Torrance's short article points out specific techniques teachers can use in the classroom to guide creativity and increase motivation.

WELCH, I., AND USHER, R. Humanistic education: The discovery of personal meaning. *Colorado Journal of Educational Research,* Vol. 17 (2), Winter 1978, pp. 17-22. Welch and Usher's article gives direct encouragement and advice to classroom teachers in a number of specific areas. It does not provide a statement of methods, but rather suggestions or guidelines to follow in dealing with such issues as how children solve problems, how they use their thinking time in school, how discussion is a major aid to learning, why teachers should listen more than they talk.

GUIDELINES FOR TEACHING

Katie Reynolds: An Example of Disciplined Motor Learning and Academic Success

Katie Reynolds is a 16-year-old currently enrolled in the twelfth grade of a large urban school. Katie lives with her middle-class, college-educated parents and three younger siblings in a large private home situated not far from the city campus of the university where her father works. Katie has an IQ of 153. She is the only member of the family who, until the tenth grade at least, hated school, never studied, and was consistently an underachiever.

When Katie was in the eighth grade, her parents arranged to have her placed in a special program for gifted children. Placement in the program was usually based on a combination of scores on IQ tests and school performance. In Katie's case, however, the counselor decided that her poor academic record was probably due to boredom. But Katie's performance in the gifted class did not improve, and, at the end of the ninth grade, she was asked to leave the program and return to regular classes.

Katie entered tenth grade with misgivings. Her parents were upset, and she felt that the classes were even more uninteresting than they had been before. In September, however, she met a group of students with strong interest in ice skating. They invited her to join a group that took weekly lessons with a professional skater at an indoor rink in the city. Katie was surprised to discover that she could excel at this sport and that she had far greater ability than her friends. She discovered that there was a skating club at school and began attending their meetings and classes. Katie's gym teacher suggested that, if she worked hard, she might even make the Olympic team one day. Katie took the suggestion in earnest, and her parents, delighted that, she was at last seriously involved in a major activity, hired a private teacher for her. She began a difficult regimen of exercise, beginning daily at 6 A.M. with a four-mile jog before school and ending with a three-hour practice every afternoon before beginning her evening studying.

The Reynoldses were delighted with Katie's sudden discipline. Katie never missed an exercise or a practice session. More than that, the discipline that she exerted in her skating carried over into her other activities. Her eleventh-grade teachers reported that she was more alert and interested in what was going on in her classes. She developed excellent study habits, and her grades improved dramatically. Katie still didn't find her courses particularly interesting, but she realized that she had to discipline herself properly if she expected to have enough time to work out at her skating. At the end of the eleventh grade, the school counselor suggested that Katie enroll in the special classes for gifted twelfth-grade students.

In the twelfth grade, Katie's grades were excellent. Her teachers reported that her A grades certainly offset the earlier poor grades, and they were certain that she would be able to enter a good college. Katie, disciplined to increase her motor skills, had learned to think realistically about academic skills and future life planning.

Up to this point, we have been talking mainly about the different ways that students develop and learn and about how those differences affect the way teachers teach. While we have stressed the need to adapt teaching methods to the individual student, there are several general rules to effective teaching that apply to all students. In this chapter, we talk about these general rules and see how they apply to the teaching of the specific skills on which all school learning is based.

Katie's story shows how achievement in one area can be generalized to cover others. But it also shows the importance of certain basic skills for overall academic performance. Perceptual skills like reading, motor skills like ice skating, cognitive skills like fluency in verbal and written language, and good problem-solving skills are the basic building blocks of competence in all academic subjects. Probably the most important of these—as well as the one most often neglected by teachers—is the development of attitudes that enhance classroom learning. None of Katie's success would have been possible without her change in attitute toward herself and her schoolwork.

the importance of planning

Planning is an important aspect of effective teaching as well as effective learning. If a lesson is well planned, students will learn it faster and remember it longer. A well-planned unit will be much more meaningful to students than one that whimsically skips from here to there and back again. A well-planned course will give students a better understanding of the subject and a better basis for later learning. A well-planned arrangement of courses results in an effective program of instruction in which all the component parts are meaningful and organized.

Planning helps the teacher in more subtle ways as well. One positive side effect of good planning is self-confidence. A teacher who comes into class with a well-thought-out plan projects self-confidence. Students are very sensitive to their teachers' emotions, particularly during the first days of a school year, and they are much more apt to respect teachers who show clearly that they know what they are doing.

New teachers often worry about being able to control their classes. Planning helps here, too. Teachers who plan their lessons well have less trouble with their classes because a good plan minimizes tha amount of "dead time" when breaks in the flow of teaching give students time to act up. Keeping the students' attention on what they are learning is the first step toward keeping control.

general aids to effective teaching

An effective plan is built on clearly stated goals. Every program of instruction has one or more learning objectives even though these objectives are not always explicitly stated. In fact, the majority of teachers probably do not outline their objectives at all. But recently, a growing number of teachers are realizing that outlining learning objectives has important effects on teaching and learning. The various ways in which instructional planning can help teachers and students was summarized by Gagné and Briggs (1974).

Reasons for Using Learning Objectives

One important reason for using learning objectives that are specified in behavioral terms is simply that teachers need to know the nature of the behavior they are hoping ultimately to establish; this is called the **terminal behavior.** Terminal behavior answers such questions as "What should the student enrolled in a particular class be able to do after leaving the class that he or she could not do previously?" "What should the student be able to do as a result of a particular unit or lesson covered in the class that he or she might not have been able to do previously?" Knowing the answers—clearly defining the terminal behavior—makes it easier to plan lessons sensibly and effectively.

Most instruction should be capable of modifying several aspects of behavior simultaneously. This fact makes the behavioral specification of learning objectives all the more necessary. It is important to distinguish between the different classes of behavior changes being sought, because different techniques of instruction probably will be necessary to successfully produce learning in all of these areas.

Another important reason for specifying learning objectives is that often they are the only means of properly evaluating the effectiveness of what the teacher is doing in the classroom. If the teacher and students don't know the goals of the lesson, a test score by itself tells them little about whether the instruction was effective. Moreover, clear learning objectives help distinguish between teacher behaviors that lead to increased learning and those that are irrelevant or counterproductive.

Specifying learning objectives in behavioral terms make the students and the teacher aware of the purpose of the instruction and of what should be derived from it (Gagné, 1965a). According to motivation theorists, this information heightens the students' motivation and gives them more incentive to actively participate in the learning process. It also provides important feedback, since it tells the students whether or not they are making progress and learning, understanding, and responding appropriately.

In order for a learning objective to be valuable, it must have two characteristics: clarity and importance (Vargas, 1972). The clarity can be achieved by stating objectives in terms of observable behaviors. But an objective, no matter how well stated, is not worthwhile unless it also makes some important contribution to the overall goals of education

Therefore, the task of specifying learning objectives should not be approached as if each learning experience demanded some unique form of behavior not found in any other learning experience. Such an approach tends to lead to the learning of petty details and trivia. A much more effective approach is to determine the general classes or categories of behavior that are desired in a given situation or, in other words, to plan on the basis of a **taxonomy of objectives** (Merrill, 1971b, 1972).

A taxonomy of learning objectives tells the teacher at a glance the fullest possible range of objectives that are available in a learning situation. Obviously, it is neither feasible nor appropriate to try to achieve all of them for every topic and for each lesson. But the teacher does have a helpful reminder of the possibilities and can use the taxonomy systematically to check off the kinds of objectives that would be most appropriate and important to emphasize for any given topic.

Bloom's Taxonomy of Objectives for Cognitive Learning

Benjamin Bloom and his associates (Bloom, Englehart, Furst, and Krathwohl, 1956) have developed a taxonomy of learning objectives useful to the classroom teacher. The first part of the taxonomy applies to cognition, or the ability to think and understand, and includes six main categories: knowledge, comprehension, application, analysis, synthesis, and evaluation. The first four of these categories of objectives apply to skills involving understanding and concept formation; the last two apply to skills involving creativity. The various classes of behavior are arranged in hierarchical order from simple to complex and from concrete to abstract. An outline of Bloom's taxonomy of cognitive learning objectives follows.*

*Adapted from pp. 201-207, *Taxonomy of Educational Objectives: The Classification of Educational Goals, Handbook I: Cognitive Domain*, edited by Benjamin S. Bloom et al. Copyright © 1965 by Longman, Inc. Reprinted by permission of Longman, Inc., New York.

1. **Knowledge** includes what is usually referred to as rote memory. The student reproduces, with little or no change, the material presented during the instruction phase. Some common examples include memorizing definitions, reciting a poem, and stating specific facts and rules. Knowledge should not be confused with comprehension, since it is quite possible to learn and repeat something by rote, without having any idea of its meaning.

2. **Comprehension** means being able to restate or identify restatements of written or pictorial information in a form that is *not* an exact replica of the original. Examples include such activities as paraphrasing, summarizing, answering direct questions based on material in a paragraph, and translating from one language to another. Comprehension can still reflect a very low level of understanding, since it does not require the ability to grasp the full implications of the material presented or the ability to relate old material to new material.

3. **Application** means being able to solve problems that are similar in principle or method but different in form from ones seen previously. Thus, for example, a student might be asked to apply the rules of English grammar to the construction of sentences with nonsense words. In order for a learning objective to qualify as an application objective, there must be some application of principles or conceptual relations. If all that is involved is the application of simple concepts, the task, strictly speaking, is comprehension, not application.

4. **Analysis** involves being able to break down an entity into its component parts. Examples include such activities as interpreting a poem by stanza and comparing one food with another in terms of their component nutrients. As in the application objective, the examples given by the student (on a test, for instance) should not be identical to those used teaching. Otherwise the learning task is reduced to mere rote memory, and the skill being displayed is knowledge rather than analysis.

5. **Synthesis** means being able to combine knowledge, skills, ideas, and experiences to create a new and original product. Examples include

Laboratory experiments provide students with opportunities for application of principles, analysis, synthesis, and evaluation skills.

Lynn McLaren, Rapho/Photo Researchers, Inc.

such diverse activities as writing an essay, drawing a picture to depict the four seasons of the year, constructing an exhibit for the school science fair, and designing a dress. Unlike most instances of the preceding learning objectives, synthesis does not involve a correct or best possible solution. Any product that meets acceptable standards of workmanship in combination with the student's expression of creativity meets this objective.

6. **Evaluation** involves the ability to judge whether or not a person's work meets the specified criterion, or the ability to compare it against someone else's work. What distinguishes this activity from both comprehension and application is that expression of an individual viewpoint is required. As with synthesis, there is not any one "right answer," but the person involved in evaluation should be able to give some rationale as to why he or she thinks as he or she does. One example of evaluation is giving a critical opinion of a book, along with one's reasons for holding such an opinion. Another example is comparing the advantages and disadvantages and the overall serviceability of two different learning theories (stimulus-response behaviorism versus the Gestalt approach, for instance)—again with the ability to state the underlying reasons for one's opinion.

Classifying the objectives for a given area of instruction according to these different levels lets the teacher see what kinds of learning

---

Matching Learning Objectives
to Bloom's Taxonomy:
An Exercise For Prospective Teachers

The following are six behaviorally stated learning objectives taken from Vargas (1972, pp. 119,121,123,130). Try to match each of them with one of the levels in Bloom's taxonomy. Then check your answers.

1. Tell in one sentence the meaning of the poem "The Oak Tree."
2. Design and construct a poster to communicate at least two of your views on school rules concerning dress.
3. Criticize a research study on the appropriateness of statistical methods for the problem selected, using the text as a reference.
4. Spell correctly at least 80 percent of the words in the sixth-grade speller.
5. Pronounce unfamiliar words or nonsense syllables that follow the silent "e" rule.
6. Trace the main theme and secondary theme of a play such as one by Shakespeare, citing the characters involved, the conflicts and allegiances, and the ways in which the themes are developed.

Answers
1. Comprehension
2. Synthesis
3. Evaluation
4. Knowledge
5. Application
6. Analysis

outcomes are likely to result from the instruction as planned and whether or not these are all the outcomes that are desired. Teachers may find, for example, that their original lesson plan places very heavy emphasis on the acquisition of knowledge and the technique of analysis, and very little on other important learning outcomes such as application and synthesis. In such instances, the teacher might want to modify the plan somewhat to incorporate a wider range of objectives.

It is particularly easy to think of knowledge objectives and, consequently, to design and teach a unit or even an entire course requiring little more than the rote memorization of facts (Vargas, 1972). But these objectives alone rarely capture all that is useful and important about a subject. Therefore, whenever possible, objectives should be carefully designed so as to incorporate all the relevant skills.

For example, in teaching the concept of hypothesis testing as related to the scientific method, confining the class to simple memorization of the terms and steps in the process is not a sensible way to teach higher-level objectives. Students can be encouraged to describe the procedure in their own words and to give examples of both positive and negative instances. Afterward, each of them can be asked to design an original experiment, using what they have learned in a creative and innovative way. The class as a whole can then discuss these experiments and take turns evaluating each other's work.

*Planning
Objectives for
Other Types of
Learning*

Bloom's taxonomy of learning objectives is particularly useful in describing the cognitive skills involved in concept learning and problem solving. The other sorts of classroom skills discussed in this chapter can also be defined by learning objectives. Desired perceptual and motor skill outcomes, for example, can be defined with relatively little effort in behavioral terms. Language communication skills can also be behaviorally defined. Defining learning objectives for attitude learning, at first glance, however, is not so clear.

Attitude learning, in marked contrast to cognitive learning, tends to be greatly neglected by teachers or, at least, is not as openly discussed. Ideally, cognitive and attitude learning should be complementary, but, in practice, political and social forces dictate that our school be very cautious about the role they should play in disseminating attitudes. Many teachers feel that this position is self-defeating. Unless knowledge is related to the learner's attitude toward everything he or she does, there is little likelihood that it will have a long-term effect on behavior. According to these teachers, in addition to increasing knowledge and other cognitive skills, education also should foster positive attitudes toward learning, both in and out of the classroom. Therefore, there are similar reasons for planning instruction on the basis of a taxonomy of learning objectives for attitude learning as well as for cognitive skills. The teacher can help the student to learn positive attitudes toward school by designing classroom activities that are realistic in terms of their level of difficulty and enjoyable for the learner. In other words, as both behavioral and motivation theorists remind us, students tend to have positive attitudes toward courses and subjects that are at the appropriate level for them and that provide rewarding experiences instead of frustrating ones.

However, not all educators agree that it is important or even appropriate to define learning objectives in behavioral terms. Critics of behavioral learning objectives feel that teachers should not limit their concern to behavior changes that might occur by the end of the school year; they should also plan for permanent changes that might be expected at some unspecified time in the future. For example, a good teacher might prepare an excellent lesson on ecology that the students remember years later and make use of when they plan gardens or develop solar heating systems for their new homes (see, for example, DeCecco and Crawford, 1974; Ebel, 1963, 1970).

Gagné (1965b) is not opposed to formulating hypotheses about behavior in the distant future, if that is the only desired goal. He does point out, however, that, for most students, indication of more immediate learning is usually a requirement for demonstrable change in behavior in the future. For this reason, he would probably not suggest designing a lesson on ecology on the basis of what the students will be doing some twenty years hence. Instead, the lesson should be designed so that students can outline the criteria for establishing good gardens or good solar heating units now. Students will be more apt to remember a lesson later when they have a chance to put the learning to work if that lesson teaches them something *now*.

Humanistic critics say that there appears to be something mechanistic, dehumanizing, and dictatorial about the learning objectives approach. Using learning objectives puts the teacher, rather than the student, in control of the kinds of learning that take place in school. The taxonomists answer that because teachers have such an important role in the socialization process, they have a responsibility to transmit the ideals and values of the larger society, as well as the knowledge and abilities students will need as responsible adults. In addition, teaching is not necessarily mechanical simply because objectives are planned—many different techniques of teaching and testing exist.

Another point against stating learning objectives in behavioral terms is based on the feeling that, because trivial aspects of behavior are easier to translate into learning objectives, they will receive more attention than the really important outcomes of education. This argument holds some weight, particularly when the task of preparing objectives is sloppily or hastily done. It is not easy to write a set of good and useful learning objectives, and many teachers do indeed specify outcomes that are petty and insignificant. According to the taxonomists, however, well-written, explicitly stated objectives actually make the discovery of important instructional outcomes easier. Because they are so explicit, the teacher can study them carefully and can identify and eliminate any objective that seems irrelevant or unimportant.

A related argument states that expecting teachers to specify learning objectives in terms of measurable behaviors is unrealistic. Very few teachers actually do this, and most of those that do set unrealistic objectives, considering the specific learning situation. This is a serious problem because researchers have shown that unachievable objectives do lead to lower performance (Rothkopf and Koether, 1978). The reply of the advocates of objectives is simple.

> There is obviously a difference between identifying the status quo and applauding it. Most of us would readily concede that few teachers specify their instructional aims in terms of measurable learned behaviors; *but they ought to*. What we have to do is to mount a widespread campaign to modify this aspect of teacher behavior. . . . The way teaching really is at the moment just isn't good enough. (Popham, 1968, p. 517)

What Teachers Can Do to Prepare Good Learning Objectives

Most teachers plan their instruction by dividing the entire course into several major topics that are in turn divided into subtopics and lessons (Gagné, 1974). The rules that apply to planning the objectives of a course are similar to those involved in preparing an outline for a story. The broader, more inclusive areas are broken down into subdivisions, and all divisions are organized into a pattern that has some sort of internal logic such as beginning, middle, and end.

Most courses, topics, and even subtopics are designed with more than one learning outcome in mind. To assure that all of the learning outcomes are accomplished, careful planning is necessary at the beginning. Otherwise, the instruction may overemphasize one learning outcome at the expense of another.

Gagné's prerequisite skills for optimal learning An important part of this planning should be a consideration of prerequisites (Gagné, 1965b, 1974; Tyler, 1964). It is important that the students have all the learning they need to be able to understand new instruction. According to Robert Gagné (1970), learning occurs under these eight conditions (arranged in order of increasing complexity).

1. *Signal learning.* Learning caused by simple connections, as in classical conditioning.
2. *Stimulus-response learning.* Learning caused by associations between stimuli and responses, as in operant conditioning.
3. *Chaining.* Learning involving a sequence of responses, each associated one with the other in a specified order, as in learning to count from one to ten.

4. *Verbal association learning*. Learning in which new words are first associated with objects, and then with old words as language develops.
5. *Discrimination learning*. Learning in which differences between stimuli are the cues for the correct response.
6. *Concept learning.*Learning in which objects or events are responded to as a class, as in the concept "gas."
7. *Rule learning*. Learning a chain of concepts in such a way that they may be applied to a variety of new situations.
8. *Problem solving*. Learning in which rules are applied to brand new situations.

More advanced forms of learning occur only after students have acquired more simple forms. For example, students must master many different types of verbal associations before they can learn discrimination or conceptual tasks. The learning of verbal associations is based in turn on basic stimulus-response learning. Students are more likely to understand new concepts if they are first acquainted with a variety of verbal associations. This is why it's difficult for students who are not familiar with the English language to learn new concepts in school. It also explains why it is difficult for some students to learn to read; if they have not developed meaningful verbal associations, many words that appear on the pages of their readers are meaningless to them. Students are more likely to understand rule learning if they previously grasped the appropriate concepts. Once they understand rules, it is much more simple for them to solve new and advanced problems.

Gagné uses these eight conditions of learning as the basis for curriculum design. He advises teachers to map plans for teaching that begin with the simplest learning conditions and continue to more advanced forms. When a student can't solve a particular problem, the teacher should check back to see whether the student has achieved the more simple conditions; if not, the teacher should begin at a lower level. Only then will the student and teacher achieve their goals.

Mager's characteristics of well-stated learning objectives Many teachers who are unskilled in the design of learning objectives make them too vague. The following example of an objective for a high school geometry course is typical: The purpose of instruction is to have the students know the basic principles of Euclidean geometry. That probably is the main goal of the course, but as written, this objective gives us no idea how a given teacher is supposed to actually achieve that goal. Nor does the statement communicate what the student will actually learn. Learning objectives expressed in behavioral terms, on the other hand, tell the teacher exactly what observable skills a student should have as a result of instruction.

According to Mager (1962), a well-stated learning objective has the following three characteristics:

1. It describes in behavioral terms what the student will be able to do when instruction has been completed.
2. It describes the conditions or circumstances under which the learned behavior will occur.
3. It describes the extent to which the specified behavior can be expected; in other words, it suggests an acceptable criterion level for performance.

Learning objectives are sometimes confused with classroom activities because both are often described in similar behavioral terms. But there is an important distinction between them: Learning objectives are considered the ends of instruction; classroom activities are the means that are used to achieve those ends. For this reason, objectives should not be tied to any one reference book or exercise. They should be stated in terms that permit the use of a variety of procedures, although a given text or exercise might be used as an example to clarify the kinds of behavior the objective entails. Of the following four statements, only the last one meets all Mager's criteria for learning objectives.

1. Read the play *Othello* and pay special attention to Shakespeare's use of character. (This is an activity, not an objective.)
2. Understand the concept of "tragic hero" as used by Shakespeare. (This could be an objective of learning, but it is not expressed in behavioral terms.)
3. Be able to explain the reasons for Othello's downfall. (This objective is expressed in behavioral terms, but it is specifically tied to only one task.)
4. Demonstrate an understanding of the Shakespearean concept of "tragic hero" by describing, in essay form, three different factors that lead to the downfall of a figure such as Othello.

The following is another example of an explicitly stated learning objective. It was suggested by Esbensen (1967) for an area of instruction much simpler than a Shakespearean play. It is included here to demonstrate the point that explicitly stated learning objectives can be written for both complex and simple tasks.

Shown the letters of the alphabet in random order (in both upper and lower case form), the student is able to say the name of each letter with 100 percent accuracy. (Esbensen, 1967, p. 247)

This objective is clear and precise and is stated in behavioral terms. We know exactly what the student should be able to do as a result of instruction, under what conditions, and according to what criterion of performance. We know the technique of measurement the teacher is planning to use to determine if the desired learning has taken place. At the same time, the specified behavior is not limited to one question exclusively.

Studying test items is one technique that might help a teacher to prepare meaningful and appropriate learning objectives. For example, the following arithmetic items all seem to be testing the same kind of skill:

$$43 \qquad 55 \qquad 72$$
$$+27 \qquad +65 \qquad +19$$

The skill they are testing is the ability to add a two-digit number by means of the carrying principle. This is the learning objective for which the test items were designed.

Studying test items will also help a teacher to identify the format in which the class should be able to apply their learning. Choosing from a set of alternatives on a multiple-choice test, for example, is easier than the less-structured free recall, but it does not measure the same ability. Many students prefer multiple-choice tests, but, in real life, they will more likely be responsible for recall than for recognition of learned material.

Objectives should contribute to the broad goals of both teacher and student, and no important objectives should be omitted. The use of a taxonomy of learning objectives, such as the one by Bloom, should make this task easier by indicating the kinds of objectives that are being emphasized, as compared to the kinds that are not being emphasized. Then, if a given taxonomic category that seems important is underrepresented, the set of objectives and consequent activities can be revised.

Competency-based Instruction

Once teachers have developed learning objectives, they may decide to use them for **competency-based instruction,** in which teachers supply each student with a list of objectives to be met through the learning process, and then provide a series of alternative approaches that students may use to meet these objectives. Competency-based instruction reduces classroom anxiety for students who are afraid of not knowing what the teacher wants. Elaborate programs may be built using this method of instruction. For example, in many cases teachers and students together may select the objectives for the course. We call these individualized **student-teacher contracts.** Many teachers find that developing these contracts is itself a major learning experience. The contracts specify in detail what behaviors will be rewarded and how. Students must decide what is important for them to do and what is not important.

Frieder (1970) has suggested several guidelines for making the most effective use of these student-teacher contracts: (1) The contract should be very specific and clear. The students must always know exactly what and how much they must do in order to receive a specified reward. (2) The contract must be fair. That is, the reward itself must be appropriate to the action required to obtain it. The exact details of what is fair must, of course, be negotiated between the student and teacher. (3) The contract should always be stated in positive terms, so that students are made aware of what they can do in order to get a reward, rather than what will happen if they don't live up to the contract. In other words, the contract should be based exclusively on positive reinforcement. Finally, teachers should agree only to those terms that they can realistically and systematically fulfill. Teachers should consider this point very carefully, for if they break the contract, the trust that has been established with the student will be seriously damaged. For competency-based instruction to work, students should be able to select from a variety of alternative instructional approaches that have been individualized for students of different backgrounds. Evaluation of final performance must depend on mastery of the initial objectives.

Task Analysis

Cognitive psychologists have recently emphasized that the use of learning objectives, by themselves, does not explain the total learning process and therefore cannot explain to the teacher what specific steps students should go through to learn specific skills (see, for example, Scandura (1977). Cognitive psychologists stress the necessity of defining the specific process through which the student must go in order to learn. They call this "task structure." For instruction to be effective, analysis of the task of learning is as necessary as a description of the desired outcome.

Scandura describes his approach as a "structural/process/systems approach to instructional science" and points out that the teaching-learning process cannot be properly understood unless it is treated as a whole. It is not adequate, according to Scandura, "to develop theories that deal with just one aspect of teaching or learning (e. g. content analysis, task analysis, cognitive processing, criterion-referencing testing) without taking into account overall relationships" (Scandura, 1977, p. 33). Task analysis is a major part of the teaching-learning process.

Because what a student can learn depends on what he or she already knows, teachers cannot optimize skill learning in the classroom unless they have an idea of what the student's current level of ability is. This can be determined by *pretesting:* the administration of criterion-referenced tests at the beginning, rather than at the end of a learning situation. Scores on such tests should be interpreted diagnostically—as showing strengths and weaknesses, rather than passing or failing.

Once they know what their students do and do not know, teachers need to determine the steps through which these students must go to reach the desired outcome. This is not a simple task; in many problem-solving situations, even researchers do not know exactly what takes place when children learn. That's why there are so many different theories of learning. However, experience can help teachers to correctly predict which steps are useful and which are useless or detrimental. It is important to note that all students do not necessarily go through the same steps in solving any particular problem. Some students can solve problems using shortcut methods that other students appear unable to use. Some students clearly are able to skip over some prerequisite skills, never learn them at all, and still solve complex problems with no trouble, while others must learn each and every prerequisite the teacher has listed (Resnick, 1972).

According to cognitive psychologists, this type of individual difference in the ability to learn to solve new types of problems might be related to the individual student's past experience in learning rules for problem-solving. The more experience a teacher gives students in discovering new rules, as happens when teachers use the discovery method of teaching, the more ability they develop later to generate new rules in new learning situations (Scandura, 1977).

Thus, in addition to outlining the objectives of any learning situation, teachers need to consider the specific procedures their students should go through in developing the desired skill. To do this in the most effective manner possible, teachers need to plan for students' individual differences in capability to learn in each of the specific situations in which they will be working in the classroom.

Helping Students to Learn Specific Classroom Skills

Teachers agree that all students must learn a series of basic skills before they can succeed at higher-level school learning. For example, perceptual and language skills are both basic to the development and mastery of reading and writing skills, and these, in turn, are necessary to all later learning.

At first glance, motor skills appear to receive insufficient attention in our schools. This is unfortunate because they are also critical to learning, particularly at early grade levels, but in the upper grades as

Michael Philip Manheim, Photo Researchers, Inc.

The reading, writing, and language skills learned in the early grades are essential to success at the higher levels of schooling.

well. Learning how to print the alphabet, which is a motor skill, is essential if children are to profit from further education. Developing the discipline to learn motor skills can also aid in learning of other subjects, as the case of Katie Reynolds demonstrates. In addition, a child's social adjustment often depends on how well he or she performs motor tasks.

Conceptual learning and problem-solving are obviously essential if students are to learn most of the subjects required of the K-12 curriculum. These skills can be enhanced or retarded, depending on the type of teaching method used.

The last type of skill learning that is discussed here is attitude learning. The development of socially desirable attitudes—such as respect for oneself and for others, responsibility and cooperativeness, and a positive attitude toward learning and education—is one of the principal, though controversial, functions of public schools today.

Helping Students to Learn Perceptual Skills

The teaching of perceptual skills is the core of the elementary school curriculum. Students who fail to learn such skills in elementary school cannot do well at the middle or high school level. Perceptual processes are important in many different kinds of learning situations, ranging from simple sensory discrimination tasks to complex acts with many component parts such as reading. In fact, the widespread problem of learning disabilities in reading and other academic areas has often been attributed to defects in visual and auditory perception (Glaser and Resnick, 1972).

Gibson's approach to perceptual learning   E. J. Gibson maintains that successful teachers help students to increase their perceptual skills by extracting and identifying the unchanging properties of their environment. For example, because each musical instrument has unique tonal properties, a person with a trained ear can differentiate among them when an orchestra plays a symphony. The properties remain constant, and the trained individual can identify each instrument under any circumstances. The objects we use in daily life are often more complex, and teachers must help students to differentiate among their distinctive features on the basis of combinations of properties. For example, when a student picks up a book to read, he or she extracts many different and complex properties: Is it a novel or a textbook? Is it written in English or a foreign language? Does it contain material that can be learned by quick skimming, or does it require slow and intensive study? All these discriminative properties can be learned, and, therefore, all of them can be taught.

Developmental differences between students   In the course of learning and development, many perceptions become less generalized and more precise as a person learns to discriminate the subtle differences among stimuli. This might explain why high school students are less variable in their perceptual judgments and have shorter reaction times in discrimination tasks than elementary school students do. In other instances, though, our perceptions may be more generalized as we detect additional structural relationships and commonalities. For example, after hearing an unfamiliar symphony, you might recognize by its many similar qualities to other works that it was composed by Mozart.

Considerable evidence suggests that the effectiveness with which students learn to make perceptual discriminations is related to age and intelligence (see, for example, Honkavaara, 1958; House, 1966; Spitz, 1964). In addition, it has been found that cognitive style—in particular, field dependence and field independence—is directly related to perceptual ability. Field-independent school-age children, for example, were found to perform more effectively on both perceptual and mathematics tasks (Satterly, 1976).

What teachers can do about developmental differences Piaget's notion of matching the task to the perceptual ability of the child is clearly important in compensating for individual differences in perceptual ability. Teachers know that perceptual skills can best be taught to younger students by providing them with material less complex than they would use with older students, since too much information will confuse young children's processes of selection. Actually, children begin to appreciate stimulus material that has a few essential details at very early ages. For example, the famous educator Maria Montessori was able to teach children well under the age of 6 the perceptual skills necessary in learning to read by using simple cut-out letters of interesting textures that the children could touch and feel as well as examine visually. The early lessons involved simple discriminations among letters. Later lessons involved associating each letter with a particular sound and, eventually, building individual sounds into words.

Another example of children's early appreciation of stimulus material with few essential details is their fondness for cartoons and comic books. Many teachers have found that cartoons and comic books are useful teaching devices for children of all ages. In addition, slow learners and learners who have not previously mastered perceptual skills enjoy using these materials for basic learning.

Reading: An example of an important perceptual skill The importance of learning to read and the difficulties encountered by anyone who can't, cannot be overestimated. The inability of students to read satisfactorily is one of the major educational problems of our time. In fact, it is cited as the single most common cause for dropping out of school before graduation (J. Gibson, 1972). The essential role of perceptual skills in learning to read thus deserves the special attention of any teacher.

Young children need materials to work with that match their level of perceptual ability.

Suzanne Szasz, Photo Researchers, Inc.

Many teachers believe that trying to teach children to read is pointless until they have demonstrated by their performance that they have reached an appropriate level of maturity. Children who fail initial reading-readiness tests are generally unable to keep up, but simply waiting for them to "mature" before giving them any reading instruction at all may be just as detrimental as teaching them before they are ready. Time alone cannot turn a nonreader into a reader if a sufficient amount of environmental stimulation and experience is lacking.

E. J. Gibson (1965, 1968) has analyzed the task of learning to read in terms of a specific hierarchy involving four stages:

1. Learning to speak.
2. Learning to discriminate printed letters.
3. Learning to decode letters to sound (a very difficult process in the English language, since there is no one-to-one spelling-sound correspondence).
4. Learning to perceive higher-order units (which is what distinguishes good readers from poor readers).

Gibson's research on discrimination in learning to read (stage 2) has been concerned largely with identifying the distinctive features (horizontal lines, vertical lines, and so on) of each of the 26 letters. According to Gibson, letters vary in the degree to which their identifying features are the same as or different from other letters. Using a list of 12 possible distinguishing features, she constructed a chart, showing for each letter in the alphabet which features are present and which are absent. Gibson then asked a sample of children to "read" the chart. She found that the number of features two or more letters shared was directly related to the number of errors caused by confusion (Gibson, 1965, 1968). These data suggest that perceptual learning is a major factor in being able to discriminate one printed letter from another, and, ultimately, in learning to read.

Gibson, Pick, Osser, and Hammond (1962) investigated the perceptual processes used by older students learning to convert letters to sounds. Nonsense words were projected one at a time on a screen to a group of college students, who were directed to write down each word as it appeared. Half of the words were pronounceable, having a high spelling-to-sound correlation (for instance, "glurk"), and the other half were unpronounceable, having a low spelling-to-sound correlation (for example, "krlg"). As expected, the pronounceable words were correctly perceived much more often than the unpronounceable words. Good readers especially perceived the pseudo-words that fit spelling-syntactical rules better than those pseudo-words that did not.

According to E. J. Gibson (1965), pointing out word structure generalizations using spelling-syntactical rules can be a help to students in learning new words. One teacher of a remedial reading class used this method by encouraging her students to create new "words" with a variety of different vowel-consonant patterns. With these new "words," they created nonsense sentences, eventually working out pleasant-sounding rhymes. The children enjoyed this immensely. Next they started rhyming real words with their creations. In addition to improving their word-attack skills, this technique made learning fun.

One characteristic that distinguishes good readers from poor readers at any age is the ability to learn higher-order units. Evidence shows that good readers do not read each letter; they read the whole word at once. Moreover, when words are arranged in a sentence or paragraph, good readers don't read just one word at a time but a group of words (E. J. Gibson, 1968).

What teachers can do to help children to learn to read What implications do these findings have for teaching reading? The method used to teach reading has a direct relationship to reading achievement (see, for example, Kirby and Das, 1978). There are two basic methods to teach reading: a **code emphasis** or phonic emphasis, in which children learn to put sounds together to make words; and a **meaning emphasis** in which students are taught to look at a word or part of a word as a whole unit and attach meaning to it. Although these two methods are closely related in practice, some beginning readers respond better to one method or the other. Students of average intelligence whose backgrounds do not provide experience in perceptual learning probably benefit most from a code (phonic) emphasis in early reading learning (Chall, 1967). Older students who speak languages or dialects different from standard English may also benefit from special practice in discriminating sounds and letters of the English alphabet when, at the same time, they are given special language and pronunciation learning. Using a code (phonic) emphasis, students can be taught to "sound out" what they are reading.

Without related skills in perception and reading comprehension, students are not able to learn other subjects. Attention to both coding and meaning, with an understanding of the perceptual processes involved, is ultimately important for optimal learning for all students.

Helping Students to Learn Motor Skills

The importance of motor skills development to all school learning is often underestimated by American school teachers. In some foreign countries, physical culture is a major component of every school curriculum, not just an additional course. Motor learning covers much more than the skills commonly taught as part of a physical education program. A motor skill is anything we do with our bodies. Motor activities enter into every sphere of our lives—work, play, eating, washing, dressing, and performing household chores. Motor skills open up new doors to hobbies and leisure-time pursuits. For people engaged in mechanical and construction trades, motor skills are, of course, of

Children whose motor skills enable them to perform self-help tasks successfully gain in self-confidence and peer acceptance.

prime importance; the exacting and often hazardous nature of their work demands that these skills be highly developed. Nurses, doctors, teachers, office workers, and salespeople also engage in activities that call for some display of motor ability.

Without the development of motor skills, children would never be able to walk, run, jump, hop, or skip. Children with poor motor skills often have low social status in the eyes of their peers. Even the basic activities of reading, writing, and speaking would be impossible because these also depend on motor skills.

Katie Reynolds, when she developed high ability in ice skating, increased her academic grades as well. The fact that Katie Reynolds's academic skills increased with her skill at ice skating isn't surprising. Researchers have found that students taught gross motor skills develop greater self-assurance and improved self-concepts (Platzer, 1976). Scales have been developed to help teachers assess perceptual-motor competencies of their students in order to give them broad descriptions of what to expect in the classroom (Aliberto, 1975). But because educators usually think of these more advanced activities in terms of their association with verbal and perceptual skills, we tend to overlook the important motor component that is involved as well.

A taxonomy of motor skills based on subject matter Because motor learning encompasses such a variety of behaviors, Merrill (1972) found it useful to construct a **motor skills taxonomy** or classification scheme based on subject matter taught in school. The five different areas of motor skills he identified include physical education, communication, fine arts, language, and vocational skills. Each of these five categories is in turn broken down into smaller categories. The five major categories of motor skills and their subdivisions are listed in Figure 7–1.

All five of these categories are taught in American schools. For the vast majority of students, *physical education* is a required part of the curriculum from elementary school through college. The skills taught by physical education teachers include swimming, soccer, tennis, volleyball, and calisthenics.

Other teachers contribute to the development of *communication* and *language* skills. In junior high and high school, special courses are offered in typing and shorthand. Speech is also an important part of the curriculum and all students know the experience of participating in class discussions and presenting oral reports. In addition, schools provide extensive instruction in foreign languages, and an important part of any good foreign language course is practice in conversation. From elementary school on, children are taught to express themselves through gestures and facial expressions in dancing and pantomime.

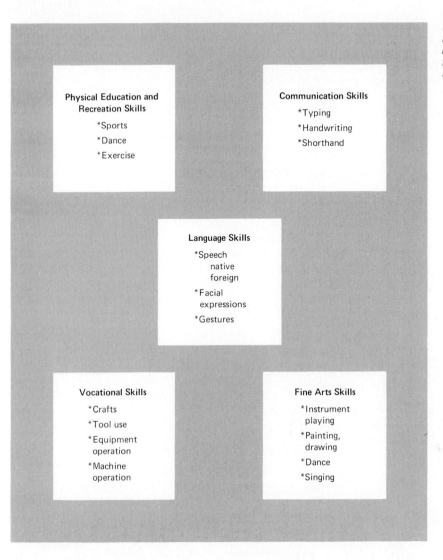

Figure 7-1 Five areas in which motor skills are important. (Adapted from Merrill, 1972, p. 388).

Physical Education and Recreation Skills

*Sports

*Dance

*Exercise

Communication Skills

*Typing

*Handwriting

*Shorthand

Language Skills

*Speech
native
foreign

*Facial
expressions

*Gestures

Vocational Skills

*Crafts

*Tool use

*Equipment
operation

*Machine
operation

Fine Arts Skills

*Instrument
playing

*Painting,
drawing

*Dance

*Singing

Similarly, the teaching of *vocational* and *fine arts* skills is found in many segments of the school curriculum. Students in junior high or high school commonly take at least one shop course, in which special skills such as cooking, sewing, woodworking, and electrical wiring are taught. Most adolescents also take driver education courses. Many adolescents and young adults who do not plan to attend college go to vocational or trade schools, where they receive special training in various kinds of manual labor. Finally, many schools provide specialized instruction in music, art, drama, and dance. For students with interest and talent, extracurricular activities such as the glee club, orchestra, theater club, and art club are also available.

Every spring in the Sports Palace in Tokyo, up to 5,000 very small and very beautiful Japanese children give a fantastic mass violin concert—without rehearsal or even a fixed program (Pronko, 1969). This concert is the work of Sinichi Suzuki, founder of the Talent Education Institute that bears his name. About thirty years ago, Suzuki, a violinist and teacher, was asked to accept a 4-year-old as one of his students. "Too young" was his initial reaction. But, because the child understood and spoke the Japanese language very well, Suzuki reasoned that he could also master the violin. After all, no one learns his or her native language from a printed text; we all begin by babbling, before going on to genuine speech that is constantly shaped and refined. This led Suzuki to a listen-and-play method of teaching the violin.

Students using the Suzuki method may start violin lessons at as young as 2½ years of age. Their motivation often comes from a background rich in fine music. Parents must have an appreciation of music, and music must be an intrinsic part of the home environment. Lessons are private and flexible; a lesson may terminate at the first yawn. There are no music stands or practice books. No coaxing, forcing, or threatening is used. Suzuki also rejects all extrinsic rewards. There is no rivalry for prizes, no city or state contests. The child finds reinforcement in his or her developing skill (much the same process as in language development). The child's models are concert violinists he or she hears on records or tapes. Later, as the child's bowing, fingering, and other techniques become refined, the transition from playing by ear to note reading is made in gradual stages. This transition occurs in much the same way as a first grader learns to read words he or she has spoken for years; the notes logically constitute the visual pattern of the child's musical native tongue.

Through these analogues of language development, Suzuki's institute has taught some 15,000 children to play the violin over the past thirty years. What happened to the 4-year-old who was the guinea pig for Suzuki's system? Toshiyo Eto later became a master violinist at the Curtis Institute of Music in Philadelphia and an international concert performer.

New techniques of music instruction pioneered in Japan have been successful even with very young children.

Basic principles of motor learning The basic principles of motor learning are in many instances the same ones that apply to other kinds of learning. Among them are the usefulness of verbal descriptions and demonstrations, emphasis on selective attention, discrimination of relevant distinguishing features such as those described by Eleanor Gibson in her alphabet chart, and the importance of reinforcement—including feedback about the quality of performance.

Children who are first learning to control the hand and arm movements needed to print and write in the first grade are helped considerably if the teacher gives them descriptions of what the finished product should look like and tells them how close their own efforts are to the desired end product. Similarly, high school students first learning to play tennis are helped by first observing other people as they practice the various kinds of strokes and play a competitive game. The newcomer to the sport would also be helped by learning the rules of the game and how to keep score. Being able to hit the ball and get it over the net is an important part of mastering tennis, but higher-level proficiency will probably depend on some additional guidance and suggestions from an expert, not to mention a great deal of practice. The old saying that "practice makes perfect" is not necessarily true, but in the development of complex motor skills, practice with knowledge of results (feedback) is the only way that high levels of proficiency can be attained (Merrill, 1971b).

Motor learning and movement theory Motor learning does have certain characteristics that distinguish it from other kinds of learning. **Movement theory** is based on these distinctive characteristics.

The basic principle of movement theory is that most learned behavior involves movement of one kind or another. For example, the infant learns through movement to differentiate between "me" and "not me." This distinction is essential to perceptual development. Furthermore, because motor behavior is observable and indicates that learning has taken place, motor behavior is the major channel through which cognitive and emotional growth become apparent (Hunter, 1972).

Movement theory is based on the premise that readiness does not simply develop; it is the result of appropriate experience in movement. The learner needs instruction in the kinds of movement and other skills that are conducive to readiness. Once the condition of readiness has been established, movement theory can be used to analyze the complex skill according to its component elements. For instance, a certain amount of maturation is necessary before a child is physically able to catch a football. But catching a football also involves the appropriate positioning of the body in space and time, and opening and closing one's hands at the precise moment that the ball can be caught. Only when all these steps have been accomplished can we say that the individual has learned to catch a football.

Movement theory can be very helpful to the teacher in planning a curriculum. However, as Gentile (1972) has pointed out, placing the major emphasis of instruction on movement may result in confusion. The student must be taught not only how to execute the required movements, but also how to recognize and process the relevant information about the environmental conditions that control those movements. Otherwise, there is no guarantee that the actual motor behavior engaged in will be appropriate for the situation. For example, a baseball player may be taught how to catch a ball quite accurately when in a simple game of catch. However, unless he or she is also taught how to judge the timing of the ball's arrival by the speed with which it is thrown together with its height and direction, there will be a lot of blunders on the ball field.

What teachers can do to increase motor skills The teaching of complex motor skills, whether in physical education, typing, shop, driver education, or any other part of the curriculum, is a difficult and demanding responsibility. Teachers who take on such assignments should be experts in the performance of the same skills themselves in order to be able to demonstrate to their students what is to be done. Katie Reynolds's first iceskating teacher—the teacher who motivated her so highly—was a professional skater.

According to Gentile (1972), teachers can aid the learning of all motor skills by dividing the learning process into two broad stages. Stage 1 involves getting the idea of the movement—learning what has to be done. Stage 2 is called the "fixation/diversification" stage. As students fixate or concentrate on those aspects that must be learned, they diversify their movements, that is, they increase the number and kinds of responses they make.

During *Stage 1,* the teacher's major function is helping students to understand the goal of the activity. Learning and refinement of most complex skills, including motor skills, require thinking about the task. It is best if this cognitive aspect of the learning activity is introduced at the beginning in order to avoid unnecessary confusion on the part of newcomers to the task. Learning a motor skill can be extremely frustrating because we can't always get our bodies to cooperate and because it often takes time to develop even a minimum level of proficiency. Thus, the teacher needs to be something of a cheerleader during this stage to keep the students' spirits up.

The teacher is also responsible for appropriately structuring the learning environment and helping the student to identify and selectively attend to the features of the environment important to a particular task. Only when it appears that the learner genuinely understands the basic purpose of the task and the crucial relationships involved should he or she be shown how to perform it. Pictures, diagrams, movies, and models are all helpful in displaying appropriate form. To maximize understanding, however, verbal instruction is always necessary.

Once the learner has performed the required movement, his or her performance needs to be evaluated. Sometimes the student receives this feedback from the act itself—getting a basketball through the hoop for the first time is generally rewarding to most students—but sometimes additional feedback from the teacher is needed, too. In general, the learner provides the cues as to whether this additional information is needed; teachers often show a tendency to give a student unnecessary assistance too quickly.

Stage 2 in the learning of motor skills involves a combination of fixation and diversification. During this phase of learning, as the student successively concentrates or fixates on different aspects of the total task, his or her repertoire of responses becomes much more diversified. The student increases the number of responses that he or she makes and, at the same time, learns to vary them according to environmental conditions. A major role of the teacher in this stage is to arrange for sufficient practice.

A characteristic feature of Stage 2 is the elimination of certain components of a motor task from practice and the addition of other, more sophisticated elements. Once students find that they no longer have to concentrate on the crude or general kinds of movement that characterized their early learning, they are ready to refine their skills by focusing on the secondary tasks that contribute to a smoother and more polished performance. Learning to drive a car reflects this progression of skills. Most people are extremely cautious their first few times at the wheel and drive very slowly for fear of an accident. However, with increased practice the clumsiness is diminished, and the driver gradually becomes expert in all the required manipulations. Skilled and experienced drivers usually have enough confidence in their ability to handle their vehicle to willingly engage in other activities simultaneously, such as listening to the radio and carrying on a conversation.

In learning to drive, Stage 1 can often be covered in a few days, but Stage 2 may take weeks, months, or even years. It usually takes a lot of time and practice to progress from the slow, hesitant, awkward movements that characterize initial learning to the rapid, precise, and seemingly involuntary movements that characterize the skilled performer. Katie Reynolds, with her disciplined practicing, took more than two years to begin to approach expertise. Often, developing even minimal expertise at a complex motor task takes far longer. In a high school typing class, it may take most of the students a whole semester to learn to touch-type rapidly and accurately. With some complex skills—for example, playing the flute—years of intensive training may be required to reach desired levels of proficiency. This is certainly true for those who wish to become professional athletes or accomplished musicians. (Fitts, 1962).

Practice Throughout our discussion of motor skills, we have emphasized the importance of practice. Everyone knows that neat, readable handwriting skills, for example, cannot be taught to students without a great deal of often laborious practice. Katie Reynolds's success would not have happened if she had not put in those long hours at the skating rink. But researchers and teachers differ in their opinions about how much practice students need and how it should be organized. Practice can occur mentally as well as physically. In one study (Johnston, 1971), for example, female high school students actually improved at the motor skills involved in volleyball by practicing *thinking* about each movement in sessions before the games.

A number of experts believe that overpractice, rather than just practice to the point of a specified achievement level, is the best way to learn a motor skill. According to some authorities, training in complex motor skills, regardless of the amount of practice, should always be programmed to provide extensive practice in the various component parts separately, rather than in the whole task at once (Fitts, 1962). In a swimming class, for example, the students might concentrate on kicking in one session, arm movements in another, and breathing in a third—before attempting to coordinate all three of these skills. This kind of instruction is sometimes called the *progressive part method,* because the various component movements are developed separately and sequentially. However, unless an effort is made to integrate these parts into a psychological whole, performance is likely to become mechanical (J. Travers, 1972).

In order for practice to be effective, conditions provided for learning should resemble, as much as possible, the conditions under

Movement theory indicates that children need both physical maturation and practice in movement to learn complex motor activities. These Soviet children begin their practice in motor skills at a very early age.

Tass from Sovfoto

which performance actually takes place once the skill is developed. The frequency and duration of practice should be adapted to individual levels of proficiency, as well as to the difficulty of the task itself. The amount of practice required varies with the degree of complexity of the skill.

Practice distributed over a period of time is preferable to massed practice. Early in learning, practice periods should be brief and carefully spaced to minimize frustration and fatigue. Later, as the learner's skill and confidence increase, the practice periods can be longer and more frequent until a satisfactory level of proficiency has been displayed. Then, in order to maintain that level of proficiency, engaging in a small amount of practice occasionally would be most helpful. Now that you know this, perhaps you will do yourself a favor and avoid having to cram for exams by studying as you go along.

Teaching manual dexterity Manual dexterity, which is necessary for printing, writing, and drawing, is a skill required of all students. The development of motor skills follows the flow of maturation, which progresses in *cephalocaudal* (head to tail) and *proximodistal* (from the central nervous system to the body extremities) directions (see Figure 7-2). For this reason, babies learn to control their arms long before they can manipulate their fingers. Most young children, in our country, at least, cannot control their fingertips well enough to make the fine movements required in writing until they are about six years old (J. Gibson, 1978, pp. 50-51). Older elementary school students fre-

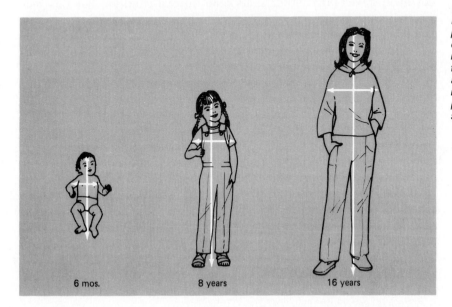

6 mos.   8 years   16 years

Figure 7-2 Maturation proceeds from the head downward and from the interior of the body to the extremities. A certain amount of physical maturation is a prerequisite for motor skill learning.

quently have difficulty controlling their fingers for neat handwriting. High school teachers complain that high school students have the same problem.

Taking students' individual differences into consideration Even when all the basic guidelines for teaching motor skills are followed, a difficult problem remains: What should the teacher do about individual differences in abilities? Many physical education teachers insist that everyone in the class engage in the same activity despite obvious differences in personality and motivation and the fact that some students far outshine others in strength, motor coordination, and agility. This is a bad mistake because it does not give the poor student a chance to succeed. Many students become nearly phobic about athletics because they have been embarrassed in front of their classmates by insensitive coaches and physical education teachers. Many youngsters and adults admit that "brain work" like math is hard, but feel that any idiot ought to be able to use his or her body. These unfortunate attitudes need to be changed. Children who have difficulty mastering any type of skill need encouragement, not ridicule.

Age differences are important in motor learning and in the development of athletic skills. Older children can generally run faster and jump and throw farther than younger children. Six-year olds can hop and skip or throw and catch a ball. But they haven't developed the dexterity or coordination yet to play a good game of softball. This won't come for a few years.

Physically and mentally handicapped children are frequently slower in developing motor skills than normal children. For this reason, federal legislation enacted in 1976 (Public Law 94-142, The Education of all Handicapped Children Act) includes instruction of physical education within the definition of required special education services. Special elements of adapted physical education services include corrective training, therapeutic training, and remedial training. Sports and games are modified for impaired, disabled, or handicapped persons as well (Stein, 1977).

Because of the new emphasis on special education services, the annual field day in one suburban middle school was reorganized to accommodate handicapped students. Rather than having only strenuous, skill-coordinated events, the event now includes many activities which use an element of luck, such as balloon blowing and breaking contests. The students choose their own events in which to participate, coach, or score, in advance. They may practice at home and change to another event if they find that they can't do the one they had signed up for. This change according to the teachers has made the field day a happy occasion for all students, not just for those who are well coordinated.

Sex differences: Do they exist?   One major cause noted in past years for differences in motor development is sex. In the elementary school years, boys and girls are quite similar in their motor skill performance. Tests of specific motor skills or general athletic ability show few differences between the sexes. This similarity lasts until children are approximately 10 to 12 years old. Past the age of 12, however, boys have been shown to become more proficient in almost all motor skills. Researchers have shown that differences in athletic performance between high school boys and girls are related to differences primarily in strength and cardiovascular endurance.

One of the great concerns relative to high school female participation in athletics has been in the area of gynecological considerations and menstruation. Researchers have found a high degree of variability among females with regard particularly to exercise and competition during the various phases of the menstrual cycle. Most recent studies, however, have shown that, regardless of these factors, if given the same training and opportunity to practice as males, females should not be expected to be different from their male counterparts (Witmore, 1977). For this reason, many teachers today point out that, with the advent of the feminist movement and new freedom for girls to take part in physical activities once provided only for boys, there is little or no reason to advocate different training programs on the basis of sex.

Whatever decisions are made in the future, though, safeguards for health will be taken into consideration. Every young athlete, boy or girl, has the right to expect certain safeguards for health, what one physician call a "kind of bill of rights" (Schaffer, 1977). Whether dealing with males or females, according to Schaffer, the well-planned health program must include policies and procedures to provide:

1. Proper conditioning
2. Intelligent coaching
3. The best possible equipment and facilities
4. Capable officiating
5. Competent medical care (Schaffer, 1977, p. 223)

Whether this can be done with coeducational interscholastic activities is still an issue. The feminist movement has opened interesting legal questions related to discrimination in the role of males and females in athletics, particularly in interscholastic activities.

Language is the vehicle through which all other skills are acquired and mastered. An individual's ability to adapt to all aspects of the environment depends on how well he or she speaks, reads, and writes. Students who have not learned basic language skills before coming to school usually have trouble learning most subjects in the curriculum.

Helping Students
To Learn
Language Skills

This is true whether the difficulty comes from inability to speak any language at all or from speaking a language other than English, when English is used as the language of communication in school.

A Japanese family recently enrolled their children Kim, a 13-year-old boy, and his sister Kami, who was 11, in a middle school in a large urban community. Neither child spoke much English when they arrived. Both were teamed with students who were friendly and outgoing. Kami quickly picked up words and phrases. By the end of the year, she was well established in her sixth-grade class and was learning many different subjects. However, Kim apparently did not have the interest or the ability to acquire a large collection of English words. Although he seemed to be as friendly as his sister, he found it difficult to make friends. He also had difficulty learning his school subjects. At the end of the year, the teacher suggested that he repeat the grade. In the meantime, she suggested that his parents arrange for special language tutoring. Lack of English language was a serious learning barrier for Kim.

Language as a productive system   Human language is by definition a productive system, because each utterance is a creative act. In the course of just a single day, for instance, one reads, hears, or constructs hundreds of sentences, no two of which are alike. The exceptions to this rule are expressions such as "How are you?" and other formal salutations, which are repeated over and over again out of habit. However, under most conditions, we usually create new sentences instead of repeating ones we have used previously.

According to psycholinguist Noam Chomsky, we are able to generate an infinite number of sentences using a finite number of words because we have mastered the basic principles of the language, the manner in which words are effectively and meaningfully combined. However, we all know that many combinations of words heard in everyday conversation, which are intended to be sentences, are far from perfect grammatically, and, in many cases, may not even be very meaningful. Many people use a kind of verbal shorthand, especially with friends, colleagues, and family. From time to time, all of us make slips of the tongue, jump from one topic to another, or start a sentence but never finish it because we forgot what we wanted to say. These mistakes do not necessarily mean that a person has an inadequate knowledge of the principles of sentence structure. The person may be tired, distracted, or untrained in organizing his or her thoughts.

In other words, there is a distinction between linguistic competence (knowledge of principles) and linguistic performance (translation of that knowledge into action). This distinction leads us to a discussion of the interests and concerns of experts on language—linguists and psycholinguists.

Linguists and psycholinguists **Linguistics** is a branch of science dealing with the fundamental structural principles of languages. These principles are believed to enable someone who knows a language to use it in a meaningful, productive, and innovative way.

People who specialize in this area of study are called linguists, and those among them who are concerned with the psychological aspects of language structure are called **psycholinguists.** Both the linguist and the psycholinguist are interested in determining the roots of a person's knowledge of language (linguistic competence), but the psycholinguist is also interested in the performance aspects of language use. Pure linguists are not particularly concerned with the everyday use of language, but rather with the underlying abilities that determine language competence. Psycholinguists, on the other hand, do consider the everyday use of language, because they are attempting to understand psychological factors that can account for discrepancies between knowledge and performance.

The contemporary approach in America to linguistics was first developed by Noam Chomsky (1957, 1968), one of the most influential figures of our time in the field of linguistics. Chomsky theorizes that human beings have an innate capability to process language, construct language rules, and understand complex speech. According to Chomsky, humans begin to construct new sentences and to relate them to other, already learned sentences by means of underlying rules of syntax called **transformational grammar,** or **transformations.** One common example of a transformation is the change in the meaning of a word from positive to negative by the addition of a contraction, such as the suffix "n't." ("Would" becomes "wouldn't," "could" becomes "couldn't," "is" becomes "isn't," and so on.) Because we are familiar with the language that we speak, we tend to use it without explicitly identifying most of these rules. According to Chomsky, we seem to have an intuitive mastery of them, because we consistently apply them in a prescribed manner, usually without being specifically taught to do so. For example, a little girl holds up a new dress and says, "Look what I bringed home from Grandma's!" This sentence is not simply a result of copying adult speech because adults say "brought" instead of "bringed.' According to Chomsky, this sentence represents the child's creative attempt to apply her intuitive understanding of the transformation of present to past tense by the addition of -ed.

You might wonder why we need to study grammar in school if we have this innate capacity to understand and apply grammatical rules. The primary purpose of studying grammar is to identify and explain the basic principles affecting the production and understanding of meaningful sentences. Grammar explains how we distinguish between sentences and nonsentences, relate sentence structure to both meaning and sound, and account for any possible sentence that might be constructed. A knowledge of grammar helps us to understand and construct more complex sentences than we would be able to on our own.

There are other explanations of language development. B. F. Skinner and his colleagues suggest that language develops through selective reinforcement, initially through parental attention to infant vocalizations, and later through reinforcement supplied by teachers and other adults for more complex speech. Learning theorists also emphasize the extreme importance of imitation and modeling in language development. The Soviet environmentalists Lev Vygotsky and A. S. Luria accept this environmental approach to language development, but stress its simplicity and limitations. In addition, they criticize what they consider to be the serious limitations of Chomsky's view of the inherited nature of linguistic structures. According to Vygotsky and Luria, language is a system of learned codes used to express the relation of a child with the outside world. Linguistic competence, in their eyes, is the result of a long series of dramatic interactions with the outside world, rather than an innate characteristic. Piaget uses another approach and describes the development of language in terms of a series of stages characterized by cognitive qualities related directly to ability to think and solve problems. Bruner relates language development to a parallel development of interests and needs.

Regardless of the theory of language development you prefer, research on teaching language in school clearly shows that, without adequate language learning in the preschool years, language development of school-age children will be retarded. In the United States, preschool children's teachers usually are their mothers. Learning takes place at home. Socioeconomic conditions, education, intelligence, general experience, and attitude of these parent-teachers thus clearly affect the ability of school children to communicate. According to researchers, if adequate stimulation is provided by these early parent-teachers, children will learn to master language structure and various transformations before entering the first grade. L. Berko, for example, reported in 1958 that most preschool and first-grade children appear to have a basic knowledge of the rules for forming plurals, possessives, and other transformations. In this study, children were shown stimulus cards, each containing an unfamiliar nonsense word, a picture, and a question (in form of an incomplete sentence) designed to test the child's knowledge of a certain grammatical principle. (See Figure 7-3 for a sample card using the nonsense word "wug" to test the child's knowledge of the rule for forming plurals.) The children's verbal responses to these cards, according to Berko, showed that knowledge of English grammar is not a matter of simple memorization. If it were, the subjects would have refused to take the test on the grounds that they had never heard the words. Instead, they proceeded to apply relevant grammatical principles to these nonsense words.

Figure 7-3

This is a wug.

Now there is another one.
There are two of them.
There are two_____.

According to Carol Chomsky (1969), a complete knowledge and understanding of grammatical rules does not take place until sometime between the ages of 5 and 10. In general, the results of a multitude of studies suggest a gradual consolidation of language structure from kindergarten to adolescence, but also indicate abrupt shifts in performance between kindergarten and first grade and between the fifth grade and seventh grade (Palermo and Molfese, 1972).

What teachers can do to increase language competence in the classroom The evironmental approach to language development is important in answering this question. Teachers should provide opportunity for students to talk and write as much as possible in class. This is true whether language development has innate origins in human beings or not. According to the behavioral approach to language development, it is important for teachers to provide students with feedback related to their use of language. Teachers should let students know when they are using language in useful (or correct) ways and when they are not communicating what they think they are. Teachers also need to remember that their own use of language serves as a model in the classroom. One important way for teachers to show students how to use the English language is to have them listen to what the teachers say and imitate by repeating words they hear in similar contexts.

According to the developmental stage approach of Piaget, children's language development parallels cognitive development; according to Bruner, it parallels developing interests. Use of new vocabulary and new ways to use old vocabulary can more easily be taught when the language used in classroom communication is related directly to topics that students are interested in and are able to understand. It is all well and good to provide spelling bees in which students learn to spell words without making errors, and perhaps provide dictionary definitions to go with the spelling. But, if the new words have not dealt with concepts that are interesting to the students, the teacher can expect the learning to be quickly forgotten. In fact, teaching spelling as a subject may have been one of the biggest mistakes of curriculum makers. Informal studies indicate that learning to spell is reflective of the usefulness of the given words in a child's life. Irrelevant lists of words discourage retention.

Providing language learning that deals with topics that interest the students is particularly important when teachers are dealing with older minority-group students who haven't learned proper English because they have always spoken some other language or dialect in their homes. Teachers can make language lessons more interesting for these students by making them deal with words they use in their day-to-day lives. Kim, for example, would enjoy lessons that involve extracurricular activities and sports that he plays daily with other children in his neighborhood. Learning these words would help him learn to get along better socially, another problem that this Japanese boy must deal with in learning to live in his new country.

Practice is as critical to the teaching of language skills as it is to the teaching of all other skills (see for example, Hall, 1978). Students learn language through practice in both talking and listening. The more opportunity the teacher provides for students to use words—in class discussions, debates, recitations, and papers—the more opportunity the students will have to commit the language to use for the remainder of their lives.

Another interesting way that teachers can get students to practice communication skills is to present them with very specific problems that require them to use English language precisely and correctly. An eighth-grade English teacher was having trouble teaching the recognition and use of concise language. She gave her students a home assignment of writing very specific directions for making peanut butter and jelly sandwiches. The following day she brought the supplies for the sandwiches to school and instructed the students to pair themselves up. One pair after another tried out their own directions. One student read the directions while the other was directed to follow them exactly. They were thwarted in their efforts by such statements as, "then spread the peanut butter on the bread" (without first opening the jar) or "next, put jelly on one slice" (without taking the bread from the wrapper). That day only two sandwiches were made, one without jelly. The same assignment was given for the following day, and this time all the students made and ate their sandwiches. They had learned from practical experience the importance of concise language.

What teachers can do about individual differences in language development The importance of language learning in the preschool years to language development during the school years cannot be overestimated. Teachers must remember that children arriving in a first-grade class have differing abilities to communicate with one another. The differences in communication skills are even greater when students are older. Some students who do not speak English in their homes have more difficulty learning to speak English in school. Students who speak English dialects other than standard white middle-class English frequently have problems in both spelling and reading. Communication difficulties between student and teacher or student and textbook because of discrepancies in both speech patterns and environmental experience can easily lead to problems. A variety of special programs,—for example, Project Upgrade, a program conducted in Kansas City in which children were taught how to read with material prepared from stories that they told themselves in their own vocabularies—have proven highly successful. The high level of interest and motivation that resulted from Project Upgrade produced dramatic improvement in reading skills as well as vocabulary (J. Gibson, 1972).

Using language competence to teach other skills   The language abilities of students have important implications for other classroom instruction, particularly instruction involving skills that require understanding words. We have already discussed the teaching of reading at some length. Reading ability is strongly affected by children's ability to use language. To give an example, recognizing written words is much easier when a word's **phonemes** (the smallest distinguishable units of sound) correspond to the printed symbols in the alphabet **(graphemes)** (Bloomfield, 1933; Fries, 1963). Many words in our language, particularly the easy words, can be classified according to a characteristic phoneme-grapheme pattern—for example, book, look, cook; cake, make, take; bell, sell, tell. By presenting basic patterns like these to their students, teachers can help beginning readers of all ages acquire a feeling for important sound-to-spelling relationships, which will, in turn, assist them in reading independently (Dale, 1972). Teachers then must provide instruction in combining words into sentences that are meaningful as well as grammatically correct.

Language competence also has implications for spelling instruction (Dale, 1972). Teachers can increase speaking and spelling abilities by pointing out whenever possible that the spelling of many words is not purely arbitrary, but understandable in terms of the spelling of a related word. For example, a student would be more likely to spell the word *medicine* with a *c* instead of an *s* after being shown the relation of this word to the word *medical*.

A fourth skill that students must develop in order to succeed in school is dealing with concepts and solving new problems.

*Helping Students
to Learn to Deal
with Concepts and
Solve Problems*

What is a concept?   A **concept** is an abstraction or idea that permits the learner to classify a variety of related phenomena into a convenient, meaningful category. For example, once a young child learns the meaning of the concept "pet," he or she can make a category of widely different animals like dogs, cats, canaries, and goldfish and can tell them apart from wolves, lions, owls, and sharks. Concepts enable the consolidation and systematization of huge quantities of data and allow communication and discussion of complex issues between individuals. Once a second-grader understands the concept of "measure," he or she can learn the concepts of "greater than" and "less than." Later, in high school, he or she can use these concepts to solve algebraic equations.

Concepts provide order and stability in an uncertain and ever-changing world. The student who has learned the concepts of "greater than" and "less than" understands that 3 is greater than 2, that a gallon bottle holds more than a quart, and that the algebraic equation $a > b$ means the same thing as $b < a$. According to Gagné (1965c), concept learning produces a certain fundamental change in human performance that is independent of subject or content.

Concepts can be divided into two broad categories: concrete and abstract. **Concrete concepts** are ideas that can be linked to a class of observable objects (for example, house, book, furniture) or object qualities (for example, color, size, shape). As students acquire concepts of this sort, they realize that they are grouping together various objects or object qualities that are very different in appearance. But they are also responding to these stimuli in terms of some property they all have in common; this makes classification possible. **Abstract concepts** such as "greater than" and "less than" cannot be directly linked to observable objects or object qualities in this manner; they are definitional. The physical concepts of force and work; the language concepts of noun, verb, adjective, and adverb; and the mathematical concepts of fractions, decimals, and percentages are just a few of the many extremely important abstract concepts taught in school.

Teaching concept formation is a continual process. Simple concepts such as work and play can be taught to young children in relatively few lessons. Advanced abstract concepts in such areas as physics, economics, and psychology, however, require many lessons and often many years to develop. With increased learning and experience, students can change their concepts to accommodate their new store of knowledge.

It is important to distinguish between concepts and rules or principles. Although related and interdependent, these terms represent two different kinds of capacity and call for different methods of instruction. Basically, teaching a concept means teaching students to give a common name or reponse to a class of stimuli that vary in appearance but are related in some way. It also means teaching them to recognize the dimensions of a stimulus that determine whether or not it belongs in a particular conceptual category. For instance, when an American child learns that there is a common bond between a fire engine and an apple, and that this bond is the color red, he or she has learned the concept of color. Learning a rule or principle, on the other hand, means being able to combine related concepts into rules that say something about those concepts. When the same child learns that by mixing different colors together he can develop new colors, he is learning the rule of color mixing.

Foundations of skill learning in concepts and problem-solving
Learning concepts and problem-solving is closely related to language learning. Language facilitates the task of concept learning considerably. It serves as an economical and convenient way of ordering and classify-

ing many different sets of observations. Language also contributes to greater uniformity in the use of concepts by different people. In addition, students are constantly encountering new words that serve as cues to the existence of concepts they don't yet know about, but perhaps should. Their natural curiosity leads them to learn the meaning of the word, and to place that word in a conceptual category. Finally, language enables the learner to grasp the relationships among different concepts and express these relationships in a meaningful, precise, and understandable way.

Once the learner has become involved in the discovery and expression of relationships among a set of concepts, his or her attention shifts from concept learning to rule or principle learning. Rule-learning, in turn, has an important bearing on the learning of problem-solving. When a student discovers how a complex problem is solved, he or she often learns a higher-order rule at the same time. When this happens, the student can use the higher-order rule to solve new, but similar problems. A high school student who learns how to read a computer language may use the new-found knowledge to read and understand computer printouts. He or she may also use that knowledge to learn other computer languages. Changes in behavior associated with succesful problem-solving tend, as a rule, to be long-lasting and readily applicable to new situations.

How do students actually acquire concepts, rules, and problem-solving abilities, and what, if anything, can the schools do to help? On this issue, as on many others in psychology, there are two opposing theories. The first is the developmental-stage view held by Piaget, Kohlberg, and others, which states that concept development progresses through a series of stages that occur in a fixed and determined order. The second theory is the learning-environmental approach, exemplified by the work of Bandura and Gagné, which maintains that concepts are primarily products of experience and that the order of development is not necessarily invariant or fixed according to a determined time scale, since different children have different experiences at different times in their lives, depending on both individual learning situations and on cultural experiences.

What teachers can do to help students to deal with concepts and problem-solving Teachers may teach concept learning in school by inductive or deductive methods. The **inductive method** consists of presenting a series of positive and negative instances of a concept and allowing the learner to infer the concept by discovering what all these instances have in common. The teacher might ask, for example, "What is a pet?" and then give the class the following examples: "A dog that lives in a house with a family is a pet. A dog that lives in the forest with a pack of dogs is not a pet. A snake kept in a cage may be a pet. A snake that lives in the woods is not a pet," and so on. In contrast, the **deductive method** involves presenting concepts by verbal definition and description. Here, the teacher might begin with, "A pet is a domesticated animal kept for pleasure and not utility." Then he or she would ask, "Can you think of some examples of pets you know about?"

Jerome Bruner's discovery teaching is built on the inductive method. According to Bruner, discovery learning leads to greater retention and greater transfer to new situations. This method takes a great deal of time, but teaching by purely deductive methods might not be sufficient for a student to identify all the critical aspects needed to understand a concept in its totality. Perhaps the best approach to the teaching of concepts is to use a combination of both methods.

The purpose of teaching concepts in school is, in part, to provide the student with definitive meanings for various terms, but this should not be considered the only purpose. Teachers should also provide practical experience in using concepts and in discovering the higher-order relationships or principles that give a set of concepts their underlying structure. In addition, teachers ought to transmit the ability to modify concepts as necessary and organize one's experience so that it makes sense in terms of one's existing concepts.

Teachers can facilitate concept learning by presenting material in a lucid but interesting manner and by using books, films, and other instructional aids, which make the subject seem interesting and relevant. For the most effective results, however, an organized plan of approach is advisable. The following procedures and guidelines were designed for this purpose by psychologists:

1. A general rule for teaching any new concept is that several illustrations, differing in appearance, should always be presented. The teacher just described might continue her discussion of pets: "A dog that is wild is *not* a pet. A kitten that lives in a garbage can is *not* a pet. A lion in the wilds of Africa is *not* a pet. A lion that stays in a house and goes for walks on a leash *is* a pet." Otherwise, the concept that actually emerges from the instruction is apt to be incomplete, and the learning process is closer to mere rote memory (Gagné, 1965c, 1970).
2. After the lesson has been completed, the teacher needs to determine whether or not the designated learning has taken place. The acquisition of a concept is best demonstrated by seeing if the student can apply it to a new situation not directly encountered during the learning phase. The teacher might ask, "is a lion at the zoo a pet?" If the student can give only an exact replica of what the teacher said in the lesson, the goals of the instruction have not been accomplished (Gagné, 1965c; Markle and Tiemann, 1970).

In addition to these two general points, the following are some specific guidelines for the teaching of concepts suggested by R. M. Travers (1967):

1. Carefully plan the lesson to reduce the number of irrelevant characteristics in the examples presented. When only the most important characteristics are discussed, they will stand out more clearly in the student's memory.
2. Be as precise and explicit as possible in presenting the relevant attributes. Use concrete examples and simplified representations. Avoid presenting concepts in such abstract terms that they lose their meaning.
3. Give the learner additional time to view the material after giving feedback as well as before. This procedure enables students to review the information according to its appropriate interpretation and thus to generate hypotheses.
4. Help students to code new information verbally by having them state it in their own words.
5. Present the concepts in an order that is consistent with their structure. General concepts which are closely tied to observable qualities and have a relatively low level of abstraction should be taught first. (For example, a student should have a general concept of direction before being asked to find different places on a map, and he or she should have the ability to read a map before being taught about latitude and longitude.)
6. Illustrate both positive and negative instances of the concept in question. (For example, in teaching the meaning of the physical concept "work"—which is different from the everyday usage of this term—illustrations should be given not only of activities that constitute "work" for the physicist, but also of those that do not.)

Travers's last point is particularly important and is often overlooked by teachers. Satisfactory demonstration that a new concept has really been learned includes not only correct generalization to situations showing similar instances but also correct discrimination of noninstances. Teachers should keep this point in mind when they are preparing examinations to test understanding of concepts. However, any test items that are intended as noninstances of a concept should have at least some resemblance to test items that do illustrate the concept, or the task becomes too easy. (Thus, for example, on a multiple-choice question relating to the concept "treaty," names of other kinds of historical documents would be far better noninstances than names of people or places.)

In addition to these guidelines, we must add one more—the need to consider individual differences, in both ability and learning style, and to adapt methods of instruction accordingly. Simple and straightforward methods of teaching concepts may very well be the only ones suitable for children of limited ability, but children capable of independent reasoning and high levels of abstraction should be able to benefit from greater emphasis on inquiry and discussion and less emphasis on drills and definitions. Another useful approach might be to call on the more able learners to help explain and demonstrate a difficult concept to the rest of the class.

Learning Complex Concepts

Bruner's proposal that children, depending on how they are taught, can learn difficult concepts before prescribed stages of cognitive development, seems to have been illustrated in a Princeton University laboratory in which 4-year-olds perform intellectual feats that theoretically only adults can do ("Toddler Logic: New Findings," *Society*, 1974). The program, designed by a specialist in cognitive psychology, Thomas Trabasso, refutes the assumption that reasoning abilities develop in discrete stages and that each stage is dependent on the previous one. He feels that this theory omits such factors as memory, perception, language, and personal experience. Trabasso's preschoolers were able to reason deductively—for example, Fred is bigger than John; John is bigger than George; therefore, Fred is also bigger than George. They succeeded because the experimenters made sure that the children remembered the people and their relative sizes. The previous failures of children on such tasks, asserts Trabasso, were due not to the lack of reasoning ability but to memory—the children forgot the names and sizes of Fred, John, and George. Five-year-olds were also able to group things into categories (presumably impossible before age 9) when the categories used in the problems were ones with which the children were already familiar. Thus, experience played a role in their success. Such experiments suggest that, if their learning environments are arranged in certain ways, very young children are capable of solving logical problems and that they can reason deductively just as adults can.

Chisanbop: A New Method for Teaching Math Simply

Chisanbop, a method to solve mathematics problems by using one's ten fingers, was the invention of Sung Jin Pai, an eminent South Korean mathematician and authority on the use of the abacus. Pai devised Chi San Bop, a method to teach Korean students of the abacus to use their fingers to make rapid and accurate finger calculations. After a period of time using this method, Pai reports students internalize the system and gradually develop the ability to make calculations with no external movement (Pearson, 1978). The method for teaching elementary arithmetic involves having children make computations almost as if they themselves were the abacus. They press down each finger on the right hand in turn to add a number in the digits column and use the fingers of the left hand for the tens columns. Multidigit computations can be taught to advanced students, and, according to reports of teachers, many children have developed the ability to solve complex problems quickly and correctly. Equally important, the children reported that using their fingers to solve the problems was fun. Early in 1978, the method began to make big news: children using their fingers were showing up as TV regulars on "Westinghouse Evening Magazine," the "Mike Douglas Show," and the "Today Show." In April, 1978, a Canadian TV crew filmed a New York class using the method; the BBC picked the segment up for showing in England.

Why has the method developed popularity so quickly? With hand calculators showing up in classrooms across the country, developmental psychologists suggest that the possibilities for children being provided opportunity to use concrete solutions to problems seems to have diminished considerably. In addition, modern mathematics methods seem to be spending a great deal of time on abstract explanations of why mathematics works and less time on concrete ways of making it work. Some people suggest that Chisanbop works because it offers children the possibility of modeling numbers, of getting the feel of what happens in a numbering system. Piagetian stage theorists would recommend the method because it provides concrete methods of problem-solving that are particularly appropriate to young elementary school students first beginning the study of mathematics, but the method appeals to older students as well. Students announce that they prefer exercises in physical and mental swiftness and going into "the way numbers feel and what they mean" instead of memorizing "number facts."

Does Chisanbop work? In 1978, the first year of experimental work with the program, children in Chisanbop experimental classrooms were tested and compared with children learning by traditional methods. The Chisanbop children clearly enjoyed their mathematics lessons and astounded both parents and teachers with their ability to solve complicated problems without pencil and paper. But it remains to be seen whether or not the method produces long-term results that prove that the method works better than others and whether it produces the same good results for all students. Teachers were saying, however, that Chisanbop works—it offers students a gamelike sense of genuine, satisfying competence, and it makes learning arithmetic fun.

Cognitive style also must be taken into consideration. Researchers have shown that students who have impulsive cognitive styles learn more effectively than reflective children when teachers use multidimensional (complex) stimuli; the reverse is true when simple, noncomplex teaching devices are used (Rollins and Genser, 1977).

Individualization of instruction is also important to children with differing mental abilities. One middle school teacher whose students represented a wide range of mental abilities tried a variety of approaches to teach the class why and when quotation marks are used. Some children cut out the bubbles from comic strips and labeled them with the speaker's name. Other students underlined the words in a paragraph that represented dialogue. During a class discussion, volunteers took down the exact words of some of the students as they spoke. After they had grown used to recognizing the use of quotations, they made up their own comic strips, small playlets, and finally short stories, using formal quotation marks.

In this section, we take a closer look at the learning of attitudes and, specifically, at the importance of school-related variables in shaping and changing the student's.

Helping Students to Learn Attitudes Conducive to School Learning

We cannot see an attitude directly. We must infer it from people's observable behavior. For example, if a student has a good attendance record, does his or her homework regularly, participates in class discussions, and volunteers for special projects, we can reasonably infer that he or she has a favorable attitude toward school. On the other hand, a student who is frequently absent or late, does not do his or her homework regularly or pay attention in class, and never volunteers for extra assignments probably has a poor or indifferent attitude toward school. Behavior thus serves as a convenient indicator of attitude.

The effects of attitudes, both toward school and toward particular subjects, on learning in general cannot be overestimated. Even the attitudes students have toward themselves (their self-concepts) are important to learning. Katie Reynolds, the adolescent girl described in the case history at the beginning of this chapter, had a poor self-concept in the early grades, and, as a result, she did poorly in school. According to the school psychologist, her major success at skating increased her self-esteem, and, in turn, her ability to do academic work. Two researchers showed that students with high self-concepts learned material they liked more efficiently in the classroom than material they didn't like; the reverse was true for students with low self-concepts (August and Rychlak, 1978).

Many studies have been conducted to determine to what extent the schools can influence attitude change. Unfortunately, however, most classroom studies have limited value, because they provide little information about the specific mechanisms involved and do not distinguish between aspects of the curriculum that are responsible for producing such changes and those that are not.

One approach to the study of attitude formation involves determining whether or not verbally reinforcing a statement that people did not initially agree with would result in their changing their attitudes. Scott (1957) explored this possibility by having students engage in debates, taking positions that were opposed to their existing beliefs. Presentation was followed by verbal reinforcement, which was meant to indicate that one of the speakers had won the debate. The results of posttests indicated that those students who had won the debate, as compared with those who had lost, showed a significant change in their attitudes toward the original statement.

In another study demonstrating a similar phenomenon, Festinger and Carlsmith (1959) exposed students to a boring set of tasks and then paid them to tell other students that the tasks had been interesting and enjoyable. On a subsequent test of their enjoyment of the tasks, the original students, who earlier displayed a negative (noninterested) attitude, appeared to have shifted to what the researchers termed a positive (interested attitude).

Other investigators, also using a reinforcement model, have indicated parallels between the learning of attitudes and the learning of concepts. According to Rhine and Silun (1958), for instance, many of the concepts we learn tend to have definite positive or negative values associated with them; these values can be strengthened when others reinforce the desired behavior and one's attitude toward it. Prejudice, thrift, and laziness are a few examples that readily come to mind.

All these early studies and many others since then suggest that attitudes are learned and that teachers, parents, or peers can either establish or modify them under conditions of appropriate reinforcement. On the other hand, not all of the published data seems to be consistent with the notion that extrinsic reinforcement is a necessary condition. For example, Rosenberg (1960) suggested to people under hypnosis that they take more liberal views on various controversial issues and succeeded in modifying their behavior without providing them with extrinsic reinforcement. The explanation that is usually given for data of this sort is that most human beings do not like to perceive inconsistencies in themselves and will therefore try to change in a direction that will reduce them.

There are many other factors affecting attitude. The extent of praise and encouragement given by the teacher also appears to be important to some students, as indicated in a study by Morrison (1966). Assessments of the teachers' behavior obtained by trained outside observers were correlated with students' shifts in attitudes toward school as determined by attitude inventories. The results indicated that students whose teachers rarely used praise and encouragement tended to shift their attitudes in a negative direction much more so than children whose teachers often used praise and encouragement.

Humanist educators suggest that one way to affect student attitudes in a direction that improves school learning is to make classroom learning as human a situation as possible. One way to do this, according to some humanist educators, is through a procedure known as **values clarification.** Students will probably develop values that will help them to become more self-confident and make decisions more easily in classroom situations if teachers help them to define and select their beliefs by carefully considering these beliefs as well as their alternatives (Raths, Harmin, and Simon, 1966). Teachers can help students to value their own beliefs by allowing students to discuss their beliefs openly and act on them in classroom situations. Values clarification strategies can be incorporated directly into teachers' presentations of different subject matters, and such presentations should ultimately lead to positive classroom attitudes (Harmin, Kirschenbaum, and Simon, 1972). Students who are happy within themselves and in expressing their own values and beliefs make better all-around students.

How can I help my children do better in school? Teachers and school administrators have heard this question from parents since schooling began. Up to now, some standard answers have been: "Keep in touch with what's going on in your child's school life"; "Meet the teacher"; "Join the P.T.A."; "Do volunteer work at school."

All of these are good suggestions, and thank goodness for parents who are involved in school activities. But parents can do *much more* to help their children do better in school—particularly with basic reading and pre-reading skills.

Following are ways you can suggest for parents to help their children and, in the process, become partners in learning with the school. Though employing these techniques takes no educational training, it does take time. It's worth it. Some of the suggestions may seem obvious, but there's no reason to assume that most parents follow them all. If presented as answers to parents' specific questions or as general, non-condescending reminders, they can serve you well. Consider sending all parents a checklist similar to this one and include a letter to introduce it.

Twenty-five Ways to Help Your Children in School
1. Keep your children healthy. Should the school nurse or doctor inform you that your child has a health problem, discuss it. He or she can help get the assistance you need. Seeing, hearing and feeling well are essential to learning.
2. Talk with your children. Talk naturally. Don't use baby talk no matter how young the child. The more words a child can understand and say, the easier it will be for him or her to learn to read and to understand.
3. Listen to your children. Encourage them to talk about their everyday activities. Make sure you give them the chance to initiate conversation during meals and on other suitable occasions. Your children will learn to express themselves if they know you will give them your attention.
4. Praise your children. Praise and recognition reinforce learning. Reading, for example, is enjoyable, but it's also hard work for children. They need your support and encouragement. Praise them when they succeed and help them when they are having problems.
5. Be patient with your children. Even though you work with them and help them with their homework, they may make the same mistakes many times. Don't despair. Some experts say that new learning sometimes requires more than 15 repetitions before it is absorbed. It's most important that you do not become angry or impatient, since learning cannot take place in a tense atmosphere. If you find yourself "losing your cool," just stop and do something else for a while.
6. Avoid comparing your children. Each child is unique. Some children learn faster than others. If your children seem to be moving at a slow rate, don't blame them or worry them about it. It's too early to make comparisons anyway, for your children may have an as yet untapped reserve of attributes and talents. Let them know you love

them for what they are and that you will continue to love them no matter how they do in school.

7. Set the stage for good homework habits. Try to provide a quiet, well-lighted place for study, and make sure there is room for books, dictionaries, papers, pens, pencils and other homework tools.

8. Schedule home study on a regular basis. To succeed in school many children need a regular study time each night free of interruptions and distractions. If your children are not given a homework assignment, this scheduled time can be used for review, reading for pleasure or some type of family or learning activity. It's a good idea to provide each of your children with a notebook so that he or she—and you—will always know exactly what the assignments are. This notebook will also serve as a written record of all assignments and will help to organize review and study of previous material.

.9. Set a bedtime and stick to it. Learning is hard work and requires full use of all faculties. Your children will be in the proper frame of mind and otherwise ready for learning only if they report to school each morning well-rested.

10. See that your children's school attendance is excellent. When children miss school, they may miss the presentation of new information or the mastery of a difficult concept. Once they fall behind their group, it's especially hard to catch up. Some children can never quite adjust after frequent or extended absences from school.

11. Know exactly how your children are doing in school. If you find out that they are having academic or other problems, don't wait to be contacted by the school. Take the initiative by making an appointment to talk it over with the teacher. If you can't get to school, send a note asking the teacher to contact you by telephone. Find out how you can help. Perhaps you can provide information about your children and family that will help school people respond with greater understanding to your child's situation.

12. Make family mealtimes meaningful. Mealtime can provide the ideal setting for talking together, sharing events of the day and discussing individual problems and aspirations. In a relaxed, family atmosphere, youngsters have a chance to test their debating skills in friendly arguments and to talk out their differences of opinion. Such discussions will help develop your children's self-confidence and encourage them to speak up in the classroom. Don't allow TV to interfere with this perfect opportunity for family communication.

13. Make television your servant, not your master. Children learn a lot from television—both good and bad. Help them choose appropriate programs to watch. Then watch with them and, afterwards, discuss what you've seen. This approach to television can help your children develop new interests that you can encourage them to read about.

One system for choosing programs carefully is to get the family together once a week to consider the television listings. Go over the listings as you would a restaurant menu. (In a restaurant you wouldn't order just anything.) By choosing carefully in advance, you'll help your children form the habit of considering television as only one of many entertainment/learning tools available, and you'll give them a valuable thinking and decision-making experience.

14. Take your children places. Visits to nature and science centers, art museums, train and subway stations, airports, farms, factories, shipyards, supermarkets, pet shops and so on will help broaden their experiences. Such diverse activities are vital in readying young children for reading.

15. Read with your children. It's a rare child who is not delighted to be read to by a parent or older friend, but it's important to read *with* your children, not only *to* them. Not long ago, I saw a young teacher trying to read a book to a small group of five-year-olds. The children kept interrupting with questions and comments, frequently turning back a page or two and saying such things as "Let me see the lion again" and "See the mouse with the hat?" Finally the teacher said in an angry tone, "Do you want me to read this story or not? If so, hush!" That teacher's scolding kept her students quiet, but from that point on the youngsters were spectators of the reading process, not participants in it. The experience lost its excitement and the story wasn't personal anymore. It was just ink on paper.

    As irritating as interruptions can sometimes become, it's important to remember that children's comments during a story signal that they are making connections between new material and something they already know—the essence of the learning process. So read *with* your children and welcome interruptions. They tell you that you are doing your job well.

16. Help your children read. If your children are beginning readers, tell them the words they can't yet read so that they can move along and maintain interest. Later, you can assist them in figuring out the harder words for themselves.

17. Have your children read to you. Encourage them to read a story to themselves before they read it to you. This practice will help give them confidence and a greater understanding of what they have read. It will also make the story more interesting to them.

18. Listen as your children tell you about what they have read. Reading is not reading unless it's accompanied by understanding. Therefore, when your child shows understanding by wanting to tell you about what he or she has read, it's extremely important to show you are interested.

19. Provide a wide variety of reading materials in your home. Children learn by example rather than by precept. If you have books, magazines and newspapers readily available and in use, your children will see that reading is a source of pleasure and information. It's infinitely more effective for your children to see you reading often than it is for you to tell them to read.

20. Give your children books as birthday or holiday gifts. Children who have books they can call their very own are motivated toward reading. The arrival of books mailed directly to your children—with their names on the labels or cartons—provides a strong inducement for reading.

21. Tempt your children with paperbacks. For a number of

young readers, there is something formidable about hardcover books; for them, paperbacks are much more attractive. Also, because paperbacks are less costly, you can provide many more and a greater variety.

22. Intrigue your children with their own magazine subscriptions. Few youngsters—even those not keen on the idea of reading anything at all—can resist the appeal of the arrival in the mail of their own magazine. Reluctant readers suddenly find themselves poring over instructions for easy do-it-yourself projects, riddles, puzzles and stories. Before they know it, they're "hooked" on reading—anxiously awaiting the next issue of *their* magazine.

23. Get your children interested in daily newpapers. The writing communicates a sense of vitality and immediacy that piques children's interest. Clip articles that will appeal to them. Also point out that newpaper advertisements provide a service for the consumer—whatever his or her age. Encourage the children to read ads in the newspaper and especially in "their" magazines for products that interest them.

24. Join and use the free public library. Take your children to the library. Help them get their own cards and select and take out their own books. Ask the librarian to suggest good books to suit your children's ages and interests.

25. Encourage a wide variety of reading experiences. The fact that children read is sometimes more important than what they read. For example:

    Kitchen Reading. Labels on food cans and boxes can make interesting reading. The contests and free gifts advertised on labels are strong reading motivators. Reading these labels can also lead to writing contest entry letters or filling out forms for free merchandise.

    Medicine Cabinet Reading. Labels on jars, bottles and boxes found in the bathroom (excluding dangerous medicines and poisons, of course) can be just as interesting as those found in the kitchen and may also include contests and special inducements.

    Rock Record Reading. If your children are between the ages of 10 and 14, they probably have a collection of rock records. Listening time can also be reading time. Album jackets are filled with information about the kids' favorite rock stars, and sometimes the words to the songs are included. Many record shops sell songbooks that have the lyrics to all the new rock records. Encourage your children to read along as they play the records. (Strannix, 1978, pp. 89-90)

summary

1. Effective teaching and effective learning both depend on how well a teacher plans. An effective plan is built on clearly stated goals which are usually stated in terms of learning objectives. Learning objectives stated in behavioral terms define the terminal behavior students should have developed by the end of a lesson, unit, or course. Learning objectives are often the only way to properly evaluate how effective the teacher is. Specifying learning objectives in behavioral terms can increase students' mo-

tivation because they have a clearer idea of the instruction's purpose. A valuable learning objective must be clear and important. Clarity comes from stating objectives in terms of observable behaviors. Using a taxonomy of objectives can help the teacher to increase an objective's importance by widening the range of objectives available in each learning situation.

2. Benjamin Bloom's taxonomy of learning objectives for cognitive learning involves six main categories of behavior: *Knowledge,* essentially rote memory; *comprehension,* restating material in original terms; *application,* being able to solve similar but new problems; *analysis,* breaking an entity down into its component parts; *synthesis,* combining past learning to create a new and original product; and *evaluation,* being able to judge a person's work against some specified criterion or against someone else's work. Whenever possible, objectives should include as many of these behaviors as possible. Although these behavioral objectives were designed for cognitive learning, they can be adapted to the learning of other skills as well.

3. Critics of behavioral learning objectives say that they lead teachers into ignoring longer-term goals, but advocates argue that learning that is meaningful now will be more apt to be remembered and used later. Humanists see the whole approach as mechanistic and authoritarian, but supporters of learning objectives feel that they help teachers to be better socializers of children. Because it is easier to write behavioral objectives for the more trivial aspects of learning, some educators feel that the really important goals of education will get short shrift. According to taxonomists, however, well-written, explicitly stated objectives can make irrelevant or unimportant objectives easier to identify.

4. According to Robert Gagné, prerequisite learning is an important consideration in planning. Gagné described eight basic types of learning (in order of increasing complexity): *signal learning,* such as classical conditioning; *stimulus-response learning,* such as operant conditioning; *chaining,* learning that involves a specific sequence of connected responses; *verbal association learning,* involved in the development of language as words are first associated with objects and then with new words; *discrimination learning,* which emphasizes the differences between stimuli; *concept learning,* in which objects or events are responded to as a class of similar phenomena; *rule learning,* learning a chain of concepts and applying them to new situations; *problem-solving,* the application of rules to new situations. Because students must master the simple forms before they can understand those that are more complex, Gagné urges curriculum planners to follow this list.

5. Most teachers write objectives that are too vague. According to Mager, a well-written learning objective states in behavioral terms what the students should be able to do after instruction, the conditions under which they should be able to do it, and a criterion for acceptable performance. A classroom activity should not be confused with a learning objective, even though both may be stated in behavioral terms.

6. Task analysis helps the teacher to understand the steps a student must go through in order to achieve a learning objective. Teachers should also pretest their students to see what their current level of ability is before deciding on a reasonable objective. Teachers need to plan for students' individual differences in the way students learn as well as what they already know.

7. Perceptual skills, motor skills, language skills, conceptual learning, problem solving, and attitudes conducive to learning are the basic building blocks of competence in all academic subjects. Of these, motor skills usually get the least attention, which is unfortunate because they enhance a child's social adjustment as well as academic achievement.

8. The teaching of perceptual skills is the core of the elementary school curriculum. According to E. J. Gibson, teachers can increase children's perceptual skills by showing them how objects in the environment have similar and distinguishing features. As children develop, some of their perceptions become more precise, while others become more general. The effectiveness with which children learn to make perceptual discriminations is related to their age, intelligence, and cognitive style. Activities used to teach perceptual skills should be matched to the child's stage of perceptual and cognitive development. Probably the most important perceptual skill is reading; reading difficulties are probably the most important cause of dropping out before graduation. According to E. J. Gibson, four stages are involved in learning to read: learning to speak, learning to discriminate printed letters, learning to attach sounds to the letters, and learning to perceive higher-order units. There are two basic ways to teach reading: the code (phonic) emphasis and the meaning emphasis. Some students initially respond better to one or the other, but both are needed for optimal learning.

9. Motor skills are usually thought of in terms of the games and activities taught by physical education teachers, but in fact a motor skill is anything we do with our bodies. In Merrill's taxonomy, there are five areas of motor skills: physical education, communication, fine arts, language, and vocational skills. The basic principles of motor learning are the same as those for other learning: descriptions and demonstrations, selective attention, discrimination, reinforcement, and feedback. However, there are some principles peculiar to motor learning; these form the basis of movement theory. The basic principle of movement theory is that most learned behavior involves some kind of movement. Readiness does not simply develop; it is the result of appropriate experience in movement. Movement theory can also be used to analyze the component elements involved in the performance of a motor skill. In addition to learning the required movements, students must also learn to recognize and process relevant environmental cues.

10. The teaching of motor skills is best divided into two stages. In Stage 1, the learner is shown what has to be done. Stage 2 is called the "fixation/diversification stage." In Stage 2, the learner practices the skill by fixating on it and, as competence increases, making more sophisticated varia-

tions of the response. Once the student has performed the skill, his or her performance needs to be evaluated, though teachers should be sensitive enough to save their feedback until the student indicates that it is needed.

11. Practice can occur mentally or physically. Some authorities advise students to overpractice, while others recommend the progressive part method in which the various component movements are taught and practiced separately and then integrated after they have been mastered. A skill should be practiced under conditions that are similar to those in which it will be performed. Practice distributed over time is better than massed practice.

12. Many teachers try to ignore individual differences in teaching motor skills, but that is a mistake. Age differences and physical handicaps obviously need to be taken into consideration. The one difference that has been stressed in the past is sex, but research has shown that before the age of 12 there is little difference between boys and girls. The primary justification for applying different standards to females in high school and college was women's supposed gynecological delicacy, but actually there seems to be little or no reason for basing different training programs on sex.

13. Language skills are important because a person's adaption to all aspects of the environment depends on how well he or she speaks, reads, and writes. Language is seen as a productive system because each utterance is a creative act. Except for ritualized expressions of social discourse, few of our sentences are ever repeated.

14. There is a difference between linguistic competence (knowledge of principles) and linguistic performance (translating this knowledge into action). The study of the basic structural principles of language is called linguistics. Linguists are interested in the knowledge aspect of language competence, while psycholinguists are more interested in how people use language in everyday life.

15. According to linguist Noam Chomsky, humans have an innate capacity to understand and apply grammatical rules (called transformations). Behaviorists, however, suggest that language develops through selective reinforcement and emphasize the importance of modeling and imitation. Jean Piaget related language development to the stages of cognitive development, while Jerome Bruner related it to a parallel development of interests and needs. The preschool period is a critical time for language development and has a great impact on linguistic abilities in school. Most American preschoolers are taught by their parents, whose characteristics exert a great influence and account for the diversity of ability among school children. Teachers can help students to develop their language skills by giving them opportunities to practice and feedback on their performance, and by being good models. Topics used for language learning should be interesting to students. Teachers should also take individual differences into account. Reading ability is based on linguistic compe-

tence. Using words with a high phoneme-grapheme correspondence in the early stages makes learning to read easier for students.

16. A concept is an idea that allows us to classify a variety of related phenomena into a meaningful category. Concrete concepts can be linked to observable objects; abstract concepts are definitional. A concept is a category; the combination of related concepts is a rule. Rules have an important bearing on learning to solve problems.

17. Piaget, Kohlberg, and other developmental-stage theorists believe that concept development goes through a fixed series of stages. The learning environmentalists, such as Bandura and Gagné, maintain that concepts are primarily products of experience, which means that a fixed order is unlikely as we all have different sets of experiences.

18. There are two ways to teach concepts. In the inductive method, the general concept must be inferred from specific instances. In the deductive method, students are provided with a general definition of the concept and asked to provide their own examples. The best approach may be a combination of the two methods. Several illustrations of a concept should always be presented. Asking the student to apply the concept to a new situation is the best way to see how well he or she has learned it. Specific procedures for teaching concepts include reducing the number of irrelevant characteristics in the instances chosen to illustrate the concept; using concrete examples and keeping explanations simple; letting the learner view the material after feedback as well as before; letting the student restate the concept in his or her own words; doing the more general concepts first; and illustrating positive and negative instances of the concept. Teachers will need to adapt these methods to students' individual differences in ability, learning style, cognitive style, and intelligence.

19. Attitudes must be inferred from observable behavior. Students' attitudes toward themselves (self-concept), a particular subject, and school in general have an incalculable effect on learning. Attitudes are learned and therefore they can be modified under proper conditions. Reinforcements such as praise and encouragement can lead to attitude change, as can exercises in values clarification. These exercises can be incorporated into the learning objectives of nearly all academic subjects.

for students who want to read further

BLOOM, B. S., KRATHWOHL, D. R., et al. A taxonomy of educational objectives. *Handbook 1, The Cognitive Domain,* 1956; *Handbook 2, The Affective Domain,* 1964, New York: McKay, (one-volume edition, 1969). These two texts are the classic books on classification of education into specific areas. They are excellent reference material for developing learning objectives.

HALL, E. T. Why Americans can't write. *Human Nature,* 1(8), August 1978, pp. 74-79. Edward T. Hall taught English in the United States for 28 years before going to Botswana to teach English to African students. In this report, he describes how, with his instruction, African students studying English as a second language learned to communicate through writing far more effectively than many students taught in the United States whose native language is English. Hall's practical solutions should be of interest to English teachers.

MYERS, M. Five approaches to the teaching of writing. *Learning*, 6(8), April 1978, pp. 38-41. This brief article designed specifically for classroom teachers presents a variety of positions on how to teach students to write in such a way that they communicate their feelings and ideas to others. The article contains positions of educational psychologists as well as of successful writers and points out advantages and disadvantages of all of them. Particularly useful to the teacher who wants to establish a meaningful writing curriculum is the resource list provided at the end of the article.

PAI, H. Y., AND LIEBERTHAL, E. (Chisanbop Enterprises, Inc.). *The Chisanbop Home Study Book.* New York: Van Nostrand Reinhold, 1978. This book presents methods by which basic computational operations and even simple algebra can be done by the ten-finger Chisanbop method. The authors caution that the procedures described simply "scratch the surface" of what can be done by the method and indicate that Chisanbop is not as simplistic as some back-to-basics proponents may suggest. However, it is useful for the teacher who would like to experiment with the beginning procedures. For those who wish to develop courses using the method, Chisanbop Enterprises suggest contacting them directly for information about workshop courses.

SPERRY, L. (Ed.). *Learning Performance and Individual Differences.* Glenview, Ill.: Scott, Foresman, 1972. This is an excellent collection of readings relating to individual differences in the learning situation. Teacher expectations, learning and cognitive styles, and instructional styles are the major topics covered.

VARGAS, J. S. *Writing Worthwhile Behavioral Objectives.* New York: Harper & Row, 1972. Vargas has developed extremely clear examples of how a teacher can build behavioral objectives. This self-instructional book should prove to be an excellent aid in developing worthwhile objectives in the cognitive domain. It is an invaluable aid for the teacher.

THE EFFECTS
OF
INDIVIDUAL
DIFFERENCES
ON
LEARNING
AND
TEACHING

Throughout this book we have emphasized the importance of approaching and understanding your students as individuals, since each one has distinct needs, problems, abilities, interests, and past histories of reinforcement. Family, peer group, school, mass media, social class, and sex—each serves as an important transmitter and interpreter of culture. Since the combined influence of all these variables is never precisely the same for any two people, each growing child develops into a unique cultural product and learns in a unique way. In additon, you must consider each student's age, intelligence, physical and emotional health, general adjustment and attitude, and past history of achievement when designing instruction. The key to dealing successfully with all these differences is flexibility.

All major approaches to development and learning take individual differences into consideration, although some approaches emphasize them much more than others. Each chapter in this section deals with children who are significantly different from most other children, and who, because of this difference, need special help from their teachers in order to succeed in school.

Children who exhibit what we call "problem behavior" in the classroom are one group in need of special help. Such children may be shy and overly withdrawn or, conversely, they may be excessively aggressive and hostile. Chapter 8 discusses family, school, and social factors that lead to different problem behaviors. Because of increasing concern in recent years about the increase in aggression and violence in schools, Chapter 8 suggests ways that teachers can manage aggression most effectively.

Chapter 9 deals with children often referred to as children with "special needs." For the most part, these children are handicapped either mentally or physically. Some children are handicapped mentally because of physiological problems. We call these children "mentally retarded." Other children, commonly referred to as "learning-disabled" have normal intelligence, but, for a variety of reasons, have difficulty learning in school. Still others have trouble learning because they don't speak the language taught in school. All these children, as well as physically handicapped children, need special help. Another group of children, those we call "gifted," also should be considered as having special needs. These children need special attention in order to learn to their fullest capacity. Chapter 9 outlines special programs and techniques to help both students and their teachers.

In September, 1978, Public Law 94-142, which requires the mainstreaming of all handicapped children into regular classrooms whenever possible, took effect. Since that date, in addition to their other duties, teachers have had to learn how to deal with the varieties of special needs that physically, mentally, and emotionally handicapped children have. Chapter 10 deals with mainstreaming and its effects on both teachers and students. It describes approaches that teachers can take to increase the chances that mainstreaming will be successful.

Joey was 15 years old when his homeroom teacher first sent him to the principal's office for hitting one of the other students with a handmade blackjack. The principal had seen Joey often in detention, where he was sent regularly for cutting class, but this was the first time that Joey had been violent.

The principal asked him why. Joey screamed, "What's it to you?" He got up from his seat, ran out of the office, and slammed the door so hard that the glass window at the top of the door shattered. One of the teachers tried to stop Joey, but he kicked his way free.

When the police found Joey the next day, he was high on heroin. He said he was glad that he didn't have to go to school anymore, and that he was glad that his mother would be "upset and embarrassed." Joey's mother cried. She said he had always been a good student until he entered high school. She thought that his problem probably had to do with the tough kids he met there.

* * * *

Roy, a 7-year-old boy, was sent to the school psychologist because, despite his above-average intelligence, he was unresponsive in class. Roy's parents told the psychologist that they fought a lot at home, but that Roy didn't seem disturbed by it. Roy, however, reported that he felt considerable pressure to take sides. He protected himself from this pressure by forcing himself to ignore what was going on, first at home, and then, later, at school as well (Resnick, 1978).

* * * *

Eleven-year-old Carol, pressured by her parents to succeed and extremely afraid of letting them down, developed a succession of mysterious illnesses that kept her home from school. Although she was highly intelligent, Carol's standards were unrealistically high and she saw herself as unable to do anything right. Being ill seemed to her to be the easiest way to avoid the anxiety aroused by going to school (Resnick, 1978).

Students with personal and social problems are not necessarily what we think of as "seriously emotionally disturbed": They may simply be having some trouble adjusting to some aspect of their environments. School may be the arena in which the students express the results of difficulties in other areas of their lives.

There are many different types of problem behaviors, but they all have one thing in common: Students with problems don't learn. Some students, like Joey, keep other students from learning as well. Carol and Roy don't disturb others, but they aren't learning either. Any student who isn't learning for any reason is a problem for the teacher.

Just as we need to know how digestion works before we can understand why we get indigestion, a look at successful adjustment can shed light on the types of maladjustments that generate problem behavior.

A Clinical Approach to Interpreting Problem Behaviors

A useful view of the happy student—the one with the "well-adjusted personality"—was presented by Havighurst (1953). He described good adjustment in terms of being able to perform certain **developmental tasks** of life. Learning to perform these tasks is essential for what Havighurst called "healthy growth." These tasks vary from society to society; what is acceptable in one society may not be acceptable in another. In our society, for instance, the developmental tasks of the middle years of childhood include learning the physical skills needed for games; getting along with peers; and developing competence in reading, writing, and arithmetic. In adolescence, the tasks include establishing mature relationships with peers of both sexes, achieving emotional independence from parents and other adults, and preparing for economic independence later in life. Mastering the developmental tasks of a particular stage usually leads a person to success in future tasks and, presumably, is the basis of a well-adjusted personality. Failure in these tasks leads to difficulty with future tasks, social disapproval, unhappiness, and, ultimately, problem behavior of various sorts. Children of poverty backgrounds often have greater difficulty accomplishing developmental tasks in relation to school than do middle-class children (Kohn, 1977).

One developmental task that is important to children in elementary, middle, and high schools alike is the learning of interpersonal skills necessary for good peer relationships. The importance that children attach to friendships changes as they get older (Selman and Jaquette, 1976). In the early elementary school years, children are just beginning to differentiate between the way they look at things and the viewpoints of their peers. Later, most students gradually develop the ability to see relations as mutual compromises between subjective viewpoints. By high school, they are learning to consider the development of friendships as a step-by-step process in which one comes to know the other person as an individual with mutual and common interests. According to Havighurst, high school students who do not reach this stage have failed at an important developmental task. Such students are likely to have difficulty getting along with others and will probably exhibit unhappiness and various sorts of problem behaviors.

The adolescent's life is further complicated by the need to learn things related to becoming an autonomous adult. This includes developing the abilities to think critically, to verify facts, and not to accept all information at face value. One-half of adolescents fail to reach Piaget's formal stage of operations (Miller, 1978). Because these students solve problems most easily at the concrete level, they often fail at abstract tasks. Such adolescents naturally feel inadequate, are angry at their inability to solve day-to-day problems, and are apt to exhibit problem behaviors instead of adult-accepted and well-adjusted behavior.

There are many other theories about what constitutes a well-adjusted personality. Some of these define personality in terms of what is sometimes called "mental health." Mental health "refers to the processes of living a full, happy, harmonious and effective existence" (Bernard, 1973, p. 242). To Journard (1971), an individual with a healthy personality receives personal satisfaction from playing his or her role well and will continually grow emotionally. An extension of personal adjustment is "comprehensive mental health" the total health and well-being of the family, community, and society as well as the individual (Coleman and Broen, 1972).

In this book, I have avoided the terms "mental health and "mental illness" because I feel that their association with physical health will lead you to a false analogy that is inappropriate and oversimplified. Physical problems have organic bases and respond to organic remedies. Problem behaviors on the other hand, are often related to past learning experiences and, in many cases, must be treated with educational and therapeutic techniques.

To a great extent, the problem behaviors discussed in this chapter appear to be a function of social values and conflicts. Social standards or norms are considered the model for well-adjusted behavior, and those who follow the norms are rewarded by society. Deviation from the norm is considered problem behavior. This distinction would be clear-cut except for the fact that social values, attitudes, and norms are not constant. They vary from period to period and from one society to another. A girl who wore slacks or jeans to school fifteen years ago might have been punished and sent home to change. What is considered exceptional or problem behavior today may be considered normal in 1995. Other societies have different definitions of problem behaviors. A 10-year-old who is withdrawn and does not play well with his or her peers or an adolescent who exhibits extreme emotional dependence on his or her parents are thought of as showing problem behavior. But, if withdrawal for 10-year-olds and adolescent dependence were acceptable in our society, this behavior would not be considered a problem. Thus, as social values change, our definition of problem behaviors changes, too.

Problem Behaviors Typical of American School Children

According to the National Institute of Mental Health, approximately 10 to 12 percent of the 50 million elementary school children in the United States have some sort of problem behavior that requires therapy. Furthermore, among the 15 million children being raised in poverty environments, one out of three falls in this category. The results in the classroom are discussed regularly on radio and TV and in newspapers and magazines: violence and a breakdown of discipline as well as lack of learning among aggressive, withdrawn, and unhappy children.

Among the most significant types of problem behavior in our society are unsocialized aggression, hyperactivity, withdrawal, overanxiousness, and the runaway reaction.

Violence and other forms of aggression   Violence toward people and property has become a major problem in American schools. In 1976, the U.S. Senate Subcommittee to Investigate Juvenile Delinquency released major reports on the nature, extent, and cost of school violence and vandalism (Bayh, 1978). In 1978, the National Institute of Education published a similar report that included descriptions of personal violence, vandalism, theft, and attacks against students and teachers. Many teachers are talking about teacher "burnout," feelings of frustration and apathy that accompany excessive nervous strain in violent or potentially violent situations. Burnout is essentially the same psychological state associated with soldiers in wartime —battle fatigue. Unsocialized, aggressive children, like Joey, who turn schools into battlefields are generally hostile, disobedient, destructive, and violent. They frequently disrupt classes and attack other students and teachers.

Fighting among very young children may give way to more violent forms of aggression later in life.

Jan Lukas, Rapho/Photo Researchers, Inc.

They may also steal, vandalize, fight (sometimes with deadly weapons), and set fires. Paradoxically, they often feel "picked on" and disliked. They believe people are mean and meet the anticipated aggression of others with aggressive acts of their own. If such behaviors occur in the context of group activity, especially during adolescent years, the aggressive child is referred to as a "group delinquent."

Some children get along well with peers but actively dislike adults. Such children frequently come from homes where arguments, fighting, and other types of aggression are commonplace. In American society, family-related factors seem particularly critical in causing aggressive behavior in children. In one study (McCord, McCord, and Howard, 1961) several factors that led boys to become aggressive were brought out. Generally, the parents of excessively aggressive boys were found to be rejecting, unaffectionate, and punishment-oriented. Athough they frequently threatened their sons, they did not supervise them closely and were inconsistent in their use and methods of discipline. They made few demands on the boys, perhaps reflecting a low level of parental expectation. The parents themselves were often socially deviant, and in many cases the relationship between the parents was filled with conflict and dissatisfaction.

The family environment of nonaggressive boys was quite different. Their parents were warm and affectionate with them. Their manner was rarely threatening or punishing, although they firmly supervised their children and disciplined them in consistent ways. High demands were placed on the boys, which may suggest a high level of parental expectation. The parents of nonaggressive boys tended to be socially conforming rather than deviant. The relationship between the parents was affectionate and characterized by mutual respect and a low degree of conflict.

One implication of such studies is that punishment intensifies aggression. Many teachers believe that discipline and obedience can be maintained only through the threat of punishment. Such teachers employ various types of punishment to keep students in line, including detention, extra assignments, public criticism and humiliation, and corporal punishment. However, punishment may actually increase students' inclination toward antisocial conduct, instead of reducing it.

Children whose home lives are unhappy often have low self-esteem. A child's level of self-esteem has a significant effect on his or her performance in school and relationships to others. Coopersmith (1968) compared students with high and low self-esteem and found that youngsters with high self-esteem were active, expressive, eager to voice their opinions, and relatively free of anxiety. They trusted their own perceptions and expected to be treated well by others. They were confident and optimistic about their lives and rarely developed psychosomatic conditions such as insomnia or headaches.

Students with low self-esteem were discouraged and depressed. They felt isolated, unloved, and unable to solve their problems. Many were shy, hesitant, and afraid of antagonizing others. They remained in the background of their peer groups. They tended to be self-conscious and preoccupied. They dwelled on their own difficulties, which only added to their isolation from their peers. Other children with low self-esteem were more likely to be aggressive. These children's behavior was often spontaneously destructive. They might rob hallway lockers or set fires in wastebaskets.

Low self-esteem students tend to come from families with rejecting, punitive parents who have low expectations for their children. By contrast, high self-esteem students tend to come from families in which parents have high expectations. High self-esteem youngsters usually develop solid and positive self-concepts.

Children with low self-esteem can often be helped by sympathetic adults who act in ways that make them feel that they are, in fact, important human beings. Horace, a foster child, announced to his teacher on his first day in the middle school, "I'm really bad news! You'll be sorry I'm in your class!" The teacher responded with a rather surprised, "Oh, really? What makes you think so?" He gleefully told her about some of the "bad" things he'd done the previous year and said that his teachers "sure didn't like me." Later, when the teacher could talk with him privately, she asked if he enjoyed his reputation, if he liked his teachers last year, if he liked school, and so on. She told him that starting in a new school gave him a clean slate. No one in this school thought he was bad, and, as long as he earned a good reputation, no one would blame him for things he had done in the past. The teacher talked with him often about his interests, a pet rabbit and a new skateboard, and encouraged him to help with classroom jobs. Whatever his previous record had been, Horace enjoyed this year, and he didn't become the monster he'd said he was.

A low self-concept is particularly striking in students from poverty backgrounds. Many middle-class teachers consider these children's behavior strange, inappropriate, or simply "wrong." Students from poverty backgrounds often feel threatened by their teachers' judgments, and many learn to feel incompetent, inadequate, and out-of-place in middle-class institutions (Karnes, Zehrbach, and Jones, 1971).

What such students learn outside the classroom—on the street— often compounds the problem. They learn not to count on anyone but themselves and that caring about others is dangerous. They learn to act impulsively, to retaliate first, and think about it later or not at all.

Although violence is seen as the property of the lower classes, aggressive children come from every socioeconomic level. Once the problem of the inner-city teacher and community, violent crime is rapidly becoming a way of life among students in American's wealthier suburban middle and high schools as well. Today many American schools are protected from violent crime by hired guards. In some cities, these guards are equipped with guns.

What should teachers do? Solving the problem of violence in the schools depends on families and the community as well as on teachers. Teachers can help by learning more about why students behave as they do. Teachers can see what kinds of homes their students come from, how they interact with their peers, and what their goals are. Using the best principles of behavior management—being consistent, rewarding good behavior whenever it occurs, and trying to minimize punishment—and showing that you have faith in your students' abilities to solve their own problems can also help.

Hyperactivity and hyperkinesis   Hyperactivity and a similar behavior problem, hyperkinesis, are often confused. **Hyperkinesis** is motor-impaired behavior that is caused by neurological disorders. Hyperactivity, on the other hand, is related to common emotional disturbance and is psychologically oriented.

Like unsocialized, aggressive children, hyperactive or hyperkinetic children are very noticeable to the teacher. These children are generally overactive, restless, excitable, and impulsive. They are constantly in motion and never seem to sit still. In school, hyperactive children rarely complete a work assignment and tend to fool around or talk out of turn. They may also display antisocial behavior such as fighting, lying, stealing, vandalism, or even being cruel to animals.

Hyperactive and hyperkinetic children are not characterized by inferior mental ability, but they do have particular learning difficulties in school. When faced with a task in which they must choose from a number of responses, they tend to react impulsively and select quickly without thinking. If a confusing series of alternatives is presented, they will choose the most obvious answer, even if it is not the best. Their homework is likely to be sloppy and disorganized, and they may make careless mistakes in reading. They may have high intellectual potential, but their impulsiveness and restlessness prevent them from achieving this potential.

Most hyperactive children connot control their compulsive activity. Some psychologists suggest that the tendency to hyperactivity may be inborn, although many other explanations are possible. Many parents of hyperactive children have reported that their hyperactive children's behavior was noticeably different, even before age 2. Hyperactive children also tend to have many health problems in their first year, and many show poor coordination and delayed speech development.

Evidence of the biological basis of hyperactivity and hyperkinesis comes from the effects of different types of drug treatment on hyperactive children. Certain doctor-prescribed drugs, which act as stimulants for most people, paradoxically have a tranquilizing effect on some hyperactive children, who then become better able to concentrate, relate to peers, and perform school tasks. Some researchers point out that caffeine in coffee can lower the activity level of some overactive children and suggest that coffee be used daily to reduce activity to a manageable point (Resnick, 1978). On the other hand, some hyperkinetic children respond better to tranquilizers (Calhoun, 1978).

Drug therapy for hyperactive and hyperkinetic children has been a controversial issue in school systems. Although a number of studies have described the positive effects of drugs, criticism of the widespread use of drugs in the treatment of school children is growing. Stimulating drugs have only a temporary effect; when the drug wears off, the child reverts to his or her typical behavior. In addition, there is the serious danger that hyperactive children may become addicted to the drugs after they have been treated over a long period of time. This possibility frightens many parents of hyperactive children. A further criticism has been the administration of these drugs by unqualified people. Many parents, teachers, and psychologists have questioned the safety of drug use—including caffeine in coffee—as well as the implications of using drugs to control what may be considered socially undesirable behavior (see, for example, Walker, 1974).

The search for other methods of treatment has concentrated on nutrition and behavioral training. For example, there is a possibility that hyperactivity in some children might be controlled by eliminating foods with artificial colors and flavors (Feingold, 1973; Snider, 1974).

Feingold (1973) reported that 16 out of 25 hyperactive children he studied who ate foods without certain artificial colorings or flavorings became significantly less aggressive. Of these 16, the four who followed the prescribed diet most closely improved most dramatically. Although food additives seem to affect only a small percentage of hyperactive children (MacMahan, 1979), the Feingold study has prompted a full-scale revision of school menus in California.

Another method of treatment involves training hyperactive children for improved self-control. Simpson and Nelson (1974) used breathing techniques and other body controls to help hyperactive children control various motor behaviors and maintain concentration. Their findings suggested that such training can help hyperactive children to develop better self-discipline and control over their actions.

Severe anxiety Students with severe anxiety symptoms are often overactive, restless, and unable to concentrate on schoolwork. They are full of conflicts, immature, insecure, inhibited, and highly self-critical with regard to failure. Severely anxious children can literally worry themselves sick, producing strong psychophysiological problems such as vomiting, headaches, stomach aches, and diarrhea. Such children may be misdiagnosed as hyperactive and mistakenly given stimulants. Such medication unfortunately may cause even more severe symptoms in excessively anxious children.

Anxiety levels differ. A low level of anxiety is not necessarily bad; it often has good side effects, such as keying you up to study for an exam. When we speak of anxiety as a problem behavior, we mean a high level of anxiety.

There are three common types of anxiety reactions. People who have chronic anxiety appear tense and fearful over a long period of time. They are under continual strain and are usually fatigued, though the cause of their anxiety is unclear to the casual observer. If such strain becomes acute, an anxiety attack—extreme agitation for a short period of time—may occur. An extreme anxiety attack may lead to a panic reaction, the most serious type of anxiety reaction.

Children with anxiety symptoms often feel rejected by their parents (Doyal and Friedman, 1974). Take the case of Jim, a fourth grader whose negative classroom attitude seemed related to hostility toward his parents. When asked which member of his family he had the most fun with, Jim replied, "Sometimes I think it's the cat." Jim seemed angry about his father's lack of concern and commented, "I can't disturb him when he is reading, and when he is not reading, he is gone" (p. 163).

Anxiety can be a basic cause of a child's failure in school. School can be a strange and even frightening world, filled with unfamiliar academic tasks and new social roles, particularly for the young child. But the demands of the school situation can produce mild anxiety symptoms in many, if not all, children. For that small number of children who bring fears and uncertainties with them, however, the added stresses of school can lead to more severe anxiety symptoms. The sensitive teacher is alert to these symptoms and treats them by carefully and sensitively showing how school can produce rewards, and how students can succeed at school-related tasks. Acceptance at school can be at least a partial antidote for rejection at home.

School phobia   One of the most common symptoms of school-related anxiety is **school phobia.** Children with school phobia are reluctant (or refuse) to go to school. School phobia is usually caused by extreme fear of some aspect of the school situation. The child may be afraid of the teacher, a particular classmate, the recess period, the school staircases, or any number of details in the school environment. Physical symptoms, such as stomach aches, headaches, or various pains often accompany the anxiety, and the child will make these symptoms the reason for staying home.

The case study of B. provides insight into some possible causes and treatments of school phobia (Weinberger, Leventhal, and Beckman, 1973). B. had a background of poor school attendance dating back to the sixth grade. Throughout eighth grade, she had failed to attend school and had been characterized by a local clinic as "schizoid and extremely narcissistic." Like many children who are afraid of school, she was good at playing on her parents' child-rearing anxieties and guilt feelings.

B. was 15 years old and in the tenth grade by the time the school psychologist was consulted. After consulting a clinical psychologist, the school psychologist eventually took a direct approach. In a meeting with B., he gave her three rather unpleasant choices: (1) she could go to school voluntarily; (2) her parents (or the police) could forcibly bring her to school; or (3) the school could refer her to the juvenile court as a delinquent, which might lead to confinement in a state home for girls. B. smiled hostilely and replied, "I am obviously being boxed in by you and have no choice" (p. 85).

However, the problem was not yet solved. After attending school for five days, B. was absent on the sixth day. Her mother called the school to say that B. had an infected foot and could not leave the house. B's doctor told the psychologist that the abrasion that led to the infection could have been self-inflicted.

The final step in helping B. to attend school came the following week, when her father told the psychologist that he was fed up with B.'s behavior. The psychologist then asked the father to help in another direct approach to B.: He was to inform B. that she had 15 minutes to get dressed and ready for school, and that after that time had passed, he would take her to school, dressed or undressed. After various attempts to stall, B. eventually complied. The decisive stand taken by her father seemed to be the crucial element. Three months later, B. was only infrequently absent from school, and her grades were good.

What is the psychological explanation for the outcome of B.'s case? According to psychologists, B.'s school phobia derived from her earlier ability to manipulate her parents' anxiety. Children may get short-term satisfaction from having such power over their parents, but eventually they come to see their parents as weak. Weak parents make children feel vulnerable and insecure. Apparently, her father's show of strength gave B. the reassurance she needed.

Although this case study is not a model for the treatment for all school phobias, it is useful in understanding some of the causes and manifestations of school phobia. Not only was B. calculating and manipulative, she was also extremely successful in playing on her parents' anxieties in order to stay out of school. School phobia is more common in very young children than in adolescents, but even young children seem skillful at playing on their parents' anxieties in order to stay out of school.

Depression and threat of suicide Depression is another problem related to anxiety. Symptoms of **depression** include slowed motor response and reaction time, appearances of sadness, despair, and suicidal ideas or threats. Depressed students have the tendency to retreat into daydreams and are not socially active. Drastic mood swings that prevent normal functioning or grief reactions that continue for months at a time can also be symptoms of depression.

Freud and many of his followers viewed depression as anger against a loved one that has been turned inward against oneself. According to this approach, rather than express anger, the child keeps

Teenage alienation and depression are two of the most serious problems to be dealt with by educators and psychologists.

all the hostility inside and lapses into grief, sadness, or physical symptoms.

Seriously depressed children and adolescents contemplating or attempting suicide have increased significantly in our society, particularly in the past few years. The greatest increase in suicide has been in the middle and late adolescent groups, for which the rate nearly tripled between 1965 and 1975. It is still increasing. Suicide now ranks as the third most common cause of death in the 15 to 24 age group, after accidents and homicides (Williams, Hager, Moore and Witherspoon, 1978). The problem is usually caused by many long-term factors such as family problems, feelings of real or imagined rejection, and struggle for independence (Rosenkrantz, 1978). Unfortunately, many depressed and potentially suicidal children go unnoticed because they don't cause major disturbances at home or at school. A teacher alert to the right symptoms will call for immediate help.

Withdrawal Extremely withdrawn children are shy, fearful, secretive, and apathetic. They feel unable to cope with everyday problems and have trouble forming close friendships. Rather than facing the unpleasant and frightening realities of life, they turn to daydreaming and fantasy as a means of escape. This isolates them even more by cutting them off from interaction with and feedback from peers. As a result, such children's already fragile sense of reality can become even more shaky.

Just as the squeaky wheel gets the grease, antisocial, aggressive children who disrupt classroom routines get more attention than children who are shy and withdrawn. It is easy to understand how a teacher confronted with 35 students may concentrate on those who continually interfere with the normal functioning of the class. But the withdrawn student, who causes no trouble and whose worst offense is daydreaming, may benefit just as much (and perhaps more) from the assistance and counseling of a warm, supportive teacher as the aggressive, antisocial student. Gordon Q. is a case in point. Gordon was a 12-year-old loner. His work was average, and, although he was quiet and shy, he would recite when called upon. His teachers didn't take much notice of him until Gordon made them look. He stole some pills from his mother's dresser and took an overdose. Gordon's teachers discovered that his mother had been in and out of mental institutions, his father was in jail, and his brother had died the previous year from a drug overdose. Luckily, Gordon's call for help was answered and he was given much-needed counseling.

Withdrawn children often live in oppressive family atmospheres. If they are offered no supportive services in school they may become runaways. Since a psychological "flight from reality" often characterizes the withdrawn child, running away can be seen as a physical form of withdrawal reaction. The timid, fearful child escapes via fantasies and daydreams into an unthreatening, self-constructed universe. The runaway escapes in a more physical sense, hoping to find a more satisfying or less repressive living situation elsewhere. Neither child has found the ideal solutions to the problem. The daydreamer increasingly loses touch with reality, and the runaway loses touch with possible sources of help.

Adolescent Behavior Problems

Some problem behaviors are particularly typical of adolescents. Adolescence can be a time of unrest, confusion, tension, conflict, and an almost desperate search for identity, individuality, and meaning. Many adolescents become alienated or depressed, especially when family, school and peer-group values conflict. Teachers planning to work in a middle school or high school should be prepared to deal with certain problems unique to this age group.

Alcohol and drug abuse   Alcohol and drug abuse are serious problems among adolescents, and today children of progressively younger ages have been reported to use alcohol and drugs. Alcohol in particular is growing in popularity among school children. In 1978, 1 out of every 11 high school seniors was reported to be using marijuana daily (Education USA, June 1978).

While parents worry about marijuana, alcohol use is also rising. Nearly 29 percent of the boys and 25 percent of the girls in some urban high schools today are using hard liquor before twelfth grade. Amphetamines, barbiturates, and psychedelic drugs continue to be freely available to high school students.

Often parents have no idea that alcohol and drugs are so readily available. In one suburban high school, for example, an overnight trip was abruptly canceled when several dozen bottles of liquor were found in the luggage. The parents were contacted, and, although most of the students had taken the liquor from their parents' home, not one parent realized that any liquor was missing.

Unfortunately, students have easier access to alcohol and drugs than to education about the dangers involved. Teachers need to provide valid evidence of the dangers of abuse in ways that students can understand and accept. They also need to help students who seek assistance and know where to go for help from specialists.

The adolescent runaway   The number of adolescent runaways has been increasing steadily in the past decade. More that 10 percent of adolescents try running away at one time or another. In one study (Shellow, Schamp, Liebow, and Unger, 1967) runaways were separated into two distinct groups: a relatively small group of adolescents who ran away frequently; and another group who ran away occasionally or only once. The frequent runaways came from disorganized families, were failures in school, and, in some cases, had been guilty of criminal behavior. The occasional or one-time runaways were also troubled, but had less need for custodial care and individual therapy. For them, running away "may be any one of a number of things ranging from a cry of despair to a victory yell." These youths seemed to have much in common with their peers who did not run away: "A plain, forthright expression of dissatisfaction with home or school" (Shellow et al., 1967, p. 29). In more recent studies, runaways reported receiving more punishment and less support from their parents than adolescents who did not run away. Runaways also had less favorable self-concepts and were more defensive.

It is more difficult for you to help runaways than to help other problem behaviors—simply because those students aren't there to help. Sometimes, however, they return. When they do, you should remember that the runaway is often an extreme example of withdrawal—who can often be helped to stay—with signs of love, attention, and concern.

Sexual activity and early pregnancy Sexuality is an important concern for the adolescent who must come to terms with his or her sexual identity. The sexual revolution makes this task even more complex. Our traditional ideas about masculinity and femininity are changing. Sexual freedom is increasing among both adolescents and adults, and traditional norms of sexuality and relationships between boys and girls, as well as between men and women, are breaking down.

These changes place greater pressure on women and girls. A survey by Brody (1967) indicated that the female college student is much more likely to enjoy her first sexual experience and much less likely to feel guilty or worried about it than in the past. The development of a serious and outspoken women's liberation movement has changed the climate of traditional sexual relationships. Women are increasingly demanding more satisfaction from sex, career, and family life.

One sad result of these changing values has been a significant increase in the number of unmarried pregnant adolescent girls. Today, more that 10 percent of all births are illegitimate, and 94 percent of adolescent mothers keep their babies. Urban studies reveal that most unwed mothers have repeated one or more grades in school and are from two to four years below the expected norm in major achievement areas (Kipp and Briggs, 1975). Coming frequently from homes in which indifferent or busy mothers provide little help and advice, these girls bring into the world a generation of new babies to repeat the cycle of unhappiness. The solution? Sex education programs are increasing in schools throughout the country. Special schools for pregnant girls are being added. The results are still too fragmentary to make clear conclusions.

What Happens to Teenage Runaways?

Walk along a downtown street of any major American city after dark. It is there that parents and police often look for teenage runaways. And it is there that they often find them—young girls in their early teens, sometimes with young boys of the same age. Some of them are looking for handouts and might politely approach you to ask for a few dollars. Others—boys or girls—might ask if you want to purchase services. Large numbers of young people, loose and afraid in the city, resort to prostitution rather than return home to their families, who, they fear, will reject them.

Some young teenagers fall into the hands of adult pimps, who take their money and give them little in return other than the hard street life. Some find other groups of teenagers and settle together in some communal arrangement. Many settle in a drug culture that eventually leads them to robbery to meet their needs.

We interviewed one 14-year-old girl on a side street in New York City. "Won't you talk to your mother on the telephone?" we begged. "You don't have to let her know where you are—just let her know you're all right." "What good would that do?" the girl replied. "She'd only start crying again. Maybe she'd talk me into going back. Then there we'd be again—fighting about grades—fighting about dates—fighting about everything. . . . No, I'd rather make it on my own."

Many street teenagers are sick because of poor nutrition, drugs, or venereal disease. In this last respect, they are not unlike many of their peers at home, who, physicians say, are the victims of an increasing spread of venereal disease. However, unlike their peers who have their families to turn to to find help, most street teenagers don't get to physicians until the diseases have left them with serious damage.

Infants born to teenagers with venereal diseases are likely to contract the diseases themselves, making them high-risk infants with greater chance of illness and death than others born in our population. Increasing numbers of infants are being born to youngsters 15 years old and younger—the highest infant risk group in our country today.

One solution, according to educators, is programs within the school—programs to deal in meaningful ways with deadly serious issues for students. Programs are being tried out that deal with drug effects, the dangers of street life for teenagers, venereal disease, and sex education. In many cities, deep controversy surrounds these programs. Does teaching about drugs increase drug usage or lower it? Does sex education increase immoral behavior among teenagers? While the public debates the issue, many boards of education are setting up new programs to help addicts who are trying to return to normal lives or young girls who have decided to complete their pregnancies and need to learn how to deal with the new life they are bringing into the world.

Today, many cities—for example, Albuquerque, New Mexico; Austin, Texas; Boston, Massachusetts; and Grand Rapids, Michigan—have established special educational centers for unwed pregnant girls. These are funded by Title IV-C federal funds of the Innovative Programs in Elementary and Secondary Education. In these programs, pregnant adolescents can learn skills in infant care and homemaking. They are encouraged to continue their educations after the births of their children, raise the levels of their abilities in saleable skills, and change their academic profiles.

what causes problem behaviors?

Many problem behaviors have causes related to changes in our country's life styles. Families are changing; schools are changing; society is changing, sometimes with dramatic speed, as Toffler (1970) predicted in his book *Future Shock.* Each change contributes in its own way to children's behavior in the classroom.

Family-related Factors

One of the most important elements in the socialization process is child-rearing in the home. The child's personality, which is the end product of this process, is affected by the way he or she has been reared. An unsupportive, troubled, and unhappy home will have a very bad effect on the development of a child's personality. Family-related factors that can influence the development of problem behaviors include the mother-child relationship, the father-child relationship, divorce, and the overall home environment.

Mothers can influence their children's behavior by providing consistent rewards and punishments, instructing children clearly and consistently, and acting as models. Research on influences in the family related to childhood schizophrenia, for example, has led to the concept of the "schizophrenogenic mother," who is defined as being aggressive, domineering, overanxious, and oversolicitous, yet basically rejecting. Some studies suggest the approximately 50 percent of schizophrenic children have mothers who fit this description (Frank, 1965). Research has focused on the mother's role because women have traditionally had the major responsibility for child rearing. But fathers also influence their children's behavior in positive or negative ways, in similar fashion to mothers.

Although neurotic behavior in children has often been linked to parental domination and overprotection, other studies have implicated entirely different causes, such as maternal rejection. Neurotic behavior of either parent, broken homes, and parental rejection, among other factors, have been investigated with no definitive results.

Although family-related factors have a great influence on the child's personality development, problem behaviors are rarely the result of these factors alone. Other factors must be considered in drawing a complete picture of the causes of problem behaviors.

School-related Factors

Children live in school much in the same way that they live at home. They have a surrogate parent (the teacher) and a family of friends. They spend a large portion of their time in school during their early years, particularly if they attend preschool. A first grader may spend 8 hours at school and only 4 hours with his or her parents each day.

The teacher should keep in mind that the way the school shapes the child's behavior is similar to the way the family shapes it. In fact, although we have spoken of the home as the primary influence on personality development, one theorist (Zimiles, 1967) has argued that, in at least one respect, the school environment often is even more influential than the home environment. Family life follows a fairly fixed pattern to which the child can easily adapt. But school life is full of constant changes—new teachers, classmates, intellectual tasks, and social demands—that require even more sensitivity and flexibility from the child.

The child's perception of school. How does a child perceive life at school? To the very young child, school can be a great adventure or an intimidating trial. The experience of being separated from his or her mother for the first time may be traumatic for the youngster entering preschool or kindergarten. He or she must confront a highly structured environment for the first time. In this complex new environment, the child meets a new authority figure: the teacher. It is difficult for the child to determine how to relate to this stranger, since he or she may have had no previous experiences with such a person. Although this unfamiliar adult shares certain features with the child's parents and other relatives, the teacher may seem to have far greater power than the nonrelated adults he or she has known before.

In addition to dealing with a new adult authority figure and a highly structured environment, the elementary school child also confronts new social pressures. In the classroom and on the playground, he or she must meet and interact with other children. Through these interactions, the child learns new lessons about what to say and what not to say; what to say to whom; how to act and how not to act; and how to obtain friendship, respect, and affection from other children and from the teacher. As if all this weren't enough to deal with, the elementary school child is also presented with an array of subject matter and skills to master. Calculus and college chemistry notwithstanding, the most intensive and demanding educational experience in your life was first grade!

The adolescent's perception of school To many adolescents, school is a place where they have to go, whether they want to or not. Many students attend school primarily because the law says they have to.

To the very young child, the first entry into school can be a great adventure or an intimidating trial.

Lionel Martinez, Photo Researchers, Inc.

Other students choose to risk the penalties and stop going. These truants feel that young people are controlled in a way in which other groups in society are not—there is no law that says adults have to go to work every day—they therefore resent school.

In a report made by a group of high school students in Montgomery County, Maryland (Montgomery Couty Student Alliance, 1971), several stifling effects of the schools on children and adolescents were mentioned. Among them were fear (of bad grades, punishment, failure, and so one); dishonesty; destruction of eagerness to learn; alienation as a result of dishonesty and the premium put on conformity; blind obedience to authority; stifling of self-expression and honest reaction; narrowing scope of ideas; and prejudice.

> Perhaps most tragic is what the school system does to the emotional and mental attitudes and subconscious of its students. The system . . . is willing to and does label students as "failures" at age eight, twelve, or seventeen. . . . Further, tension has been shown to be an integral part of the school experience, with very damaging effects. (p. 111)

The feelings expressed by these students may seem radical, harsh, and unsupportable, but they reflect the intense feelings of distrust, alienation, and even hatred that many adolescents seem to associate with school.

The teacher's perception of students   The way teachers perceive their students is a key factor in school achievement and in problem behaviors.

A sensitive teacher can recognize a troubled child and be an important resource for help. The teacher need not be trained in therapy in order to offer assistance. Many times, a teacher's warmth, support, and willingness to listen can do the trick. When a more serious problem arises, a sensitive teacher can direct the student to professional counseling services.

In a classic study of classroom teachers replicated many times since the original, Wickman (1928) cast serious doubt on the ability of teachers to diagnose student problem behaviors. He showed that there was an extremely small relationship between ratings of problem behaviors by teachers and ratings of the same problems by clinicians. For example, teachers tended to ignore highly withdrawn children, focusing instead on aggressive youngsters. Clinicians, on the other hand, considered withdrawal a warning of more serious problems in the future and therefore a symptom that should be watched. Teachers and clinicians also had different ideas about which problem behaviors were the most serious. For teachers, the most serious problem behaviors involved immorality and action against authority (heterosexual activity, stealing, masturbation, obscene notes, impertinence, destruction of school materials, disobedience, profanity, and impudence). Clinicians were much less concerned about such behaviors and saw only one of these problems, stealing, as "making for considerable difficulty."

In a review of follow-up studies on teachers' and clinicians' attitudes toward problem behaviors, Beilen (1959) found considerable evidence to support Wickman's conclusions. Teacher attitudes had shifted in the thirty years since the Wickman study was done and this shift had narrowed the difference between the attitudes of the two groups. However, Beilen reasserted that "the teacher's role remains principally task-oriented; the clinician's more adjustment-oriented" (p. 185). He suggested that these role differences contribute to the varying perceptions each group had about children's behavior.

In a later follow-up study, Tolor, Scarpetti, and Lane (1967) found that teachers were still particularly critical of aggressive and emotionally expressive behavior. Elementary school teachers seemed most prone to categorize such behavior as pathological. Experience also proved to be a significant variable. More experienced teachers reacted to aggressive and other unwanted behaviors more like psychologists, while less experienced teachers tended to label a wider range of behavior as abnormal. A ninth-grade teacher with twenty years' experience explained how her own reaction to one unwanted behavior, note passing, had changed: "When I first started teaching, I'd be so angry when the kids passed notes. I'd read them to the class to embarrass them sometimes. Now, it embarrasses me to think I once did that. Today, I really don't always notice it, I'm sure. When I do, and I think the correspondents aren't paying attention, I'll intercept it (if I can), smile, and say, 'You can have it after class.' Sometimes they'll shriek, 'Don't read it! Please don't read it!' I assure them I'm not at all interested in reading their personal notes. I don't have much note passing anymore."

Happily, the majority of more recent studies contradict Wickman's early findings. Teachers seem to be getting better at predicting their students' future achievements and difficulties. Keogh, Tchir, and Windeguth-Behn (1974) interviewed 58 kindergarten and primary grade teachers in order to find out which behaviors teachers felt would lead to future problems. They found a consensus among teachers on what constituted high-risk symptoms. The researchers argued that, since the teacher is generally the first professional to see a child interacting with peers, he or she is probably the best person to screen a child for clinical examination.

A study by Gullotta (1974) also noted the teacher's potential importance in aiding the student with problem behaviors. Gullotta described teacher attitudes and expectations in treating a student with moderate problems. He found that the majority of teachers were willing to keep such a child in their classes as long as they were assisted by supportive services, and that they rejected institutional treatment for moderately disturbed children. These results suggest that teachers are willing to perform a counseling as well as a teaching role, as long as children with problem behaviors also receive more expert attention.

In thinking of possible relationships between teacher perceptions of their students and student problem behaviors, it is important to remember that teacher perceptions of student problem behaviors can become self-fulfilling. Teachers may treat talented students with respect and support and may write off children with learning disabilities or problem behaviors. Teachers sometimes assume that these students cannot be helped and turn their attention toward more rewarding students. The teacher who expects a child to be slow or disturbed may well intensify that child's feelings of low self-esteem. Such biases and expectations are especially damaging to children from socially disadvantaged groups. Since low self-esteem increases feelings of anxiety, such false expectations may result in an increased incidence of withdrawal or antisocial conduct on the part of the child.

The family-related and school-related factors that affect problem behaviors should be understood within the perspective of society at large. Social factors contributing to the development of problem behaviors include poverty, unemployment, racial prejudice and discrimination, violence, and alienation.

Social Factors

Social stress and "future shock"   In his book *Future Shock*, Alvin Toffler (1970) suggested that the rapidly accelerating change that characterizes modern life "is a concrete force that reaches deep into our personal lives, compels us to act out new roles, and confronts us with the danger of a new and powerfully upsetting psychological disease" (p. 10). Toffler named the new disease "future shock." Future shock can be compared to the cultural shock an African pygmy would feel if he were plunked down in the middle of Times Square during rush hour. But the cause of future shock is rapid change in our own culture, not transportation to someone else's. People can adjust to anything, given time, but, unfortunately, the world won't wait for us to catch up.

In the 1980s, "future shock" may become "present shock." Toffler suggested that our traditional bases of stability—the nuclear family, the neighborhood, the church, the school—have all been eroded. People feel cast adrift in a fluid society over which they have no control. Various behaviors today simply "reflect the everyday experience of masses of ordinary people who find they can no longer cope rationally with change" (p. 365). The stress caused by future shock is contagious—parents give it to their children, and the children bring it to school.

Socioeconomic status and prejudice   Many social factors, such as the interrelated problems of poverty, unemployment, and low socioeconomic status, can have a serious impact on a child's self-esteem and personality and can thus lead to the development of problem behaviors.

Studies have shown a high incidence of problem behavior among people with low socioeconomic status (Sarason, 1972). Such maladaptive behavior is a predictable response to poverty. Children raised in low-income homes often live in an atmosphere of fear, apathy, and normlessness. In school, such children lack a sense of hope, self-confidence, and the intellectual background necessary for success. This leads to a profound sense of alienation and to social behavior that seems rebellious in relation to middle-class standards. Problem behaviors appear to be particularly severe among victims of racial prejudice and discrimination.

Anomie is a condition that often arises in people when a social structure is disintegrating and traditional norms are eroding. Anomie leads to feelings of rootlessness, and this generally results in alienated behavior. Such alienated behavior may include racial and religious prejudice, passivity and withdrawal, or participation in extreme political or religious movements. We see the effects of anomie in adolescents, whose feelings of alienation may lead them to join criminal gangs, experiment with hard drugs, or become disciples in questionable religious cults.

managing aggression and other problem behaviors in the classroom

A great deal has been written in the past five years about what to do about problem behavior in the classroom. The Senate Subcommittee to Investigate Juvenile Delinquency has suggested, among other things, community education, curriculum reform, police/school/community liaison arrangements, school security programs, and the like, to deal with violence and acts of vandalism (Bayh, 1978). In addition, preservice and in-service programs have bombarded teachers with lists of "do's" and "don'ts" on how to deal with their recalcitrant and obstreperous students. Negotiations between school boards and teachers' unions have regularly dealt with the same issue.

With this flow of discussion and advice coming from all corners, teachers are often understandably confused. Just what should they do about behavior problems in their classrooms? Should they develop behavior modification programs? Or should they insist that the school board provide specialists to help them? The problem of deciding what to do has become even more difficult with the advent of mainstreaming. With the new programs that recently have been developed to provide equal education for all children—including those with special needs and those who exhibit problem behaviors of all sorts—today's teacher is beset on all sides with new problems.

One of the first things that teachers can do to help children with problem behaviors is to learn as much as they can about them. Why is Johnny constantly fighting with other students in the class? Is his behavior as annoying to the other students as it is to the teacher? Why is it annoying to the teacher?

Understanding and being involved Joey, the boy described at the beginning of the chapter who was acting out in the classroom, keeps the teacher from teaching and the other students from learning. When it is clear that nothing the teacher can do will stop Joey from this clearly disruptive behavior, even the strongest advocates of mainstreaming would suggest his removal—for the benefit of the rest of the class and for more intensive help than the teacher can provide. Before this happens, however, teachers should be sure that they have tried everything possible to help Joey learn to behave. Boys who behave like Joey are often motivated by a need for attention. When this is the case, simply showing interest in their needs and desires can often help. If the teacher is too busy with a large class to provide individual attention, he or she may use many different devices to provide it. One way might be to make Joey a peer teacher who provides help to other, perhaps younger, children. Sometimes showing children like Joey that an adult has faith in their ability to handle such situations will solve the problem of acting out. Peer teaching is an effective teaching device that benefits peer teachers and their students. Of course, it is important that the teacher recognize Joey's need for attention; only a teacher who attends closely and personally to the needs of the children in the class is likely to perceive this need. The teacher's attitude clearly is important.

Understanding teachers can give students attention in many different ways. The case of Manny G. is a good example. Manny was an attractive, overly active child with a knack for disturbing the class. Finally, his second-grade teacher told him, "Manny, next time you want to yell, or hit, run around, or say something nasty, tell me before you do it so I'll be prepared!" He grinned impishly and said he'd try. The teacher was surprised to realize that he believed that she actually meant what she had said. He came up to her desk in a few minutes and asked to hit Phil because he had taken his pencil. The teacher pointed to the corner top of her desk and said "That's Phil! You can hit right there, once." While he was busy hitting the desk with his fist, she retrieved his pencil. Some of the other children joined in this new game. Manny didn't become an angel, but he was less disruptive.

Having faith that students can learn and succeed Often children exhibit problem behaviors in the classroom because they haven't learned what they should have in previous years. They don't understand what is going on in class. They are bored and are acting out because there is nothing else interesting to do. Although it is very difficult to make up for the lost time, teachers' attitudes can be very important. Although education can help to resolve these children's problem behaviors, teachers must base their help on several assumptions.

The first assumption is that students with problem behaviors have the same motivation to learn, grow, explore, and discover that other children do. Consistently treating a child on this basis with an effective blend of warmth, sensitivity, firmness, and direction may help him or her settle down. Treating such children as incorrigible troublemakers certainly won't.

The second assumption is that the teacher must design teaching strategies and curricula with the needs of troubled children in mind. The child with problem behaviors needs a full education in the schools. In addition to academic training, he or she must also learn new self-concepts and methods of interacting with others. Again, the teacher must believe that the child has the desire to enjoy life and school, have friends, and develop satisfying ways of interacting. School climate, as measured in part by teachers' expectations that children can and will learn, is directly related to their doing so (Brookover, Schweitzer, Schneider, Beady, Flood, and Wisenbaker, 1978).

Understanding children's home backgrounds Teachers who do not take time to learn about the family backgrounds of their students will have a great deal of difficulty understanding why their students behave as they do. Often knowledge of a child's home life will provide a teacher with a place to start. Roy, the young boy who was withdrawn and depressed both at school and at home, and whose teacher eventually called in a psychologist for help, is a case in point.

Sometimes teachers must go to the parents for direct help. Many parents react defensively to complaints about their children, so they

Often students exhibit problem behavior because of earlier failures to learn in school. Teachers can tackle this problem by helping such students to learn the basics.

should be approached in as nonthreatening a way as possible. "A common reaction by parents will be, 'you're a teacher, teach—and don't attempt to analyze my child.'" But, "if you can point out how the child's behavior is hurting his academic success, then parents are usually more amenable to further evaluation of their child's problems" (Resnick, 1978, p. 391). Giving the parents several concrete examples of the child's maladaptive behavioral patterns can be convincing evidence that help is needed. Taking this trouble is worth it because teachers can most effectively help students with problem behaviors by getting the parents involved (Wehman, Abramson, and Norman, 1977).

Understanding the importance of peer relationships Teachers must be sensitive to their students' social needs as well as their academic ones. Some children do not develop the ability to interact in an effective manner with their peers as rapidly as others. Such children are likely to be ostracized by these peers—a punishment difficult for elementary school students and often unbearable for adolescents, whose social needs center around their age-mates. Selman and Jaquette (1976) have suggested a formal curriculum designed for emotionally disturbed children that includes interpersonal and communication skills as well as fairness and reciprocity skills. A sensitive classroom teacher who is interested in his or her students and who has an open attitude toward their behaviors can often introduce these same skills in an informal manner.

Many poor children coming from tough neighborhoods learn on the street that a person who cares about others is likely to be used and abused. A useful program for socially maladjusted children from such backgrounds was developed by Kobak (1977), who suggested teaching *all* students in the class to serve as growth models and to help each student care for one another. Kobak's curriculum involves teaching children to help each other learn. Regardless of their individual problems, each student learns that he or she can contribute and feels more worthwhile and important.

Being a good model Teachers should always remember that they serve as important models, for young children as well as adolescents. An important part of the socialization process is identification with significant adults. At first, children simply imitate their parents' behavior. But later, as their understanding grows, they come to identify with their parents and internalize their characteristics and values. Prohibition learning and identification with the aggressor (Kagan, 1958) are other types of learned behavior that occur together with the identification process. In **prohibition learning,** children have been taught certain "don'ts" by parents and other adult models; their adoption of these prohibitions is apparent to anyone who has watched a group of children playing "school." Children also learn to identify with the aggressor in situations in which the aggressor's actions provoke anxiety (A. Freud, 1937). This process has been called **defensive identification** (Mowrer, 1950). "Daddy's right, I told you not to do it," says the little boy to his brother, who is being spanked for misbehaving. Similarly, an adolescent who is reprimanded by the principal for cutting school may not always be comforted by his peers. Often he or she will be jeered at and ridiculed by those who didn't get caught. Those jeerers are identifying with the principal.

Why does a student identify with certain models and not with others? What can the teacher do to provide a model with whom students can identify? Such factors as the status of the model in the students' eyes, the model's opportunities to exercise support and control, the students' view of consequences of the model's behavior, and their view of the similarity of the model to themselves determine the level of identification (Bronfenbrenner, 1970). Through identification, the students reduce anxiety and acquire (through their imagined participation) the same positive traits that they perceive in the model. In short, the teacher who is successful in the eyes of the class, who is supportive and warm, and who does not appear too distant socially or intellectually will provide a figure with whom children can identify and from whom they can learn both prohibition learning and identification.

Recognizing creativity Many teachers have trouble distinguishing creativity from problem behaviors. Teachers tend to respond negatively to aggressive and hyperactive children whose behavior interferes with the teacher's role and with the normal classroom routine. In some instances, this negative response carries over to the creative child who may aggressively question (or reject) classroom norms and procedures. This is something that the teacher needs to watch out for. If a student's behavior interferes with normal teaching but produces useful learning, the teacher should accommodate that behavior to the best of his or her ability. Conformity is not always "good adjustment." The teacher should remember that the creative student quite frequently is unusual in his or her behavior and sometimes downright difficult to deal with when a lesson plan must be considered. If such students were just like everybody else, they wouldn't be creative.

Understanding adolescent behavior One problem common to adolescents is the inability to deal with and verify all the different sorts of inputs made available to them. Adolescents are capable of achieving Piaget's stage of formal operations, but, in fact, only about half of them do so (Miller, 1978). One reason is simply that no one has taken the time to take them through the necessary learning steps. In addition, the adolescent is besieged on all sides by varieties of contradictions in adult interactions. As Erikson (1959, pp. 90-91) pointed out:

The danger of this stage is identity diffusion; as Biff puts it in Arthur Miller's *Death of a Salesman*, "I just can't take hold, Mom, I can't take hold of some kind of life." . . .Youth after youth, bewildered by some assumed role, a role forced on him by the inexorable standardization of American adolescence, runs away in one form or another; leaving schools and jobs, staying out all night, or withdrawing into bizarre and inaccessible moods.

To help adolescents face these social dilemmas, teachers should take into consideration the advice prompted by Miller (1978) and others:

1. Remember that adolescents are at different stages of development. Consider the implications of these different developmental levels and arrange classroom conditions so that students operating at lower-than-formal-operations stages do not become "locked" into these levels.
2. Provide students with experience at resolving conflicts. They will have to solve conflicts in their day-to-day living. Anything the teacher can do to help will make adjustment easier.
3. Let students do their own learning. You can't understand them if you do all the talking.
4. Be flexible. Be a good listener. There are as many problems in your class as there are students. Let your students commit themselves temporarily to alternative roles if they are not learning in the traditional classroom. Let them explore the city or city agencies, if this helps. Let them take individual courses that offer opportunities to involve themselves in the community. Help them become committed rather than alienated.
5. Be ready to provide information on problems that adolescents are interested in. This includes sex education. As more and more adolescents experiment with sex, this may involve information about birth control and venereal disease.
6. Watch out for withdrawn adolescents; be sensitive and alert to signs of depression. Researchers at the National Insitute of Mental Health suggest that teachers are closest to young people and are best equipped to help them when they are in trouble—by talking to them, listening to their problems, and, if necessary, steering them to proper professional help. Most depressed and potentially suicidal youngsters require intensive therapy. They will never get it if their problem is not given attention.

Teachers must be sensitive to signs of depression in order to provide help when it is needed.

Developing meaningful educational and behavioral rules and goals

King and Frignac (1973) developed a series of educational and behavioral goals for teachers and parents who work with children who exhibit problem behaviors. Among the behavioral and educational goals are:

Human Relations. Goal: To develop ability to socialize with other people. Objectives: The student will:
   (a) Display socially acceptable manners.
   (b) Respect other people's property.
   (c) Understand the concept of sharing.
   (d) Work cooperatively.

Home and Family. Goal: To recognize the importance of being a responsible and contributing member of home and family.

Rohn Engh, Photo Researchers, Inc.

Objectives: The student will:
(a) Recognize and understand relationships among family members.
(b) Gain an awareness of own and other's roles.
(c) Appreciate the individual rights of family members.
(d) Recognize and respect adults in authority.
(e) Recognize that every family has its own living pattern and style.

Social Initiative. Educational Goal: The student will experience opportunities to build self-confidence through social participation. Objectives: The student will:
(a) Be given opportunities to perform as a leader.
(b) Accept reasonable rules of the group.
(c) Be given opportunities to succeed socially. (King and Frignac, 1973, pp. 2-3)

Helping the shy student   Teachers' attitudes are important for the shy student as well as for the aggressive, disruptive student. Withdrawn children tend to be ignored because they usually do not create noticeable behavior problems and often are not disruptive in the classroom. Often, they go undetected for years and do not surface with significant behavioral symptoms until late elementary, middle school, or high school. Unfortunately, these withdrawn children are most likely to become the depressed or potentially suicidal adolescents that psychologists are so concerned about today.

Heart pounding, pulse racing, blushing, perspiring, and suffering agonies, the average shy American struggles to cope with social demands. Shyness may lead to temporary self-consciousness and excessive preoccupation with personal reactions, or it may end up as an enduring isolation that forces the individual into a life of excruciating loneliness (Zimbardo, Pilkonis, and Norwood, 1975). The shy individual is rarely given attention because the chaos within is often hidden by his or her outward appearance of calm. Shyness is often interpreted as modesty, discretion, and introspection. Sometimes shy people are perceived as snobbish or stuck-up. In any case, they are not often seen as a problem to others. In fact, their public behavior often amounts to what can be characterized as nonbehavior. Unable to assert themselves, their poor self-projection allows others to overlook their real assets. By the same token, their nonbehavior may mask a lack of self-confidence and inadequate social skills, and, in extreme cases, even deep pathological problems. The example of Carol, the highly overanxious young girl described at the beginning of this chapter, is a case in point.

What can be done to free the shy individual? Researchers have suggested various kinds of guidance, modeling, and practice in social skills. But they concluded that we must "understand and change cultural values . . .for shyness is not essentially a personal problem. It is really a social problem" (Zimbardo et al., 1975, p. 70).

Zimbardo (1977) has provided a series of useful ideas for teachers who want to help their shy students. Although these activites do not provide a complete solution for all students or teachers, they do provide a general framework through which teachers can develop a variety of meaningful activities geared to the needs of their students.

1. Try to make students feel good about themselves by giving them honest and specific compliments: "I like your sense of humor. I find it an attractive quality." Encourage kids to compliment each other whenever it's appropriate to do so.

2. Use games or activites that break the ice in a nonthreatening way. For example, have kids roar like lions and then chug like the Little Engine That Could. Begin by saying:

   We are all lions in a big lion family, and we are having a roaring contest to see who is the loudest roarer. When I say, "Roar, Lion, roar," let me hear your loudest roar . . . . OK now lions, roar . . . . You call that a lion's roar? That's a pussy cat. I mean really roar.

   Now get the children moving in a line around the room by having each put one hand on the shoulder of the child in front of him. You be the Big Engine at first. Start slowly, moving in a circle, chugging and hooting as you go. When you come back to the starting point, go to the back of the train to become the caboose while the child next in line is the engine. She should chug a *little* louder and move a *little* faster. Continue around the tracks replacing engines until everyone has had a turn and the train is really chugging and moving. End with a derailment-all fall down.

3. Excessive self-preoccupation can be set aside by arranging conditions for children to express themselves through another voice, another self. Our research has shown that masks and costumes liberate behavior that is normally inhibited and restrained. If the setting you help to create is one that encourages joyful, playful exuberance, open expressions of feelings and tender sentiments, then anonymity will help make it happen. Provide masks, or have the children make them from paper bags or out of papier-mâché. Have available old clothes to use as costumes for dress-up time, especially for dressing like grown-ups. Face painting is another way to turn a shy child into whatever he or she would like to be. Don't wait for Halloween to provide an excuse for masks and costumes.

4. Encourage the open sharing not only of feelings but of talents and knowledge as well. You don't have to join the Peace Corps and go to foreign lands before you can share your abilities and specialized knowledge; you can do it here and now, and your children should be encouraged to do it with one another. Any child's gifts then become prizes for all to share and rejoice in. .Once a child has accepted this attitude about his or her talents, then "performing" is no longer shyness-inducing. It becomes an act of sharing, of entertaining others, of helping them. It does not mean basking, or suffering, in the spotlight of attention.

5. Create conditions where children learn to use other children as resources, seeking help and giving help to one another. The purpose of the exercise then is to promote cooperation, sharing and friendship by creating a democractic community of scholar-experts.

   Prepare a set of materials that can be divided into as many equal segments as there are children (in groups from two to six). Each child is to receive one piece of the total, which will be put together in the manner of a jigsaw puzzle. If there are several such groups, the same material is distributed to each. The material can, for example, be information about another society. One child gets a paragraph about geography and climate, another about economy, another learns a paragraph about political conditions, while others in the team may get information about child-rearing practices, sports or other aspects of the culture. Only by combining all the parts does a whole story of the culture emerge. Each child masters his or her paragraph and then teaches it to the others. Obviously, any materials can be used that are dividable; history lessons, stories, art projects or mechanical-electrical devices will do nicely. In addition, toys and games that require two or more players should be available to encourage cooperative play behavior.

6. Popularity can be taught to shy children who are left out of the social action. They are taught to be pleasant, to cooperate, to initiate games, and to look other children in the eye when they communicate. A research team has shown that third and fourth grade children who were rated low in acceptance by their classmates came to be accepted and chosen as friends after a month of supervised coaching and practice in social skills. You too can achieve similar results if you're willing to be an informed coach.

Recognizing and consistently rewarding appropriate behavior Thus far in the text, behavior management and classroom management have been described as techniques for changing simple, undesirable problem behaviors. But this approach may have a wider and more significant application. For example, we have seen the crucial effect that a child's self-concept has on success or failure in school. A study by Parker (1974), although limited in value because of methodological problems, indicated that a classroom management program could improve students' self-concepts. This supports the position of social learning theorists who say that one's self-concept results from a set of learning experiences and can be modified like any other behavior.

A well-planned classroom management program, based on a supportive educational environment, can significantly alter the behavior of children with a variety of problems. For example, hyperactive children and withdrawn, apathetic children respond well when they are given minimal rewards for small, progressive steps toward normal behavior. Later, the criteria for reward can be enlarged and more and more delay can be given between rewards.

One classroom management program that has been successful in dealing with hyperactive children who are difficult to manage is the Center at Oregon for Research in the Behavioral Education of the Handicapped. According to Hill Walker, the program's director:

> At six or seven years old, acting-out children (also described as hyperactive, hyperaggressive, or even emotionally disturbed) already tend to be outsiders. These children are very difficult to manage. They are accustomed to peer rejection and teacher dislike. Usually, it doesn't faze them. What's more, principally because of their acting-out behaviors, they're often below grade level in academic skills. (Hackett, 1975, p.11)

In an effort to help these youngsters, the Center at Oregon developed Contingencies for Learning Academic and Social Skills (CLASS), a program designed to change disruptive children's negative behaviors.

The CLASS program involves classroom management through standard reinforcement techniques. The children earn points and praise for proper behavior. The procedures involve the cooperative efforts of a CLASS consultant, the classroom teacher, the principal, the parents, and the child.

During the first five days of the program, the consultant assumes the major responsibility. The important thing is to get the help of the child's classmates who must work on their own assignments and not disturb the student while he or she is working. The goal is to make the child behave appropriately 80 percent of the time (a normal average)—not only in class, but also, in time, during lunch and play periods as well. When this goal is reached, the child is given a point card to take home to his or her parents, who then give further reinforcement with their praise and reward. Inappropriate behavior means being sent from the classroom. Since good behavior earns extra privileges for the entire class and thus results in class approval never experienced before, the child learns to suppress behaviors that result in exclusion.

The program works because the key elements are there—the necessary understanding of goals and techniques, full participation and cooperation by everyone involved, and the teacher's earnest desire to change their own negative attitudes and patterns of response toward the hyperactive child.

Classroom management programs have also been used successfully with aggressive children. In one successful program (Kirschner and Levin, 1975) students and the teacher negotiated a contract that consisted of a precise description of the classroom behaviors to be modified and a statement of consequences for different levels of behavioral reinforcement. For not fighting or threatening in the classroom, disturbed and aggressive children received chances to meet with their psychologist, buy games, models, balls, or more expensive presents, or receive a "good" letter to go home to their parents.

*Calling in
the Specialist*

Sometimes, even the best classroom management program doesn't work. It is impossible for the teacher to set up conditions as controlled as those used, say, at the Center at Oregon in the regular classroom. Then the teacher needs to call on a specialist for help.

The first step: Identifying the problem   The teacher's role in helping children with problem behaviors begins when he or she conducts an accurate screening of such children. The teacher is in a decisive position to identify a child's problems and recommend a form of counsel-

A Case Study of Lisa:
An Example of Effective Use
of Behavior Management

In a case study of Lisa, a 6-year-old, we can see how individual behavior management can be used (Cooper, 1973). Lisa showed symptoms of school phobia. During kindergarten, she cried daily, claimed that she was sick, and asked if she could go home. The same pattern continued for the first six weeks of first grade. Eventually, the case was reported to the school psychologist. A conference with the mother revealed that Lisa had been an unwanted pregnancy. Lisa had been severely ill on three occasions by the time she was 4 years old. During Lisa's illnesses, her mother always gave her a great deal of attention, possibly because she saw her child's illness as some kind of punishment for her being an unfit mother. The school psychologist explained to the mother that by giving Lisa special attention when she claimed to be sick at school, she was unintentionlly rewarding Lisa's undesirable behavior. They agreed to a strategy whereby the mother would attempt to reverse this process: Instead of giving Lisa special attention when she said she was ill, the mother would reward her for positive comments about school. The mother was also instructed to ignore Lisa's complaints about illness. After following through on this program for three weeks, the mother was impressed with Lisa's changed behavior, and the psychologist transferred responsibility back to the teacher. Eight months later, both the mother and the teacher reported that Lisa was happy in school and was no longer complaining of illness.

This case study presents an instance of successful intervention using a form of behavior management. However, it should be remembered that most behavior management programs in the classroom will depend on the teacher's active involvement and enthusiasm as well. If teachers are not cooperative, well organized, and systematic in their application of the techniques, the therapy will not succeed.

ing. If he or she fails to notice a troubled child, the child's problem behaviors may continue for years without treatment.

The teacher must carefully observe learning difficulties, unsatisfactory interpersonal relationships, inappropriate behavior, unhappiness, and repetitive symptoms of stress. But, while teachers are best equipped to screen their students, they should leave the diagnosis to a qualified professional. Teachers should observe and record but avoid using clinical labels. For example, your notes should read, "Paul threw a book at Jane for no apparent reason," not "Paul is an aggressive personality with paranoid tendencies." Once the teacher defines the problem and decides that help is necessary, it is time to call in the specialist.

The second step: Notifying the school's resident or consultant specialist Outside professional help may not always come from outside the school. Snapp, McNeil, and Haug (1973) have offered a model for the development of in-school services for children with behavioral problems. In their view, the school psychologist should assist school personnel in mobilizing other available resources and in developing a plan of action to deal with a child's problems when the psychologist is unable to solve them. Part of the Snapp model involves having the school psychologist develop programs whereby resource people, called "helping teachers," would be placed in each school to work with children and consult with teachers. These helping teachers would have training in psychology as well as in education. Their primary goal would be to keep difficult children in regular classrooms (mainstreaming) and to insure that these children have a productive educational experience. The helping teacher would also have a classroom in which individuals or groups of children with problem behaviors could be temporarily isolated for more focused treatment.

According to Nugent (1973), the functions of the school psychol-

Helping a student in trouble may involve the services of outside specialists who can talk the problem out and get at what it's all about.

Marion Bernstein

ogist, the social worker, and the counselor should be differentiated. School psychologists should handle involuntary referrals involving classroom difficulties between student and teacher. The social worker should handle involuntary referrals in which the critical issue seems to be family interactions or school-family tensions. Counselors would handle the voluntary cases.

Other intervention measures have been developed to help children with problem behaviors. In **crisis intervention,** a specialist comes in when a situation is intensely upset and disrupted. He or she tries to calm both the student and the school officials, and in so doing demonstrates to school personnel the way to handle an extremely agitated child. In community liaison, a school specialist acts as a go-between for the child and the school. He or she may act as an advocate for the child in court or with mental health agencies, as a coordinator of various community agencies working with the child, or as an intervening agent in the child's home or classroom.

summary

1. There are two general types of problem behaviors. Some children are actively disruptive, while others passively withdraw. Both types of children fail to learn, but those who keep others from learning generally get more attention from teachers.

2. Understanding what makes a person well adjusted can help us to understand why some children become maladjusted. The basis of good adjustment is the mastery of certain tasks essential for getting along in a particular society, such as motor skills, interpersonal interactions, and basic academic competence. In adolescence, people must also learn to establish mature relationships with both sexes and become emotionally autonomous and economically independent. Children of poverty backgrounds often have greater difficulty in mastering these tasks, but any child who fails can be expected to develop problem behaviors in response to social disapproval. While some people define adjustment in terms of mental health or illness, such terms oversimplify our understanding of the causes and treatment of problem behavior.

3. Problem behaviors are socially defined, and, as social values change, our definitions of problem behavior changes as well. What was considered a problem ten years ago may be quite acceptable today. What is considered deviant in one society may be quite acceptable in another.

4. Violence is a major problem in today's schools. This violence is directed toward school property, teachers, and other students. Violent children generally have negative attitudes about themselves and other people and see their aggressive acts as a way of hurting others before they can be hurt by them. Family-related factors, particularly aggressive arguments in the family, are a primary cause of aggressive behavior in children. Punishment intensifies aggression, instead of reducing it as many people expect. Withdrawn and depressed children, as well as those who are

openly aggressive and hostile, are apt to have low self-esteem. Helping students feel better about themselves instead of punishing them is thus more effective in dealing with problem behaviors. Children from poverty backgrounds are particularly vulnerable. They may make a negative impression on middle-class teachers and may learn not to care about people from their friends outside of school. However, violence is no longer just a lower-class problem. Although a full solution to the problem must involve the family and the community, teachers can help by trying to understand their students, using behavior management, and having faith in their students' abilities to solve their own problems.

5. Hyperkinesis, an organically based disorder, is often confused with hyperactivity, which is a psychologically oriented emotional disturbance. Both disorders are characterized by overactivity, restlessness, excitability, and impulsivity. Hyperkinetic and hyperactive children are difficult to teach, although they do not have inferior intelligence. Using drugs to treat both disorders has been the common practice until recently. Drugs can be effective in some cases: Some children are calmed down by stimulants, while others respond better to tranquilizers. But, because drugs help only temporarily, may have unpleasant side effects, and may be administered by unqualified people if the child takes medication at school, the use of drugs has been increasingly criticized. Two other approaches currently being studied are the elimination of artificial food additives from the child's diet and behaviorally training the children to increase their self-control.

6. Severely anxious children have difficulty learning and may develop physical symptoms. These children may be misdiagnosed as being hyperactive. The three common types of anxiety reactions are chronic anxiety, anxiety attack, and panic reaction. Children who suffer from anxiety often feel neglected by their parents. The added stresses of school can further increase the child's anxiety. One of the most common symptoms of school-related anxiety is school phobia. School phobia is more common among very young children and is usually treated by using behavioral principles to change the child's behavior.

7. Another anxiety-related symptom is depression. The number of school children who are seriously depressed and have suicidal tendencies has increased significantly in the last few years. Suicide is now the third most common cause of death among people aged 15 to 24. Unfortunately, because they do not cause major disturbances, many depressed and potentially suicidal students do not get the help they need.

8. Extremely withdrawn children escape a reality they can't cope with through daydreams and fantasies. Their lack of response may trouble teachers, but they tend to concentrate on students who actively disrupt the classroom routine. Running away can be seen as a physical form of withdrawal.

9. Certain behavioral problems are unique to adolescents. Alcohol and drug abuse, running away, sexual activity, and early pregnancy could all be minimized by more intensive and meaningful educational programs.

10. The basic cause of problem behaviors is rapid social change, which affects our families, schools, and the very structure of society. Family-related factors that influence the development of problem behaviors include the mother-child relationship, the father-child relationship, divorce, and the overall home environment.

11. The school can be a second family for many children and can shape a child's behavior in much the same way the child's biological family does. The school's routine is not as fixed as that at home and requires much more sensitivity and flexibility from the child. Very young children can see school as exciting or intimidating. In addition to beginning the study of academic subjects, children must adjust to a new authority figure, a highly structured environment, and the interpersonal relations required to get along with their classmates. Many adolescents resent the laws that make them go to school whether they want to or not, and school can stifle an adolescent's spirit in many ways. Adolescents striving to create an identity particularly resent forced conformity and dishonesty. The teacher's attitude toward the students is a key factor. Teachers who spot problems early can be an important part of the effort to help, but teachers who let their negative expectations influence their behavior toward troubled students can make the situation worse.

12. Social factors that contribute to problem behaviors include poverty, unemployment, racial prejudice and discrimination, violence, and alienation. The stress caused by the need to adjust to social life that changes too rapidly—called "future shock" by Alvin Toffler—is contagious. This stress is accelerating at the same time as our traditional sources of support—family, neighborhood, church, and school—are eroding.

13. Problem behavior is particularly common among people with low socioeconomic status. Poverty and unemployment have a serious effect on a child's self-esteem, and thus children from poverty backgrounds can become alienated or rebellious when their lack of intellectual preparation leads to failure in school. Anomie, an extreme form of alienation, arises when traditional norms no longer function.

14. The task of handling problem behavior in the classroom has been complicated by mainstreaming. A teacher's first step in helping children with problem behaviors is to learn as much as possible about them. Teachers should become involved with their students; have faith that even children with problem behaviors want to learn; understand the home background that has shaped these students and get the parents involved in helping efforts; understand the importance of peer relationships; be good models for their students, which encourages prohibition learning and identification with the aggressor; and be able to tell when a student has a problem or is simply expressing creativity. Understanding adolescent behavior is particularly difficult. Teachers should consider the adolescent's stage of development, provide opportunities to practice conflict resolution, be good listeners, have information on problems adolescents are interested in, and be alert for signs of depression.

15. Teachers need to develop classroom management programs to help shy,

withdrawn children as well as those who are disruptive and aggressive. Shyness is often hard to diagnose. Shy individuals may have calm exteriors and may even seem snobbish or simply reserved. Guidance, modeling, and practice in social skills can help shy people become more outgoing. Cooperative activities in which each child's assignment is necessary to the project's outcome can be a good way to integrate a shy child into classroom life.

16. Well-planned classroom management programs can significantly alter the behavior of children with a variety of problems. Programs in which positive behavior changes are consistently regarded can improve students' self-concepts as well as their behavior.

17. Sometimes even the best classroom management program fails, and a specialist must be called in. Teachers are probably in the best position to spot problem behaviors, but they should be careful to leave the diagnosis to a qualified professional. After identifying a problem, the teacher should call the specialist. Many schools have resident psychologists, social workers, or counselors, while other schools use outside consultants. "Helping teachers," who have a background in psychology as well as education, are a new approach to dealing with problem behaviors while keeping the child in the classroom. Two other approaches are crisis intervention and community liaison.

AXLINE, V. *Dibs: In Search of Self*. Boston: Houghton Mifflin, 1964. This is a case history of a small boy, and a description of the psychotherapeutic approach that helped him.

CANFIELD, J. AND WELLS, H. *100 Ways to Enhance Self-Concept in the Classroom*. Englewood Cliffs, N. J.: Prentice-Hall, 1976. Canfield and Wells provide descriptions of 105 tested classroom activities that teachers can use to foster self-image, character development, and so on.

COSTELLO, J., JANIS, M., AND SOLNIT, A. Overcoming early school difficulties. Three aspects of learning inhibition. *Elementary School Journal*, November, 1977, 78 (2), 140-148. This brief article is designed to help teachers working with elementary school children who are facing educational failure because of behavior problems.

GORDON, T. *Parent Effectiveness Training*. New York: Wyden, 1970. This how-to-do-it guide for parents describes ways to deal with conflicts with children. The approach, which is also useful for teachers, emphasizes three elements: how to listen to a child's feelings and needs and let him or her know you are really listening; how to express feelings and needs effectively to a child; and how to settle conflicts between those needs using a "no lose" method for decision making.

GROSSMAN, H. *Nine Rotten Lousy Kids*. New York: Holt, Rinehart & Winston, 1972. This interesting book describes a unique radical experimental school for delinquent boys and the successful and novel methods that a team of teachers and psychologists developed to work with the students.

KOHN, M. *Social Competence, Symptoms, and Underachievement in Childhood: A Longitudinal Perspective*. New York: Halstead Press, 1977. This is a report of a five-year longitudinal study involving approximately 1,000 children. A major concern of the author is "symptom formation" and early identification of disturbance for intervention and correction.

for students
who want to read
further

TEACHING STUDENTS WITH SPECIAL NEEDS

Johnny, a frail boy in the first grade, takes very little interest in classroom activities. He has not begun to read like the other children in the class. He refuses to talk or play with them, and he seems lost in a world of his own. The school psychologist administers an IQ test and discovers that Johnny's functional IQ is 68. Is Johnny mentally retarded, or is he suffering from a severe emotional disturbance that interferes with his achievement? Additional tests, observation, and perhaps a medical examination are necessary to determine the nature and extent of his problem as well as the best way to deal with it.

* * * *

Alice, now in the fifth grade, used to be an "A" student. Now, her work has begun to deteriorate, and the teacher is unable to determine the cause. However, she notices peculiarities in Alice's posture and observes that Alice runs and plays awkwardly during recess. The teacher requests a diagnostic evaluation by the school psychologist. Tests suggest the possibility of organic brain damage. The school psychologist then advises Alice's mother that her daughter should have a thorough medical examination.

* * * *

Philippe, a handsome boy of 11, sits quietly in his seat in the third-grade classroom. He speaks English only haltingly and has difficulty communicating with his teacher and the other members of the class. His family speaks only Vietnamese in their home and a few words of English on the street. There is no one at home who can help Philippe learn, and Philippe shows little interest in learning on his own. He spends as much time as possible alone. The school psychologist advises his mother about the importance of Philippe's learning English and also about receiving special help in reading.

* * * *

Aaron is 15 years old and in his sophomore year at a special high school for gifted students. Aaron is the son of two university professors, who began teaching him to read when he was 2 years old. By the time Aaron was 4, he was already studying mathematics and physics at home. When he was 6, his parents decided to continue teaching him at home instead of sending him to school. They thought that Aaron would have a hard time being in school with children who were just beginning to learn to read and write. This year is Aaron's first year at public school. Although he is studying with many other students his own age and capability, he is having a great deal of difficulty. He frequently gets upset when his teacher can't answer his questions in class. He says that the other students avoid him because he isn't interested in "girls or ball games." His father says that this is "a rough year for Aaron. But if he's going to live in the real world, he has to start sometime."

who are the students with special needs?

Because of various characteristics, a student with special needs requires special teaching procedures to develop to his or her fullest capacity. These students may have physical handicaps; vision, speech, or hearing problems; below-average intelligence; or, like Aaron, they may be far above average in intelligence and creativity. Students with special needs may come from average, wealthy, or poor socioeconomic backgrounds. The teacher has a serious obligation to identify all children with special needs and help them in the best way possible.

Johnny, the first case at the beginning of this chapter, has been classified as mentally retarded on the basis of his test scores. How does Johnny differ from students of average intelligence? For one thing, Johnny learns more slowly. For another, he needs more practice at each step of the way. How can we make it easier for Johnny to cope with his disability?

Alice presents potentially more severe problems: the possibility of organic—and irreversible—brain damage. Teachers, of course, cannot provide a cure for Alice's problem if it does turn out that she has brain damage. But they can provide assistance in getting her problem diagnosed. And—if her problem turns out to be severe—they may be able to offer remediation training.

Although Philippe has never had his intelligence tested, his teacher believes that he is a bright boy who is capable of learning to read. Philippe's job is far more difficult than it is for many other children. How does Philippe differ from them? For one thing, he needs help learning English before he can even begin the process of learning to read.

Aaron also has special problems learning in school, although his problems are very different from Philippe's. Aaron's father says Aaron has "to learn to live in the real world." His teachers agree. They are beginning by teaching him how to work in groups with other students, something he has never had to do before in his life. Although being special in a positive way, as Aaron is, is not the same as being special in a negative way, both sorts of "specialness" cause problems for the children and for those who teach them.

Students with Physical Handicaps

Johnny and Alice are among the small percentage of American children and adolescents who are classified as handicapped in some way. Thirty years ago, the severely handicapped were often regarded as not-quite people who were only a heavy burden to society. They were frequently placed in custodial institutions where they remained untrained, uneducated, and unprepared to lead fulfilling lives. Less severely crippled, retarded, and disturbed children were grouped together in special education classes taught by one teacher. Only very recently have laws been passed to give these and other handicapped children the same rights to education as average children by mainstreaming them into regular classrooms.

Students with sensory handicaps   Mary is a poor reader and has difficulty keeping up with classroom activities. Tests indicate that there is nothing wrong with her thinking. She simply has trouble seeing the blackboard and her textbook. Often, all that is needed to correct a problem such as Mary's is evaluation by an ophthalmologist and a pair of eyeglasses. Other students, however, are not so fortunate. They have bad eyesight even with corrective glasses. We call this group the visually handicapped.

Special arrangements are made in most schools today for physically handicapped children to learn side-by-side with others in the regular classroom.

Bernard Pierre Wolff, Photo Researchers, Inc.

Scott sits in the last row of his third-grade class and spends most of his time daydreaming. He is falling behind the rest of the class. One day his teacher realizes that he cannot hear what she is saying. All Scott needs to help him learn is a hearing aid; unfortunately he doesn't have one. *Hearing-impaired* children often display faulty speech as well. The American Speech and Hearing Association has estimated that 5 percent of all school children have speech defects serious enough to demand therapy (Karagianis and Merricks, 1973). Some children have the multiple handicaps of impaired speech and mental retardation, hearing loss, or physical deformity.

Most speech defects involve problems of articulation—omissions, substitutions, distortions, and additions of sounds. Impaired hearing is often responsible for these. Voice and pitch defects are the second most prevalent problems. The child's voice may be too high, too low, or monotonous, or it may have an unpleasant nasal quality or hoarseness. There are also rhythmic defects such as stuttering and stammering. Finally, and least prevalent, is delayed speech, which is often accompanied by a marked retardation, severe emotional disturbance, lack of environmental stimulation, neurological impairment, or loss of hearing.

The communication problems that children with speech and hearing handicaps have are often complicated by the ridicule of other

Correction of speech problems is done most effectively by calling in a specialist in speech therapy.

children, who are often insensitive and cruel to children who are different in any way. It is crucial that the teacher recognize and deal with this possibility before deep emotional scars become a part of the child's personality and drastically damage his or her self-esteem.

Students with neurological or orthopedic handicaps   Many classrooms contain one or two children like Alice described at the beginning of this chapter, who have some neurological or orthopedic handicap such as physical deformity, paralysis, or epilepsy, or who suffer from a disabling disease such as cerebral palsy or muscular dystrophy. Some of these children use crutches or wear braces; others are confined to wheelchairs. Chronic debilitating diseases such as arthritis, diabetes, heart trouble, hemophilia (a serious blood defect), cystic fibrosis, severe allergies requiring heavy medication, and asthma also affect a significant number of school children.

   Epilepsy is a noncontagious neurological disorder characterized by seizures. It is important for teachers to understand seizures so that they themselves are not frightened by them and so that they can help the epileptic child reduce his or her anxiety. There are two types of epileptic seizures, classified medically as grand mal and petit mal. During the highly dramatic grand mal seizure, the child loses consciousness, twitches convulsively, and may lapse into a coma. Petit mal seizures are less severe. The child simply loses motor control and stares blindly for a few seconds. Epileptic attacks can usually be controlled by drugs. When they cannot, teachers and students should be prepared to deal with them. The child's parents, doctors, or school nurse should give the teacher directions for helping the child if an attack occurs at school.

*Students with
Mental, Learning,
or Social
Handicaps*

Many children who appear perfectly healthy on the surface still have trouble learning in school. Because Scott's hearing problem caused him to fall behind the other children in his class, his teacher might have thought that he was mentally retarded when he wasn't. However, approximately 2 percent of the student population are significantly deficient in their thinking capacity and social behavior. There are four general classifications of retardation: profound, severe, trainable, and educable.

In addition to very low intelligence, **profoundly retarded** children often have multiple handicaps, such as blindness and deafness. They usually cannot speak, and their sensorimotor development is extremely limited. Some never even learn to walk or use a toilet. The profoundly retarded cannot take care of themselves and must be constantly supervised. Most of them require lifelong care in institutions. Because profound retardation is often accompanied by serious physical defects, many others die in childhood. Very few retarded people are profoundly retarded.

Severely retarded people also tend to have multiple handicaps. Because they too generally require constant supervision and medical care, they are often placed in institutions. After intensive and prolonged training, some severely retarded individuals can learn to help themselves and, as adults, may be able to perform simple tasks in closely supervised situations. Their sensorimotor skill development is often slow, and severely retarded children tend to be awkward and clumsy (Rogers, 1977). Speech is often absent or very limited.

Trainable students are only moderately retarded and are less likely to have multiple handicaps and obvious physical defects. They can speak, and their motor development may approach normalcy. While they are not capable of reading or doing complex arithmetic, they can learn to take care of themselves and to become more socially aware. They may eventually become partially self-supporting at jobs in sheltered workshops.

Most (85 percent) of the mentally retarded are **educable.** Their physical appearance and motor development are relatively normal, and their handicaps are often not detected until they begin school, when their poor ability becomes obvious. They generally require special programs and classes. Mildly retarded are sometimes difficult to manage in the classroom because they require a lot of individual attention and often become discipline problems. They can learn basic elementary skills in childhood; and crafts, graphic arts, and physical education in adolescence. As adults, they are capable of performing simple jobs in the community.

Learning-disabled students are often categorized by their teachers as "slow learners," but unlike the mentally retarded, they may have average or even above average IQ scores. Many different kinds of problems that involve reading ability, memory, concentration, motor ability, and disruptive behavior can lead to learning disabilities. Learning-disabled students perform significantly lower than nondisabled students on measures of motor skills. They tend to do badly on tasks involving balance, delicate hand-eye coordination, and using both sides of their bodies at the same time (Bruininks and Bruininks, 1977).

It is difficult to detect and diagnose learning disabilities because there are no clear-cut symptoms common to all cases. Many students stand out because they have a history of delayed speech and difficulty in motor coordination and memory, but many others escape detection for a long time.

Golick (1970) classified and described ten broad categories of learning disabilities that are helpful for teachers. None of these categories is exclusive; many students experience difficulty in several categories at the same time.

1. *Poor body awareness.* Confusion over the location of different parts of the body (as revealed by children's drawings showing arms extending from heads, and so on); difficulty assessing size and telling right from left; lack of fine motor coordination; inability to participate in ball games, jump rope, or put together jigsaw puzzles; difficulty in learning to print and write.
2. *Poor ability to combine movement and vision.* Poor eye-hand coordination; clumsiness; inability to follow a moving target or judge distance; inability to throw or catch a ball.
3. *Visual inefficiency.* Inability to notice particular features in the environment, even with perfect vision; inability to give selective attention or screen out competing stimuli; bad vision for both distant and near objects.

Mentally retarded and learning disabled children profit from individually prescribed instruction and attention.

Van Bucher, Photo Researchers, Inc.

4. *Poor listening ability.* Cannot process information to keep up with the speaker; easily distracted by other noises; inability to distinguish word sounds.
5. *Integrating information from several sensory channels.* Difficulty associating letters of the alphabet and their sounds, though capable of handling tasks that are primarily visual or auditory.
6. *Poor grasp of sequence.* Difficulty remembering things in order, such as days of the week, letters of a word, or word order in a compound word or sentence.
7. *Poor sense of rhythm.* Difficulty reciting a poem, singing a song, bouncing a ball, or jumping rope.
8. *Problems with concepts.* Difficulty in forming categories and recognizing differences and similarities between objects. Poorly developed concepts of time, number, and space.
9. *Problems in style of learning.* Difficulty learning and remembering names, telephone numbers, multiplication tables. Possible good performances in analytic and intuitive tasks that do not involve memory.
10. *Gaps in general knowledge.* Inability to learn basic general information such as parents' first names, what parents do for a living, names of cities, and so on.

The most noticeable learning-disabled students tend to have severe behavior problems. They often are impulsive or aggressive, have infantile tantrums, and are poorly socialized. These symptoms also characterize hyperactivity, which sometimes leads to misdiagnosis. Many hyperactive students have responded to drug therapy. Amphetamines such as Ritalin and Dexedrine have helped reduce hyperactivity and improve self-control in certain cases (Bradbury, 1972). However, use of these drugs is still enormously controversial because teachers and others who are not competent to prescribe medication have sometimes administered them routinely to disruptive children.

The largest group of learning-disabled students consists of those who have language or reading difficulties. At least 10 percent of all children with average or above intelligence suffer from the little-understood learning disorder called **dyslexia.**

Dyslexic children show a wide variety of symptoms. These symptoms are quite common in preschool-age children, even those who later become good readers. For example, both very young children and older dyslexic students may confuse spatial relationships such as left and right. They reverse the order of letters, syllables, and words. They read "b" instead of "d," "tap" instead of "pat." They also may confuse up and down and invert pairs of letters such as "m" and "w" or "d" and "p" (Bernard, 1973; Ellingson and Cass, 1966). These symptoms become important if they persist after the child is in school.

There is no known cause for the cluster of problems called dyslexia or for other learning disabilities. Neurological and genetic theories have been advanced, but there is no definite proof of genetic or physiological causes. The dyslexic or otherwise learning-disabled child behaves in ways that defy the development pattern of the so-called normal child, and none of the specific techniques that work with normal children seem to help the learning-disabled.

It is crucial for teachers to understand that there is a close and important relationship between a child's emotional adjustment and his or her readiness to learn. Students with school phobias or severe anxiety in general may be too preoccupied with themselves to be receptive and responsive to what the school has to offer. Students with low self-concepts are convinced they are going to fail before they even try. Some show basic mistrust of the educational environment and of teachers as authority figures. Because mistrust lowers both motivation and achievement, these children are likely to experience difficulties in cognitive and social development.

Gifted Students

Students who are more capable intellectually than average are considered to be gifted. Gifted children comprise approximately 3 percent of the school population when classified according to IQ (Mitchell and Erikson, 1978). Most gifted students do not have parents who choose to keep them out of school and teach them at home, as Aaron's did. Still, many have problems learning to get along with others because their capabilities set them so far apart. Often they are bored in class having to review material they already know so well and have difficulty doing regular assignments. Others who are sometimes allowed to attend classes with students much older than themselves may do fine academically but may suffer socially or emotionally. The authorization in 1974 of Section 404 of Public Law 93-380 (Amendment to the Elementary and Secondary Education Act) acknowledges that gifted children have special educational needs in order to develop to their fullest capacity. Public Law 93-380 has provided millions of dollars in the last decade to develop programs for these children.

*Students from
Poverty
Backgrounds*

A sizable subculture of low-income Americans (the bottom 15 to 20 percent of the American population) are characterized by an absence of steady employment, a low level of educational and technical skills, a dependence on government assistance programs, and, most important isolation from the remainder of society (Havighurst, 1969). According to Department of Labor Statistics, the income difference between rich and poor is growing. No single racial or ethnic group has a monopoly on poverty, although disproportionate numbers of some ethnic groups fall into the category. For example, although many black Americans fit such a description, the growing black middle class does not. The same is true for other ethnic groups.

Most people suppose that America's poor are primarily non-white. Actually, almost two thirds of this group are English-speaking whites. In 1969, some 20 million disadvantaged whites were at the bottom of America's socioeconomic structure, along with 8 million blacks, 700,000 Puerto Ricans, 2 million other Spanish-Americans, and 500,000 American Indians. In the 1970s the number of Spanish-Americans in this country increased. It is anticipated that during the next decade, they will become the single largest minority group in the United States. The vast majority of this minority group falls in the low-income level.

The poor live in what Oscar Lewis (1966) called a "culture of poverty" within a wealthy society. A culture is defined as the total pattern of behavior relating to what people eat, how they earn their livings, what interactions they have with other subcultures, and so on. According to Lewis, the culture of poverty is quite distinctive and spans all races and ethnic groups. For example, the poor live at or near subsistence levels throughout their lives. They tend to be dropouts from school and thus are limited to unskilled, low-paying jobs. By their late twenties they have already passed their peak earning years. The disadvantaged tend to have difficulty focusing on long-term goals; day-to-day existence is a hard struggle. They cannot hold out for jobs that promise security and advancement.

The stark lives of the urban poor are in marked contrast to popular images of our "affluent society."

> Peter sleeps with his brother in one bedroom. The three girls sleep in the living room which is a bedroom. . . . There is not very much furniture about. The kitchen has a table with four chairs, only two of which are sturdy. The girls sleep in one big bed. Peter shares his bed with his brother. The mother sleeps on a couch. . . . The apartment has no books, no records. There is a television set in the living room, and I have never seen it off. (Coles, 1968, p. 1320)

Rural poverty may be different in certain respects from urban poverty, but it is hardly better. Eight-year-old Sally comes from a family of migrant workers.

> (Her home) stands on four cement blocks. The cabin lacks curtains but does possess that old stove. . . . Near the stove there are three beds with mattresses but nothing else. Ten human beings use the mattresses: Sally's grandmother, her parents, and the seven children.
> These are people to whom a toothbrush is a strange instrument. Who have been to a doctor once or twice in their lives, and never to a hospital. Whose children must take turns going to school because they share the available clothing. (Van Brunt, 1972, p. 71)

Many poor children receive little guidance or supervision. It is not easy for them to develop the verbal and intellectual skills necessary for success in the educational world. Their parents often are uninterested in formal learning, and they may unknowingly pass along to their children a fear of failure and a negative self-image.

Hunger and malnutrition are widespread conditions in America as well as elsewhere in the world. The Office of Economic Opportunity estimated in 1969, even before the period of inflation in the 1970s and early 1980s, that some 14 to 15 million Americans were unable to afford a minimally adequate diet. The Select Senate Committee on Nutrition and Human Needs suggested at that time that there were 10 million hungry Americans. The federal food stamp program was one attempt to solve this problem. Still, the number of malnourished people is increasing dramatically each day.

The ability to afford a diet that provides sufficient nutrients for adequate growth and development is directly linked to income level. America's poor tend to suffer from severe health problems, many of which can be directly linked to malnutrition. Malnutrition has been directly related to mental and physical impairment and other birth defects (Guthrie, Masangkay, and Guthrie, 1976; Lester, 1976; Perkins, 1977). Malnutrition also leads to a variety of physical problems and diseases among the poor. A Seattle doctor estimated that between 50 percent and 75 percent of all children from poverty backgrounds suffer from nutritional deficiency anemia, as compared with only 5 percent of children seen in private practice (*Hunger USA*, 1968).

The health problems of socially disadvantaged students raise serious questions for teachers. Nutrition-related problems are one of the reasons that poor children often find it hard to learn at school. Physiological needs are primary in Maslow's hierarchy of needs (see Chapter 5). A hungry or sick person will not pursue needs for love and belonging, esteem, or self-actualization as readily as a well-fed or healthy person.

> A child comes to school with no breakfast—except perhaps for a cup of coffee. He has no lunch and no money for a school lunch. He may carry some candy to nibble on to appease his appetite. Teachers and principals have repeatedly told the board the obstacle which hunger places in their way—in the form of listlessness, fights over food, inattentiveness, acute hunger pangs, withdrawal, a sense of failure. (*Hunger USA*, 1968, p. 19)

The solution to the problem of hunger in the classroom? Unfortunately, this problem is easier to discuss than to solve. One solution funded by the federal government is lunches provided free or for fees on a sliding scale to children from varying income backgrounds. In some schools, particularly where all the children have similar financial backgrounds, these programs have been quite successful. In other schools, however, poor children feel stigmatized by having to apply for free lunches. In increasing numbers of schools today, free lunches are not available—simply because the funds to provide the services are not available.

Bilingual Students   Children who begin the educational process with well-developed oral language skills in standard English start off in American schools with a tremendous advantage. Such children usually come from a middle-class or upper-class background. For children coming from minority ethnic or racial backgrounds, the situation often is quite different. Such children, frequently from poverty backgrounds, commonly have language difficulties that interfere with their learning in school. As noted earlier, it has been estimated that in the 1980s the largest single ethnic minority in the United States will be Hispanic. For children from Spanish-speaking homes, the language problem is obvious. School may be their first exposure to written or spoken English. Despite the large number of Spanish-speaking children in the United States, there are fewer bilingual programs than needed.

Black children often have language problems too. Linguists have shown that many black children learn an English dialect called black English, which has marked differences from the formal, middle-class standard English of the schools.

identifying and teaching students with special needs

The importance of early identification of students with special needs cannot be overstated. In most extreme cases—for example, the severely retarded or those with major physical handicaps—the problems are identified well before the child enters school. Much more frequently, however, the child's needs do not really become apparent until he or she enters school and tries to adapt to the competitive classroom situation so common in our society. Even then, far too many children who need special help go unnoticed for too long.

Identifying and Teaching the Physically Handicapped   Although the teacher can often spot a child with special needs, he or she should also rely on the screening services of medical and educational specialists to determine the nature of the problem and what to do about it. Every state now offers services for children with special needs through the public school system, but the regulations vary drastically from state to state. The following are some general principles for identifying and helping children with particular problems in the schools.

Visual, hearing, and speech handicaps   Teachers can identify visual, speech, and hearing handicaps through regular screening tests. Before children are formally screened, however, teachers can often pick them out in the classroom. Teachers should be alert to the symptoms of the visually handicapped child—poor attention and poor reading ability, for example—and request testing as soon as they are noted.

Hanna W. Schreiber, Rupho/Photo Researchers, Inc.

Deaf or hard-of-hearing children need training to correct their pronunciation so that it is understandable.

Teachers should also be alert to the symptoms that hearing-impaired children generally display. These include inattention, failure to respond, very slow or faulty speech, and educational retardation not explainable by low intelligence. However, none of these symptoms by itself is indicative of a hearing defect. Accurate diagnosis can be made only after the child is given a hearing test in which the degree of hearing impairment is determined. Approximately 5 percent of school-age children have some hearing loss.

Children with very severe hearing impairments must be taught, in many cases, by methods that differ from those that work with children who have normal hearing (see, for example, Brogman and Hardy, 1978). Such children may need special instruction outside the regular classroom. However, those with slight to moderate impairment can remain in regular classes with the help of hearing aids or built-in amplification systems in the classroom.

Sometimes students have visual or auditory impairments so severe that teachers in regular schools cannot help them with the teaching methods at their disposal. Special schools for the deaf and blind still exist because these children require careful, methodical, and patient instruction. Precision teaching has worked successfully with blind and deaf students, both in institutions (Phillips, 1972) and at home, where children's parents are used as teachers (Young, 1972). However, many teachers believe that children with some hearing or vision and sufficient mobility should be integrated into regular schools. This is beginning to take place in many school districts and is discussed more fully in Chapter 10.

Speech problems are often, although not necessarily, associated with hearing problems. Sometimes children who do not hear well when they are young develop inappropriate methods to make the sounds that form words. Later, when these children are helped to hear more effectively, speech therapists can teach them to make language sounds correctly. Children can develop speech problems even when their hearing is excellent. Sometimes children mispronounce a few sounds, as, for example, "s," "r," "th," or "l." Other children lisp, stutter, or stammer.

Special language-instruction programs headed by speech clinicians now exist all over the country as part of regular public school programs. Children with speech problems usually spend part of the day in special classes where trained therapists provide them with help. Unfortunately, because these programs are expensive, they are increasingly being reserved for children who have only very serious difficulty communicating. Therapy for children whose speech is not so badly impaired, but who still need help, is usually provided by the classroom teacher (Mowrer, 1978).

Correcting children's speech is not an easy task even for qualified speech pathologists. Classroom teachers who want to help children with speech problems should get advice from the school's speech therapist. The best way to help a child to make a sound correctly is to demonstrate exactly what we do with our mouths and tongues to make the sound. Most of us have never developed that sort of body consciousness. We never think about what we are actually doing when we talk, and therefore find it difficult to tell others (Mowrer, 1978).

Physical and neurolgical handicaps Children with suspected or noticeable physical or neurological handicaps should be referred to specialists for complete physical, educational, and psychological evaluations. Medical specialists as well as vocational and occupational therapists can help teachers, students, and parents do what is necessary to make classroom learning as effective as possible.

Sometimes children have handicaps too severe for them to continue in regular programs. Special programs have been developed for these children both through association with hospitals and through private organizations. Decisions to place children in such programs depend on need and on the medical assistance available.

Physical and neurological handicaps that leave noticeable deficits in gross motor skills present self-concept problems for many children. Teachers can help these children to deal with their problems by reinforcing their social interactions and by helping the other children in the class to recognize and understand the problem.

By far the greatest number of children who need special help from the schools are the educable mentally retarded.

Mental retardation General intelligence and adaptive behavior are the criteria for determining what special help a child needs. In order to be considered officially educable, a retarded child must achieve a score between 51 and 75 on a standardized IQ test such as the Wechsler or the Stanford-Binet; to be considered trainable, the child must score between 25 and 50 (Florida State Department of Education, 1974).

American schools have traditionally placed educable mentally retarded children in special classes where teachers can work with them individually or in small groups. However, special education classes have posed a number of problems for teachers and students. Initially, these classes were designed for homogeneous groups of children who required the same sort of special instruction. Special education teachers have frequently found themselves faced with too many different kinds of problems in one class and not enough resources to provide for the individual needs of the students.

Special education classes have often been used to house and educate the learning-disabled or emotionally disturbed child as well as the educable mentally retarded. Critics complain that a high proportion of children who are not physically or mentally disabled are also placed in these classes. Most of these misassignments are socially disadvantaged children from poverty backgrounds.

Finally, critics complain that children in special education classes tend to be labeled as inferior by their peers. Teachers tend to think of them as "impaired," "disabled," "hopeless," or "disadvantaged." As a result of these labels, children find it difficult to regain the respect of their classmates, teachers, and, later, their employers. As we have emphasized before in this text, children commonly derive their sense of self-worth from the evaluations of others. Therefore it is not surprising that children with special needs often apply these derogatory labels to themselves. Because they have been taught to think poorly of themselves, they perform poorly in class (Algozzine, Mercer, and Countermine, 1977).

For all these reasons, many educators and parents have become convinced that special education classes are not the solution for many retarded children or children with other special needs. Instead, they have advocated mainstreaming these students into regular classrooms.

Children with IQs below 51 are not considered educable and, in most states, are not provided with regular public school education. Such children usually are cared for institutionally. Raising and caring for a seriously retarded child at home is a difficult and demanding responsibility that not all families can accept. However, institutions do not always provide the best opportunities for growth and development. The current trend is to develop community resources that can relieve the families of retarded children of some of the burden. In fact, 96 percent of all mentally retarded people in the United States are cared for outside of institutions (Karagianis and Merricks, 1973). What this statistic doesn't reveal, however, is the quality of that care, which may or may not be better than it would be in an institution.

The Eastern Nebraska Community Office of Retardation (ENCOR) is a good example of one comprehensive plan for the education and care of the retarded that utilizes both institutional and home care. The profoundly retarded receive close medical supervision in an institution; others attend developmental centers for educational and vocational training. School staff members work closely with parents, and whenever possible, the child is kept with his or her natural family (Galloway, 1972).

Learning disabilities Children with learning disabilities are often mistakenly believed to have low general intelligence and are sometimes put into classes for slow learners and into nonacademic high school programs. These children's difficulties in visual-motor perception have been associated with their apparent lack of understanding of what is happening in the classroom and their apparent disinterest in the quality of their performance and with school in general (Wallbrown and Wallbrown, 1976). Teachers sometimes consider these symptoms as signs of immaturity or emotional disturbance instead of what they really are. If tests given to these children do not disclose poor intellectual ability, other diagnostic tests —for example, medical, optometric, and audiometric examinations—should be used. If none of these show problems the children should be tested for specific learning disabilities.

There are many kinds of diagnostic tests for learning disabilities. A young child can be given just one or two or an extensive battery of them. Marianne Frostig, founder of the Frostig Center of Educational Therapy in Los Angeles, advocates testing sensorimotor abilities, language, perception, thought processes, and social and emotional behavior to diagnose the disability and form a composite picture (Frostig and Maslow, 1973). A standard IQ test such as the Wechsler Intelligence Scale for Children can reveal wide discrepancies between verbal and performance IQs. Others such as the Bender-Gestalt and the Frostig Developmental Test of Visual Perception can detect minimal brain dysfunction. Psycholinguistic tests such as the Illinois Test of Psycholinguistic Abilities can isolate visual and auditory problems. Standardized achievement tests in reading, spelling, and arithmetic can also yield useful diagnostic information.

Since reading is a subject that most learning-disabled children have serious difficulty with, we'll use it here as one example of what teachers can do to provide useful remedial instruction in the classroom.

Reading specialists agree that remedial reading should include a thorough, initial diagnosis of each student's disabilities. Classes should be limited to four or five students so that the teacher can give the necessary individual attention. Instruction should be carefully organized into realistic short-term goals, and the teacher should motivate the children by giving them concrete evidence of their progress. Basic reading skills should be developed first, then comprehension and reading rate (Woestehoff, 1970).

Research shows that remedial reading classes are more effective if they meet frequently. One study (Silberberg and Silberberg, 1973) indicated that in one project children given two hours of remedial reading instruction every day for five weeks showed a five-month reading gain.

What distinguishes remedial reading classes from regular reading classes? Special emphasis on phonetics has been found to increase comprehension of many learning-disabled students (Summerell and Brannigan, 1977). This may be related to findings that show that many learning-disabled children also have verbal encoding (visual-verbal integration) deficiencies (Swanson, 1978). Remedial reading lessons in which children are instructed in efficient memory strategies are highly successful with reading-disabled students (Thoresen, 1977).

Teachers assign all work according to individual abilities. Because reading disabilities cripple learning in all subjects, teachers have a serious responsibility to provide reading matter of appropriate levels of difficulty for each child. This does not mean that subject matter needs to be boring, as one researcher found out. Starnes (1975) described one class of fifth-grade students in a District of Columbia school who were reading at second-grade level. The teacher noted that the students sat stiffly, obviously bored with "See Spot Run" primers. Reading can and should be fun, thought the teacher. Why should there be this air of defeatism? The next day she brought one 11-year-old a rousing Jules Verne novel from her home library. The child was so entranced by Verne's adventure story that he begged her for the book. She wrote his name on the flyleaf and gave it to him. What followed was a deluge of 25 million paperback books selected by children as their own in a program aptly called Reading Is FUN-damental (RIF). Launched as a pilot program in the District of Columbia schools in 1966, in 1975 RIF had 350 chapters in 48 states and hoped to double that number in a year or two.

The response to the program has been significant. Children in the pilot program who were reading three and four years behind their grade levels became avid readers almost overnight. Parents also became enthusiastic partners in the plan. Surveys taken since indicated that more than 90 percent of the parents say the program has increased their children's reading skills; 60 percent say their children urged them to buy other books. Children are learning that reading is fun.

Although teachers can best help learning-disabled children when diagnosis is made early (Wooden, Lisowski, and Early, 1976), help still can be given to older students. Diagnosing and compensating for learning disabilities of older children and adolescents require different criterion instruments and procedures. The Wechsler Adult Intelligence Scale, the Berry-Buktenica Developmental Test of Visual Motor Integration, the Gray Standardized Oral Reading Paragraph Test, and the Peabody Individual Achievement Test may lead to the discovery of adolescents with undetected learning disabilities (D'Alonzo and Miller, 1977). In addition, teachers can develop their own instruments to explore specific achievement deficiencies in reading, mathematics, and written communication.

Helping students with learning disabilities is a complex task, as many teachers have found. Adolescents with learning disabilities have already suffered from years of school failure and resultant low self-esteem. They suffer the stigma of being "special" or "different" at a time when it is important to be as like one's peers as possible. As two educators have described it, "In a world of teenage conformity, this adolescent is a non-conformist by circumstance, rather than by choice. At an age when a case of acne can spell gloom and depression, this adolescent suffers from the anxiety that his peers might uncover the 'hidden handicap'"(Jacks and Keller, 1978, p. 61). It takes a special teacher with a great deal of sensitivity to deal with these problems.

Social-emotional handicaps are extremely difficult for teachers to deal with in regular classrooms. Since many children with special needs have multiple handicaps, and since many physical and mental handicaps are associated with social-emotional problems, it follows that large numbers of children fall into this category and provide major sources of difficulty, particularly for teachers concerned with classroom discipline.

Identifying and Teaching Gifted Students

Gifted students like Aaron are more capable than the average student in their ability to organize material, express shades of meaning, use imagery and analogies, and analyze. However, bright children also need guidance. Highly gifted children are not necessarily gifted in every subject, and the teacher should consider their strong and weak areas. Some are socially mature; others cannot get along with anybody.

Ability grouping generally separates students in a particular grade level homogeneously according to IQ scores or, in some cases, IQ scores and reading achievement scores.

Many teachers have assumed that ability grouping facilitates teaching as well as learning because it reduces the range of differences between students. Both rapid and slow learners are supposed to benefit because instruction can be geared to the capabilities of each group.

Theoretically, ability grouping motivates high-ability students to apply themselves and gives the slow learners more opportunity for success (Bayuk, 1972).

Ability grouping capitalizes on the establishment of special self-contained classrooms where gifted students can receive specialized attention and instruction. An alternative to specialized classrooms is setting an entire school aside for this purpose. One example is the Bronx High School of Science in New York City. In recent years, big cities in the United States have set up magnet school programs in which schools are set aside to provide specialized programs not only for the extremely gifted, but also the underachieving gifted and the minority-group gifted student.

Many critics suggest, however, that ability grouping by special classes or schools increases discipline problems and creates elitist, undemocratic attitudes among students and teachers. According to Urevick (1965), this kind of "artificial stratification" gives students in advanced classes a false sense of superiority and students in slower classes feelings of inferiority and a defeatist attitude toward education. Moreover, students in slow classes too often receive inferior instruction. They then score badly on tests, which reinforces the belief that they are indeed slow learners. Students in advanced classes, on the other hand, sometimes suffer from an overemphasis on competition and grades instead of learning for its own sake.

Findley and Bryan (1970) reported that, besides reinforcing unfavorable self-concepts and stigmatizing slow learners, ability grouping also reinforced the social class system. A disproportionate number of children from minority and poor backgrounds get segregated into slow classes, thereby depriving them of the stimulation they could be receiving from high-achievers in an integrated class.

Those who argue for the heterogeneous class say that it provides every child with valuable insights about others and enables students to learn from each other as well as from the teacher. Brighter students can help the slower ones academically and socially, and slower students can help the brighter ones develop compassion and understanding (Heathers, 1969; Urevick, 1965).

Acceleration generally allows a gifted student to progress more rapidly through school by skipping one or more grades. Klausmeier and Ripple (1962) studied the effects of acceleration on bright second-grade pupils in Racine, Wisconsin, and reported that accelerated students performed as well or better than an equally bright unaccelerated control group. One negative effect of acceleration was that the accelerated pupils were not readily accepted socially by older students in the higher grade. Boys seem to suffer more social ill effects than girls.

Occasionally, there is a student so exceptionally intelligent that he or she can skip several grades with no harmful effects. The case of Dr. Norbert Weiner is an excellent example of successful acceleration. Dr. Weiner graduated from high school at age 11, was awarded his Ph.D. in mathematics at the age of 18, and went on to become one of the famous researchers in his field in the century.

In 1973, researchers at Johns Hopkins University studied the effects of "radical acceleration" on extremely bright students (those who score in the top 0.5 percent of their age group on the Scholastic Aptitude Tests). These students took college courses for credit while in high school, which enabled them to skip several grades and enter college early. This study showed that these students made satisfactory personal adjustments and had no major academic problems (Stanley, 1973).

Acceleration does not always produce favorable results, however. Husen (1967) studied students in twelve countries and found that poor children who entered school earlier than other children of the same background were more likely to develop negative attitudes toward school. In addition, many educators and psychologists are concerned about social difficulties that might be encountered by bright children who are accelerated and spend all of their school time with children much older than themselves.

Enrichment programs are intended to counteract some of the bad effects of ability grouping and acceleration by allowing gifted students to remain in regular classrooms. They do this by providing gifted children with individually prescribed instruction, special classes, seminars and other activities geared to their needs. Under Project CLUE in Memphis, for example, gifted students in the fourth through sixth grades attended two optional half-day seminars each week and spent the rest of their time in the regular classroom. The seminars provided an informal, relaxed atmosphere and flexible seating arrangements. The teachers gave no grades but continuously evaluated student performance in critical thinking and creativity (Memphis City School System, 1974).

Another excellent method of developing enrichment programs is to employ a contract system, that is, a self-pacing system that places the responsibility on the student. "A contract should be constructed so that each child achieves an immense amount of proficiency in the topic he is concentrating in" (Kinslow and Patryla, 1978, p. 16).

One last method of providing enrichment programs is what one educator called the "after-school special." Students at the St. Joseph Program for the Gifted are selected on the basis of their voluntary requests and faculty recommendations. Students may choose advanced courses in humanities, math, or science (Rosenberg, 1978).

Sometimes enrichment programs of this sort are used even with children as young as 5 years old. In Marin County, California, for example, such a program was set up for gifted children. Kindergarteners

Special enrichment classes in subjects of interest to gifted students challenge them to apply their talents and intellect.

to ninth graders in this program take a variety of college-level courses such as electronics, computers, and marine biology. The courses are specifically designed for them and taught by college professors. The purpose of College for Kids is to supplement the students' education in their regular schools. It is designed to fill a void of special education for the gifted that existed in more than one-third of the local public schools when the program began. Dr. Jared Sharon, director of community and college development at College of Marin, parent school of College for Kids, explained, "Our program is not intended to advance a student beyond the grade to which he normally is assigned but rather to enrich his background. Our central purpose is to make available unique learning experiences that any single school district could not provide by itself" (Blakeslee, 1975, p. 39). College for Kids makes full use of resources that the public schools don't have—the science computer center, the marine biology laboratory, audiovisual equipment, speed reading machines, binocular microscopes, and so on.

The professors at College for Kids reported enthusiasm about the program. Vic Seegar, who taught physics to third, fourth, and fifth graders, explained the rewards of the program both to him and to the students:

> One day I was explaining nuclear energy to them, and I told them how the sun is just a great big nuclear reactor up there in the sky. One child then raised his hand and asked, "If we already have that great big nuclear reactor up in the sky, why do we need any more down here?" "What could I say?" Mr. Seeger said, smiling broadly. (p. 39)

Identifying and Teaching Students from Poverty Backgrounds

Students from poverty backgrounds arrive in school with characteristics that any teacher should notice easily. Their clothes are shabby, they are often malnourished, and they are often unhealthy. Especially significant, but possibly less obvious are the negative self-images that tend to be instilled in these children. Many qualities and customs of the poor are considered strange, inappropriate, or simply wrong by middle-class teachers. The poor child is sensitive to these judgments and quickly learns to feel incompetent, inadequate, and out of place in middle-class institutions. The problem of self-concept is serious for many minority-group children. The perceived racism of white middle-class society begins to affect their image of what they are and the value they place on their self-worth at an early age.

Various behavior patterns follow directly from poor self-concepts. Many poor youth are prone to passivity in school and find it difficult to adapt to delayed rewards (Karnes, Teska, Hodgins, and Badger, 1971). Others frequently violate middle-class social mores by being either excessively boisterous or overly withdrawn, by speaking without permission, by refusing to defer to authority figures, by using street language that is considered improper in school, by solving problems through combat and violence, and by reacting in a hostile manner to constructive criticism from the teacher (Houston-Stein, Freidrich-Cofer, and Susman, 1977). These behavior patterns, acceptable to the culture of poverty but not to the middle-class norms of the school, program the poor child for failure.

Because of these failures, poor children often drop out early, cannot find steady employment, and end up as disadvantaged adults stuck in the same pattern of poverty. Their children must then be reared under the same difficult conditions, and they also find themselves in danger of failing in school. What can teachers do to help poor children learn and possibly break out of this terrible cycle?

Providing effective reward systems The work of Robert J. Havighurst provides a useful theoretical model for understanding what we have accomplished so far in reducing the learning problems of poor children. According to Havighurst, teachers have lacked a systematic theory of the effects of rewards and punishments on poor children. He cited the findings of Davis (1965) to back up his contention that tangible, material rewards are important in stimulating poor children in school.

> Davis . . . noted that his wife, then working as a substitute teacher in the Chicago public schools, made a discovery about the way that disadvantaged children may learn arithmetic. In a second grade in a ghetto school she found several children, including one 9-year-old boy who could not count beyond two or three. The following day was Valentine's Day, and she brought some candy hearts to school. She told the children that they could have as many candy hearts as they could count. *The 9-year-old boy thereupon counted 14 candy hearts.* (Havighurst, 1970, p. 315)

The secret apparently lay simply in finding the appropriate stimulus with which to reward the child.

Havighurst also demonstrated that different groups of poor Americans have different kinds of reward systems that appear to be most effective. As an example, he cited a study by Wax (1969) of Cherokee and Sioux children, who are observed to form close-knit groups that oppose individual excellence at the expense of peers.

> In oral reading, the whole class tends to read together in audible whispers, so that the child supposed to be reciting can simply wait when he comes to a difficult word until he hears it said by his classmates. Generally, pupils like to work together and help each other. Consequently, the weak students are carried along by the stronger ones, and the stronger ones do not exert themselves to excel the weaker ones. (Havighurst, 1970, p. 315)

Reward in this group apparently is provided through feedback that is meted out primarily by peers. Havighurst contrasted these Indian children with Appalachian poor children, who get rewards mainly from the family circle rather than peers, and with poor black children, who, interestingly, depend primarily on the teacher's approval or disapproval. This may be because they are less likely than Indian and Appalachian children to have both parents at home, and according to Havighurst, they probably also receive less parental approval or disapproval.

Clearly, teachers working with poor children need to learn about their backgrounds and what rewards are most important to them so that they can use these rewards effectively in the classroom.

Teacher expectations If teachers want poor children to learn in the classroom, one thing they must do is *expect* them to learn. Many researchers have pointed to a self-fulfilling prophesy whereby the negative expectations of middle-class teachers about poor children may contribute strongly to their failure in school.

Although the original and probably most famous study demonstrating the self-fulfilling prophesy (Rosenthal and Jacobson, 1968) was severely criticized by many educational theorists, the hypothesis itself has been supported by data from many studies. One of them, a Hunter College Examination of fourteen new teachers in inner-city schools, describes an especially revealing diary of one of the young teachers (Fuchs, 1972). Her own words make the pattern of teacher socialization clear. At first she is warm, friendly and respectful toward her students. But after a talk with a more experienced teacher, she begins to assimilate the prevailing values of the school. She blames the children's family backgrounds for their failure, rather than questioning the workings of the educational system. Soon she is "tracking" her class—choosing a select few "good" students for special attention and labeling others as "slow" and thus, in her eyes, not deserving of as much attention. In merely using one term, "slow," she manages to write off most of her class as being hopeless.

The problem of teacher expectations cannot be separated from the negative self-images of poor children. When these children enter an alien school system, they are often fearful and uncertain. This is particularly true of those who come from minority groups. If they enter with self-doubts, and if they are immediately faced with a teacher who reinforces their negative self-concepts, failure is almost a certainty. It is easy for a teacher to make poor children feel inferior and out of place—whether by overt actions or by subtle, even unconscious, facial expressions and tone of voice.

Finally, teachers must remember that their own behavior can have a marked effect on student performance. A teacher who is excited about learning and who genuinely likes the students in the class may help excite the students; a teacher who is pessimistic and cynical will only feed the students' dislike of the school system.

Identifying and Teaching Bilingual Students

Most bilingual students in the United States, those who speak languages other than standard English at home, are often better at processing of verbal materials and making perceptual discriminations than are children fluent in only one language. However, they have lower vocabulary levels in English (Ben-Zeev, 1977). This lower vocabulary level can have detrimental effects on school learning.

There is now evidence that poor black children as well as Spanish-speaking (and other foreign-language-speaking) children in the United States should be thought of as bilingual. Studies by Baratz (1969), Marwit, Marwit, and Boswell (1972), and Genshaft and Hirst (1974) all suggest that these black children are learning a well-ordered dialect that is different from standard English but not deficient. The Genshaft and Hirt study showed that when black and white children were matched for social class and nonverbal intelligence, both groups performed equally well on verbal tasks involving standard English. Further, on tasks involving black English, the white children performed significantly worse. This confirms the theory that many poor

In some parts of the United States today, bilingual Spanish-English instruction is the norm, rather than the exception.

black children are learning two languages: black dialect for use at home and standard English for use in school.

These studies all point toward a need for increased bilingual education in this country. There are a number of highly successful pilot projects in bilingualism. Particularly important are the experiments in Montreal—the St. Lambert project (Brock, Lambert, and Tucher, 1973; Lambert, 1972)—and in Culver City, California (Cohen, 1974). In each of these, English-speaking children were instructed in many subject matters in a second language foreign to that spoken in their homes (French for English-speaking students in Canada; Spanish for English-speaking students in California). The children became competent in the new language, remained proficient in the native language, and performed well in nonlanguage subjects using the same curriculum as children who were not bilingual. This procedure is not new; bilingual education has been carried out extensively in many European countries, where children frequently learn several languages in school and at home.

Since the 1968 passage of the Bilingual Education Act, which calls for teaching of subject matters in English and the native language of students unfamiliar with standard English, experimental bilingual programs have expanded in America. Yet bilingual education is still a highly controversial issue in the United States, especially in the case of black English. It seems clear that if children speak a different dialect from their teachers, either the children must learn standard English, or the teacher must learn to communicate in the children's dialect, or, as many educators have come to realize, both must happen at once.

Some educators believe that there must be "total acceptance of the child's nonstandard dialect spoken at home" if any language program is to succeed (Strickland, 1972). Others insist that consideration of such dialects by teachers will make the teaching of reading more difficult (Vail, 1970). Professor Toni Cade of Rutgers, a noted black writer, poses the basic dilemma for minorities. She opposes tampering with ghetto accents, but at the same time advocates the learning of standard English, because "if you want to get ahead in this country, you must master the language of the ruling class" (Seymour, 1971).

Researchers interested in teaching second languages most efficiently to school children have carefully examined the method by which the first language was learned and used this same method successfully to teach the second language. Asher (1977), for example, reported success in teaching fifth through eighth graders a second language when he used talking and listening as the basic procedures, the method by which they had originally learned their first languages at home.

successful intervention programs

In the past decade, the federal government has sponsored the development of a variety of special intervention programs designed to help children with special needs. Most of these programs have been designed for children of the poor because the largest number of children whose needs are not met either by family or local community assistance are found among that group. A great deal of federal assistance has also gone into programming for bilingual children. In addition to the Spanish-speaking children and children who speak varieties of black dialects, children from Vietnam to the Soviet Union have come to our country and our schools in the past ten years. Developing programs to teach and improve English language speaking as well as programs to teach bilingually (in both English and the native language of these students) has become a necessity.

Early Childhood Intervention Programs

The children of America's poor frequently come from homes in which both parents work. Ten years ago, some 4.5 million women with children under the age of 6 were job holders, mostly out of economic necessity (Keyserling, 1972). Today the figure is much larger. Approximately 2 million of their children were left in homes that were not their own. Of these, only 700,000 spent the day in licensed day-care centers. Furthermore, many of the children stayed in substandard facilities supervised by untrained people. Some apartments that were licensed as proprietary day-care centers for six children were caring for as many as forty-seven.

Children of the poor need more than day care. They need early childhood education programs that will stimulate their cognitive development as well as their emotional and social well-being. Such programs could be helpful for infants and toddlers as well as older children. "The sooner the better" is not a bad rule in this situation, for once the poor children have fallen behind their more affluent peers, their educational success is in jeopardy.

One approach to remedying the learning difficulties of poor children has centered on intervention programs involving parents. Karnes, Teska, Hodgins, and Badger (1970) reported on a program in Campaign-Urbana, Illinois, in which mothers were the primary agents of intervention. Twenty mothers were recruited from inner-city neighborhoods for the pilot project. Each agreed to attend a two-hour weekly meeting during which she would be instructed in teaching techniques to use with infants (varying in age from 12 to 24 months). In addition, a portion of each meeting was reserved for discussion time, in order to build a supportive atmosphere for the mothers and foster their sense of dignity and efficacy. The aim was to stimulate the cognitive and verbal development of the children using the natural mother in place of an elaborate outside program at as low a cost as possible.

After completion of the program by fifteen mothers, IQ testing of the children revealed substantial improvement in learning skills. The results compared favorably with other studies that have relied on college graduates or professional tutors to do the same work.

Jason, Clarfield, and Cowen (1973) studied an intervention program involving ten inner-city toddlers in Rochester, New York. These children met frequently with college undergraduate "helpers" over a five-month period. In addition, home sessions were conducted at which parents were present. The program stressed cognitive and verbal development and social behavior. Jason and his colleagues found that "a saturated infant stimulation program with parent involvement helped significantly, at least in the short run" (p. 57). There were significant improvements in the children's cognitive skills and social behavior. In addition, mothers became progressively more interested in the program and more actively involved in stressing similar goals in the home.

Nimnicht and Brown (1972) developed a training course for parents in connection with their toy library at the Far West Laboratory for Educational Development. Parents were instructed in the use of certain educational toys and in the basic concepts and facts of child development. Particular emphasis was placed on the children's needs for healthy self-concepts and on positive reinforcement for the children.

One of the key findings of the program was that parents' attitudes toward their children improved noticeably. In their descriptions of their children, the parents used words that showed that they were more respectful toward their children and more confident of the children's abilities. The children showed significant improvement in nine intellectual areas: color naming, color identification, shape naming, shape identification, numerical concepts, relational concepts, problem solving, verbal communication, and verbal comprehension. This success seems attributable both to the quality of the educational toys used and to the interest and enthusiasm of the parents. In fact, several parents mentioned that the discussion sessions with other parents were the most helpful part of the course.

Schaefer (1972), after evaluating various parent intervention programs, concluded that working with mothers works effectively to produce gains in intellectual functioning. However, such programs cannot in themselves be a total educational answer for the problems of disadvantaged children, and there must be sufficient follow-through if the gains of these programs are to be preserved. Schaefer points to the need for early and continuing support to help parents educate their own children and to help them learn the theory and practice of education in the home.

One of the most interesting preschool programs is Bettye Caldwell's children's center first established in Syracuse, New York (Caldwell, 1968). The center was originally created to test the hypothesis that the first three years of a child's life constitute the optimal time for educational enrichment programs. It was designed to serve about twenty-five children between the ages of 6 months and 3 years, who generally attended the center from six to nine hours daily, five days a week. Almost all of the children were from poverty backgrounds.

The content of the Caldwell program placed heavy stress on spoken language skills. In addition, there were attempts to promote social and emotional development and perceptual, motor, and cognitive skills. Behind all these efforts was a belief that the child must feel secure and masterful in order to develop a positive self-image and succeed in the educational world.

Caldwell and her staff tested these ideas by evaluating the progress of all children who had been using the center for more than three months. Caldwell noted that these children showed IQ gains just at the age that poor children often register declining test scores. Caldwell's data suggested further that the children from the poorest families gained the most from the center's program, and that the children who had benefited most from the enrichment program had spent the longest time in it.

Another important finding was that the children showed gains in terms of social competence and no increase in symptoms of emotional problems. There had been concern by some that, due to the young age of the children, increased physical illnesses or emotional problems might result from the enrichment program. In fact, these fears seem to be unfounded, and the success of the Caldwell center seems clearly established.

Probably the best-known preschool intervention program is **Project Head Start,** originally sponsored by the federal government's Office of Economic Opportunity. Head Start came into existence in the summer of 1964 at 13,400 educational centers across the nation, serving 560,000 poor children. Initially, Head Start was an eight-week introductory program designed to prepare poor preschool children for public school education. Head Start was enthusiastically praised by parents, teachers, and pupils, and by the end of the 1960s had expanded into a broad, nationwide preschool program for inner-city children.

Head Start's growth and popularity has been reevaluated in the light of critical research on the program's educational value. For example, a study by the Westinghouse Learning Corporation and Ohio University concluded that Head Start apparently did not significantly increase the intellectual capabilities of inner-city children (Cicirelli et al., 1969).

The early evaluations did not find fault with Head Start itself, but rather with a lack of satisfactory follow-through programs. They pointed out that it makes little sense to spend large sums of money to enrich the learning experiences of poor children, only to cut them adrift when they enter the public schools. For this reason, in the past decade a series of new programs called **Follow-Through** have been designed to extend Head Start's compensatory education through third grade. In addition, the Head Start preschool programs themselves have been lengthened and extended. The results of these changes have been so successful that a long-term follow-up by the Consortium on Developmental Continuity of the Education Commission of the States reported significant educational gains that have remained over time for Head Start children (1977). Since then, the effects of Head Start have been shown in the following areas: Children in Head Start programs are less likely to enter special education classes than are their counterparts of similar background and ability who have not attended such programs. Children in Head Start programs—regardless of sex, ethnic background, early IQ, or home background—remain in their proper grade significantly more frequently than non-Head Start children. Children with Head Start educations have increased scores for at least the first several years of school on math achievement and IQ tests. Finally, these children are more likely than control children to give achievement-related reasons for being proud of themselves (Brown, 1979).

The Bereiter-Engelmann program is probably one of the most highly structured educational programs for poor children. Because of its emphasis on language development, it has been used extensively with children who speak other than standard English in their homes. Bereiter and Engelmann's program has been harshly criticized by some teachers and parents because of its strict adherence to structure, and by others because of the assumption implicit in Bereiter and Engelmann's educational theories—that these children's skills are deficient, not *different*. Nevertheless, the program has produced some startling results.

An experimental group of fifteen children was recruited from a predominantly black, poor community in Champaign-Urbana, Illinois. These children attended special classes for two hours a day, five days a week. A fairly rigid schedule was established. The class was divided into three work groups of five children each. After a 10-minute free-play period to begin the session, each work group went off for a 20-minute class in language, arithmetic, or reading.

After the initial class period, the whole group would reunite for a 30-minute break in which they could sing, snack, and use the rest rooms. This break period was followed by another 20-minute subject class. Next came another 20-minute period in which all fifteen children got together for reading and discussion of stories. A final 20-minute subject class concluded the day's schedule.

The general instructional strategy involved pattern drills conducted at a rapid pace. The language program focused on developing "the minimum essentials of language competence." At first a verbal formula was learned by rote: "This *apple* is *red*," "This is a *cup*," "This *cup* is *full*." Gradually, more complicated variations were presented to the students.

Arithmetic was viewed and taught primarily as a "science of counting." As in the language program, pattern drills were heavily stressed. Rather than formally presenting explicit rules of arithmetic, the teacher encouraged the children to learn these rules implicitly through constant repetition of various example patterns.

The reading program centered on an explicit rule system that was tied to a restricted vocabulary. Initially, the children were exposed only to three-letter (consonant-vowel-consonant) patterns. In addition, a few of the more difficult consonants were excluded, and only lower-case letters were included.

This program resulted in dramatic increases in Stanford-Binet scores (Bereiter and Engelmann, 1968). As Table 9-1 indicates, 4-year-olds in the Bereiter-Engelmann program showed consistent and significant improvement after one year. This improvement was generally greater than that of the control group, which was not part of the program. Furthermore, the 1964 and 1965 experimental groups both in-

Table 9-1 Stanford-Binet Test Results for 4-year-old Children in the Bereiter-Engelmann Program

YEAR ENTERING	PRETEST SCORE	SCORE AFTER 1 YR.	SCORE AFTER 2 YR.
1964	97.6	104.2	106.8
1965	97.0	111.5	120.4
1966	91.1	102.9	—
1965 control	94.5	102.6	99.6

J. Osborn, Teaching a teaching language to disadvantaged children. In M. A. Brottman (ed.), Language remediation for the disadvantaged preschool child. *Monographs of the Society for Research in Child Development*, 1968, 33 (8, Serial No. 124), 47.

creased their scores a second time after two years, whereas the control group's scores fell in the second year.

Bereiter and Engelmann (1968), in analyzing the results of various testing procedures, concluded that twenty minutes a day of instruction in each area over two year's time can improve the performance of disadvantaged preschool children from a year or more below average to average level in mathematics, reading, spelling, and language learning.

In the last decade, many new programs have been designed for school-aged children who need special help to learn. One program, designed particularly for poor children with special language and reading needs, that does not require special staff or equipment was developed in Kansas City, Missouri—Operation Upgrade.

Programs for School-aged Children

Operation Upgrade, a community-based reading program, used high school tutors to instruct children on a one-to-one basis. The tutors were supervised by adult program directors, and all tutors and directors were community residents. This was particularly important in helping the children to communicate verbally and to read and write in their own dialects, and later to do this in standard English (Johnson, 1973). Classroom teachers wanting to use this technique may use peer teaching instead, in which older students serve as tutors or paraprofessionals.

A crucial element in Operation Upgrade was teaching children to communicate in words and to read by using stories that they themselves had written, as well as stories written by their peers. These stories were extremely popular with the students. The following is an example of the stories written by the children and used for reading lesson material:

On my way home I seen a man run out in the street and he all most got hit by the driver of the car and the man start to kus the driver got

out and the driver jump out of the car and they start to fight and the
police can came and put them in the car and drove away on the a red
light and went down town. (Johnson, 1973)

The Operation Upgrade staff experimented with various methods
of using the children's stories to teach standard English language before settling on a workable compromise. Presentation of uncorrected
stories led students to absorb the mistakes in them. On the other
hand, using adult-corrected stories caused the students to lose interest. It is important to understand this issue from the viewpoint of the
student who, by seeing his or her own work in print, is learning for
the first time how important and worthwhile he or she really is. As
one student angrily declared after examining her corrected story,
"That ain't none of mine." If teachers fail to understand the importance of the student's work to the student as an issue of self-worth,
they can easily turn off the child.

Eventually, as a compromise, a story game system was designed
(Johnson, 1973):

MY SELF

I like myself. I like to talk to myself. When I go to bed I look funny.
My aunt think I look fat. I don't look fat. My sister think I am small. I
don't think I look small.

STORY GAME (THINKS THAT)

1. He <u>thinks that</u> he's smart.
2. My mother <u>thinks that</u> I should rest.
3. My brother <u>thinks that</u> it is going to rain.
4. My aunt _____ _____ I look fat.
5. My sister _____ _____ I am small.

The story game method allows teachers to preserve the children's original writing in its natural form, while pointing out errors in a helpful
and supportive way. In preparing a story game, the teacher will not
concentrate on all of the errors in a child's story, but rather on those
that are most important and most relevant to the child's current level
of ability.

Operation Upgrade is a good example of a special help program that functions independently and in addition to regular school
programs. Besides such supplementary programs there are special
schools that devote their entire curricula to teaching children with severe learning disabilities. These schools use innovative techniques
such as individualized instruction and intensive tutoring. In many
cases, physicians and psychiatrists are on the school staff.

An example of one successful special help school is the Laboratory School at Kingsbury Center in Washington, D.C. Many specialists
are available at the Lab School, including reading specialists; music

teachers to teach auditory discrimination; dance teachers to teach co-ordination of arms, legs, and facial expressions; and graphic arts teachers to pull together visual experiences and to teach students to visually separate foregrounds from backgrounds. The Lab School also has drama teachers who, through work with puppets, masks, and hats, in settings that simulate a radio station, spaceship, and restaurant, teach children to organize and integrate their actions, walk in certain ways, and control gestures, facial expressions, and voices. The Lab School is just one program that has used the arts as a major means of teaching academic skills to learning-disabled children. This method of teaching through art has been found effective in numerous studies (see, for example, Gair, 1975, and Gair, 1977) and should be particularly useful to the classroom teacher.

Most enrichment programs are focused on preschool or elementary school children. It is often believed that if a boy or girl has not shown academic potential by adolescence, it is too late to do anything. This line of reasoning is circular, because although most teachers and psychologists agree that the optimal age to help most children with special needs is in the first several years of life, the absence of special assistance once children have become older will only serve to ensure continued failure and thus provide "proof" that such youths were doomed from the start.

*Programs for
Older Students*

Surveys at a variety of universities support the contention that poor and minority-group students, for example, can be helped to succeed in the schools and to continue on to achievement at the college level (Green, 1969). Many youths who have entered college as high-risk students have compiled acceptable academic records when supported with tutorial and counseling assistance.

One support program, providing extensive tutorial and counseling services at Southern Illinois University in 1966, exceeded even its own predictions. The university's Counseling and Testing Office had projected that out of a group of 100 high-risk students beginning their programs, the average grade would be 2.2 (equivalent to a low D). It was predicted that 24 students of 100 would fail to make a 2.0 (D) average, and that only 1 student would score as high as 3.0 (C). In actuality, the results were quite different. Of the 74 students who remained in the program, 65 bettered their predicted grade-point levels. Thirty of the 74 were at or above 3.0 (C), while only 5 were below 2.0 (D). Similar successes with high-risk students through tutorial and counseling programs have been reported at the University of California campuses at Berkeley and Los Angeles.

Experiments at the high school level have been more frequent than college-level programs. One of the best-known has been Upward Bound, a nationwide program that has functioned as a special tutorial aid for inner-city high school students preparing for college.

One Upward Bound program particularly worthy of discussion is the innovative curriculum project at St. Louis University (Hyram, 1972). The 120 Upward Bound students were divided into six heterogeneous groups. Each was led in learning activities by a team consisting of teachers specializing in different fields.

For each week of the program, there was a specific inquiry core, consisting of a set of basic questions relevant to the students' lives. For example, the questions for the fifth week included:

> What's my greatest holdback?
> Is it really my race or religion?
> Is it the economic level in which I was born and raised?
> Is it really within me, my personality, my values, my speech, my attitudes, and my ways of acting toward people?
> Am I as limited in my opportunities as I think?

> (Hyram, 1972, p. 320)

Activities in the various subject areas for the week were structured around these core questions. Thus, the curriculum was intended as a unified search for knowledge that would be directly tied to the lives of the poverty-level students, rather than a series of fragmented academic and vocational subjects.

Some compensatory programs at this age level have been more successful than others. But it seems clearly established that adolescents should not be written off. In an effective program, a large number of these youths can make dramatic progress.

summary

1. Students with special needs require special teaching procedures to reach their potential. Special needs include physical handicaps, mental retardation, learning disabilities, social handicaps, poverty backgrounds, bilingualism, and extreme giftedness.

2. In the past, handicapped children were either institutionalized or segregated in special classes. Today, there is a greater effort to educate these children in regular classrooms.

3. Visually handicapped children have bad eyesight even with corrective eyeglasses. Hearing-impaired children may have problems speaking as well as hearing. Most speech defects involved articulation problems. Other prevalent problems are voice and pitch defects; stuttering, stammering, and lisping; and delayed speech.

4. Neurological or orthopedic handicaps include deformity, paralysis, epilepsy, cerebral palsy, muscular dystrophy, and other disabling diseases such as arthritis, diabetes, heart trouble, hemophilia, cystic fibrosis, serious allergies, and asthma. Epilepsy is a noncontagious neurological disorder. There are two types of epileptic seizures: petit mal and the more dramatic grand mal.

5. There are four general types of mental retardation: profound, severe, trainable, and educable. Profoundly retarded people generally require

life-long institutional care. Severely retarded people tend to have multiple handicaps and are often placed in institutions. Trainable people are less likely to have multiple handicaps and obvious physical defects. They can learn to become partially and sometimes fully self-supportive in sheltered situations. Most mentally retarded people are educable. Their handicaps are often not detected until they enter school, and as adults they are capable of supporting themselves as marginal workers.

6. Learning-disabled students may have average or above-average IQ scores, but they are often mistakenly described as "slow" by their teachers. Learning disabilities may be caused by problems in reading, memory, concentration, motor ability, and social behavior. It is difficult to detect and diagnose learning disabilities because there are no clear-cut symptoms common to all cases. The most noticeable learning-disabled students tend to have severe behavior problems similar to those shown by hyperactive students. The largest group of learning-disabled children have language and reading difficulties such as dyslexia.

7. Almost two-thirds of Americans who are poor are English-speaking whites; other groups with significant numbers of poor people are blacks, Puerto Ricans, other Spanish-Americans, and American Indians. According to Oscar Lewis, the poor live in a culture of poverty whose norms differ significantly from those of mainstream American culture. Poor children are prone to negative self-images and nutrition-related health problems that can both affect their performance in school.

8. Children who enter school with language difficulties get off to a slower start than children with well-developed skills in standard English. The largest single group of children with language problems currently are Spanish-speaking children. Inner-city blacks who speak black English may also encounter difficulties with standard school English.

9. Approximately 3 percent of American school children are gifted. Many gifted children have problems because there are too few challenging programs in their schools, or because their capabilities make it hard for them to get along with less-gifted students.

10. The early identification of children with special needs is often critical. Regular screening tests can be used to identify students with sensory handicaps. Sometimes such students can be kept in regular classes, though those with severe handicaps may be better off in special schools. Children with severe speech problems can be given special help within the public schools, but classroom teachers are often the only source of help for those whose speech problems are less serious.

11. Children with suspected or noticeable physical or neurological handicaps should be referred to specialists for complete physical, educational, and psychological evaluations. Some of these children may be able to stay in regular classrooms and must be helped to cope with their deficiencies and the reactions of their classmates.

12. The criteria for determining the kind of help a retarded child needs are general intelligence and adaptive behavior. Children with IQ scores be-

tween 51 and 75 are considered educable, while those whose IQs are between 25 and 50 are considered trainable. Educable retarded students have traditionally been placed in special classes, though the recent admission of emotionally disturbed and learning-disabled children to such classes has damaged their effectiveness. Mainstreaming has developed in response to the segregation and labeling inherent in the special class concept. Trainable retarded children are usually not placed in public schools; recent programs have aimed at supportive home care rather than institutionalization.

13. There are a wide variety of screening tests for learning disabilities. Many learning-disabled children are misdiagnosed as retarded, hyperactive, or simply emotionally immature. Although early identification is important, older students can also be helped to overcome their learning disabilities.

14. Social-emotional handicaps are exceptionally difficult for teachers to deal with in regular classrooms. Since many physical and mental handicaps are associated with social and emotional handicaps, children with special needs can be a major problem for classroom teachers.

15. Identifying children from poverty backgrounds is generally easy. Because much of these children's behavior is considered inadequate by middle-class norms, these children easily develop feelings of inferiority and failure. Teachers can help break the vicious cycle of poverty by providing effective rewards and having positive expectations for their students.

16. The major problem bilingual students have is lower vocabulary levels. Many poor black children have been designated as bilingual, as have Spanish-speaking children. The increasing numbers of such children have necessitated more bilingual teaching programs.

17. Several different approaches for teaching gifted children have been developed. Ability grouping places students in classes based on scores on IQ and other tests taken into consideration together. Ability grouping has been criticized as fostering elitism. Acceleration allows gifted students to go through school faster by skipping grades. Accelerated students, whose classmates may be several years older, may face social and emotional adjustment problems. Enrichment programs try to counteract some of these bad effects by allowing gifted students to stay in regular classes while providing them with individualized instruction and other challenging activities.

18. Most intervention programs have been aimed at poor and bilingual students whose needs are likely to be met by their families and localities. Many poor children need programs that provide cognitive stimulation as well as day care. The most successful intervention programs involve the parents as well as the schools. Most preschool programs are initially successful, though most lack follow-through programs to solidify long-term gains. Operation Upgrade, an example of a program for school-age children, uses children's own stories to teach reading. The Lab School in Washington, D.C., is an example of an entire school devoted to learning-disabled children. Even university-level programs have been successful, proving that it is never too late to help a student with special needs.

COLES, R. *Children of Crisis,* a series of books dealing with American children and their problems (Boston: Atlantic-Little Brown). Coles's famous series describes a psychiatrist's interpretation of the problems of children from minority-group backgrounds across our country. The complete series consists of *Children of Crisis: A Study of Courage and Fear* (1964), describing poor black children in the South; *Migrants, Mountaineers, and Sharecroppers* (1967), describing the children of another group of underprivileged Americans; *The South Goes North* (1967), describing the plight of poor children moved to northern slums; *Eskimos, Chicanos, Indians* (1977), describing minority-group children from the North and West; and, finally, *Privileged Ones* (1977), about America's rich and well-off children. Coles writes in an easy and comfortable style and explains with sensitivity the interests, values, and problems of all of these groups of children. Any book in the series is extremely useful to help teachers working with these children to understand them better and help them.

GOLICK, M. *A Parents' Guide to Learning Problems.* Montreal: Association for Children with Learning Disabilities, 1970. This book has many specific and helpful tips for teachers of students who have learning problems. Since it is intended for parents, all the advice is quite easy to understand as well as practical. The materials for the various suggested activities described in the book are readily available and inexpensive.

GOLICK, M. *She Thought I Was Dumb But I Told Her I Had a Learning Disability.* Montreal: Association for Children with Learning Disabilities, 1970. This book offers many practical tips for helping these children—both for teachers and parents. It discusses the early identification of children with learning disabilities. Golick points out that such children may have to be taught things that ordinary children pick up on their own.

HARE, B., AND HARE, J. *Teaching Young Handicapped Children.* New York: Grune & Stratton, 1977. This is an excellent text for both preservice and inservice teachers with directions and strategies for programming of handicapped children in the preschool and primary grades. Specific developmental problems are discussed.

MOWRER, D. Speech problems: What you should do and shouldn't do. *Learning,* January 1978, 6 (5), 34-35. Mowrer's extremely brief and direct article points to the problem that many classroom teachers are having today: There are many special programs in schools today for children with serious speech problems, but there are fewer and fewer services for children with minor speech problems that need correcting. Mowrer gives a series of specific hints to teachers who want to help these students.

NOLAN, R., AND CRAFT, L. Fifteen approaches to motivate the reluctant reader. *Journal of Reading,* 1976, 19, 387-391. This is a very brief and directive article written for teachers with students with reading problems. A number of different methods are described in detail, as well as a remedial reading program for students from 7 to 16 years of age that the authors have found to be very effective.

*for students
who want to read
further*

10

MAINSTREAMING

A Case History of Richie:
A Boy Labeled Mentally Retarded
and Placed in a Special Education Program

Richie was the third of four children, all of whom attended the Murray Public School system. The oldest child in the family, a boy, completed public school on schedule and then attended college. He is currently employed as an accountant. The youngest boy, two years younger than Richie, did average work in school, although he had to repeat third grade.

Richie at age 25 is a physically attractive young man; he is much stronger than either of his two brothers. However, he reads poorly and seems to tire easily after doing even a short amount of reading or writing. During all of his school years, he was never reported to act out in class or to give his teachers a difficult time.

Richie's mother completed high school at age 47 through night classes. She enrolled in a local university night program after receiving her high school degree. Richie's father received an education through eighth grade. He is currently employed in a local factory.

Richie's mother reported that he had an uneventful and seemingly happy preschool period, but that he "got a poor start in school." He didn't begin until he was 6 years old. Richie didn't want his mother to go home on the first day of school and cried for some time. His mother spent the first week or two attending classes with him. In the middle of his first year in school, the method of teaching reading was changed to phonetics.

In the second grade, Richie's teacher quit during the middle of the year. Richie was extremely upset and had difficulty adjusting to the new teacher. In the third grade, his teacher died in the middle of the school year; this provided another major trauma for Richie, who began to withdraw into himself.

Richie's teachers reported to his mother that he seemed to learn slowly. However, his mother remembers being told many times that, once he learned something, he didn't forget it. Richie had a short attention span. He would work for a time, then simply refuse to do more.

At age 12, when he was in the fifth grade, his teacher called Richie's mother to school and suggested that he be placed in a special education class "because he was a poor student." The mother reports:

"I was extremely upset and went to see the principal to find out why. I was willing to spend a lot of time with Richie, and provide tutors if he wasn't doing well. The principal told me that it would be of no use to put in the additional effort, that Richie had done poorly on tests and that he was mentally retarded. Although he hadn't failed any classes, his scores on tests that had been administered by the school psychologist were very low. I asked to see the school psychologist and then received the worst shock. The school psychologist had never met Richie in person. He had based his decision to remove Richie from regular classes on standardized tests that showed poor reading skills, inattentiveness, and what the psychologist said was short attention span. I asked the psychologist if the tests measured Richie's unusual mechanical ability. I asked how he could decide my son was mentally retarded without even seeing him. He responded, 'I have spent five years in preparation for this position; much money was spent on my training. This all makes me eligible to make such assumptions.'"

Richie's mother reported that she was so upset after the interview with the school psychologist that she remained sick in bed for three days. When she told her son that he was to be taken out of regular classes and placed in the special program, he reacted strongly. Later, he became extremely shy and withdrawn; his mother felt that he had been pushed "into a world of loneliness."

Several of Richie's friends were placed in the special class at the same time that he was. His best friend, however, remained in regular classes. Richie and his mother both remember that gradually, during the following year, the boy "shied away" from Richie. Richie says today that he remembers sensing this; he feels that this is one of the happenings that led him to build a "safety wall" around himself. He tended to spend as much time as possible by himself. Often he lashed out against his younger brother, Billy. Until Richie was placed in the special class, the two boys had been close friends. After the special placement, they grew apart.

Richie's mother remembers being terribly worried about her two youngest boys. She tutored both Richie and Billy herself every night. They both remember hating the tutoring and did their best to escape it. Their mother was determined, however, and their nightly sessions continued until Richie finally graduated from the special education program and Billy showed marked improvement in his grades in the regular class he attended. When Richie was ready to graduate, his mother went to the school board and asked permission to put her son into a regular program so that he could obtain a regular high school diploma. Permission was refused.

Today, Richie works on a farm. He reports that he gave up his battle to fight the system once he reached high school age, and he decided that he would instead find peace in "my own world where no one bothers me." He spends as much time as possible today out-of-doors by himself and enjoys hunting and fishing. His brother Billy is currently a student at the University of Pittsburgh (Seeley, 1978).

a rationale for mainstreaming

Special education classes were initially designed to teach children who were diagnosed as needing homogeneous grouping and special instruction. These classes were meant to deal with only problem learners—but, as time went by, special education teachers found themselves facing children with an amazing variety of problems and special needs. In many special education classes, crippled, emotionally disturbed, and learning-disabled children have been included together with slow learners. As noted in the case history of Richie, such classes cannot always provide adequate solutions to all these sorts of learning problems.

Some educators have suggested that homogeneous groupings have not improved the academic performance or social development of children with special needs. Teachers of special classes for handicapped pupils find it impossible to adapt the curriculum to each child's level when children are segregated according to physical handicap instead of mental ability and social maturity (Karagianis and Merricks, 1973). It has also been shown that educable retarded children do not necessarily benefit from being placed in special classes (Pedrini and Pedrini, 1973). In the great majority of cases, educators suggest, the special physical and medical needs of crippled children can be met in the regular classroom (Karagianis and Merricks, 1973). Black and Spanish-American children with special needs suffer the double penalty of being separated because of their ethnic status as well as because of their special needs. Many of their parents complain that their children are denied the specialized instruction that was the original rationale for the segregation.

Recently, parents of children with special needs have brought court suits against school boards that advocate what they consider uncritical homogeneous grouping, claiming that their children have the same rights as average children to education in a regular classroom. The courts have responded by mandating the integration of these students into regular classes whenever such placement does not interfere with the education of others. This has given rise to the procedure known as **mainstreaming**—bringing students with special needs of all kinds into the mainstream of American education.

There are valid arguments for and against keeping children with problem behaviors in regular classes. Many of these children improve considerably by remaining in ordinary classrooms where they are exposed daily to the positive influence of children who are better adjusted. However, very aggressive children not only drain the teacher's energy, but, without proper supervision, they may disrupt the entire class. A compromise has been to place these children in a special class two or three times a week temporarily until they show by their behavior that they can participate in the regular program (Central Advisory Council for Education, 1967; Karagianis and Merricks, 1973).

Research in British schools suggests that mainstreaming is beneficial and that many handicapped children are able to make a satisfactory academic adjustment in ordinary classes (Anderson, 1973). Most British educators feel that segregating the handicapped does not serve anyone's best interest and may actually make it more difficult for them to accept and live with their disabilities (Central Advisory Council for Education, 1967).

mainstreaming and the law

The concept of mainstreaming has interested psychologists and educators for a number of years, but was not until a series of class-action lawsuits were filed by American parents in the early 1970s, that the concept actually began to be taken seriously in American school systems.

Litigation begun in the past decade has had two major thrusts (Gearhart and Weishahn, 1976). The first involves court cases in which it has been alleged that special education classes (usually classes for the educable mentally retarded) lead to stigma, inadequate education, and irreparable injury. Suits have been brought on behalf of special plaintiffs and "all others similarly situated." A majority of these suits were brought on behalf of black or Mexican-American children and were in part the result of placement of children like Richie in special classes on the basis of what parents considered grossly inadequate evaluation. Most of these class-action suits alleged that the tests used for placement were culturally biased and that class placement based on these inadequate tests led to inadequate education. In addition, some suits claimed that the stigma of mental retardation was suffered by children who were not mentally retarded. In an interview with Richie's mother, she reported that she had no idea what her son's IQ score was, nor what test had been administered in order to determine the score. Richie's case history suggests that the problems often encountered by poor minority-group members apply to white children whose parents have low levels of education as well.

A second type of litigation begun in the past decade appeared to be going in a different direction from the first (Gearhart and Weishahn, 1976). The first thrust had been aimed primarily at programs for children scoring low on IQ tests; the second related specifically to *all* handicapped children who required special assistance to have a chance to succeed at school. The result of the second thrust has been monumental. As many educators have described it, it has brought special education and children with special needs in the forefront of the news and out of the closet.

In 1975, Public Law 94-142, the Education for All Handicapped Children Act, was passed by huge margins by Congress. Effective September 1, 1978, Public Law 94-142 guarantees basic rights to all children with special needs. These include the right to a "free and appropriate" public education, as well as the rights to due process, nondiscriminatory testing and labeling, and confidential handling of personal records and files.

Local school districts must use several screening procedures before placing students in special classes and must review their decision every year. State departments of education are to act as liasions between the federal government and local school districts, checking to make sure that local agencies obey the law and securing federal support for localities that need it. Local and state plans must be submitted to the federal government for approval.

One important aspect of P.L. 94-142 is the Individualized Education Plan. The **Individualized Education Plan (IEP)** for children with special needs requires clear-cut assessment of children's performance levels, annual goals, including short-term measurable objectives related to long-term goals, specific educational services, specification of the extent to which such children will be able to participate in regular educational programs, and "appropriate objective criteria and evaluation procedures and schedules" verifying annual review of the instructional objectives (Cole and Dunn, 1977). Goals outlined in the IEPs may be nonacademic—being able to sit quietly and listen to a story— or may consist of lists of three or four math objectives or an entire reading book. The IEP is based on what teachers believe that certain children can achieve, rather than what they know they will do. Teachers are not held responsible if they try their best and their goals are not met. If this happens, teachers are obligated to reassess the situation, define new goals, and then go on from there. Some teachers and administrators complain about the additional time and effort involved in implementing the IEPs; yet had the IEP been mandated when Richie was in the fifth grade, he might have had a much better chance at succeeding in school.

One result of Public Law 94–142 has been the teaching of children with differing mental and physical abilities by the same teachers in the same classrooms. According to one expert in mainstreaming, the central idea behind this concept is that every student has the right to receive an "individually appropriate combination of regular and special education" while attending regular classes. Each school system is obligated by public policy to arrange that, to the extent that modern instructional practices allow. Moreover, school systems today are being encouraged to create new educational configurations to make mainstreaming a reality. According to Birch (1978), "Some have done so; others are trying."

In some cases, the result of Public Law 94–142 has been the development of special classes and assistance with special problems by experts in addition to the mainstreamed classes. In all cases, administrators, often for the first time, are required to be accountable for the decisions made regarding each individual student (Gibson, 1979). Such accountability was not a requirement when Richie attended fifth grade at Murray Elementary School.

The passing of Public Law 94–142 has posed a multitude of problems for administrators and teachers. States have had to develop special task forces to provide leaders for in-service training concerning the act, its requirements and intent, as well as its implications for teachers. In-service workshops have been developed across the country to train school personnel to work under the mandates of the new law. Diagnosticians have been selected and trained to perform the required evaluations of students and programs. Workshops have been established for principals, classroom supervisors, and teachers to help them individualize instruction based on team diagnoses and establish long-range goals for each student. Parents have been educated and informed of their and their children's rights under the new law. Since evidence shows that standardized tests often are inaccurate and inappropriate for children under stress and therefore cannot always be useful for children with special needs, teachers have been taught new methods of evaluation based on observation and experience with each student.

mainstreaming: new problems for teachers

Most school systems are taking mainstreaming seriously. In-service training is being organized for teachers who are being faced with problems for which they have not received advance preparation. The new problems for classroom teachers are numerous. Teachers of children with orthopedic handicaps or with cerebral palsy now need to learn ways to handle wheelchairs in their classrooms and to teach the other children how to help. Teachers of retarded children placed in regular classes need to use, and in some cases to develop, district-mandated learning materials, provide for the special needs of the retarded, and, at the same time, help these children handle newly encountered social adjustment problems. Teachers dealing with blind children need to learn how to help them move around the classroom and through the school; learning independent orientation and travel skills is particularly important to these children. Teachers of deaf children need to learn how to get their attention and encourage development of their communication skills, including speech, speechreading, finger spelling, and manual communication. Autistic children, previously kept in special classes, more and more frequently are being placed in regular classes (Sage, 1975). Teachers of these children need, among other things, to help with language lessons and behavior modification. Moreover, teachers must do all these things without neglecting the educations of their nonhandicapped students.

Mainstreaming does not do away with the need for specialized services—it makes them more urgently needed than before. Although many of the requirements that students with special needs have can be met in the regular classroom, careful attention is needed to determine the best curriculum for each child. Teachers with various special skills will have to coordinate their efforts to deal with all the unusual problems that will arise. All school personnel—regular and special education teachers, resource specialists, administrators, psychologists, social workers—and parents will have to act as a team. Regular classroom teachers will have to train themselves for a much wider variety of student interaction and group dynamics in order to promote the acceptance of children with exceptional needs in regular classes. Additional personnel—paraprofessionals, case managers, tutors, and specialists in child development, instruction, resource learning, and diagnosis—will have to be introduced to give children with special needs the individualized instruction they require. If mainstreaming is to be a success, teachers will require innovations in the old curriculum, instructional methods, and even school architecture (Birch, 1971).

Mainstreaming means bringing into the regular classroom children with physical handicaps as well as children with other kinds of problems.

Freda Leinwand, Monkmeyer

The day David learned to write disproved all my preconceived notions about mainstreaming. He was born without arms and legs. All he had for arms were short, uneven stubs. He was confined to a wheelchair. Yet he had a healthy outlook about his handicap. . . .

Most of the kids in our second-third-grade combination were seven- and eight-year-olds. David was 12. I was bothered about the age difference, especially because David seemed more mature even than most 12-year-olds. He was very inquisitive and eager to answer many questions the second and third graders posed. On his own, David asked his teacher in the orthopedic unit if he could join my class a couple of times a week to participate in the science lessons.

My initial reaction to his request was negative. After all, I felt, 32 children were enough. Another student, particularly David, would be an added burden, one I wasn't at all sure I could deal with. . . . It was tough enough to work with the so-called "average" child. And my teaching credentials did not include work with exceptional children.

David gained permission from our principal to participate in my class on a trial basis for two science periods a week. . . .

David volunteered information on plant structure at his first lesson. He raised his stubs and wheeled his odd wheelchair over to the cabinet where the plants grew profusely. Most of the thriving plants had grown from his own seeds. He asked if he could tell about the structure of one plant he was particularly fond of. The children listened intently. Thursday came and David brought in some exotic plants from Africa to talk about. His Mom came with him and held the plants while David told about them. David's resourcefulness stimulated children who had not previously been too eager to participate.

As one challenge after another arose, David became comfortable with his new-found leadership and acceptance. Gradually, he became less awkward. For two years he had been in the unit with other handicapped children. But now things were changing. He wanted to spend more time with us, so he went to his homeroom teacher asking to come to our room for social studies. He was convincing. David was now a part of our class, with us three days a week for social studies and two days a week for science.

We were studying various areas of the world—those with both warm and cold climates. We planned to do an art project, a food project and a music project for each of five locales—Norway, Alaska, Hawaii, Mexico and Egypt—contrasting cultures with both warm and cold climates. David insisted on going with us for our regular once-a-week library period in order to help a friend get the information for his country. His friend, a poor reader, loved social studies. David was scheduled for physical therapy during our library period, but the therapist, after talking to David about the time conflict, arranged his therapy for a different time.

At this point I was becoming alarmed. David seemed to be running his own life. He had told his homeroom teacher that it was OK with me for him to go to the library, but I hadn't even been consulted. David had assumed that it would be OK. So David and I talked at length about correct "procedures" before making decisions. We both understood that he must consult others before he made any further assumptions.

David wheeled his special wheelchair around the library as

though he were the research librarian—to the amazement of the school librarian. He located the books on Hawaii for his friend, and since Warren couldn't read most of the books, David read parts aloud in a quiet corner. When he finished reading, Warren started asking questions and expecting answers—from David, not the librarian!

A milestone had been reached. I had always needed an assistant in the library and now David could fill the bill. He was at home in the library, read well and obviously loved books.

For the next several weeks, our classroom looked like a disaster area as we tackled one ambitious project after another. We built a papier-mâché volcano. David thought of making it explode with dry ice. We made dioramas featuring hula dancers. David suggested a way to cut a hole in the back of the box and put a fan behind the dancers to make them move. It worked! I found myself feeling jealous, upset that David was so ingenious.

Then came the day when David announced that he wanted to *write* a report. . . . At this point my third graders were just learning to make cursive letters. And David wanted to learn too. . . .

Two days later, David joined our morning penmanship classes. My dilemma: How could I teach someone who had no arms to write? Keeping him after school for individual help was impossible since he rode on the school bus. Where to begin? David couldn't hold a pencil, the school-issued chalk was too short and his wheelchair didn't reach the chalkboard. The law (PL 94–142) required an "appropriate education" for all children aged 3 through 17. David certainly fit into that category. But I was feeling increasingly insecure.

Two weeks passed. Then David helped me solve the problem. His father had made some plastic-covered metal braces to fit around his stubs. Now he could reach the chalkboard, but the chalk needed a

Children with physical handicaps can learn as effectively as children who are physically able to get about without any assistance.

tight clamp. Before the day was over, David had talked with the school custodian and the school principal. Together they contrived a chalk clamp that could be wired onto the braces. David was thrilled! The first step in learning to write had been conquered.

Five weeks had gone by since David had first declared his intention to learn to write. Most of the other class members were already writing short sentences by this time. David watched new strokes being taught every day. He could tell Warren what was wrong with his letters, and Warren listened. They were helping each other. The more Warren learned, the more David intensified his efforts.

Another couple of weeks went by before David and I arranged to work on a one-to-one basis. His parents agreed to pick him up late a couple of nights after school. We started in February, and by the end of May David could write small words on the board. He was impatient and upset because he felt he wasn't progressing fast enough. We both almost gave up time and time again. Warren was the buffer, always telling David that he could do it. . . .

David and I continued to work together until the second week in June. In two weeks time, he had learned to write short sentences on the board. As he mastered the writing skills, other boys and girls learned new vocabulary through his work. Warren could read almost at grade level by the end of the school year. David could write on the chalkboard. I had found out that mainstreaming could be successful if attitudes were right. . . .

Not every exceptional child will be as successful as David in the regular classroom—"the mainstream." For some children, the regular classroom is a "restrictive" environment. And I discovered, as many of you have, that I was the key "partner" in the success of mainstreaming. David, with my help and that of his parents and peers, made mainstreaming work for us. We all learned from David. (Hogan, 1978, pp. 49–50)

According to law, teachers must develop and use Individual Education Plans. The IEP is a way of ensuring that the teacher and others have properly translated the federal goal of an appropriate education for every handicapped child into reality. Each IEP must contain the following elements (Hayden and Edgar, 1978):

Designing and Implementing Individual Education Plans

1. A summary of present levels of the child's performance
2. Yearly goals
3. Short-term objectives for each yearly goal
4. A list of the specific educational and support services needed to meet each objective
5. Evaluation criteria for each objective
6. Procedures for reevaluating the IEP

The teacher ordinarily does not have to do all the work involved in developing an appropriate IEP. Planning committees composed of teachers, representatives of school districts, and parents usually plan the IEPs together. However, teachers do have the primary responsibility for the IEPs' implementation. To do the job satisfactorily, planning committees must collect relevant assessment information, including medical and physical data as well as current functioning level. They must establish main priorities. They must determine methods of implementing the IEP as well as evaluating the teacher's efforts. Because parents must be involved in the process, meetings must be scheduled at convenient times for them to attend.

In addition to listing what teachers will try to do in the classroom, the IEP also details the special help and materials teachers and students will need. To do the complex job spelled out by the IEP, teachers frequently need the aid of special educators as well as school psychologists, counselors, social workers, physical and occupational therapists, speech therapists, physicians, and others. In addition, they must learn how to use the specialized instructional materials handicapped children need and how to handle crisis situations.

Helping Students with Special Needs Gain Social Acceptance

Teachers must spend a great deal of time dealing with new problems related to the social adjustment of their students with special needs. Psychologists have shown that young children's skill in using their bodies is directly related to their self-concept (Platzer, 1976). Children with physical or motor handicaps are therefore likely to enter regular classrooms with lower self-concepts than other children. Rejection by their nonhandicapped peers can lower their self-esteem considerably.

In addition to helping the handicapped student adjust to his or her new surroundings, the classroom teacher must teach other children in the class how to deal with handicaps most of them have never seen before. Researchers have shown that children who are seen as academically incompetent are met with low levels of social acceptance, and that peers reject children who are seen as misbehaving (Gottlieb, Semmel, and Veldman, 1978). Handicapped children are frequently rejected by their peers because of these misperceptions.

Actually, studies have shown that most children have views about the handicapped, but really know very little about them. In a study designed by the Workshop on Children's Awareness, a division of the American Institutes for Research in Cambridge, Massachusetts, researchers interviewed a group of children whose average age was 10. They discovered that less than 25 percent of the children knew more than two disabled people; more than 25 percent knew no one with a disability; the rest knew one or two but not always of their own age. However, the fact that the children's exposure to the disabled was limited did not mean that their opinions were. Eighty percent of those interviewed said they agreed with the statement "Disabled people are generally sad most of the time" (Hoyt, 1978a).

Simply exposing children to handicapped peers doesn't change their attitudes. They need to be introduced to handicapped children in

David S. Strickler, Monkmeyer

Handicapped children need to be introduced to their peers in ways that will help the regular students to empathize with them.

such a way that they will empathize with them. The task of assisting children to do this is not an easy one. One study (Ballard, Corman, Gottlieb, and Kaufman, 1977) showed that teachers can help normal children to accept handicapped children and help handicapped children to gain social acceptance by placing them together in small groups of from four to six to work on highly structured manipulative tasks. In this case, the handicapped children were mentally retarded. Changes in the attitudes of the nonretarded classmates came in from two to four weeks, with, of course, a great deal of attention and intervention during that time by the teacher.

Another approach is to provide special programming. The Workshop on Children's Awareness developed a TV film series, *Feeling Free*, for this purpose. The aim of the series was "to show nondisabled children that the disabled are more like them than different" (Hoyt, 1978 b, p. 25). The series was set up in a magazine format with five children, each with a different handicap, as regulars. Five types of segments were provided: mini-documentary on each child; a chance for guests to ask more about the regulars; sharing of a skill or hobby; a discussion involving the whole group; and a modification of familiar games that everyone, including the handicapped children, could play.

The results, in terms of increasing awareness, were positive. Children's letters to the editors included such comments as:

> My cousin is handicapped. He has trouble walking but he is getting better and he is doing very good now. I love him handicapped or not. It is very true.

> I think just because they aren't the same they can sometimes do better things. Maybe because they can't jump they can draw better or explain better than other people.

> People think that kids with such problems can't do anything but they can really do almost more than us. (Hoyt, 1978, p. 28)

Dealing with Parents Teachers must spend a great deal of time working with parents. Public Law 94–142 clearly stipulates that parents of handicapped children be involved in the development of educational programs. This law affords them certain safeguards, including due process, in the evaluation, placement, and programming of their children. When parents or guardians are unknown or unavailable, when they do not answer the telephone or ignore letters sent from school, or when the children involved are wards of the state, the school must arrange for the assignment of surrogate guardians who will represent the children in all proceedings. Teachers are not usually involved in court proceedings, but their presence is necessary in committee planning, developing the IEPs, and explaining how the program works to the parents or legal surrogates. Teachers must also involve parents of normal children in the planning and development of effective programs if the classmates of the mainstreamed children are to play helpful roles.

Parents have many important roles to play. They should consult with the teachers and provide important information concerning the child's activities and development, work with the social worker and school psychologist, submit written reports, even participate in family therapy sessions when necessary. They can help by joining parent-awareness groups to discuss common problems and attending lectures and films presented by special education teams (Bernauer and Jackson, 1974).

services to make mainstreaming work

If teachers are to make mainstreaming work, a number of special services are necessary. In many cases, school architecture can affect whether or not mainstreaming will work. If a new school is being built, many of these services can be built in at the outset. In other cases, special services can be provided by additional personnel.

Architects must consider many aspects in designing a building to accommodate children with handicaps. For example, does the school have elevator facilities that can be used easily by children in wheelchairs? New buildings are being supplied with elevators. New and old buildings are also being supplied with ramps as well as stairs so children in wheelchairs or with locomotor disabilities can get from floor to floor. Often, special equipment is needed.

How School Architecture Can Help the Handicapped

The Rachel Carson Intermediate School in New York City was designed as a prototype school for educating the handicapped (Solomon, 1977). The school had ramps and elevator, but other special features were needed. A special education center was designed for the new students who were to be mainstreamed in order to wean them from "their dependence and isolation." Special resource rooms with equipment available for children with special needs were also planned and provided.

For effective mainstreaming, supportive services must be designed to allow mildly handicapped children to remain in ordinary classes. These services can also be extended to more severely handicapped children who receive part of their instruction in special classes, but attend regular classes the rest of the time. Some, but not all, of these services and service personnel are found in most school districts, and they vary tremendously from state to state.

Supportive Services for Teachers and Students

Special education teachers Mainstreaming has not done away with the need for special education teachers. Teachers cannot implement or even plan an IEP without the continual assistance of special education teachers. Before Public Law 94–142, special education teachers spent their time in special education classes. They were segregated from the regular programs and, often, had little interaction with regular teachers. In the mainstreamed classroom, however, special education teachers may work side by side with regular teachers. In some cases, they show regular teachers different ways to teach children with specific handicaps. In other cases, special education teachers do some of the actual teaching.

School staff redeployment often is necessary to do the job adequately. Whenever possible, handicapped children should be allowed to remain in regular classrooms rather than being sent to special teachers in different parts of the building. Instead, special education teachers should plan special activities and bring special equipment in to the regular classrooms. In this way, everyone in the class can be a "visual participant" (Birch, 1978), and the activity can become an ordinary part of the day-to-day schedule. Cooperation between the regular teacher and the special education teacher can ensure that each child receives attention at least equivalent to that supplied by a system of special education.

Psychological services The role of the school psychologist typically involves assessment, intervention, and evaluation of severe student problems, as well as consultation and administrative work. The requirements established for the preparation of the IEPs extend the school psychologist's responsibilities. The psychologist integrates information from his or her own analysis with that of teachers, parents, and community agencies to form a composite picture of the child. Having made a diagnosis, the psychologist recommends a course of action to help the child make a better adjustment. He or she then determines whether that intervention has been effective by evaluating feedback from teachers and parents.

Counseling services Although counselors often work closely with the school psychologist, they focus mostly on important educational decisions, not on therapy.

Counselors are of particular importance in designing IEPs and in advising students, teachers, and parents about available alternatives. When behavior problems become serious in the mainstreamed classroom, both counselors and school psychologists may provide major help through one of three principal types of therapy: individual counseling, individual behavior therapy, and group-centered approaches.

Individual counseling may follow the *nondirective* approach, in which the therapist assumes that the handicapped child is able to solve his or her own problems with the support and assistance (but not the *direction*) of the therapist. Nondirective therapy is *child-centered* in that the child is responsible for much of the process of change.

The *directive* approach maintains that a trained professional's direction of the therapeutic process is crucial to the child's progress. Directive counselors believe that constant nondirectiveness on the part of the therapist might not get to the heart of the problem.

Many therapeutic approaches used with school children can be categorized as **group centered.** Most are based on the theory that a group supplies an individual with more acceptance and encouragement than an individual therapist can. A group offers the child the opportunity to work out personality changes within an interpersonal context. A therapist is always present in the group, and he or she can clarify matters or intervene when necessary.

Although the techniques and procedures of groups vary, children generally are encouraged to speak frankly about their personal feelings, including self-doubts and hostilities. In the course of such revelations, angry clashes, moments of deep warmth and affection, laughter, weeping, and bold confessions may occur.

Another group-centered approach is *family therapy* (Harper, 1974), in which the therapist treats the entire family rather than the individual. The theory underlying this approach is that balancing and opposing types of problems tend to exist within a family. These problems can best be addressed by treating the family unit as a whole rather than treating each family member (or one of them) separately.

Social workers   The school social worker arranges meetings with the child, the parents, and the teachers in a cooperative effort to help the child adjust to school. In severe or pathological cases, the social worker, together with the psychologist, teacher, and parents, might decide to place the child in a special school or residential institution. The social workers must help parents, particularly, to understand the nature of their children's problems as well as what ways they have available to deal with them.

Physical therapists   The physical therapist helps children with bone, muscular, or joint defects by providing individual exercise and treatment programs on the recommendation of a medical specialist.

Occupational therapists   Handicapped children also may require an occupational therapist to help them develop their sensorimotor abilities and, later during adolescence, to help them fit these abilities with available employment or careers. Occupational therapists help students form good work habits and develop a sense of personal responsibility, particularly in self-care skills. Even severely handicapped children should learn to dress and bathe themselves, attend to personal and health needs, and learn basic social and safety principles.

Speech correctionists and audiologists   The speech correctionist helps children with articulation problems, stuttering, and defective speech due to cleft palates and hearing impairments. Hearing-impaired children may also require the service of an audiologist.

Physicians   No diagnosis of a handicapped child is complete without a medical examination by a qualified physician. Some children will also require the services of an ophthalmologist or neurologist. Schools that do not have these medical services should make the necessary referrals.

Director of special services   All special programs for children with special needs should be under the close supervision of a special education director. The director should have previous teaching experience in both regular and special classrooms and be able to help with curriculum planning, learning materials, and testing methods. He or she should also be able to help teachers manage classrooms, write behavioral objectives, and prescribe and evaluate individual instruction programs required by the IEPs.

*Using Special
Programs for
Students with
Special Needs*

Even with mainstreamed classes, no school can effectively provide for all its students without some special classes. Two examples of such classes are *reading* and *speech correction.* Some children have difficulty learning the basic skills of reading. These children need special lessons, often with individualized instruction, to gain the knowledge required to read, write, and understand what is going on in their classes. *Speech therapy* classes are designed to correct problems in articulation, voice, and rhythm. Speech therapists often use behavior modification techniques.

Often technological innovations provide special help to schools accepting handicapped children in regular classrooms. For example, technological innovation is proving a boon to visually handicapped children in the Madison Elementary School in Santa Monica, California ("Closed-Circuit Sight," *Human Behavior,* 1975). The nearby RAND Corporation has developed an individualized, closed-circuit TV system, called Randsight, which the Madison School is using. The experimental model can be used by a teacher and three students. Each student has his or her own closed-circuit TV screen, camera, and a lighted, movable platform. An additional camera, suspended from the ceiling, can pick up images from any location in the room. Essentially, the system works like a giant magnifying glass, producing a bright, high-contrast image of whatever the cameras focus on—the teacher, the blackboard, or a book or paper on the student's desk. The images picked up by the cameras can be used full-screen, split-screen, or superimposed—with a flick of the master controls operated by the teacher. Depending on how the cameras are manipulated, the teacher can give individual attention or encourage group interaction.

With the help of this machine, the visually handicapped are learning to read and write like their normal peers. Many are able to share the visual experience of their classmates for the first time, and they now can take an active part in class discussions. As their teacher notes, "It makes them feel really good about themselves" (p. 30). Says the system's designer, Samuel Genensky, an engineer who is himself legally blind, "Kids who might have had to use Braille all their lives can now enter the mainstream of sighted society" (p. 30). The project has sparked international interest, and researchers at RAND are presently contemplating an eight-station model that would be cheaper to build as well as more practical for larger classes.

Another innovation, this one requiring special programming, was successful in mainstreaming an autistic child into regular classes. Hoyt (1978b) reported a program in Lexington, Massachusetts, that successfully educated a 14-year-old autistic child and helped her to make "dramatic changes" in her behavior in just the first year. Hoyt (p. 13) reported that "from outbursts and total inattentiveness she progressed to orderliness and proper classroom behavior." At the time of writing the article, Hoyt reported that the student had learned to raise her hand before speaking, to type a business letter, and to develop a Spanish vocabulary that her teacher proudly termed "immense."

The program at Clarke Junior High in Lexington, Massachusetts, began by educating the teachers. They provided a greal deal of information about the new student—for example, a description of her home life, the kinds of behavior she was likely to exhibit, and what to do about it. Teachers each then developed and implemented IEPs for the student in their courses and changed their expectations and goals regularly as they learned what she could and could not do. Resource teachers made themselves available for assistance in behavior management, and an art therapist provided art therapy to help with behavior problems. The consensus at Clarke Junior High is that mainstreaming for this autistic child was definitely worth the team effort expended by the faculty.

making mainstreaming work: some approaches for the teacher

Mainstreaming puts heavy demands on the classroom teacher. Handicapped, learning-disabled, retarded, and gifted children, as well as children with problem behaviors, enter regular classes knowing that they have special needs and are different in some way. Because of this, the teacher must have a special set of capabilities in order to build an effective and therapeutic learning environment.

Handicapped children are likely to have poor self-concepts and other feelings of inadequacy. These show up in a variety of ways, such as lack of consideration for the rights of others and other problem behaviors such as withdrawal. These children may have reached widely varying levels of cognitive development, and their classroom performances vary accordingly. The teacher, therefore, must develop a set of behaviors that will reduce fear and tension in these children, be familiar with the principles of child psychology, and know how to use appropriate methods of teaching to assess each child's learning problems.

Developing Attitudes, Characteristics, and Behaviors that Help Children with Special Needs

According to specialists in educating young children, successful teachers must have characteristics that allow them to "work productively, without dogmatism or disorganization" in promoting a child's growth (Rabinow, 1964). Other characteristics include skill in working with individual students and small groups; openness to new ideas and methods; acceptance of individual learning differences; ease in a structured classroom; and a combination of warmth, patience, and firmness. The teacher must know how to help children overcome their problem behavior by using classroom activities to improve self-concepts and build academic skills. This calls for constant self-control, honest and constructive expression of feelings, and a helping attitude that is not too approving or permissive.

Many specific techniques have been shown to be highly effective in working with handicapped children. Art therapy is only one of many approaches the sensitive teacher might try.

Teachers' attitudes toward their students are more important than the specific teaching techniques they employ. Narang pointed out the following attitudes, characteristics, and behaviors of teachers who are successful in teaching children with special needs.

1. *They like children in spite of their faults.* They realize that children who are singled out for special help have already experienced more than their share of failure, and need a teacher who will be warm, accepting, and understanding.
2. *They base remediation on diagnosis of each child's problems and needs.* They carefully consider individual strengths and weaknesses, likes and dislikes.
3. *They start their instructional program at the child's present level of functioning.* They build the child's self-confidence because the initial task leads to success.
4. *They break down the learning task into small, manageable steps* and encourage success with various kinds of reinforcement (tangible and intangible), especially praise.
5. They are *flexible* in adapting a variety of remedial techniques to the needs of different children.
6. They realize that diagnosis and remediation are complex tasks that require the *cooperation* of a physician, psychologist, social worker, other teachers, and parents.

(Narang, 1973, pp. 49–51)

Many specific suggestions have also been made to help teachers dealing with many different kinds of handicaps.

Overcoming anxiety   Teachers need to overcome their own anxiety as well as that of their students (Swartz, 1978). Psychological evidence suggests that highly anxious teachers are less efficient in the classroom (see, for example, the extensive review of the literature by Coates and Thoresen, 1976). This is particularly true when teachers are dealing with handicapped children. Many teachers are afraid that nothing will work with their new charges, but, in fact, many of the teaching techniques that work successfully with regular children work with handicapped children, too.

Maintaining a positive attitude   (Although the term "positive attitude" may be a cliché (Swartz, 1978), the impact of the teacher's attitude is critical. Narang pointed out that teachers should "like" chil-

Olson (1978, p. 111) provided the following advice for teachers who have blind students in their classrooms:

1. Identify yourself by name when you walk up to a visually handicapped student. Do not walk away without telling the child that you are going.
2. Use the sighted-guide technique for helping the blind student through unfamiliar territory. Have him grasp your arm just above the elbow with his four fingers on the inside of your arm and his thumb on the outside. Walk a half step ahead with the blind student's left shoulder behind your right shoulder (or vice versa). When going through doorways or other narrow areas, drop your guiding arm down behind you to let the student know that he should step behind you.
3. When describing the location of an object on a flat surface, use clock directions. "Your book is at 3 o' clock."
4. If you give the blind student verbal directions to a specific destination, make certain the directions are nonvisual and are given from where he is. Use compass directions and left-right cues as well as familiar landmarks. "Turn left by the drinking fountain."
5. Don't leave any doors ajar, and if there has been a rearrangement of a particular classroom corridor, advise the blind student of the change.
6. Guide the hand of the blind student to an object if it is near and in danger of being knocked over.

dren, but it is equally important that teachers begin with the assumption that all children can learn.

Being involved Involvement—recognizing and treating children as human beings, regardless of their specific abilities or handicaps, by sharing mutual feelings, frustrations, and expectations—is a prerequisite to any successful educational program for children with special needs. It is particularly important in the mainstreamed classroom. Involvement can be expressed in concrete ways. For example, percentages can be taught by having a student compute his or her favorite baseball player's average, or asking a blind child to count the number of different sounds in a piece of music. Involved teachers know their students' abilities and capitalize on them.

Employing classroom management principles Teachers who are successful with handicapped children never forget the basic principles of classroom management. They recognize appropriate behavior when it occurs and are quick to reward it, ignore unwanted behavior whenever possible, and are consistent in use of rewards, punishments, and extinction.

Involving students in decision making The chances that decisions will be implemented are much stronger when students have a say in what they are doing in a classroom. Group discussion sessions, particularly when a teacher is trying to help the students in the class understand one another, are extremely useful. Rap sessions can provide an excellent format for obtaining student reactions. The teacher serves as a guide, moderator, and arbitrator, instead of dictator.

Redefining goals Finally, many goals that are established parts of the regular school curriculum are inappropriate for handicapped children. Teachers should understand this fact at the outset and should be prepared to evaluate and reevaluate each goal as they go along. Methods and materials will also have to be evaluated and reevaluated in order to make learning meaningful and useful to children whose learning needs differ from others in the classroom.

Special educators have provided very specific advice to teachers on how to deal with special handicaps. Since teaching blind and hearing-impaired children is new to most regular classroom teachers, these are used as examples here.

Teaching the Deaf Student

Culhane and Curwin (1978, pp. 111–117) offer the following suggestions for teachers with deaf or hearing impaired children in their classrooms:

1. Do not allow initial awkwardness to develop into lingering, uncomfortable feelings. Acquaint yourself with other hearing impaired individuals before meeting your new students for the first time. Many cities have schools for the deaf that would welcome a visit from an interested teacher. . . . A call to your local vocational rehabilitation agency might provide you with another opportunity for meeting hearing impaired individuals. . . . Occasionally, one or both parents of a hearing impaired child may be deaf, and these experiences will help you develop positive relationships with both students and parents.
2. Understand that all hearing losses are not the same. They can be mild or profound and involve one or both ears. Different kinds of losses produce different effects on students. Find out the nature of each student's problem and learn the best way to deal with the individual rather than attempt to find general ways of dealing with deafness.
3. Do not assume that deaf students are mute. A large majority of deaf people have no physical problem with their sound-producing mechanisms. But because these individuals cannot monitor their voices, they may sound different with respect to loudness, pitch, tone and discrimination of specific sounds. Many hearing impaired people do not like to use their voices because they lack training or fear embarrassment. Differences in speech and communication modes can create the misconception that deaf persons are somehow less intelligent.

In teaching deaf students, teachers need to be ready to accept a wide variety of communication skills.

Miriam Reinhart, Photo Researchers, Inc.

This, of course, is nonsense—intelligence is distributed normally among deaf students.

4. Do not expect all deaf students to speechread (lipread) well. Not every deaf child learns to be a good speechreader, and even those who are highly skilled cannot depend on speechreading alone. Good speechreaders can comprehend 25 to 30 percent of the spoken message.

5. Be ready to accept a wide variety of communication skills from deaf students. Those students who come to you from "oral" schools, or schools that stress speech and speechreading, have different skills from those who were trained to use sign language.

6. Do not expect all deaf students to be exceptional readers. And don't think that deaf students will understand a concept by merely reading it. Most deaf children do not read as well as their hearing peers, and just giving a deaf child reading material will not guarantee understanding any more than it will with most children. In fact, deaf youngsters might have difficulty with reading comprehension because of poor vocabulary development and problems with English sentence structure.

7. Reject all the other misconceptions, such as: deaf people see better, cannot appreciate music or dance, cannot drive. These give false impressions about deaf students and can limit what might be done to meet their needs and educational requirements.

If mainstreaming is going to succeed, the regular classroom teacher must be competent to deal with a child who has a variety of disabilities. For example, a child with reading disabilities is also likely to have emotional and communication problems. "Resource teachers," who are able to deal with many disabilities and who can assist the regular teacher in meeting all of the special needs of these children, are necessary to help the regular teacher.

Making the Best Use of Resource Personnel

395

Using
Individualized
Instruction and
Other Special
Programs and
Materials
Because of the uniqueness of these students' needs, teachers should be prepared to use a variety of teaching methods. Individualized instruction methods and computer-assisted instruction may be very useful for children with learning difficulties. Precision teaching methods have been shown to be very successful with the educable mentally retarded and blind and institutionalized children with behavior problems (Phillips, 1972). They are also effective with learning-disabled and gifted children.

Using charts and audiovisual tape recordings of classroom behavior to make precise records of changes in student performance is very helpful (Galloway, 1972; McDonald, 1971; Phillips, 1972; Starlin, 1971). This method furnishes an accurate record of how a child is actually performing in a particular situation and enables the teacher to evaluate his or her influence and plan more effective programs (Cohen and Martin, 1971).

A humanistic approach to teaching children with special needs was described by Jacks and Keller, 1978. Educational programs for these children should focus on fostering independence because self-esteem is derived from economic, physical, and emotional independence. Jacks and Keller designed a series of modules dealing with building maintenance, photography, video operation, consumer services, and the like. Each module was designed to provide practical experience as well as understanding. Teachers were assisted by a series of resource personnel, including a psychologist who was responsible for individual and group counseling, peer counselors, and parents. The entire staff was committed to fostering career development, with two faculty members having direct responsibility for career education and vocational placement. A career education intern designed special mini-programs to teach self-awareness, career awareness, economic awareness, decision-making, and employability skills.

Another reportedly effective program that mainstreams children with problem behaviors is Project RE-ED (Zax and Cowen, 1972). This project is based on the idea that effective education is the best form of therapy. The program uses a 24-hour-a-day treatment approach over a six-month period. During the week the children live in two residential centers; on weekends they go home to their families.

Project RE-ED aims at short-term, concrete educational goals, rather than long-term therapy or rehabilitation. The school day is focused on instruction in basic academic skills such as reading, arithmetic, and language (Lewis, 1967). Most teaching is individualized. In addition, the children are helped to develop simple socially useful skills such as roller skating, swimming, or bicycle riding. A specific goal of the program is to teach children with problem behaviors skills that help them to interact more easily with their peers. The overall goal is to prepare the children for functioning in a normal school and home environment.

Special programs have been developed to teach normal children how to empathize with their handicapped peers. Some involve special TV films designed to teach students in mainstreamed classrooms what their handicapped peers feel like. Another program, designed by Kobak (1977), teaches what she calls the "CQ" or "caring quality." Kobak worked with severely emotionally and socially maladjusted children. One problem with these children, she noted, was the inability to care about or for others. Kobak used psychodrama, a method in which one child played the part of another in different day-to-day situations. Kobak videotaped the psychodrama and reenacted it for class discussion. Response to the videotape was excellent. Children freely expressed their feelings from others' points of view. Kobak followed these sessions with art therapy in which the same children were allowed to express their feelings in clay and other materials they could manipulate creatively. Kobak reports:

> It is *desirable* to teach children to care!
> It is *possible* to teach children to care!
> It is *essential* to teach to care! (p. 102)

Such programs can be particularly important. Teachers and the other students may learn to care about their handicapped classmates, but, in the long run, successful mainstreaming may depend on helping the handicapped to care about themselves.

summary

1. As special education classes became open to children with an increasing variety of handicaps and problems, such classes became less able to provide their students with the best possible education. Even when special classes were able to stay more homogeneous, many educators and parents questioned the benefit of segregating these students from nonhandicapped students. Parent-sponsored litigation has led to the legal requirement to mainstream students with special needs into regular classrooms.

2. Mainstreaming is embodied in the Education for All Handicapped Children Act (Public Law 94–142). This law grew out of class-action suits that charged that children in special classes were unfairly stigmatized, given inferior educations, and were assigned to such classes on the basis of inadequate screening procedures. These charges, which were mainly brought on behalf of children with low IQ test scores, were later expanded to cover children with every conceivable sort of special problem. As a result of P.L. 94–142, local and state authorities must satisfy the federal government that such children will be educated in the least restrictive possible environment and that they will spend as much time in regular classes as possible.

3. An important part of P.L. 94–142 requires the construction of an Individualized Education Plan (IEP) for each child. The IEP is based on what teachers think the child can do and is drawn up by a planning committee that includes the parents as well as teachers and specialists. IEPs clearly assess the child's level of competence, set annual goals, detail specific

educational services, specify the child's ability to join regular educational programs, and set up specific procedures for evaluation of the child's performance and review of the objectives.

4. The implementation of P.L. 94–142 has required a major reordering of our educational system. Special education teachers, administrators, and regular classroom teachers have had to reeducate themselves in order to educate handicapped students and their parents. In-service workshops are organized to prepare teachers to deal with the variety of special problems they will encounter in the mainstreamed classes.

5. Mainstreaming has not done away with the need for special education. Designing the best curriculum for each child depends on teamwork from all school personnel and the child's parents. Although teachers do not have the sole responsibility in the development of an IEP, they do have primary responsibility for its implementation.

6. Teachers must learn to deal with their students' social needs as well as their academic ones. This involves raising the self-concepts of handicapped children as well as teaching their nonhandicapped peers to be more empathetic and helpful.

7. Parents are an integral part of the mainstreaming approach. When parents are voluntarily or involuntarily unavailable, legal surrogates will be appointed for them.

8. Mainstreaming's success depends on many special services. School architecture can be an important factor in the handicapped child's adjustment to regular school life. Supportive services for teachers include special education teachers, school psychologists, counselors, social workers, physical therapists, occupational therapists, speech correctionists, audiologists, physicians, and the school's director of special services. Counseling approaches include nondirective and directive individual counseling, group-centered counseling, and family therapy.

9. Special classes for reading and speech correction are usually necessary even in a highly mainstreamed school. Technological innovations like Randsight help handicapped children participate in regular classroom activities.

10. To cope with the variety of special problems in learning and social development, teachers must be able to reduce their students' fear and tension, be familiar with the principles of child psychology, and use appropriate methods of teaching and assessment. Although many specific techniques exist that are effective with handicapped students, the teacher's attitude is probably the key to successful mainstreaming. Teachers need to control their own anxiety, maintain a positive attitude, get involved with their students, use classroom management principles, involve their students in decision making, and redefine their goals as necessary. Teachers should also avoid the feeling that they are in this alone: Resource personnel should be freely called on for help.

11. Teachers need to be prepared to use a wide variety of teaching methods such as individualized instruction, computer-assisted instruction, and

precision teaching. Careful records of classroom behavior can be a good source of information for evaluating a child's performance and planning more effective programs. A humanistic approach to teaching children with special needs emphasizes the importance of independence to a positive self-concept and teaching handicapped children to care about themselves.

BAKER, B., BRIGHTMAN, A., HEIFETZ, L. AND MURPHY, D. *Steps to Independence: A Skills Training Series for Children with Special Needs.* Champaign, Ill.: Research Press, 1976. This text provides how-to-do-it help for anyone working with early, intermediate, or advanced self-help skills, as well as behavior problems.

KAUFMAN, B. *Son Rise.* New York: Harper & Row, 1976. This is a personal story of an autistic child and his development, written by the boy's father. In addition to describing the child's behavior, it also describes the intense emotional reactions of both his parents and others who dealt with him. Kaufman relates the team efforts designed to help the boy to learn.

VERNON, M., AND PRICKETT, H. Mainstreaming: Issues and a Model Plan, *Audiology & Hearing Education*, 1976, 2, 5–11. This article is a brief description of the issues involved in mainstreaming as those who must implement mainstreaming have to deal with them. A plan is provided to show what can be done, as well as some of the problems involved.

WEBSTER, E. *Counseling with Parents of Handicapped Children.* New York: Grune & Stratton, 1977. This brief text was designed to increase the effectiveness of teachers and others who must deal with parents of handicapped children. Guidelines for improving communication with individuals or groups are outlined.

for students
who want to read
further

The following children's books are among many designed to help children in mainstreamed classrooms form realistic pictures of what children with particular handicaps can and cannot do. These and other examples are listed in *Learning*, October 1978, pp. 119–120.

LITTLE, J. *Take Wing.* Boston: Little, Brown. This is a story of a girl who takes care of her mentally retarded brother. It shows what love and courage can do to help the retarded. (Grades 3–6)

SPLAVER, S. *Your Handicap: Don't Let It Handicap You.* New York: Julian Messner. This book offers encouragement to the handicapped child, role models, and a positive path from disabilities to abilities, and career and college information. (Grades 6–8)

STEIN, S. *About Handicaps.* New York: Walker & Co. This is a story about a child with cerebral palsy and his friend. The friend learns how to deal with his fears. (Grades K–4)

TATE, J. *Ben and Annie.* New York: Doubleday. An 11-year-old boy befriends a 13-year-old girl who lives in his building and is confined to a wheelchair. He talks to her and plays with her. When he and his friends roll her wheelchair down a hill, her parents forbid her to play with her new friends, and she is doomed again to isolation. (Grades 4–8)

IV

USES AND METHODS OF EVALUATION

The only way that teachers and students can find out whether learning has taken place in the classroom is to evaluate it in some way. Testing is important to evaluate student progress and evaluate teacher success, diagnose student strengths and weaknesses, and assess learning while it is taking place so that both student and teacher know where to go next. Today, however, there is a great deal of disagreement among teachers, students, and the public over the real value of testing. The issue is not whether we should test but how we should do it.

Chapter 11 deals with ways that teachers can develop meaningful classroom tests. Both norm-referenced and criterion-referenced testing are described, together with simple statistics necessary to understand what test scores really mean. Competency-based instruction is described in detail. Other innovations such as contract teaching are discussed. Chapter 11 also deals with ways to use the grading system to increase learning and motivation.

Chapter 12 describes another type of testing used extensively in American schools today. Standardized tests of ability and achievement are both described, as are ways to interpret scores obtained on these tests. Standardized tests can be used to the advantage of both student and teacher. If misinterpreted, they can, however, lead to disastrous results. Chapter 12 therefore discusses ways by which teachers can determine the reliability and validity of these tests, as well as ways to interpret individual scores.

II

THE TEST AS A TEACHING AND LEARNING TOOL

Mrs. Roberts, an eighth-grade teacher, reports that she began to use testing in a new way with her students. Instead of using tests to decide what grades to give, she gave the tests at the beginning of the semester. The first time she did this, the students were very upset. They were all afraid that they didn't know enough to "pass." "It's not to 'pass you' or to 'fail you,'" Mrs. Roberts explained. "I want to use the test scores to help me arrange my lesson plans for the next two weeks. Let's look at the test scores and see what we will be studying." The students crowded around her desk as she scored their papers. Everyone in the class had missed the question about environmental pollution. "Tomorrow's lesson will be on acid rainfall," reported Mrs. Roberts. "I want you all to go home this evening and see if you can find out what it is."

* * * *

In one state where achievement testing had been mandated on an annual basis, a sixth-grade teacher became disturbed at the unfinished answer sheets her student handed in. She felt convinced that the students knew the material—in this case math—and was puzzled that they had worked so slowly. She found that, instead of placing the scratch paper next to the problem on the test and working out the solution, her students had been copying the entire problem, often a column of eight or ten numbers, before working out the solution. Since these were timed tests, they naturally failed to finish.

A deeper look into the students' test-taking skills revealed that they knew very little about how to approach the test. The teacher launched a unit on how to take tests, with the result that their next year's scores rose considerably, and most of the students finished each section, many with time to spare.

Testing, when used to its best advantage, is an integral part of teaching and learning. Some teachers, like Mrs. Roberts, use testing even before teaching has begun in order to select learning activities appropriate to their students' strengths and weaknesses. Testing can also be used at the end of the course as a means of evaluating what effects the course had on the class and which areas of the course need to be improved. Finally, testing is a useful way to assess students' progress while learning is actually taking place. The results of such testing can be used in ways that will help the teacher in instructional planning and help the students in the actual learning process.

Psychologists and teachers agree that knowledge of student progress is crucial for the teacher in planning any kind of instruction. The teacher can use tests to discover which teaching methods are most effective in changing student behavior and in meeting student and teacher goals. For example, a first-grade teacher's goal is teaching her students to read. She tries the basic reader assigned to her class and uses it for several weeks, then gives the class a test to find out whether they understand what they're reading. To her dismay, after reading out loud three pages from the basic reader, most of the children in the class can't tell her what the story is about. The teacher doesn't give up, but uses this information as the reason for selecting another set of reading materials. She thinks that another book, which has stories about urban children, will be more interesting for her class.

There are many teaching systems that depend on testing. Some systems are adaptable to all subjects, while others have more limited applications. Some are more suited to certain types of teachers, just as some are better suited to certain types of students. Some systems depend on computers and take up a lot of the teacher's time, while others that are equally effective are extremely informal and demand a flexible attitude rather than expensive equipment. What all these systems have in common is the use of tests to help students learn, not to punish them for failing to learn. This positive use of testing transforms tests into opportunities for growth instead of anxiety.

The use of classroom testing for diagnostic purposes has a long history. Pressey (1932) and his colleague at Ohio State University (Little, 1934) were the first Americans to dramatize this. They showed that frequently administered tests can be highly effective teaching instruments when they are used as a source of constant feedback. Pressey initially developed an elaborate device that he called a "multiple-choice teaching-testing apparatus." This device provided immediate knowledge of one's results. Later, the punchboard, a small board in which holes were provided corresponding to each answer, was developed. Because only correct choices could be punched through the board, the student received immediate feedback indicating whether he or she was right or wrong. The punchboard gave results similar to the initial teaching-testing apparatus and also demonstrated that feedback provided by tests can increase student learning (Angell and Troyer, 1948).

Tools for diagnostic teaching have been developed that do not depend on the special equipment and settings used by Pressey and his colleagues. For example, child-centered testing that is concerned with detecting learning and developmental changes is an effective form of diagnostic testing (Rowland, 1978). According to Rowland, such testing occurs most effectively within the context of the student's learning environment. It also measures much more than memorization of facts. Because children should do more in school than memorize facts, a good test should measure students' ability to interpret and form concepts as well as store information.

Good diagnostic testing can be very informal. Consider the following examples of much less formal types of evaluation that we all perform often without thinking about it.

> "Martha, let's see how long it takes you to run half a mile," says her gym teacher. Outside on the baseball diamond, Mark's coach tells him to "hit me another grounder." Each instructor is giving an impromptu "test" to determine the learner's level of proficiency. They will not give grades; rather, their observations will provide the basis for corrections and appropriate guidance in developing higher levels of proficiency. Their students may not even be aware that they are being tested or that tests are an important part of their learning.

Martha's teacher and Mark's coach are engaging in diagnostic teaching. Another word for this type of evaluation is **formative evaluation,** evaluation that is used to help form the students' new behaviors. This kind of testing for the purposes of diagnosis and remediation of student errors is familiar. We have all experienced it, though more often in terms of physical rather than intellectual activities. In terms of the learning process, these teachers have clearly in mind the behaviors (in this case, physical activities) their students should be demonstrating. By attending to what their students do wrong, they can prescribe alterations in their students' learning procedures. For diagnostic teaching, clear objectives are a necessity. It seems easy to develop behavioral objectives that describe physical activities. With practice, it is just as easy to develop behavioral objectives that describe mental activities.

Supplying Feedback

Teachers making use of diagnostic techniques help their students by supplying feedback as to when they are responding correctly or incorrectly. Feedback is a critical variable in good teaching as well as in good learning. When teachers are not using the appropriate methods or when they are making mistakes of some kind, their students' errors will point out areas in which the teachers need to improve. Dodd, Jones, and Lamb (1975), in a study of the teaching of elementary mathematics, showed that student teachers improved their ability to develop remedial instruction through describing and illustrating their students' errors.

Feedback from questions is important in instruction whether the questions come from teachers or students. Researchers studying the effects of questions as part of the learning-teaching process showed, in fact, that one very effective way to increase classroom retention is to have children ask the questions and teachers provide the correct answers—a reversal of traditional classroom procedure (Ross and Killey, 1977).

Adkins (1975) reports that letting students provide test questions was also highly effective in increasing student motivation. To put the

Feedback can be supplied informally through the teacher's verbal evaluation of student work.

Carmine L. Galasso

emphasis where it belongs, Adkins had made the following suggestion:

> Tests are ordinarily made by teachers (I am not speaking of standardized tests at the moment). What if students made them? Mine do. They write test items, both essay and multiple choice. . . . My students write these items on assigned areas of the course they are taking, . . . on facts or concepts within that area which they consider important. They do this because I think that formulating a test question on an important fact or idea is a learning experience. They also do it because, frankly, I believe that a teacher should do nothing which he or she can get students to do, whether it is to ask a question or to answer it. (p. 271)

Adkins gives his high school students models to use in developing test questions. Then, working in groups of three or four, they mutually decide on item content and phrasing, offering criticism and suggestions for revision. Writing multiple-choice items is fairly easy for students, Adkins has found, since students often know what the trickiest alternative answers would be better than the teacher does. Writing essay questions is somewhat harder. Selection of content and clarity of phrasing are important here, too, but often, Adkins says, students discover that "what seems like a good question for an essay exam turns out to be unanswerable or unscorable in any reasonably objective manner" (p. 272). Such questions are then used for discussion or study.

Once the various groups' test items are selected and refined, they are assembled into a test, duplicated, and administered to the class as a whole. Taking the test supplies a further learning experience, and scoring it adds another. Multiple-choice tests are easy to score, because the method of scoring is objective. (It is this, rather than content, Adkins reminds us, that is necessarily objective.) Adkins groups students for scoring the essay test in much the same way as he does for writing the items and the scoring guides. Often he asks them to score responses using someone else's guide. Analyzing and evaluating the test, he says, is indispensable: "Why should item analysis be an exercise reserved for teachers or computers or experts in measurement? It is a chore, but it is the one best way to improve tests and test items. It can be done in class, it can be done by students, it can be fun" (p. 273). And most important, he concludes, it is a valuable learning experience at any level.

Diagnostic Testing: Part of Task Analysis

Many teachers today are interested in a new approach to the teaching-learning process that involves carefully defining the specific process that occurs when students learn. **Task analysis** involves determining just what steps a learner goes through in the total learning task. Teachers utilizing task analysis in the classroom need to make extensive use of diagnostic testing. First, they must test the skills that students bring to the situation. Once they know exactly what their students know and do not know how to do, they can determine the necessary steps to reach the desired outcome. Continued testing in some form or another at each step along the way determines whether or not a student should go on to further steps or backtrack. The process is a complex one if the teaching-learning process is to be thoroughly understood (Scandura, 1977).

using norm-referenced tests

Traditionally, American schools have been concerned primarily with norm-referenced testing. A **norm-referenced test** is used as a means of comparing scores within a group. In other words, schools compare students with each other and rank them in order of their comparative excellence in academic achievement.

An illustration of this is a testing system in which students are assigned grades on the basis of a comparison with other students in the class. Teachers refer to what is really an improper classroom use of norm-referenced testing as "marking on the curve." This usually means arranging raw test scores (original number of questions answered correctly by the student) in order from high to low and assigning different grades to predetermined proportions of each rank. For example, the top five students in history class, whose last test scores ranged from 83 to 97, may all be given an A, the next ten students, whose grades ranged from 75 to 82, a B, and so on. Usually the largest proportion get the middle mark, a C. Johnny, who has a C average, is considered "an average student."

Teachers who mark on the curve base their grades on the assumption that in every classroom, raw test scores are distributed in the same manner as those scores obtained by hypothetical infinitely large statistical sample, the normal curve. Teachers need to understand the normal curve and another statistical concept, measures of average, to understand just what is involved in norm-referenced testing.

Understanding the Normal Curve and Measures of Average

The normal curve The **normal curve,** or the **normal distribution,** as it is sometimes called, describes the scores of a hypothetical infinitely large number of students. Just what should it mean to the teacher? To answer this question, let us make the following assumption: Suppose that we were to randomly select an infinitely large number of students and measure differences in their performances on a specified examination of 1,000 questions. The horizontal axis of the graph in Figure 11–1 would show the number of correct answers out of 1,000. The vertical axis would show the number of people who answered the questions correctly. With an infinitely large number of peo-

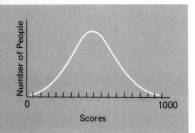

Figure 11-1 The curve of scores on a test with an infinitely large population.

ple, the curve of scores would look like the curve in Figure 11–1. The normal distribution is symmetrical—the left and right halves are mirror images of each other. The hypothetical normal curve never quite meets the base line on either side, but continues to infinity in what we call the **asymptote**. This is to show that—in theory, at least—there is no limit on how low or high the scores can be in normal distribution. The smoothness and regularity of this curve are the result of the large number of people being measured.

In the normal distribution we know the percentage of scores that will fall under each part of the curve. If two vertical lines are drawn from the base line to the two points where the curve changes slope from convex to concave, then 68 percent of the total area under the curve is cut off, as shown in Figure 11–2. This tells us that 68 percent of the scores fall within that area.

When we understand the derivation of the normal distribution, we realize immediately that the validity of the assumption of normality is directly related to the size of the population. The more students that take an examination, the more likely it is that their grades will be normally distributed. When teachers grade on the curve, they are making the assumption that their classes of 20 or 30 students will have scores that match the shape of the normal curve. The problem is that this assumption may be false. Teachers who grade on a curve that does not exist naturally in their small classrooms (as it would if the population were infinitely large) often force students into molds in which they do not belong. Let's take an extreme example. Suppose a teacher gave a test to a very bright class of students. The lowest grade was 90 and the highest grade was 100. The largest proportion of students received 95. If the teacher were marking on a curve and assigning letter grades, a 95 would be a C! This means that a C student did average work in relation to the rest of that particular class, but it does not show that in this case "average" means 95 percent correct. The problem with norm-referenced testing in classroom settings is that the only evaluation made is based on each student's rank in relation to the other students in the class. No attempt is made to evaluate whether or not each individual student has met the learning objectives.

The normal curve is extremely important in psychology. When social scientists measure a trait in a large number of people, the resulting distribution is often normal, or approximately normal, provided that the number of people used is large enough.

The normal curve and measures of average Johnny has a C average in history. What does this mean? Statisticians have shown that there are many different ways to determine averages. The most common method of determining the average score in a given group of scores is to take the **mean**. Johnny's teacher got the mean by adding up all the scores and dividing the total by the number of students. Only nine

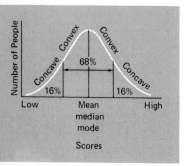

Figure 11-2 Normal distribution of scores.

412

students took the test. The total of their scores was 630 points. Dividing 630 by 9 gives a mean score of 70; which also happened to be Johnny's score on the test (see Figure 11–3).

Another way to determine the average score in the class is to find the **median.** The median is the score that falls in the exact middle of the group. A teacher using the median as the measure of average usually will rank-order all the test scores from the highest to the lowest and then pick out the score that falls right at the middle. Figure 11–3 shows that Johnny's score of 70 was the median score of the group as well as the mean score.

The **mode** is still another measure of average. This measure refers to the score that occurs most frequently. The modal score shown in Figure 11–3 is 65—the score obtained by Lynn, Sarah, and Sam.

In small classes of students, like Johnny's, the three measures of average—the mean, median, and mode—may fall at different scores. This is because the scores in Johnny's class are not normally distributed. In the normal distribution, with an infinitely large number of scores being considered, the mean, median, and mode all have the same value and fall at the same point on the distribution (see Figure 11–2).

Understanding the Social Implications of Norm-referencing

What are the social implications of norm-referenced testing? Certainly this kind of testing fosters competition rather than cooperation among classmates. The bright students in a class may need to battle each other for a few points on a test. Students competing for class rank in high school sometimes reject the opportunity to go into a special honors class. Usually this happens when students know that the teacher grades on a curve. It is to their advantage, if they want a good class standing, to remain in classes where the other students are not so likely to get good grades. This kind of thinking ruins the effectiveness of honors classes. Nevertheless, some teachers report that norm-referenced testing does provide the incentive for those who are good at academic subjects to work hard for success, and in a sense that kind of incentive supports the ideals of academic achievement.

Does norm-referenced testing have the effect of encouraging students to work only for marks and not for knowledge? Some teachers say no, that such a result could come only from a failure on the teacher's part to define the goals of instruction or else from careless procedures of evaluation. The incentive for some students, however, even bright ones with high motivations to achieve, will sometimes be to cheat rather than to study. Furthermore, students who receive average grades without effort may not be motivated to learn more than they need to get by. Perhaps the negative effects of norm-referenced testing, particularly when grading is done on the curve, are most severe for the slow student—the one who, like Tom in Figure 11–3, is always at the bottom of the curve. A student's level of aspiration is

Figure 11-3 Grades of 9 students on a history test

Alice	90
Dick	88
Bill	80
Marie	75
Johnny	70 (mean, median)
Lynn	65
Sarah	65 }(mode)
Sam	65
Tom	32
Total	630

based on his or her history of success and failure. It is likely, then, that the student who is always at the bottom of the curve will become convinced that he or she will always fail. On the other hand, a slow student who fails a test may be given a passing grade if others in the class also do poorly. The increasing numbers of functionally illiterate high school graduates may well be one result of this practice.

Although norm-referenced testing may serve some purposes for some students (and may make the teacher look better), teachers must be aware of its drawbacks. Many teachers feel that a more humane approach, and one more in line with the basic aims of education, is to give all students a chance to succeed in their own way and at their own pace and so move on to their top level of achievement. Norm-referenced testing often does not permit this.

using criterion-referenced tests

A **criterion-referenced test** is used to show which pupils have mastered the learning objectives and which need more help. It also shows what each individual student can and cannot do. The teacher needs such knowledge to assign the correct plan of instruction. This is especially important when individualized instruction is used.

An important problem in criterion-referenced testing is determining the tasks that should be selected for mastery. In other words, how do you choose the learning objectives for each student? What tasks must be mastered before further learning takes place? For safe performance in a laboratory or when driving a car? For job proficiency? What does a student need to know for everyday life? Are the skills being called for appropriate to the students' developmental level?

The objectives selected should not be arbitrary choices. If possible, Gronlund (1973) suggests, the teachers in a school should cooperate in deciding what kinds of learning are to be mastered. The teachers should strive toward arranging learning objectives in sequence and identifying the minimal skills needed at each stage before going to the next. In addition to working with each other, teachers should consult authorities in subject matter and curriculum for assistance. Airasian (1971) found that groups of teachers working together on the measurement of competency-based learning could quickly define the order of objectives, construct test items, and develop corrective exercises.

Understanding the Social Implications of Criterion-referencing Teachers, using norm-referenced evaluation, used to expect that one-third of a class would be superior in performance, one-third would be passable, and one-third would fail. But this assumption is changing. We now state more objectively that almost everyone can learn—if the teacher can teach. This is the assumption behind competency-based instruction.

Of course, people differ in many ways. Many ask, "Isn't it true that not everyone has the aptitudes needed for learning?" Others respond by saying, "An aptitude is merely an ability to learn quickly, everyone can learn if given enough time." There is in fact evidence that some children learn more slowly than others, or have particular problems learning certain kinds of skills. These children can profit particularly well from instruction and evaluation that are not norm-referenced. D'Alonzo and Miller (1977) point out that a criterion-referenced, competency-based program is essential for these students if they are to succeed beyond the domain of the school setting. Such a system is implied in the requirements for the Individual Education Programs (IEPs) for handicapped children mandated by Public Law 94–142.

Criterion-referenced testing can be used to diagnose individual difficulties so that the teacher may modify instruction for a particular student. We have already referred to this kind of ongoing evaluation as formative evaluation. A final evaluation, **summative evaluation,** is done at the end of the term, to measure either a student's success or the success of the program of instruction, in order to decide whether or not it should be repeated, and, if so, how it can be improved. Criterion-referenced teaching lends itself well to summative evaluation.

Finally, not all educators agree that criterion-referenced testing by itself adequately performs all the functions listed. Ebel (1971), for

Does testing tend to encourage or discourage learning? Criterion-referenced testing can be used to show which students need more help in overcoming specific weaknesses.

example, believes that, despite the seeming paradox, this kind of testing does not really tell us what students can do. He thinks that norm-referenced tests do that job better because "excellence or deficiency are necessarily relative concepts" (p. 283). According to Ebel, the learning objectives required in advance by criterion-referenced testing actually suppress good teaching because, although establishing learning objectives beforehand is a very good thing to do, the learning objectives required by criterion-referenced testing are too narrow and inflexible. Criterion-referenced testing is suited to measuring basic skills, Ebel concludes, but basic skills make up only a small portion of what we teach.

Developing Criterion-referencing with Competency-based Instruction

In **competency-based instruction,** students are first given a specific set of competencies to be attained during learning. Good competency-based instruction requires that the objectives of instruction be carefully defined well before instruction begins. The students are allowed to select from an instructional approach that will meet those objectives. Later, after instruction, students are evaluated on their abilities. That evaluation is dependent on the students' mastery of the same objectives they were given in the beginning.

Glaser (1962) presents a model of teaching in which learning objectives are based on the students' behavior before instruction begins. However, many classroom teachers have to design learning objectives before they even meet their students. In this case, when learning objectives have to be preset, the entering behavior of the student can be used to design appropriate methods of instruction.

Popham's (1973) model is very similar. Learning objectives lead to preassessment (criterion-referenced testing), instruction follows, and then evaluation (more criterion-referenced testing) provides feedback and leads to new decisions about curriculum and methods of instruction.

Gronlund (1973) has made a number of recommendations for constructing criterion-referenced tests. His basic idea is keeping the unit of study to be covered by a test brief, so that the test will not be too long. This will necessarily lead to frequent testing, which may result in more immediate feedback, more frequent diagnosis of problems, and more effective assignment of remedial work.

Each task included in the test must coincide with a particular performance specified under the heading of a general learning objective. For the sake of reliability, several examples of each type of task should be included. Exactly which tasks the students are to perform must be clearly and precisely stated in planning the test. Are the students to spell words of a certain degree of difficulty? Add three-digit numbers with carrying?

The standard of performance that is to be met must also be stated exactly. How much must the student know before you are satisfied that the learning objective has been achieved? Is the student to solve correctly 90 percent of the arithmetic problems? 80 percent? In determining this percentage, the teacher must decide what level of mastery is needed for the next stage of instruction or for safe performance of an activity such as driving. The teacher can then adjust the percentages up or down when experience indicates the necessity.

In such a system, the purpose of evaluation is not to rank students in order to give them grades, but to let them know what stage of learning they have reached, and how they should continue from there in order to develop to their fullest capacity. When a student is able to learn—through a system in which everyone can learn—positive attitudes toward the self are fostered.

other approaches to classroom testing

Some educators argue that the contributions students make to their own education—that is, the ideas they create for themselves from the content of the course or the thinking of the teacher—are the most important. If this is so, then it is appropriate for students to cooperate in selecting the methods of their own instruction and testing.

Contract Teaching and Testing

In some cases, **student-teacher contracts** are used to determine objectives in competency-based instruction. Contracts can be used effectively in most situations in which the student differs in some way from the average. A successful contract should include significant input from both teacher and student, clear-cut data that indicate how well the criteria have been met, and comparison between the data and the criteria. Curwin (1978) cautions that the student, either alone or in conjunction with the teacher, should determine the final evaluation in order for it to be meaningful. One sixth-grade teacher decided to teach math using student-teacher contracts. He and his students agreed that any student who could answer 75 percent of the questions correctly on a test administered at the end of the unit and also turned in at least 80 percent of the homework papers would get a C. Any student who wanted a B had to turn in at least ten special problems assigned by the teacher as optional homework. To get an A, students had to answer at least 85 percent of the questions on the test correctly, turn in all the homework assignments, and complete at least 15 optional special problems. Students who received 95 percent to 100 percent on the examination would get As without having to do the optional extra problems. The students all graded their own test papers, computed their scores, and turned them in, together with their course grade, the homework problems, and the extra problems.

Jensen (1973) describes how undergraduates at the University of Nebraska successfully cooperated in selecting the method of instruction in a large class in introductory psychology. No lectures were given in the course; instead, mimeographed material was handed out regularly. Films were presented regularly; each film was shown many times during one week, and students were free to choose when to attend it. Either the instructor or a graduate assistant was always in attendance in a discussion room, and students could ask questions or discuss the course at any time. Students also chose when they would take tests. From a pool of test items, a computer produced a few thousand variations of the same weekly test. If a student did badly on a test, he or she could take it again and again until he or she did well; only the highest score was counted. (This system of testing depends on the existence of a very large number of very well written test items.) Each week's work had to be completed within the week, but within this limitation, students had the freedom to choose their own study and testing time. The end-of-term grade depended on how well a student did above what would be pure chance; 50 percent above the score expected by pure chance led to a D, 90 percent above pure chance to an A. The most common grade was an A, failure was reduced to less than 10 percent, and enrollment doubled.

Under certain circumstances, student cooperation can extend even to having students grade their own papers. Ackerman (1971) found that letting students in psychology classes grade their own tests (after having listened to a talk on the evils of cheating) produced no increase in the amount of cheating. The primary advantage of honor grading to the students is the feedback of a greater sense of integrity. Perhaps, under appropriate teaching-learning conditions in which stress on grades is eliminated, this added sense of integrity will lead to the elimination of cheating.

Keller (1968) has designed a course in general psychology in which students move at their own pace. Some students may not necessarily finish a term's work in a single term, while others may finish it in less than a term. Lectures and demonstrations are provided to students only when they have demonstrated that they are ready for them by passing a test. There are 30 tests, in addition to a final examination.

In this type of program, a mimeographed list of study questions is given to each student to be used in preparing for a readiness test. Any test in the series of 30 can be taken at any of several times during any week. The student chooses both the week and hour he or she will take a particular test. The test is given and scored by a proctor who has already finished the course. The proctor is assigned to several students for the term and helps each one as needed. The proctor usually scores and returns the test paper immediately and discusses the wrong answers, and sometimes a few of the right ones, with the student. This inevitably leads to the proctor's becoming a kind of tutor who provides help with the course and advice about further study. Failure to pass a readiness test at any point does not count against a student. A student may be tested as many as 40 to 50 times during one semester. He or she always gets an opportunity to defend any answer that has been marked wrong and is given an opportunity to learn how to make the correct response. One of the benefits of the program has been a more favorable attitude among the students toward tests because of the benefits they receive from taking them.

The Keller system of instruction can be facilitated by the use of a computer. In an applied mathematics course taught in a similar system at Oakland University in Rochester, Michigan, a computer was used to produce the tests given after each unit of work (Young, 1978). In addition to taking the tests, students sometimes used the computer terminals to generate extra problems on which they worked individually or in groups. Young notes that the computer could also have been used when diagnostic pretests were given at the beginning of the course.

Student peers can be used as proctors in this method of instruction. Tosti (1973) uses students who are only one unit ahead of the others as tutors in a program of instruction in arithmetic. Peer proctors, also in use in some other adaptations of Keller's method, are selected from the students who receive superior grades from the instructor on the first-unit tests. Tosti reports that one professor rotates the proctorships so that most of the class have a chance to act as proctor before the term ends. Some instructors use students in advanced courses to supervise the peer proctors. As a result of his own experiences and those of others, Tosti recommends the use of peer proctors. He feels that students take a more enthusiastic interest in their own learning when they have the opportunity to proctor the learning of their peers.

Self-paced evaluation has been used with elementary school students as well as college-level students (Klausmeier, Sorenson, and Ghatala, 1971). In most of the studies in which elementary school students have been used, students all worked at their own pace and teachers were available to provide answers to questions. When students decided they were ready to be tested, they presented themselves to the teacher, who sent them off to the testing area with a test designed for their particular learning level. In some studies, students with the best grades served effectively as tutors to provide assistance for students who were having trouble at one step of the way. In each situation, both tutors and learners were helped.

Novel Situation Testing

Most effective systems of evaluation, such as Keller's, can be used with any course. A set of study questions can be designed for any course, and tests designed for use with those study questions. But, what if the goal of instruction is to produce new types of responding in novel situations? With such a goal, there is no one single correct

Table 11.1 Examples of Novel Situation Testing

Course	Objective	Novel situation
Literature	How to attach meaning to poetry, including an attitude that poetry is a form of communication.	Popular songs (if teaching has dealt with traditional poetry) with open-ended measurement requesting an interpretation and the basis of the interpretation.
Home Economics	How to plan a meal as a part of a total nutritional plan, including an attitude that foods complement each other nutritionally.	Loss of planned food or unexpected diet restrictions with objective measurement requesting identification of the optimal combination of available foods.
Physical Education	How to play some sport according to a set of rules, including an attitude that motor-skill learning has some pattern.	A new sport to be learned or a limitation on an existing sport with open-ended measurement of the approach to the new motor skills and objective measurement of what the new rules would have to be because of the limitation.
History	How to interpret historical data, including an attitude that historical data gain meaning through inter-relatedness of events.	Real or hypothetical news programs or reports of legislative action with either open-ended measurement or objective measurement, requesting identification of logical consequences.

R. W. Young, "Novel Situation Testing," *Contemporary Education* (Winter 1978, *48*(2), 76–80. Copyright 1977 by R. W. Young and *Contemporary Education*.

answer. Young (1977) has suggested an approach to evaluation in which students are tested in situations that require broad competence for solution. Instruction in such situations involves presenting data and asking the students to provide ideas about what the data seem to mean. Once they have formulated ideas, they are then asked to check them against other data for verification. To test whether students achieve this goal, Young proposed what he called "novel situation testing," in which students, after discussing the objective with the instructor, are given novel situations and asked to meet that objective in the new situation; some examples are shown in Table 11.1.

judging the quality of a classroom test

Whether norm-referenced or criterion-referenced tests are used, all the purposes of evaluation cannot be fulfilled unless the tests have certain desirable characteristics. The two most important of these are **reliability** and **validity**.

Reliability is the extent to which everyone gets the same raw score (number of correct answers) when the test is repeated. In the case of norm-referenced tests, reliability may mean that if the raw scores of a group are arranged in order from high to low, on repeated testing everyone will keep the same rank in the group. In other words, a test is reliable if it measures consistently. Reliable tests require a large amount of care and thought in development.

Deciding Whether a Test Is Reliable

Many influences affect reliability. Some are related to the specific type of test used and are discussed in a later section. But others involve the students themselves or the immediate testing situation. Assuming that a student's knowledge of a subject has not changed, a different score on a retest (or, what is usually more practical, a second test on the same subject but in a different form) may be caused by differences in the student. He or she may be in good health one day, but may not feel well another day. He or she may concentrate well on one occasion, but be distracted by emotional problems or some future event on the next occasion. In addition, the classroom may be quiet during the first testing and noisy during the second. Some of these influences, such as varying health, will affect some members of the class and not others. Other influences, such as variations in noise, will affect all students in the class, but not to the same degree. The general tendency will be changes in scores. There will probably be changes in the raw scores of individuals, and there may also be changes in an individual's place in relation to others in the group, so that the top student of the first testing may no longer be on top the second time. To the extent that these influences affect test scores, the test measures less consistently and, thus, is less reliable.

A test may measure reliably. This does not, however, mean that the test is valid. A test has validity if it measures what it is supposed to measure. No one would give students a set of arithmetic examples to measure their knowledge of geography. An arithmetic test is not a valid measure of knowledge of geography because it does not measure what it is supposed to measure. But even something that seems to be testing geography may not be doing its job as well as it should. A teacher-made test in geography that includes questions from only about half of the topics covered in class is not a very valid test of what was taught in that class. A test designed to measure students' ability to use concepts in new situations is not valid if it tests only their ability to memorize. An achievement test is valid if its questions representatively cover the area of knowledge that the test is intended to measure. This kind of validity is called **content validity** and is the measure usually used by teachers to judge their own classroom tests.

Deciding Whether a Test Is Valid

The teacher should try to create tests that are both reliable and valid, that measure consistently and that measure what they are intended to measure. The example of using an arithmetic test to measure knowledge of geography shows that a reliable test may not be valid for the purpose chosen. The most reliable arithmetic test in the world will not measure knowledge of geography. On the other hand, a valid test, by definition, must also be reliable; it will always measure consistently.

*Evaluating Test
Results*

It is the teacher's responsibility to remain as detached and fair as possible in evaluating test results. Even a valid and reliable test becomes an invalid indicator of what a student has learned if it is not evaluated fairly. Teachers should guard against factors that might affect their judgment. For example, the teacher should avoid what is called the *halo effect*, where a student's poor performance may be given a better grade because he or she has done well in the past. The teacher should also be very careful not to build expectations on irrelevant issues. Johnny, who is neat and well behaved, is not necessarily learning more than Bobby, who is sloppy and rude. Alice, who is good in one subject, is not necessarily good in another. Suzie, who has worked hard in the past, may be lazy now. The teacher who fails to recognize these truths and thus imagines that the neat, polite child is automatically clever and studies hard has been blinded by the halo effect.

developing and improving your own classroom tests

Construction of a valid classroom test requires preparation and planning. The test will be used to measure achievement in some area of a school subject, so the teacher must first break that area down into smaller content areas, or subtopics, and decide how important each subtopic is. The more important subtopics should have more questions devoted to them.

If the teacher has been conscientious in developing learning objectives at the outset of the unit, the goals of the test will be clear: The test will be used as a means of evaluating whether or not these objectives have been achieved. The learning objectives will affect the types of questions chosen and how each question is phrased. The teacher should know whether he or she wants to test for an understanding of facts and the ability to apply them. He or she could also test to see if students can organize facts and ideas or develop an argument. Whatever the goal of the lesson, questions should be designed to measure that goal. Here, too, the more important behaviors should have more questions devoted to them.

*Selecting
a Test Format*

To develop a proper test to use in the classroom, the teacher must understand the kinds of questions that test each kind of behavior. For example, Young's method for novel situation testing provides a unique way of testing students in situations that require broad competence for solution. Other types of tests and test items are available for the teacher's use. The following are some of the most typical.

The essay format   Most likely you are familiar with the **essay test.** To answer an essay question, the student is expected to write some connected prose ranging in length from a few paragraphs to several pages. The essay test can be used to test memory of facts, understanding of them, and the ability to apply them. This kind of test, however, is at its best when used to do what no other test can do—test the ability to organize material or to develop an argument. Here are two examples of essay questions.

> State your position for or against the tax bill recently proposed in the state legislature. Support your position by developing an argument from the relevant facts.

> Develop an argument to convince your mother that there should be a Children's Day as well as a Mother's Day and a Father's Day. List as many specific reasons as you can.

Essay questions help students to sharpen their reading and writing abilities. A major disadvantage of the essay test is that, because it takes so long to develop the answers, only a few questions can be answered during the usual testing period. As a result, essay tests cannot provide a representative sampling of content. Furthermore, the grading of essay tests is often subjective and unreliable. Two different teachers grading the same set of essay papers may not assign the same grades to them, nor may the same teacher grading the papers twice assign the same marks both times. Also, teachers may be prejudiced against students whose handwriting is illegible, whose paper is untidy, or whose grammar or spelling is faulty. Such a prejudice may be reliable (that is, consistent), but it is not valid—unless the test is designed to measure tidiness, grammar, or spelling. A test that is supposed to measure competence in history should not be measuring neatness.

There are techniques for increasing the reliability of essay test grading. Most of these are considered in a later section, but one of them should be considered here. The problem of representative sampling of content can be solved by using a series of short-essay questions. In taking this type of test, the student needs to write only one or two sentences in answer to each question. For example,

> Beginning with the mouth, briefly describe the process of digestion.

In this short-essay type of test a great deal more content can be sampled than by the extended essay question method, and the grading will be more reliable. However, testing for the ability to develop an argument or organize a large body of material may not be possible using this method.

The objective format   The *multiple-choice question* is known to most American students. If properly written, this kind of question can be used to test not only memory of facts but also mental processes such as reasoning ability. For example, if the actual example used in the following question had not been discussed in course work, selecting the correct answer to the question would require an application of knowledge rather than just memory of a fact.

> A baby begins to whimper. The mother rushes to bring its bottle in order to keep the baby from crying. The baby learns from then on that when it wants a bottle, it should whimper. The behavior of the mother is an example of
>
> A. operant conditioning.   C. avoidance conditioning.
> B. retroactive inhibition.   D. generalization.

The great advantages of the multiple-choice test are its flexibility, the wide sampling of content possible on a single test, and the ease and objectivity of scoring. However, a multiple-choice item is difficult to write so that the correct response is a good measure of the teacher's goals and the incorrect choices are equally valid indicators of inappropriate learning.

Other objective tests are useful for special purposes. The following is an example of a *true-false item*.

> Achievement evaluation should be designed to determine if, and to what extent, learning objectives have been met.   T   F

True-false items have some merit. A very large number of items can be answered in one testing period, and the scoring is easy and reliable. However, it is difficult to use true-false tests to measure anything but memory of facts, often minor facts, and it is difficult to write true-false items well. Furthermore, with the multiple-choice question with four choices, the student has only a 25 percent chance of guessing the correct answer. The true-false item's two choices bring this probability to 50 percent.

The *matching item* can also be used to provide variety in tests.

> Each of the authors listed on the left wrote one of the books listed on the right. Match the letter of the book with the name of its author.

_____ Jane Austen	A. Wuthering Heights
_____ Emily Bronte	B. David Copperfield
_____ Henry James	C. Pride and Prejudice
_____ Ernest Hemingway	D. Look Homeward Angel
_____ Thomas Wolfe	E. Vanity Fair
	F. Mrs. Dalloway
	G. A Farewell to Arms
	H. The Ambassadors

A *short-answer question* (not the same as a short-essay question) asks the student to fill in a blank after a direct question.

What is the process through which children learn what is socially acceptable? _____

If the blank is part of a sentence, the item is called a *completion item.*

Children learn what is socially acceptable through what is called _____ _____.

Oral testing allows students who may have difficulty reading test questions to overcome that disadvantage.

Scoring both short-answer questions and completion questions is easy and reliable if the questions are clear. Both types are quite limited in what they can test for, however; they usually test only for memory of facts.

Not all tests, of course, have to be written. Oral tests are particularly useful for the teacher with students who are poor readers. Often the reason why students perform poorly on tests is because they can't read the questions. With young children for whom reading might be a problem, it is an excellent idea for the teacher to read the test questions aloud and have the pupils write down the answers. Sometimes teachers of young students find it practical to give oral tests in which each student, in turn, stands up and answers a question asked out loud by the teacher. Spelling bees are examples of this sort of testing. Oral tests are also useful with older students because answers can be challenged and discussed. Often doctoral exams are oral for this reason. The oral exam allows considerable flexibility.

Developing good test questions is a major task on which the reliability and validity of a test depend.

Preparing Test Questions

Preparing essay questions Essay tests are sometimes called subjective tests because grading is often unreliable or even unfair. Marshall (1967) found that minor errors in English accounted for lower grades on an American history test, although the grading supposedly measured only the content of the answers. In a similar study by Marshall and Powers (1969), it was found that neatly written answers were graded higher on the average than those that were only fairly neat. Similarly, papers without errors in spelling and grammar were graded higher on the average than those with such errors. According to a study by Huck and Bounds (1972), neatness made a difference in the grades assigned to essay tests by graders who were neat, but graders who were untidy were not biased against untidy papers. Follman, Lowe, and Miller (1971) found no difference in the grades assigned to typed themes and those assigned to written themes, but they did find that themes graded last received higher grades than those graded first. Such a finding might suggest that graders tend to become less rigorous as they become fatigued or that, midway through grading, they realize that their standards are excessively high.

Teachers can make essay tests more objective by taking certain precautions, some of them in the grading itself, and some in writing the test questions. In constructing an essay test, the teacher must take care to clearly define the question the student is supposed to answer. For example, the following question is too vague.

> Tell what you know about attempts to raise silkworms as a commercial venture in the United States.

The same question is more sharply phrased in this manner.

> Explain why raising silkworms has never been a commercial success in the United States.

Teachers should also be careful not to ask too many essay questions for the testing time allowed.

When it comes to grading, various authorities recommend grading papers without looking at the students' names. Read all the papers through at one sitting. In addition, read all the answers to one question first, then go back and read all the answers to the second question, and so on. Perhaps most important of all, prepare in advance a set of model answers to all the questions so that there is a fixed standard to judge the students' answers by. Ahmann and Glock (1971) recommend an analytical system of scoring in which each model answer is broken down into component parts and a number of points assigned to each part. Irrelevant material is corrected but not scored, regardless of whether it is right or wrong.

Preparing objective questions Writing good objective test items (multiple-choice, true-false, matching, short-answer, and completion) is extremely difficult, but can be learned through practice. Thought and care in the construction of questions will be well repaid in the increased validity of the test. Some hints for improving the construction of test items follow, with multiple choice items considered first.*

State each item in as few words as possible. Here is an example of a wordy item:

Among the many great plays written by William Shakespeare are several famous and beautiful tragedies. An example of one of the tragedies that he wrote is

A. *Macbeth.*   C. *A Winter's Tale.*
B. *Dr. Faustus.*   D. *Measure for Measure.*

The students' time would be saved if they only had to read

Shakespeare wrote the tragedy

A. *Macbeth.*   C. *A Winter's Tale.*
B. *Dr. Faustus.*   D. *Measure for Measure.*

The reading level of the items should not be too difficult for any member of the class, unless reading ability is what is being tested. Obviously, no one would write an item like the following one for children, but even many older students would find it difficult to understand.

An explanation of the observable preference of many persons for wearing light-colored apparel during the summer months is to be sought in the phenomenon of heat transference known as

A. conduction.   C. radiation.
B. convection.   D. none of these.

A test in science should not turn into a test of reading comprehension. Written more simply, the item looks like this:

Many people wear light-colored clothing in the summer because light-colored clothing takes up less heat through

A. conduction   C. radiation.
B. convection.   D. none of these.

As much of the item as possible should be contained in the lead-

---

*The hints outlined here apply to both norm-referenced and criterion-referenced tests. However, specific recommendations on constructing the latter are discussed later in this chapter.

in to the choices. This lead-in is called the *stem*. Besides helping to make the wording economical and the reading easier, this rule guides the teacher in defining the question to be answered at the outset. The following shows what happens when this is *not* done.

A nerve has been

A. defined as a bundle of axons, dendrites, and cell bodies.
B. defined as a bundle of axons.
C. defined as a bundle of dendrites.
D. defined as a bundle of synapses.

The item has been improved in this version.

A nerve has been defined as a bundle of

A. axons, dendrites, and cell bodies.   C. dendrites.
B. axons.   D. synapses.

The wording of an item must be clear. The answer to the following question depends on exact knowledge of what is meant by "origin" and by "printing."

The origin of printing is to be found in

A. an adaptation of the wine press.
B. Gutenberg's invention of movable type.
C. the Chinese invention of movable type.
D. the need to reproduce documents and books easily.

Actually, any of the choices might be considered the right answer, because the stem does not state the question clearly.

All the choices should seem at least possible and should attract some responses. Otherwise, the number of effective choices is reduced, and the probability of getting the right answer by chance is increased.

A little boy is putting coins in a machine in order to obtain candy bars. At first he obtains a few bars, but then the machine, having been emptied, keeps returning the coins. After several unsuccessful attempts, the child walks away in disgust. This situation best illustrates

A. projection.   C. instrumental conditioning.
B. avoidance conditioning.   D. extinction.

All the choices here are terms from learning theory except the first, which comes from psychoanalysis. Because choice A is from a different field, it will be eliminated more readily than the others and should be replaced by another term from learning theory—for example, "negative reinforcement."

Be careful to avoid clues that unintentionally give the answer away.

HC1 is the formula for an

A. base.   C. polymer.
B. free radical. D. acid.

The word "an" in the stem reveals the answer, "acid." The same item would be better written this way.

HC1 is the formula for

A. a base.   C. a polymer.
B. a free radical. D. an acid.

Avoid using the word "not" or any other negative if you can; negatives often confuse unnecessarily. If you must use "not" in either the stem or the options, underline it so that students will not make a mistake in reading.

Homeostasis does <u>not</u> occur when someone

A. suffers from diabetes.
B. drinks a lot of water after exercise on a hot day.
C. shivers on a cold day.
D. manufactures ribonucleic acid.

Make sure the items are independent of one another. It is not fair to have the answer to one item depend on the answer to another. For example, it would be unfair to use both of the following questions in the same test.

The Would-Be Gentleman was written by

A. Corneille.   C. Molière.
B. Racine.   D. Marivaux.

The author of *The Would-Be Gentleman* also wrote

A. *The Cid*.   C. *The Miser*.
B. *Phaedra*.   D. *The Game of Love and Chance*.

Your students might know that Corneille wrote *The Cid*, that Racine wrote *Phaedra*, that Molière wrote *The Miser* and that Marivaux wrote *The Game of Love and Chance*, but if they did not also know that Molière wrote *The Would-Be Gentleman*, they might well answer both questions incorrectly.

Even well-written multiple-choice items sometimes have more than one correct or true answer; this is why the test directions should tell the student to choose the single *best* answer. Make sure that each question does indeed have a single best answer.

The most impressive theme of *The Remembrance of Things Past* is

A. time.   C. love.
B. memory.   D. social change.

The meaning of "most impressive" is sufficiently clear, but what impresses one reader may not impress another. Thus, this question has no single best answer.

Some of these hints for multiple-choice items apply to true-false items as well. In fact, in writing any sort of test the teacher should try to be brief, make the reading level easy for all members of the class, and the questions unambiguous. There are three other points to remember in making up true-false tests:

First, do not be unclear. Each statement must be either true or false.

Sigmund Freud originated our idea of the unconscious mind.   T   F

The idea of the unconscious mind was not really original with Freud; on the other hand, his work shaped our ideas on the subject to such an extent that it could be argued that the statement is true.

Second, do not give away the true statements by making them noticeably long. The following is not a good statement for a true-false test.

Although *a cappella* originally had a narrower meaning, drawn from reference to the style of singing in the large chapels of Europe, today the phrase is usually used to refer to any choral music that is unaccompanied.   T   F

Third, put only one idea in each statement.

Michelangelo did not admire Titian's genius and regretted that Titian did not paint in Michelangelo's style.   T   F

Of the two ideas expressed here, the first is false and the second is true; this is a confusing, deceptive item.

A few more observations are in order about other types of short-answer tests. A matching item should not involve a very long list of choices. If the list is long, the student will spend too much time reading and checking one list against the other. The choices should be all of one kind. In the matching example given earlier, the choices are all authors who wrote in English. Note that the authors are presented in chronological order so that the item has a basic framework, and that there are more works listed than authors so that guessing will not be too easy for the student. Other matching items will suggest their own ways of ordering the choices. It is all right to have an answer used more than once in a matching item if this possibility is made clear to the student in the test directions.

In short-answer or completion items, the blanks should all be the same length, otherwise the length of the blank can be a clue to the answer. It is especially important to make completion items clear.

The first U.S. President was ⸺.

The blank could be filled in with "George Washington," "a Virginian," or "a man of British descent," and all would have to be counted correct because the question did not specifically ask for the man's name.

After a short-answer test has been given and scored, the information obtained from the scores can help the teacher improve future testing. Each item has to be examined separately to discover its characteristics. How difficult was the item? (That is, what percentage of students answered it correctly?) How well did the item discriminate between those who had learned and those who hadn't? (That is, when the students who received a high-score on the total test are compared with those who received a low score on the total test, did more of the high scorers get the item right?) If the item is multiple-choice, did all the choices attract responses?

The difficulty of an item can be determined by calculating the percentage of students who got it right. If 90 percent of the students got the item right, it was easy, if 15 percent got it right, it was hard. In constructing a test designed to positively reinforce the students, a teacher might want all the items to be easy, but this would not be so on a norm-referenced test, which compares students with one another. If everyone gets all the items right, it is impossible to compare them. But all the items can't be very difficult. If no one gets more than a few items right, again there will be no basis for comparison. A blend of easy, difficult, and in-between items, with most of them in-between, will produce the spread of scores desired on a norm-referenced test.

If the low scorers on the test tended to get the item right and the high scorers tended to get it wrong, something is wrong, either with the item or with the way the subject was taught. Such an item is said to discriminate in the wrong direction. Items discriminate in the right direction when questions are answered correctly by more high scorers than low scorers.

Using a Simple Item Analysis to Test Your Test

It is useful for the teacher to be able to determine whether any particular test question is doing its job of discriminating between those who have learned the material and those who have not. Garrett (1965) devised a simple test-item analysis for calculating this important evaluative index. He called a test item's power of discrimination its validity index. This index, also called the **index of discrimination,** can easily be calculated by the teacher in the following manner:

Step 1. Rank all the test papers from low to high. Take the top quarter and the bottom quarter and put them aside for analysis. If there are 100 students in the class, set aside the 25 best papers and the 25 worst papers. (If there are less than 50 students in the class, set aside a larger proportion, such as the top third and the bottom third.)

Step 2. Count the number of students in the top quarter who answered the first test item correctly. Then do the same for the bottom quarter.

Step 3. Fill in the following formula.

$$\text{Index of discrimination} = \frac{\#\ \text{right in top quarter} - \#\ \text{right in bottom quarter}}{\text{total}\ \#\ \text{in top quarter}}$$

Suppose that there are 30 students in the top quarter and that all of them answered the test item correctly. Suppose also that there are 30 students in the bottom quarter and that 10 of them answered the test item correctly.

$$\text{Index of discrimination} = \frac{30 - 10}{30} = \frac{20}{30} = .67$$

Suppose that in another class there are five students in the top quarter and that all of them answered the test item correctly. Of the five students in the bottom quarter, one student answered it correctly.

$$\text{Index of discrimination} = \frac{5 - 1}{5} = \frac{4}{5} = .80$$

The index of discrimination in the first example is lower than the one in the second. This means that the second example is one of a more valid test item.

The validity of a particular test item can range from +1 to −1. An item is completely valid (index of +1) when all the students in the top quarter get it right and all the students in the bottom quarter get it wrong. It is completely invalid (index of −1) when the opposite situation occurs. To determine the validity of the whole test, the teacher can go through a test item by item, repeating steps 2 and 3 of this process.

Once teachers have obtained this kind of statistical information, they can learn still more by discussing any questionable items with the class. They may discover ways to revise items to make them better— to make them easier or harder, to cause them to discriminate in the right direction, to replace easy or misleading choices with better ones. In this way, teachers can reword and thus rescue ineffective items for a future file of test questions. They should continue to make counts of responses and to calculate indices in the future, since a single class is a small sample of students, and, in any case, the index may change as teaching changes. Sometimes what needs revision is not the item itself but the way the course is taught.

deciding about grading

Although testing procedures and other methods of evaluation have been questioned for some time, present-day teachers rarely debate the question of whether or not to evaluate student learning. Instead, they ask, "What are the most meaningful ways to evaluate?" Another question asked frequently is how to record and communicate the results of classroom evaluation. The method most commonly used is the grading system. Recording is done by assigning a letter evaluation. In the United States, grading is done on an A–F basis. Recording of evaluations can be done either in terms of a student's achievement of learning objectives (criterion-referenced grading) or in terms of a student's achievement as compared with that of other students (norm-referenced grading).

Why Grade?

Much controversy about the question of whether or not to grade has centered around norm-referenced grading. Many educators and psychologists point out that determining students' grades by comparing them with other students creates an unhealthy and competitive atmosphere. These critics aruge that motivation should come from learning itself, not from the need to prove to oneself and to others that one is better than one's classmates.

Other critics report that grading may be effective if it actually conveys meaning. But, as Curwin (1978) points out, grades must have the same meaning for the person who gets them as they do for the person who gives them. Grades, like tests, should be valid and reliable, but according to Curwin, they often aren't. In some situations, as, for example, in subjective grading of essay examinations, grades may depend on who is doing the evaluation and who is being evaluated. Even true-false and multiple-choice tests can result in subjective

Grading has also been criticized as a process that causes student cheating. Cheating is one of those subjects that occasionally rises to claim local or even national attention—Regents exams are stolen in New York, service academy classmen defy the honor code, students in another university openly buy term papers and theses—and a public outcry goes up. And down. Nobody applauds cheating, but its prevalence has become commonplace and is all too often accepted—at least by the students. One editor of a weekly educational publication regularly visits schools. On his return from one of these visits, he wrote the following to a friend, a high school principal:

> I wonder if the high school I visited recently is typical of high schools elsewhere in the U.S. . . . . If it is, then teachers and administrators had better take notice: THE EDUCATIONAL SYSTEM IN THEIR CHARGE MAY BE IN SERIOUS TROUBLE.
>
> The students I spoke with said that everyone in school makes a practice of cheating on tests. Not just many or most—so they claim—but EVERYONE. Could this be true? (*Senior Scholastic*, May 8, 1972, p. 4)

Many teachers echo the editor's question. They cannot close their eyes to the answer. Cheating, as two educators have pointed out, has become a part of the school experience as a result of "the stress on grades, on passing, on good results at all costs" (Georgiady and Romano, 1971, p. 272). Behind this emphasis on grades stands that most American of concepts—competition. To win has become the name of the game—any game. If you're not counted among the winners, you're not counted. Individual uniqueness, as a result, has been demeaned.

Recently, another criticism has been added to the list. This is the relatively new phenomenon of grade inflation, which has been occurring in our schools and which, critics say, has erased the meaning of grades (see, for example, Winsor, 1977). Grade inflation occurs most frequently at the college level but appears in high schools too. It began during the 1960s when low grades meant a loss of one's student deferment and a ticket to Vietnam. But faculty are still increasingly hesitant to give grades of C or below because it makes them and their institution look bad and may further decrease our dwindling college enrollment.

grading if the teacher does not carefully attempt to sample the subject matter objectively. Curwin also complains that traditional methods of letter grading serve to perpetuate the halo effect. Students who have received high grades in the past will tend to be given higher grades than students who haven't been doing as well. Thus, teacher expectations affect student achievement and grades as well.

Why Not Grade? The first, and many feel the most important, function of grades is to serve as formal feedback to students about their achievement. Without this feedback, students might find it difficult to decide on their future course of study and, ultimately, their careers. Furthermore, some types of grades, such as letter grades, help students to see their achievement in comparison with others. This will help them to adjust to the competition inherent in the adult world of work.

Finally, grading is the meaningful end product of the teaching-learning situation. Because teachers are increasingly being held accountable for their students' level of achievement, they have had to develop more clearly defined learning objectives. The record of a student's performance on a criterion-referenced test will show exactly what each student has achieved. But, we pointed out at the beginning of this chapter, a good test is a marking tool for the teacher as well as for the student. It is a meaningful measure of both teaching and learning, and, in the end, a means for improving both.

Thus, when used properly, grades can perform valuable functions. What educators need to strive for is a more objective system of grading, one in which competition is not so severe that it results in lowering the students' ability to achieve.

Selecting a Grading System

There are many types of grading frameworks. Ahmann and Glock (1971) and Terwilliger (1971) distinguish between grading students in terms of their *development*, taking into account their ability, background, experience, and so on, and grading students in absolute terms according to their *achievement*, what they know now, regardless of their ability and background.

Generally, the teacher must give the student a single grade. This forces the teacher to choose between these two frameworks. One way of changing this is for schools to adopt multiple marking systems, which would take both frameworks into account (Terwilliger, 1971). Thus students would receive one grade based on their achievement and another based on their growth.

Regardless of the framework chosen, grades are frequently reported either by letters or by numbers representing letter equivalents (1 = A, 2 = B, 3 = C, 4 = D, 5 = F). Many teachers feel that even though they cannot communicate everything of interest through the use of letter or number grades, such grades are simple, concise, and convenient (Ebel, 1964). According to Feldmesser (1972), letter grades help a college student to decide whether he or she should stay in college and what he or she should study, and they provide extrinsic motivation for those who may not realize the importance of what they are studying at the time.

Many educators feel, however, that the kind of motivation that results from traditional five-point or letter grading is often undesirable, particularly when students are younger. Extreme competition, sometimes leading to cheating even in the primary grades, is too often the result.

An alternative to the traditional five-point grading system is that of pass/fail or pass/no credit. This system was originally developed to relieve students of the pressure of competition and to remove grades as a motivation for study. This system results in added pressure for the teacher, however. The teacher must very clearly define exactly what criteria must be met if the grading is to be fair and objective. In addition, students who have not received traditional grades in college sometimes are at a disadvantage when trying for admission to graduate or professional schools (Stevens, 1973). In such cases, added weight can be given to scores on standardized tests, but these tests are not always accurate measures of a student's potential and actual achievement.

A three-point grading system using honors, pass, and fail is a compromise between these two systems. Such a three-point system was compared with the traditional five-point system by undergraduates, graduate students, and faculty members in a study by Goldstein and Tilker (1971). The three-point system was favored because it supposedly encouraged what the authors called creativity, learning, and fairness. On the other hand, the five-point system was seen as giving better feedback and greater help with admission to graduate school. Some universities have tried out variations of all these systems. Goldstein and Tilker's particular favorite was a dual system in which students could choose the kind of grading system that best suited their needs.

Many other types of grading systems are used in elementary and high schools. Elementary school teachers are frequently required to give grades for character traits and attitudes as well as academic achievement. This kind of marking often becomes subjective and su-

Parent-student-teacher conferences bring together all the important people in a teaching-learning situation to determine just what is being accomplished in school.

Michael Uffer, Photo Researchers, Inc.

perficial, however (Ahmann and Glock, 1971). To make such grading meaningful, the teacher must be careful to avoid the halo effect and to overcome our socialized prejudices against saying negative things about a persons' character.

Teachers may also write letters to parents as reports. If the teacher has adequate data on which to base such letters, the comments can be helpful. But like a checklist of traits of character and attitudes, these letters may be superficial. Writing truly informative letters takes a great deal of time and thought.

Conferences between parents and teachers are another means of reporting evaluations. Although they too take up considerable time, they can be a good means of communication. Of course, this can be true only if the teacher prepares detailed information in advance of the conference. In addition, many parents are reluctant to attend such conferences. In fact, many high school students are opposed to them, because they feel that they, not their parents, should be receiving the feedback from their teachers. And, of course, students do not receive the direct feedback that results from other grading systems (Richardson, 1955).

Resolving Grading Problems

Combining data from different kinds of work—tests, homework assignments, reports, laboratory exercises, and so on—can be a problem, because the units of measurement from the different sources (sometimes even from different tests) may not be truly comparable. To overcome this lack of comparability, Ahmann and Glock (1971) have suggested a system of weighting that must be determined by the teacher in relation to learning objectives. They also suggest using standardized achievement test scores to supplement final grades. But these tests, which may not have been designed with the same objectives that the teacher had in mind, may not be precisely comparable to the teacher's own exams.

To sum up the problems: Grades may not reflect actual achievement; clear objective criteria for assigning grades are often lacking; the halo effect too often influences grades; teachers are occasionally biased against individuals; and grades may be based on insufficient data. To counteract these difficulties, Green (1963) suggests collecting sufficient data to increase the teacher's objectivity through frequent testing and various kinds of written assignments.

Holt (1970) has suggested the following ways to make grading less harmful to elementary school children.

1. Don't fail a child. Holt believes that all children have the ability to learn. Therefore, if a child doesn't achieve, the failure is the teacher's.
2. Base your grades on a cross section of the child's best work. If a student does badly on a paper, it might be that this was the wrong paper for him. He suggests that you give a wide enough variety of

choices and opportunities for writing, reading, and talking so that everyone has a fairly good chance of showing his best talents.

3. Grade privately—let no one know what mark someone else has received. This will, of course, help to control competition and the negative effects that result from it.

4. Don't fail a child against his or her will. This will add to the child's sense of insecurity and lower his or her level of aspiration. This, in turn, will make learning even more difficult the following year.

5. Don't assume that someone in a class for slow students can't do superior work. This attitude can result in a self-fulfilling prophecy.

Managing School Grades and Records

There has been much controversy over what constitutes appropriate management (that is, collection and maintenance) of student grades and records. Some interesting proposals have been made in this regard. Wellington and Wellington (1966) argue that teachers should never have direct access to student records because records prejudice teachers, and students tend to live up to or down to teacher expectations. In contrast, however Lawton (1966) maintains that the extra information from previous records can be of considerable help to a teacher in guiding children; she suggests, however, that teachers be trained to prepare and use records properly.

The Russell Sage Foundation (1970) has published a set of proposed principles for the management of school records which urge that no information be collected about students without the prior informed consent of students and their parents. The Foundation's report argues for the careful preservation of confidentiality.

A federal law passed in 1974 (commonly known as the Buckley amendment) allows access to school records to all students over the age of 18 and to the parents of students under the age of 18. For the first time, students who feel that teachers, counselors, or other school administrators have evaluated their behavior in a less-than-objective manner can examine their own records and publicly prove their belief. Today it is necessary for teachers to be prepared to back up evaluations with facts—another aspect of teacher accountability.

summary

1. Testing can be an integral part of the teaching and learning process. Testing can be used for diagnosis at the start of a course, for final evaluation of student learning and teacher ability at the end of a course, and for periodic checks on student progress while learning is taking place.

2. Pressey first demonstrated the use of tests for diagnostic purposes in 1932 when he developed testing devices that gave immediate feedback. Since that time research has shown that frequent testing with constant feedback is an effective way to enhance learning.

3. A common type of diagnostic testing is formative evaluation, which is used to help form students' new behaviors.

4. Feedback can help the teacher as well as the student by highlighting areas where the teacher needs to improve. Some research indicates that having students ask the questions and teachers provide the answers is an effective way to increase students' retention.

5. Through task analysis, teachers can discover the steps students go through in mastering a particular activity. Task analysis depends on frequent testing.

6. Norm-referenced tests compare a student's performance against his or her classmates'. Grades are based on comparative achievement rather than on an absolute standard of accomplishment. Marking on the curve is a commonly used but improper use of norm-referenced testing.

7. Norm-referenced testing is based on the normal curve and measures of average. The normal curve is a statistical concept that describes the scores of an infinitely large population of students. Its distinguishing feature is its symmetry—each side is the mirror image of the other. In addition, the curve is asymtotic, never crossing the base line on either side.

8. Measures of average include the mean, the median, and the mode. To get the mean, you add up all the scores and divide the total by the number of scores. The median is the score that falls precisely in the middle of a rank-ordered group of scores. The mode is the most frequently occurring score. In a normal distribution, mean, median, and mode all fall in the same place.

9. Norm-referenced testing fosters competition. Some critics also argue that such tests lead to working for grades rather than knowledge and remove students' incentive to do better than average work.

10. Criterion-referenced tests must be based on clearly stated learning objectives and need to cover all necessary tasks. Performance standards should be clear. Short, frequent tests are preferable to longer ones given less often.

11. Several new approaches to teaching depend on input from the students. Student-teacher contracts have been used to establish objectives in competency-based instruction. College students have been allowed to choose the method of instruction in certain courses. The Keller system of instruction, which depends on frequent testing and immediate feedback, allows students to work at their own pace.

12. Novel situation testing tests students' ability to make judgments rather than repeat memorized facts.

13. Even the best of tests can become invalid and unreliable if they are not graded properly. Teachers should take particular care to avoid the halo effect, in which a student's past performance influences the teacher's appraisal of current work.

14. The learning objectives chosen often determine the type of test and the format of the questions. Essay questions are the best test of students' ability to organize material and develop an argument, although the time

required to answer such questions limits the number of topics that can be tested during one exam. In addition, grading essay tests is a subjective and often unreliable process. Objective formats include multiple-choice, true-false, matching, short-answer, and completion questions. All require careful planning and writing and generally elicit memorized facts, but can cover a great many topics in each test. In addition, if these types of questions are carefully written, grading such exams is usually clear cut and unbiased by the halo effect. Oral tests are often just as effective as written tests.

15. Item analysis can help teachers determine which test questions are effective and which need to be improved. Teachers can calculate the index of discrimination by subtracting the number of students in the bottom quarter who got an item right from the number of right answers in the top quarter and dividing the result by the total number of students in the top quarter. The validity of a test item can range from $+1$ (completely valid) to -1 (completely invalid). Open discussions with class members can also give teachers ideas about proper test construction.

16. In America, grading is usually done on an A to F basis, either in terms of a student's achievement of learning objectives (criterion-referenced grading) or in comparison to the other students' performance (norm-referenced grading). Grading has been criticized for creating an unhealthy and competitive atmosphere, being overly subjective and thus unreliable, and leading to cheating. A recent criticism reflects the growing trend toward grade inflation. On the positive side, grades are formal feedback about student achievement and can be a meaningful measure of teaching and learning and a means for improving both.

17. The two most common bases for grading are achievement (what students know) and development (how much they increase in achievement during their lessons). Some schools have developed multiple grading systems so that both achievement and development can be measured.

18. Letter grades are simple and convenient, but some educators consider them too limited. Alternative grading systems include pass/fail or pass/no credit; honors, pass, and fail; and written remarks. However, such nontraditional systems can complicate matters when students apply to graduate or professional schools.

19. Grades are especially important in elementary school when children are developing their first feelings of competence at school. Elementary school children should not be failed if at all possible. Instead, they should be provided help to learn. Grades should be based on a cross section of the child's best work and should be confidential. Teachers should also avoid firm expectations about a child's ability as these tend to become self-fulfilling prophecies with children of all ages.

20. As a result of the Buckley amendment (1974), students and their parents have the right to examine their own school records. Teachers should carefully record all grades and the reasons for their evaluations.

AHMANN, J. S., AND GLOCK, M. D. *Evaluating Pupil Growth* (4th ed.). Boston: Allyn & Bacon, 1971. This book is probably the classic source book for all research on classroom evaluation of students. Many of the topics covered in this chapter are more fully discussed in this book. It should help teachers to have a better understanding of the issues involved in testing.

CURWIN, R. The grapes of wrath: Some alternatives. *Learning*, February 1978, 6 (6), 60-64. This article criticizes grading as it currently is used in American schools. The alternatives Curwin proposes are self-grading, contract grading, peer grading, and blanket grading. He describes each in detail sufficient to allow the teacher to try them out.

FELDMESSER, R. The positive function of grades. In Hamacheck, D. (Ed.). *Human Dynamics in Psychology and Education*. Boston: Allyn & Bacon, 1977. Feldmesser discusses the pros and cons of classroom grading and comes out strongly on the pro side.

NAGEL, T. AND RICHMAN, *Competency Based Instruction*. Columbus, Ohio: Charles E. Merrill, 1972. This is a brief branching program designed to teach the teacher how to develop good competency-based instruction for the classroom.

YOUNG, R. W. Novel situation testing. *Contemporary Education*, Winter 1977, 48 (2), 76-80. In this brief but carefully thought-out article, Young presents a rationale for developing not only a new approach to teaching, but a clever testing method that serves as a major component of the teaching-learning process. Teachers who are interested in teaching for creative, constructive responses will find the approach meaningful.

for students
who want to read
further

12

MAKING USE
OF
STANDARDIZED
TESTS

Frank: A Boy Who Used His Standardized Test Scores
to Plan His Education

In June of his sophomore year at Pleasant Hills High School, Frank, like many
of his classmates, took the Scholastic Aptitude Test (SAT).

The College Board Admissions Testing Program sent a copy of his scores to
his home and to his guidance counselor at school. Frank's scores looked
something like this:

| Standard Scores | Verbal | Verbal Subscores | | Math | TSWE |
		Reading	Vocabulary		
Percentiles	470	49	45	590	47
National High School Sample	80			93	
College-Bound Seniors	63	69	55	82	58

His father was pleased. "Frank, these are good: you're above average on all
the tests. You're even above average when your scores are compared only
with college-bound seniors! You'll do really well after you have your junior year
behind you."

Frank made an appointment the next day to talk over his scores with his
guidance counselor. Mr. Higgins was as encouraging as Frank's parents. But
he pointed to the fact that some parts of Frank's total score were weaker than
others. "I wonder why your vocabulary score is so much lower than your
reading subscore and your math subscore," he commented. "And look at your
Test of Standard Written English (TSWE). It's just above the mean.
I expected your math score to be highest, considering your leadership in the
math club and the chess club. But we'll have to see about helping you pull up
your vocabulary and your writing." Mr. Higgins and Frank's English teacher
decided that Frank should take a creative writing course in his junior year. The
English teacher said that the creative writing teacher was a great language
builder. "Not that that score was bad, mind you," she hastened to add.
"Frank did do better than the mean. But I know that his parents want to send
him to Jayson College, where they were students. And Jayson places a lot of

what are standardized tests?

In Chapter 11, we discussed tests that teachers can develop themselves. These tests are sometimes limited because classroom teachers are not professional test writers. Teachers usually do not have the time or facilities to develop the objectivity in test items that professional test writers are capable of. Furthermore, the results of teacher-made tests cannot be used to compare children across the nation or even across a city. Standardized tests like the one that Frank took to prepare for college were developed for these purposes.

Standardized tests are those whose procedures for administration and scoring have been made uniform or standard. This uniformity makes it possible to compare the scores of students from different parts of the country. For example, Frank's math score of 590 falls in the ninety-third percentile of high school students. This tells Frank that 93 percent of students taking the test got scores the same or lower than he—no matter where they lived or went to school.

A standardized test is written by a test publisher, who produces the test for a national market. The publisher also provides a manual of instructions on administration and scoring. In addition, before releasing the test, the publisher administers it to a sample of the kind of students for whom it is intended. This is done in order to obtain **norms** or standards—by which scores on the test may be interpreted.

Types of Standardized Tests Available to Classroom Teachers

Today, in classrooms across the country, teachers use many different types of standardized tests. Some, like the Scholastic Aptitude Test (SAT) and the Achievement Test administered by the Admissions Testing Program of the College Entrance Examination Board (CEEB), are designed to measure student ability and student achievement. They have been designed to test both verbal and nonverbal behavior. Some tests can be administered in group or individual situations. Some tests, like the SAT, measure the speed with which students take tests; others measure the students' power, that is, their ability to answer test questions properly. Test makers have attempted to develop tests they call "culture-fair." Such tests are supposed to measure children's abilities accurately, regardless of the culture in which the children were raised. Whether or not these tests succeed in that mission is not clear.

On July 13, 1979, Governor Carey of New York signed into law a bill to regulate standardized admission testing. One section of the bill requires that test questions be disclosed shortly after a test is given. That destroys the security of each test form. Similar bills have been introduced in other states, including Pennsylvania, and at the federal level. Many questions have been raised by this legislation, and it is receiving widespread attention from many sources—the press, elected officials, public interest groups, students, higher education administrators, test publishers, and national educational organizations (Bond, Cole, and Linhart, 1980). One reason for the passage of the New York ruling was the possibility of unfairness of the tests to some children; another reason was new federal legislation (the Buckley amendment) that mandates the release of information on student records to both students and their parents.

Finally, standardized tests are used as the basis for the admission of thousands of students every year into colleges and universities in most states in this country. Many private colleges and universities belong to the CEEB and require applicants for admission to take the College Board's Scholastic Aptitude Test. (New York State is a relatively new exception to this rule. Many testing services no longer send test results to New York State since the ruling there that students must be allowed to see the correct answers to test items.) Frank's scores on the SAT—his verbal score from a subtest made up for the most part of reading comprehension, and his mathematical score from a subtest of mathematical reasoning, reading tables, and such—count heavily in admissions, along with achievement test scores and high school grades. The ACT, the scholastic aptitude test of the American College Testing Program, is taken by applicants to public colleges and universities. The ACT is more closely tied than the SAT to learning in school. Answering the questions requires reading comprehension, reasoning in mathematics and science, scientific judgment, and the ability to use clear and correct language.

By their nature, standardized tests are norm-referenced, as opposed to criterion-referenced (see Chapter 11). If a student's score on a test is compared with the scores of other people taking the same test, the test is called norm-referenced. If the person's score is based on his or her achievement of specified learning objectives, the test is called criterion-referenced. Although classroom tests are usually designed for one purpose or the other, sometimes scores from a single test can be used either way. Each type of test measures something different and should be understood by teachers before they administer them.

Ability tests One very important and common type of standardized test is the test of ability, the student's potential maximum performance. **Ability tests** are designed to help teachers know how well their students are capable of performing.

Abilities can be divided into general and specific skills. Tests of general ability are sometimes referred to as mental tests or **intelligence tests.** Measures of specialized abilities such as mechanical comprehension, sense of pitch, and manual dexterity also exist.

What are often referred to as **aptitude tests** are really only a special kind of ability test. Aptitude tests are intended to predict success in a specific occupation or training program. Frank took the SAT in order to predict how well he would do in college. Other aptitude tests measure engineering aptitude, musical aptitude, aptitude for algebra, and so on. A single aptitude test may include separate sections that measure general mental ability and special abilities. Thus, an engineering aptitude test may have subtests of general mental ability as well as subtests of special abilities such as mechanical reasoning and spatial reasoning.

Achievement tests Many standardized tests are tests of what has been learned in a particular school subject. How are such standardized **achievement tests** used? Teachers can use a standardized achievement test as a check to ensure that they have been emphasizing the important skills or, at least, those skills the test designers think are important. The College Board achievement tests measure how well students preparing to go to college have learned their high school subjects. If the students do poorly on a standardized test, the teacher might ask if important knowledge and skills covered by the test have been omit-

Standardized achievement tests can be used to measure student progress and also to indicate whether the teacher has presented the material effectively.

Mimi Forsyth, Monkmeyer

ted from the course work. For example, Frank may have gotten his relatively low vocabulary score because his English teacher hadn't emphasized the learning of new words.

Many educators also recommend the use of standardized achievement tests to determine student progress. Progress within a given term can be determined when there are available equivalent forms of the same test, one of which can be given at the beginning of the term (pretest) and the other at the end (posttest). Interpretations of differences in individual scores must be tentative because many extraneous factors, such as mood and health, can affect them. But, if the group does better as a whole, the teacher can assume that progress has been made in the skills measured by the test. Standardized achievement tests can also be used to diagnose individual difficulties in achievement. They help to predict whether a student will do well in a particular course. Students with similar levels of ability can then be grouped accordingly.

There is an important distinction between ability and achievement tests. An achievement test is used primarily to examine the person's success in past study. An ability test is used to forecast that person's success in some future course or assignment. In other words, an achievement test looks backward, and an ability test looks forward. This does not mean that achievement tests do not help predict behavior. Achievement tests can predict future success on the basis of present knowledge of the student's already acquired skills. Ability and aptitude tests, on the other hand, attempt to measure what people think of as potential, regardless of the person's present level of scholastic achievement.

Individual and group tests   Some standardized tests are designed to be administered to only one individual at a time. Others, like the SAT, are designed for groups of any size. When an **individual standardized test** is given, a trained examiner asks the questions one by one, or directs the test-taker by words or gestures to perform certain tasks. The test-taker usually does not have to read the questions, and sometimes he or she does not need to use language at all. Their lack of extensive reliance on language abilities makes individual tests especially useful for measuring the abilities of students who have trouble speaking English or do not speak standard English at all.

Group standardized tests are usually paper-and-pencil tests and often require the test-takers to read the questions to themselves. Group tests are economical and convenient. The whole class can be tested at once and need not be interrupted when one child at a time is taken out for testing. Furthermore, a trained examiner is usually not needed, because the classroom teacher can read the test's manual of instructions on giving and scoring the test. With an individual test, however, a skillful examiner is often better able to help the person being tested to relax and thus do his or her best.

Verbal and nonverbal tests A group test that relies heavily on the use of words is an example of a **verbal test**. A **nonverbal test** does not rely as much on words in the questions, but may still use words in giving the test directions. Since Frank seems to do better on nonverbal problems, he might get a higher score on a nonverbal test. Tests that make use of apparatus—equipment, machinery, materials, implements, and other instruments—are also considered nonverbal tests. These tests may be called nonlanguage or **performance tests.** Such tests are usually individual tests. Nonverbal tests can be used for measuring the general mental ability of anyone who may have a language handicap.

Speed and power tests A **speed test** is made up of a very large number of questions of a uniform level of difficulty. The score on such a test depends on the total number of questions the test-taker answers correctly in a restricted time period. (There are too many questions for anyone to be able to answer all of them.) The SAT is a speed test.

Other individual tests, such as the Stanford-Binet Test of Intelligence, are **power tests.** A power test is made up of questions of varying degrees of difficulty. Scores on this test depend on the test-taker's ability to answer correctly. Ideally, there is no time limit, but giving a test-taker unlimited time to answer does not necessarily increase his or her score on this type of test. Therefore, a time limit is often set up, designed to allow a certain percentage of the test-takers (usually 90 percent is the minimum) to attempt to answer all questions.

The Standardization Process: What Test-Makers Do

As with teacher-made tests, the general content to be covered and the students for whom the test is intended must be decided on before constructing a standardized test. For example, suppose that you are a professional test-writer who has been hired to produce an achievement test in American history for students from the fifth through the eighth grades. Your first step would be to make a detailed list of the content that should be covered by the test. This list should break the content down into subtopics and should indicate the percentage of test questions to be devoted to each subtopic. You would also list the behaviors the test-takers are expected to perform.

In order to construct a test for a wide market, the test publisher must analyze the content of many programs, textbooks, courses of study, and sets of examinations. Some of the writers who produce the items will be specialists in American history; if necessary, the publisher will train them in the techniques of item writing. Other writers will be specialists in testing. A different group of both kinds of specialists will edit the items looking for content errors and technical imperfections in measurement.

A much larger pool of items than will be needed in the test is put together in this way. The items are then tried out on a group of students who have backgrounds similar to those of the students for whom the test is intended. This pretesting will reveal whether or not the items discriminate in the right direction (that is, whether or not difficult items tend to be answered correctly by students with high overall scores and incorrectly by students with low overall scores), whether all the choices in a multiple-choice item are working, and how difficult each item is. This information is used to choose the items that will be used in the final test. When most of the items chosen are answered correctly by about half the students, a spread of scores results, with total scores all along the line from very low to very high. For a norm-referenced test and a sufficiently large test population, these scores would fall in the shape of a normal curve.

Developing norms: Using a standardization sample   When the items selected have been assembled as a final test, the test-maker administers the test to another group of students that is also representative of those for whom the test is intended. This second group is called the **standardization sample.** The process of administering the test to the sample is known as standardizing the test. The test must be standardized in this way so that norms can be obtained. Norms are information about scores that are typical for the kind of students who were sampled (see Chapter 11).

Usually when scores on standardized tests are reported to students or to others, corresponding norms rather than raw scores (number of correct answers on the test) are given. For example, suppose that a student in the tenth grade got 65 correct answers out of 100 on an achievement test in American literature, and that this is a better score than 90 percent of the tenth-grade students received. To tell the student that his or her raw score was 65 would be meaningless. Instead, we would normally report the percentile rank of 90, and the student understands that his performance was in the top 10 percent.

Percentile ranks   The **percentile rank** tells the percent of scores in the standardization sample that fall at or below a given raw score. For example, Philip, a fifth grader at Cornelius Elementary School, receives a percentile rank of 80. Philip's teacher knows that 80 percent of students in the standardization sample received scores lower than Philip did.

Age or grade norms   An age or grade norm refers to the age or grade for which a raw score is typical. Thus, a student who receives a raw score on a standardized achievement test that matches an age norm of 10 scores as an average 10-year-old. A student whose raw score matches a grade norm of fifth grade, 0 months, is performing at a level comparable to that of an average fifth grader at the beginning of the school year.

Providing information for the test-user Test publishers should tell test-users how the norms used to determine the scores were arrived at. Such norms are based on only a sample of the nation's school children, and the validity of the norms depends on the validity of the sample the test publisher has chosen.

For instance, when testing items intended for the upper years of grade school, it is not possible to sample all school children in every fifth, sixth, seventh, and eighth grade in the country. Thus, test publishers cannot possibly arrive at truly universal norms for children. The publisher must, therefore, define the sample so that the teacher and administrator can see whether it is a suitable one for comparison with their own group of students.

Sometimes the publisher will provide several tables of norms for different groups. One sample may be drawn from middle-class eastern urban schools, one from rural western schools, and so on. Each sample should be clearly described in the instruction manual. The teacher or administrator must keep in mind, however, that such variables as region, density of population, and socioeconomic status all affect the performance that can be expected on a test.

Percentile ranks, age norms, and grade norms are only a few of the many different possible scores from standardized tests. In order to understand the different scores and what they mean, it is necessary to go back to our description of the normal curve.

Understanding test scores in relation to the normal curve In Chapter 11, we learned that the *normal curve* is the distribution that results when we measure a trait such as achievement or intelligence in an infinitely large population of subjects. The normal curve is symmetrical; the left and right halves are mirror images of each other. All measures of average—the *mean, median,* and *mode*—have the same value in the normal curve.

The reason that the normal curve is so important to standardized test developers is that we know the percentage of scores that will fall under each part of the curve in this distribution. If two vertical lines are drawn from the base line to the two points where the curve changes slope from convex to concave, then 68 percent of the total area under the curve is cut off, as shown in Figure 12-1.

The standard deviation and the normal curve The distance along the base line from the center of the distribution to one or the other of the solid lines perpendicular to the base is called a **standard deviation (SD).** It is shown in Figure 12-2.

Since the mean, the median, and the mode cut the normal distribution in half, 34 percent (half of 68 percent) of the scores fall be-

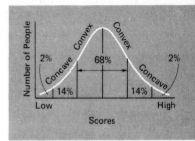

Figure 12.1 Normal distribution showing percentage of the population falling within concave and convex portions of the normal curve.

Interpreting Scores on Standardized Tests: What Teachers Need to Know

Figure 12.2 Normal distribution showing percentages of the population falling above or below ±1, and ±2 standard deviations.

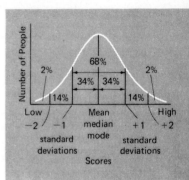

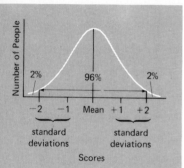

tween the mean and the point that represents one standard deviation above the mean. Thirty-four percent of the scores fall between the mean and the point that represents one standard deviation below the mean. (We speak of plus one standard deviation and minus one standard deviation from the mean.) Frank, the student described at the opening of this chapter, had a reading subscore that fell just above +1 SD from the mean.

If we double the distance along the base line that represents one standard deviation, we then include two standard deviations, as in Figure 12-3. In this figure, we see that 96 percent of the scores in a normal distribution fall between the point two standard deviations above the mean and the point two standard deviations below the mean. Statisticians working with the normal curve have drawn up tables giving the percentages of scores that fall above or below a point any fractional number of standard deviations from the mean. These tables have important uses in the interpretation of standardized test scores. With them, a teacher knowing a student's raw score on a test (number of correct items) and the standard deviation of that test can determine the percentage of scores falling above or below that score.

Figure 12.3 Normal distribution showing percentages of the population falling between 0 and ±2 standard deviations.

It is important to remember that not all distributions that otherwise would be approximately normal will look normal because too few people were used in gathering the data. Figure 12-4, for instance, shows the curve for a classroom test that was too difficult for the class. This is an example of what is called a **skewed distribution.** Because not many students did well on this test, the scores have piled up at the low end of the base line. If a test is too easy for a class, the curve will be skewed in the opposite direction. (Figure 12-5 shows this kind of curve.) A major advantage of standardized tests is that they are tested on populations that are large enough for the resulting curves to be normal and not skewed.

The z score and the normal curve A common score used on standardized tests is the standard score, or z score. A **z score** is a score given in terms of numbers of standard deviations. A z score tells how far from the average a given raw score is. A student whose raw score is above the average of the standardization group will receive a positive z score; one whose raw score falls below the average will receive a negative z score.

Figure 12.4 Example of a distribution with a negative skew.

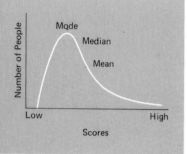
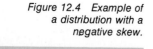

Let us consider the distribution of scores on a hypothetical test. This hypothetical distribution of scores has a mean of 80. We want to make a value statement about a score of 85 on this test. This score is 5 points above the mean. On this hypothetical test, the distance of one standard deviation from the mean is also 5 points. Therefore, we can say that a raw score of 85 is one standard deviation above the mean, and is thus equivalent to a z score of +1.

Suppose that someone has a raw score of 62 on the same test. This is 18 points below the mean of 80. Since one standard deviation on this test is 5 points, this raw score is 3.6 standard deviations below the mean (18 ÷ 5 = 3.6). We say, therefore, that a raw score of 62 is equivalent to a z score of −3.6.

The use of z scores makes it possible to compare scores from different tests because all scores describe performance in the same terms: the amount of deviation from the mean.

Transformation of z scores on aptitude and ability tests The use of z scores sometimes requires using unwieldy decimals. In such cases, z scores can be transformed to less confusing numbers.

A well-known type of transformation is that used by the College Board. Since the College Board figures z scores on its Scholastic Aptitude Test to two decimal places, multiplying all the z scores by 100 gets rid of the decimal points. (A z score of +1.43 becomes a +143.) College Board scores have a normal curve, so, practically speaking, virtually all scores fall between the z scores of −3.00 and +3.00. After multiplication to get rid of the decimal points, these z scores equal −300 and +300. In order to get rid of the minus signs, 500 is added to these already multiplied scores. The mean (which is equivalent to a z score of 0) now approximates 500.*

Virtually all students receive scores between 200 and 800. Frank had a verbal score of 470, below the mean. He had a math score of 590, above the mean. A score of 600 on the College Board Aptitude Test falls one standard deviation above the mean. Frank's math score of 590 doesn't quite place him in this bracket. Because the scores have a normal distribution, a score of 600 equals or surpasses 84 percent of the population and is thus a good score. Any score in the 700s is very good; such scores surpass 96 percent or more of the population who take the test.

The College Board standard scores are designed to have a mean of 500 and a standard deviation of 100. Other systems of transformation have produced other well-known types of standard scores. The Wechsler Adult Intelligence Scale (WAIS) has a mean of 100 and a standard deviation of 15, so that a score of 85 on the WAIS indicates a z score of −1; it surpasses only 16 percent of the population (intelligence is believed to be normally distributed). The Stanford-Binet Intelligence Test has a mean of 100 and a standard deviation of 16. A score of 140 on the Stanford-Binet is the equivalent of a z score of +2.5. Tables of the normal curve tell us that this score surpasses 99.4 percent of the population.

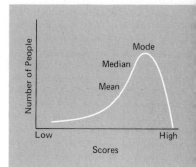

Figure 12.5 Example of a distribution with a positive skew.

*Because the population of students applying to college has changed since the College Board Aptitude Test was last normed, the mean has now sunk to below 500.

The reliability of any test is the extent to which it measures consistently. The reliability of a standardized test is estimated by means of a *correlation coefficient,* the mathematical measure of the degree of a relationship. In this case, the relationship being measured is the one between the scores obtained by the same person on two different administrations of the same test. The closer the two scores are, the higher the correlation coefficient. The higher the correlation coefficient, the more reliable the test.

The correlation coefficient as an index of reliability There are various methods for obtaining a correlation coefficient. All of them naturally involve two lists of scores. The list of scores from one administration of a test can be correlated with a second list of scores from a second administration of the same test to the same students, but this is not usually practical. A better way to estimate the reliability of a test is to give two equivalent forms of the same test to the same students and use the two lists of scores to obtain a correlation coefficient. It is best to allow a short time interval, perhaps a few weeks, between the two testings.

Since test manuals frequently discuss correlations, teachers ought to know just what this term means. The correlation coefficient (symbolized by r) is a decimal fraction between 0 and $+1$ or -1. On two administrations of the same test, we know that the correlation coefficient could not be 0 or close to 0 because there is clearly some relationship between two administrations of the same test to the same

The validity and reliability of the numerous tests taken by students today affect the validity of the entire grading system. Their importance cannot be overestimated.

Miriam Reinhart, Photo Researchers, Inc.

student. Our correlation coefficient probably would not be +1, either. An *r* of +1 would mean that there was a perfect correlation between the two testings, and it is highly unlikely that everyone would get exactly the same score both times. Thus, we would expect an *r* that was much higher than 0 and much lower than +1. Negative correlations also exist, but rarely, if ever, occur on measures of test reliability. A negative *r* would mean that students who got high scores on one test would tend to low scores on the next. This situation is theoretically possible, but is highly unlikely.

The sign—whether *r* is plus or minus—does not tell us anything about the strength of the relationship. In judging the strength of the correlation between two sets of test scores, we are guided by the absolute value of the correlation coefficient. Thus, an *r* of either +0.90 or −0.90 is very substantial, one of either +0.70 or −0.70 is fair, and one of +0.30 is usually quite low.

One last fact that teachers should remember about *r*: People often assume that, if two sets of numbers are highly correlated, there must be a cause-and-effect relationship between them. This is not necessarily so. It is extremely important never to assume a cause-and-effect relationship from a high correlation alone. For example, in one study of large American cities, a substantial positive correlation was found between the birth rate and the amount of street paving—more babies were born in those months when more street paving was done. Are we then to assume that street paving causes babies to be born?

Even when we feel confident that some cause and effect do underlie the correlation, we can never be certain which is the cause and which is the effect. For example, the incidence of smoking among grammar school children has been found to be positively correlated with low grades. Despite this correlation, we cannot prove that cigarette smoking causes low grades. Why? We can never establish cause and effect from a correlation alone because a correlation tells us nothing about outside influences. For example, young children may smoke cigarettes and, at the same time, get low grades because their parents give them little attention.

Teachers should keep in mind that there are always outside factors that may affect a student's ability to perform in different ways each time he or she is tested. Teachers should also remember that no test has a coefficient correlation of +1 and, therefore, that no test is perfectly reliable.

The standard error as a measure of reliability The test manual of a standardized test may report a measure called the **standard error** (SE) of the test. Knowledge of the standard error, which is calculated from the reliability of the test as well as from other figures, helps a teacher to remember the fact that no test is perfectly reliable and to adjust for it. Assume that the standard error on a certain test is reported as 6 points. This means that, if a student could retake the test, the chances are about 7 out of 10 that the new score would fall between 6 points below and 6 points above the old score. Thus, if the student got a score of 78 the first time, his or her score would probably fall between 72 and 84 the second time. But there are about 3 chances in 10 that the second score would differ even more widely from the first one and would fall somewhere below 72 or above 84 on the second test.

*Determing Test
Validity*

A reliable test measures the same thing, or nearly the same thing, each time it is administered. A reliable test is not necessarily a valid test. A valid test measures what it is supposed to measure. For example, if the standardization sample for a test meant for poor urban students was drawn from middle-class suburban students, then we would say that the test is invalid, even if a student gets the same score over and over. Using another example, suppose a test is meant to measure ability to add using word problems. The word problems, however, use everyday situations from white middle-class America. Socially disadvantaged students may not be familiar with such situations and may therefore be unable to answer the questions. But this does not mean that they don't know how to add. It means only that they are not familiar with white middle-class America and have wasted some time taking an invalid test.

Content validity   A test has content validity if it contains an adequate sample of the knowledge to be tested. For example, a test of verbal ability that leaves out reading comprehension would not have content validity, because an important part of the subject's content has been omitted. Another example of a test that lacks content validity would be a general biology test that had twelve questions on the life-style of the amoeba and only one question on genetics. The space a topic is given on a test must reflect the time given to it in the actual class.

Predictive validity   The validity of standardized ability tests, particularly group tests, is measured in a different way. This special kind of validity is called **predictive validity** and can best be explained by giving an example: It is common for students like Frank to take tests of general mental ability (or scholastic aptitude) in high school as part of the process of applying for college. The test score for each student is used to predict his or her college grade point average. Frank got fairly good scores on the test. How likely is it that he will also have a high college grade point average? A correlation coefficient relating test scores and grade point averages gives us the answer: The higher the correlation coefficient between scores on a standardized aptitude test and college grades, the more valid that test is to predict future college students' grades.

In a sample of 520 graduating college seniors taking the Scholastic

Aptitude Test, the correlation of their college grade point averages and Scholastic Aptitude Test-Verbal (SAT-V) and Scholastic Aptitude Quantitative (SAT-M) taken prior to college were .26 and .22, respectively (Mauger and Kolmodin, 1975). For this study, at least, the SAT, probably the most important determinant of college admission after high school grades, showed very low predictive validity.

Construct validity In some cases, the validity of an ability test is determined by correlating scores on that test with some other currently accepted criterion of ability. For example, the validity of most group tests of intelligence is determined by correlating scores on those tests with scores on the most reliable and widely accepted individual test of intelligence, the **Stanford-Binet Intelligence Test.** In this case, the correlation coefficient is a quantitative statement of what is know as the *construct validity* of the test. Construct validity essentially means that the definition of the ability to be tested is fairly standard. This is especially important in psychological testing. For example, someone might define intelligence as the ability to get along with other people and might construct a perfectly reliable test on the basis of that definition. But, because not many other people define intelligence that way, the test would not be considered to have construct validity.

The effects of student "prepping" on test validity No matter how the validity of a standardized test is measured, a test is valid only when it measures what it is intended to measure. Thus, a test of ability is valid only when it measures ability; a test of achievement in school is valid only when it measures achievement in school.

Because standardized tests have such an important influence on students' careers, many classroom teachers, as well as parents and others interested in school children, have begun to prepare them to take such tests. Frank is not alone in preparing for the SATs early in his high school career.

McCall's is a national magazine aimed at that stratum of society known as the middle class. Many important tips are given in its pages on how children (and often their parents) can be helped to cope with current trends. One issue, for example, described how youngsters can overcome "the traumas of test taking" (Chan, 1975). The author stated that it is never too early to begin teaching children how to cope with standardized tests, for "the skills of test taking are really a necessary survival strategy." The most important part of this strategy is making a child more comfortable and confident about taking tests by helping him or her to understand that tests are not a measure of personal worth.

Teachers can help to prepare students for taking tests by giving elementary classes sample answer sheets to play with, by giving them the required #2 pencils to use on exercises where they practice darkening boxes for the correct answer, and by changing their seating arrangements from time to time. It also helps if, once in a while, the teacher uses the language of the test administrator. It is important that children understand the meaning of such words as "match," "missing," and "identify."

Standardized Tests: Friend or Enemy?

Elise, a 17-year-old senior at Wesley High School, wanted very much to enter Jayson College. Both her parents were Jayson alumni, and Elise wanted to continue the family tradition. Elise's English teacher reported in her letter of recommendation to the admissions office at Jayson that Elise was a creative writer, one of the best English students in class that year. "Her writing expresses a large number of novel ideas," the teacher pointed out, "and she's not afraid to take on controversial issues." Elise was also extremely interested in history; her history teacher wrote that he believed that she could probably be very successful in the honors program if she enrolled in it, but Elise was doing A work in the regular program, and he was satisfied with her progress.

In the fall of Elise's senior year, she took the SAT examinations. Unfortunately, in spite of her good work in history and in English, she fell far below the mean of seniors applying to college. Jayson College decided not to admit her on this basis. "'Not only was her verbal score just below average," the admissions officer told her parents, "but her math score was in the bottom thirtieth percentile." He advised her to apply to a smaller, less prestigious college.

Elise was heartbroken. Her father suggested that she practice taking the examination again and try for entrance the following year. "What will my friends think? That I'm a dodo?" Elise wailed. Studying hard and doing everything required of her at Wesley High had not compensated for the terrible test anxiety generated by the SAT. Because of that anxiety, the test didn't really measure what she knew, and as a result, her entire career may well have been affected. Elise considered the SAT her enemy. "And," she said, "I have good reason to believe it is."

John, on the other hand, told quite a different story about the SAT. "Without that exam, I would never be at an Ivy League College now. I wasn't a *bad* student in high school—that is, my grades were above average, but not good enough, certainly, to be admitted to this college. And my high school was not a recognized one. It was in a very small town; it did not have an honors program; and few of its graduates went on to college. But my parents traveled a lot while I was growing up. I lived in a number of different countries over a five-year period when my father worked abroad for an overseas corporation. I learned a lot more in my travels than the kids back at home did—things that didn't show up on the math exams in my junior year or on the physics tests in my senior year. They did show, however, in my general knowledge and probably gave me my high SAT score. I was in the top 3 percent of the country. And even though I had only good, not excellent, high school grades, the college admissions committee decided to give me a second look. They called me in for an interview, and, well, here I am! I think the standardized tests are the best friend I ever had!"

"Prepping" for standardized testing—which is what Frank did when he took the SAT in his sophomore year—is not simply child's play, as can be seen from the many ads for schools specializing in preparing high school and college students for standardized tests. However, because such training is available for some children and not for others, many test makers fear that the validity of their tests will be reduced.

The Advantages and Disadvantages of Standardized Testing in the Classroom

The use of standardized ability and achievement tests to select students for college, graduate, and professional schools is widespread. A standardized ability test can be used to predict a child's or a class's future achievement. A standardized achievement test can identify strengths and weaknesses. As we saw in the description of Frank, it can serve as an important diagnostic tool for teachers and students. It can identify subject matter objectives that should be given curricular emphasis and thus serve a major guidance function.

The standardized test also has disadvantages that the teacher should understand. First, such tests are inflexible and cannot be adapted to special local needs. If local objectives are not covered by a standardized achievement test, the test should not be used. Teachers should carefully study the manual accompanying any test before deciding whether or not to use it.

Second, even if the objectives of the standardized test are the same as local objectives, the table of norms may not be satisfactory. No matter how satisfactory the table of norms is, local norms are needed for some purposes. For instance, a first-grade child who scores at the twentieth percentile when his or her raw score on a standardized test is compared with national first-grade urban norms may be only at the second percentile in the first grade of a very select school. Of course, the exact opposite may be true for children in poverty neighborhoods. A poverty-area minority student taking a standardized math test may score at the ninetieth percentile in his Puerto Rican neighborhood in New York City, but only at the fiftieth percentile according to the nationwide table of norms. Achievement tests and ability tests have similar problems in this respect.

A few years ago, because of the problems inherent in the testing of minority-group students, Congress directed the Office of Education to develop an achievement test that would be fair to minority-group students and that could be used to evaluate newly desegregated schools. The Office of Education selected certain reading and mathematics achievement tests for grades 3 through 5 and then improved their sensitivity, reliability, and validity for students in schools with a minority enrollment of 50 percent or more (Schuchat, 1975). This process of restandardization produced a test battery referenced to two sets of norms. The score of a student or a school can be compared to the norms for students and schools in general and also to norms for minority students and schools with heavy enrollments of minority-group students.

Some 9,000 minority-group children were tested during the process. To no one's surprise, about 80 percent of elementary school students in general achieved at a higher level than those in the restandardization sample. Nevertheless, now there is a test battery that can be used to evaluate the effect, if any, of the considerable amount of funds the federal government is providing for improvement of schooling of minority-group children (Schuchat, 1975, p. 63).

Teachers who want to be fair judges of all their students, particularly minority-group students, need to keep the standardization factor in mind. If they still elect to judge these students on the basis of the same standardization used for more advantaged children, they can, of course, do so. But, to determine the validity of the test for *their* students, they must collect local norms.

A third disadvantage of using standardized tests in the classroom, according to some critics, lies in the fact that so few organizations are responsible for their development. These critics raise serious questions about what they term "abuse and misuse of unregulated power." Testing is big business in America. More than a quarter of a million dollars is spent on tests in a year (Sherwood, 1978). The focus on one investigation has been the Educational Testing Service (ETS). ETS holds a near-monopoly on "the development of tests which classify candidates for pre-secondary school, secondary school, college, graduate school, business school, and law school" (Brill, 1974, p. 67). For many students, ETS exams serve as vehicles of forward movement. Others, however, are carried to a dead end, because low scores deny them access to further education at schools of their choice. ETS has a contract "in perpetuity" to produce, consolidate, and administer the SAT, or College Boards, which in 1974 constituted $24 million in income, which was 42 percent of ETS's annual revenues (Rodriguez, 1974, p. 7). Critics of ETS, in increasing numbers today, are charging that "the way ETS 'aptitude' and 'achievement' tests are evaluated and interpreted is a classic model of unaccountable power" (p. 79).

using standardized tests of intelligence

American psychologists have a long history of interest in measuring differences between children in the ability to think and solve problems. It is not surprising that standardized intelligence testing has become a major (and controversial) part of American education.

What Is Intelligence? Before we begin talking about IQ tests, it is important to understand what these tests are supposed to be testing. Teachers frequently talk about mentally retarded or gifted children, or about low or high IQ scores. Very often, however, they don't stop to give serious thought to what these terms mean. What is intelligence?

The developers of two of the most widely used IQ tests, Alfred Binet and David Wechsler, had the same definition of intelligence. They suggested, simply, that intelligence was the general ability to adjust to the environment. This definition is similar to that used by Jean Piaget. Other psychologists, who attach a much more specific definition to the term, insist that intelligence is the ability to perform academic tasks (Keating, 1978). Still others consider intelligence as the ability to learn. Some early psychologists, such as Spearman (1904), thought that intelligence was a composite of many separate abilities to perform specialized tasks. Spearman believed that it was impossible to describe intelligence with a single number. He preferred subtests of different mental abilities, similar in many respects to the aptitude tests described at the beginning of this chapter. Many present-day psychologists agree (see, for example, Cattell, 1963; Labouvie-Vief, Levin, and Urberg, 1975; Stankov, 1978). With all these very different views of intelligence, it isn't surprising that teachers have difficulty understanding what intelligence is and interpreting IQ scores. It is no surprise that standardized intelligence testing is so controversial. If people do not agree on what intelligence is, they will not agree that standardized tests do, in fact, measure intelligence.

*Understanding
What IQ Scores
Measure:
What Teachers
Need to Know*

Just what do intelligence tests measure? Psychologists who believe that IQ tests are valid measures of intelligence say that the IQ is a valid index of how smart a person is and thus deserves the name "intelligence" quotient. But other psychologists, who question the validity of standardized intelligence tests, prefer to define IQ as "whatever the quality is that IQ tests measure." With this controversy in mind, let us examine the tests closely and see what they do, in fact, measure.

The IQ tests used in the United States today grew out of the work of Alfred Binet, a French psychologist. In 1905, Binet developed the first Binet Scale of Intelligence. This early test was designed to identify those children in the Paris schools who, because of apparently lower ability, could not benefit from ordinary instruction and so were to be taken out of regular classes and given a simpler education. In developing his scale, Binet tried many ways of distinguishing the bright children from the dull. He finally arrived at the conclusion that intelligence is "the tendency to take and maintain a definite direction; the capacity to make adaptations for the purpose of attaining a desired end" (Terman, 1916, p. 45). This was the definition that shaped Binet's final scale.

Binet's early test has long since been revised for use in other countries. The American revision, known as the Stanford-Binet Intelligence Test, uses many items similar in content and form to the early Binet scale. The general purpose of the later revisions of the test has been the same: to measure differences among children in ability to learn.

The difference between the ratio and the deviation IQ   The IQ obtained from the Stanford-Binet scale was at first an actual quotient. It was the person's mental age divided by his or her chronological age and multiplied by 100.

Mental age was obtained by comparing the test-taker's raw score with the standardization sample scores typical of different ages. The age that an individual's score matched was called his or her mental age. For example, suppose that Johnny, an 8-year-old third grader, has a mental age of 10. This would mean that Johnny can answer as many questions correctly as the typical 10-year-old in the standardization sample. To get Johnny's IQ, his mental age is divided by his chronological age of 8 years. The quotient is then multiplied by 100. Johnny's IQ found this way is called a **ratio IQ:** $10/8 \times 100 = 125$.

In the 1960 revision of the Stanford-Binet Scale, another kind of IQ score was added. This is called a **deviation IQ.** A deviation IQ is determined by comparing the individual's raw score only with those raw scores of individuals from the standardization sample who are of the same chronological age as the person being tested. For the Stanford-Binet scale deviation IQ, the average score at each age is arbitrarily set at 100. The student's score is computed by measuring how much above or below the student is compared to those of his or her own age, or how much he or she deviates from the norm.**

Test-makers with different understandings of what intelligence is develop different types of tests and different types of IQ scores. For example, a score of a mental age IQ test has a different meaning from a score on a deviation IQ test. Ratio IQs were replaced because they varied in meaning from age to age. Deviation IQs, on the other hand, have the advantage of being comparable from age to age. A deviation IQ of, say, 135 means the same thing from age to age, in that it indicates the same degree of superiority relative to the average score for the age of the individual.

The differences between tests and what they measure   The Stanford-Binet Intelligence Test has many levels of questions to cover the years from 2 through 14, some levels covering only six months. There are adult levels as well.

At each level, there are several subtests of different types. The subtests vary widely in content, depending on the age level. For instance, very young test-takers are asked to identify objects ("Show me the dolly's hair"). Those a little older are asked to trace mazes. Vocabulary is tested at all age levels. Picture and verbal absurdities are presented, and the person taking the test must explain what is wrong

---

**The distance between the average score and the actual score is divided into 16-point groups. Each group of 16 points is called a standard deviation. Therefore, a child who is one standard deviation above 100, the average score for his age, has an IQ of 100+ 16, or 116.

with them (for example, the shadow is going in the wrong direction). The examiner recites a set of digits, and the test-taker must say them backwards. Adults are asked to explain essential differences ("What is the principal difference between work and play?").

The Stanford-Binet Intelligence Test is in some ways a test of scholastic ability, and the tests are predominantly verbal, especially at the older age levels. This bias is understandable when one remembers that Binet's original purpose in developing the scale was to discriminate among children's differing levels of ability to succeed in school.

The Stanford-Binet Intelligence Test is an individual test. A specially trained examiner records and scores the test-taker's responses. This is necessary because the examiner must know which subtests to present—no one takes them all. An important part of the examiner's job is to establish rapport with the child being tested, so that he or she will be relaxed enough to perform well.

Although the Stanford-Binet Scale was adapted for American use, some psychologists were still dissatisfied with it. A test that eventually came to rival the Stanford-Binet was developed by David Wechsler, who felt that the single total score of general mental ability that comes from the Stanford-Binet Test did not provide enough information. Wechsler constructed ten or more subtests for each of several age levels, each subtest devoted to one kind of task. Some of the subtests were primarily verbally oriented, yielding what Wechsler termed a *verbal measure* of intelligence. Others, which required little or no verbal ability, gave what Wechsler termed a *performance measure* of intelligence. One way he used the test was in diagnosis. Wechsler noted

The Wechsler Intelligence Scales provide subtests that measure verbal and performance abilities. A trained examiner can measure the intellectual ability of students who may have verbal or language problems more easily with this test than with some other IQ tests.

Sing-Si Schwartz

that particular patterns of scores corresponded to certain types of intellectual problems. In addition, Wechsler's test was the first intelligence test that gave a deviation IQ.

The Wechsler-Bellevue Intelligence Scale was originally developed in 1939. Wechsler has since updated his original scales and developed the Wechsler Intelligence Scale for Children (WISC) and the Wechsler Adult Intelligence Scale (WAIS). He also developed an additional scale for children from 4 to 6 years of age, the Weschler Preprimary and Primary Intelligence Scale (WPPIS). In these tests, the subtests are divided into verbal tests and performance tests. For example, in the WISC, the verbal subtests are Information, Comprehension, Arithmetic, Similarities, and Vocabulary; the performance subtests are Block Design, Picture Completion, Picture Arrangement, Object Assembly, Mazes, and Coding. Separate verbal and performance deviation IQs are obtained. There is also a combined total deviation IQ score.

The Wechsler Scales all are individual tests of intelligence. As with the Stanford-Binet test, the examiner must keep a record of the test-taker's responses and score them as he or she goes along. The performance subtests are useful with those whose difficulties with language make other tests unsuitable. Much attention has been paid to different patterns of response on the verbal and performance subtests, but, according to Cronbach (1970), this kind of analysis has not proved sound and should not be depended on. Nevertheless, as with the Stanford-Binet test, a trained examiner can make diagnostic inferences about intellectual performance and perhaps even emotional problems by observing how the test-taker works.

Other individual tests of ability measure different things and are used for different purposes. The Goodenough-Harris Drawing Test, which uses drawing to test general mental ability, is often employed with children from different cultures, even though it is not wholly free of cultural influence.

In the Peabody Picture Vocabulary Test, the examiner says a word, and the child being tested points to the right picture. Without requiring the child to use language, this measuring instrument can test his or her knowledge of vocabulary. Although it is not very comprehensive, this test can be used with the retarded or handicapped (Cronbach, 1970).

Psychologists prefer such individual tests as the Stanford-Binet and the WISC, which have greater reliability, to group tests of general mental ability. But individual tests are expensive to administer because they require trained examiners. As a result, most testing of intelligence in the schools relies on group tests. Among the better-known group tests are the Lorge-Thorndike Intelligence Tests, for grades 3 through 13, which include both verbal and nonverbal subtests. A

Lorge-Thorndike Test can be given quickly; it takes only 62 minutes, plus time for distributing materials and explaining directions. Furthermore, a carefully planned national sample was used to obtain the norms (Cronbach, 1970).

If the same child took a group test and an individual IQ test, he or she would probably not get exactly the same score both times because group and individual tests, by their very nature, test different kinds of abilities. Group tests usually do not eliminate verbal skills entirely, because the person taking the test must write down the answers. In addition, group tests are usually timed tests, while individual tests are not.

Are stable scores obtained from tests of general mental ability? Will one IQ score predict another one, obtained years later?

Using IQ Tests to Predict Future Ability

Regardless of how it is obtained, IQ is not very stable during the first years of life. It had been thought at first that a person's IQ would remain the same as he or she got older. It was later discovered, however, that test scores obtained in the first few months of life were not related to scores at the end of the first year (Bayley, 1955). In fact, if infants and young children are given two tests a year or so apart, the correlation between the two scores is very low.

It is now well established that later intelligence cannot be predicted from test scores in infancy. This is logical: What is a valid test for an infant will not be so for an older child. Infants do not perform many different tasks, and so there are only a few ways to test their abilities. At first, all that can be done is to see whether their senses act as they should. Does a 1-month-old infant look at a dangling ring? Does a sharp sound make him or her blink? At 6 months, motor coordination can be tested. Can the infant pick up a 1-inch cube in easy reach? As time goes on, the development of language can be observed. Does the infant use relatively complex language? Is it meaningful (Bayley, 1955)?

More than thirty years ago, Honzik, MacFarlane, and Allen (1948) studied the IQs of 252 urban children between the ages of 21 months and 18 years. They obtained a correlation between scores at the age of 2 years and scores at the age of 5 years that was only slightly better than what would be expected by pure chance. To some extent, the changes in IQ came from the low reliability of testing in very young children, as well as from certain technical problems in the study.

These investigators reported other dramatic changes: Between the ages of 6 and 18, the IQs of almost 60 percent of the group changed 20 or more points, and the IQs of 9 percent of the group changed 30 or more points. Some individuals showed a change of more than 50 points. The IQs of only 15 percent of the group changed less than 10 points. On the whole, children tended to change in the direction that brought them more in line with the average IQ of people of the same educational and socioeconomic status as their parents.

Some startling case histories were related in this study. One girl went from an IQ of 133 down to an IQ of 77. The investigators could give no sufficient explanation of the decrease, but did say that "she was always overindulged by the mother, who lived to feed her and keep her young, and who was always complaining that her daughter never gave her enough affection" (Honzik et al., 1948, p. 77).

In contrast, a boy in the study whose score deviated significantly below the average raised his IQ to even more of a deviation above the average. As Honzik and his colleagues (1948) described him:

> He is small-statured, thin, with very poor musculature, and presents a history of early ear infections and chronic bronchitis from infancy—headaches (early glasses), stomach pains (appendectomy); he has had three operations and three serious accidents. He has had only one six-month period in his life free of illness. In spite of a frail frame, which has suffered many serious indignities, an early strained family situation, and relatively low mental test scores in his early, preschool years, his tested ability steadily increased until 9, from which time he has maintained high and fairly stable scores. (p. 77)

These investigators found, however, that the briefer the interval between testings and the older the child when the two testings were done, the more likely it was that the IQ score would stay the same or close to the same.

Later, Cronbach (1970) observed that IQ scores tend to become more stable when children get older. Test scores obtained in adolescence have been closely related, with a correlation of .75 to scores obtained twenty to forty years later. Nevertheless, as he points out, there are some late bloomers, whose high ability becomes apparent relatively late in life. In general, no matter what the age, Cronbach (1970) recommends that if a decision is to be made about a student on the basis of a test score, only a recent score should be used. Furthermore, he cautions, we should watch out for children who are not used to being tested. Scores on tests improve just with practice in taking tests.

interpreting the controversies about IQ testing in the school

The primary advantage of IQ testing is that it attempts to identify those students with special needs—the gifted or the mentally retarded. Tests of general mental ability can also be used for diagnosis of learning disabilities, although additional diagnostic procedures are often needed.

But the teacher must keep in mind the limitations of mental tests. These tests are not infallible. IQs do not always remain stable, and the longer the interval since the last testing, the less faith we can put in the score. Tests that require reading will be unfair to children with reading difficulties—no matter how intelligent they are, they will not get a high score. Most intelligence tests are heavily verbal and are therefore unfair to the child who does not speak English well or has other verbal problems. In such cases, the only fair test would be a nonverbal or performance test.

Much has been written about the unfairness of intelligence tests to some children, particularly those from minority groups. In the past, ability grouping that used verbally oriented tests as criteria for placement frequently led many of these children into low-ability special education classes. In these classes, according to litigation against the school boards in the early 1970s, children often did not receive the kind of stimulation they needed. Furthermore, stigma attached to their placement made it difficult for them to adjust to school. Public outcry against such procedures led eventually to the passing of Public Law 94–142, that now guarantees, among other things, a multifactored assessment to determine the appropriate educational program for all handicapped children.

The Jensen Controversy: Is Intelligence Inherited?

In 1969, Arthur Jensen, a California psychologist, published a highly controversial article in the *Harvard Educational Review* that stated that large portions of what the IQ tests measure are, in fact, hereditary abilities. Jensen considers IQ tests fair measures of ability. He has suggested (in 1969 and in later writings) that some groups of children get lower scores on such tests for the same reason that early compensatory education programs like Head Start have been ineffective: Those children's abilities simply are inferior. Jensen's articles caused an immediate furor, and he was vigorously attacked by many environmentalists, who quickly cited evidence that the environment, not heredity, is the prime factor determining ability to perform on these tests. Other critics have argued that there is no way to be certain how much of any test score is due to heredity and how much to environment. They pointed out what they consider a dangerous result of Jensen's statements: They can be used as an excuse to decrease government's commitment to early intervention efforts. (For a discussion of the arguments presented at the time of Jensen's 1969 writing, see Crow, 1969; Hebb, 1970; Jensen, 1969, Bodmer and Cavalli-Sforza, 1970.)

In the years since Jensen's article first appeared, the nature/nurture controversy, as it relates to intelligence tests, has bloomed. Textbooks in psychology and educational psychology have discussed the argument in detail (Miller, 1978). Environmental psychologists have presented arguments to back up their position that, since environment plays such a major role in the development of the cognitive processes, teachers should take full responsibility for classroom learning and not hide behind the statement that some of their students "just aren't smart" (see, for example, Dlugokinski et al., 1976; Samuel, 1977).

The Burt-Kamin Controversy: Shooting Down a Classic Study

One of the major arguments posed on Jensen's behalf was made by Sir Cyril Burt, a British psychologist. Over a period of many years, Burt presented a series of papers that argued strongly for a genetic theory of intelligence and a genetic theory of social class. The strongest data Burt presented to prove his point were a series of studies that showed that the correlation between IQs of identical twins separated at early ages and reared apart under different environmental conditions was extremely high—above +.77. The correlation between IQs of siblings reared in the same household was much lower. Burt's study had been described as a classic study of twins and was included in most textbook discussions of basic twin research.

In the early 1970s, however, a Princeton environmental psychologist, Leon Kamin, examined Burt's data closely and reported a number of ambiguities and oddities, the most remarkable being some kinship correlations that did not change with increasing sample size. In *The Science and Politics of IQ* (1974) Kamin charged that Burt had fabricated his data. Further analysis by other researchers showed a great many more oddities in Burt's data that could not possibly have occurred by accident (Burt, 1978; Dorfman, 1978). It was the first time that a researcher of Burt's prominence had been accused of making up data to support an argument.

What Should Be Done about IQ Testing?

Does this evidence suggest that IQ tests should be dropped from use in American schools? Some psychologists and educators say yes. Some cities have already done so. New York City, for example, dropped the use of IQ testing in its schools well before the Burt-Kamin controversy and even before Public Law 94–142 was passed.

Not all educators agree with this position. They say that IQ tests have so many uses that dropping them would amount to throwing the baby out with the bath water. Cronbach (1970), for example, remarks:

> The opposition to tests rests in part on the belief that the test is designed for the white middle-class child, and does not give the slum child a fair chance. The middle-class child is encouraged to develop verbal abilities and to reason critically; such training is much less common in lower-class homes. This does not show the tests to be unfair; abstract and critical reasoning is indispensable for full participation in a complex and technical civilization. But *it justifies our thinking of the low-scoring slum children as culturally handicapped rather than as inferior from birth* [italics added]. (p. 303)

To support his argument, Cronbach quotes two test questions from Davis (1951):

A symphony is to a composer as a book is to what?
      paper   sculptor   author   musician   man

A baker goes with bread like a carpenter goes with what?
      a saw   a house   a spoon   a nail   a man

Answering the first question requires knowledge that only advantaged children are likely to have, but the second is based on information children of all social strata are equally likely to know. When children were divided into two groups according to socioeconomic status, 81 percent of the advantaged group got the first question right, but only 51 percent of the disadvantaged group did so. Fifty percent of both groups got the the second question right. Cronbach concludes that "the critical problem is not one of modifying tests but of inventing educational procedures suitable for children who are prepared neither intellectually nor motivationally for the traditional school" (p. 306).

Many other educators agree. According to Zach (1972), our real problem is not the tests themselves but how we use them. Are we going to continue to use tests only to make divisions between the fast learners and the slow, or are we going to use them to determine children's state of intellectual development so that we can use this information to help them develop further?

A student's test score is meaningful only when compared with norms, but no just comparison is possible unless the norms were drawn from a group similar to the student's own group. Because totally culture-free tests do not exist, a low score on an IQ test should be considered only in light of both the test-taker's background and the background of the standardization sample. If a student's cultural and intellectual background differ greatly from that of the standardization sample, comparing his or her score with the published norms is inappropriate and unfair. Not all educators agree that it is possible objectively to evaluate a minority-group student's low score in light of his or her cultural background and that of the standardization sample.

DeAvila and Havassy (1974) have suggested that test developers consider an alternative assessment model derived from the work of Jean Piaget. Such a model was used, along with standardized achievement and IQ tests, on 1,100 Mexican-American and other children in four southwestern states. Results of the pilot study show that the four Piagetian stages of cognitive development are exhibited in a developmental progression of performance scores appropriate to each age, regardless of ethnicity. The minority children failed to perform as well as the Anglo-Americans on the traditional capacity and achievement measures, but the difference was perhaps a result of poorly designed curriculum, language usage, and so on, rather than cognitive inferiority.

DeAvila and Havassy have also demonstrated that administrators and teachers could use the information provided by the neo-Piagetian approach on a daily basis. To help teachers do this, they designed a computerized system, which

> at the administrative level. . .provides group statistical data for program evaluation and needs assessment and, at the teacher level, provides classroom recommendations rather than scores.

> This system simultaneously takes into account achievement and developmental scores for both the individual child and the child's referent group. It thus becomes possible to determine all of the possible test outcomes and, thereby, to design individual computerized program prescriptions for each child tested. Workshops are then held with the teachers involved to discuss the implementation of these prescriptions. A copy of these recommendations can also be sent to the home so that parents are aware of what the teacher is trying to accomplish with the child and can, with guidance from the teacher, participate in the child's education. (p.75)

This system, called Program Assessment Pupil Instruction (PAPI), has been used successfully in the four states where the data were gathered.

using standardized achievement tests

Standardized achievement tests exist in profusion—they cover almost every school subject, and many other subjects as well.

*Who Uses
Standardized
Achievement Tests
and What Do They
Use Them For?*

The public schools rely on standardized achievement tests for placement, prediction, and planning. As students now move more and more freely among school systems, this form of standardized measurement is needed to determine which classes the transferring students should be placed in. A standardized achievement test can provide a teacher with a rough estimate of where to begin course work with either an individual or a class. These tests, along with standardized aptitude and ability tests, provide information needed in counseling individual students. They can be used in comparing different methods of teaching and in comparing a group with national norms. They have some value in diagnosis of learning problems.

Some educators recommend still other uses. Standardized achievement tests, they say, can be used to compare an individual's or a group's achievement and aptitude with their potential. Frank's SAT scores can be used to compare his verbal and math aptitudes. Test scores can be used to compare classes and schools and to study student growth over time (presumably with equivalent forms being used for pretest and posttest).

Many colleges and universities still employ standardized achievement tests, along with standardized ability tests and high school grades, as a means for predicting the college grade point averages of applicants for admission.

No matter what the purpose is, in selecting a standardized achievement test a teacher should examine the test manual to see what evidence the publisher presents about the reliability and validity of the test. He or she should also examine the tables or norms to see if they are appropriate and check the instructions for administration and scoring to determine their practicality. Most important, teachers should examine the test objectives to see if they match their own. Because

With Education in Washington:
Restandardization

Critics of standardized achievement tests often point to the bias of such tests in favor of white middle-class Americans. Such critics feel that minority-group students are underrepresented in the test-development process and, as a result, often have low scores when these tests are used. Defenders of the tests, on the other hand, argue that white middle-class standards, which represent those of the majority, are necessary for comparison of schools and students. The tests, they say, serve as a measure of a minority student's ability to compete with the majority and, perhaps, to join the mainstream. Now the United States government has stepped into the picture, as Theodore Schuchat (1975, p. 63) reports:

Congress directed the Office of Education to develop an achievement test that would satisfy both viewpoints and could be used to evaluate newly desegregated schools. The OE selected certain reading and mathematics achievement tests for grades 3–5 and then improved their sensitivity, reliability, and validity for students in schools with a minority enrollment of 50 percent or more.

This process of restandardization produced a test battery referenced to two sets of norms. The score of a student or a school can be compared to the norms for students and schools in general and also to norms for minority students and schools with heavy enrollments of minority-group students.

Some 9,000 minority-group children were tested during the process. To no one's surprise, about 80 percent of elementary school students in general achieved at a higher level than those in the restandardization sample. Nevertheless, now there is a test battery that can be used to evaluate the effect, if any, of the not inconsiderable amount of funds the federal government is providing for improvement of their schooling. (p.63)

Is this a compromise? A solution? What might the ramifications of "two sets of norms" be? And perhaps, above all, should the federal government assume any role in respect to the complex issues facing American educators today?

standardized achievement tests cover the large segments of subject matter and the broad aims common to many schools, they are not suitable for evaluating achievement in a limited unit of instruction or judging how well a strictly local learning objective has been accomplished.

*What Do
Achievement Tests
Measure?*

One of the most frequent uses of achievement tests is to predict future achievement. Teachers often want to predict the future success of their students—even as early as preschool. One group of tests that attempts to measure prereading achievement is the Metropolitan Readiness Tests (MRT). These tests have been used with moderate success with preschool children to predict what their reading, spelling, and arithmetic achievement will be in the latter part of first grade. Tests like the MRT can be useful in identifying children with learning problems when they first enter school. They can also be used to identify those children who should enter school early and those who should not. Furthermore, kindergarten programs in reading readiness can be evaluated through the use of pretest and posttest scores (Rubin, 1974).

Many of you may remember a battery of achievement tests called the Iowa Tests of Educational Development. These tests have given better prediction of college grade point average than the usual scholastic ability test. In fact, these tests have been as useful in predicting future achievement as a combination of high school grades and scholastic ability tests (Harris, 1940; Science Research Associates, 1957).

In their study, Burnham and Hewitt (1971) showed that scores on the College Board's Mathematics Achievement Test were successful in evaluating a student's readiness to pursue college-level mathematics and quantitative science work. When used in conjunction with the College Board's test of scholastic verbal ability (the SAT-V), these scores were also successful predictors of general academic success.

Although such tests appear to be reliable predictors, it is unwise to put all our eggs in one basket. The best prediction of a student's future success will most likely be obtained by using a combination of a few good predictors.

*The Advantages
and Disadvantages
of Standardized
Achievement
Testing:
What Teachers
Need to Know*

Highly reliable and valid standardized tests, just like well-constructed standardized ability tests, have much to offer. They are used in placement, planning, and evaluation. They can also be invaluable in diagnosis and in the individualization of instruction.

However, like standardized IQ tests, standardized achievement tests often do a poorer job of long-term prediction than many educators would like to admit. They are invalid for students whose backgrounds or current school curricula do not match those of the standardization sample. It is unjust for large groups of students to have their achievement assessed by these exams. In order for a test to be a truly suitable measure, the sample on which the test is standardized must be similar in all important respects to the population for whom the test is designed.

Because of the stress placed on achievement tests by the community, many teachers find themselves teaching for achievement on the standardized achievement tests. In recent years many colleges have allowed students to practice on the College Board achievement tests by taking them in both their junior and senior years of high school, which perhaps gives them an unfair advantage. Some students take the test many times in order to become "test-wise."

By concentrating their teaching on the standardized tests, teachers have handed over to the test developers the right to select what will be taught to their students. The United States has been noted for its insistence on local control of schools as a necessary measure to prevent centralized political control of education. Curriculum has long been selected by the communities in which students live in order to prevent excessive federal control. However, although we have carefully protected ourselves from control by politicians in the field of education, we have inadvertently given much of this control to the testing centers responsible for developing standardized achievement tests. In many cases, the learning objectives of a school or class do not match those of a particular standardized achievement test. When we judge achievement by the scores obtained on such a test, we have abandoned local control.

Standardized tests of achievement can be extremely valuable when they are flexible enough to deal differentially with individual students, aims, and instructional facilities. But invalid tests that force students and teachers into predetermined molds do not achieve these goals.

Interpreting test scores on standardized tests often calls for the assistance of specialists trained in this field.

Most teachers today understand the problems of using standardized achievement tests with children of varying socioeconomic backgrounds, just as they understand many of the problems associated with the use of IQ tests on the same population. They are less likely, however, to be able to explain a decline in achievement among all American students, as measured by standardized test scores, that has taken place over the past fifteen years.

It is a fact that the average scores of students who take the SAT have declined steadily and noticeably over the past fifteen years, after having remained relatively stable during the preceding decade. Verbal scores on the SAT dropped 49 points from 1963 to 1977; math scores dropped 32 points (Ryor, 1977). Although in 1978, for the first time in ten years, the average verbal score of seniors taking the test did not decline further, the math score went down that year still another two points.

Just as there was a public uproar over the use of intelligence tests in the schools, this evidence of what many see as a decline in the learn-

Lower Standardized Test Scores: What Do They Mean?

ing of our students has created a new public furor. At first, people echoed the anti-IQ testers and claimed that the tests were bad. But other critics complained that falling test scores reflected our schools' lack of ability to teach, not bad tests. There have been complaints of increasing illiteracy among our teachers as well as among our students. The public outcry has given rise to a "back to basics" movement and a call for competency tests. Arguments for increased emphasis on academic rigor were backed in 1978 by the National Association of Secondary School Principals, who noted that schools that emphasize math and English have not shown evidence of score decreases.

Are Our Students Illiterate?

Literacy advocates place most of the blame for the poorer test scores of today's students on inadequate teaching. Critics suggest that students coming out of today's schools lack the basic knowledge necessary to receive and express ideas through reading and writing and to relate the content of verbal communication to the continual stream of events that are shaping their futures. Books published years ago, such as Rudolf Flesch's famous book, *Why Johnny Can't Read* (1955), have suddenly become popular among critics of present-day schools.

A close look at the data and the tests that were used to collect them shows that the issue of lower standardized test scores is not a simple one. The College Entrance Examination Board commissioned a two-year study to investigate the decline. Its report, published in 1977, identified several causes of the decline. First, between 1963 and 1970, there was a sharp increase in the proportion of students taking college entrance examinations who came from groups that have always registered substantially lower than average scores in scholastic aptitude. In other words, the population of students taking the test during that period changed drastically because of widespread extension of educational opportunities to students from poor and minority backgrounds. A second cause of the decline, the study reported, was due to social factors: The period of sharpest decline in the test scores, 1967 to 1975, was marked by the Vietnam War, political assassinations, the burning of U.S. cities, and corruption of national leadership. The study suggested that these external factors contributed to a decrease in motivation among young people. Researchers also found clear relationships between home environment and scholastic achievement (Kellaghan 1977; Trotman, 1977).

Other causal factors noted by the CEEB study were changes in the role of the family in the educational process, the impact of television, an increase in elective as opposed to required courses in the schools, and diminishing importance in our society of academic scholarship (Shane and Wirtz, 1977).

Some educators point out that other evidence shows that this decline has not occurred in all instances. Farr, Fay, and Negley (1978), for example, demonstrated that students in Indiana schools showed no significant differences and even, in some cases, slight gains in scores at certain age levels over a span of years. In another study, 63,900 9-year-olds were given tests on literal and inferential comprehension and reference skills. Significant improvement was found in all three abilities when the students were tested again four years later (National Assessment of Educational Progress, 1978).

Other investigators have questioned the tests themselves. For example, in a study of the Stanford Diagnostic Reading Test, Allen (1978) concluded that this popular test does not actually test the reading that teachers think it does. Allen pointed out that only 42 of the 255 items were designed specifically to find out how well pupils comprehended printed prose (p. 89).

Clearly, the problem is complex and has tremendous importance for all of us. Standardized tests will no doubt continue to be an important yardstick of student growth and teacher effectiveness in many schools. At present, they are carrying more weight than they can comfortably bear, but they remain a potentially valuable part of the educational process.

summary

1. Standardized tests have uniform procedures for administration and scoring. They are used in many parts of the country to compare students' scores from different areas and schools. They are written by professional test specialists and sold by test publishers.

2. Standardized tests can measure student ability, achievement, verbal and nonverbal behavior, speed, and power. Such tests are an important basis for admission to college and graduate and professional schools. By their nature, all standardized tests are norm-referenced.

3. Standardized ability tests are designed to measure a student's potential maximum performance. Abilities may be general or specific. Aptitude tests are a special type of ability test.

4. Achievement tests are designed to measure what a student has learned in a particular school subject. Such tests can be used to evaluate a course's effectiveness, determine student progress, and diagnose individual differences. In general, achievement tests measure past learning, while ability tests measure the potential to learn.

5. Some standardized tests are designed to be administered to one individual at a time, while others are designed for groups of any size. Individual tests may not use language at all and are thus important for students who have language difficulties. Group tests are usually paper-and-pencil tests. Group tests are economical and convenient and do not require trained administrators.

6. A test that relies heavily on words is a verbal test. Nonverbal tests do not depend very much on words, except possibly for the test instructions. Tests that require equipment are called nonlanguage or performance tests.

7. A speed test measures how many questions a student can answer correctly in a restricted time period. A power test generally has no time limit and tests the student's ability to answer correctly.

8. The standardization process begins with a list of the test's content (broken down into weighted subtopics) and the behavior test-takers will be expected to perform. Specialists in testing and experts in the subject to be tested work together to generate the questions. Test items are then tested on a representative sample of students, and a group of items is selected for the final published form of the test. This final test is then given to a second group of students called the standardization sample. The scores of this sample, which is also representative of the students for whom the test is intended, become the norms for the test. Several sorts of norms are possible. Based on a student's raw score (the number of correct answers), percentile rank, an age norm, and a grade norm all can be provided. The validity of these norms depends on how representative the standardization sample was, and this sample must be described in the test's instruction manual.

9. The basis for interpreting the scores on a standardized test is the normal curve. The standard deviation (SD) from the mean is derived from the normal curve. The standard deviation is the basis for the z score, which tells how far from the average a given raw score is in terms of standard deviations. The z score lets us compare scores from different tests.

10. The reliability of a standardized test—its ability to measure consistently—is determined by giving the test twice and finding the correlation coefficient (r) between the two scores. The higher the correlation coefficient, the more reliable the test. Because no test is perfectly reliable, no test has a correlation coefficient of +1. The correlation coefficient measures only the strength and direction of a relationship; it tell us nothing about causes and effects because it does not take into account outside factors that might influence the relationship.

11. The standard error (SE) of a test enables us to adjust for a test's imperfect reliability by projecting what students would get on a second administration of the same test.

12. A reliable test is not necessarily a valid test. A valid test measures what it is supposed to measure. A test has content validity when it contains an adequate sample of the knowledge to be tested. A special sort of validity relevant to ability tests is called predictive validity and refers to the correlation between scores on the test and some other measure of future success such as college grade point average. A test has construct validity when it is based on a generally agreed-upon definition of the ability to be tested. Because standardized tests have such an impact on students' careers, many teachers and parents have begun to prepare students to take such tests. Many test makers fear that the validity of their tests will be reduced because such special preparation is not available to all students.

13. Standardized tests can diagnose students' strengths and weaknesses, identify weak areas in teaching, and predict students' future achieve-

ment. But such tests are inflexible and hard to adapt to local needs. Tables of norms may be inappropriate, particularly for minority-group children, and many teachers will want to make their own tables of local norms to more fairly judge their students' performance.

14. Standardized intelligence testing is a major and controversial part of American education. Much of the controversy stems from the fact that there is no single agreed-upon definition of what intelligence is. Binet and Wechsler defined intelligence as a general ability to adapt to the environment. Other psychologists see it as the ability to perform specific academic tasks. Spearman felt that intelligence was a composite of many separate abilities and that it was impossible to describe it with a single number. Some psychologists today feel that IQ tests are valid measures of intelligence, while others feel that they are valid measures of IQ.

15. The first intelligence test was developed by Alfred Binet in 1905; the revised American version is called the Stanford-Binet Scale of Intelligence. The IQ, or intelligence quotient, was first derived by dividing a person's mental age by his or her chronological age, and multiplying by 100. This is called a ratio IQ. The deviation IQ is obtained by comparing an individual's raw score with the scores of individuals who are the same age as the person being tested.

16. The Stanford-Binet test is largely verbal and is individually administered. David Wechsler's intelligence tests, which were the first to provide a deviation IQ, combine performance tasks and verbal tasks and are also individually administered. Other individual ability tests include the Goodenough-Harris Drawing Test and the Peabody Picture Vocabulary Test. One of the better-known group tests is the Lorge-Thorndike Intelligence Test.

17. Childhood or adult intelligence test scores cannot be predicted with any degree of accuracy from test scores in infancy. IQs are not stable, and the longer the interval since the last test, the less relevant the earlier IQ is likely to be. Predictions based on a single testing are usually inaccurate and are especially unfair to children who do not have test-taking experience.

18. Arthur Jensen and some of his colleagues who believe in the hereditability of IQ have stated that most of what IQ tests measure is inherited ability. These theoreticians have suggested, among other things, that blacks have done less well on such tests and have not responded as expected to compensatory education because their inherited abilities tended to be lower than those of whites. Jensen's critics blame him for ignoring environmental influences, giving fuel to racists, and weakening the government's commitment to compensatory education.

19. Cyril Burt's studies of twins seemed to prove the heritability of intelligence and were cited as classics in their field, until Leon Kamin provided evidence to show that Burt had made up some of the data to support his argument.

20. Because of these controversies, some states and cities are curtailing the

use of intelligence and other standardized tests in schools. Many educators and psychologists say that this reaction is extreme. IQ tests have several positive functions, and the problem may be in the way we use the tests, not in the tests themselves.

21. Standardized achievement tests are used for placement, prediction, and planning. They are an important basis for admission to college in many states. Teachers who use such tests should be sure that the norms are appropriate and that the test objectives match their own.

22. Achievement tests are mainly used to predict future success. The Metropolitan Readiness Tests (MRT) can be used to test preschool children's readiness for kindergarten. A particularly useful battery of achievement tests for school-age children are the Iowa Tests of Educational Development. But no single test is a reliable predictor. The best predictor of success is derived from a combination of good predictors.

23. Standard achievement tests are invalid for students whose backgrounds and current school curricula do not match those of the standardization sample. The importance people place on such tests has the unfortunate result of causing teachers to teach for the tests, not for the sake of knowledge. Teachers who do this are abdicating to the test makers their right to determine learning objectives.

24. Students' scores on standard achievement tests such as the SAT have dropped steadily during the last decade. Some people blame the tests, but others blame the schools. The public is increasingly demanding basic competency tests as a requirement for graduation and a return to basics in teaching. A study by the College Entrance Examination Board, however, suggested that the decline in scores was mainly caused by an increasing number of students from groups that have always scored lower in scholastic aptitude taking the tests and by social factors such as the Vietnam War, Watergate, and political assassinations, which have led to a decrease in motivation among young people. The home environment and television were also implicated.

**for students
who want to read
further**

BLUMENFIELD, S. *The New Illiterates—And How You Can Keep Your Child from Becoming One.* New Rochelle, N. Y.: Arlington House, 1973. Blumenfield reports on statistical figures of illiteracy in the United States and presents a case for the return to the teaching of phonics. He also advises parents on how to prepare their children for school.

KAMIN, L. J. *The Science and Politics of IQ.* Potomac, Md: Lawrence Erlbaum, 1974. Kamin's review of the political problems plaguing the IQ question since the inception of IQ testing in the United States is quite fascinating. His attack on Sir Cyril Burt is written in an interesting fashion and presents the reader with a brand new approach to psychology. Kamin plays the role of a historical detective in his interpretation and analysis of Burt's data.

LYMAN, H. B. *Test Scores and What They Mean,* 3rd ed. Englewood Cliffs, N. J.: Prentice-Hall, 1978. This is an easy-to-read guide to understanding standardized test scores. The basic attributes of a test as well as types of tests and scores are explained.

SHANE, H. G., AND WIRTZ, W. "The academic score decline: Are facts the enemy of truth?" *Phi Delta Kappan*, October 1977, pp. 83–86. This short article is basically an interview with W. Willard Wirtz, Chairman of the National Manpower Institute, who served for two years as chairman of the 21-member advisory panel charged with investigating the decline in the Scholastic Aptitude Test (SAT) scores. H. G. Shane is University Professor of Education at Indiana University. The interview presents Shane's questions about the meaning of the score decline and Wirtz's answers as the panel saw them.

EPILOGUE: SO, YOU STILL WANT TO BE A TEACHER?

**Excerpts From "A Love Letter
To A Dead Teacher"**

Dear Mr. Stock:

You probably wouldn't remember me, even if you were alive. I sat in the third row back in your English 512 class in South Side High School in Newark, New Jersey. You gave me an A minus for being unprepared.

You had asked us to write a composition in class about one of Hardy's heroines, but I had neglected to read the book assigned. Caught off guard, writing frantically against the clock, I described a young woman, the room she sat in, the beam of light from the high window, her hands in her lap, the thoughts in her head. I anticipated failure, disgrace, worst of all—your disappointment. Instead, you gave me a minus for being unprepared and an A for something uniquely mine. Your scrawled comment in red ink on my paper read, "This isn't Hardy's character, but you've made yours very real."

Startled into gratitude, I became aware of my own possibilities.
You *recognized* me. . . .

I don't think you knew what you did for me, Mr. Stock. We teachers seldom know whom we influence or even why. It was not my defects you emphasized, but my worth.

Other teachers dealt differently with us, demanding discipline or wooing us with false camaraderie.

You assumed one simple fact: If the lesson was interesting, we would be attentive. We were more than attentive. We hated to see the period end, for you knew when to ask the provocative, unexpected "Why?" which tumbled upside down our whole cluttered cart of preconceptions and set us thinking long after the dismissal bell. You did not try to charm or to beguile us. You never pretended to be a pal. You were a *teacher*. Your dignity was unassailable. Because you respected yourself and us, we were able to respect ourselves. . . .

When one of us returned after an absence, you would say, "We missed you." When one was unprepared, you would shake your head: "Too bad; we were hoping to know what *you* think." You treated us as adults, your equals, and so—in your class—we were. . . .

And you shared with us your loves. "Listen to this!" you would say, eagerly opening a book, unashamed to be moved by a poem, unafraid to use words like "magnificent.". . .

Are teachers like you really dead? I think not—as long as there are people who can still say: "I had a teacher once . . . who made that difference!" Perhaps at this very moment someone, someplace, is saying this about one of us. That is our immortality.

You former pupil,
Bel Kaufman

B. Kaufman, "A Love Letter to a Dead Teacher," condensed from *Today's Education*, March-April 1975, 20–23.

so you still want to be a teacher?

All of us preparing to be teachers set out with grand plans. We would all like to affect our students in positive ways so that we will be remembered the way Mr. Stock was remembered by Bel Kaufman. We would like to be good teachers and hope (and expect) to be rewarded for our efforts at reaching this goal.

This new edition of *Psychology for the Classroom* was designed to help you learn the skills necessary for good teaching. Good teachers need to learn more than the subject matter they teach and how to communicate information. Really successful teachers like Mr. Stock, teachers that students remember fondly long after they have gone on to other pursuits, know how to apply psychological principles. They understand the instructional process and know what to do when it isn't going right. They can adapt quickly to new situations. When teaching innovations are called for, they learn to use them. When they are told suddenly that, without receiving special training, they will be expected to accept handicapped children into their classrooms, they learn to teach them. They also are prepared for attacks by aggressive students, angry parents, and unhappy community members. Newspapers frequently describe teachers' difficulties in reducing classroom aggression. Student violence directed against other students and teachers is no longer uncommon. Some teachers complain that the question that teachers must face is not "How do we reduce aggression in the classroom?" Instead it is, "Teaching--or surviving?" (Woods, 1977). In spite of all of this, truly effective teachers feel rewarded by their successes (when they occur) and by the rewards inherent in watching children grow and observing the small changes that are the fruit of grueling teacher efforts.

Teaching is still a rewarding profession for those who, like Mr. Stock, enjoy helping children learn, are unafraid of the changes that are taking place today in education, are prepared for adversity and for some failures, and learn from their successes when they come. Teaching is a difficult job, even for those who are truly successful. If you decide, after completing this course, that you still want to be a teacher, be prepared for plain hard work and new problems every day.

what specific problems should you be prepared for?

In this text, we have reviewed some specific problems that new teachers will need to deal with. Violence is one problem. There are many others. Our list must be incomplete; we have no crystal ball to tell us what issues will present themselves tomorrow. But the teacher who is prepared to face those problems we can foresee has a greater chance of success than one who is not.

Remaining Up-to-Date on What You're Teaching

No teacher can perform well without a solid background in the subject that he or she is teaching. Today, the public is complaining that teachers are not equipped to do the jobs they are hired to do. Specifically, the charge is that many teachers do not have adequate knowledge of the subject matter or sufficient communication skills to do decent jobs in the classroom. A Gallup poll has shown that the public is concerned with a number of issues. In order of importance, these are lack of discipline, use of drugs, poor curriculum, poor standards, and difficulty in getting good teachers (Gallup, 1978). In some states, the public has asked for literacy tests for teachers as well as for graduating students. (Literacy in general is a growing problem. In one state, the bill ordering basic competency tests for teachers had three misspelled words in it.)

Applying Psychological Principles to Classroom Learning

Besides knowing what to say and how to say it, teachers need to know who they are talking to. Social and economic conditions in America are changing, and the rates and ways that children develop are also changing. For example, the high school teacher of the 1940s was terribly concerned about students who chewed bubble gum in class and wrote notes to their friends. The teacher of the 1970s and 1980s, in contrast, has had to be continually alert for dangerous drugs and weapons in the school building.

The principles of learning and teaching put forth by behavioral or motivational theorists generally hold true despite changes in social and economic conditions. But, although reinforcement, for example, is still a valid technique, the specific reinforcers that work with students change over time; the goals of students also change with changing

Van Bucher, Photo Researchers, Inc.

times. Teachers who do not keep up with current events are not likely to understand what is going on in the classroom, or why procedure that worked well two years ago turns students off today.

New teachers in the 1980s can expect to deal more with individual differences in ability, aptitude, and interests than teachers, like Mr. Stock, who taught in the two previous decades. They can expect that mainstreaming will bring changes to the classroom in the 1980s that were not anticipated in the 1970s before Public Law 94-142 was passed. They can expect continued use of classroom testing; if they have not learned how to use tests to increase their knowledge of their students, they will be less successful than those who have learned how to make best use of these diagnostic tools.

Because teachers in our society are subject to many contradictory demands and constraints from the schools, the community, and society in general, it is difficult to state specifically what they are expected to do and what model of behavior they should present to their students. One way to look at this problem is in terms of conflict of roles teachers are expected to play. The basic confusion lies in whether teachers should preserve current cultural standards by reinforcing and trans-

Teachers have to make many decisions related to demands from the school, the community, and society. Some of these decisions are hammered out at faculty meetings; others must be made privately by each teacher.

Dealing with Conflicting Roles

mitting them to the young, or whether they should try to improve those standards when this involves breaking down traditional ideas and attitudes (Denno, 1977).

The teacher's role as improver of culture Some teachers find certain attitudes and values in our society objectionable and would rather not pass them on to their students. Such teachers are disillusioned with things as they are and would like to help create a better society through educational reform. However, because of the emphasis on individual rights in this country, teachers who see themselves as improvers of culture are frequently criticized for overstepping their roles, because they often impose middle-class values on children from non-middle-class subcultures. The real problems for these teachers are how to teach basic learning skills to both privileged and poor students so that all have an equal chance to learn and how to decide on the important areas of learning in a school setting in which it is agreed that parents should have a strong say in what is taught. These problems of giving optimal education to all and still meeting the needs of parents seem to be peculiar to our society and its democratic value system.

The teacher's role as preserver of culture A contrasting position is taken by many people who feel that the teacher's role is to transmit and preserve society's prevailing traditional attitudes and values. Teachers with this attitude tend to be more conservative than the "improvers." They recognize that our culture is changing rapidly, but they do not feel that they should promote change, and they are bothered by unconventional attitudes and behavior. These teachers feel that they have only a limited right to judge society and limited authority to try to change it. They too are caught in a conflict because our culture is full of contradictions, and this makes it difficult for them to identify what the prevailing attitudes are.

Other sources of role conflict in teachers Young, married teachers; those who teach in communities different from those in which they grew up; and those who do not have many friends or are dissatisfied with their school administration are more troubled by role conflicts than others. All teachers, however, must deal with some incompatible demands from various segments of the community and the school administration. Getzels (1963) listed a series of conflicts that existed for teachers about twenty years ago. A review of these conflicts shows them to exist for teachers of the 1980s as well.

1. *Conflict between cultural values and institutional expectations.* Parents expect schools to teach children to be studious, hard-working, and independent; however, our culture expects them to be sociable, popular, well-rounded, and considerate.

2. *Conflict between role expectation and personality.* An authoritarian teacher may find himself or herself in a school where the principal promotes permissiveness, and vice versa. A teacher who sacrifices his or her own preferences in order to conform to others' expectations will resent this situation; one who tries to fulfill his or her own needs and ignores the community's and administration's wishes will be looked on as inefficient and ineffective.

3. *Disagreement on role expectations among different reference groups.* The school principal expects the teacher to cover the prescribed curriculum in the time allowed; the parents expect him or her to appreciate the uniqueness of each child and give individualized instruction.

4. *Conflict caused by inconsistent role expectations.* A teacher may have his or her professional judgment challenged and have to submit to the decisions of people who do not have comparable training or experience. Teachers are expected to be good citizens, yet they are not allowed to be outspoken about their political activities or participation in controversial social movements.

What should the new teacher do? There is no simple answer to this question. A teacher may choose to be a "preserver," an "improver," or both. Whatever role he or she chooses, however, the successful teacher will be primarily concerned with what students should be learning, how it should be taught, and how it should be tested. According to Carl Rogers (1971), teachers can help students learn by showing a concern for what subjects interest students and by creating a psychological climate in the classroom in which learning is enjoyable. "Preserver" or "improver"? The right approach might lie in striking a balance. Teachers should have some control over what subject matter is taught, but they have an equal responsibility to make learning stimulating and exciting for the learner. They must consider the needs and values of students in their classes, but at the same time give weight to those of the school administration and the community.

The Teacher's Effect on Classroom Achievement

Teachers strongly influence their students' self-concepts as well as their academic achievement. Teachers, as significant others, are key variables in the self-concept formation of school children (Curtis and Altmann, 1977). Anxious, unhappy teachers tend to adversely affect their students' performance (Coates and Thoresen, 1976; Denno, 1977; White, 1975). Students can easily tell how a teacher regards them when they compare the way the teacher behaves toward them with the way he or she behaves toward their classmates.

Teachers' expectations of how well a student will perform have a considerable impact on academic performance. For example, Rosenthal and Jacobson's study (1966) showed that when teacher expectations were communicated to pupils the result was changed student behavior.

A teacher's predisposition will ultimately affect the way in which he or she reacts to students. This, in turn, will affect student achievement. A student who senses that the teacher has low expectations is more likely to perform poorly in class than a student who senses that the teacher has high expectations. Thus, a teacher's expectations are easily transformed into self-fulfilling prophecies. Murphy (1979) demonstrated the influence of self-fulfilling prophecies in a study of the effects of personality testing on children's independence. In Murphy's study, first and second graders were administered portions of a personality questionnaire purportedly measuring independence. Their teachers were given false test results of a few randomly selected children from each classroom. On a posttest personality questionnaire, those children whose teachers had been told that they were more independent (regardless of their true scores) scored considerably higher than those whose teachers were not given this information.

Teachers' attitudes toward students and expectations for success or failure are based in part on the sex of both teacher and student. Goebes and Shore (1975) showed that female teachers tended to rate the behavior of female students as closer to what they termed the "ideal student." Male teachers did not have such sex-linked attitudes.

Teacher expectations are not always logical. Often, as Harari and McDavid (1973) demonstrated, they are based on stereotypes and emotions. Harari and McDavid found that teachers were influenced in their grading of students by the students' names. Those students with more common names actually received higher grades than those with unusual names. Clearly, the teacher's important role in determining student achievement cannot be underestimated. Neither can the effect of parental attitudes.

The teacher's style of instruction also has a great influence on student performance. Domino (1971) found that college students who were taught by professors with teaching styles consistent with the students' achievement orientation—"conformity" (preservation) or "independence" (improvement)—learned significantly more and were more satisfied with the curriculum. It is crucial, then, that we understand how teachers develop their predispositions.

considering yourself as a teacher and as a human being

More than most citizens in this country, teachers come face to face with contemporary social issues such as sex and race biases, censorship, personal freedom, and so on. They must take stands on controversial issues that directly involve the school, such as busing and textbook censorship. Teachers who fight restrictions on personal freedom and student rights often come into conflict with school authorities and community leaders.

A major political issue in the 1970s that directly affected teachers and students was school desegregation and busing. In 1972, at a public expense of $1.5 billion a year, approximately 20 million children (43 percent of the total public school enrollment) were bused to school in order to facilitate racial desegregation (Pettigrew, 1973). The primary purpose of busing was to counteract the educational inequalities in overcrowded inner-city schools. Experimental busing programs in several Northern cities showed that minority-group children who were bused to integrated schools made significant academic gains, while white middle-class children who were bused to integrated schools performed as well as, or better than, those who remained in segregated white schools (Green, Smith, and Schweitzer, 1972). Furthermore, research showed that people who attended integrated schools as children had far more positive racial attitudes than those who grew up racially isolated (Green, Smith, and Schweitzer, 1972).

School Desegregation and Busing

Despite these advantages of busing, a strong antibusing movement arose in the early 1970s. This movement expressed deeply rooted racial prejudice as well as persistent doubts about maintaining educational quality in the public schools. The issue has become so controversial that the Supreme Court (in *Swann* v. *Charlotte-Mecklenburg Board of Education*) had to uphold federal court rulings and declare busing constitutional for the purposes of dismantling dual school systems (Harvey and Holmes, 1972).

However, the Supreme Court's *Swann* decision did not provide clear guidelines for desegregating schools in the cities and the suburbs. As the 1970s progressed, more and more white students and their families fled to the suburbs. Suburbs generally have their own school districts, and busing regulations that apply to city schools do not apply there. Many white students were enrolled in private schools to avoid busing and, in some cases, to escape the increasing violence of the public schools. The result today is that, despite busing, inner-city schools continue to be predominantly black and those in the suburbs almost all white. In 1980, in some major cities both black and white parents were still voicing their disapproval of busing and desegregation plans, requesting in many cases "better schools instead of desegregated schools."

Why has there been so much trouble for so little gain? For various reasons, it has been much more difficult to desegregate schools in the North than in the South. The dual school systems in the South were the result of specific state laws (de jure segregation) that are now unconstitutional. When the laws were gone, the basis for segregation was gone too. The dual systems in the North, on the other hand, were the result of segregated residential patterns (de facto segregation). Thus, to achieve integration in the North, people would actually have to be moved. As a result, the courts have been able to force integration while limiting the need for busing in the South much more

Four years ago, the all-black elementary school was ready to shut down. Situated across the street from Milwaukee's Schlitz brewery, the shabby building suffered from decades of neglect, and enrollment had steadily slumped. But today the Golda Meir School draws youngsters from 90 city schools—and 400 students are crammed on its waiting list. It has become a new magnet school, designed to attract gifted children. Two-thirds of the students take piano or violin lessons. Recess activities range from chess to science projects, and local celebrities are invited to chat with youngsters over lunch. And these days, Golda Meir is over 50 per cent white.

Golda Meir offers one of two thousand magnet programs springing up in elementary and secondary schools across the nation. As separate specialty schools or "schools-within-schools," magnets try to stimulate voluntary desegregation—and improve the quality of inner-city schools, They offer wide—sometimes dazzling—educational benefits, and admit students on the basis of racial quotas. Their success varies. "In most cases, magnet schools cannot stand alone as desegregation tools," says U. S. education official David Lerch. But they can complement busing. And by giving parents a choice in selecting schools, they blunt hostility to court-ordered integration.

Lure: In elementary schools, the most popular magnet programs are aimed at talented kids. The lure may be one course, such as Chinese or German, or an impressive array of electives. In Houston, for example, black, white, and Hispanic youngsters may qualify for Wainwright School's early-morning math-science program. At 7:30, students arrive from all over the city and bustle into a special magnet wing. Every three weeks, they select a new thematic course—from sharks to stamps—out of a table of 64 electives. Wainwright stresses active participation: to study astronomy, youngsters talk to scientists at the local museums; to get a feel for the workplace, they hear craftsmen describe their trade in class. Basic academics aren't shortchanged; the students join regular classes later in the morning.

Many high-school magnets provide high-powered curricula, but the most popular programs concentrate on vocational skills to help graduates get good jobs. In San Francisco and Pittsburgh, schools and companies have teamed to teach secretarial, computer, and accounting skills. Students go to magnets to become cops, nurses, actors—or to pick up early ROTC training with an eye to a military career. Boston's four-year-old Umana School, assisted by experts from Logan airport and the Massachusetts Institute of Technology, specializes in aviation. Says Charles Glenn, the state Equal Educational Opportunity director: "A magnet school should create a program that will benefit all students. Those who become aerospace engineers and those who become baggage handlers ought to take courses together."

Many cities have even used magnet schools to found old-fashioned academies. "They are much like the schools that parents remember," says Pittsburgh assistant superintendent Helen Faison. Pittsburgh requires academy students at all grade levels to sign a contract to abide by school rules and meet stiff academic obligations. If a student skips homework, dresses sloppily, cuts classes or smokes on campus, he gets demerits. Too many demerits mean expulsion from the academy.

While magnets often work wonders, their impact in desegregation is limited. Milwaukee's twenty specialty schools have contributed to racial balance—70 percent of its entire system has integrated in the last four years—but integration really depends on citywide busing to succeed. "Boston's magnets have prospered because of a desegregation mandate from the courts," says MIT Prof. Stanley Russell, a consultant for Umana. Magnet schools draw less than 10 per cent of the students in most cities—and the white exodus to suburban and private schools continues to gain momentum. Los Angeles decided last month to halt eleven of 54 magnet programs because they could not attract enough white students.

Critics argue that magnet programs may create more problems than cures. Hoping to avoid court-ordered desegregation, some cities have tried to install magnets as a cosmetic subterfuge. Faculties in regular schools resent the magnets' smaller classes and superior equipment—and "schools-within-schools" sometimes spark civil wars among teachers. Even more troubling, some educators contend that selective specialty schools encourage a two-tiered educational system, skimming off top students and teachers who work in elite havens while the rest of the public schools decay. "Magnet schools benefit liberal whites and middle-class blacks, and what's left behind is the dregs," says EEO's Charles Glenn.

Support: But many parents think magnets are wonderful. Having more control over the education their children receive, they support them readily, and their enthusiasm rubs off on the kids. Black parents think magnet programs offer a better education for their children. White families don't feel trapped by mandatory busing. Consequently, hostility over desegregation is softened. "When I first heard about busing, I had visions of blacks molesting my child," says Milwaukee's Pat Luckert, whose daughter attends Golda Meir. "But magnet schools have diminished my prejudices and my child doesn't look at color."

Magnet schools may some day exert a stronger pull on the middle-class whites who still shun them. But the hope that such voluntary desegregation programs will soon replace forced busing remains highly unlikely. The magnets' most valuable contribution so far has been to offer parents and children something more than mediocrity at the end of the bus ride to the inner-city school. That is less than magnet-school advocates used to claim. Yet it is also much more than the descent into hell that white parents expect their children to face when kids leave their neighborhood schools.

Newsweek, January 7, 1980, p 68. Copyright 1980 by Newsweek, Inc. All rights reserved. Reprinted by permission.

than in the North (Sinowitz, 1973). Desegregation orders have not been easy to enforce in Northern cities. In fact, in 1980, the Supreme Court was still intervening to force many communities to cooperate.

School boards in Northern cities have attempted a variety of solutions to the problem. Some of these plans have been successful. For example, in one urban area, white children were bused to predominantly black schools, while at the same time black children were bused to predominantly white schools—using both state and local financial support for the program. Children were bused only to schools whose facilities and instruction were considered at least as good as (and preferably superior to) those of the neighborhood schools they would have attended without busing. Even programs like this are not always accepted favorably, as demonstrated by the tension over the introduction of busing in Boston in the mid-1970s.

At the end of the 1970s, a new approach was being taken. Instead of trying to bus children across city areas to schools offering curricula similar to what the children could get in their own neighborhoods, school administrators began to establish what came to be known as **magnet schools**—schools that could attract students voluntarily on the basis of their unique curricular offerings. The enrollment of these magnet schools was supposed to match the city population by race, but, in fact, they tended to offer different opportunities for black and white students. In Pittsburgh, for example, a brand new middle school, Florence Reizenstein School, was developed as a magnet school. A unique scholar's program, designed for the school, provided gifted children with special classes and an opportunity to go to one of the "best" high schools in the city when they graduated Reizenstein. However, because the school board restricted the number of black children entering the school in order to "maintain a racial balance," many black children who wanted to enroll were not allowed to do so. The program resulted in many difficulties. An increase in violence in the school, destruction of property, and graffiti on the walls served as mute evidence of the problems that lay inside. By the middle of 1978, Jerry Olsen, the Superintendent of Schools in Pittsburgh, reported, "I am out of ideas; only a court order will desegregate the school system" (*Pittsburgh Press,* June 9, 1978).

As the 1980s approached, court orders were indeed used to increase the speed of desegregation. Attitudes toward the different solutions to the problem today vary widely, depending on the community. Teachers get caught up in the controversy but are relatively powerless to do much about the ensuing ill effects on students without taking strong stands as "improvers" of society.

Mainstreaming   Another controversy that today's teachers are getting caught up in is mainstreaming. Mainstreaming is based on the assumption that handicapped and normal children both benefit from being assigned to the same classes. Critics of mainstreaming, however, worry that neither group of children will receive as good an education as if they had been placed in entirely separate, specialized programs. Public Law 94-142 has mandated mainstreaming whenever possible in regular public classrooms, so educators who do not support it must learn to live with it anyway as long as they want the advantage of federal funding.

In the 1980s a great deal of effort and money will be expended by school districts and the federal government in an attempt to make mainstreaming work. It isn't clear how much of this extra help will go to the teachers responsible for making it work. Although teachers are caught up in the controversy, they are relatively powerless to do very much about mainstreaming's effects on students without taking strong stands as "improvers" of society.

Censorship

Two examples of censorship and community action illustrate how a teacher's activities can be limited. The first involved a massive protest in 1974 by families in an isolated coal-mining section of Kanawha Valley, West Virginia. They insisted that $400,000 worth of English textbooks be removed from the local school on the grounds that the books were un-American, anti-Christian, and obscene. Hundreds of students boycotted classes, and many people were arrested during the controversy. The Board of Education finally restored the books with the provision that any student who found them objectionable would not be required to read them. Despite the concession, boycotting and violence continued (Franklin, 1974; "Those Books Are Restored in West Virginia," *New York Times*, November 10, 1974).

   The second case involved a new ninth-grade textbook on Mississippi history that the State Textbook Purchasing Board rejected, allegedly because of the amount of attention it gave to the black experience. The book was intended to replace an earlier segregationist textbook that ignored the civil rights movement and black contributions in Mississippi. School districts were eventually permitted to use the new book, but they had to use their own money, not state funds, to buy it ("Bias Charged in Book Rejection," *New York Times*, November 10, 1974). As a result, a revised version of the old book, which mentions only 13 blacks and 365 whites, was readopted.

   Such decisions by school boards ultimately affect what teachers and students do in the classroom. Teachers, acting in their roles as citizens, must take a stand on such issues. But the way they act in their roles as teachers will depend on whether they consider themselves "preservers" or "improvers."

*Sex Bias
in the Schools*

The issue of sex bias has affected many areas of American life, including education. Laws eliminating racial segregation in education have been followed by laws against sex bias as well. The Equal Pay Act of 1963 (an amendment to the Fair Labor Standards Act) requires equal pay for equal work. The Civil Rights Act of 1964 (amended in 1972 to include teachers) under Title VII has enabled teachers to sue school districts and institutions for sexual discrimination in hiring. Title IX of the Higher Education Act of 1972 prohibits educational institutions from engaging in sexual discrimination in educational programs and activities. Title IX of the Education Amendment of 1972 and the proposed Equal Rights Amendment both begin by providing specific guidelines for eliminating sex bias in schools.

Feminists and child-development specialists have called attention to the many ways in which schools perpetuate stereotyped sex-role expectations for boys and girls. For example, teachers pay more attention—both positive and negative—to boys than to girls and are more concerned with boys' social adjustment (Levy, 1972). Teachers also tend to expect boys to excel in math and science and girls to excel in English. Although most schools are gradually changing their curricula to include both males and females in all classes, some schools today still have sex-segregated classes and activities such as physical education, home economics, shop, and so on.

In the early 1970s, a special task force of the National Organization for Women (NOW) conducted a two-year study of sex stereotyping in children's textbooks. They found that males were in 69 percent of these books' illustrations, while females appeared in only 31 percent. The illustrations frequently depicted boys as strong, brave, and competitive and girls as small, fearful, and helpless. The stories in these textbooks gave a much greater range of activities to boys than to girls, who were invariably portrayed as passive observers. Boy-centered stories outnumbered girl-centered stories by a ratio of 5 to 2, and adult male characters outnumbered adult females by a ratio of 3 to 1 (Jacobs and Eaton, 1972). The National Education Association (NEA) has recommended that all instructional material should provide a positive self-image for every student, regardless of sex or race, and should avoid suggesting that one group is inferior or superior to another (Dorros and Browne, 1973; Wise, 1974). Although texts are expected to change as publishers are pressured to decrease sex stereotyping, this change is coming slowly.

The importance of the results of these studies is twofold. First, students are strongly affected by teacher expectations. Sex bias is another subtle influence on those expectations. Even teachers who try to avoid bias on the basis of race or social class may unwittingly display sex bias toward their students. Second, the female teacher herself is often a victim of sex bias. In education, as in many other occupations, women hold fewer administrative jobs than men and often earn less pay for an equal amount of work. In the early 1970s, 85 percent of elementary teachers were women, while 79 percent of elementary school principals were men (Levy, 1972). These figures did not change very much in the past decade.

What effects does this have on classroom teachers? Since teachers serve as models for students, a female teacher's situation becomes contradictory. Female teachers must teach students the importance of equality, yet they themselves are often proof that equality is not always realized.

For years union activity and federal legislation have been aimed at equalizing women's pay and reducing sex discrimination. In spite of the gradual advances, female teachers are still faced with sex bias in the behavior of their male colleagues and even in their own attitudes. School counselors who adopt the "preserver" role still steer female students into homemaking or traditionally feminine occupations. Many teachers claim to treat both sexes equally, but most teachers still want to see male students become dominant, independent, and assertive, while they expect female students to be submissive, emotional, and concerned with dating and their appearance. Teachers must attempt to change their own biased attitudes before sexism can be reduced in the schools. Prospective teachers can enroll in women's studies courses, join consciousness-raising discussion groups with their colleagues, and participate in workshops and in-service training programs.

Assertiveness training can be valuable for male teachers, too, but it is especially important for women to learn how to stick up for themselves in a constructive way. Hundreds of such courses have sprung up around the country in the 1970s at universities and counseling centers. Their proliferation attests to the wide demand for this kind of training. As one teacher explained ("Assignment Assertion," 1975). "Traditionally, women have been unassertive. They have played the roles men and society have given them rather than seeking their own" (p. 65). Often they are the victims of the "compassion trap—the need to serve others and provide tenderness and compassion at all times." Because women have been taught that speaking up on their own behalf is "pushy" and "unladylike," their wishes are frequently the last to be considered or, worse yet, are simply ignored: Mom has a few dollars she'd like to spend on herself, but daughter sees a blouse she absolutely must have, so Mom buys it. Junior has been home sick all day wearing Mom to a frazzle, and Dad calls to say that five of his friends are coming over after dinner to play cards. "Oh dear," says Mom—and puts up with it. What else can she do?

Plenty. Assertiveness can be learned and practiced like any other skill. Through hypothetical conflicts, students and teachers can learn such techniques as the "broken record"—a simple, repeated "no"—and "fogging"—saying "no" while generously agreeing with one's adversary. ("I agree with you absolutely that you need to have that blouse. But I'm not going to buy it.") If assertiveness classes and the NEA's recommendations have the desired effects, female teachers in the 1980s will be voicing their concerns more clearly and loudly. For true success, existing biases toward female teachers must be removed. As long as such bias exists—as long as most principals and administrators are men—teacher behavior and, in turn, students' attitudes, will be adversely affected.

Your Personal Freedoms as a Teacher

American teachers have never had the same personal freedom as other professionals. Ever since Socrates was forced to drink hemlock as punishment for "corrupting" the youth of Athens, teachers have been carefully watched, lest they place dangerous ideas in their students'

The issue of tenure is an important one in protecting the freedom of public school teachers. Tenure guarantees that a teacher cannot be fired on grounds other than inadequate performance on the job.

impressionable minds through their teaching or by example in their lives outside of school. Teachers' political activities, organization membership, sex lives, marital status, and recreational activities have always been the subject of public scrutiny. Furthermore, many school boards prefer that teachers play the role of "preservers" only, thereby forcing them to conform to community values and standards. The Supreme Court has held that school boards who fire nonconformist teachers often violate the due process clause of the Fourteenth Amendment as well as the First Amendment rights of freedom of association and privacy, especially if the teacher's conduct does not interfere with his or her ability in the classroom.

The case of *Pickering* v. *Board of Education* provides an interesting test of whether or not a teacher's atypical behavior interferes with school operations or classroom performance. Mr. Pickering was dismissed by the community school board for writing a long, sarcastic letter to the local newspaper criticizing the way the board raised and allocated funds. The board claimed not only that Pickering's accusations were false, but also that they were "detrimental to the efficient operation and administration of the schools of the district" (Schimmel, 1972, p. 258). The Supreme Court ruled in Pickering's favor. The Court maintained that his criticism was not part of a personal crusade, but simply amounted to a difference of opinion that had no effect on Pickering's ability as a teacher. The Court concluded that "a teacher's exercise of his right to speak on issues of public importance may not furnish the basis for his dismissal" (Schimmel, 1972, p. 259).

The American Federation of Teachers (AFT) holds that teachers as professionals have unconditional freedom of speech in the classroom. The AFT takes the position that teachers as citizens have the same constitutional rights and freedoms as any other American citizen (AFT, 1977).

Students are beginning to gain personal freedoms that they did not have before. Today federal law gives college students and parents of elementary and high school students full access to their school records (Fields, 1974). This law was partially based on the premise that students have a right to know what their records say, since school authorities use that information to make important decisions about them throughout their school careers and afterwards. The fact that this right has now been made law will undoubtedly affect teacher behavior. Confidential information must now be stated very carefully so that it does not imply something other than the truth. Teachers must be prepared to justify every judgment to people who may be less competent to interpret test scores, medical diagnoses, and psychiatric evaluations, and who may be hostile as well.

Your Students' Personal Freedoms

Students also have gained the right to practice their religion anywhere they wish, including school, but the school does not have the right to force religion on any student. The Supreme Court ruled in 1962 that all laws requiring religious practices in the schools were unconstitutional because they violated the First Amendment provision that the government must maintain strict separation between church and state (Pancopf, 1974).

Understanding what other teachers have voiced as their most serious concerns in the classroom can be of help to the new teacher. According to one NEA research specialist, teachers most frequently list bad working conditions as their primary dissatisfaction with teaching. The most common complaint in the early 1970s was overcrowded classes ("Finding Out," 1972). Today, although enrollment has decreased, many schools have lost teachers and classes are still crowded. Overcrowded classrooms, with all the attendant management problems, reduce teaching efficiency and optimum learning. An uncrowded classroom provides a relaxed environment, increases attentiveness and participation, allows more individual instruction, and reduces discipline problems.

Understanding the Major Dissatisfactions of Being a Teacher

Overcrowded classrooms are largely caused by the spiraling costs of education. Shortages of funds have produced layoffs, cut out special programs and services, and canceled proposed innovations and improvements. These economic measures have compromised the quality of education and reduced teachers' salaries and fringe benefits. Although the unionization movement has helped to combat salary reductions, teachers often still have grounds to complain about salaries.

Maternity leave policies have aroused as much concern as salaries. Many school districts have traditionally forced pregnant teachers to take a leave of absence or resign from the school system upon reaching a certain stage in pregnancy. However, the courts declared forced maternity leave unconstitutional in 1971, having decided that it was arbitrary, discriminatory, and violated the Fourteenth Amendment. Title VII of the Civil Rights Act of 1964 also protects pregnant teachers and grants them the same benefits, including sick leave pay, that apply to any other "temporary disability." A pregnant teacher can now continue working as close to the end of her pregnancy as she chooses, providing she can fulfill her duties in the classroom.

According to nationwide surveys conducted by the NEA in 1968 and 1972, many teachers felt left out of school policy making. In the 1972 survey, 52 percent of the respondents wanted more say in the selection of school principals; and between 40 and 50 percent wanted more influence in teacher evaluation procedures, salaries, fringe benefits, curriculum and school calendar planning, textbook selection, and student discipline.

Another very common complaint involves the accountability of teachers, who, while being held accountable to themselves and their students, are at the same time under continual pressure to conform to community standards and expectations. These dual demands of accountability reflect the conflicting roles of the teacher that we discussed earlier in this chapter. Certainly, the teacher should be entitled to freedom of expression, but, as the Supreme Court pointed out, this freedom must not interfere with the teacher's ability to perform in the classroom. Certainly, teachers must be accountable for what students learn. If they are not, who should be? Accountability is an important and controversial issue for teachers today.

In 1974 the NEA conducted a survey among teachers to determine which problems they felt kept them from teaching more effectively. The following is a list of the problems they felt had considerable or some impact:

Considerable

Parents apathetic about their children's education*
Too many students indifferent to school*
Physical facilities limiting the kinds of student programs*
The wide range of student achievement
Working with too many students each day
Too many noninstructional duties
The values and attitudes of the current generation

Some

Diagnosing student learning problems
The lack of instructional materials
The quality of instructional materials
Disruption of classes by students
Little help with instruction-related problems from school administrators
The psychological climate of the school*

(Bartholomew, 1974, p. 79)

*These problems appear to affect secondary teachers more than elementary teachers.

Teachers today are quite articulate about how these problems can be solved. All over the United States teachers are concerned with their working conditions, their personal freedom, and their salaries, and they are insisting more and more frequently that their grievances be discussed at the bargaining table.

the impact of unionization on the teaching profession

While there has been considerable controversy over the role of teachers' unions, unionization is now a well-established part of our educational system. It affects not only elementary and secondary schools but community colleges and universities as well.

One large and powerful national teachers' union is the American Federation of Teachers (AFT), an affiliate of the AFL-CIO; its members include preschool, elementary, secondary, and college teachers from all parts of the United States. The union does not accept administrators, superintendents, principals, or anyone else who has the power to hire, fire, or discipline a teacher.

The AFT's aim is to improve the status and welfare of teachers and to provide better educational opportunities for students. Some of its specific goals include:

1. A salary schedule that provides adequate pay differentials based on training and experience. (However, the AFT is opposed to merit pay.
2. Adequate state tenure laws that protect teachers from being discharged without demonstrable cause after a reasonable probationary period.
3. Improved pension plans, sick leave pay, and other benefits.
4. Programs to reduce class size.

Collective Bargaining

The unionization movement was built on the belief that unions can accomplish more than an individual acting alone because they are able to use collective bargaining. **Collective bargaining** is a process by which wages, hours, and conditions of employment are determined by a joint committee of union workers' representatives and the employer, rather than simply imposed on the workers without their consent. Representatives of both sides present their respective proposals and discuss and negotiate terms. Meetings continue until they are able to draw up a mutually agreeable contract. When an impasse occurs, with either or both parties refusing to compromise, it can be handled by mediation, fact finding, arbitration, and—as a last resort—a strike. Collective bargaining does not prevent teachers, or any other unionized workers, from taking up their grievances with their employers directly.

Union contracts, made possible by collective bargaining, now set

Collective bargaining has provided teachers with the opportunity to improve their working conditions. Teacher unions have become a major factor in politics today.

teachers' salaries and are also a means of redressing grievances and conferring recognition. Many teachers attribute reduced class loads, more adequate staffing, and a larger say for teachers in determining school policy to collective bargaining.

Collective bargaining operates at the state and local levels as well as the national level; it is legally sanctioned for teachers in most states but is used more often in large cities.

Strikes The legal and ethical questions involved in the increasing numbers of teachers' strikes in recent years have been heavily debated (Hetenyi, 1978). Regardless of their controversiality, strikes are today a major economic force in the United States. Ultimately they affect the teacher's ability to teach and, therefore, the student's opportunity to learn. The major issue in teachers' strikes is usually salary. Other issues have included class size and teacher involvement in school policy decisions.

Whether or not to strike poses a new dilemma for teachers. Some teachers, as citizens, believe that no public employee should strike. Such teachers may privately feel that too many innocent people are hurt when firemen, policemen, garbagemen, and teachers strike. Teachers who accept any exploited group's right to bargain for better treatment may still feel a conflict between their natural desire to provide a better life for themselves and their families and their professional commitment to their students. As teachers' strikes become more commonplace in our larger cities, more and more teachers will have to find an answer to this dilemma.

your role as a leader of young people

Effective leadership—knowing how to guide and help students to acquire the skills, knowledge, attitudes, and values necessary for appropriate adjustment to society—is not easy to develop. We first discuss some factors that contribute to effective leadership in teachers, then some serious problems that prevent teachers from acting in the best interests of their students, and, finally, some solutions to these problems.

The Factors Needed for Effective Leadership

Some teachers have an attractive, pleasant, friendly manner that students cannot help but like. Others are overly strict, efficient, and brisk—they command respect, but students are less likely to appreciate them. The teacher's behavior determines students' behavior. According to one study, a teacher who is understanding, friendly, organized, businesslike, stimulating, and original will have alert, active, confident, responsible, self-controlled students (Ryans, 1960).

Teachers' classroom behavior also varies according to their views on how students learn. Teachers who believe in using positive reinforcement are generous with their praise. Other teachers believe that a quiet, orderly classroom and respect for authority promote learning; they tend to be strict and demanding, and some use punishment to maintain discipline. These views on learning determine the decisions teachers make in conducting their classes. For example, whenever a student asks a question, the teacher must decide whether that question is important enough to stop and answer. A teacher who repeatedly dismisses students' questions is likely to inhibit their curiosity. On the other hand, students may regard a teacher who stops to answer every question as disorganized and inefficient.

Cultural variables from the community, combined with the teacher's predispositions, may influence student behavior in particular situations. For instance, the effectiveness of a teacher's style will

Teachers' duties extend far beyond the end of the school day, and their influence reaches much farther than the grade book and the classroom.

sometimes depend on whether the school is located in a small, medium-sized, or large town. Mattsson (1974) found that introverted and reserved teachers were most successful in small towns, while extroverted and outgoing teachers were most successful in large towns.

Characteristics of Teachers Who Are Effective Leaders

According to Pearl (1972), the teacher who is a true leader shows the following characteristics:

1. *Appreciation for diversity.* A teacher should always be willing to hear new ideas and should therefore encourage full and open debate in the classroom.
2. *Willingness to be energetically accountable.* A teacher should be prepared to defend his or her beliefs when challenged.
3. *Willingness to negotiate honestly.* Conflicts are inevitable in any educational system, but they can be resolved beneficially if the teacher is willing to negotiate.
4. *Recognition that some conflicts are irreconcilable.* A teacher should be able to handle conflict intelligently and know how to prevent violence. When a conflict cannot be resolved, the teacher should not push for a pseudo-agreement, but should instead use common sense. If there is a serious conflict between student and teacher, the teacher might request to have the student transferred; if the conflict is between two students, the teacher should separate them.
5. *Ability to view rules in the context of ends.* Instead of being slaves to rules, teachers should be concerned with what is just and fair.

Problems Stemming from Poor Leadership

Teachers who have too little understanding of their students will never be good leaders. Teachers must be sensitive to their students' needs and feelings. All children—the bright and the not-so-bright, the well-behaved and the unruly—need regular support and encouragement. Criticism is important but becomes destructive if it is overdone. Children are notorious for their cruelty to one another: They tattle, insult, ridicule, and are capable of giving precise, malicious criticisms of each other. They can also be quite sensitive to one another, and the degree to which they are depends largely on the model set by teachers and the image they project.

Teachers who inadvertently reinforce competition will not be successful in their teaching roles. Although America is a competitive society, the teacher must guard against reinforcing competition that may be destructive. The teacher must be aware that each child seeks approval and attention from the teacher at the expense of other children. The following example shows a teacher whose actions reinforce competition.

> Boris had trouble reducing 12/16 to its lowest terms, and could get only as far as 6/8. Much excitement. Teacher asked him quietly if that was as far as he could reduce it. . . . Much heaving up and down from the other children, all frantic to correct him. Boris pretty unhappy. Teacher, patient, quiet, ignoring others, and concentrating with look and voice on Boris. She says, "Is there a bigger number than 2 you can divide into the two parts of the fraction?" . . . No response from Boris. She then turns to the class and says, "Well, who can tell Boris what the number is?" Forest of hands. (Henry, 1957, p. 123)

In this example, the teacher is reinforcing classroom competition at Boris's expense. It is crucial that the teacher realize the negative effects that classroom competition can have, especially on children like Boris.

Teachers who inadvertently reinforce docility may have polite and docile classrooms but may still fail in their roles as teachers. Many children quickly learn to hide their true feelings by putting on an act. The name of the game is "please the teacher by telling him or her what he or she wants to hear." Children easily find out what the teacher wants to hear by paying close attention to the kinds of answers the teacher has reinforced in the past. A highly competitive classroom atmosphere generates considerable anxiety. One way students cope with that anxiety involves getting the teacher's approval through docile, compliant behavior. Some teachers encourage this puppetlike behavior because it bolsters their own self-esteem, power, and importance.

The successful teacher does not often lose control of the classroom. Teachers often use positive reinforcement as a means of establishing their leadership in the classroom. The effectiveness of this procedure becomes diluted at times, however, particularly in a poorly established and designed open classroom. Unwanted student behavior is often the result of this uncertain social context, in which the teacher sometimes expects too much self-discipline of students and at other times ignores inappropriate behavior. Instead of specifying learning objectives, the teacher has a mistaken faith in the ability of students to totally direct their own learning.

It is very important to realize that the comparatively free atmosphere of the open classroom, in which the student is allowed to select the learning materials and specific behaviors through which he or she will learn specified skills, does not have to be incompatible with the teacher's maintaining control. A teacher in any kind of classroom can and must provide some structure to the learning situation. Teachers should help students to plan and evaluate their work and schedule their activities so that there is a realistic balance between self-direction and teacher guidance.

Many researchers have studied the contrasting effects of authoritarian and democratic leadership on students. "Authoritarian leadership" is a vague term that encompasses a wide range of behavior, not all of it harsh, brutal, or ineffective. A classic study by Lewin (1953) found less conflict and aggression and higher morale in groups with democratic leaders, but greater productivity in groups with authoritarian leaders. However, this increased productivity appeared when the teacher was present to oversee the work. Other researchers have not been able to find any clear-cut evidence that either style of teaching consistently produces high productivity or superior learning. Some investigators have suggested that authoritarian leadership is most effective for simple, concrete tasks, while democratic leadership is most effective for complex ones (Anderson, 1959). There are many problems with the research in this area. The most serious problem comes from many investigators' oversimplifying the two types of leadership. Neither extreme indicates how ordinary teachers behave in an everyday classroom.

Authoritarian leadership does tend to be harmful when a teacher fails to consider the class as a group. Students' superficial compliance toward this kind of teacher often masks their deep inner resistance. The group loses its cohesiveness, and the teacher becomes ineffective as a leader (Flanders and Havumaki, 1960).

Punitive leadership is ineffective in reaching its goal. The use of punishment, especially corporal punishment, is not effective in teaching. In fact, it is often detrimental. Child psychologists and educators are concerned over the continued use of punishment in the schools despite the mounting evidence against it. They feel that is produces long-term psychological damage.

Teachers and school administrators sometimes inflict punishment to an outrageous extent. The following is a child's statement of his own experience in the Dallas public schools:

> Oh, we get lots of licks. In one class, for every minute you're late, you get a lick. And in another class, a teacher took me down to the assistant principal to get some licks because I'd been chewing on my pen and there was ink on my mouth. The assistant principal, he used three paddles on me, and he broke two of them. (Hentoff, 1973, p. 20)

Continual punishment in school leads children to associate anxiety and hostility with learning. Moreover, although punishment may subdue a child temporarily, it does not produce any lasting positive change. Children may bury their aggressive and antisocial tendencies for a while, but they are likely to erupt later in more serious forms. Punishment also teaches the child that abusive behavior, such as nagging, criticizing, even the use of physical force, is a socially accepted way of solving problems. For these reasons, an NEA task force urged all teachers to end the practice of "inflicting pain on students, except for purposes of restraint, or protection of self or other students" (Hechinger and Hechinger, 1974, p. 84). Punishment remains widespread in American schools. The NEA task force reported that students and teachers have changed their attitudes toward corporal punishment very little over the last decade. A study by Kounin and Gump (1961) showed that children with punitive teachers tend to be preoccupied with aggression and are more inclined to misbehave. Children with nonpunitive teachers have greater trust and faith in the "rightness" of what their teacher tells them and are more concerned with the effects of misbehavior on learning and achievement.

Teachers can avoid many of these problems by getting to know each of their students' interests, concerns, and problems. One method is to have students evaluate themselves and discuss their problems openly. Whenever possible, the teacher should get to know something about a child's background and family through conferences with parents, or with parents and child together.

Becoming an Effective Leader

We have repeatedly emphasized the importance of using positive reinforcement whenever possible to shape student behavior, instead of punishment. Although teachers are aware of the value of tangible and intangible positive reinforcers in promoting desired behavior, many teachers forget to use them, particularly when they themselves are harried and pressured. A study by Byalick and Bersoff (1974) revealed that only 32 percent of the teachers in their sample actually used the forms of positive reinforcement they said they preferred. An earlier study by DeGroat and Thompson (1949) revealed that most teachers directed their approval and disapproval toward just a few students and gave little feedback of any kind to the majority.

Teachers need to be alert to the kinds of interactions that occur between themselves and their students. In most classrooms, the teacher initiates more interactions than the students do (Bellack and Antell, 1974). Most of these interactions consist of lecturing, instructing, and criticizing by the teacher (Flanders, 1970). According to one study, a "superior" teacher talks and directs less and encourages the students to participate more (Amidon and Giammatteo, 1965). One effective way of communicating with younger children and engaging their participation is to touch them (Dunaway, 1974). Warmth, kind words, friendliness, and helpfulness promote more active participation in older children (Cogan, 1958; Ryans, 1960).

The Flanders system of **interaction analysis** can help teachers to assess the patterns of interaction in their classes (Flanders, 1963; Kryspin and Feldhusen, 1974). Flanders has identified several categories of verbal communication in the classroom. Of these he distinguishes between **indirect teacher talk** and **direct teacher talk** and finds that indirect talk gives students a much wider range of responses and encourages participation to a greater degree than direct talk. Direct teacher talk consists mostly of explaining and informing, giving directions and comments, scolding and reprimanding, and defending authority. Although indirect techniques are clearly superior, many teachers continue to rely on direct techniques.

Flanders's categories of indirect teacher talk are

1. *Accepting Feeling:* Acknowledging and accepting a student's expression of emotion without making judgments about it.
Examples: "I understand how you feel." "We all feel that way sometimes."
2. *Praise and Encouragement:* Praise consists of statements like "That's right," "Fine," "Terrific." Encouragement, "Go on," "You've got the idea," "Tell me more."
3. *Accepting and Using Ideas:* Clarifying or elaborating an idea provided by a student.
Examples: "I see your point." "I think what Mary is trying to say is the following."
4. *Asking Questions:* A range of specific and broad open-ended questions such as "What is photosynthesis?" and "What is the relationship between force and work?" will promote greater student interaction. (Flanders, 1963, p. 255)

Students exposed to such positive behaviors do better scholastically and develop better attitudes toward learning (Amidon and Flanders, 1967; Flanders, 1970; Flanders and Simon, 1969; Kryspin and Feldhusen, 1974; Morrison, 1966).

Analysis of the kinds of talk taking place in the classroom can provide the teacher with valuable clues about his or her intentions and actual behavior and the means to reduce the discrepancies between them (Amidon and Flanders, 1967; Flanders, 1963, 1970). However, self-evaluation does not necessarily make the teacher a better instructor (Doyle and Redwine, 1974). No matter how much we talk about the teacher as a leader, we should also remember that the teacher as a human being is constantly being influenced by all the students in the class.

teacher accountability: how does it affect you?

In the 1970s, a new way of thinking about public education began to spread across the United States. School communities began to accept the idea of **teacher accountability:** that the teacher, not the student, is ultimately responsible for what and how much a student learns.

Several factors are responsible for this recent change in thinking. There is a growing body of knowledge that demonstrates how much we can change children's behavior through exciting and stimulating learning environments. The premise that all children have the ability to learn is partially responsible for bringing teacher accountability to the forefront. If all children have the ability to learn, then it is the teacher, not the student, who is responsible when learning does not occur. Thus, the community and the school board are increasingly apt to blame the teachers for what they call "deteriorated standards" (see, for example, *Education USA*, March 13, 1978). They suggest that high grades today are due to grade inflation rather than increased learning (Bromley, Crow, and Gibson, 1978).

The taxpayers' revolt that became famous in 1978 with the passing of Proposition 13 in California has also given impetus to the accountability movement. The public has become increasingly concerned with what local, state, and federal governments are doing with education funds. During the last ten years, the push to improve the quality of instruction has resulted in huge expenditures for educational "inputs," such as books, instructional techniques, in-service training programs, and other resources. With costs higher than ever before, the public is demanding proof that the "outputs"—objective results of improved learning based on such factors as standardized test scores and the number of students graduating from high school—are worth the expense.

Testing Minimal Compentency of Students and Teacher Accountability

The movement toward teacher accountability is related to the passing of laws in many states that require all students who graduate from high school to have minimal competency in certain basic skills. When large numbers of students failed during the first year these tests were administered, a tremendous hue and cry about the quality of teaching in our schools erupted.

Teachers found themselves besieged by an angry public demanding to know where their money was going and why so many students were failing. Minimal competency testing is a particularly serious problem to students who always fall at the bottom of the barrel and have been graduated more on the basis of their efforts than of their achievement. Teachers, pushed for years to develop "well-rounded individuals," are now being told to "go back to basics." But, while competency testing does provide evidence of inadequate learning, it doesn't answer the important question of why the students did not learn in the first place. The apparent answer—that our teachers aren't doing their jobs—unfairly ignores other influences on student performance such as home environment.

Of course, not everyone is unhappy with the idea of minimal competency requirements. Some states that have these new requirements report good results. For example, *Education USA* (May 29, 1978) reported that Oregon's new high school graduation requirements led to "healthy rethinking of curriculum" and "design of stronger course requirements." Critics disagree, although many admit that the examinations have given the diplomas granted in that state more credibility with the public.

Understanding
the Implications
of Teacher
Accountability

The accountability movement is causing many changes in the schools. Instead of judging a school's quality by its classrooms and equipment, the public now may judge it by its output in student achievement. Some school districts must justify their expenses by showing how much the students actually accomplish (Barro, 1970; Lessinger, 1970; Rosenshine and McGaw, 1972). Not only must schools be committed to providing equal educational opportunity for all children, now they must be committed to the idea that every student must learn something and be willing to experiment with many different programs to insure better student performance. Teachers are making greater use of learning objectives in their instruction and testing students more frequently to determine whether they have attained those objectives.

Accountability has become a very controversial issue, and there are many compelling arguments for and against it. Both sides need to be considered.

Arguments for accountability Those who favor accountability claim advantages such as:

1. Making teachers responsible to see that all students learn to the best of their abilities will be helpful to disadvantaged and minority-group students, who would have been allowed to fail under the traditional system.
2. Students will be highly motivated to learn because now they will be less likely to blame their difficulties on their lack of ability.
3. The emphasis on results will motivate teachers and students to keep trying new approaches until they find one that works.
4. School facilities will become more open, flexible, and oriented toward the individual instead of the group.
5. Testing will become more objective and rely more on proven ways to increase learning. Staff, facilities, and equipment will be used more efficiently.
6. Accountability will inform the public on what is happening in the schools to a greater degree and create closer ties between school and community.

Arguments against accountability Those who are against accountability claim that:

1. The idea of accountability is too simplistic. Parents and students should also be held accountable. Teachers have no control over what a student does outside school.

2. Accountability overemphasizes test scores. Teachers may simply "teach to test" and ignore other important aspects of a subject. Students may become so involved in getting good scores that they will ignore learning for its own sake.

3. Accountability reduces education to a series of inputs and outputs instead of treating it as a complex, dynamic process that involves individual needs and feelings. The new curriculum considers only the student's rate of learning and ignores individual differences in interest and ability.

4. Accountability prevents teachers from using their professional judgment in carrying out instruction programs by setting arbitrary, "inhumane" performance requirements.

5. Learning objectives set too narrow a limit on instruction when teachers are asked to make a list of objectives. The ones that find their way into the teaching plan are likely to be ones that are most easily measureable, not necessarily those that are the most important to learn.

6. Accountability is just an excuse to coerce teachers and slash education budgets.

The idea of accountability and the radical changes it implies raise difficult questions for which there are no clear answers. Who should be accountable to whom and under what conditions? Who should assess teacher competency and how should it be done? Who should receive the results of an evaluation? What effect should these results have on salary and tenure? Who is to blame if students fail tests because they haven't done their homework? Who is to blame if a highly recommended textbook fails to live up to expectations? According to a 1972 Gallup poll, many parents and educators feel that the teacher is not primarily to blame for educational failures. They feel that the cause is the child's home life.

If we grant, however, that teachers are partially accountable for what students learn, we must then decide which evaluating and rating procedures will yield the fairest and most accurate assessment. Table 13-1 provides a revealing comparison between teacher evaluations as they are and as they ought to be. We can see that evaluations fail to account for working conditions, parents' aspirations, and children's readiness to learn. Teachers with large classes or learning-disabled children might receive poorer ratings than they deserve if the evaluator ignores these considerations. Teachers who have no control over curriculum and teaching strategies are not necessarily accountable for performance results.

Who should evaluate a teacher's performance is another difficult question. In practice, many people—students, parents, other teachers, supervisors—informally evaluate a teacher on the basis of their own observations or hearsay, and they do this from a unique point of view that severely limits their ability to accurately assess a teacher's competence.

Table 13-1 A Comparison between Teacher Evaluations as They Usually Are and as They Should Be

THE WAY IT USUALLY IS	THE WAY IT OUGHT TO BE
Evaluation is threatening to teachers.	Evaluation should be something that teachers anticipate and want because it gives them insight into their own performance.
They see it as something that is done to them by someone else.	It should be something in which teachers have a part along with students, parents, and administrators.
It is used mostly for determining teacher status relative to dismissal, tenure, and promotion, even though instructional improvement is often advertised as its major purpose.	Evaluation should be used to diagnose teachers' performance so they can strengthen their weaknesses through in-service education.
Teachers often are unaware of the criteria used to judge them.	Teachers should take part in developing or selecting evaluation instruments so that they know the criteria against which they are judged.

B. H. McKenna, Teacher Evaluation, *Today's Education,* February 1973, p. 55.

Some feel that students are the best judges of a teacher's effectiveness because they are in daily contact with the teacher and are most affected by his or her abilities. Although students can readily say whether they find a teacher stimulating or boring, they cannot necessarily judge which teachers actually help them learn. Students are not in the best position to identify a teacher's weak areas or to suggest improvements in instructional methods. They are also biased by their own attitudes and by grades.

Wicks (1973) suggests voluntary self-appraisal and mutual appraisal with colleagues and supervisors; then having another person compare the two. The teacher should have some say about who this independent evaluator will be and about which instruments and criteria the evaluator will use. The teacher has a right to be fully informed of the evaluator's recommendations and to discuss and challenge them if necessary.

*Tenure and
Merit Pay*

If evaluation results show that some teachers are clearly more effective than others, should they be paid more? Should tenure laws be modified so that inadequate teachers can be dismissed?

State tenure laws now provide job security to most teachers by protecting them from arbitrary demotion and dismissal. School boards must abide by due process procedures and show sufficient cause before they can discharge a teacher. Many people consider these policies a breakthrough for education and teachers' rights. Others, especially school administrators who resent the loss of power and taxpayers who resent paying salaries to teachers they consider inadequate, would like to see them abandoned. The AFT and the NEA, who would like to see tenure provisions extended (Sinowitz, 1973b), point out that incompetent teachers are supposed to be screened out during their probationary periods, or during their formal training and student teaching.

Those against the tenure system would like to substitute merit pay in place of tenure. They argue that merit pay will attract better teachers and weed out the unqualified. Since other professions and businesses give merit increases, why shouldn't the schools?

The NEA and AFT are opposed to merit pay for several reasons. One is that ratings are a matter of personal judgment and bias on the part of the rater. Because teaching involves so many different capabilities, supervisors would be unable to agree on a precise dollar value for any one of them. Moreover, every teacher has both good and bad qualities (Fondy, 1973; Wilson, 1962). Merit pay might also produce competitiveness, suspicion, distrust, and resentment in an environment that should be based on mutual trust and cooperation. It might also ruin the relationship between teachers and supervisors by putting too much power in the hands of administrators.

*Accountability
to Oneself*

In the final analysis, teachers may be accountable to principals, school boards, communities, and students, but most of all they are accountable to themselves. Everyone would like to be a model teacher like Mr. Stock. Not all of us will reach that goal. However, those of us who enjoy what we are doing will have a better chance of reaching it than those who don't. Teachers who are dissatisfied with their role should analyze the causes to see if they can do something about them. If they cannot avoid certain problems, they must determine whether or not they can live with them. Teaching, like any other job, can be frustrating and unpleasant. A teacher who finds the job unpleasant nearly all the time should not be in the classroom.

Kuhlen (1963) has shown that when teachers believe that teaching satisfies their inner needs, they will always find it rewarding; if teaching does not, they are bound to find it unpleasant. Clearly, teachers who are personally satisfied with their work will be far more effective with their students than those who are not. Successful teaching and high-quality education, therefore, depend as much on self-accountability as on any other factor.

1. Teaching is a difficult job, even for successful teachers. Two problems teachers can easily avoid are inadequate grounding in subject matter and poor communications skills. Teachers' competence in basic verbal skills is becoming an object of public concern. Teachers also need to know their students and be able to apply psychological principles to classroom situations.

2. Teachers have to cope with many conflicting roles. The most basic dilemma teachers have to solve involves their roles as transmitters of culture. Some teachers must choose between being "preservers" or "improvers," while other teachers must learn to cope with school administrators who don't give them a choice.

3. Teachers have an important influence on children's developing self-concepts. Teachers' expectations can easily become self-fulfilling prophecies. Emotional biases, stereotypes, and even children's names can cause a teacher to respond differently to some of his or her students.

4. More than most citizens, teachers must face contemporary social issues that affect our schools such as sex and race bias, censorship, and personal freedom.

5. A major tool in the effort to desegregate American schools has been busing. Despite its advantages, busing has numerous critics. White flight to the suburbs has left many inner-city schools predominantly black, and many white and black parents are urging that efforts be directed toward improving all schools and away from busing. Busing is more of an issue in the North, where segregation was de facto rather than de jure. As an alternative to busing, some school districts have established magnet schools whose unique curricula and facilities are designed to attract students voluntarily. Magnet schools have received mixed reviews from educators and other professionals, but most parents and students like them.

6. Another current controversy involves mainstreaming. Not all educators agree that teaching normal and handicapped children together is a good idea, but, because Public Law 94-142 has made mainstreaming the rule instead of the exception, all teachers must expect to face this issue.

7. Teachers' activities can also be affected by community attempts to censor educational materials and subject matter. Teachers' attitudes as citizens and their chosen roles as teachers may come into conflict over community interference in the educational process.

8. Teachers have traditionally been given less personal freedom than other professionals. Restrictions have been placed on the way teachers live as well as teach. In *Pickering* v. *Board of Education,* however, the Supreme Court ruled that a teacher could not be fired if his or her nonconformist conduct did not interfere with his or her ability in the classroom.

9. Today, federal law gives college students and parents of elementary and high school students full access to their school records. Teachers must therefore be prepared to justify their judgments of students. Students

have also gained the right to practice their religion in school, though schools are not allowed to impose religion on the child.

10. Teachers' most frequently voiced complaints about teaching are bad working conditions and overcrowded classes. Teachers also complain about salaries and fringe benefits, particularly maternity leave policies. However, since the Supreme Court's 1971 decision that forced maternity leave was unconstitutional, pregnant teachers are now able to work as long as they can fulfill their classroom duties. Teachers also complain about being left out of school policy making. Accountability is another major source of discord and conflict.

11. Unionization is now a well-established part of our educational system. The American Federation of Teachers (AFT) is the major teachers' union. Unions are favored by those who feel that collective bargaining can accomplish more for teachers than individual negotiation. Teachers' strikes are increasingly common, but have legal and ethical problems. Teachers are particularly concerned about the damage that strikes do to their students.

12. Teachers' personalities and views of learning will influence they way they conduct their classes and how their students respond to them. Teachers who are effective leaders appreciate diversity, are energetically accountable, negotiate honestly, recognize that some conflicts are irreconcilable, and can view rules in the context of ends. They are also sensitive to their students' needs and feelings. Teachers must take care not to overdo criticism and not to reinforce competition among their students.

13. The comparative freedom of the open classroom is not necessarily incompatible with the teacher's maintenance of control. Teachers must structure all learning situations, though, in general, a democratic leadership style is more effective than authoritarianism. Punitive leadership is ineffective. Punishment makes children anxious and hostile and does not produce lasting changes in behavior. Punishment remains widespread in American schools despite research that indicates that it is generally harmful as well as ineffective.

14. Teachers can improve their abilities as leaders by getting to know their students individually, using positive reinforcement, and using indirect teacher talk more than direct teacher talk. Indirect teacher talk involves acknowledging students' feelings, giving praise and encouragement, accepting and using ideas, and asking questions instead of giving answers.

15. Teachers are increasingly being held accountable for what and how much their students learn. Communities and school boards are increasingly apt to blame teachers for declining student performance, particularly since the taxpayers' revolt that has made people more conscious of where their tax dollars go. A related development is the establishment of minimum competency standards for high school graduation. Competency testing does prove that students have or have not learned, but does not say why. The accountability movement is leading people to view schools

in terms of their students' achievement, rather than in terms of facilities and curricula.

16. Supporters of accountability say that it will ensure that minority children get a fairer shake, increase students' motivation, encourage the use of new teaching techniques, focus attention on the individual, make testing more objective and use of facilities more efficient, and encourage greater interaction between the school and the community.

17. Opponents of accountability say that teachers are bearing too much responsibility for students' failures; parents and the students themselves should also be held accountable. Overemphasis on test scores leads to "teaching to test" and learning to do well on a test, not learning for the sake of learning. Accountability oversimplifies the teaching process and prevents teachers from exercising their professional judgment. Learning objectives are apt to be selected for easy measurement, not for their importance in understanding the subject. Accountability has also been called an excuse to coerce teachers and slash education budgets.

18. The accountability movement has led to an increasing emphasis on teacher evaluation. It has been suggested that teachers who are rated highly should be paid more and that tenure laws should be changed to allow the dismissal of low-rated teachers. The NEA and the AFT want to see tenure protection extended and disapprove of merit pay. Administrators and taxpayers, on the other hand, generally favor merit pay and would like to see tenure laws repealed.

19. In the final analysis, teachers are accountable to themselves. Teachers who enjoy teaching will obviously be more successful than those who don't. Teachers who don't enjoy teaching do a disservice to their students as well as to themselves.

for students who want to read further

COATES, T. J., AND THORESEN, C. E. Teacher anxiety: A review with recommendations. *Review of Educational Research*, Spring 1976, 46 (2), 159-184. Coates and Thoresen's scholarly article provides a number of insights into ways that teachers' feelings affect those of their students. It also talks in some detail about research designed to determine what can be done about this phenomenon.

DENYER, B. Diary of a nonstriking teacher. *Learning*, August-September 1978, 7 (1), 152-154. Bill Denyer presents an antistrike position based on his belief that children whose teachers are striking are, in fact, being used as pawns in a game played between two groups of adults.

REILLY, W. Competency-based instruction: Pros and Cons. *American Education*, April 1978, 14 (3), 21-22. Wayne Reilly, education reporter from the Bangor, Maine, *Daily News*, spent a leave of absence as Ford Fellow in Educational Journalism observing competency-based instruction in a large number of cities throughout the country. His description of the advantages and disadvantages of the reforms in education related to competency is a useful one for teachers learning to deal with this procedure.

RUBIN, D. The rights of teachers. Washington, D. C.: *The American Civil Liberties Union*, 1972. This book outlines the legal rights of teachers. It also tells how teachers can investigate to determine whether any of their rights have been denied to them, and what they can do about it.

WINSOR, J. L. A's B's, but not C's? A comment. *Contemporary Education*, Winter 1977, 48 (2), 82-84. Winsor's brief commentary is interesting reading for teachers concerned with the dilemmas involved in grading students in meaningful ways and, at the same time, dealing with competency-based instruction.

ability grouping   the grouping of students in a particular grade into homogeneous classes based on IQ and reading achievement scores.

ability tests   tests of maximum performance, used to find out how well the person is capable of performing.

abstract concept   an idea that involves abstraction or symbols and that cannot be linked directly to observable objects or object qualities.

acceleration   a school program in which a gifted student can skip one or more grades and progress more rapidly through school.

accommodation   according to Piaget, a cognitive process that occurs when we add a new activity to what we already know, or modify an old behavior.

achievement motivation   a persistent attempt to achieve what is thought to be excellence.

achievement- or success-oriented   an enduring personality characteristic in which the individual is predisposed toward success and relatively unconcerned with failure.

achievement tests   tests of what has been learned in a school subject.

acquisition   the process of obtaining new information that can be used to either replace or refine something known previously, the first step in learning, according to Bruner.

adaptation   according to Piaget, the intellectual activity by which we can alter the ways we deal with the environment, either by changing ourselves (accommodation) or changing the environment (assimilation).

aggression   quarrelsome or attacking behavior that may be self-assertive, self-protective, or hostile to oneself or others.

alienation   withdrawal, diversion, or estrangement of emotional contact.

analysis   breaking down an entity into its component parts, a middle level in Bloom's taxonomy.

anomie   a subjective feeling of separation of oneself from societal norms.

anxiety   an internal fear response that has generalized from the original feared stimulus to many stimuli.

application   the ability to solve problems that are similar in principle, but different in form from those seen previously; a middle level in Bloom's taxonomy.

aptitude test   a special kind of ability test intended to predict success in a specific occupation or training course.

assimilation   part of the Piagetian process of adaptation. Assimilation occurs when new objects are treated in the same way familiar objects are treated.

associationism   a psychological theory that explains behavior in terms of stimulus and response, based on the premise that people naturally tend to associate their behavior with stimuli in the environment. Also known as the stimulus-response approach (SR).

asymptote   a straight line associated with a curve such that it approaches but never reaches another line.

attachment   a durable tie or affection oriented toward one particular person; observed in such behaviors as clinging, following, smiling, etc.

autism   a mental disorder characterized, among other attributes, by withdrawal from communication with others.

avoidance learning   a type of classical conditioning in which the subject learns to make a response after the presentation of a stimulus in order to avoid some unpleasant occurrence.

basic research   research conducted under controlled conditions for the purpose of answering basic questions that may or may not be applicable in applied situations.

behavior   a collection of stimulus-response associations, according to associationist theorists; a meaningful product of perceptual change due to interactions between the individual and his environment, according to the cognitive-field theorists.

behavior management the process of taking conscious and active control of the environment by rewarding desirable behavior and ignoring or punishing undesirable behavior.

behavior therapy behavior management designed to deal specifically with serious behavior problems.

behavioral objectives learning objectives for a course of study or a unit that are defined in terms of desired student behavioral outcome.

behaviorism or **behavioral psychology** the approach to studying learning that assumes that human behavior is real, objective, and practical, and that psychologists should study behavior as the means of understanding how learning takes place.

bilingual ability ability to communicate in more than one language with equal ease.

Bilingual Education Act an Act passed by Congress in 1968 that calls for the teaching of subject matters in both English and native language for students unfamiliar with standard English.

black English a dialect of English very different from the formal middle-class "standard English" of the schools.

branching programming routes each student individually, depending on his or her responses at preselected choice points.

Buckley Amendment law passed in 1974 that makes student files open to students or their parents, and that provides recourse to students whose teachers, counselors, or other school administrators might have evaluated student behavior in nonobjective ways.

capabilities the precise behaviors the teacher wants a student to master; the objectives of a lesson, according to Gagné.

chaining higher-order learning in which the subject learns to make a series of responses in a specified order before reinforcement occurs.

circular reactions Piaget's term for the repetitious actions performed by babies for the sake of the action, itself, or to observe the results of actions.

classical conditioning the procedure in which a subject learns to respond to a new stimulus by associating it with a stimulus that elicited the desired response automatically. In classical conditioning, the response occurs *after* a stimulus is presented.

classification the ability to sort according to some quality.

classroom management the process of taking active control of the classroom environment by rewarding desirable behavior and extinguishing or punishing undesirable behavior.

code emphasis in reading instruction children are taught to "sound out" what they are reading in their earliest reading instruction.

cognitive development the development of thought processes; a spontaneous process that occurs as a function of total development.

cognitive process the intellectual processes involved in thinking, understanding, and solving problems.

cognitive psychology the approach to psychology that emphasizes thought processes rather than behavior alone.

cognitive style style of learning developed early in life that pervades most learning situations.

collective bargaining a process by which organized groups of employees, acting through representatives, jointly determine with their employer conditions of employment.

compensatory education educational programs designed to prepare students who have not learned the prerequisite skills for satisfactory school learning.

competence motivation White's idea that an individual has an intrinsic need to deal effectively with the environment.

competency-based instruction a type of instruction that is geared toward achieving specific learning objectives.

comprehension the ability to identify or restate information in a form that is not an exact replica of the original; the second level of cognitive learning, according to Bloom's taxonomy.

computer-assisted instruction (CAI) the computer itself instructs the students and prescribes learning materials on an individual basis.

computer-managed instruction (CMI) the computer assists teachers and students in planning and record keeping, but does not instruct students.

concept an abstraction or idea that permits the learner to classify a variety of related phenomena into a convenient, meaningful category.

concrete concept an idea that can be linked to a class of observable objects.

concrete operations according to Piaget, the stage of cognitive development from about 7 to 11 years of age, at which a child has the ability to deal with concrete objects in a logical fashion.

conditioned response response in a classical or operant learning situation that is learned by association.

conditioned stimulus stimulus in a classical conditioning-learning situation, which, at the outset of learning, does not elicit the learned response.

consequence the term used in precision teaching for a reinforcer such as a gold star or being leader in the line.

conservation according to Piaget, the cognitive ability of children in the concrete operations stage to realize that an object remains constant or the same regardless of its changes in form.

construct validity the validity of a test, determined by correlating scores on that test with some other currently accepted criterion measure for that area.

content validity a measure of the representativeness of the sample of knowledge that the test is intended to measure.

contiguity the temporal (time) relationship between a stimulus and a response.

contingency contract an agreement arranged between students and teachers stipulating specific reinforcers for specified behaviors or levels of achievement.

continuous reinforcement reinforcement that follows every response and leads to a regular pattern of responding.

contract teaching agreements between groups offering instruction and schools needing such services. The group offering instruction is paid in proportion to student achievement on standarized tests.

control group the group that is compared with the experimental group but does not receive the treatment that the experimental group does.

cooperative planning a method of instruction used in some schools in which students cooperate in selecting the teaching method.

correlation a mathematical measure of the degree of relationship. Correlations do *not* indicate cause-and-effect relationships.

creativity the ability to solve new and different problems in new and innovative ways.

crisis intervention professional intervention at the moment of intensive upset and disruption.

criterion-referenced tests measures whether or not a student has mastered specified learning objectives. This type of testing does not tell the student how he did in relation to other students.

culture-fair tests tests designed to ask questions that do not discriminate against any particular culture or subculture.

cybernetic theories a group of theories that compare the functioning of the human brain with similar processes in a computer.

deductive method of teaching this method involves presenting concepts by verbal definition and description.

defensive identification identification through which

individuals internalize the prohibitions of a model figure.

delayed reinforcement reinforcement that occurs after a period of time has elapsed since the behavior was exhibited.

dependency behaviors that seek help, attention, and approval from others.

depression a problem behavior related to anxiety. Clinical symptoms include psychomotor retardation, sadness, hopelessness, and suicidal ideas or threats.

deschooling Illich's idea to eliminate the need for schools, placing learning in the community through individual interactions.

developmental psychologist psychologist whose research interests involve the changes that take place in individuals as they increase in chronological age.

developmental-stage theories theories of development that characterize the various stages through which humans go as they increase in age. Stage theorists are observational researchers who study what people do under "normal" circumstances, rather than manipulate the environment to change behavior.

developmental task term used by Havighurst to describe the age-related, culture-bound activities a person must learn for successful adjustment.

deviation IQ the type of IQ score currently used on the Stanford-Binet and Wechsler tests. The deviation IQ score is determined by comparing the individual's raw score with those raw scores of people from the standardization sample who are of the same chronological age.

diagnostic teaching teaching based on testing in which teachers first determine the skills students need to know but have not yet learned, and then design the curriculum to teach these skills.

diagnostic testing testing used for diagnostic purposes rather than for grading.

differentiation the process of responding differently to two or more similar stimuli. Differentiation is a fundamental aspect of perceptual learning, according to E. J. Gibson.

direct teacher talk the category in Flanders's interaction analysis that includes explaining information, giving directions, and scolding.

directive counseling counseling in which the trained professional directs the therapeutic process.

discipline control of behavior through training.

discovery teaching a teaching method endorsed by Bruner that requires rearranging the subject matter structure so that the learner is able to go beyond the evidence presented to newly gained insights.

discrimination the process of learning whereby an individual responds in a certain way to one set of circumstances and in a different way to another, similar set of circumstances. Discrimination occurs when two or more stimuli are responded to differently.

distributive justice Piaget's term for older children's way of deciding rewards and punishments on the basis of fairness of treatment.

drive the internal state or compulsion that generates activity. Drive is inferred from measurable circumstances.

drive reduction the reduction of drive strength as measured by the amount of energized activity.

drive strength the amount of energized behavior or the measure of a drive.

dyslexia a type of learning disability characterized by language difficulties, particularly in reading.

economy the amount of information a person must learn and remember in order to understand a subject. The larger the amount, the less the economy. Bruner uses the term in relation to the structure of a subject.

educable mentally retarded the least severe level of mental retardation; the educable mentally retarded are capable of learning skills necessary to hold relatively simple jobs.

educational television (ETV) programs on noncommercial TV channels that the Federal Communications Commission has specifically allocated for educational purpose.

efficacy White's term for competence. The goal of such behavior is getting to know what the environment is all about.

egocentric speech according to Piaget, an early form of speech seemingly intended to serve one's own purposes rather than to communicate information to others.

egocentrism the inability of a child to see viewpoints (either in perception or in conception) other than his own, according to Piaget.

enactive mode according to Bruner, the most basic way of representing the environment. The enactive mode is a set of actions appropriate for achieving a certain result.

encoding the process that enables people to reduce or abbreviate the amount of information stored in the brain (or in a computer) for a particular item.

enculturation the process by which an individual learns the traditional content of a culture and assimilates its practices and values (also referred to as socialization).

enrichment programs programs that allow gifted children to remain in regular classrooms but still receive the extra stimulation and challenge they need to learn to the best of their abilities.

environmental approaches to development approaches taken by researchers concerned primarily with manipulating the environment and studying the effects on development.

epilepsy a neurological disorder characterized by grand mal and petit mal seizures. During a grand mal seizure the person loses consciousness, twitches convulsively, and may even lapse into a coma. Petit mal seizures are less severe and may cause the individual to lose motor control temporarily.

equilibration the transforming process in Piaget's cognitive developmental theory which goes from simple to more complex conceptual thinking.

equilibrium the balance between assimilation and accommodation as a function of a person's level of cognitive development, according to Piaget.

essay test requires the student to organize material and write the answer in a sentence form. This test is graded more subjectively than other types of tests.

evaluation (1) indication of whether or not a person's work meets the specified criterion, or a comparison with someone else's work. (2) Ability to evaluate is the most complex type of learning, according to Bloom's taxonomy, and the final step of the learning process, according to Bruner. (3) Evaluation is the process of checking whether the acquired information has been manipulated appropriately.

"exchange games" the language interactions that take place between children and their care-givers, and that Jerome Bruner suggests are significant for first mastery of the language.

exploratory drive the intrinsic human need to explore whatever is novel or unfamiliar, according to Berlyne.

extended family a household unit consisting of parents, children, and close relatives living together.

extinction the process in operant conditioning in which a nonreinforced behavior will gradually occur less and less frequently and eventually return to the rate of occurrence before conditioning was first begun.

extrinsic motivation doing something for the sole purpose of an external reward without any inherent reinforcement.

fading the representation of items in the memory, called traces, gradually fade with time and forgetting occurs.

failure-oriented an enduring personality characteristic in which the individual is concerned more with possible failures than with successes.

feedback knowledge of the correctness of one's responses.

field dependence inability to discriminate between figure and ground; that is, to isolate items from a surrounding context.

field independence ability to make fine discriminations and to isolate items from a surrounding context.

figure-ground perception according to Gestalt psychologists, perception of an object (figure) as clearly standing out from its background (ground).

fixation a condition in which learners cling to incorrect assumptions and are unable to perceive the essential elements required for problem solving.

fixed schedule of reinforcement reinforcement is given according to a consistent and set pattern. Both interval and ratio schedules may be fixed schedules.

Follow-Through education program designed to "follow through" on early intervention programs, and to insure that required educational support is continued.

foreign hull the term Lewin used to describe those things in a person's external environment that do not affect his or her behavior.

forgetting inability to retain information after learning has taken place.

formal operations Piaget's last stage to cognitive development, which is characterized by the ability to use formal or abstract logic and reason through the use of hypotheses.

formative evaluation a type of evaluation used to improve instruction or to diagnose student weaknesses while the course is being taught.

"free" schools alternative schools, often staffed both by teachers and community volunteers, designed for students who cannot learn in the traditional program.

functional invariants intellectual functions, such as organization and adaptation, that do not change with development, according to Piaget's theory of intelligence.

future shock the internal force, described by Alvin Toffler, that compels us to act out new roles and confronts us with the dangers of a new and powerfully upsetting disease; due to economic, sexual, racial, youth, and technological revolutions which, Toffler suggests, we are experiencing simultaneously.

generalization the process in learning whereby an individual responds in an identical way to two or more separate stimuli. Generalization also occurs when a particular stimulus evokes responses that are similar or related to the desired response. (See also **stimulus generalization** and **response generalization**.)

generative grammar rules and principles governing the relationships between sound and meaning.

Gestalt psychology school of psychology that investigates learning by examination of the perceptions of the learner.

gifted individuals who fall in the top 3 percent of the population when classified according to IQ.

goal in motivation theory, an object that will reduce a need.

grades the recording of student performance after it has been evaluated.

graphemes the printed symbols in an alphabet.

group-centered therapy therapy based on the theory that students can benefit from acceptance and encouragement of all group members rather than just the therapist; family therapy is one example of group therapy.

group reinforcement reinforcing a group for its collective behavior rather than individual behavior.

group standardized tests tests that many people can take at one time. Group tests are usually paper-and-pencil tests often requiring the use of language and reading.

guided discovery teaching method of teaching that allows the learners to formulate for themselves the principles that are to be learned. The instructor in guided discovery teaching plays the role of director and provides the cues that will allow the solution to the problem to be found.

Head Start a well known, federally funded enrichment program for preschool children.

hierarchy of needs according to Maslow, there are five hierarchical types of needs: physiological, safety, love and belonging, esteem, and self-actualization.

homeostasis the tendency of individuals to resist deviation from an optimally steady state. People act to reduce their needs so as to maintain a steady or balanced internal state of being.

humanistic psychologists educators whose methods take into consideration the individual needs, motives, and capacities of each student, and who use those individual qualities to help students discover for themselves what there is to be learned as well as what they want to learn.

hyperactivity a child who is hyperactive is characteristically overactive, restless, excitable, impulsive, and seems never to sit still. Hyperactivity may also be seen as a learning disability.

hyperkinesis motor-impaired behavior that results from neurological disorders.

iconic mode Bruner's term for a pictorial representation that stands for a concept without fully defining it.

identification more than imitation of a model, a cognitive process in which persons adopt for themselves the standards of the model by which they can judge their own behavior. Identification requires internalization.

identity   the personality factor that makes each person unique.

identity crisis   according to Eriksonian theory, a crisis that takes place when an individual becomes unsure of his own identity and place in life.

identity diffusion   Erikson's term for the lack of a clear answer to the question "Who am I?"

imitation   occurs when children's behavior very closely matches the behavior of other people in certain situations.

immanent justice   Piaget's term for young children's belief that punishment is a natural consequence and must follow when they have done something wrong.

immediate feedback   immediate knowledge of results or correctness of a response; often serves as reinforcement in learning.

impulsivity   an attitude toward problem-solving that shows a tendency to report answers without first thinking through the problem and considering alternatives.

index of discrimination   the degree to which a question discriminates between high scorers and low scorers. Items discriminate in the right direction when questions are answered correctly by more high scorers than low scorers.

indirect teacher talk   the category in Flanders's interaction analysis that includes praise, asking questions, and clarifying ideas.

individual standardized tests   tests in which the trained examiner asks the test-taker questions, one by one, or directs him or her to perform tasks. The test-taker usually does not have to read the question.

Individualized Education Plan (IEP)   requirement, enforced by Public Law 94-142, that assessment of performance levels, annual goals (inclucling both short and long-term goals), specific educational services, and evaluation procedures be specified for all handicapped children in the school system.

individualized instruction   offers special individualized plans of study based on the individual's needs, abilities, and interests. Individualized instruction is often individually paced.

inductive method of teaching   consists of presenting a series of positive and negative instances of a concept and allowing the learner to make inferences from the invariant attributes. This is similar to Bruner's discovery approach.

indulgence   kindness and warm attention meted out in the course of childrearing.

information-processing theories   (see **cybernetic theories**).

information retrieval   according to cybernetic theory of remembering and forgetting, material that is retrieved from the memory bank for use.

information storage   according to cybernetic theory of remembering and forgetting, material that is learned and placed in the memory bank.

Initial Teaching Alphabet (ITA)   an artificial, printed English language, in which there is a one-to-one phoneme-grapheme relationship. Used for the purpose of early reading instruction.

innate capability theory   Chomsky's theory that human beings have "innate mechanisms" built in that enable them to comprehend and use complex speech.

insight   a form of discovery learning in which the end results are finding a solution that works and developing an understanding as to why it works. One may achieve insight when there is a reorganization or transformation of stimuli. It can be both a product and a process.

instructional television (ITV)   special TV broadcasts that provide formal course instruction in a logical sequence; usually offered during school hours and shown in school classes.

instrumental conditioning   (see **operant conditioning**).

intelligence quotient (IQ)   score obtained on an intelligence test; may be found either by deviation or ratio methods.

intelligence tests   mental tests of general ability.

interaction analysis   a system developed by Flanders to help teachers assess the patterns of interaction in their classes. Verbal communications are broken down into several categories and a frequency count of each is made based upon classroom observations.

interference—a theory of forgetting   in which new learning and old learning are seen to compete and interfere with one another.

intermittent reinforcement   reinforcement given on the basis of a specified number of responses (ratio) or a specified amount of time after the last reinforcement (interval).

interval schedule   reinforcement that depends on the amount of time that has elapsed since the previous reinforcement.

intervening variable   a theoretical construct that cannot be observed but is used to explain behavior. The presence of an intervening variable is inferred by performance.

intervention programs   educational programs designed to "intervene" in the learning process in order to give extra help to children with special needs.

intrinsic motivation   the reward in a task is intrinsic to the behavior itself, without need for external reinforcers.

intuition immedate apprehension or cognition, according to Bruner. Intuitive thinking is characterized by the development of hunches and hypotheses, by perceptions that seem to appear suddenly and dramatically.

intuitive stage of cognitive development according to Piaget, the stage of thought involving image-based thinking.

item analysis analysis of test scores, item-by-item, to determine which items are answered correctly and which are not by students who are high and low scorers on the total tests.

kernel grammar early grammar that, according to Chomsky, consists of the main parts of speech and rules for creating simple sentences, and that precedes the ability to develop more complex grammatical rules.

knowledge the simplest type of learning, according to Bloom's taxonomy. Knowlege includes rote memory. One may have knowledge without comprehension or understanding.

law of closure the Gestalt principle that closed figures are more stable (remembered better) than open figures.

law of continuation the Gestalt principle that the way in which the first part of a stimulus is perceived determines how a continuation of that stimulus is perceived.

law of effect E. L. Thorndike's principle that the associative bond is strengthened or weakened, depending on whether a satisfier (reward) or an annoyer (punishment) follows a response. (See also **truncated law of effect**.)

learner-centered approach (as opposed to teacher-centered approach) concept used first by Carl Rogers to define education based on the premise that the student should determine and be responsible for his or her own behavior.

learning the process whereby the perceptual field is organized, according to Gestalt psychologists. A relatively permanent change in behavior as a result of reinforced practice, according to associationist psychologists.

learning disability learning problem unrelated to intelligence; often characterized by inability to learn to read and write, left-right reversals and the like.

learning-environmental theories of development theories that explain cognitive development through focusing directly on the environmental stimulation and learning experiences that are possible.

learning objectives instructional objectives that describe in behavioral terms what the student should be able to do, the conditions under which the task is to be performed, and the criterion for acceptable performance.

learning styles different ways in which people process information in the course of learning, including individual preferences in both perceptual organization and conceptual categorization. Also called cognitive styles.

learning to learn Harlow's theory that teaching by presenting a series of new problems increases ability to learn because the student learns "how" to learn.

level of aspiration the individual's expectation of his or her own future success or failure, based upon his or her evalution of past performance and his or her desire to perform better in the future.

linear programming the questions in a lesson are arranged in a single line from simple to complex; all students answer the same questions in the same order.

linguistics branch of science dealing with the fundamental structural principles of languages.

long-term memory a permanent memory store of almost unlimited capacity. Stores information only after it has been processed or rehearsed.

Lorge-Thorndike Intelligence Test widely used, reliable group test of intelligence for children that includes both verbal and nonverbal subtests.

magnet school a school, usually in an urban area, that provides exciting special programs not available in other schools in the city. Magnet schools are designed to increase voluntary desegregation by providing programs of interest to all.

mainstreaming the incorporation of students with special needs into regular classes.

maintenance systems the economic, political, and social structures necessary to uphold a society.

manipulation drive an independent but nonphysiological drive to investigate and control the environment. Harlow believes that this drive is independent because it is not associated with any primary drives.

matching Piaget's concept that states that the only stimuli that will produce a change in the assimilation-accommodation process are those matched to the cognitive level of the learner.

maturation the development of the body, or mind, regardless of outside influences.

mean a statistical measure of average determined by adding all the scores in a group and dividing by the number of scores.

meaning emphasis in reading instruction attention given in early reading instruction to semantics, or the meaning of words, rather than the sounds of the letters.

meaningfulness measures of meaningfulness include number of associations, familiarity, and frequency of use. The more meaningful something is, the more easily it will be learned and remembered.

median the statistical measure of average found by determining the score that falls in the exact middle of the group.

memory traces structural changes in the nervous system that are associated with learning.

mental age obtained by comparing the test-taker's raw score with the typical age of those of the standardization sample who obtained the same raw score.

mental combinations Piaget's term for children's ability to represent to themselves the outcome of actions before they take them.

mental discipline doctrine that states that the mind is composed of a series of faculties analogous to muscles in that they need exercise to function adequately and become strengthened.

mentally retarded those individuals who are significantly deficient in both thinking capacity and behavioral adaptation to society. The four classifications of retardation are (in order of decreasing intelligence): the educable, trainable, severely retarded, and profoundly retarded.

minimal competency testing a strategy in which students are required to pass examinations demonstrating minimal competency in specified subject matters in order to go on to a higher grade or to graduate.

mnemonics special strategies for rote memorization, such as associating one word with another, associating words with geographical locations, or forming a sentence using words from the first letters of the terms to be remembered.

mode the statistical measure of average found by determining the single score that occurs most frequently.

mode of representation Bruner's term for the basic method by which people understand and make use of their environment. The three modes are enactive, iconic, and symbolic.

modeling or model building a process in which children exhibit symbolic equivalents of observed behavior, not exact replications. Children generalize their behavior to situations other than the exact ones observed.

modular instruction individualized instruction programs structured around separate sequential units of study known as models. Students play an active role in their own learning with modular instruction.

Montessori method an instructional program within a planned environment; emphasizes action, sensorimotor materials, self-learning, and self-reinforcement or feedback.

morality aspect of personality that includes the development and expression of conscience, or the internalization of values accepted by society.

morality of constraint Piaget's term for young children's morality, in which parental and other authority figures' decisions are accepted as moral absolutes. It is based on unilateral respect.

morality of cooperation Piaget's term for a more mature basis of morality, which grows out of mutual respect. The individual is personally responsible for his or her own actions.

morpheme any word or part of a word that conveys meaning and cannot be divided into a smaller form conveying meaning.

motivation the internal factors that cause a person to act, the goals or purposes underlying an individual's behavior. Motivation includes both energizing and directional properties.

motor skills taxonomy a classification scheme of motor skills based on subject matter, developed by Merrill. The five different motor skills he identified include physical education, communication, fine arts, language, and vocational skills.

movement theory most learned behavior involves movement of one kind or another. Motor behavior is the major channel through which cognitive and affective behavior become apparent to oneself and others.

multiple mothering or multiple care-giving the child-rearing practice whereby the child is cared for, to a large extent, by more than one mother or more than one primary care-giver.

need a requirement that must be met by an organism for optimal adjustment to the environment.

negative reinforcer reinforcer that is meant to increase the frequency of escape behavior. Negative reinforcers are effective only when there is an opportunity to escape and the opportunity is obvious to the person.

negative transfer the interference to learning in one area with learning in another area.

neurosis a functional disorder manifested by anxiety, phobias, obsessions, or compulsions.

neutral stimulus a stimulus that by itself would be incapable of eliciting a response. Through repeated associations with unconditioned stimuli, neutral stimuli themselves elicit responses and become conditioned stimuli.

nondirective counseling counseling in which the therapist assumes that the student can solve problems with support and assistance (not *direction*) of the therapist; also called child-centered therapy.

nongraded classrooms a heterogeneous age grouping of students, based on the premise that children of the same age are capable of learning the same things.

nonverbal test test that is completely without words; usually administered individually.

norm-referenced test a test used to compare students' scores within a group.

normal curve the distribution of a human trait when measured in sufficiently large numbers of people. The normal curve is a symmetrical, bell-shaped curve.

normal distribution (see **normal curve**).

norms information about typical scores for the kinds of students who made up the standardization sample. Norms can be percentile ranks or age or grade norms.

nuclear family a household unit consisting of two parents and their offspring.

objective tests tests requiring the student to write a short answer or to choose the correct answer. Multiple-choice, true-false, matching items, short-answer, and completion questions are examples of objective tests.

open classroom (1) a nontraditional approach to teaching in which the room is divided into functional areas for specific subjects (learning resource centers). The students work individually or in small groups. Children have a great deal to say in determining their own learning. (2) An underlying flexible attitude toward education with an informal style of teaching and individualized instruction.

operant conditioning the process of modifying behavior by reinforcers; involves responses that occur before any stimulus is presented.

operants behaviors that request (or make) a change in the environment.

operant strength the strength of the response, such as the increase in the number of bar-pressings.

organization the intellectual activity, whereby we arrange and systematize perceptual and cognitive data into units and patterns that have meaning for us.

overgeneralization generalization to such an extent that it distorts reality.

overlearning learning that continues after material appears to be learned and remembered. Overlearning reduces forgetting, especially of factual material.

parallel play play in which preschool children perform the same activities at the same time, aware of one another but independent of one another.

peer group people of about the same age and status in a society or neighborhood.

peer teaching the educational process in which children work together and teach each other.

percentile rank a statistic telling the percent of scores in the standardization sample falling below a certain given raw score.

perception sensation, as it is given meaning through the learning experiences of the developing mind.

perceptual learning an increase in one's ability to extract meaningful and relevant information from one's environment as a result of practice and experience, according to E. J. Gibson.

performance tests tests that use apparati such as equipment, machinery, material, implements, and other instruments. They are also called nonlanguage tests. They may measure both general and specialized abilities.

phoneme the smallest unit of speech that distinguishes one utterance from another.

phonetics the system of teaching reading in which letters are the basic units, beginning with instruction in how to sound or pronounce various letters.

planned environment a learning environment designed specifically to meet the individual needs of children.

Plowden Report a comprehensive analysis of modern British primary school practices conducted by the British Central Advisory Council for Education.

positive reinforcers stimuli that follow operant behavior and increase its frequency.

positive transfer occurs when learning in one activity facilitates learning in a new or similar activity.

power the term Bruner used to describe the value of the material being learned in terms of its applicability.

power tests tests composed of questions of varying degrees of difficulty. The score of a power test depends on the ability of the test-taker to answer the questions correctly.

precision teaching a behavior management program of individualized instruction that emphasizes monitoring of a child's performance, which is clearly pinpointed and charted on daily progress records.

preconceptual stage of cognitive development according to Piaget, an early stage of thinking characterized by reliance on only partially complete concepts to solve problems.

predictive validity a measure of the ability of a test to predict future success in a field or in a school. Predictive validity is also called *statistical validity* or *empirical validity*.

Premack principle allows children to select their own reinforcers; teachers use school activities that the students enjoy as reinforcers.

preoperational stage Piaget's second stage of development, occurring between the ages of 2 and 7. Children learn to use language effectively during this stage; however, their thought is still very egocentric.

primary needs those requirements that must be met in

order for the organism to survive, such as the need for food or water.

primary reinforcers stimuli that are of prime importance to the physical survival of the organism such as food and water.

principle learning learning to combine related concepts into rules that say something about these concepts; the most advanced method of problem solving.

proactive inhibition occurs when prior learning interferes with the ability to remember new learning.

problem behaviors behaviors exhibited as a result of poor personal and social adjustment to the environment.

productive thinking Wertheimer's approach to creating genuine understanding of solutions to problems.

profoundly mentally retarded the most extreme level of mental retardation; the profoundly retarded are helpless and require lifelong care.

programmed instuction an active learning process in which students are constantly asked questions as they progress through the unit. The material is presented in a progressive stepwise order of difficulty. Immediate feedback as to the correctness of the answers is given.

prohibition learning a type of learned behavior that occurs together with the identification process. A child is taught certain "don'ts" by parents and other models.

psychoanalytic theory first developed by Sigmund Freud; a stage approach that assumes that what happens in early childhood is critical in determining future personality and ability to adjust.

psycholinguists specialists in a branch of science that deals with the psychological aspects of language structure.

psychological principles principles that have been ascertained on the basis of psychological research and that can be applied to explain human behavior.

psychosocial theory developed by E. Erikson; a developmental-stage theory that assumes that social-cultural influences have a great deal of effect on the stages of developing personality.

Public Law 94-142 The Education for All Handicapped Children Act, a programmatic bill passed by the federal government in 1975 that guarantees basic rights to all children with special needs.

punishment the administration of an aversive stimulus for the purpose of inhibiting the preceding response.

Pygmalion effect (see **self-fulfilling prophecy**).

ratio IQ IQ determined by dividing mental age by chronological age and multiplying by 100.

ratio schedule reinforcement given only after the subject makes a specified number of desired responses.

raw score the number of correct answers attained by an individual on a test.

reading-readiness tests tests designed to measure ability to learn to read; include largely perceptual and discrimination learning tasks.

recall a fairly insensitive method of measuring remembering that requires the student to remember as much information as possible with only minimum number of cues or suggestions as to the correct answer.

reception teaching/learning a method of teaching in which the material is presented in more or less final form to the student. The student learns the information in that form without greatly transforming it; the student's learning is guided closely by the teacher.

recognition a measure of remembering in which many cues are given. The multiple-choice question is the most frequently used type of recognition question.

reduction of uncertainty the reinforcing aspect of learning, according to E. J. Gibson's perceptual learning theory. It helps the student to transform what would otherwise be confusing into meaningful stimulation.

reflectivity an attitude toward selecting responses that demonstrates a tendency to consider various possibilities before deciding on an answer.

reinforcement stimulus that increases the future probability of a particular response occurring.

relearning the most sensitive measure of remembering, in which one measures the number of trials needed to learn material at a later date and compares that number to the original number of trials needed to learn the material.

reliability one of the most important criteria for a good test. A test is reliable if it gives the same scores on repeated testing.

remembering the retention of information after learning has taken place; the availability of previously learned information.

repression a psychoanalytic explanation for the inability to recall some learned information. We push painful experiences out of our conciousness as a way of preserving our self-esteem.

respondent conditioning (see **classical conditioning**).

response generalization occurs when a particular stimulus evokes responses that are similar or related to the desired response.

retroactive inhibition interference in which subsequent learning interferes with earlier learning.

role playing when people assume other or new roles and portray these in common situations.

rote learning learning by memorization without meaning.

schizophrenia a psychotic disorder of unknown complex etiology; researchers have related this disorder both to chemical imbalances within the body system and to environmental factors.

schizophrenogenic mother mother who is aggressive, domineering, overanxious, and overly solicitous, yet basically rejecting; 50 percent of schizophrenic children have schizophrenogenic mothers.

school counselor works with school psychologists; usually focuses on educational decisions.

school phobia reluctance or refusal to go to school, usually as a result of an extreme fear about some aspect of the school situation; a school-related anxiety.

school psychologist works with students in assessing, intervening, and evaluating student learning and emotional problems.

secondary needs requirements that are not needed for survival but that optimize a person's adjustment to a complex learned, social, and physical environment. Secondary needs develop from association with primary needs.

secondary reinforcers stimuli that in themselves are not rewarding but come to be rewarding when they are associated with primary reinforcers. Secondary reinforcers such as approval or money are created by the process of conditioning.

self-actualization Maslow's "highest" and most far-reaching need, involving, among other attributes, ability to perceive reality, accept others, feel freedom, think and act creatively, and enjoy work and living.

self-adequacy Arthur Combs's goal for students taught by humanistic methods.

self-concept, self-image the unified mental picture every individual has of himself. Includes self-evaluation, a self-enhancing aspect.

self-discovery the educational approach of Maslow that suggests that the role of the teacher is to help students discover who they are and what they can become. The entire process involves self-discovery, self-acceptance, and self-making.

self-esteem an individual's attitude regarding his or her own worth as a person.

self-fulfilling prophecy the fact that teachers' attitudes and behaviors can influence students' self-evaluations and behaviors.

self-management of contingencies regarding oneself after one has achieved certain previously determined subgoals.

self-paced evaluation a method of evaluation in which students move at their own pace and are evaluated when they believe they are ready. The Keller plan was based on self-paced evaluation.

sensation a state of consciousness produced by impingement of an external condition or object on the sensory organs of the body—as in sight, hearing, and the like.

sensorimotor stage Piaget's earliest stage of cognitive development, usually from birth to about 2 years old. This is an action-oriented stage, which occurs prior to the development of language.

sensory information storage an extremely short-lived memory storage, it refers to our perception of the world through our senses.

seriation the ability to order a series of objects along some dimension.

severely mentally retarded mentally retarded individuals who, with intensive training, may be able to learn some self-help skills.

sex-role identification the way in which children learn how to feel and act the role of a particular sex. Parental rewards, imitation, and modeling contribute to sex-role identification.

shaping the process of conditioning in which successive reinforcements are given for closer approaches to the desired behavior. At first any improvement is reinforced; later, only more correct or more precise responses are reinforced.

short-term memory material that is stored as an immediate and direct interpretation of sensory stimuli. This memory is short-lived and of limited capacity.

skewed distribution non-normal distribution, usually occurs with small samples.

Skinner box an enclosed box containing a bar or a lever and a device for providing reinforcers; designed by B. F. Skinner for his operant conditioning research.

socialization the learning process whereby children learn the behaviors, ideas, attitudes, and values that are socially acceptable in their culture.

socialized speech a form of speech designed to communicate information accurately to another person, often taking into account the listener's point of view.

special education classes special classes where children with special needs are segregated from the others in order to receive special instruction.

special education teachers teachers trained specially to meet the needs of and provide instruction for handicapped students.

speed test a type of test that is made up of a very large number of questions of a uniform level of difficulty. A speed test score depends on the total number of questions the test taker answers correctly in a restricted time period.

spiral curriculum Jerome Bruner's concept in which there is a logical progression from the simple to the complex in the structural representation of the subject matter.

standard deviation statistical term referring to the distance along the baseline from the center of the normal curve to a point that cuts off 34 percent of the sample.

standard error (SE) statistic calculated from the reliability of a test as well as from other statistics that tells by how many points we may expect a given score to vary in a second testing.

standard score (see **z score**).

standardization sample the group of people given the final version of a standardized test. This sample should be representative of those people for whom the test is intended. Norms are obtained from the standardization sample.

standardized test a test for which the procedures for administering and scoring have been made uniform or standard.

Stanford-Binet Intelligence Test the most reliable and widely accepted individually administered, standardized test of intelligence currently in use.

stimulus generalization the same or similar response is made to two or more stimuli.

structure of a subject in a curriculum the fundamental ideas and relationships that are inherent in the subject matter.

student-teacher contracts used in contract teaching; students and teachers agree formally on objectives prior to learning.

subsumption Ausubel's principle that learning general principles will help a student organize new material.

summative evaluation a type of evaluation done at the end of a course to assign grades or to measure the success of the instruction.

superstitious behavior a response or series of responses that occur before reinforcement but yet do not have any relationship to the reinforcement. There is no causal link between the behavior and the reinforcement.

Suzuki method a method used to teach violin playing to very young children; developed by Sinichi Suzuki, founder of Suzuki Talent Education Institute.

symbolic mode according to Bruner, the most advanced mode of representation, because it provides a means of going beyond what is immediately perceptible in a situation. Language plays a major role in the symbolic mode.

synthesis the ability to combine knowledge, skills, ideas, and experiences to create a new and original product. A most complex type of learning in the cognitive domain, according to Bloom.

task analysis determination of the specific individual steps through which a learner goes to solve a given problem.

taxonomy of objectives an instructional plan for determining what general class or category of behavior is desired in a given situation; gives the full possible range of objectives that are available in a learning situation.

teacher accountability the idea that the teacher, not the student, is ultimately responsible for what and how much a student learns.

teaching-learning unit (TLU) a unit of instruction designed to contain all components necessary for learning.

teaching machines instructional devices that students can operate and then be reinforced, depending on the appropriateness of their response.

team teaching a variety of teaching techniques in which a number of teachers share responsibility for teaching students and subject materials.

terminal behavior the behavior that teachers ultimately wish to establish in a learning situation.

theory of generalized principles Judd's ideas that transfer is based upon an understanding of the principle underlying two or more activities. Understanding a general principle makes it possible to interrelate and interpret a whole body of varied experiences.

theory of identical elements E. L. Thorndike's belief that transfer occurs only within a restricted range of conditions. Transfer occurs to the extent that two activities share composite elements.

token reinforcers immediate reinforcement for a desired response is given in the form of some sort of token. After a number of tokens have been accumulated the child can cash them in for a desired object or privilege.

trainable mentally retarded the level of mental retardation in which the individual can learn sufficient self-care skills to live successfully in the community rather than in an institution.

transfer the application of knowledge from one area to another.

transfer of learning the process that occurs whenever the existence of a previously established habit has an influence upon the acquisition, performance, or relearning of a second habit.

transformation the manipulation of information to make it fit new situations; the second step of the learning process, according to Bruner.

transformational grammar the contemporary approach to linguistics developed by Noam Chomsky. Sentences are constructed and related to one another by means of underlying syntactical rules called *transformations.*

transposition the Gestalt term for application of learned solutions to new situations or the transfer of training.

truncated law of effect E. L. Thorndike's revised law of effect: although satisfiers always strengthen the bond between the stimulus and the response, annoyers (punishment) do not necessarily weaken it—they may have little effect upon it at all.

unconditioned response an automatic response. When bright light is directed toward someone's eyes, that person automatically blinks. The blink is an unconditioned response.

unconditioned stimulus a stimulus, such as noise, light, etc., that produces a response without learning having to take place.

undirected speech Vygotsky's explanation of what Piaget termed "egocentric speech"; a tool that young children use to help them direct their own cognitive processes.

validity one of the important criteria for a good test. A test has validity if it measures what it is designed to measure.

values clarification a psychological procedure designed to produce understanding of one's relationships to others in teaching-learning situations.

variable schedule of reinforcement the average number (ratio) or average time period (interval) of responses, rather than a specific number of responses or specific time period, determines the reinforcement schedule.

verbal tests tests that rely on the use of words in the questions or directions. Group tests are usually verbal tests.

Wechsler Intelligence Scales individual, standardized intelligence tests for children and adults that yield both a verbal and a performance subscore and a total deviation IQ score.

withdrawal a problem behavior characterized by shyness, fear, secretiveness, apathy, daydreaming, and isolation.

Zeigarnik effect recalling an incomplete task more readily than a completed one due to motivation.

z score or standard score a statistic that tells how far from the average a given raw score is. z scores may be positive (raw score above the average), negative (raw score below the average of the standardization group), or zero (raw score the same as the average of the standardization group).

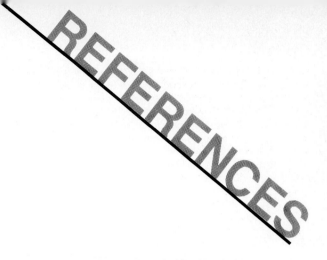

ACKERMAN, P. D. The effects of honor-grading on students' test scores. *American Educational Research Journal*, 1971, *8*, 321–333.

ADKINS, A. Testing: Alternative to grading. *Educational Leadership*, January 1975, pp. 271–273.

AHLSTROM, K. G. *Motivation and achievement*. Uppsala, Sweden: Institute of Education, Uppsala University, 1957.

AHMANN, J. S., AND GLOCK, M. D. *Evaluating pupil growth* (4th ed.). Boston: Allyn & Bacon, 1971.

AINSWORTH, M. D. S. *Infancy in Uganda*. Baltimore: Johns Hopkins University Press, 1967.

AIRASIAN, P. W. The role of mastery learning. In J. H. Block (ed.), *Mastery learning*. New York: Holt, Rinehart and Winston, 1971.

ALGOZZINE, B., MERCER, C. D., AND COUNTERMINE, T. The effects of labels and behavior on teacher expectation. *Exceptional Children*, 44(2), October 1977, 131–132.

ALIBERTO, C. A. Assessing perceptual-motor competency. *Academic Therapy*, 1975, *10*, 355–359.

ALLEN, V. F. Riddle: What does a reading test test? *Learning*, November 1978, 87–89.

ALSCHULER, A. S. *How to increase motivation through climate and structure* (Achievement Motivation Development Project Working Paper No. 8). Cambridge, Mass,: Harvard University Graduate School of Education, 1968.

ALSTON, F. *Early childrearing patterns in the People's Republic of China*. Paper delivered at the annual meeting of the American Educational Research Association, San Francisco, April 1976.

American Federation of Teachers, AFL-CIO. *Academic freedom and the rights of faculty* (Position paper). Unpublished manuscript, 1977. (Available from 1012 14th St., N.W., Washington, D.C. 20005).

AMES, C. Children's achievement attributions and self-reinforcement: Effects of self-concept and competitive reward structure. *Journal of Educational Psychology*, 1978 *70* (3), 345–354.

AMIDON, E. J., AND FLANDERS, N. *The role of the teacher in the classroom* (Rev. ed.). Minneapolis: Association for Productive Teaching, 1967.

AMIDON, E. J., AND GIAMMATTEO, M. The verbal behavior of superior teachers. *Elementary School Journal*, 1965, *65*, 283–285.

ANDERSON, E. M. *The disabled schoolchild*. London: Methuen, 1973.

ANDERSON, L. W. An empirical investigation of individual differences in time to learn. *Journal of Educational Psychology*, 1976, *68* (2), 226–233.

ANDERSON, R. C. Learning in Discussions: A resume of the authoritarian-democratic studies. *Harvard Educational Review*, 1959, *29*, 201–215.

ANDERSON, R. P. *The child with learning disabilities and guidance*. Boston: Houghton Mifflin, 1970.

ANDREWS, G. R., AND DEBUS, R. L. Persistence and the causal perception of failure: Modifying cognitive attributions. *Journal of Educational Psychology*, 1978, *70*(2), 154–165.

ANDREWS, T. G., AND CRONBACH, L. J. Transfer of training. In W. S. Munroe (Ed.), *Encyclopedia of educational research* (2nd ed.). New York: Macmillan, 1950.

ANGELL, G. W. AND TROYER, M. E. A new self-scoring test device for improving instruction. *School and Society*, 1948, *67*, 84–85.

Animals go to Northgate School. *Pittsburgh Press*, March 4, 1975, p. 9.

ASHER, J. J. Children learning another language: A developmental hypothesis. *Child Development*, 1977, *48*, 1040–1048.

Assignment: Assertion. *Time*, May 19, 1975, p. 65.

ATKINSON, J. (Ed.). *Motives in fantasy, action, and society*. Princeton, N. J.: Van Nostrand, 1958.

AUGUST, G. J., AND RYCHLAK, J. F. Role of intelligence and task difficulty in the affective learning styles of children with high and low self-concepts. *Journal of Educational Psychology*, 1978, *70*(3), 406–413.

AUSUBEL, D. P. *Theory and problems of adolescent development*. New York: Grune & Stratton, 1954.

AUSUBEL, D. P. *The psychology of meaningful verbal learning*. New York: Grune & Stratton, 1963.

AUSUBEL, D. P. *Learning theory and classroom practice* (Bulletin No. 1). Toronto: Ontario Institute for Studies in Education, 1967. (a)

AUSUBEL, D. P. A cognitive-structure theory of school learning. In L. Siegel (Ed.), *Instruction: Some contemporary viewpoints*, San Francisco: Chandler: 1967. (b)

AUSUBEL, D. P. *Educational psychology: A cognitive view*. New York: Holt, Rinehart and Winston, 1968.

AUSUBEL, D. P., NOVAK, J. D., AND HANESIAN, H., *Educational psychology: A cognitive view* (2nd ed.). New York: Holt, Rinehart and Winston, 1978.

AUSUBEL, D. P., AND ROBINSON, F. G. *School learning: An introduction to educational psychology*. New York: Holt, Rinehart and Winston, 1969.

AUSUBEL, D. P., AND SULLIVAN, E. V. *Theory and problems of child development (2nd ed.)*. New York: Grune & Stratton, 1970.

BACHRACH, A., CANDLAND, D., and GIBSON, J. Group reinforcement of individual response experiments in verbal behavior. In I. Berg and B. Bass (Eds.), *Conformity and deviation*. New York: Harper & Brothers, 1961.

BACK, K. W. *Beyond words: The story of sensitivity training and the encounter movement*. New York: Russell Sage Foundation, 1972.

Back to basics in the schools. *Newsweek*, October 21, 1974, 87–88 ff.

BAHRICK, H. P., BAHRICK, P. O., AND WITTLINGER, R. P. Longterm memory. *Psychology Today*, December 1974, 50–56.

BAILYN, L. Mass media and children. *Psychological Monographs*, 1959, 73 (1, Whole No. 471).

BALLARD, M., CORMAN, L., GOTTLIEB, J. AND KAUFMAN, M. J. Improving the social status of mainstreamed retarded children. *Journal of Educational Psychology*, 1977, 69(5), 605–611.

BANDURA, A. Behavioral psychotherapy. *Scientific American*, March 1967, 78–86.

BANDURA, A. Social-learning theory of identificatory processes. In D. A. Goslin (Ed.), *Handbook of socialization theory and research*. Chicago: Rand McNally, 1969.

BANDURA, A., AND McDONALD, F. J. Influence of social reinforcement and the behavior of models in shaping children's moral judgments. *Journal of Abnormal and Social Psychology*, 1963, 67, 274–281.

BARATZ, J. C. A bi-dialectal task for determining language proficiency in economically disadvantaged Negro children. *Child Development*, 1969, 40, 889–901.

BARBER, T. X., CALVERLEY, D. S., FORGIONE, A., McPEAKE, J. D., CHAVES, J. F., AND BOWEN, B. Five attempts to replicate the experimenter bias effect. *Journal of Consulting and Clinical Psychology*, 1969, 33, 1–6.

BARBER, T. X., AND SILVER, M. J. Fact, fiction, and the experimenter bias effect. *Psychological Bulletin Monograph*, 1968, 70(6, Pt. 2), 1–29.

BARENBOIM, C. Developmental changes in the interpersonal cognitive system from middle childhood to adolescence. *Child Development*, 1977, 48, 1467–1474.

BARNES, B. R. AND CLAWSON, E. U. Do advance organizers facilitate learning? Recommendations for further research based on an analysis of 32 studies. *Review of Educational Research*, Fall 1975, 45 (4), 637–659.

BARRO, S. M. An approach to developing accountability measures for the public schools. *Phi Delta Kappan*, 1970, 52, 196–205.

BARTHOLOMEW, B. R. Teachers' instructional problems, 1974. *Today's Education*, September 1974, 78–80.

BAYARD-DE-VOLO, C. L., AND FIEBERT, M. S. Creativity in the preschool child and its relationship to parental authoritarianism. *Perceptual and Motor Skills*, 1977, 45, 170.

BAYH, B. Seeking solutions to school violence and vandalism. *Phi Delta Kappan*, January 1978, 299–302.

BAYLEY, N. On the growth of intelligence. *American Psychologist*, 1955, 10, 805–818.

BAYUK, Z. The case for elitism. *Clearing House*, 1972, 46, 506–507.

BECHTEREV, V. M. [*General principles of human reflexology*] (E. Murphy and W. Murphy, trans.). New York: International Publishers, 1928.

BECKER, M. Sixth graders and first graders sharpen skills together. *Learning*, January 1978, 6(5), 32–33.

BECKER, W. C., et al. *Teaching I: Classroom management*. Chicago: Science Research Associates, 1975.

BEILEN, H. Teachers' and clinicians' attitudes toward the behavior problems of children. *Child Development*, 1959, 30, 9–25.

BELL, T. H. What makes a good teacher? *American Educator*, 1977, 1(1) 16–18.

BELLACK, L., AND ANTELL M. An intercultural study of aggressive behavior on children's playgrounds. *American Journal of Orthopsychiatry* 44, no. 4 (July 1974), 503–508.

BEN-ZEEV, S. The influence of bilingualism on cognitive strategy and cognitive development. *Child Development*, 1977, 48, 1009–1018.

BEREITER, C. AND ENGELMANN, S. *Teaching disadvantaged children in the preschool*. Englewood Cliffs, N. J.: Prentice-Hall, 1966.

BEREITER, C., AND ENGELMANN, S. An academically

oriented preschool for disadvantaged children. In *Psychology and early childhood education*. Toronto: Ontario Institute for Studies in Education, 1968, 17–36.

BERKO, L. The child's learning of English morphology. *Word*, 1958, *14*, 150–177.

BERLINER, D. *Successful classroom teaching and learning*. Invited address at the Learning, Research, and Development Center, University of Pittsburgh, January 25, 1979.

BERLYNE, D. E. Conflict and information-theory variables as determinants of human perceptual curiosity. *Journal of Experimental Psychology*, 1957, *53*, 399–404.

BERLYNE, D. E. Notes on intrinsic motivation and intrinsic reward in relation to instruction. In J. S. Bruner (Ed.), *Learning about learning* (Cooperative Research Monograph No. 15). Washington, D.C.: U. S. Department of Health, Education, and Welfare, Office of Education, 1966.

BERNARD, H. W. *Child development and learning*. Boston: Allyn & Bacon, 1973.

BERNAUER, M., AND JACKSON, J. H. Review of school psychology for 1973. *Professional Psychology*, 1974, *5*, 155–165.

BERNSTEIN, B. Some sociological determinants of perception. *British Journal of Sociology*, 1958, *9*, 159–174.

BERNSTEIN, B. Language and social class. *British Journal of Sociology*, 1960, *11*, 271–276.

BERRYMAN, C., AND PERRY, B. *A manual for teachers of learning disabled children*. Bristol City, Tenn.: Bristol City Board of Education, 1974. (ERIC Document Reproduction Service No. ED 085 958)

BETTELHEIM, B. *The children of the dream*. New York: Macmillan, 1969.

Bias charged in book rejection. *New York Times*, November 10, 1974, 53.

BIGGE, M. L. *Learning theories for teachers* (2nd ed). New York: Harper & Row, 1964.

BIRCH, J. Mainstreaming that works in elementary and secondary schools. *Journal of Teacher Education*, November-December 1978, *29*(6), 18–21.

BIRCH, J. Special education for exceptional children through regular school personnel and programs. In M. C. Reynolds and M. D. Davis (Eds.), *Exceptional children in regular classrooms*. Minneapolis: University of Minnesota Press, 1971.

BLAKESLEE, S. Challenge for the very bright: A "college for kids." *New York Times*, May 21, 1975, 39.

BLANK, M. AND SOLOMON, F. A tutorial language program to develop abstract thinking in socially disadvantaged preschool children. *Child Development*, 1968, *39*, 379–389.

BLOOM, B. S. *Stability and change in human characteristics*. New York: Wiley, 1964.

BLOOM, B. S., ENGLEHART, M. D., FURST, E. J., AND KRATHWOHL, D. R. *A taxonomy of educational objectives* (Handbook 1). New York: David McKay, 1956.

BLOOMFIELD, L. *Language*. New York: Holt, 1933.

BODMER, W. F., AND CAVALLI-SFORZA, L. L. Intelligence and race. *Scientific American*, October 1970, 19–30.

BOGATZ, G. A. AND BALL, S. *The second year of Sesame Street* (Vol. 1). Princeton: Educational Testing Service, November 1971.

BOND, L., COLE, N., AND LINHART C. Truth in testing: Their laws and their implications. Invited address, program in Educational Research Methodology Seminar series, University of Pittsburgh, February 15, 1980.

BOWER, G. H. Analysis of a mnemonic device. *American Scientist*, 1970, *58*, 496–510.

BOWERMAN, C. E., AND KINCH, J. W. Changes in family and peer orientation of children between the 4th and 10th grades. *Social Forces*, 1959, *37*, 206–211.

BOWERS, N. P. Rule learning and transfer in oddity and discrimination problems. *Child Development*, 1976, *47*, 1130–1137.

BRADBURY, W. An agony of learning. *Life*, October 6, 1972, p. 57–78 ff.

BRADY, E. To test or not to test. *American Education*, 1977, *1*(1), 3–14.

BRAINERD, C. J. Feedback, rule knowledge, and conservation learning. *Child Development*, 1977, *48* (1), 404–410.

BREUNING, S. E. Precision teaching in the high school classroom: A necessary step toward maximizing teacher effectiveness and student performance. *American Educational Research Journal*, Winter 1978, *15*, (1), 125–140.

BRILL, S. The secrecy behind the college boards. *New York Magazine*, October 7, 1974, 67–83.

BROCK, M., LAMBERT, W., AND TUCHER, G. *Cognitive and attitudinal consequences of bilingual schooling: The St. Lambert Project through Grade 6*. Unpublished manuscript, McGill University, 1973.

BROD, R. L. *The computer as an authority figure* (Technical Report No. 29). Stanford: Stanford Center for Research and Development in Teaching, Stanford University, August 1972.

BRODY, G. H., AND HENDERSON, R. W. Effects of multiple model variations and rationale provisions on the moral judgements and explanations of young children. *Child Development*, 1977, *48*, 1117–1120.

BRODY, J. E. More coeds find less guilt in sex. *New York Times*, December 30, 1967, p. 1.

BROGMAN, R., AND HARDY, R. *Pattern recognition in deaf children*. Paper delivered at the annual meeting of the Northeastern Educational Research Association, October 1978.

BROMLEY, D. G., CROW, M. L., AND GIBSON, M. S. Grade

inflation: Trends, causes, and implications. *Phi Delta Kappan,* June 1978, *59*(10), 694–697.

BRONFENBRENNER, U. Soviet methods of character education. *American Psychologist, 1962, 17,* 550–564.

BRONFENBRENNER, U. The dream of the kibbutz. *Saturday Review,* September 20, 1969, 72–73 ff.

BRONFENBRENNER, U. *Two worlds of childhood: U.S. and U.S.S.R.* New York: Basic Books, 1970.

BRONFENBRENNER, U. Some familial antecedents of responsibility and leadership in adolescents. In L. Petrullo and B. Bass (Eds.), *Leadership and interpersonal behavior.* New York: Holt, Rinehart & Winston, 1961.

BRONFENBRENNER, U. The roots of alienation. In U. Bronfenbrenner (Ed.), *Influences on human development.* Hinsdale, Ill.: Dryden, 1972.

BRONFENBRENNER, U. Who cares for America's children? *New York Times Educational Supplement,* December 16, 1977, pp. 15–17.

BROOKOVER W. B., SCHWEITZER, J. H., SCHNEIDER, J. M., BEADY, C. H., FLOOD, P. K. AND WISENBAKER, J. M. *American Educational Research Journal,* Spring 1978 15(2), 301–318.

BROOKS, H. Piano lessons: Striking a new chord. *McCall's,* August 1974, p. 48.

BROWN, B. *How social research changed public policy: A history of debate on Head Start.* Unpublished manuscript, 1979. (Available from Administration for Children, Youth and Families, Office of Child Development, Washington D. C.)

BROWN, B., AND FRASER, C. The acquisition of syntax. In U. Bellugi and R. Brown (Eds.), *The acquisition of language.* Monographs of the Society for Research in Child Development, 1964, *29,* 43–79.

BROWN, B., AND KULIK, J. Flashbulb memories, *Cognition,* 1977, *5*(1), 73–79.

BROZAN, N. Film and TV violence: A nursery school takes a stand. *New York Times,* June 3, 1975, 28.

BRUININKS, V. L., AND BRUININKS, R. H. Motor proficiency of learning disabled and nondisabled students. *Perceptual and Motor Skills,* 1977, *44*(3), 1131–1136.

BRUNER, J. S. Learning and thinking. *Harvard Educational Review,* 1959, *29,* 184–192.

BRUNER J. S. *The process of education.* New York: Vintage, 1960.

BRUNER, J. S. *On knowing: Essays for the left hand.* Cambridge, Mass.: Belknap Press, 1962.

BRUNER, J. S. The course of cognitive growth. *American Psychologist,* 1964, *19,* 1–15.

BRUNER, J. S. The growth of the mind. *American Psychologist,* 1965, *20,* 1007–1017.

BRUNER, J. S. *Toward a theory of instruction.* Cambridge, Mass.: Harvard University Press, 1966.

BRUNER, J. S. Organization of early skilled action. *Child Development,* 1973, *44*(1), 1–10.

BRUNER, J. S. Child development: Play is serious business. *Psychology Today,* January 1975, 81–83.

BRUNER, J. S. The act of discovery, *Harvard Educational Review,* 1961, *31,* 21–32.

BRUNER, J. S. The nature and uses of immaturity. *The growth of competence,* 1974, 11–45.

BRUNER, J. Learning the mother tongue, *Human Nature,* September 1978, *1*(9), 42–49.

BRUNER, J. S., OLVER, R. R., GREENFIELD, P. M., AND OTHERS. *Studies in cognitive growth.* New York: Wiley, 1966.

BUELL, M. A. A peaceful coexistence? Behaviorism vs. humanism. *Delta Kappa Gamma Bulletin,* Winter 1978, *44*(2), 29–31.

BURNHAM, P. S., AND HEWITT, B. A. Advanced placement scores: Their predictive validity. *Educational and Psychological Measurement,* 1971, *31,* 939–945.

BUSK, P. L., FORD, R. C., AND SCHULMAN, J. L. Effects of schools' racial composition on the self-concept of black and white students. *Journal of Educational Research,* 1973, *67,* 57–63.

BYALICK, R., AND BERSOFF, D. N. Reinforcement practices of black and white teachers in integrated classrooms. *Journal of Educational Psychology,* 1974, *66,* 473–480.

CALDWELL, B. M. The fourth dimension in early childhood education. In R. D. Hess and R. M. Bear (Eds.), *Early education.* Chicago: Aldine, 1968.

CALHOUN, G. Hyperactive emotionally disturbed and hyperkinetic learning disabilities: A challenge for the regular classroom. *Adolescence,* 1978, *13*(50), 335–338.

CARLSON, J. S. Children's probability judgments as related to age, intelligence, socio-economic level, and sex. *Human Development,* 1969, *12,* 192–203.

CASTANEDA, A., PALERMO, D. S., AND MCCANDLESS, B. R. Complex learning and performance as a function of anxiety in children and task difficulty. *Child Development,* 1956, *27,* 327–332,

CATTELL, R. B. Theory of fluid and crystallized intelligence: A critical experiment. *Journal of Educational Psychology,* 1963, *54*(1), 1–22.

CAUDILL, W., AND WEINSTEIN, H. Maternal care and infant behavior in Japan and America. *Psychiatry,* 1969, *32,* 12–43.

CAZDEN, C. The Electric Company turns-on to reading. *Harvard Graduate School of Education Bulletin,* Spring 1972, *16,* 2–3.

Central Advisory Council for Education. *Children and their primary schools* (Vols. 1 and 2). London: Her Majesty's Stationery Office, 1967.

CHALL, J. S. *Learning to read: The great debate.* New York: McGraw-Hill, 1967.

CHAN, J. The art of test taking. *McCall's,* April 1975, p. 38.

Choice in Quincy. *Time,* March 10, 1975, p. 73

CHOMSKY, C. *The acquisition of syntax in children from five to ten.* Cambridge, Mass:, MIT Press, 1969.

CHOMSKY, N. *Syntactic structures.*The Hague: Mouton, 1957.

CHOMSKY, N. Language and the mind. *Psychology Today,* February 1968, 48–51 ff.

CICCONE, D. S. Massed and distributed item repetition in verbal discrimination learning. *Journal of Experimental Psychology,* 1973, *101,* 396–397.

CICIRELLI, V., AND OTHERS. *The impact of Head Start: An evaluation of the effects of Head Start on children's cognitive and affective development.* The report of a study undertaken by Westinghouse Learning Corporation and Ohio University under DED contract B 89–4536, Washington, D.C., 1969.

Citizens' Board of Inquiry into Hunger and Malnutrition in the U.S. *Hunger U.S.A.* (A report). Boston: Beacon, 1968.

CLAIBORN, W. L. Expectancy effects in the classroom. *Journal of Educational Psychology,* 1969, *60,* 377–383.

CLARK, D. H. (Ed.). *The psychology of education.* New York: Free Press, 1967.

CLARK, K. *An appendix to a possible reality.* New York: Metropolitan Applied Research Center, 1970.

CLARKE-STEWART, K. A. Interactions between mothers and their young children. *Monographs of the Society for Research in Child Development,* 1973, *38* (6–7, Serial No. 153).

CLIFFORD, J. O. Kids check out pets at library. *Pittsburgh Press,* April 27, 1975, p. E–1.

CLIFFORD, M. M., CLEARY, T. A., WALSTER, G. W. Effects of emphasizing competition in classroom-testing procedures. *Journal of Educational Research,* 1972, *65,* 234–238.

Closed-circuit sight. *Human Behavior,* February 1975, 30.

COATES, T. J., AND THORESEN, C. E. Teacher anxiety: A review with recommendations. *Review of Educational Research,* Spring 1976, *46*(2), 159–184.

COGAN, M. L. The behavior of teachers and the productive behavior of their pupils. *Journal of Experimental Education,* 1958, *27,* 89–124.

COHEN, A. The Culver City Spanish Immersion Program: The first two years. *Modern Language Journal,* 1974, *58,* 95–103.

COHEN, A. L., AND FILIPCZAK, J. *A new learning environment.* San Francisco: Jossey-Bass, 1971.

COHEN, M. A., AND MARTIN, G. L. Applying precision teaching to academic assessment. *Teaching Exceptional Children,* 1971, *3,* 147–150.

COHEN, P. S., AND COHEN, L. R. Computer generated tests for a student paced course. *Educational Technology,* March 1973, 18–19.

COLE, N. *Studies of recent declines in test scores.* Symposium presented at the Northeast Educational Research Association, Ellenville, N.Y., October 1977.

COLE, R. W., AND DUNN, R. A new lease on life for education of the handicapped. *Phi Delta Kappan,* September 1977, *59*(1), 3–10.

COLEMAN, J., AND BROEN, W. E., Jr. *Abnormal psychology and modern life* (4th ed.). Glenview, Ill.: Scott, Foresman, 1972.

COLES, R. Like it is in the alley. *Daedalus,* 1968, *97,* 1315–1330.

College Entrance Examination Board. *On Further Examination.* New York: Author, 1977.

COLQUHOUN, W. P., BLAKE, M. J. F., AND EDWARDS, R. S. Experimental studies of shift work I: A comparison of 'rotating' and 'stabilized' four hour shift systems. *Economics,* 1968, *11* 437–453.

COMBS, A. W. *The professional education of teachers.* Boston: Allyn & Bacon, 1965.

COMBS, A. W. Humanistic goals of education. In D. A. Read and S. B. Simon (Eds.), *Humanistic education sourcebook.* Englewood Cliffs, N. J.: Prentice-Hall, 1975.

Consortium on Developmental Continuity. *The persistence of preschool effects.* Final report to the Administration on Children, Youth and Families, September 1977.

COOK, A. M. Alternative schools as a solution for the back-to-basics-antibasics-feud. *Delta Kappa Gamma Bulletin,* Winter 1978, *44*(2), 61–63

COOLEY, W. W., AND GLASER, R. The computer and individualized instruction. *Science,* 1969, *166,* 574–579.

COOPER, H. M. Controlling personal rewards: Professional teachers' differential use of feedback and the effects of feedback on the students' motivation to perform. *Journal of Educational Psychology,* 1977, *69*(4), 419–427.

COOPER, J. A. Application of the consultant role to parent-teacher management of school avoidance behavior. *Psychology in the Schools,* 1973, *10,* 259–262.

COOPERSMITH, S. *The antecedents of self-esteem.* San Francisco: Freeman, 1967.

COOPERSMITH, S. Studies in self-esteem. *Scientific American,* February, 1968, 96–100 ff.

COSTANZO, P. R., AND SHAW, M. E. Conformity as a function of age level. *Child Development,* 1966, *37,* 967–975.

CRAIK, F.I.M., AND BLANKSTEIN, K. K. Psychophysiology and human memory. In P. H. Venables and M. J. Christie (Eds.), *Research in Psychophysiology.* London: Wiley, 1975.

CRANO, W., AND Mellon, P. M. Causal influence of teachers' expectations on children's academic performance: A cross-logged panel analysis. *Journal of Educational Psychology,* 1978, *70*(1), 39–48.

CRAWFORD, J. (Ed.). *CORD national research training manual* (2nd ed.). Monmouth, Ore.: Training Research Division of the Oregon State System of Higher Education, 1969.

CRONBACH, L. J. How can instruction be adapted to individual differences? In R. M. Gagné (Ed.), *Learning and individual differences.* Columbus, Ohio: Merrill, 1967.

CRONBACH, L. J. *Essentials of Psychological Testing* (3rd ed.). New York: Harper & Row, 1970.

CROW, J. F. Genetic theories and influences. *Harvard Educational Review,* 1969, *39,* 301–309.

CULHANE, B. R., AND CURWIN, R. There's a deaf child in my class. *Learning,* October 1978, *7(2),* 111–117.

CURTIS, J., AND ALTMANN, H. The relationship between the teacher's self-concept and the self-concept of students. *Child Study Journal,* 1977, *7(1),* 17–25.

CURWIN, R. The grapes of wrath: Some alternatives. *Learning,* February 1978, *6(60),* 60–64.

CUSIMANO, V. J. The test as a teaching and learning tool. *American Biology Teacher,* March 1975, 176 f.

DALE, P. S. *Language development.* Hinsdale, Ill.: Dryden, 1972.

D'ALONZO, B. J., AND MILLER, S. R. A management model for learning disabled adolescents. *Teaching Exceptional Children,* Spring 1977, *9(3),* 58–60.

DAMICO, S. B., AND PURKEY, W. W. Class clowns: A study of middle school students. *American Educational Research Journal,* Summer 1978, *15,(3),* 391–398.

DANNER, F. W., AND Day, M. C. Eliciting formal operations. *Child Development,* 1977, *48,* 1600–1606.

DAVIS, A. Socio-economic influences upon children's learning. *Understanding the Child,* 1951, *20,* 10–16.

DAVIS, A. Cultural factors in remediation. *Educational Horizons,* 1965, *43,* 231–251.

DAVIS, R., AND BUCHWALD, A. M. An exploration of somatic response patterns. *Journal of Comparative and Physiological Psychology,* 1957, *50,* 44–52.

Day care? In France, it's a science. *New York Times,* December 20, 1970, Section 2, p. 18.

DAY, W. F., AND MOWRER, O. H. Beyond bondage and regimentation. (Review of *Beyond freedom and dignity,* by B. F. Skinner.) *Contemporary Psychology,* 1972, *17,* 465–472.

DEAVILA, E. A., AND HAVASSY, B. The testing of minority children: A neo-Piagetian approach. *Today's Education,* November-December 1974, pp. 72–75.

DECECCO, J. P., AND CRAWFORD, W. R. *The psychology of learning and instruction: Educational psychology* (2nd ed.). Englewood Cliffs, N.J.: Prentice-Hall, 1974.

DEGROAT, A. F., AND THOMPSON, G. G. A study of the distribution of teacher approval and disapproval among sixth-grade pupils. *Journal of Experimental Education,* 1949, *18,* 57–75.

DENNO, D. The elementary school teacher: Conformity and maladjustment in a prefabricated role. *Adolescence,* 1977, *12(46),* 247–258.

DeVRIES, D. L., EDWARDS, K. J., AND SLAVIN, R. E. Biracial learning teams and race relations in the classroom: Four field experiments using teams-games-tournament. *Journal of Educational Psychology,* 1978, *70(3),* 356–362.

Divorce course. *Time,* December 2, 1974, 92.

DLUGOKINSKI, E., WEISS, S., AND JOHNSTON, S. Preschoolers at risk: Social, emotional, and cognitive considerations. *Psychology in the Schools,* 1976, *13,* 134–138.

DOCTOROW, M., WITTROCK, M. C., AND MARKS, C. Generative processes in reading comprehension. *Journal of Educational Psychology,* 1979, *70(2),* 109–118.

DODD, C. A., JONES, G. A., AND LAMB, C. E. Diagnosis and remediation of pupil errors. *School Science and Mathematics,* March 1975, pp. 270–276.

DOMINO, G. Interactive effects of achievement orientation and teaching style on academic achievement. *Journal of Educational Psychology,* 1971, *62,* 427–431.

DORFMAN, D. The Cyril Burt question: New findings. *Science,* September 29, 1978, *201* (4362), 1177–1186.

DORROS, S., AND BROWNE, J. What you can do now. *Today's Education,* January 1973, 41–42.

DORSEY, M. F., AND HOPKINS, L. T. The influence of attitude upon transfer. *Journal of Educational Psychology,* 1930, *21,* 410–417.

DOUGLAS, J., AND WONG, A. Formal operations: Age and sex differences in Chinese and American children. *Child Development,* 1977, *48,* 689–692.

DOUVAN, E., AND ADELSON, J. B. *The Adolescent Experience.* New York: Wiley, 1966.

DOYAL, G. T., AND FRIEDMAN, R. J. Anxiety in children: Some observations for the school psychologist. *Psychology in the Schools,* 1974, *11,* 161–164.

DOYLE, K. O., AND MOEN, R. E.. Toward the definition of a domain of academic motivation. *Journal of Educational Psychology,* 1978, *70(2),* 231–235.

DOYLE, W., AND REDWINE, J. McN. Effect of intent-action discrepency and student performance feedback on teacher behavior change. *Journal of Educational Psychology,* 1974, *66,* 750–755.

DREYFUS, H. L. *What computers can't do: A critique of artificial reason.* New York: Harper & Row, 1972.

DUKE, D. L. How the adults in your schools cause student discipline problems—and what to do about it. *American School Board Journal*, June 1978, *165*(6), 29–46.

DUNAWAY, J. How to cut discipline problems in half. *Today's Education*, September-October 1974, 75–77.

DWYER, F. M. *A Guide for Improving Visualized Instruction*. State College, Pa.: Learning Services, 1972.

EBBINGHAUS, H. *Memory: A contribution to experimental psychology* (H. A. Ruger and C. E. Bussenius, trans.). New York: Teachers College, Columbia University, 1913. (Originally published, 1885)

EBEL, R. L. The relation of testing programs to educational goals. In W. G. Findley (Ed.), *The impact and improvement of school testing programs* (62nd Yearbook of the National Society for the Study of Education, Part 2). Chicago: University of Chicago Press, 1963.

EBEL, R. L. Should school marks be abolished? *Michigan Journal of Secondary Education*, 1964, *6*, 12–18.

EBEL, R. L. Behavioral objectives. *Phi Delta Kappan*, 1970, *52*, 171–173.

EBEL, R. L. Criterion-referenced measurements. *School Review*, 1971, *79*, 282–288.

Education USA. Schools don't need to go back to basics; they need to go "back to complexity." February 20, 1978, *20*(25), 187.

Education USA. Schools don't need to go back to basics. March 13, 1978, *20*(28), 210.

Education USA. From those who've done it: How to get those SAT scores up. April 3, 1978, *20*(31), 233.

Education USA. Are competency tests for teachers the next step? May 1, 1978, *20*(35), 265.

Education USA. Board members say standards went down. May 13, 1978, *20*(28), 210.

Education USA. Oregon competencies—Process was worth it. May 29, 1978, *20*(39), 300.

Education USA. Daily 'pot' rate climbing among youth. June 12, 1978, *20*(37), 282.

Education USA. NEA leaders want halt to state competency testing. July 10, 1978, *20*(45), 335.

Education USA. PTA may challenge TV licenses. August 28, 1978, *20*(52), 379.

Education USA. New SAT scores: Has the decline ended? September 1978, *20*(3).

EISNER, E. W. Emerging models for educational evaluation. *School Review*, 1972, *80*, 573–590.

ELKIND, D. Children's conceptions of brother and sister: Piaget replication study V. *Journal of Genetic Psychology*, 1962, *100*, 129–136.

ELLINGSON, C., AND CASS, J. Teaching the dyslexic child: New hope for non-readers. *Saturday Review*, April 16, 1966, 82–85 f.

ELLIS, H. *The transfer of learning*. New York: Macmillan, 1967.

ELLIS, H. C. *Fundamentals of human learning and cognition*. Dubuque, Iowa: William C. Brown, 1972.

ELLIS, J. A. Transfer failure and proactive interference in short-term memory. *Journal of Experimental Psychology: Human Learning and Memory*, 1977, *3*(2), 211–221.

ENGEL, B. S. A sensible alternative to standardized reading tests. *Learning*, November 1978, 94–95.

Enterprise: Cheating, Inc. *Newsweek*, March 20, 1972, 89–90.

ERIKSON, E. H. Identity and the life cycle: Selected papers. *Psychological Issues*, 1959, *1*(1), 90–91.

ERIKSON, E. H. *Childhood and society*. New York: Norton, 1963.

ERIKSON, E. H. *Identity: Youth and crisis*. New York: Norton, 1968.

ERVIN-TRIPP, S. Language and thought. In S. Tax (Ed.), *Horizons of anthropology*. Chicago: Aldine, 1964.

ESBENSEN, T. Writing instructional objectives. *Phi Delta Kappan*, 1967, *48*, 246–247.

Evaluation and Advisory Service. *Short-cut statistics for teacher-made tests*. Princeton, N.J.: Educational Testing Service, 1964.

FAGOT, B. I. Consequences of moderate cross-gender behavior in pre-school children. *Child Development*, 1977, *48*(3), 902–907.

FARR, B., FAY, L., AND NEGLEY, H. *Then and now: Reading achievement in Indiana (1944–45 and 1976)*. Bloomington, Indiana School of Education, Indiana University, 1978.

FEATHER, N. T. Persistence at a difficult task with alternative task of intermediate difficulty. *Journal of Abnormal and Social Psychology*, 1963, *66*, 604–609.

FEATHERSTONE, J. *Schools where children learn*. New York: Liveright, 1971.

FEINGOLD, B. F. *Introduction to clinical allergy*. Springfield, Ill: Charles C Thomas, 1973.

FEINGOLD, B. F. *Why your child is hyperactive*. New York: Random House, 1975.

FELDMESSER, R. A. The positive functions of grades. *Educational Record*, 1972, *53*, 66–72.

FELKER, D. W. *Building positive self-concepts*. Minneapolis: Burgess, 1974.

FESHBACH, N. D. Cross-cultural studies of teaching styles in four-year-olds and their mothers. In A. D. Pick (Ed.), *Minnesota Symposium on Child Psychology* (Vol. 7.) Minneapolis: University of Minnesota Press, 1972.

FESTINGER, L., AND CARLSMITH, J. M. Cognitive consequences of forced compliance. *Journal of Abnormal and Social Psychology*, 1959, *58*, 203–210.

FIELDS, C. M. Students' rights versus confidential files. *Chronicle of Higher Education*, October 7, 1974, 1 f.

Finding out what teachers need and want. *Today's Education*, October 1972, 31–35.

FINDLEY, W. G., AND BRYAN, M. M. Ability grouping:

1970. Athens: Center for Educational Improvement, University of Georgia, 1970.

FISHER, R. J. *Learning how to learn*. New York: Harcourt Brace Jovanovich, 1972.

FITTS, P. M. Factors in complex skill training. In R. Glaser (Ed.), *Training research and education*. Pittsburgh: University of Pittsburgh Press, 1962.

FLANDERS, N. A. Intent, action and feedback: A preparation for teaching. *Journal of Teacher Education*, 1963, *14*, 251–260.

FLANDERS, N. A. *Analyzing teaching behavior*. Reading, Mass: Addison-Wesley, 1970.

FLANDERS, N. A., AND HAVUMAKI, S. Group compliance to dominative teacher influence. *Human Relations*, 1960, *13*, 67–82.

FLANDERS, N. A., AND SIMON, A. Teacher effectiveness. In R. L. Ebel (Ed.), *Encyclopedia of educational research* (4th ed.). New York: Macmillan, 1969.

FLAVELL, H. J. *The developmental psychology of Jean Piaget*. Princeton: Van Nostrand, 1963.

FLEMING, E. S., AND ANTTONEN, R. G. Teacher expectancy or My Fair Lady. *American Educational Research Journal*, 1971, *8*, 241–252.

FLESCH, R. *Why Johnny can't read and what you can do about it*. New York: Harper & Row, 1955.

Florida State Department of Education, Division of Elementary and Secondary Education. *District Procedures for Providing Special Education for Exceptional Students: 1974 Guidelines* (Vol. 2). Tallahassee, Fla.: Author, 1974. (ERIC Document Reproduction Service No. ED 087 164).

FOELLINGER, D. B., AND TRABASSO, T. Seeing, hearing and doing: A developmental study of memory for actions. *Child Development*, 1977, *48*(4), 1482–1488.

FOLKARD, S., MONK, T. H., BRADBURY, R., AND ROSENTHAL, J. Time of day effects in school children's immediate and delayed recall of meaningful material. *British Journal of Psychology*, 1977, *68*, 45–50.

FOLLMAN, J., LOWE, A. J., AND MILLER, W. Graphics variables and reliability and level of essay grades. *American Educational Research Journal*, 1971, *8*, 365–373.

FONDY, A. *The "merit pay" mirage*. Pittsburgh: Pittsburgh Federation of Teachers, June 1973.

FONTANA, G. L. J. An investigation into the dynamics of achievement motivation in women (Doctoral dissertation, University of Michigan, 1970). *Dissertation Abstracts International*, 1971, *32B*, 1821B. (University Microfilms No. 71–23, 754)

FRANK, G. H. The role of the family in the development of psychopathology. *Psychological Bulletin*, 1965, *64*, 191–205.

FRANKLIN, B. A. The Appalachian creekers: Literally, a world apart. *New York Times*, October 27, 1974, 10.

FREEMAN, G. L., AND HOVLAND, C. I. Diurnal variations in performance and related physiological processes. *Psychological Bulletin*, 1934, *31*, 777–799.

FREUD, A. *The ego and the mechanisms of defence* (C. Baines, trans.). London: Hogarth, 1937.

FREUD, A., AND BURLINGHAM, D.T. *War and children*. New York: International Universities Press, 1943

FREUD, A., AND BURLINGHAM, D. T. *Infants without families*. New York: International Universities Press, 1944.

FREUD, S. *The basic writings of Sigmund Freud* (A. A. Brill, Ed. and trans.). New York: Modern Library, 1938.

FREUD, S. *An outline of psychoanalysis* (J. Strachey, trans.). New York: Norton, 1949.

FREUD, S. Three essays on the theory of sexuality. In the *Complete psychological works of Sigmund Freud*. Standard edition, Vol. 5, 1905. Reprint. London: Hogarth Press, 1953.

FREYBERG, J. T. Increasing children's fantasies. *Psychology Today*, February 1975, 63–64.

FRIEDER, B. Motivator: Least developed of teacher roles. *Educational Technology*, February 1970, 28–36.

FRIEDMAN, R. J., AND DOYAL, G. T. Depression in children. *Psychology in the Schools*, 1974, *11*, 19–23.

FRIEDMAN, W. J. The development of children's understanding of cyclic aspects of time. *Child Development*, 1977, *48*, 1593–1599.

FRIEDRICH, L. K., AND STEIN, A. H. Aggressive and prosocial television programs and the natural behavior of preschool children. *Monographs of the Society for Research in Child Development*, 1973, *38*(4, Serial No. 151).

FRIES, C. C. *Linguistics and reading*. New York: Holt, Rinehart and Winston, 1963.

From a student—William (Mannix) Smith. In J. Bremer and M. von Moschzisker (Eds.), *The school without walls: Philadelphia's Parkway Program*. New York: Holt, Rinehart and Winston, 1971.

FROSTIG, M., AND MASLOW, P. *Learning problems in the classroom*. New York: Grune & Stratton, 1973.

FUCHS, E. How teachers learn to help children fail. In J. McV. Hunt (Ed.), *Human intelligence*. New Brunswick, N.J.: Transaction Books, 1972.

FURTH, H. *Piaget for teachers*. Englewood Cliffs, N.J.: Prentice-Hall, 1970.

FURTH, W., AND WACHS, H. *Thinking goes to school*. New York: Oxford University Press, 1975.

GAGNÉ, E. D., BING, S. B., AND BING, J. R. Combined effect of goal organization and test expectations on organization in free recall following learning from text. *Journal of Educational Psychology*, 1977, *69*(4), 428–431.

GAGNÉ, R. M. The acquisition of knowledge. *Psychological Review*, 1962, *69*, 355–365.

GAGNÉ, R. M. The analysis of instructional objectives for the design of instruction. In R. Glaser (Ed.), *Teaching machines and programmed learning. II: Data and Directions.* Washington, D.C.: National Educational Association, 1965.(a)

GAGNÉ, R. M. Educational objectives and human performance. In J. D. Krumboltz (Ed.), *Learning and the educational process.* Chicago: Rand McNally, 1965. (b).

GAGNÉ, R. M. The learning of concepts. *School Review*, 1965, *73*, 187–196. (c).

GAGNÉ, R. M. Contributions of learning to human development. *Psychological Review*, 1968, *75*, 177–191.

GAGNÉ, R. M. Context, isolation, and interference effects on the retention of fact. *Journal of Educational Psychology*, 1969, *60*, 408–414.

GAGNÉ, R. M. *The conditions of learning* (2nd ed.). New York: Holt, Rinehart and Winston, 1970.

GAGNÉ, R. M. *Essentials of learning for instruction.* Hinsdale, Ill.: Dryden, 1974.

GAGNÉ, R. M., AND BRIGGS, L. J. *Principles of instructional design.* New York: Holt, Rinehart and Winston, 1974.

GAIR, S. B. An art-based remediation program for children with learning disabilities, *Studies in Art Education*, 1975, *17*(1), 55–67.

GAIR, S. B. Form and function: Teaching problem learners through art. *Teaching Exceptional Children*, Winter 1977, *9*(2), 30–32.

GALL, M. D., WARD, B. A., BERLINER, D. C., COHEN, L. S., WINNE, P. H., ELASHOFF, J. D., AND STANTON, G. C. Effects of questioning techniques and recitation on student learning. *American Educational Research Journal*, Spring 1978, *15*(2), 175–199.

GALLOWAY, C. Precision parents and the development of retarded behavior. In J. B. Jordan and L. S. Robbins (Eds.), *Let's try doing something else kind of thing: Behavioral principles and the exceptional child.* Arlington, Va.: Council for Exceptional Children, 1972.

GALLUP, G. H. Fourth annual Gallup poll of public attitudes toward education. *Phi Delta Kappan*, 1972, *54*, 33–46.

GALLUP, G. H. The tenth annual Gallup poll of the public's attitude toward the public schools. *Phi Delta Kappan*, September 1978, *60*(1), 33–45.

GARRETT, H. E. *Testing for teachers.* New York: American Book, 1965.

GATES, A. I. Variations in efficiency during the day, together with practice effects, sex differences and correlations. *University of California Publications in Psychology*, 1916, *2*, 1–156.

GEARHART, B. R., AND WEISHAHN, M. W. *The handicapped child in the regular classroom.* St. Louis, Mo.: C. V. Mosby, 1976.

GENSHAFT, J. L., AND HIRST, M. Language differences between black children and white children. *Developmental Psychology*, 1974, *10*, 451–456.

GENTILE, A. M. A working model of skill acquisition with application to teaching. *Quest*, 1972, *17*, 1–23.

GEORGIADY, N. P., AND ROMANO, L. G. Ulcerville, U.S.A. *Educational Leadership*, December 1971, 269–272.

GERBNER, G. Drama: Trends and symbolic violence in television functions. In G. A. Comstock and E. A. Rubenstein (Eds.), *Television and social behavior: Media content and control.* Washington, D.C.: U.S. Government Printing Office, 1972.

GESELL, A., Ilg, F., AMES, L., AND RODELL, JR. *Infant and child in the culture of today* (rev. ed). New York: Harper & Row, 1974.

GETZELS, J. W. Conflict and role behavior in the educational setting. In W. W. Charters, Jr., and N. L. Gage (Eds.), *Readings in the social psychology of education.* Boston: Allyn & Bacon, 1963.

GIBSON, E. J. The ontogeny of reading. *American Psychologist*, 1970, 25, 136–143.

GIBSON, E. J. Learning to read. *Science*, 1965, *148*, 1066–1072.

GIBSON, E. J. Perceptual learning in educational situations. In R. M. Gagné and W. J. Gephart (Eds.), *Learning research and school subjects.* Itasca, Ill.: Peacock, 1968.

GIBSON, E. J. *Principles of perceptual learning and development.* New York: Appleton-Century-Crofts, 1969.

GIBSON, E. J. The development of perception as an adaptive process. *American Scientist*, 1970, *58*, 98–107.

GIBSON, E. J., PICK, A., OSSER, H., AND HAMMOND, M. The role of grapheme-phoneme correspondence in the perception of words. *American Journal of Psychology*, 1962, *75*, 554–570.

GIBSON, J. *Educational psychology: A programmed text.* New York: Appleton-Century-Crofts, 1968.

GIBSON, J. *Educational psychology: A programmed text* (2nd ed.). Englewood Cliffs, N.J.: Prentice-Hall, Inc., 1972.

GIBSON, J. *Experiencing the inner city.* New York: Harper & Row, 1973. (a)

GIBSON, J. *Principles of instruction.* Pittsburgh: University of Pittsburgh Press, 1973. (b)

GIBSON, J. *Goals of educational psychology in teacher preparation.* Paper presented at meeting of the American Educational Research Association, Washington, D.C., March 1975.

GIBSON, J. Goals of educational psychology: A discipline approach. *Contemporary Educational Psychology*, Spring 1976.

GIBSON, J. *Growing up: A study of children*. Reading, Mass.: Addison-Wesley, 1978.

GIBSON, J. A current view of Soviet research in cognitive psychology. *Contemporary Educational Psychology*, Spring 1980, *5*, 184–191.

GIBSON, J. The special child: A cross-cultural view. *Phi Delta Kappan*, December, 1980.

GIBSON, J., AND VINOGRADOFF, E. *Growing up in Moscow*. In Press.

GIBSON, J., WURST, K., AND CANNONITO, M. *Caretaker-child interactions in three societies*. In preparation.

GILBERT, N., SPRING, C., AND SASSENRATH, J. Effects of overlearning and similarity on transfer in word recognition. *Perceptual and Motor Skills*, 1977, *44*, 591–598.

GINOTT, H. G. *Between parent and child*. New York: Macmillan, 1965.

GLASER, R. Psychology and instructional technology. In R. Glaser (Ed.), *Training research and education*. Pittsburgh: University of Pittsburgh Press, 1962.

GLASER, R., AND RESNICK, L. B. Instructional psychology. *Annual Review of Psychology*, 1972, *23*, 207–276.

GLYNN, S. M., AND DiVESTA, F. J. Outline and hierarchical organization as aids for study and retrieval. *Journal of Educational Psychology*, 1977, *69*(2), 89–95.

GODSAVE, B. F. What not to do for the hearing impaired child. *Learning*, October 1978, *7*(2), 117–118.

GOEBES, D. S., AND SHORE, M. F. Behavioral expectations of students as related to the sex of the teacher. *Psychology in the Schools*, 1975, *12*(2), 222–224.

GOLDBERG, C. Some effects of fear of failure in the academic setting. *Journal of Psychology*, 1973, *84*, 323–331.

GOLDFARB A. F. Puberty and menarche. *Clinical Obstetrics and Gynecology*, 1977, *20*(3), 625–631.

GOLDSTEIN, K. M., AND TILKER, H. A. Attitudes toward A-B-C-D-F and honors-pass-fail grading systems. *Journal of Educational Research*, 1971, *65*, 99–100.

GOLICK, M. *A parent's guide to learning problems*. Montreal, Quebec: Association for Children with Learning Disabilities, 1970.

GOOD, T. L., AND BECKERMAN, T. M. An examination of teachers' effects on high, middle, and low aptitude performance on a standardized achievement test. *American Educational Research Journal*, Summer 1978, *15*(3), 477–482.

GORES, H. B. Schools in the 70's. *National Association of Secondary School Principals Bulletin*, May 1970, *54*, 134–138.

GOTTLIEB, J., SEMMEL, M. I., AND VELDMAN, D. J. Correlates of social status among mainstreamed mentally retarded children. *Journal of Educational Psychology*, 1978, *70*(3), 396–405.

Grade-school philosophers. *Time*, November 18, 1974, p. 74.

GRAUBARD, A. The free school movement. *Harvard Educational Review*, 1972, *42*, 351–373.

GRAY, F., GRAUBARD, P. S., AND ROSENBERG, H. Little brother is changing you. *Psychology Today*, March 1974, 42–46.

GREEN, J. A. *Teacher-made tests*. New York: Harper & Row, 1963.

GREEN, R. L. The black quest for higher education. *Personnel and Guidance Journal*, 1969, *47*. 905–911.

GREEN, R. L., SMITH, E., AND SCHWEITZER, J. H. Busing and the multiracial classroom. *Phi Delta Kappan*, 1972, *53*, 543–547.

GREENO, J. G., JAMES, C. T., AND DaPOLITO, F. J. A cognitive interpretation of negative transfer and forgetting of paired associates. *Journal of Verbal Learning and Verbal Behavior*, 1971, *10*, 331–345.

GRIER, W. H., AND COBBS, P. M. *Black rage*. New York: Basic Books, 1968.

GRIMES, J. W., AND ALLINSMITH, W. Compulsivity, anxiety, and school achievement. *Merrill-Palmer Quarterly*, 1961, *7*, 247–271.

GRONLUND, N. E. *Preparing criterion-referenced tests for classroom instruction*. New York: Macmillan, 1973.

GRUNAU, R. V. Effects of elaborative prompt condition and developmental level on the performance of additional problems by kindergarten children. *Journal of Educational Psychology*, 1978, *70*(3), 422–432.

GULLOTTA, T. P. Teacher attitudes toward the moderately disturbed child. *Exceptional Children*, 1974, *41*, 49–50.

GUTHRIE, E. R. *The psychology of learning* (Rev. ed.). New York: Harper & Brothers, 1952.

GUTHRIE, G. M., MASANGKAY, Z. AND GUTHRIE, H. A. Behavior, malnutrition, and mental development. *Journal of Cross-Cultural Psychology*, June 1976, *7*(2), 169–180.

HACKETT, R. In praise of praise. *American Education*, March 1975, pp. 11–15.

HALES, L. W., BAIN, P. T., AND RAND, L. P. The pass-fail option. *Journal of Educational Research*, 1973, *66*, 295–298.

HALL, J. W., AND PRESSLEY, G. M. *Free recall and recognition memory in young children*. Paper presented at the Annual Meeting of the Psychonomic Society, St. Louis, November 1973.

HALL, R. V., AXELROD, S., FOUNDOPOULOS, M., SHELL-

MAN, J., CAMPBELL, R. A., AND CRANSTON, S. S. The effective use of punishment to modify behavior in the classroom. *Educational Technology,* April 1971, 24–26.

HALL, V. C. Why Americans can't write. *Human Nature.* August 1978, *1*(8), 74–79.

HALL, V. C., AND KAYE, D. B. Patterns of early cognitive development among boys in four subcultural groups. *Journal of Educational Psychology,* 1977. *69,* 66–88

HAMBLEN, A. A. *Investigation to determine the extent to which the effect of the study of Latin upon a knowledge of English derivatives can be increased by conscious adaptation of content and method to the attainment of this objective.* Philadelphia: University of Pennsylvania Press, 1925.

HAMM, N. H., AND HOVING, K. L. Conformity of children in an ambiguous perceptual situation. *Child Development,* 1969, *40,* 773–784.

HARARI, H., AND McDAVID, J. W. Name stereotypes and teachers' expectations. *Journal of Educational Psychology,* 1973, *65,* 222–225.

HARDIE, C. D. Measurement in education. *Educational Theory,* Winter 1978, *28*(1), 54–61.

HARLOW, H. F. The formation of learning sets. *Psychological Review,* 1949, *56,* 51–65.

HARLOW, H. F. The nature of love. *American Psychologist,* 1958, *13,* 673–685

HARLOW, H. F., AND HARLOW, M. K. Learning to love. *American Scientist,* 1966, *54,* 244–272.

HARLOW, H. F., HARLOW, M. K., AND MEYER, D. R. Learning motivated by a manipulation drive. *Journal of Experimental Psychology,* 1950, *40,* 228–234.

HARLOW, H. F., AND ZIMMERMANN, R. R. Affectional responses in the infant monkey. *Science,* 1959, *130,* 421–432.

HARMIN, M., KIRSCHENBAUM, H., AND SIMON, S. *Clarifying values through subject matter.* Minneapolis: Winston Press, 1972.

HARPER, R. A. *Psychoanalysis and psychotherapy.* New York: Jason Aronson, 1974.

HARRINGTON, C., AND WHITING, J. W. M Socialization process and personality. In F. L. K. Hsu (Ed.), *Psychological anthropology* (2nd ed.). Cambridge, Mass.: Schenkman, 1972.

HARRIS, D. Factors affecting college grades: A review of the literature, 1930–1937. *Psychological Bulletin,* 1940, *37,* 125–166.

HARRISON, M. *Instant reading: The story of the Initial Teaching Alphabet.* London: Pitman, 1964.

HART, L. A. The new 'brain' concept of learning. *Phi Delta Kappan,* February 1978, *59*(6), 393–396.

HARTSHORNE, H., AND MAY, M. A. *Studies in the organization of character.* New York: Macmillan, 1930.

HARTUP, W. W. Peer interaction and social organization. In P. H. Mussen (Ed.), *Carmichael's manual of child psychology* (3rd ed.) (Vol. 2). New York: Wiley, 1970.

HARVEY, J. C. AND HOLMES, C. H. Busing and school desegregation. *Phi Delta Kappan,* 1972, *53,* 540–542.

HASLERUD, G. M., AND MEYERS, S. The transfer value of given and individually derived principles. *Journal of Educational Psychology,* 1958, *49,* 293–298.

HAVIGHURST, R. J. *Developmental tasks and education* (2nd ed.). New York: Longmans, Green, 1952.

HAVIGHURST, R. J. *Human development and education.* New York: Longmans, Green, 1953.

HAVIGHURST, R. J. Minority subcultures and the law of effect. *American Psychologist,* 1969, *25,* 313–322.

HAVIS, A. L., AND YAWKEY, T. D. "Back-to-basics" in early childhood education: A re-examination of "good old rithmetic." *Education,* Winter 1977, *98*(2), 135–140.

HAYDEN, A. H., AND EDGAR, E. Developing individualized education programs for young handicapped children. *Teaching Exceptional Children,* Spring 1978, *10*(3), 67–70.

HEATHERS, G. Grouping. In R. L. Ebel (Ed.), *Encyclopedia of educational research* (4th ed.). New York: Macmillan, 1969.

HEBB, D. O. A return to Jensen and his social science critics. *American Psychologist,* 1970, *25,* 568.

HECHINGER, F. M. About education. *New York Times,* May 1, 1979, C5.

HECHINGER, G., AND HECHINGER, F. M. The corporal punishment debate, updated. *New York Times Magazine,* October 6, 1974, pp. 84 ff.

HENRY, J. Attitude organization in elementary school classrooms. *American Journal of Orthopsychiatry,* 1957, *27,* 117–133.

HENRY, J. Of achievement, hope, and time in poverty. In J. McV. Hunt (Ed.), *Human intelligence.* New Brunswick, N.J.: Transaction Books, 1972.

HENTOFF, N. A parent-teacher's view of corporal punishment. *Today's Education,* May 1973, 18–21.

HETENYI, L. Unionism: The ethics of it. *Educational Theory,* Spring 1978, *28*(2), 90–95.

HEWETT, F. M. Teaching speech to an autistic child through operant conditioning. *American Journal of Orthopsychiatry,* 1965, *35,* 927–936.

HILGARD, E. R., AND BOWER, G. H. *Theories of learning* (4th ed.). Englewood Cliffs, N.J.: Prentice-Hall, 1975.

HOFFMAN, M. L. Moral development. In P. H. Mussen (Ed.). *Carmichael's manual of child psychology* (3rd ed.) (Vol. 2). New York: Wiley, 1970.

HOGAN, I. M. David mainstreams himself. *Teacher,* December 1978, *96*(44), 49–50.

HOHN, R. L., AND MEINKE, D. L. Competency-based education and educational psychology. *Contemporary Education*, Summer 1978, *49*(4), 211–213.

HOLLAND, J. G. *Behavior modification for prisoners, patients, and other people as a prescription for the planned society*. Paper presented at the meeting of the Eastern Psychological Association, Philadelphia, April 1974.

HOLSTEIN, C. E. *The relation of children's moral judgment level to that of their parents and to communication patterns in the family*. Paper presented at the Biennial Meeting of the Society for Research in Child Development, Santa Monica, Calif., 1969.

HOLT, J. *What do I do Monday?* New York: Dutton, 1970.

HOLZMAN, P. S. AND KLEIN, G. S. Cognitive system principles of leveling and sharpening: Individual differences in assimilation effects in visual time-error. *Journal of Psychology*, 1954, *37*, 105–122.

HONZIK, M. P., MACFARLANE, J. W., AND ALLEN, L. The stability of mental test performance between two and eighteen years. *Journal of Experimental Education*, 1948, *17*, 309–324.

HORNER, M. S. Toward an understanding of achievement-related conflicts in women. *Journal of Social Issues*, 1972, *28*(2), 157–175.

HOUSE, B. J. Discrimination of symmetrical and asymmetrical dot patterns by retardates. *Journal of Experimental Child Psychology*, 1966, *3*, 377–389.

HOUSTON-STEIN, A., FRIEDRICH-COFER, L., AND SUSMAN, E. J. The relation of classroom structure to social behavior, imaginative play, and self-regulation of economically disadvantaged children. *Child Development*, 1977, *48*, 908–916.

HOUTS, P. S., AND ENTWISTLE, D. R. Academic achievement effort among females. *Journal of Counseling Psychology*, 1968, *15*, 284–286.

HOVING, K. L., HAMM, N., AND GALVIN, P. Social influence as a function of stimulus ambiguity at three age levels. *Developmental Psychology*, 1969, *1*, 631–636.

HOYT, J. H., Feeling free. *American Education*, November 1978, *14*(9), 24–28.(a)

HOYT, J. H. Mainstreaming Mary Ann. *American Education*, November 1978, *14* (9), 13–17.(b)

HSU, T. C, AND CARLSON, M. *Oakleaf School Project: Computer-assisted achievement testing*. Pittsburgh: Learning Research and Development Center, University of Pittsburgh, February 1972.

HUCK, S., AND BOUNDS, W. Essay grades: An interaction between graders' handwriting clarity and the neatness of examination papers. *American Educational Research Journal*, 1972, *9*, 279–283.

HUMMEL-ROSSI, B., AND MERRIFIELD, P. Student personality factors related to teacher reports of their interactions with students. *Journal of Educational Psychology*, 1977, *69*(4), 375–380.

Hunger USA: *A report by the citizen's board of inquiry into hunger and malnutrition in the U. S.* Boston: Beacon' Press, 1968, 10–31.

HUNT, D. E. Teachers are psychologists, too: On the application of psychology to education. *Canadian Psychological Review*, July 1976, *17*(3), 210–218.

HUNT, J. McV. *Development and the educational enterprise*. Paper delivered at the College of Education at Hofstra University, Hempstead, N.Y., November 15, 1973.

HUNTER, I.M.L. An exceptional memory. *British Journal of Psychology*, 1977, *68*, 155–164.

HUNTER, M. C. The role of physical education in child development and learning. In H. D. Behrens, and G. Maynard (Eds.) *The changing child*. Glenview, Ill,: Scott, Foresman, 1972.

HUSEN, T. *International study of achievement in mathematics* (Vol. 2). Uppsala, Sweden: Almquist and Wiksells, 1967.

HYRAM, G. H. *Socio-psychological concepts related to teaching the culturally disadvantaged*. New York: Pageant-Poseidon, 1972.

If you want to give up cigarettes. New York: American Cancer Society, 1970.

ILLICH, I. *Deschooling Society*. New York: Harper & Row, 1971.

IMEDADZE, N. V. On the psychological nature of child speech formation under conditions of exposure to two languages. *International Journal of Psychology*, 1967, *2*(2), 129–132.

Instamatic therapy. *Human Behavior*, February 1973, 30.

ISRAEL, B. Success grows in Brooklyn. *Audiovisual Instruction*, December 1969, 40–42.

JACKS, K. B., AND KELLER, M. E. A humanistic approach to the adolescent with learning disabilities: An educational, psychological, and vocational model. *Adolescence*, 1978, *13*(49), 59–68.

JACOBS, C., AND EATON, C. Sexism in the elementary school. *Today's Education*, December 1972, 20–22.

JAMES, W. *Principles of psychology*. New York: Holt, 1890.

JASON, L., CLARFIELD, S., AND COWEN, E. L. Preventative intervention with young disadvantaged children. *American Journal of Community Psychology*, 1973, *1*(1), 50–61.

JENKINS, J. G., AND DALLENBACH, K. M. Oblivescence during sleep and waking. *American Journal of Psychology*, 1924, *35*, 605–612.

JENSEN, A. How much can we boost IQ and scholastic achievement? *Harvard Educational Review*, 1969, *39*, 1–123.

JENSEN, D. D. Toward efficient, effective and humane

instruction in large classes: Student scheduled involvement in films, discussions and computer generated repeatable tests. *Educational Technology,* March 1973, 28–29.

JOHNSON, E. C. Precision teaching helps children learn. *Teaching Exceptional Children,* 1971, *3,* 106–110.

JOHNSON, N.J.A. *Four steps to precision teaching.* Unpublished manuscript, Western Illinois University, 1973.

JOHNSON, R. C. A study of children's moral judgements. *Child Development,* 1962, *33,* 327–354.

JOHNSTON, J. E. Effects of imagery on learning the volleyball pass (Doctoral dissertation, Temple University, 1971). *Dissertation Abstracts International,* 1972, *32A,* 772A. (University Microfilms No. 71-19, 985)

JOSÉ, J., AND CODY, J. J. Teacher-pupil interaction as it relates to attempted changes in teacher expectancy of academic ability and achievement. *American Educational Research Journal,* 1971, *8,* 39–49.

JOURNARD, S. M. *The transparent self.* New York: Van Nostrand-Reinhold, 1971.

JUDD, C. The relation of special training to general intelligence. *Educational Review,* 1908, *36,* 28–42.

JUDD, C. H. *Educational psychology.* Boston: Houghton Mifflin, 1939.

KAGAN, J. The concept of identification. *Psychological Review,* 1958, *65,* 296–305.

KAMII, C. An application of Piaget's theory to the conceptualization of a preschool curriculum. In R. K. Parker (Ed.) *Exploring early childhood programs.* Boston: Allyn & Bacon, 1972.

KAMII, C. K., AND RADIN, N. L. Class differences in the socialization practices of Negro mothers. *Journal of Marriage and the Family,* 1967, *29,* 302–310.

KAMIN, L. *The science and politics of IQ.* Potomac, Md.: Lawrence Erlbaum Associates, 1974.

KAMIN, L. *The politics of IQ.* Keynote address, meeting of the Northeastern Educational Research Association, Ellenville, N.Y., October 1978.

KARAGIANIS, L. D., AND MERRICKS, D. L. (Eds.). *Where the action is: Teaching exceptional children.* St. John's, Newfoundland: Memorial University, 1973. (ERIC Document Reproduction Service No. ED 084 764)

KARNES, M. B., TESKA, J. A., HODGINS, A. S., AND BADGER, E. D. Educational intervention at home by mothers of disadvantaged infants. *Child Development,* 1970, *41,* 925–935.

KARNES, M. B., ZEHRBACH, R. R., AND JONES G. R. *The culturally disadvantaged student and guidance.* Boston: Houghton Mifflin, 1971.

KAUFMAN, B. A love letter to a dead teacher. *Today's Education,* March–April 1975, 20–23.

KEATING, D. A search for social intelligence. *Journal of Educational Psychology,* 1978, *70*(2), 218–223.

KELLAGHAN, T. Relationships between home environment and scholastic behavior in a disadvantaged population. *Journal of Educational Psychology,* 1977, *69*(6), 754–760.

KELLER, F. S. Goodby, teacher . . . *Journal of Applied Behavior Analysis,* 1968, *1,* 79–89.

KENNAN, K. Open school according to St. Paul. *American Education,* October 1978, *14*(8), 38–42.

KEOGH, B. K., TCHIR, C., AND WINDEGUTH-BEHN, A. Teachers' perceptions of educationally high-risk children. *Journal of Learning Disabilities,* 1974, *7,* 367–374.

KEYSERLING, M. D. *Windows on day care.* New York: National Council of Jewish Women, 1972.

KING, S., AND FRIGNAC, D. *Teaching objectives for the emotionally handicapped.* Phoenix, Ariz.: Creighton School District No. 14, 1973. (ERIC Document Reproduction Service No. ED 081 144)

KINKADE, K. Commune: A Walden Two experiment. *Psychology Today,* January 1973, 35–42 ff.

KINSLOW, K. M., AND PATRYLA, V. How do the gifted grow? *School and Community,* November 1978, *65*(3), 14–16.

KIPP, M., AND BRIGGS, S. A. Special education centers for unwed pregnant girls. *School Counselor,* May 1975, *22*(5), 342–346.

KIRBY, J. R., AND DAS, J. P. Reading achievement, IQ, and simultaneous-successive processing. *Journal of Educational Psychology,* 1977, *69*(5), 564–570.

KIRBY, J. R. AND DAS, J. P. Information processing and human abilities. *Journal of Educational Psychology.* 1978, *70*(1), 58–65.

KIRSCHNER, N. M., AND LEVIN, L. A direct school intervention program for the modification of aggressive behavior. *Psychology in the Schools,* April 1975, *12*(2), 202–208.

KLAUSMEIER, H. J., AND RIPPLE, R. E. Effects of accelerating bright older pupils from second to fourth grade. *Journal of Educational Psychology,* 1962, *53,* 93–100.

KLAUSMEIER, H. J., SORENSON, J. S., AND GHATALA, E. S. Individually guided motivation. *Elementary School Journal,* 1971, *71,* 339–350.

KLEIN, G. S., GARDNER, R. W., AND SCHLESINGER, H. J. Tolerance for unrealistic experiences. *British Journal of Psychology,* 1962, *53,* 41–55.

KLEIN, P. S. Effect of open vs. structured teacher-student interaction on creativity of children with different levels of anxiety. *Psychology in the Schools,* July 1975, *12*(3), 286–288.

KLEIN, R. D., AND SCHULER, C. F. *Increasing academic performance through the contingent use of self-*

evaluation. Paper presented at the annual meeting of the American Educational Research Association, Chicago, April 1974.

KLEITMAN, N. *Sleep and wakefulness.* Chicago: University of Chicago Press, 1963.

KOBAK, D. "Edu-caring—teaching children to care": Developing the "CQ" or caring quality in children. *Adolescence,* 1977, *12*(45), 97–102.

KOFFKA, K. *Principles of Gestalt psychology.* New York: Harcourt, Brace, 1935.

KOHL, H. R. *The open classroom.* New York: Vintage, 1969.

KOHLBERG, L. The development of children's orientation toward a moral order: Sequence in the development of moral thought. *Vita Humana,* 1963, *6,* 11–33.

KOHLBERG, L. Development of moral character and moral ideology. In M. L. Hoffman and L. W. Hoffman (Eds.), *Review of child development research* (Vol. 1). New York: Russell Sage Foundation, 1964.

KOHLBERG, L. Stages of moral development as a basis for moral education. In C. M. Beck, B. S. Crittenden, and E. V. Sullivan (Eds.), *Moral Education.* Toronto: University of Toronto Press, 1971.

KOHLER, W. *The mentality of apes]* (E. Winter, trans.). New York: Harcourt, Brace, 1925.

KOHN, M. *Social competence, symptoms, and underachievement in childhood: A longitudinal perspective.* New York: Halstead Press, 1977.

KOLESNIK, W. *Motivation.* Boston: Allyn & Bacon, 1978.

KOSMOSKI, G. J., AND VOCKELL, E. L. The learning center: Stimulus to cognitive and affective growth. *The Elementary School Journal,* 1978, *79*(1), 42–54.

KOUNIN, J. S. *Discipline and group management in classrooms.* New York: Holt, Rinehart & Winston, 1970.

KOUNIN, J. S., AND GUMP, P. V. The comparative influence of punitive and nonpunitive teachers upon children's concepts of school misconduct. *Journal of Educational Psychology,* 1961, *52,* 44–49.

KRATHWOHL, D. R., BLOOM, B. S., AND MASIA, B. B. *A taxonomy of educational objectives* (Handbook 2). New York: David McKay, 1964.

KROGMAN, W. M. *Child growth.* Ann Arbor: University of Michigan Press, 1972.

KRYSPIN, W. J., AND FELDHUSEN, J. F. *Analyzing verbal classroom interaction.* Minneapolis: Burgess, 1974.

KUHLEN, R. G. Needs, perceived need satisfaction opportunities, and satisfaction with occupation. *Journal of Applied Psychology,* 1963, *47,* 56–64.

LABOUVIE-VIEF, G., LEVIN, J. R, AND URBERG, K. A. The relationship between selected cognitive abilities and learning: A second look. *Journal of Educational Psychology,* 1975, *67*(4), 558–569.

LAMBERT, W. E. *Language, psychology, and culture: Essays by Wallace E. Lambert* (A. S. Dil, Ed.). Stanford: Stanford University Press, 1972.

LANDIS, J. T. The trauma of children when parents divorce. *Marriage and Family Living,* 1960, *22,* 7–13.

LANGDON, J. S. Court rules girls can compete with boys in PIAA. *Pittsburgh Press,* March 19, 1975, 1.

LAWTON, E. Should teachers see student records? Yes. *National Education Association Journal,* October 1966, 35–37.

LAZAR, I., AND DARLINGTON, R. *Lasting effects after preschool, A report of the Central Staff of the Consortium for Longitudinal Studies.* Washington, D.C.: U.S. Department of Health, Education and Welfare, Office of Human Development Services, Administration for Children, Youth, and Families, DHEW Publication No. (OHDS) 79-30179, September 1979.

LEACOCK, E. B. *Teaching and learning in city schools.* New York: Basic Books, 1969.

LENNON, R. T. *Accountability and performance contracting.* Paper presented at the annual meeting of the American Educational Research Association, New York, February 1971.

LESSINGER, L. M. The powerful notion of accountability in education. *Journal of Secondary Education,* 1970, *45,* 339–347.

LESTER, B. M. Psychological and central nervous system consequences of protein-calorie malnutrition: A review of research findings and some implications. *Interamerican Journal of Psychology,* 1976, *10,* 17–31.

LEVENSON, D. Make phys ed fit. *Teacher,* February 1975, 58–60 ff.

LEVY, B. Do teachers sell girls short? *Today's Education,* December 1972, 27–29.

LEWIN, K. Studies in group decision. In D. Cartwright and A. Zander (Eds.), *Group dynamics: Research and theory.* Evanston, Ill.: Row, Peterson, 1953.

LEWIS, O. The culture of poverty. *Scientific American,* October 1966, 19–25.

LEWIS, W. W., Project RE-ED: Educational intervention in discordant child rearing systems. In E. L Cowen, E. A. Gardner, and M. Zax (Eds.), *Emergent approaches to mental health problems.* New York: Appleton-Century-Crofts, 1967.

LINDSAY, P. H., AND NORMAN, D. A. *Human information processing.* New York: Academic Press, 1972.

LINDSEY, B. L., AND CUNNINGHAM, J. W. Behavior modification: Some doubts and dangers. *Phi Delta Kappan,* 1973, *54,* 596–597.

LITTLE, J. K. Results of use of machines for testing and for drill upon learning in educational psychology. *Journal of Experimental Education,* 1934, *3,* 45–49.

LOFTUS, E. Reconstructing memory. *Psychology Today,* December 1974, 116–119.

LONG, N. J., MORSE, W. C., AND NEWMAN, R. G. *Conflict in the classroom: The education of emotionally disturbed children* (2nd ed.) Belmont, Calif: Wadsworth, 1971.

LOVAAS, O. I., VARNI, J. W., KOEGEL, R. L., AND LORSCH, N. Some observations on the nonextinguishability of children's speech. *Child development,* 1977, *48,* 1121–1127.

LOVELL, K., AND OGILVIE, E. A study of the conservation of substance in the Junior School child. *British Journal of Educational Psychology,* 1960, *30,* 109–118.

LOWE, W. T. *Structure and the social studies.* Ithaca: Cornell University Press, 1969.

LOWELL, J. *Dear Folks.* New York: Putnam's, 1960.

LUCAS, C. J. On the possible meaning of "Back to Basics." *Educational Theory,* Summer 1978, *28(3),* 231–237.

LURIA, A. K. Towards the problem of the historical nature of psychological processes. *International Journal of Psychology,* 1971, *6,* 259–272.

LURIA, A. K. Scientific perspectives and philosophical dead ends in modern linguistics. *Cognition,* 1974-75, *3(4),* 377–386.

LYNN, D. B. *The father: His role in child development.* Monterey, Calif.: Brooks-Cole, 1974.

MACCOBY, E. *Sex differences revisited, myth and reality.* Address presented at the annual meeting of the American Educational Research Association, Chicago, 1974.

MACMAHAN, J. *Hyperactivity.* Paper read at the meeting of the Council for Exceptional Children, University of Maine, Farmington, Maine, April 1979.

MACROFF, G. School science struggles less successfully than ever. *New York Times,* July 2, 1978, 16E.

MADDEN, P. C. Skinner and the open classroom. *School Review,* 1972, *81,* 100–107.

MAEHR, M. L. Continuing motivation: An analysis of a seldom considered educational outcome. *Review of Educational Research,* Fall 1976, *46(3)* 443–462.

MAEHR, M. L., AND SJOGREN, D. D. Atkinson's theory of achievement motivation: First step toward a theory of academic motivation? *Review of Educational Research,* 1971, *41,* 143–161.

MAGER, R. F. *Preparing instructional objectives.* Belmont, Calif.: Fearon, 1962.

MARGOLIN, E. *Sociocultural elements in early childhood education,* New York: Macmillan, 1974.

MARINO, C., AND MCCOWAN, R. The effects of parent absence on children. *Child Study Journal,* 1976, *6(3),* 165–181.

MARKLE, S. M., AND TIEMANN, P. W. Problems of conceptual learning. *British Journal of Educational Technology,* 1970, *1,* 52–62.

MARSHALL, J. C. Composition errors and essay examination grades re-examined. *American Educational Research Journal,* 1967, *4,* 375–385.

MARSHALL, J. C., AND POWERS, J. M. Writing neatness, composition errors, and essay grades. *Journal of Educational Measurement,* 1969, *6,* 97–101.

MARWIT, S. J., MARWIT, K. L., AND BOSWELL, J. J. Negro children's use of nonstandard grammar. *Journal of Educational Psychology,* 1972, *63,* 218–224.

MASLOW, A. H. A theory of human motivation. *Psychological Review,* 1943, *50,* 370–396.

MASLOW, A. H. *Motivation and personality.* New York: Harper & Brothers, 1954.

MASLOW, A. H. Some educational implications of the humanistic psychologies. *Harvard Educational Review,* 1968, *38(4),* 685–696.(a)

MASLOW, A. H. *Toward a psychology of being* (2nd ed.). Princeton: Van Nostrand-Reinhold, 1968.(b)

MASLOW, A. H. *Farther reaches of human nature.* New York: Viking Press, 1971.

MATTSSON, K. D. Personality traits associated with effective teaching in rural and urban secondary schools. *Journal of Educational Psychology,* 1974, *66,* 123–128.

MAUGER, P. A., AND KOLMODIN, C. A. Long-term predictive validity of the Scholastic Aptitude Test. *Journal of Educational Psychology,* 1975, *67(6),* 847–851.

MCCANDLESS, B. R. Adolescents: Behavior and development. Hinsdale, Ill.: Dryden, 1970.

MCCLEAN, P. D. Induced arousal and time of recall as determinants of paired-associate recall. *British Journal of Psychology,* 1969, *60,* 57–62.

MCCLELLAND, D. C. Toward a theory of motive acquisition. *American Psychologist,* 1965, *20,* 321–333.

MCCLELLAND, D. C. What is the effect of achievement motivation training in the schools? *Teachers College Record,* 1972, *74,* 129–145.

MCCLELLAND, D. C., ATKINSON, J. W., CLARK, R. A., AND LOWELL, E. L. *The achievement motive.* New York: Appleton-Century-Crofts, 1953.

MCCORD, W., MCCORD, J., AND HOWARD, A. Familial correlates of aggression in nondelinquent male children. *Journal of Abnormal and Social Psychology,* 1961, *62,* 79–93.

MCCORMICK, M., SHEEHY, N., AND MITCHEL, J. Tradiional vs. open classroom structure and examiner style: The effect on creativity in children. *Child Study Journal,* 1978, *8(2),* 75–81.

MCDADE, C. E. Subsumption versus educational set: Implications for sequencing of instructional material. *Journal of Educational Psychology,* *70(2),* 1978, 137–141.

McDonald, P. Media offer new charting possibilities. *Teaching Exceptional Children*, 1971, *3*, 151.

McGeogh, J. A., and Irion, A. L. *The psychology of human learning*. New York: David McKay, 1956.

McKenna, B. H. Teacher evaluation. *Today's Education*, February 1973, 55–56.

Mecklenburger, J. A., and Wilson, J. A. Learning C.O.D.: Can the schools buy success? *Saturday Review*, September 18, 1971, 62–65.

Memphis City School System. *Report for Diffusion: Project CLUE, Memphis Component*. Memphis, Tenn.: Author, 1974. (ERIC Document Reproduction Service No. ED 083 773)

Meredith, G. M. Evaluation of attitudes toward learning resources in higher education. *Perceptual and Motor Skills*, 1977, *44*, 1093–1094.

Merrill, M. D. Necessary psychological conditions for defining instructional outcomes. *Educational Technology*, August 1971, 34–39. (a)

Merrill, M. D. Psychomotor and memorization behavior. In M. D. Merrill (Ed.), *Instructional design*. Englewood Cliffs, N. J.: Prentice-Hall, 1971. (b)

Merrill, M.D. Psychomotor taxonomies, classifications and instructional theory. In R. N. Singer (Ed.), *The psychomotor domain*. Philadelphia: Lea & Febiger, 1972.

Messick, S. The criterion problem in the evaluation of instruction. In M. C. Wittrock and D. E. Wiley (Eds.), *The evaluation of instruction: Issues and problems*. New York: Holt, Rinehart and Winston, 1970.

The metrics are coming! The metrics are coming! *Changing Times*, May 1974, pp. 33–34.

Michaels, J. W. Effects of differential rewarding and sex on math performance. *Journal of Educational Psychology*, 1978, *70*(4), 565–572.

Milgram, R. M., and Milgram, N. A. Creative thinking and creative performance in Israeli students. *Journal of Educational Psychology*, 1976, *68*(3), 255–259.

Milgram, S. Behavioral study of obedience. *Journal of Abnormal and Social Psychology*, 1963, *67*, 371–378.

Miller, A. Learning miniature linguistic systems. *Journal of General Psychology*, 1973, *89*, 15–25.

Miller, D. R. Nature/nurture and intelligence in current introductory educational psychology textbooks. *Educational Psychologist*, 1978, *13*, 87–92.

Miller, G. A. The magical number seven, plus or minus two: Some limits on our capacity for processing information. *Psychological Review*, 1956, *63*, 81–97.

Miller, G. A., Galanter, E., and Pribram, K. *Plans and the structure of behavior*. New York: Holt, Rinehart and Winston, 1960.

Miller, J. P. Piaget, Kohlberg, and Erikson: Developmental implications for secondary education. *Adolescence*, Summer 1978, Vol. XIII, No. 50.

Miller, N. E. Studies of fear as an acquirable drive: I. Fear as motivation and fear-reduction as reinforcement in the learning of new responses. *Journal of Experimental Psychology*, 1948, *38*, 89–101.

Mitchell, P. B., and Erikson, D. K. The education of gifted and talented children: A status report. *Exceptional Children*, September 1978, *45*(1), 12–16.

Montague, E. K. The role of anxiety in serial rote learning. *Journal of Experimental Psychology*, 1953, *45* 91–96.

Montessori, M. *The Montessori method* (Rev. ed.). New York: Schocken Books, 1964. (Originally published, 1909)

Montessori, M. *The absorbent mind* (C. A. Claremont, trans.). New York: Holt, Rinehart and Winston, 1967.

Montgomery County Student Alliance. Wanted: A humane education. In R. Gross and P. Osterman (Eds.), *High school*. New York: Simon and Schuster, 1971.

Moore, J. W., Schaut, J., and Fritzges, C. Evaluation of the effects of feedback associated with a problem-solving approach to instruction on teacher and student behavior. *Journal of Educational Psychology*, 1978, *70*(2), 200–208.

Moore, O. K. Autotelic responsive environments and exceptional children. In O. J. Harvey (Ed.), *Experience, structure and adaptability*. New York: Springer, 1966.

Moore, O. K., and Anderson, A. R. The responsive environments project. In R. D. Hess and R. M. Bear (Eds.), *Early education*. Chicago: Aldine, 1968.

Moore, O. K., and Anderson, A. R. Some principles for the design of clarifying educational environments. In D. A. Goslin (Ed.), *Handbook of socialization theory and research*. Chicago: Rand McNally, 1969.

Morelli, G., and Schwartz, S. Picture mediation in abstract-concrete paired associates. *Perceptual and Motor Skills*, 1977, *45*, 551–554.

Morrelli, G., and Atkinson, D. R. Effects of breakfast program on school performance and attendance of elementary school children. *Education*, Winter 1977, *98*(2), 111–116.

Morris, E. K., Surber, C. F., and Bijou, S. W. Self-pacing versus instructor-pacing: Achievement, evaluations and retention. *Journal of Educational Psychology*, 1978, *70*(2), 224–230.

Morrison, B. M. The reactions of external and internal pupils to patterns of teacher behavior (Doctoral dissertation, University of Michigan, 1966). *Dis-*

sertation *Abstracts International*, 1967, 27A, 2072A. (University Microfilms No. 66–14, 560)

MOSBY, R. S. *A seminar for teachers of the culturally disadvantaged*. New York: Pageant-Poseidon, 1971.

MOULDS, H. To grade or not to grade: A futile question. *Intellect*, Summer 1974, *102*, 501–504.

MOWRER, D. Speech problems: What you should do and shouldn't do. *Learning*, January 1978, *6*(5), 34–35.

MOWRER, O. H. *Learning theory and personality dynamics: Selected papers*. New York: Ronald Press, 1950.

The mural message. *Time*, April 7, 1975, p. 79.

MURPHY, T. F. *Self-fulfilling prophecies and the effects of personality testing upon children's independence*. Unpublished doctoral dissertation, University of Pittsburgh, 1979.

MUSON, H. Teenage violence and the telly. *Psychology Today*, March 1978, 50–54.

MUUSS, R. Kohlberg's cognitive-developmental approach to adolescent morality. *Adolescence*, Spring 1976, Vol. XI, No. 41.

NARANG, H. L. Characteristics of a remedial teacher. In L. D. Karagianis and D. L. Merricks (Eds.), *Where the action is: Teaching exceptional children*. St. John's, Newfoundland: Memorial University, 1973. (ERIC Document Reproduction Service No. ED 084 764)

National Assessment of Educational Progress. *Reading in America: A perspective of two assessments*, 1978.

National Education Association, Division of Instruction and Professional Development. *Accountability*. Washington, D. C.: Author, December 1972. (ERIC Document Reproduction Service No. ED 077 894)

National Institute of Education. *Violent Schools—Safe Schools*. Washington, D.C.: U.S. Government Printing Office, January 1978.

NATIONS, J. E. *Caring for individual differences in reading through non-grading*. Lecture at the Seattle Public Schools, May 13, 1967.

NAUMANN, N. Anatomy of a reading problem and its solution. *Learning*, May–June 1978, *6*(9), 81–83.

NEILL, A. S. *Summerhill: A radical approach to child rearing*. New York: Hart, 1960.

NEWELL, A., AND SIMON, H. A. *Human problem-solving*. Englewood Cliffs, N.J.: Prentice-Hall, 1972.

NEWMAN, P. R., AND NEWMAN, B. M. Early adolescence and its conflict: Group identity vs. alienation. *Adolescence*, Summer 1976, Vol. XI, No. 42.

NEWMAN, P. Social settings and their significance for adolescent development. *Adolescence*, Fall 1976, Vol. XI. No. 43.

New tool: Reinforcement for good work. *Psychology Today*, April 1972, 68–69.

NIMNICHT, G. P. AND BROWN, E. The parent-child toy library programme. *British Journal of Educational Technology*, 1972, *3*, 75–81.

NUGENT, F. A. School counselors, psychologists, and social workers. *Psychology in the Schools*, 1973, *10*, 327–333.

OAKLAND, T., AND WILLIAMS, F. An evaluation of two methods of peer tutoring. *Psychology in the Schools*, 1975, *12*(2), 166–171.

OKUN, M. A., AND SASFY, J. H. Adolescence, the self-concept, and formal operations. *Adolescence*, Fall 1977, Vol. XII, No. 47, 373–379.

OLSON, M. N. Ways to achieve quality in school classrooms. *Phi Delta Kappan*, 1971, *53*, 63–65.

OLSON, M. R. Orienting the blind student. *Learning*, October 1978, *7*(2), 110–111.

OSBORN, J. Teaching a teaching language to disadvantaged children. In M. A. Brottman (Ed.), *Language remediation for the disadvantaged preschool child*. *Monographs of the Society for Research in Child Development*, 1968, *33* (8, Serial No. 124).

OSGOOD, C. E. *Method and theory in experimental psychology*. New York: Oxford University Press, 1953.

OVERING, R. L. R., AND TRAVERS, R. M. W. Effect upon transfer of variations in training conditions. *Journal of Educational Psychology*, 1966, *57*, 179–188.

PALERMO, D. S., AND MOLFESE, D. L. Language acquisition from age five onward. *Psychological Bulletin*, 1972, *78*, 409–428.

PANKOPF, J. *Free Learning Environment Program* (Year-end report, 1972-1973). Pittsburgh: Washington Education Center, Pittsburgh Public Schools, 1974.

PARKER, H. C. Contingency management and concomitant changes in elementary-school students' self-concepts. *Psychology in the Schools*, 1974, *11*, 70–79.

PASSANTINO, R. Swedish preschools: environments of sensitivity. *Childhood Education*, May 1971, 406–411.

PAVLOV, I. P. Conditioned reflexes (G. V. Anrep, Ed. and trans.). London: Oxford University Press, 1927.

PEARL, A. There is nothing more loco than loco parentis. *Phi Delta Kappan*, 1972, *53*, 629–631.

PEARSON, C. Do you know how to chisanbop? *Learning*, August-September 1978, *7*(1), 134–138.

PEDRINI, B. C., AND PEDRINI, D. T. *Special Education*. 1973. (ERIC Document Reproduction Service No. ED 085 927)

PERKINS, S. A. Malnutrition and mental development. *Exceptional Children*, January 1977, *43*, 214–219.

PETTIGREW, T. F. The measurement and correlates of category width as a cognitive variable. *Journal of Personality*, 1958, *26*, 532–544.

PETTIGREW, T. F. On busing and race relations. *Today's Education*, November–December 1973, 37.

PETTY, N. E., AND HARRELL, E. H. Effect of programmed instruction related to motivation, anxiety and test wiseness on group IQ performance. *Journal of Educational Psychology*, 1977, *69*(5), 630–635.

PHILLIPS, D. We have a successful tool now—Let's use it. In J. B. Jordan and L. S. Robbins (Eds.) *Let's try doing something else kind of thing: Behavioral principles and the exceptional child.* Arlington, Va.: Council for Exceptional Children, 1972.

PIAGET, J. The moral judgement of the child (M. Gabain, trans.). New York: Free Press, 1965. (Originally published, 1933)

PIAGET, J. The origins of intelligence in children (M. Cook, trans.). New York: International Universities Press, 1952. (Originally published, 1936)

PIAGET, J. The psychology of intelligence (M. Percy and D. E. Berlyne, trans.). London: Routledge and Kegan Paul, 1950.

PIAGET, J. Development and learning. In R. E. Ripple and V. N. Rockcastle (Eds.), *Piaget Rediscovered.* Ithaca: School of Education, Cornell University, 1964.

PIAGET, J. Intellectual evolution from adolescence to adulthood (J. Bliss and H. Furth, trans.). *Human Development*, 1972, *15*, 1–12.

PIAGET, J. *To understand is to invent.* New York: Grossman, 1973.

PIAGET, J, AND INHELDER, B. *The psychology of the child.* New York: Basic Books, 1969.

PINES, M. *Revolution in learning.* New York: Harper & Row, 1967.

PITMAN, J., AND ST. JOHN, J. *Alphabets and reading.* New York: Pitman, 1969.

PLATZER, W. S. Effect of perceptual motor training on gross-motor skills and self-concepts of young children. *American Journal of Occupational Therapy*, August 1976, *30*(7), 423–428.

POPHAM, W. J. *Probing the validity of arguments against behavioral goals.* Paper presented at the annual meeting of the American Educational Research Association, Chicago, February 1968.

POPHAM, W. J. *Criterion-referenced instruction.* Belmont Cal.; Fearon, 1973.

POPHAM, W. J. Teacher evaluation and domain-referenced measurement. *Educational Technology*, June 1974, 35–37.

PRANGESHVILI, A. S. *Learning and set.* Paper presented at the International Congress of Psychology, Prague, 1973.

Precision teaching perspective: An interview with Ogden R. Lindsley. *Teaching Exceptional Children*, 1971, *3*, 114–119.

PREMACK, D. Toward empirical behavior laws: I. Positive reinforcement. *Psychological Review*, 1959, *66*, 219–233.

PRESSEY, S. L. A third and fourth contribution toward the coming "industrial revolution" in education. *School and Society*, 1932, *36*, 668–672.

PRONKO, N. H. On learning to play the violin at the age of four without tears. *Psychology Today*, May 1969, 52–53 ff.

PROSCURA, E. V. The role of teaching in the formation of seriation actions in pre-school children. *Voprosy Psychologee*, 1969, *15*, 37–45. (I. A. Holowinsky, Seriation actions of pre-school children. *Journal of Learning Disabilities*, 1970, *3*, 34–35).

PYLSHYN, Z. W. Minds, machines, and phenomenology: Some reflections on Dreyfus' "What Computer's Can't Do." *Cognition*, 1974–75, *3*(1), 57–76.

RABINOW, B. *The training and supervision of teaching of emotionally disturbed children.* Albany: University of the State of New York, State Department of Education, Bureau of Teacher Education, 1964.

RAFFERTY, M. An analysis of Summerhill—Con, *Summerhill: For and against.* New York: Hart, 1970.

RAMELLA, R. The anatomy of discipline: Should punishment be corporal? *PTA Magazine*, June 1973, 24–27.

RANDOLF, A. The robot who teaches in the Bronx. *PTA Magazine*, June 1974, 28–29.

RATHBONE, C. H. Examining the open education classroom. *School Review*, 1972, *80*, 521–549.

RATHS, L., HARMIN, M., AND SIMON, S. *Values and teaching.* Columbus, Ohio: Charles E. Merrill, 1966.

REBELSKY, F. G., ALLINSMITH, W., AND GRINDER, R. E. Resistance to temptation and sex differences in children's use of fantasy confession. *Child Development*, 1963, *34*, 955–962.

REISS, I. L. America's sex standards—How and why they're changing. *Trans-action*, 1968, *5*, 26-32.

REISSMAN, F. The "helper" therapy principle. *Social Work*, 1965, *10*(2), 27–32.

REISSMAN, F. Styles of learning. *National Education Association Journal*, March 1966, 15–17.

RESNICK, D. P., AND RESNICK, L. B. The nature of literacy: An historical exploration. *Harvard Educational Review*, 1977, *47*(3), 370–385.

RESNICK, L. B. *Teacher behavior in an informal British Infant School.* Pittsburgh: Learning Research and Development Center, University of Pittsburgh, 1971.

RESNICK, L. B. Open education: Some tasks for technology. *Educational Technology*, 1972, *12*(1), 70–76.

RESNICK, R. J. The primary teacher and the emotionally disabled child. *Education*, Summer 1978, *98*(4), 387–391.

RESNIK, H. Parkway: A school without walls. In R.

Gross and P. Osterman (Eds.), *High school.* New York: Simon and Schuster, 1971.

RHINE, R. J., AND SILUN, B. A. Acquisition and change of a concept attitude as a function of consistency of reinforcement. *Journal of Experimental Psychology,* 1958, *55,* 524–529.

RHODES, W. C. Curriculum and disordered behavior. *Exceptional Children,* 1963, *30,* 61–66.

RHODES, W. C. *The emotionally disturbed student and guidance.* Boston: Houghton Mifflin, 1970.

RICHARDSON, S. K. How do children feel about reports to parents? *California Journal of Elementary Education,* 1955, *24,* 98–111.

ROBERTS, J. M., AND SUTTON-SMITH, B. Child training and game involvement. *Ethnology,* 1962, *1,* 166–185.

RODRIGUEZ, E. Inside ETS: Or the plot to multiple-choice us from cradle to grave. *Washington Monthly,* March 1974, 5–12.

ROGERS, C. Forget you are a teacher. *Instructor,* August-September 1971, *81,* 65–66.

ROGERS, C. R. Learning to be free. In C. R. Rogers and B. Steven (Eds.), *Person to person: The problem of being human.* Lafayette, Calif.: Real People Press, 1967.

ROGERS, C. R. The interpersonal relationship in the facilitation of learning. In D. A. Read and S. B. Simon (Eds.), *Humanistic education source book.* Englewood-Cliffs, N. J. : Prentice-Hall, 1975.

ROGERS, C. R., AND SKINNER, B. F. Some issues concerning the control of human behavior. *Science,* 1956, *74,* 1057–1066.

ROGERS, S. J. Characteristics of the cognitive development of profoundly retarded children. *Child Development,* 1977, *48*(3), 837–843.

ROLLINS, H. A., AND GENSER, L. Role of cognitive style in a cognitive task: A case favoring the impulsive approach to problem-solving. *Journal of Educational Psychology,* 1977, *69*(3), 281–287.

ROSEN, S., POWELL, E. R., SCHUBOT, D.B., AND ROLLINS, P. Competence and tutorial role as status variables affecting peer-tutoring outcomes in public school settings. *Journal of Educational Psychology,* 1978, *70*(4), 602–612.

ROSENBERG, E. After-school special. *School and Community,* November 1978, *65*(3), 10–11.

ROSENBERG, M. J. Cognitive reorganization in response to the hypnotic reversal of attitudinal affect. *Journal of Personality,* 1960, *28,* 39–63.

ROSENHAM, D. The kindnesses of children. *Young Children,* 1969, *25,* 30–44.

ROSENKRANTZ, A. L. A note on adolescent suicide: Incidence, dynamics and some suggestions for treatment. *Adolescence,* 1978, *13*(50), 209–214.

ROSENSHINE, B. AND McGAW, B. Issues in assessing

teacher accountability in public education. *Phi Delta Kappan,* 1972, *53,* 640–643.

ROSENSWEET, A. Head Start wears off. *Pittsburgh Post-Gazette,* February 24, 1971, Section 2, 24.

ROSENTHAL, R., AND JACOBSON, L. Teachers' expectancies: Determinants of pupils' IQ gains. *Psychological Reports,* 1966, *19,* 115–118.

ROSENTHAL, R., AND JACOBSON, L. *Pygmalion in the classroom.* New York: Holt, Rinehart and Winston, 1968.

ROSS, H. S., AND KILLEY, J. C. The effect of questioning on retention. *Child Development,* 1977, *48*(1), 312–314.

ROTHBART, M., DALFEN, S., AND BARRETT, R. Effects of teachers' expectancy on student-teacher interaction. *Journal of Educational Psychology,* 1971, *62,* 49–54.

ROTHKOPF, E. Z., AND KOETHER, M.E. Instructional effects of discrepancies in content and organization between study goals and information sources. *Journal of Educational Psychology,* 1978, *70*(1), 67–71.

ROWLAND, S. Assessment in the primary school. *Forum for discussion of NEA trends in Education Teaching Issue,* Summer 1978, *20*((3), 78–80.

RUBIN, L. B. White against white: School desegregation and the revolt of middle America. *School Review,* May 1976, *84*(3), 373–388.

RUBIN, R. A. Preschool application of the Metropolitan Readiness Tests: Validity, reliability, and preschool norms. *Educational and Psychological Measurement,* 1974, *34,* 417–422.

Russell Sage Foundation. *Guidelines for the collection, maintenance, and dissemination of pupil records.* New York: Author, 1970.

RYANS, D. G. *Characteristics of teachers.* Washington, D.C.: American Council on Education, 1961.

RYOR, J. Declining SAT scores. (Editorial) *Today's Education,* 1977, *66*(4).

SAGARIA, S.D., AND DiVESTA, F. J. Learner expectations induced by adjunct questions and the retrieval of intentional and incidental information. *Journal of Educational Psychology,* 1978, *70*(3), 280–288.

SAGE, W. Classrooms for the autistic child. *Human Behavior,* March 1975, 39–42.

SAMUEL, W. Observed IQ as a function of test atmosphere, tester expectation, and race of tester: A replication for female subjects. *Journal of Educational Psychology,* 1977, *69*(5), 593–604.

SARSON, J. G. *Abnormal psychology.* New York: Appleton-Century-Crofts, 1972.

SATTERLY, D. J. Cognitive styles, spatial ability, and school achievement. *Journal of Educational Psychology,* 1976, *68*(1), 36–42.

SCANDURA, J. M. Structural approach to instructional

problems. *American Psychologist,* 1977, *32*(1), 33–52.

SCANDURA, J. M., FRASE, L. T., GAGNÉ, R. M., STOLU-ROW, K.A.C., STOLUROW, L. M., AND GROEN, G. J. Current status and future directions of educational psychology as a discipline. *Educational Psychologist,* 1978, *13,* 43–56.

SCHAEFER, E.S. Parents as educators. In W.W. Hartup (Ed.), *The young child: Review of research* (Vol. 2). Washington, D.C.: National Association for the Education of Young Children, 1972.

SCHAFFER, T. E. The young athlete. *The Journal of School Health,* April 1977, 222–226.

SCHEERER, M. Problem-solving. *Scientific American,* April 1963, 118–128.

SCHIMMEL, D. To speak out freely: Do teachers have the right? *Phi Delta Kappan,* 1972, *54,* 258–260.

SCHNEIR, W., AND SCHNEIR, M. The joy of learning in the open corridor. *New York Times Magazine,* April 4, 1971, 30 ff.

SCHUCHAT, T. With education in Washington. *Educational Digest,* May 1975, 63.

Science Research Associates. *Using the Iowa Tests of Educational Development for college planning.* Chicago: Author, 1957.

SCOTT, W. A. Attitude change through reward of verbal behavior. *Journal of Abnormal and Social Psychology,* 1957, *55,* 72–75.

SEELEY, C. *A case history of Richie: A boy labeled mentally retarded and placed in a special education program.* Unpublished manuscript, University of Pittsburgh, 1978.

SEIDNER, C. J., LEWIS, S. C., SHERWIN, N. V., AND TROLL, E. W. Cognitive and affective outcomes for pupils in an open-space elementary school: A comparative study. *The Elementary School Journal,* 1978, *78*(3), 208–218.

SELMAN, R. L., AND JAQUETTE, D. To understand and to help: Implications of developmental research for the education of children with interpersonal problems. *Contemporary Education,* Fall 1976, *48*(1), 42–51.

SEYMOUR, D. Z. Black children, black speech. *Commonweal,* November 19, 1971, pp. 175–178.

SHANE, H. G., AND WIRTZ, W. W. The academic score decline: Are facts the enemy of truth? *Phi Delta Kappan,* October 1977, *59*(2), 83–86.

SHAW, M. E. Some motivational factors in cooperation and competition. *Journal of Personality,* 1958, *26,* 155–169.

SHELLOW, R., SCHAMP, J. R., LIEBOW, E., AND UNGER, E. Suburban runaways of the 1960's. *Monographs of the Society for Research in Child Development,* 1967, *32*(3, Serial No. 111).

SHERWOOD, P. The testing invasion. *Forum for Discussion*

of NEA Trends in Education, Summer 1978, *20*(3), 72–83.

SHORE, A. L. Confirmation of expectancy and changes in teachers' evaluations of student behavior (Doctoral dissertation, University of Southern California, 1969). *Dissertation Abstracts International,* 1969, 30A, 1878A. (University Microfilms No. 69-19, 402).

SILBERBERG, N. E., AND SILBERBERG, M. C. Myths in remedial education. In L. D. Karagianis and D. L. Merricks (Eds.), *Where the action is: Teaching exceptional children.* St. John's Newfoundland: Memorial University, 1973. (ERIC Document Reproduction Service No. ED 084 764)

SILLICK, J. Is anything happening under their hair? *American Educator,* 1977, *1*(1), 32–34.

SIMON, H. A. On the development of the processor. In S. Farnham-Diggory (Ed.), *Information processing in children.* New York: Academic Press, 1972.

SIMPSON, D. D., AND NELSON, A. L. Attention training through breathing control to modify hyperactivity. *Journal of Learning Disabilities,* 1974, *7,* 274–283.

SINOWITZ, B. E. School integration and the teacher. *Today's Education,* May, 1973, 30–33.(a).

SINOWITZ, B. E. The teacher's right to privacy. *Today's Education,* November-December 1973, 89–90. (b)

SKINNER, B. F. "Superstition" in the pigeon. *Journal of Experimental Psychology,* 1948, *38,* 168–172. (a)

SKINNER, B. F. *Walden two.* New York: Macmillan, 1948. (b)

SKINNER, B. F. *Contingency management in the classroom.* Paper presented at Western Washington State College, October 2, 1969.

SKINNER, B. F. *Beyond freedom and dignity.* New York: Knopf, 1971.

SKINNER, B. F. (Ed.). *Cumulative record* (3rd ed.). New York: Appleton-Century-Crofts, 1972.

Skinner's Utopia: Panacea or path to hell? *Time,* September 20, 1971, 47–53.

SLOBIN, D. Seven questions about language development. In P. Dadwell (Ed.), *New Horizons in Psychology,* No. 2. Baltimore: Penguin, 1972.

SMART, M. S., AND SMART, R. C. *Children: Development and relationships* (2nd ed.). New York: Macmillan, 1972.

SMEDSLUND, J. Educational psychology. *Annual Review of Psychology,* 1964, *15,* 251–276.

SNADOWSKY, A. (Ed.). *Child and adolescent development.* New York: Free Press, 1973.

SNAPP, M., MCNEIL, D. C., AND HAUG, D. Development of in-school psychoeducational services for emotionally disturbed children. *Psychology in the Schools,* 1973, *10,* 392–396.

SNIDER, A. J. Hyperactivity. *Pittsburgh Press*, July 1, 1974, 13.

SOLOMON, E. L. New York City's prototype school for educating the handicapped. *Phi Delta Kappan*, September 1977, *59*(1), 7–10.

SOLOMON, G., AND COHEN, A. A. Television formats, mastery of mental skills, and the acquisition of knowledge. *Journal of Educational Psychology*, 1977, *69*(5), 612–619.

SOLTER, A., AND MAYER, R. E. Broader transfer produced by guided discovery of number concepts with preschool children. *Journal of Educational Psychology*, 1978, *70*(3), 363–370.

SOLZHENITSYN, A. I. *The Gulag Archipelago* (T. P. Whitney, trans.). New York: Harper & Row, 1973.

SPEARMAN, C. "General intelligence," objectively determined and measured. *American Journal of Psychology*, 1904, *15*, 201–293.

SPERRY, L. (Ed.). *Learning performance and individual differences*. Glenview, Ill.: Scott, Foresman, 1972.

SPITZ, H. H. Effects of symmetry on the reproduction of dot patterns by mental retardates and equal MA normals. *American Journal of Mental Deficiency*, 1964, *69*, 101–106.

SPITZ, R. A. Hospitalism: An inquiry into the genesis of psychiatric conditions in early childhood. *Psychoanalytic Study of the Child*, 1945, *1*, 53–74.

SPITZ, R. A. Hospitalism: A follow-up report. *Psychoanalytic Study of the Child*, 1946, *2*, 113–117.

STANKOV, L. Fluid and crystallized intelligence and broad perceptual factors among 11 to 12 year olds. *Journal of Educational Psychology*, 1978, *70*(3), 324–334.

STANLEY, J. C. Accelerating the educational progress of intellectually gifted youths. *Educational Psychologist*, 1973, *10*, 133–146.

STARLIN, C. Peers and precision. *Teaching Exceptional Children*, 1971, *3*,129–133 ff.

STARNES, R. "Johnny" proves he can read. *Pittsburgh Press*, April 7, 1975, 23.

STEIN, J. S. Physical education, recreation, and sports for special populations. *Education and Training of the Mentally Retarded*, February 1977, *12*, 4–12.

STEVENS, E. I. Grading systems and student mobility. *Educational Record*, 1973, *54*, 308–312.

STILLWELL, L. Students slip but grades rise. *Pittsburgh Press*, July 15, 1974, 19.

STRANIX, E. L. How can I help my children do better in school? *Teacher*, September 1978, *96*(1), 89–90.

STRICKLAND, D. S. Black is beautiful vs. white is right. *Elementary English*, 1972, *49*, 220–223.

STRIKE, K. A. The logic of learning by discovery. *Review of Educational Research*, Summer 1975, *45*(3), 461–483.

STRONG, C. H. Motivation related to performance on physical fitness tests. *Research Quarterly*, 1963, *34*, 197–207.

STURGIS, P. T. Delay of informative feedback in computer-assisted testing. *Journal of Educational Testing*, 1978, *70*(3), 378–387.

Suing for not learning. *Time*, March 3, 1975, 73.

SUMMERELL, S., AND BRANNIGAN, G. J. Comparrison of reading programs for children with low levels of reading readiness. *Perceptual and Motor Skills*, 1977, *44*(3), 743–746.

SWANSON, L. Verbal encoding effects on the visual short-term memory of learning disabled and normal readers. *Journal of Educational Psychology*, 1978, *70*(4), 539–544.

SWARTZ, S. L. Zero reject—the public law regarding handicapped children. *Curriculum Review: A Special Issue on Mainstreaming*, October 1978, *17*(4), 251–284.

TANNER, J. M. Earlier maturation in man. *Scientific American*, January 1968, 21–27.

TAYLOR, J. A. The relationship of anxiety to the conditioned eyelid response. *Journal of Experimental Psychology*, 1951, *41*, 81–92.

TEMPLETON, I. Class size. *Educational Management Review Series*, 1972, *8*, 1–7.

TERMAN, L. M. *The measurement of intelligence*. Boston: Houghton Mifflin, 1916.

TERWILLIGER, J. S. *Assigning grades to students*. Glenview, Ill.: Scott, Foresman, 1971.

THOMPSON, M., BRASSELL, W. R., PERSONS, S., TUCKER, R., AND ROLLINS, H. Contingency management in the schools. *American Educational Research Journal*, 1974, *11*, 19–28.

THORESEN, J. K. Memorization processes in reading disabled children. *Journal of Educational Psychology*, 1977, *69*(5), 571–578.

THORNBURG, H. D. (Ed.). *School learning and instruction*. Monterey, Calif.: Brooks-Cole, 1973.

THORNDIKE, E. L. Animal intelligence. *Psychological Review Monograph Supplement*, 1898, *2* (4, Whole No. 8).

THORNDIKE, E. L. *Educational psychology* (Vol. 1). New York: Teachers College, Columbia University, 1913.

THORNDIKE, E. L. Mental discipline in high school studies. *Journal of Educational Psychology*, 1924, *15*, 83–98.

THORNDIKE, E. L. *The fundamentals of learning*. New York: Teachers College, Columbia University, 1932.

THORNDIKE, R. L. Review of *Pygmalion in the classroom* by R. Rosenthal and L. Jacobson. *American Educational Research Journal*, 1968, *5*, 708–711.

Those books are restored in West Virginia. *New York Times*, November 10, 1974, Section 4, 9.

TIMKO, H. The effects of three variables on the discrimination of letters. *Journal of Educational Research*, 1977, *70*(5), 269–271.

Toddler logic: New findings. *Society*, September 1974, 10 f.

TOFFLER, A. *Future Shock.* New York: Random House, 1970.

TOLMAN, E. C. *Purposive behavior in animals and men.* New York: Century, 1932.

TOLMAN, E. C. A psychological model. In T. Parsons and E. A. Shils (Eds.), *Toward a general theory of action.* Cambridge, Mass.: Harvard University Press, 1951.

TOLOR, A., SCARPETTI, W. L., AND LANE, P. A. Teachers' attitudes toward children's behavior revisited. *Journal of Educational Psychology*, 1967, *58*, 175–180.

TORRANCE, E. P. Explorations in creative thinking. *Education*, 1960, *81*, 216–220.

TORRANCE, E. P. Motivation and creativity. In E. P. Torrance and W. F. White (Eds.), *Issues and advances in educational psychology* (2nd ed.). Itasca, Ill.: F. E. Peacock, 1975.

TOSTI, D. T. The peer-proctor in individualized programs. *Educational Technology*, August 1973, 29–30.

TRAVERS, J. *Learning: Analysis and application* (2nd ed.). New York: David McKay, 1972.

TRAVERS, R. M. W. *Essentials of learning* (2nd ed.). New York: Macmillan, 1967.

TROTMAN, F. K. Race, IQ and the middle class. *Journal of Educational Psychology*, 1977, *69*(3), 266–273.

TULVING, E. Episodic and semantic memory. In E. Tulving and W. Donaldson (Eds.), *Organization of memory.* New York: Academic Press, 1972.

TYLER, R. W. Some persistent questions on the defining of objectives. In C. M. Lindvall (Ed.), *Defining educational objectives.* Pittsburgh: University of Pittsburgh Press, 1964.

UREVICK, S. J. Ability grouping: Why is it undemocratic? *Clearing House*, 1965, *39*, 530–532.

U. S. Department of Health, Education, and Welfare. *The health of children. I. The world that greets the infant.* Washington, D.C.: U.S. Government Printing Office, 1970.

VAIL, E. O. What will it be? Reading or machismo and soul? *Clearing House*, 1970, *45*, 92–96.

VAN BRUNT, H. L. Review of *Children of Crisis*, Vols. 2 & 3, by R. Coles. *Saturday Review*, April 8, 1972, 69–72.

VARGAS, J. S. *Writing worthwhile behavioral objectives.* New York: Harper & Row, 1972.

VASUDEV, J. *An exercise testing a Piagetian-type task.* Unpublished manuscript, University of Pittsburgh, 1976.

VENEZKY, R. L. Research on reading processes: A historical perspective. *American Psychologist*, 1977, *32*(5), 339–344.

VEROFF, J., WILCOX, S., AND ATKINSON, J. W. The achievement motive in high school and college age women. *Journal of Abnormal and Social Psychology*, 1953, *48*, 108–119.

VINCENT, W. S. *Further clarification of the class size question* (IAR Research Bulletin 9). New York: Institute of Administrative Research, Columbia University, November 1968.

VYGOTSKY, L. S. [*Thought and Language*] (E. Hanfmann and G. Vakar, trans.). Cambridge, Mass.: MIT Press, 1962. (Originally published, 1934)

WALKER, H. M., AND HOPS, H. Increasing academic achievement by reinforcing direct academic performance and/or facilitative nonacademic responses. *Journal of Educational Psychology*, 1976, *68*(2), 218–225.

WALKER, S., III. Drugging the American child. We're too cavalier about hyperactivity. *Psychology Today*, December 1974, 43–48.

WALLBROWN, J. D., AND WALLBROWN, F. H. Classroom behaviors associated with difficulties in visual-motor perception. *Psychology in the Schools*, January 1976, *13*(1), 20–24.

WARBURTON, F. W., AND SOUTHGATE, V. *I.T.A.: An independent evaluation.* London: Murray and Chambers, 1969.

WATERS, C. R. Thank God something has finally reached Him. *TV Guide*, January 19, 1974, 6–9.

WATSON, J. B. Psychology as the behaviorist views it. *Psychological Review*, 1913, *20*, 158–177.

WATSON, J. B. *Psychology from the standpoint of a behaviorist.* Philadelphia: Lippincott, 1919.

WATSON, J. B., AND RAYNER, R. Conditioned emotional reactions. *Journal of Experimental Psychology*, 1920, *3*, 1–14.

WAX, M. L. *Indian education in Eastern Oklahoma* (Research contract report No. O.E. 6–10–260 and B.I.A. No. 5–0565–1–12–1). Washington, D.C.: U.S. Office of Education, 1969.

WEHMAN, P., ABRAMSON, M., AND NORMAN, C. Transfer of training in behavior modification programs. *Journal of Special Education*, Summer 1977, *11* (2), 217–231.

WEINBERGER, G., LEVENTHAL, T., AND BECKMAN, G. The management of a chronic school phobic through the use of consultation with school personnel. *Psychology in the Schools*, 1973, *10*, 83–88.

WELCH, I. D. AND USHER, R. H. Humanistic education: The discovery of personal meaning. *Colorado Journal of Educational Research*, Winter 1978, *17*(2), 17–22.

WELLINGTON, J., AND WELLINGTON, C. B. Should teachers see student records? No. *National Education Association Journal*, October 1966, 35–37.

WERTHEIMER, M. *Productive thinking* (Rev. ed.). New York: Harper & Brothers, 1959.

WESTLAKE, H. *Children: A study in individual behavior.* Lexington, Mass.: Ginn and Co., 1973.

WHITE, W. The teacher's personality is the primary motive in the classroom. In E. Torrance and W. White (Eds.), *Issues and advances in educational psychology.* Itasca, Ill.: Peacock, 1975.

WHITEHURST, G. J., AND MERKUR, A. E. The development of communication: Modeling and contrast failure. *Child Development,* 1977, *48,* 993–1001.

WHITING, J.W.M. Socialization process and personality. In F.L.K. Hsu (Ed.), *Psychological anthropology.* Homewood, Ill.: Dorsey Press, 1961.

WICKMAN, E. *Children's behavior and teachers' attitudes.* New York: Commonwealth Fund, 1928.

WICKS, L. E. Teacher evaluation. *Today's Education,* March 1973, 42–43.

WILLIAMS, P. A., HAGER, M., MOORE, S., AND WITHERSPOON, D. Teen-age suicide. *Newsweek,* August 28, 1978, 74–77.

WILLIAMS, T. Childrearing practices of young mothers: What we know, how it matters, why it's so little. *American Journal of Orthopsychiatry,* 44,1 (January 1974), 70–75.

WILSON, C. H. The case against merit pay. *Saturday Review,* January 20, 1962, 44 ff.

WINETT, R. A., AND WINKLER, R. C. Current behavior modification in the classroom: Be still, be quiet, be docile. *Journal of Applied Behavioral Analysis,* 1972, 5,499–504.

WINSOR, J. L. A's, B's, but not C's?: A comment. *Contemporary Education,* 1977, 48(2), 82–84.

WINTER, J.S.D., FAIMAN, C., AND REYES, F. I. Normal and abnormal pubertal development. *Clinical Obstetrics and Gynecology,* March 1978, 21(1), 67–86.

WISE, H. D. How teachers can promote equality. *Today's Education,* March-April 1974, 75.

WITKIN, H. A., DYK, R. B., PATTERSON, H. F., GOODENOUGH, D. R., AND KARP, S. A. *Psychological differentiation.* New York: Wiley, 1962.

WITKIN, H. A., GOODENOUGH, D. R., AND Karp, S. A. Stability of cognitive style from childhood to young adulthood. *Journal of Personality and Social Psychology,* 1967, *7,* 291–300.

WITKIN, H. A., MOORE, C. A., GOODENOUGH, D. R., AND COX, P. W. Field-dependent and field-independent cognitive styles and their educational implications. *Review of Educational Research,* Winter 1977, 47(1), 1–64. (a)

WITKIN, H. A., MOORE, C. A., OLTMAN, P. K., GOODENOUGH, D. R., FRIEDMAN, F., OWEN, D. R., AND RASKIN, E. Role of the field-dependent and field-independent cognitive styles in academic evaluation: A longitudinal study. *Journal of Educational Psychology,* 1977, 69(3), 197–211. (b)

WITMORE, H. J. The female athlete. *The Journal of School Health,* April 1977, 47, 227–233.

WOESTEHOFF, E. S. *Students with reading disabilities and guidance.* Boston: Houghton Mifflin, 1970.

WOOD, G. Organizational processes and free recall. In E. Tulving and W. Donaldson (Eds.), *Organization of memory.* New York: Academic Press, 1972.

WOODEN, H. E., LISOWSKI, S., AND EARLY, F. Volunteers, Head Start children, and development. *Academic Therapy,* 1976, *11,* 449–453.

WOODS, P. Teaching or surviving? *American Educator,* 1977, 1(2), 12–14.

WOOLFOLK, A. E. Student learning and performance under varying conditions of teacher verbal and nonverbal communication. *Journal of Educational Psychology,* 1978, 70(1), 87–94.

WULF, F. Tendencies in figural variation. In W. D. Ellis (Ed. and trans.), *A source book of Gestalt psychology.* New York: Harcourt, Brace, 1938. (Translated and condensed from *Psychol. Forsch.,* 1922, *1,* 333–373.)

WURST, K. *Caretaker-child interactions in Greek and American cultures.* Paper presented at the annual meeting of the Northeastern Educational Research Association meetings. Ellenville, N.Y., October 25-27, 1978.

YERKES, R. M. *Chimpanzees: A laboratory colony.* New Haven: Yale University Press, 1943.

YOUNG, B. J. Imagine you're the parent of a deaf-blind child. In J. B. Jordan and L. S. Robbins (Eds.), *Let's try doing something else kind of things: Behavioral principles and the exceptional child.* Arlington, Va.: Council for Exceptional Children, 1972.

YOUNG, J. I., AND VAN MONDFRANS, A. P. Psychological implications of competency-based education. *Educational Technology,* November 1972, 15–18.

YOUNG, K. C. Using a computer to help implement the Keller method of instruction. *Educational Technology,* October 1974, 53–55.

YOUNG, R. W. Novel situation testing. *Contemporary Education,* Winter 1978, 48(2), 76–80.

ZACH, L. The IQ debate. *Today's Education,* September 1972, 40–43 ff.

ZAX, M., AND COWEN, E. L. *Abnormal psychology.* New York: Holt, Rinehart & Winston, 1972.

ZIMBARDO, P. Shyness can be a quiet yet devastating problem. *Learning,* 1978, 6(1), 68–72.

ZIMBARDO, P. G., PILKONIS, P. A., AND NORWOOD, R. M. The social disease called shyness. *Psychology Today,* May 1975, 69–72.

ZIMILES, H. Preventive aspects of school experience. In E. L. Cowen, E. A. Gardner, and M. Zax (Eds.), *Emergent approaches to mental health problems.* New York: Appleton-Century-Crofts, 1967.

ZIV, A. Facilitating effects of humor on creativity. *Journal of Educational Psychology,* 1976, 68(3), 318–322.

author index

Abramson, M., 321
Ackerman, P.D., 418
Adkins, A., 409–10
Ahlstrom, K. G., 221
Ahmann, J. S., 426, 435, 437
Ainsworth, M. D. S., 17, 18
Aitken, A. C., 160–61, 163, 168
Algozzine, B., 349
Aliberto, C. A., 260
Allen, L., 466–67
Allen, V. F., 475
Alschuler, A. S., 213
Alston, F., 21
Altmann, H., 217, 487
Ames, C., 96, 212
Ames, L., 8
Amidon, E. J., 505, 506
Anderson, E. M., 377
Anderson, R. C., 503
Andrews, G. R., 215
Andrews, T. G., 196
Angell, G. W., 408
Antell, M., 505
Anttonen, R. G., 215
Asher, J. J., 360
Atkinson, John W., 212, 213
August, G. J., 282
Ausubel, David, 24, 120, 136–38, 146, 149–50, 197

Bachrach, A., 87
Badger, E. D., 356, 361
Bahrick, H. P., 164
Bahrick, P. O., 164
Bain, P. T., 228
Ballard, M., 385
Bandura, A., 26, 277
Baratz, J. C., 358
Barber, T. X., 215
Barenboim, C., 53

Barnes, B. R., 179
Barrett, R., 215
Barro, S. M., 508
Bayard-de-Volo, C. L., 233
Bayh, B., 301, 318
Bayley, N., 465
Beady, C. H., 320
Bechterev, V. M., 77
Becker, M., 142
Becker, W. C., 102
Beckman, G., 307
Beilen, H., 316
Bellack, M., 505
Bereiter, C., 63, 364–65
Berko, L., 272
Berlyne, D. E., 216, 231, 232
Bernard, H. W., 300, 342
Bernauer, M., 386
Bernstein, B., 60
Bersoff, D. N., 505
Bigge, M. L., 145, 181, 186
Binet, Alfred, 461
Bing, J. R., 179
Bing, S. J., 179
Birch, J., 379, 380, 387
Blake, M. J. F., 171
Blakelee, S., 355
Blank, M., 60
Blankstein, K. K., 171
Bloom, Benjamin, 245–49
Bloomfield, L., 275
Bodmer, W. F., 467
Bond, L., 446
Boswell, J. J., 358
Bounds, W., 426
Bowen, B., 215
Bower, G. H., 97, 182
Bowerman, C. E., 23
Bowers, N. P., 189
Bradbury, R., 171–72
Bradbury, W., 392
Brannigan, G. J., 352

Wittlinger, R. P., 164
Wittrock, M. C., 151
Woestehoff, E. S., 352
Wood, G., 135
Wooden, H. E., 351
Woods, P., 483
Woolfolk, A. E., 94
Wurst, K., 18, 23

Yawkey, T. D., 62
Yerkes, R. M., 121

Young, B. J., 347
Young, J. L., 228
Young, R. W., 419, 420

Zach, L., 469
Zax, M., 396
Zehrbach, R. R., 304
Zimbardo, P. G., 324, 325–26
Zimiles, H., 314
Zimmerman, R. R., 19
Ziv, A., 235

subject index

Merit pay, 511
Metric system, 195
Metropolitan Readiness Tests (MRT), 472
Middle schools, 9-10
Milwaukee, Wisc. 490-91
Minimal competency, 507-8, 523
Minority groups (racial problems), 318. *See also* Blacks;
    Language skills, Poverty
  and standardized testing, 459-60, 467
Mississippi, 493
Mnemonics, 182-84, 523
Mode, 413, 451, 523
Modeling (model building), 23, 272. *See also specific
    skills*
  defined, 523
  and language, 43
Models. *See also* Leadership; Roles
  teachers as, and problem behaviors, 321-22
Mode of representation, 126, 523
Modular instruction, defined, 523
Monkeys, 19, 194, 216
Montessori method, 61-63, 523
Montgomery County, Md., 315
Montreal, 359
Morality, 523. *See also* Values
Morality of constraint, defined, 523
Morality of cooperation, defined, 523
Morpheme, defined, 523
Moscow, 51
Mothers, 17-18, 19, 80, 94, 272, 313. *See also* Day care;
    Intervention programs
  and exchange games, 44-45
  schizophrenogenic, 526
  teen-age, 20
Motivation, 125, 203-39, 523
Motivation theory, 170-72, 205, 245
Motor development, 8-10
Motor skills (motor learning), 242-43, 255-256, 259-69
Motor skills taxonomy, 260, 523
Movement theory, 263-64, 523
MRT. *See* Metropolitan Readiness Tests
Multiple-choice tests, 410, 424, 427-30, 433-34
Multiple-mothering; multiple caregiving, defined, 523
Multiplication, 145
Music, 173, 262

Names, and grading, 448
National Assessment of Educational Progress, 475
National Association of Secondary School Principals,
    474
National Education Association (NEA), 494, 495, 498,
    505, 511
National Institute of Education, 301
National Institute of Mental Health, 301, 323
National Organization for Women (NOW), 494
National Training School for Boys, 221
NEA. *See* National Education Association
Nebraska, University of, 418
Needs, 205-10, 216-19, 222-24, 523
Negative reinforcement, 81-85, 86, 94-95, 523. *See also*
    Reinforcements

Negative self-concepts. *See* Achievement; Self-esteem
Negative transfer, 523. *See also* Interference
Neurological handicaps, 339-40, 348
Neurosis, 523. *See also* Problem behaviors
Newsweek, 491
New York City, 100, 312, 353, 468
New York State, 446
New York Times, 493
Nondirective counseling, defined, 523
Nongraded classes, 228-30, 523
Nonverbal tests, 449, 524
Normal curve (normal distribution), 411-12, 451-53, 524
Norm-referenced tests (grades), 411-14, 433, 524
Norms, 524. *See also* Problem behaviors; Standardized
    tests
North Philadelphia, Penn., 229
Novel situation testing, 419-20
NOW. *See* National Organization for Women
Nuclear family, 16, 17, 524
Nutrition, 345
  hunger, 208, 223, 345
  and problem behavior, 305-6

Oakland University, 419
Obedience, 22, 30. *See also* Punishment; Values
Object concept, 47
Objectives, learning, 244-53, 522. *See also* Goals
Objective tests, 424-25, 426-32, 524
Occupational therapists, 389
Office of Education, 459, 470
Ohio University, 363
Open classrooms, 55, 147-49, 234-35, 503-4, 524
Open-space schools, 148
Operant conditioning, 43, 79-92, 93-96, 524
Operants, 80, 524
Operant strength, 80, 524
Operation Upgrade (Project Upgrade), 274-75, 365-66
Oral recitation, 174, 182
Oral tests, 425
Oregon, 508
Organization, 135, 167-68, 180, 190, 524. *See also*
    Curriculum
Orthopedic handicaps, 339, 379
Overgeneralization, 91, 524
Overlearning, 173-74, 182, 195-96, 266, 524

Panic reaction, 306
PAPI. See Program Assessment Pupil Instruction
Parallel play, 23, 524
Parents, 24, 284-85. *See also* Environment; Families;
    Preschoolers; Socialization
  and alternatives to grading, 437
  deprivation of, 19-20
  and intervention programs, 361-62
  and magnet schools, 491
  and mainstreaming, 377, 388
  and problem behaviors. *See under* Families
Paris, 461
Peabody Individual Achievement Test, 351
Peabody Picture Vocabulary Test, 464